VOLUME THREE

A COUNTERINTELLIGENCE READER

POST-WORLD WAR II TO CLOSING THE 20TH CENTURY

FRANK J. RAFALKO (EDITOR)
NATIONAL COUNTERINTELLIGENCE CENTER

Published by Books Express Publishing
Copyright © Books Express, 2011
ISBN 978-1-78039-537-1

Books Express publications are available from all good retail and online booksellers. For publishing proposals and direct ordering please contact us at: info@books-express.com

TABLE OF CONTENTS

Chapter 1–*Cold War Counterintelligence* 1
    Introduction 3
Military Security 5
The Communist Party and Soviet Intelligence 20
    Whittaker Chambers and Alger Hiss 28
    Elizabeth Bentley 30
Indictment of Communists - January 1949 31
Information Relating to Domestic Espionage, Sabotage, Subversive Activities and Related Matters 33
Klaus Fuchs 33
The Rosenbergs 34
The Rosenberg Spy Apparatus 38
    Morton Sobell 38
    Theodore Alvin Hall 40
    Joel Barr and Al Sarrant 41
Other Spies in the Rosenberg Net 42
    Max Elitcher 42
    Harry Gold 44
    William Perl 47
US Senator Joseph R. McCarthy 47
William August Fisher–"Rudolph Ivanovich Abel" 49
    Reino Hayhanen 51
The Case of the Substitute Colonel 55
Other Spies 57
    Giuseppe E. Cascio 57
    Jack Edward Dunlap 58
    George H. French 58
    Valentin Alekseyevich Gubichev 59
    John P. Jones 60
    Hans Kessler 60
    Gustav Adolph Mueller 61
    Joseph Sidney Petersen, Jr. 61
    Roy Adair Rhodes 62
    James Sattler 62
    Otto Verber 62
    Sybille Wambach 63
The Soble Spy Ring 64
    Jacob Albam 64
    Jack Soble 64
    Myra Soble 64
    Mr. and Mrs. George M. Zlatovski 65
    Mr. and Mrs. Alfred K. Stern 65

Mark Zborowski	66
Defectors	66
Yuriy Aleksandrovich Rastvorov	66
Ivan Vasilyevich Ovchinnikov	67
Ismail Gusseynovich Akhmedov	68
Anatoliy Mikhaylovich Granovskiy	69
Petr Sergeyevich Deryabin	69
Grigoriy Stepanovich Burlutskiy	71
Cold War Counterintelligence Bibliography	72
Cold War Counterintelligence Chronology	74
Cold War Counterintelligence End Notes	425
Chapter 2–*Counterintelligence in the Turbulent 1960s and 1970s*	83
Introduction	85
Administratively Confidential	88
Memorandum for the Heads of Executive Departments and Agencies	88
US Double Agent Thwarts State Department Bugging	88
Military Surveillance	90
Central Intelligence Agency Testimony on Domestic Spying	94
The CIA, Authority and Background	94
Security and Counterintelligence	96
Activities Within the United States	97
Allegations and Some Details	99
CIA Relationships With Other Government Agencies	104
The Angleton Era in CIA	109
The Philby Connection	110
Angleton Named Chief of CI Staff	112
Anatoliy Golitsyn, Angleton's Rasputin	112
The Nosenko-Golitsyn Debate	113
The Angleton Legacy and Deception	114
The Trust Operation and Its Impact on the CI Staff's View of Deception	114
The Monster Plan vs. The Master Plan	115
The Loginov Affair	115
The Cold Warrior	116
FBI Counterintelligence Programs	117
Counterintelligence Program–Background Material	117
Central Intelligency Agency Mail Openings	121
Inspector General's Survey of the Office of Security Annex II	121
Project SGPOINTER/HTLINGUAL	121
FBI Mail Opening	125
Introduction and Major Facts	125
Description of FBI Mail Opening Programs	128
Nature and Value of the Product	133
Internal Authorization and Controls	137

  External Authorizations 139
  Termination of the FBI Mail Opening Programs 145
  Legal and Security Considerations Within the FBI 147
Warrantless National Security Electronic Surveillance 150
Agreement Governing the Conduct of Defense Department Counterintelligence Activities in Conjunction With the Federal Bureau of Investigation 158
  SECTION 1 Purpose 158
  SECTION 2 Defense Components Authorized to Conduct Counterintelligence Activities 159
  SECTION 3 Federal Bureau of Investigation Coordination with the Department of Defense 159
  SECTION 4 Definitions 159
  SECTION 5 Policy 159
  SECTION 6 Delineation of Responsibility for Counterintelligence Investigations 160
  SECTION 7 Coordination of Counterintelligence Operations 161
  SECTION 8 Implementation 161
Executive Order No. 12139, Exercise of Certain Authority Respecting Electronic Surveillance 161
Congressional Committees and Executive Commissions 1934-75 162
  Special Committee To Investigate Un-American Activities 162
  Special House Committee for the Investigation of Un-American Activities 163
  Commission on the Organization of the Executive Branch of the Government 163
  The Doolittle Review 164
  The Rockefeller Commission 164
  Select Committee to Study Government Operations With Respect to Intelligence Activities 165
  The House Select Committee on Intelligence 166
In the United States District Court For the District of Maryland-David Henry Barnett 166
Operation Lemonaid 176
Other Spies 177
  Joseph B. Attardi 177
  Herbert W. Boeckenhaupt 177
  Harold N. Borger 179
  Christopher J. Boyce and Andrew Dalton Lee 179
  John William Butenko 180
  Morris and Lona Cohen a.k.a. Peter and Helen Kroger 181
  Raymond George DeChamplain 181
  Nelson Cornelious Drummond 183
  George John Gessner 184
  Oliver Everett Grunden 184
  Robert Lee Johnson 185
  William Kampiles 186
  Joseph Patrick Kauffman 186
  Erich Englehardt and Karl Heinz Kiefer 187
  Kurt Kuehn 187
  Joseph Werner Leben 187
  Gary Lee Ledbetter 188
  Lee Eugene Madsen 188

Edwin G. Moore II	189
Walter T. Perkins	189
Leonard Jenkins Safford and Ulysses L. Harris	189
Irvin C. Scarbeck	190
Robert Glenn Thompson	190
William Henry Whalen	191
Defectors	192
Michal Goleniewski	192
Frantisek August	193
Ladislav Bittman	194
Joseph Frolik	194
Vaclav Marous	194
Yuriy Vasilyevich Krotkov	195
Aleksandr Nikolayevich Cherepanov	195
Rupert Sigl	196
Yuriy Ivanovich Nosenko	196
Olga Aleksandrovna Farmakovskaya	197
Oleg Vladimirovich Penkovskiy	199
Defection of Bernon F. Mitchell and William H. Martin	200
CI in the Turbulent 1960s and 1970s: Bibliography	202
CI in the Turbulent 1960s and 1970s: Chronology	205
CI in the Turbulent 1960s and 1970s: End Notes	429

Chapter 3–*Decade of the Spy* 215

Introduction	217
Executive Order 12333	219
National Security Decision Directive Number 84 – 11 March, 1983	231
The Walker Spy Ring	233
Jerry Alfred Whitworth	234
Arthur James Walker	235
Michael Lance Walker	236
Meeting the Espionage Challenge: Review of US Counterintelligence and Security Programs	236
Operation Station Zebra	251
Spies	253
Michael Hahn Allen	253
Stephen Anthony Baba	253
William Holden Bell	254
Edward Owen Buchanan	254
Thomas Patrick Cavanagh	255
Larry Wu-Tai Chin	257
Clyde Lee Conrad	257
Christopher M. Cooke	258
Robert Ernest Cordrey	260

John Allen Davies	260
Sahag K. Dedeyan	260
Hou Desheng	261
Thomas Joseph Dolce	261
Waldo H. Dubberstein	261
Robert Wade Ellis	261
David Fleming	262
Ernst Forbrich	262
Wilfredo Garcia	262
Otto Attila Gilbert	263
Robert Dean Haguewood	263
James Hall III	263
James Durward Harper, Jr. and Ruby Louise Schuler	264
Stephen Dwayne Hawkins	265
Joseph George Helmich	265
Rudolph Albert Herrmann	267
Brian Patrick Horton	267
Edward Lee Howard	268
Ronald Louis Humphrey	269
Vladimir Izmaylov	269
Randy Miles Jeffries	269
Mikhail Katkov	270
Bruce Leland Kearn	270
Karl F. Koecher	270
Penyu B. Kostadinov	270
Craig Dee Kunkle	271
Yuriy P. Leonov	271
Clayton John Lonetree	271
John Raymond Maynard	272
Alice Michelson	272
Richard Miller	272
Francisco de Asis Mira	273
Samuel Loring Morison	274
Tommaso Mortati	274
Michael R. Murphy	275
Frank Arnold Nesbitt	275
Bruce Damian Ott	275
Yuriy N. Pakhtusov	276
Leslie J. Payne	276
Ronald William Pelton	276
Michael A. Peri	277
Jeffrey Loring Pickering	278
Jonathan Jay Pollard	278
Daniel Walter Richardson	280

  Ivan N. Rogalsky 280
  Sharon Marie Scranage 280
  Brian Everett Slavens 281
  Glenn Michael Souther 281
  Michael Timothy Tobias 282
  Arne Treholt 283
  Douglas Tsou 283
  James R. Wilmoth and Russell Paul Brown 283
  Edward Hilledon Wine 284
  Hans Palmer Wold 284
  Ronald Craig Wolf 285
  Jay Clyde Wolff 285
  James D. Wood 285
  Gennadiy F. Zakharov 286
  Alfred Zehe 286
Defectors 287
  Artush Sergeyevich Oganesyan 287
  Nikolay Grigoryevich Petrov 287
Decade of the Spy: Bibliography 290
Decade of the Spy: Chronology 292

Chapter 4-*Counterintelligence at the End of the 20th Century* 299
  Introduction 301
The Jacobs Panel 303
The White House Executive Order 12863 304
United States of America v. Aldrich Hazen Ames 306
Central Intelligence Agency 311
The Ames Notebook 313
Statement of the Director of Central Intelligence on the Clandestine Services and the Damage
Caused by Aldrich Ames 314
  The Actual Damage 315
  Conclusions 319
Unclassified Abstract of the CIA Inspector Generals Report on the Aldrich H. Ames Case 320
  Preface to the Report from the IG 320
  Summary 322
The White House Office of the Press Secretary May 3, 1994 334
  Fact Sheet Counterintelligence Effectiveness 335
  National Counterintelligence Policy Coordination 335
  Counterintelligence Integration and Cooperation 336
Preparing for the 21st Century: An Appraisal of U.S. Intelligence 337
  Background 337
  The Goal of the Report 337
  The Commission's View of Counterintelligence 337

- Three Overarching Themes 337
- Summary of the Commission's Key Recommendations 338
- Robert Chaegon Kim 341
- Robert Stephan Lipka 347
- UNITED STATES OF AMERICA V. ROBERT STEPHAN LIPKA, A/K/A "ROOK" 347
- Phillip Tyler Seldon 350
- UNITED STATES OF AMERICA V. PHILLIP TYLER SELDON 351
- The Nicholson Chronology 353
- Harold J. Nicholson 354
  - Background 355
  - The Investigation–Polygraphs 356
- Pitts Affidavit 363
- AFFIDAVIT IN SUPPORT OF CRIMINAL COMPLAINT, ARREST WARRANT, AND SEARCH WARRANTS 364
  - Summary 365
  - Background on Earl Edwin Pitts 366
- Russian Commentary on Pitts' Arrest 389
- Economic Espionage Act of 1996 390
- Cold War Espionage in Germany 393
- Department of Defense Directive *May 22, 1997* 399
- Spies 406
  - Charles Lee Francis Anzalone 406
  - Joseph Garfield Brown and Virginia Jean Baynes 407
  - Jeffrey M. Carney 407
  - Mark Goldberg 407
  - Douglas Frederick Groat 408
  - Jeff E. Gregory 409
  - Frederick Christopher Hamilton 410
  - Geneva Jones and Dominic Ntube 410
  - Peter H. Lee 410
  - Kurt G. Lessenthien 411
  - Aluru J. Prasad 411
  - Yen Men Kao 412
  - Steven J. Lalas 412
  - Roderick James Ramsay 412
  - Jeffrey Stephen Rondeau 413
  - Albert T. Sombolay 413
  - Jeffrey Schevitz 414
  - Three Taiwan Nationals Indicted for Espionage 414
  - Daniel and Patrick Worthing 415
  - Charles Schoof and John Haeger 415
- CI at the End of the 20th Century: Bibliography 417
- CI at the End of the 20th Century: Chronology 419
- CI at the End of the 20th Century: End Notes 435

CHAPTER 1

Cold War Counterintelligence

Introduction

The distinguished American historian Richard Hofstadter suggested that periodically in American history, during times of great worry, many individuals turn to "conspiracy theories" to explain away their anxieties. The early post–World War II scene was such a period. To some Americans, President Franklin Roosevelt sold out the European nations that fell victim to the Communists. The peace that Americans expected after fighting the Nazi attempt to subvert the European continent was not there. Unable to rationally explain why they failed to achieve any security, the American public believed the answer was the result of widespread treason and subversion within the nation.

President Harry Truman was bogged down in Korea but unwilling to commit the resources to win because the United States had to build up NATO to defend Europe. Because of Truman's actions in promoting loyalty oaths for the US Government, some rightwing Republicans in Congress accused the Democrats of being soft on Communism. there were indeed traitors in the country, then the Democratic Party was responsible for them because they had controlled the government since 1932.

In 1948, Whittaker Chambers, a journalist who admitted he was a Communist Party member and Soviet spy, accused Alger Hiss, a middle-level aide to President Roosevelt, as having provided classified documents to the Soviets. The case might have faded into the dustpan of history except that Hiss lied about knowing Chambers. Caught in that lie he was convicted of perjury. Elizabeth Bentley, another former Soviet spy, also came forward at this time with her story of Soviet intelligence penetration of the government.

The next event fueling American anxiety was the Soviet Union's detonation of the atomic bomb. The US intelligence community had convinced American leaders that the United States was five years ahead of the Soviets in this area yet the country now faced this new menace. The arrests of Julius and Ethel Rosenberg, Harry Gold, and several other Americans revealed that through them Soviet intelligence had penetrated the Manhattan Project, as the A-Bomb program was called.

A senator from Wisconsin by the name of Joseph McCarthy rode the nation's apprehension about Communist subversion to political stardom. McCarthy constantly told people he had the names of Communists within the government. Yet, he never released a single name to the press nor did he identify a single

Communist in the government. He actually had nothing but was able to convince people that what he said was true. McCarthy was an alarming symbol of just how anxious American society had become. In the end he went down in flames.

The identification of the Communist party spy rings caused Soviet intelligence to end this recruitment practice. The intelligence services looked to running "illegals"— a Soviet national documented as a citizen of another country who emigrates to the targeted nation. This practice was revealed when Rudolph Ivanovich Abel was arrested by the FBI in 1957.

It was the start of the Cold War. Every presidential administration beginning with Harry Truman had to design its foreign policy around the overwhelming fact that the United States was locked into a deadly competition with the Soviet Union that left very little room to maneuver. To the Counterintelligence Community, this meant its resources and energy had to be focused on that threat.

Military Security

The sudden Korean outbreak found the military security (counterintelligence) effort of the Office of the Acting Chief of Staff Intelligence Division, Department of the Army (OACofS G-2, D/A), in a noticeably unsatisfactory state. Although the new conditions of Cold War had served to increase all phases of this effort to a marked degree, the Army had not only been prevented by higher authority from carrying out the domestic intelligence operations it needed to support prior planning for the possible use of federal troops in local emergencies but had also been denied any direct control over the establishment of policies and procedures aimed at uncovering subversion or sabotage within its own ranks. Moreover, due mainly to defense economy considerations, the total authorized strength of the two security branches that formed part of the earlier merged Security and Training Division had been reduced to 36 officers and 41 civilian employees just when the demands of the security clearance program for personnel, requiring access to classified information of the Government, had reached a new peak in intensity. On 25 June 1950, under the terms of a special regulation dated 14 September 1949, which was still in force, these branches were being called upon to perform the following functions:

Operations Branch—Formulates, promulgates, and supervises counterintelligence programs pertaining to the Army; establishes countermeasures against efforts to gain unauthorized access to classified information pertaining to plans, operations, and capabilities of the Army; and initiates, controls, reviews, and recommends final action on certain types of security investigations of military and civilian personnel connected with the Army.

Security of Military Information Branch—Formulates, promulgates, and exercises supervision over measures for censorship and for safeguarding classified military information; and promulgates and interprets policy on the disclosure of classified military information to foreign governments and their nationals, the United States Government, nongovernmental agencies, and individuals.[1]

The most pressing counterintelligence problem right after the opening of the Korean Conflict had to do with the establishment of military censorship, especially armed forces and public information media censorship. This was the case despite the fact that anticipatory planning both for national and military censorship in the event of an emergency had been accomplished during the previous Cold War period. Furthermore, on 7 February 1950, the Secretary of Defense had formally directed the Secretary of the Army to assume primary responsibility for:

Coordinating all aspects of censorship planning, as it concerns the Department of Defense, with a view to developing censorship programs which are soundly conceived and integrated with those of the Federal Agency having primary responsibility for censorship.

Providing consultation and coordination with the National Security Resources Board through a working group compromising appropriate representation from each military department and such representation as the NSRB may desire.

Informing the Secretary of Defense from time to time of programs and developments in the field of censorship planning.[2]

One result of this timely directive from the Secretary of Defense was the prompt creation of a working group on censorship planning, which came to be known as the National Censorship Readiness Measures Coordination Committee (NCRMCC). Enjoying appropriate National Security Resources Board (NSRB), Office of Secretary of Defense (OSD), Army, Navy, and Air Force representation, the NRCMCC started without delay to prepare an emergency plan for armed forces participation in the implementation of national censorship if it was ever ordered into effect.[3] Even though the letter of instructions to the field regarding that plan could not be actually issued until 29 August 1950,[4] it was already in the process of Army–Air Force staff coordination at the time of the Korean outbreak, so its chief provisions were generally understood and accepted by all concerned.

This planning effort had been founded on the thesis that national censorship would be immediately imposed by the Chief Executive following some kind of declaration of war. The Korean conflict, however, was then being officially regarded as a United Nations police action led by the United States, which presented an entirely new concept in the matter. Besides, neither the Air Force nor the Navy seemed to feel in 1950 there was any compelling need for the establishment of censorship and the National Censorship Adviser to the NSB had already expressed an opinion that "in view of the diplomatic and political implications, the President would not give his approval to the imposition of national censorship."[5]

Nevertheless, the problem of affording a suitable military security for troop movements, combat operations, and the introduction of new weapons into the Korean conflict soon became both real and acute. Since there were at first almost no curbs at all on reporting about those matters, serious security breaches repeatedly occurred during the early weeks of the fighting. These security breaches thoroughly alarmed the operating personnel within the OACofS G-3, D/A, and prompted the G-2 security officials to undertake a comprehensive study of the entire censorship situation.

Upon completion, this study reached the rather indefinite conclusion that only total national censorship embracing the armed forces, mail, and public information media could possibly hope to solve the problem effectively; but, under the existing conditions such a course of action was plainly out of the question. The three major press services in the United States, though, were persuaded to agree not "to compile or publish state or national round-ups of National Guard or Reserve units being called to active duty." Additionally, on 9 August 1950, when the Secretary of Defense cabled Commander-in-Chief Far East (CINCFE) to express his grave concern over the recurring breaches of security displayed in dispatches emanating from Korea, General MacArthur stated that he preferred a code of voluntary press control to one calling for an imposed censorship and also noted as follows:

In Tokyo previous directives from Washington forbade such direct procedure but something of the same general effect has been accomplished by constantly calling attention to correspondents to published dispatches which jeopardized security. The results are progressively encouraging. The practical difficulties involved with nearly 300 correspondents representing 19 foreign countries of varying attitudes and with the constant demands for more rapid transmission of copy to their home offices render the problem of arbitrarily checking dispatches almost insurmountable. Of course, whatever system is applied here will not prevent violations through stateside or other foreign outlets and unless something of the same sort is applied there articles violating security can rapidly be transmitted by airmail delivery or even faster methods of communication. To attempt a complete censorship in Japan would require the employment of thousands of persons to check the various communications systems involved. This is completely beyond the resources of this command. In addition it would involve international complications which would be practically insurmountable. If any change in the present system is to be made I suggest that for general coordination and understanding it be formulated and announced by the government from Washington after due consultation with other nations involved.[6]

Military security problems bearing upon the establishment of armed forces and public information media censorship then continued to plague the Army authorities both in Washington and the Far East. They were soon made even more difficult when a heated dispute broke out in the Department of the Army over whether the press censorship function should be performed within a theater of operations by G-2 or Public Information Office personnel. This particular

Interrogating a North Korean.

dispute was presumably settled on 30 January 1951, at least for the Department of the Army, with general staff responsibility for supervising press censorship being definitely assigned to the OACofS G-2, D/A, but the Chief of Information (CINFO) was also designated as a "proponent agent" for such matters.[7] In the meantime, Gen. A. R. Bolling had submitted a recommendation through channels to the Chief of Staff that military censorship, including press censorship, should be ordered into effect without delay in Korea.[8]

The Chief of Staff, Gen. J. Lawton Collins, disagreed with the G-2 proposal for establishing an armed forces censorship in Korea but did feel that press censorship ought to be imposed there just as soon as possible, and he promptly forwarded a recommendation along those lines to the JCS. On 8 September 1950, the JCS informed CINCFE they considered his voluntary press censorship system ineffective and intended to notify the Secretary of Defense that a more positive censorship of all public information media in FECOM was now necessary. General MacArthur then sharply reminded them he had no personnel trained or available to perform detailed censorship work and reiterated an earlier belief that the implementation of censorship should be a United Nations activity. On the basis of this reply and numerous indicated problems concerned with personnel requirements, shipping space, and day-to-day regulation of some 60 non-English-speaking war correspondents, the JCS finally decided to forego any further moves toward imposing censorship on public information media in the Far East. CINCFE was carefully cautioned, however, to continue "positive pressure in support of the principles of voluntary censorship at all levels in order to provide maximum security of force deployment."[9]

Another major counterintelligence problem that confronted the departmental intelligence agency of the Army during the early part of the Korean Conflict period was connected with developing more effective removal procedures for personnel, both civilian and military, who were found to be either serious security risks or disloyal. In January 1950, the Secretary of the Army had asked the Personnel Policy Board, Office of the Secretary of Defense, to make a study of the procedures currently in use for that purpose by the three Service Departments, so more uniform policies could be established regarding the dismissal of such employees. The Army, for example, was still utilizing the summary authority contained in the Public Law 808 to process both its security risk and disloyalty cases but the Navy and Air Force were now using that particular authority only for security risk cases and EO 9835 procedures, through the Civil Service Commission, for handling their disloyalty cases. One result of this study, therefore, was to have the Secretary of the Army, on 12 May 1950, notify the Chairman of the Personnel Policy Board that in the future the Army would conform to the Navy and Air Force system for all removal cases.[10]

Meanwhile, at an Armed Forces Policy Council meeting held on 10 May 1950, the Secretary of Defense himself had requested the Chairman of the Personnel Policy Board "to undertake a general review of the present policies and procedures for determining the loyalty and security of Department of Defense civilian personnel." The Korean outbreak thus found the OACofS G-2, D/A, in the midst of preparing several informative memorandums dealing with this complicated subject for the guidance of Army representatives participating in two major personnel security reviews.[11] Less than two weeks later and before either review could be actually concluded, though, Mr. Johnson, the Secretary of Defense, ordered the service secretaries to take immediate steps to accomplish pre-employment investigations for all civilian employees being assigned to sensitive positions requiring access to Top Secret, Secret, or Confidential material in their respective departments.[12] These early actions were then strongly influenced by other closely related developments within the personnel security field as follows:

1. Passage of Public Law 733, 81st Congress, on 26 August 1950, not only repealing the initial suspension section of PL 808 but also providing for the establishment of Loyalty-Security Hearing Boards to receive testimony from civilian employees who were answering charges for their removal on loyalty-security grounds.

2. Passage by Congress, on 20 September 1950, over President Truman's veto, of a new Internal Security Act (PL 831, 81st Congress, commonly known as the McCarran Act), which was intended to furnish an effective legal basis for prosecuting members of the Communist Party seeking to subvert the US Government.

3. Issuance of Army-wide directive by the Adjutant General, dated 20 September 1950, covering the establishment of Loyalty-Security Hearing Boards in compliance with PL 733 and also giving official notice that the existing Special Regulation 620-220-1, Civilian Personnel, Loyalty-Security Adjudication, was being rewritten to conform to this new law.

4. Approval by Secretary of Defense George Marshall, on 2 October 1950, of a recommended list from the Personnel Policy Board of "Criteria for Determining Eligibility for Employment for Sensitive and Non-Sensitive Duties in the Department of Defense". Among other things, this list indicated the need for a special regulation to assist the appropriate commanders in determining security qualifications and requirements for the employment or assignment of personnel to sensitive positions throughout the US Army.[13]

Since these measures were all aimed primarily at establishing effective procedures for handling civilian loyalty and security risk cases, they did not alter in any significant degree the currently prescribed methods for disposing of disloyal, disaffected, or subversive military personnel. To serve that latter purpose, the Army had already devised a workable program based upon the provisions of a Special Regulation 600-220-1, originally issued on 10 November 1948 and then slightly revised in January 1950, supplemented by additional instructions contained in a Special Regulation 600-220-2 (SECRET) dated 9 June 1949. This program normally involved one or more of the following administrative actions:

1. Each Army inductee or enlistee was initially called upon to fill out and sign a standard Loyalty Certificate (NME Form 98). If that certificate failed to mention membership in any organization designated by the Attorney General as being inimical to the US Government, no further action was taken. When it did so indicate, however, then more security checks were accomplished and proper authority eventually made a decision on the enlistment of continued induction of the person in light of them.

2. Similar procedures were utilized to eliminate disloyal or subversive Regular Army personnel and Army Reserve personnel either on active duty or in an inactive duty status, under the terms of a 615-370, Enlisted Personnel, Discharge, Disloyal, or Subversive.

3. Army Reserve personnel on whom fragmentary disloyal or subversive information was already known were deliberately not recalled to active duty until such time as a suitable investigation could be conducted to determine whether or not they should be eliminated through AR 615-370 procedures.

4. Under the provisions of SR 600-220-2 (Secret), the duty assignments of suspected military and civilian personnel were fittingly restricted pending the completion of a full-scale investigation to determine whether or not they should be eliminated through AR 615-70 procedures.[14]

While the departmental military security officials were not entirely satisfied with the powers they possessed under this adopted program for eliminating known or suspected subversives from the Army, they had generally come to accept the situation in that respect by the time the Korean conflict started. As a matter of fact, during its total period of operation from 10 November 1948 to early August 1950, the program did succeed in producing some interesting statistics, as follows:

Action Under SR 600-220-1
Cases Received 107
Cases pending (discharge recommended) 15
Personnel discharged 55
Cases returned for further investigative action ..
.... 100

Action Under Reserve Recall Program
Total cases 1147

(a) Derogatory cases (will not be recalled until investigations can be conducted or may be discharged under SR 600-220 -1) 480

(b) Derogatory cases (may be recalled but will be placed under surveillance) 420

(c) Derogatory cases not identified to persons of Army service 68

(d) Pending classification to (a) or (b) above 179

Action Under SR 600-220-2 (Regular Army Personnel)
Class "A" Restrictees – 21
Class "B" Restrictees – 45[15]

The advent of the Korean conflict made it virtually imperative, of course, to eliminate all disloyal or subversive persons from the US military establishment as soon as possible. At a meeting of the Armed Forces Policy Council held on 8 August 1950, therefore, Secretary of Defense Johnson not only requested the three Services to review their security files and separate any personnel with Communist leanings but also announced he intended to advise the White House when this action had been completed. Because the Army felt that its existing program was well suited for such purpose, no important changes were recommended in it. Nevertheless, all four of the basic special regulations supporting the program were promptly revised in order to render them more applicable, and they were reissued before the end of the year, as follows:

SR 600-220-2 (S), Personnel, Disposition of Subversive and Disaffected Personnel, 6 September 1950.

SR 620-220-1, Civilian Personnel, Loyalty-Security Adjudication, 13 November 1950.

SR 600-220-1, Personnel, Disloyal and Subversive Military Personnel, 6 December 1950.

SR 380-160-2, Military Security, Determining Eligibility for Employment on Sensitive Duties, 28 December 1950.[16]

Other events bearing upon the military security field that occurred during the early Korean conflict period and appear to warrant special mention were, as follows:

1. The IIC, on 8 June 1950, had approved a change in the current Delimitations Agreement on Security activities by governmental agencies, which was designed to transfer responsibility for performing certain counterintelligence investigations aboard Military Sea Transport Services (MSTS) ships from the Army and the Navy. This change then necessitated a corresponding revision of the latest SR 380-320-2, "Military Security, Counterintelligence Investigative Agencies, Supplementary Agreements" that was duly accomplished, effective 16 August 1950.[17]

2. Congress, on 16 June 1950, had passed a law (PL 555, 81st Congress) amending the Displaced Persons Act of 1948, in order to permit the entrance into the United States of 500 additional DPs as "national interest cases" provided they were recommended by both the Secretary of Defense and Secretary of State. Investigating the DP applicants for such entrance from the security viewpoint, however, presented some almost insuperable problems for all concerned. With the Army CIC representing the only possible means of performing satisfactory overseas investigations for that purpose, the Secretary of Defense chose to delegate his own assigned responsibility in the matter to the Secretary of the Army. Col. William H. Brunke, Chief of the Exploitation Branch, ID, OACofS G-2, D/A, was then selected to organize this new Army effort. Representative committees were also soon formed to develop and coordinate workable procedures for clearing the DP applicants, so that, late in November 1950, detailed instructions could be sent out to the various occupation commanders covering the entire conduct of screening operations in the field.[18] Shortly thereafter, arrangements were likewise concluded to speed up the local DP processing by establishing joint Army-State clearance committees in Frankfurt, Germany, and Salzburg, Austria.

3. The Informant and Observer system that had been in force during WWII was abolished, effective 20 August 1945, and not replaced. While the need for a similar system without some of the

more objectionable features of this earlier organization had become clearly apparent during the subsequent Cold War period, no attempt was made to introduce another one into the Army until after the Korean outbreak. On 20 October 1950, the deputy Chief of Staff for Administration did approve, but for planning purposes only, the distribution of a G-2 sponsored "Counter-subversive Plan" to be instituted in all units of the Army Field Establishment upon specific direction by the Secretary of the Army. Regardless of the fact that this new system had been most carefully designed to operate through the regular chain of command and was plainly "non-punitive, non-investigative and non-mandatory if other coverage existed," it was never put into actual effect.[19]

4. Having been beset by many serious personnel problems throughout the entire preceding Cold War period, the CIC was finally able to get a new AR 600-148, "Personnel, Assignment to Counter Intelligence Corps (CIC)" published in August 1950, which served to tighten up several of the mandatory qualification requirements governing the selection of personnel for CIC assignment. Notwithstanding, the sudden Korean emergency had found the CIC with a shortage in officer strength of 15 lieutenant colonels and 55 majors and needing five lieutenant colonels and 50 majors for immediate duty in the Far East. The desired raising of CIC personnel standards, therefore, especially for field grade officers in most cases again had to be postponed.[20]

5. Under the current SR 10-5-1, "Organization and Functions, Department of the Army," date 11 April 1950, the OACofS G-2, D/A, had been charged with "planning, coordinating and supervising the collection, evaluation and dissemination of intelligence information concerning the strategic vulnerability of the United States and its possessions." Because the term "strategic vulnerability" was so broad and elastic, though, the other three general staff divisions continued to remain deeply involved in activities impinging directly upon that function. During December 1950, for example, the ACofS G-3, D/A, addresses a letter to the six Continental Army Commanders on the subject of "Department of the Army Responsibility for Industrial Security" and instructed them to accomplish a "Facility Security Survey" for the industrial plants located within their respective areas that were being carried as "Key Facilities" by the national Munitions Board. Since these surveys might well produce some valuable information both from the strategic vulnerability and military security (sabotage) standpoint, the ACofS G-2, D/A, not only arranged to receive a copy of each for use in the departmental military intelligence agency but also advised the ACofS G-2s of the Continental Armies to make similar arrangements at their own headquarters.[21]

6. A law (PL 679, 81st Congress) was passed on 9 August 1950 that authorized the President to prescribe regulations for safeguarding American ports and waterfront facilities. President Truman then issued an Executive Order (EO 10173), dated 18 October 1950, establishing a limited port security program to be implemented by the US Coast Guard of the Treasury Department. In accordance with a written request from the Secretary of the Treasury to the Secretary of the Army, therefore, the ACofS G-2, D/A, in January 1951, was called upon to take necessary steps to ensure that all the Army Commanders and Attaches would urgently report any information which might give:

(a) Warning of the actual or suspected departure for the United States or approach to the United States of any vessel known or suspected of carrying materials for attack.

(b) Warning of the actual or suspected departure for the US vessels owned, controlled, or in the service of the USSR, Poland, Czechoslovakia, Hungary, Albania, Romania, Bulgaria, Communist China, Outer Mongolia, North Korea, Eastern Germany, or Eastern Austria.

(c) Any other information of value to the Coast Guard in carrying out its tasks.[22]

7. Early in January 1951, the Director of Administration, Office of the Secretary of Defense, proposed to make the formation of a joint

Service agency to develop needed equipment for physical or investigative security use. The Army did not favor the formation of such an agency because the Joint Intelligence Committee (JIC) had already taken action in the same matter, which included the CIA. Nevertheless, the Department of Defense ignored this obvious duplication and announced the establishment of Physical Security Equipment Agency (PSEA), effective 6 February 1951. Under management direction of the Secretary of the Air Force, the PSEA was then held responsible to provide for the "development of physical security and related investigative equipment as a common service for all agencies of the Department of Defense." Army participation in the new agency was subsequently covered by the publication of SR 380-410-1, dated 23 February 1951.[23]

The establishment of the G-2 Central Records Facilities (CRF) at Fort Holabird, Maryland, on 17 August 1951, was a most progressive step in the direction of improving the Army's entire counterintelligence effort. Not to be confused with the Central CIC Files, which had recently been microfilmed and consolidated in the CIC Center at Fort Holabird, this new field facility was originally intended to furnish a centralized repository for all closed personnel security cases of the Continental Armies, Military District of Washington (MDW), and OACofS G-2, D/A. Remaining under G-2 control but supervised directly by the Commanding General, Fort Holabird, who was also Chief, CIC, the CRF was officially charged with the "maintenance, processing, and administration" of the files in its custody. It was not in any sense an investigative agency nor was it capable of making any loyalty evaluations. In January 1952, its specific functions could thus be described to the Commanding Generals of the Continental Armies and MDW, as follows:

   a. To provide a central repository for all intelligence investigations which have been or are being conducted by the above-named commands.

   b. To provide a master index to all intelligence investigations which have been or are being conducted by the above named commands, which will be furnished a copy thereof, including changes when issued.

   c. To consolidate all intelligence information that has been developed on an individual by the above-named commands, eliminating duplicate and nonessential material.

   d. To prevent duplication of intelligence investigative effort by investigative agencies of the above-named commands.

   e. To provide a standardized filing system for all intelligence personality investigative files within the above-named commands.

   f. To facilitate the use of personality investigative files by furnishing the files or information therefrom to the above named commands.[24]

While the new CRF was promptly recognized by all concerned as representing a major contribution in simplifying and facilitating procedures for checking the security background of persons who had previously come under the cognizance of an Army counterintelligence investigative agency, it soon ran into severe personnel difficulties of its own. Initially, the CRF was allocated just eight military and 32 civilian spaces; these totals were raised to 11 military and 86 civilian on 29 October 1952, in view of the increased emphasis that was being placed upon personnel clearance matters throughout the US Government. This favorable action did not provide much real relief for the CRF, however, because it could only employ trained civilians possessing the highest possible security qualifications, and by that time there were very few such persons readily available for such procurement. The facility was thus forced to operate during most of the Korean conflict period by utilizing whatever "pipeline" military personnel happened to be passing through the CIC Center from time to time on temporary duty or other transient status.[25]

Early in 1951, the Secretary of Defense had queried the Secretary of the Army with reference to the current security status of the Panama Canal. The result was that Secretary Pace ordered Maj. Gen. John K. Rice, Chief, CIC, and Col. Duncan S. Somerville, from the OACofS G-3, D/A, to visit the Canal Zone as his personal representatives for the purpose of examining the "question of counterintelligence measures...now being taken to provide for the protection and security of the Panama Canal." During their visit, they discovered that CIA activity within the Canal Zone and surrounding areas had been quite limited, and most of the required counterintelligence operations were being performed by CIC personnel assigned to Headquarters, United States Army, Caribbean (USARCARIB). This was an Army command that functioned under the Commander in Chief, Caribbean (CINCARIB), who acted in the capacity of Executive Agent for the JCS.[26]

After Lt. Gen. Horace L. McBride, U.S.A., became CINCARIB on 1 April 1952, the question of responsibility and means for conducting counterintelligence operations within his command again came to the fore. He felt that because of his JCS mission he ought to assume operational control of the 470th CIC Detachment, Headquarters, USARCARIB, but this view was not shared by either Maj. Gen. Lester G. Whitlock, CG, USCARCARIB or Maj. Gen. Richard C. Partridge, the newly appointed ACofS G-2, D/A.[27] Following an exchange of several unyielding letters on the subject between Washington, DC and Quarry Heights, CZ, it appeared that the problem could probably best be settled through personal contact. On 22 October 1952, therefore, Generals McBride, Whitlock, and Partridge, along with Brig. Gen. Martin F. Hass, Chief of Staff, Caribbean Command, conferred together at Quarry Heights in the matter and reached an agreement that:

1. CINCARIB would assume direct control of the 470th CIC Detachment but leave a small group of its personnel with CG USARCARIB for his own investigative use. CINCARIB would then not only be responsible for the "investigation, collection, and reporting of intelligence matters in the Republic of Panama and the Canal Zone" but also "accept requests for information on these areas from the Department of the Army" while acting as Executive Agent for the JCS.

2. Utilizing his retained group of personnel from the 470th CIC Detachment for such purpose, CG USRCARIB would continue to undertake the reporting of "purely Army intelligence matters."

3. This new CIC organization was to remain on a trial basis until the end of March 1953. At that time, it would revert back to the prior organization if the ACofS G-2, D/A or CG USCARIB felt "things were not working out properly."[28]

With military security problems thus continuing to demand a large share of attention within the departmental intelligence agency of the Army, the Security Division, OACofS G-2,[29] now formed into four functional branches designed respectively as Personal Security, Special Operations, Security of Military Information, and Censorship, was mainly engaged during the periods from 9 September 1951 to 31 December 1952 in supervising the following activities:

Personal Security Branch—called upon to handle all matters relating to policies and procedures for the investigation and clearance of personnel from the military security standpoint; this branch was faced with these principal problems:

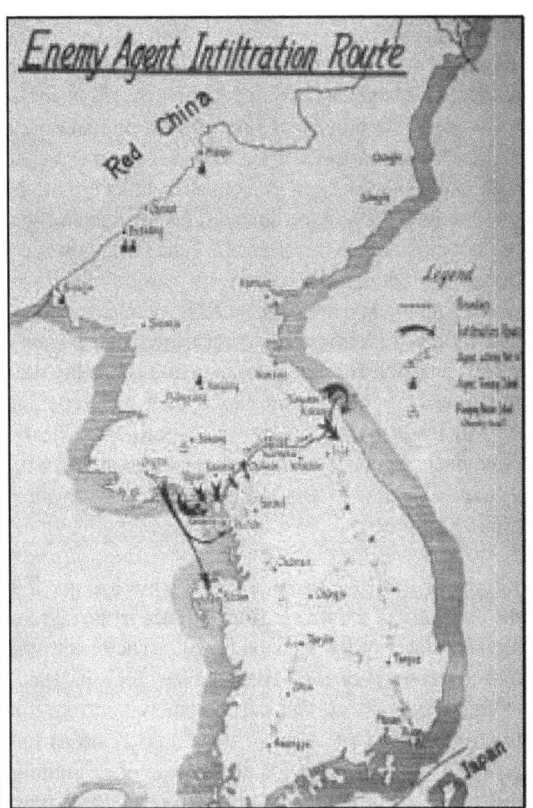

K–Map

a. Investigation and Clearance of Foreign Personnel for Entrance into the United States under Auspices of the Joint Intelligence Objectives Agency (JIOA)—On 8 May 1952, a new SR 380-160-12 (C) was issued to govern the granting of "limited access" security clearances to foreign personnel brought into the United States under JIOA auspices. One noteworthy feature of this regulation was that it authorized the substitution of a polygraph test for such components of the required background investigation as could not be properly accomplished due to inaccessibility of the geographic area from which the subject personnel had originated. Moreover, an announced aim of the regulation was to ensure that the respective skills of these foreign personnel would be exploited by the Military Departments concerned to the fullest extent possible.

b. Security Clearance of Aliens by Private Industry—While the publication of SR 380-160-12 (C) did help to ease the security clearance problem in connection with the employment of foreign personnel by the Military Departments, the polygraph substitution that it authorized still could not be applied to aliens who were under consideration for employment within private industry. Feeling that some of these latter aliens were probably being denied advantageous employment from the US viewpoint on classified contracts by private industry, the ACofS G-2, D/A, asked the Department of Defense Munitions Board to grant the same type of exemption to them as the others. Even though this request had been concurred in by all the Army agencies concerned, the Munitions Board, on 13 June 1952, chose to act unfavorably upon it.

c. Investigation and Clearance of Aliens Serving in the US Army—Strongly indicated at this time was a need to have the polygraph exemption also cover enlisted aliens serving in the US Army, so that their individual skills could be fully utilized within the appropriate military commands. After a G-2 recommendation to permit such an exemption had been approved first by the Department of Defense and then by the Munitions Board, a new SR 380-160-13 (C) was issued, on 15 August 1952, to implement it.

d. Armed Forces Industrial Security Regulation—Because the three Military Department were now dealing with private industry on an ever-increasing scale, the necessity for having a single Armed Forces Security regulation to control it soon became plainly apparent. During May 1952, therefore, the Munitions Board decided to form an Armed Forces Industrial Security Regulations Committee to accomplish that particular task. This committee was composed of two members from the Munitions Board staff plus two representatives from each of the three Military Departments. Initially, the two Army representatives on it were Lt. Col. Donald C. Landon, OACofS G-2, D/A, and Lt. Col. David G. Fitch, OACofS G-4, D/A. Capt. A.H. Ladner, OACofS G-3, D/A, however, was later permitted to attend the committee meetings and to receive copies of its agenda and minutes without holding a formal membership. The eventual result was the publication of a far-reaching SR 380-405-5 in January 1953, designed to establish a single personnel investigative and clearance system at all private industrial plants performing classified contracts for any of the Military Departments. It also returned to the OACofS, D/A, several functions bearing upon safeguarding classified information, which had been given to the Provost Marshal General's Office during World War II, in order that administration of the Army part of the new Industrial Security Program would come under complete control by the departmental military intelligence agency. This work then soon grew to be so demanding that a separate Industrial Security Branch, Security Division, was formed in March 1953, in accordance with a directive received from the Secretary of Defense.

Special Operations Branch—Until 19 September 1951, the entire counterintelligence responsibility for the Pentagon Building had rested with a small 118th CIC Detachment functioning directly under the Special Operations Branch, OACofS G-2, D/A. On that date, the Secretary of Defense instructed the Secretary of the Army to install a much more comprehensive program, which would not only encompass the Pentagon Building proper, but also its "grounds and appurtenant buildings." In view of these additional demands, the 118th Detachment was inactivated, effective 8 January 1952, and replaced by a larger Sub-Detachment "A" from the 902nd CIC Detachment that had recently been organized at Fort Holabird, MD, to execute special counterintelligence missions for the ACofS, D/A. On 1 December 1952, the Special Operations Branch was renamed the Special Investigation Section, Security Division, but its duties continued to remain essentially unchanged.

Security of Military Information (SMI) Branch- Held responsible for handling all Army matters concerned with the security of classified military information; this branch was involved in a remarkably wide variety of activities along such lines, as follows:

a. Tripartite (US-UK-France) Security Agreement—The US Government, in August 1951, formally accepted a set of "principles and standards" for safeguarding information that had been agreed upon by a Tripartite Security Working Group made up of top-level security experts from the United States, United Kingdom, and France. This Working Group, with Col. Gordon E. Dawson, Chief of the SMI Branch, OACofS G-2, D/A, acting as Chairman, had completed a detailed survey of the regulations and methods in current use within those three countries for that particular purpose. By May 1952, both the United Kingdom and France had also announced similar notice of acceptance in the same matter. The Tripartite Security Working Group, with its Army representation now consisting of Brig. Gen. J. H. Phillips, Deputy ACofS G-2, D/A, as Principal, and Col. John F. Schmelzer, newly appointed Chief of the SMI Branch as Alternate, then met successively in Washington, London, and Paris during the period from October to December 1952 to examine and judge at firsthand the progress stemming from this key international security of information agreement. The true significance of these meetings becomes well illustrated by the fact that they ultimately led to the military security arrangements that were adopted for NATO.

b. Eligibility of Foreign Representatives to Receive Classified Security Information- In compliance with a National Security Council (NSC) directive issued during November 1950, the security officials of the member agencies of the Interdepartmental Committee on Internal Security (ICIS) were finally able some two years later to agree upon a proposed list of procedures for determining the eligibility of individual representatives of foreign governments to receive US classified information. As recommended to the ICIS, each individual representative would be required to furnish an identification document, including a suitable photograph, for check by the FBI and other appropriate internal security agencies before any classified information could be given to him. While certain exceptions were authorized for high-ranking foreign diplomatic or consular personnel and invited guests of the American Government, the procedures were meant to apply fully to all Foreign Service Attaches. No definite action was taken by the ICIS on this touchy position, however, prior to the end of the Korean conflict period.

c. Security Agreement Between the Departments of Defense of the United States and New Zealand—In September 1952, the United States and New Zealand Department of Defense concluded an agreement with reference to taking coordinated measures for the security of their own military information. This agreement called for each De-partment to maintain military security classifi-cations based upon mutually approved criteria and to disclose classified information to other nationals only under regularly established rules and procedures.

d. Security Policy Toward the European Defense Community (EDC)—The signing of the EDC Treaty, in May 1952, posed a new and difficult security of information problem to the US authorities because the German Federal Republic, a non-NATO member, was included in it. Moreover, the treaty itself provided for the formation of an advance Interim Committee to get the EDC ready to function effectively just as soon as it had been ratified by the legislative bodies of the nations concerned and also activated a staff organization to commence immediate EDC military planning under the direct guidance of Supreme Headquarters, Allied Powers in Europe (SHAPE). In July 1952, therefore the ACofS G–2, D/A, forwarded a request to the State-

Defense Military Information Control Committee (S–DMICC) recommending the establishment of a temporary disclosure policy toward the EDC to be maintained strictly on a "need to know" basis. The S–DMICC then officially approved the disclosure of the US information classified as high as SECRET on that limited basis to the Interim Committee of the EDC, if such information was deemed necessary for accomplishing its defense planning objections.

e. Security Policy toward the German Federal Republic—With the advent of German participation in the European Defense Forces of EDC, it became clearly evident that West Germany would soon have to be included within the framework of the national disclosure policies being formulated by S-DMICC. Arrangements were thus made for a combined State-Defense team to visit West Germany during October 1952 and examine the security of information system currently in use therein. Published by the State Department on 3 December 1952, the report of this team expressed general satisfaction regarding the legal basis of West German security, a lesser satisfaction with the actual security of some of its governmental agencies, and no satisfaction at all with West German industrial security. On the other hand, because of the sound legal basis and strong will to achieve suitable information security it had observed in West Germany, the team felt that S-DMICC should "proceed with those measures which may be expected to bring about rapid improvements in the German security picture."

f. Security Policy Toward Japan—The establishment of an adequate policy covering the disclosure of US military information to Japan had been under active consideration ever since 1949. At that time, the Japanese Diet (legislature) had enacted a National Public Service Law, which provided stiff penalties for divulging government information and rendered members of the subversive organizations ineligible for government employment. This law, though, promptly came under heavy internal attack and was never firmly implemented. Nevertheless, in October 1951, the ACofS G-2, D/A, did recommend the adoption of a limited information disclosure policy toward Japan on an interim basis, and a course of action along those lines was duly approved by S-DMICC. With the Japanese passing of additional laws aimed at tightening their security producers in May and July 1952, the situation appeared to be clearing up but the country shortly experienced another serious political crisis. S–DMICC then decided to postpone any further action in the matter, at least until after this latest governmental crisis had been successfully resolved.

g. Executive Order 10290—Designed to establish basic standards throughout the Executive Branch of the Government for safeguarding information affecting the security of the United States, this EO became effective on 27 October 1951 and caused several changes in the current Army security regulations. It required, for example, that all information of such nature should be positively identified as "Security Information." Changes in AR 380-5 incorporating the minimum requirements of EO 10290 were published without delay, but a rewritten version thereof, covering the entire provisions of EO 10290, could not be prepared and issued until 6 June 1952.

Censorship Branch—Being primarily a planning group, this branch was seldom called upon to perform any actual operation or supervisory censorship functions. Its activities from 9 September 1951 through 31 December 1952 were, thus principally, as follows:

a. Civil Censorship—Although US policy had for some time been to encourage the unconditional abolishment of civil censorship throughout Austria, there was still a small island of it remaining in Vienna. The main reason for this anomaly was that the Soviet element within the Censorship Technical Committee of the quadpatriate Allied Council for Austria kept pressing for numerous "compromises," which were obviously calculated to assure Soviet control over all Austrian communications. It was felt best, therefore, to allow the original situation to continue unchanged.

b. National Censorship—As Executive Agent for the Secretary of Defense in connection with planning for the imposition of National Censorship, the Censorship Branch was required to monitor the active duty training of Army and Air Force Reserve Officers holding national censorship mobilization assignments. Arrangements were thus made to have appropriate training courses in censorship work conducted for these personnel at Fort Benning, Georgia, from 1-15 June 1952, and at the Presidio of San Francisco, California, from 16-30 June 1952. A special activities course was also given to selected censorship military reservists at Washington, DC, on methods of detecting messages written in code, cipher, or secret ink. Other important events relating to national censorship planning at this same time were the submission of a detailed staff study to the Secretary of Defense, which recommended the completion of needed censorship agreements with several Western Hemisphere countries and the initiation of coordinated planning between the Censorship Branch and all governmental agencies engaged in psychological warfare.

c. Armed Forces Censorship—Censorship activities within this field were centered mostly upon accomplishing the following three tasks:

1. Arranging for the training of censorship units at Fort Bragg, North Carolina.

2. Shipping the 1st Military Censorship Organization to EUSOM so it would be readily available there to open Armed Forces censorship in the event of hostilities.

3. Developing the Armed Forces Censorship Play for Exercise Long Horn, scheduled to be held at Fort Hood, Texas, during March-April 1952. This exercise not only uncovered a number of valuable indoctrination procedures but also furnished an excellent guide for the reassessment of previously accepted censorship personnel qualifications.[30]

The first mention of mail being received within the United States from American Prisoners of War held in North Korea or Red China was contained in a report forwarded to Washington by the ACofS G-2, Fifth Army, dated 5 April 1951. It stated that according to the Post S-2 at Camp Carson, Colorado, Mr. and Mrs. R. W. Wegner of Denver, Colorado, had recently received a letter from their POW son along with 23 other letters written by America's POWs in North Korean or Red Chinese prison camps. The Wegners had proceeded to remail the enclosed letters to the respective addresses shown on them, as requested. Shortly thereafter, the ACofS G-2, Second Army, took note of a similar report that 11 POW letters had been received at Mayfield, Kentucky, accompanied by the same sort of remailing instructions. This sudden POW mail influx plainly represented an integral part of a vigorous Communist psychological warfare offensive, which was also featuring anti-American propaganda disseminated through radio broadcasts, news organs, typical hate pamphlets, and undercover agents on a global basis.[31] The offensive undoubtedly aimed at gaining a cease-fire with complete exchange of all POWs for the Communist truce negotiations at Panmunjam, regardless of whether or not the North Korean or Red Chinese POWs in UN prison camps wished to be repatriated. As a matter of fact, a large number of these prisoners had actually signified a desire to refuse such repatriation and to remain on the Free World side of the Iron Curtain.[32]

In May 1951, the ACofS G-2, D/A, forwarded a summary sheet to the Chief of Staff on the subject of POW mail, the terms of which had already been discussed with the ACofS G-1, D/A, and the interested CIA, FBI, ONI, and Air Force Office of Intelligence (AFOIN) officials. It not only called attention to the favorable worldwide reaction that the publication of POW lists in Communist news organs was receiving but also pointed out that the Chinese were encouraging correspondence between selected POW's and their relatives within the United States for the obvious purpose of distributing Communist propaganda. The feeling was, therefore, that an appropriate explanatory statement should be devised and forwarded to the next of kin of American POWs, in order to offset any psychological warfare gains the Chinese may have achieved by releasing their POW lists in a seemingly forthright manner. The Communist propaganda drive then showed signs of becoming so increasingly successful that the departmental military security officials, during March 1952, joined with the CIA in preparing a plan for the censorship of all communica-tions, including POW mail, passing between the United States and the Chinese mainland. A series of representative conferences were soon held under Army G-2 sponsorship to inquire into the feasibility of establishing that type of censorship without further delay. On 11 August 1952, though, it was decided that two separate studies ought to be initiated in the matter, one to cover just the censorship of the POW mail problem and the other to explore "larger-scale censorship."[33]

Meanwhile, late in December 1951, the Chief of Staff had approved an intelligence project authorizing the ACofS G-2, FECOM, to read and microfilm prior to remailing, all POW mail turned over to the UN negotiators by the Communists during the truce talks, which were taking place at Panmunjam. Although most of the propaganda included in these letters was so specious that it could be considered dangerous, some of them did contain invidious remarks or potentially valuable military information, and they were sent directly to the ACofS G-2 to D/A for final review and disposition. This mail inspection effort promptly proved to be such a major drain on G-2 FECOM's limited personnel resources, however, that he was forced to request permission to discontinue it. In May 1952, General Bolling did grant permission for G-2 FECOM to cease examining by not microfilming the POW mail, and at the same time, forwarded a so-called "Watch List" to him presenting the names of seven officers and 24 enlisted men who had either given "definite evidence of Communist indoctrination" or were "suspects of successful indoctrination." Any letters received from them were to be placed at the beginning of the microfilm and after that handled in a special manner.[34] The Watch List, which was carefully kept up to date in accordance with the latest available information, then served to provided the initial indication to the departmental military intelligence authorities of the true nature and extent of the indoctrination being given to the UN POWs held by the Communists.[35]

With ACOofS G-2, D/A, having thus already embarked upon a program of seeking to collect as much information as possible about the Communist indoctrination of American POWs held in North Korea and Red China, that distressful subject suddenly became of serious national concern late in 1952, when the truce talks at Panmunjam gave distinct promise of yielding an agreement for the large-scale exchange of captured personnel from both sides. Since no firm policies had as yet been announced for handling such returnees, the Secretary of the Army, during January 1953, addressed a number of pertinent questions to the Secretary of Defense regarding the Communist employment of "brain washing" techniques on the US military personnel, in order to obtain proper guidance. Secretary Wilson's[36] reply dated 19 February 1953, first took note that the Department of the Army had a primary interest in the matter and then requested it to "develop immediate screening and deindoctrination procedures designed to both determine and overcome any adverse mental effects found to exist among personnel of any of the services who have been released or escaped from prisoner of war camps in Korea." He further asked the Department of the Army to supply the national Psychological Strategy Board with any data it managed to obtain from the screening of returned prisoners of war."[37]

Although the OACofS G-1, D/A, was designed to be the staff agency for monitoring the entire program involving the return and reassignment of the US POWs from Korea, now officially known as the "Returned or Exchanged Captured American Prisoners–Korea (RECAP-K) Program," the OACofS G-2, D/A, continued to remain fully aware of its own fundamental intelligence and security responsibilities in connection therewith. These responsibilities not only called for deriving all possible intelligence of tactical or strategic value from it but also collecting information on Communist indoctrination means and methods, which might serve as a basis for developing effective counter-measures.[38]

Having recently prepared detailed letters of instruction to CINCFE and the Commanding Generals of all Major Commands relative to the intelligence processing of RECAP-K personnel, which had first been carefully coordinated with G-1, G-3, G-4, Chief Psy-War, TAG, CINFO, and the Surgeon General, and then duly approved by the Chiefs of Staff, these letters were dispatched on 13 March 1953.[39] Shortly thereafter, Maj. Gen. (later Lt. Gen.) Robert N. Young, the ACofS G-1, D/A, appointed an ad hoc committee, composed of representatives from the Offices of the ACofS G-2, Surgeon General, Chief of Psychological Warfare and Chief of Information, to "study and prepare methods and procedures for deindoctrination of U.S. personnel" being returned from POW camps in North Korea or Red China. The proposed plan was to have the members of this committee assigned to Valley Forge General Hospital, Phoenixville, Pennsylvania, where they would be able to observe personnel suffering from Communist "brain washing" techniques and, after studying the problem, submit to the OACofS G-1, D/A, adequate deindoctrination procedures "for immediate use to overcome any adverse mental efforts found to exist among those present and recommend disposition in each case."[40]

It soon became imperative that some sort of a definite plan should be agreed upon by all concerned for handling returnees from Korea, because the initial exchange operation of captured personnel who were sick and wounded, subsequently known as "Little Switch," had already begun on 19 April 1953 and the American ex-POWs involved were scheduled to start to arrive by air at designated ports of debarkation in the Sixth Army Area within a few days. During a meeting held in the Office of the Chief of Staff on 20 April 1953, therefore, General Collins first asked several pointed questions in the matter and then approved an information seeking program calling for a preliminary interrogation at Valley Forge General Hospital or in the proper Continental Army area, depending principally upon the physical condition of the individual returnee concerned. It was also understood that when these returnees were finally discharged from the Army their respective security files would be turned over to the FBI if an additional investigation seemed indicated.[41]

Of the 149 American persons processed under this Operation "Little Switch," a total of 127 (three officers and 124 enlisted men) were from the Army. Only 21 of this total required special Army or FBI investigations but one person did turn out to be a "hard core" Communist and was eventually discharged without honor for "security reasons" in the Sixth Army Area.[42] It was however, most productive from the standpoint of collecting information for both future intelligence and counterintelligence use.[43]

The close of the Korean conflict period thus found the OACofS G-2, D/A, not only faced with an ever-mounting number of difficult military security problems but also right in the midst of conducting a highly sensitive counterintelligence operation that was fraught with disquieting implications. The most striking development of the entire period, though, had undoubtedly been the rapid growth of a vast personnel loyalty-security program, which demanded numerous and varied investigations by many different agencies before appropriate clearance could be granted for an individual to have access to certain classified information of the US Government. The inordinate growth of these investigative activities after the Korean outbreak becomes clearly apparent from the following table, designed to compare the average weekly load of security cases in six different categories handled within the Security Division, OACofS G-2, D/A, during the months of June 1950 and June 1951:

	1950	1951
Civilian Removal Recommendations	3	18
Military Discharge Recommendations	3	10
National Agency Checks	750	2000
FBI Loyalty Investigations	3	17
G-2 File Checks	5000	13250
CIC Investigations	940	2280[44]

One of the chief results of this huge expansion in counterintelligence activities during the first year of the Korean conflict period was to render the already difficult CIC personnel procurement problem almost insolvable. Although from June 1950 to August 1952 the total worldwide strength of the CIC did increase by approximately 1,200 enlisted men, it also decreased over the same period by 100 officers. Furthermore, most of the new enlisted men could only be hastily trained on an emergency basis and the existing qualification standards for CIC duty assignment had to be habitually lowered in order to procure them. This adverse personnel situation unquestionably contributed materially to the fact that the backlog of unfinished clearance cases kept getting larger and larger while the conflict progressed. The tremendous extent of that backlog seems aptly illustrated by a report forwarded from the CIC Center to the OACofS G-2, D/A, on 21 August 1952, giving the average number of personnel clearance cases completed per month within the ZI and Overseas Theaters, along with the companion backlog, during a nine-month period ending 31 March 1952, as follows:

Average number of ZI cases
closed per month 18,694

Average number of Overseas cases
closed per month 102,363

Average backlog of ZI cases
per month 28,441

Average backlog of Overseas cases
per month .... 61,428[45]

Not all of these listed investigative cases, of course, fell under the same category. Of a total caseload of 42,889 ZI cases current on 15 November 1952, for example, 25,301 were Background Investigations, 16,776 National Agency Checks, and 812 Complaint Type Investigations. The latter investigations were the least numerous by far but they represented the more serious cases and always required special handling. The bulk of the normal backlog was ordinarily made up of National Agency Checks, due to the large number of different agencies that had to be consulted before an individual clearance could be granted. Brig. Gen. P. E. Gallagher thus described the system then in use for that particular purpose, Chief CIC, at an Army Command Conference held in December 1952, as follows:

> *This National Agency Check, in brief, is initiated by the requesting agency or facility and is processed to the G-2 of the Army Area. From this office it is sent to the ACofS, G-2, Department of the Army, who, in addition to checking their own files, obtains a check from the FBI and the House Committee on Un-American Activities. When leads so indicate, the Office of Naval Intelligence, the Office of Special Investigation, Civil Service Commission, Central Intelligence Agency, State Department, and Bureau of Immigration and Naturalization are also checked. In many cases it has been found that a bottleneck often occurs, as far as time is concerned, in clearing a name through some of the National Agencies which I have outlined.*[46]

By the end of 1952, the number of investigative cases assigned to the CIC had finally commenced to decline, especially within the ZI. The effort was still a major undertaking, however, and, on 31 December 1952, the CIC called for the full services of a total of 7,030 persons, including the 1,428 officers, 384 warrant officers, 4,622 enlisted men and 596 civilians. At that time, the caseload status of all CIC investigations for the past six months was officially estimated to be, as follows:

Personnel Security Investigations
Pending 1 July 52 21,677
Opened these 6 mos. 50,420
Closed these 6 mos. 44,611
Pending 31 December 52 27,486

Contractor Personnel and Facility Clearance Investigation
Pending 1 July 52 5,739
Opened these 6 mos. 13,123
Closed these 6 mos. 11,286
Pending 31 December 52 7,576

Other Personnel Investigatins
Pending 1 July 52 20,273
Opened these 6 mos. 37,848
Closed these 6 mos. 40,386
Pending 31 December 52 17,735

Counterintelligence Investigations
Pending 1 July 52. 1,898
Opened these 6 mos. 6,529
Closed these 6 mos. 7,080
Pending 31 December 52 1,347

All other types of Investigations
Pending 1 July 52 8,689
Opened these 6 mos. 43,726
Closed these 6 mos. 45,203
Pending 31 December 52 7,212

Grand Total
Pending 1 July 52 58,276
Opened these 6 mos. 151,646
Closed these 6 mos. 148,566
Pending 31 Decembers 52 .... 62,356[47]

The military security function was intimately connected in a great many different ways during the Korean conflict period with the intelligence training effort. Training considerations were not only an important influence in limiting the prompt execution of all CIC investigations but also represented a controlling factor in proper development of such basic counterintelligence measures as censorship, industrial security, and the security of military information. Since there were not nearly enough intelligence specialists on hand at the opening of the conflict to satisfy the sudden demands of a major Army expansion, in most cases they had to be immediately procured regardless of established qualification standards and then hastily trained on the job. Unfortunately, the matter of agency or staff responsibility for supervising the conduct of intelligence training remained so obscurely drawn that training along those lines was often badly neglected.

The Communist Party and Soviet Intelligence

Soviet intelligence activities in the United States apparently began in 1919 when Ludwig Martens, a Russian-born communist residing in the United States, assumed the mantle of representative of the new revolutionary Soviet government. The United States, like most other nations at the time, did not extend diplomatic recognition to the regime that had in effect, declared war on other nation states and called for violent revolution to overthrow the existing order. The attitude of the United States, like most other states at the time, was generally hostile. It must be remembered that it seemed that the worldwide convulsion that the Soviet Government called for was in fact a real possibility.

In the period following World War I, Marxist revolutions and leftist agitation that spread to virtually all countries shook Europe and the United States. The Soviet Government had established an organization known as the Comintern to coordinate and direct revolutionary movements and communist parties around the world. It is against this historical backdrop that Marten's activities must be viewed.

In the absence of diplomatic relations, which extended to 1933, the Soviets operated unofficially through envoys like Martens and Amtorg, a corporation that ostensibly was to facilitate US–Soviet trade. At this time, around 1920, espionage against the United States was not the highest priority of the Soviet intelligence apparatus. The activities of Russian anti-Communist expatriates, operating primarily from European nations, especially France, commanded their interest. However, the United States did not escape the attention of the Soviet leadership as a valuable target for their intelligence services. Lenin had specifically directed that the intelligence arms of the Soviet state function in the United States.

Probably the first identified Soviet intelligence officer operating in the United States was Arthur Adams, who was described officially as director of the unofficial embassy's "technical department." Adams was deeply involved with the theft of American technology and would appear periodically in the United States over the next 30 years. Both Adams and Martens were deported in 1920 as aliens affiliated with an organization that advocated the overthrow by force or violence of the Government of the United States.

It is important to describe the beginnings of the American Communist Party (CPUSA) that was developing at the same time as the Soviet espionage apparatus in the United States. The CPUSA was founded in 1919 in Chicago and was an outgrowth of the Socialist Party, founded in 1900. The early CPUSA was noteworthy for several reasons, among them was the fact that the overwhelming majority of members were foreign born and did not speak English. Most of the early members were Russian or emigrants from other Eastern European nations, and a large number also were Jews.

Nick Dozenberg

From its earliest beginning, the party was wracked by severe divisions. Some were ideological, and some were linguistic. Another aspect of the party was its slavish devotion to Moscow. The CPUSA never deviated from the Moscow line at any time in its history.

In 1920 with the CPUSA badly divided, the Comintern, acting as sort of a referee, dispatched functionaries with orders to the party to reunite. At a series of secret meetings, the different wings of the party were fused into one organization. During the early 1920s, the party apparatus was to a great extent underground, with a small legal aboveground element, the Workers Party.

As the Red Scare and deportations of the early 1920s ebbed, the party became bolder and more open. By 1930 it adopted the title Communist Party, USA. However, an element of the party remained underground permanently. It was through this underground party, often commanded by a Soviet official operating as an illegal in the United States, that Soviet intelligence coopted CPUSA members.

The Soviet intelligence apparatus, which was introduced into the United States around the same time as the CPUSA was founded, maintained intimate relations with the party from the start. The CPUSA provided a ready pool of eager volunteers, anxious to be of service to the revolutionary state. Party members such as Nick Dozenberg found themselves assigned to Soviet intelligence by party leaders. Usually, when this occurred, the party member was instructed not to engage in open party work or associations.

By the mid to late 1920s, there were three elements of Soviet power operating in the United States, despite the absence of formal diplomatic relations. They were the Comintern, military intelligence, and the forerunner of the KGB, the GPU. It appears that during the early 1920s, the Comintern was the dominant arm of service in the United States, although it was not unusual at that time for agents or officers to be switched from one service to another.

What was US counterintelligence doing? After the Red Scare collapsed in 1924, the Department of Justice and its investigative arm, the Bureau of Investigation, declined to investigate "radicalism." The US military intelligence services, ONI and MID, to a certain extent filled the void, but these organizations were poorly funded after the war and not able to counter the scope of activities of the Soviets in the United States. The US State Department was investigating international communism and also had jurisdiction over investigations of passport fraud. However, there was no central direction or focus to countering or investigating Soviet espionage during the 1920s and early 1930s. As a result, the Soviets had almost free run for about 12 years before the FBI was given the task again of monitoring Communist and Fascist activities in the United States.

The fact is that few Americans had any awareness of the existence of Soviet espionage in the United States and would have been shocked if such a thing were to be made known. At that time, no state openly admitted engaging in peacetime spying, which was considered disreputable and underhanded.

During the 1920s, Soviet intelligence in the United States focused on industry, specifically the aircraft and munitions industries, and to penetrating the mainline federal government bureaucracies such as the Departments of State and War. A favorite Soviet tactic in gathering intelligence on US industry was to exploit the desire of US firms to do business in Russia.

A Soviet representative would call on an American business and dangle the possibility of a lucrative contract with the USSR. However, the Soviets would insist on extensive plant inspections prior to actually signing a contract. After numerous visits and inspections by Soviet representatives, actually intelligence officers, some excuse for not doing business would be found. By then the Soviets would have extracted whatever technical information they were seeking. This tactic was repeated scores of times over the 1920s.

Another success of Soviet military intelligence in the United States was obtaining of the complete plans of the British warship, *Royal Oak,* from the Navy Department. The Soviets recruited an American, Robert Switz, as an agent, along with a US Army corporal, Robert Osman. The two provided US military information to the GRU. Osman was tried in 1933 for illegal possession of secret documents relating to national defense. He was convicted, but the conviction was overturned on appeal.

The role of Amtorg (a Soviet trading company) in Soviet intelligence operations was first revealed in 1929 by the first senior Soviet intelligence officer to defect to the West. Using the name George Agabekov, he had served in Turkey in the GPU residency. After his defection he wrote, "The first GPU resident in the U.S. was Tschatzky. As there was no Soviet diplomatic representation in the US, he was known as an employee of Amtorg...."

The case of William Disch alerted some in the United States to what the Soviets were doing behind the doors of Amtorg in New York. A US Navy defense contractor working on fire-control mechanisms employed Disch as a draftsman. An Amtorg employee who called himself Mr. Herb approached Disch. Herb told Disch that he was willing to pay two thousand dollars a year, a considerable sum in 1931, for classified information on the fire-control apparatus. Disch informed the company what had transpired and Naval Intelligence conducted a surveillance of meetings between Disch and Herb, who was identified as Moshe Stern, alias Mark Zilbert, of Amtorg. Eventually, Stern broke contact with Disch, but no legal proceedings against Herb or Stern were forthcoming.

The decade of the 1930s saw a dramatic increase in activities of both the Soviet intelligence apparatus in the United States and the CPUSA. There were several factors at work that gave impetus to both phenomena. The economic depression, which gripped the industrial world, seemed to bear out Marxist predictions of the impending collapse of capitalism. Many American intellectuals embraced Marxism as the inevitable wave of the future. The international scene also worked to the Communists' favor. The rise of Fascist and Nazi dictatorships seemed threatening to many, and the anti-Semitic nature of both regimes seemed to many Jewish Americans cause to defend the interests of the USSR, and by extension, the CPUSA.

Another boost to Soviet prestige, and also to Soviet intelligence in the United States, was the establishment of diplomatic relations in 1933. At last the Soviet intelligence organs in the United States could function under the protection and cover of diplomatic immunity. At the time, the United States had no real intelligence service operating in Moscow, other than a few military attachés. Aside from the embassy in Washington, the Soviets also established consulates in several large cities, including San Francisco and New York.

The relationship between the CPUSA and the Soviet espionage apparatus is best illustrated by the examples of Elizabeth Bentley and Whittaker Chambers.[48] Both cases exemplify the success the CPUSA, and by extension the Soviet espionage services, had in attracting bright, well educated native born Americans to do their bidding.

Whittaker Chambers was a remarkable intellectual. He had translated the German novel *Bambi* into English. As a result of his literary ability, Chambers was named editor of the Communist party magazine, *New Masses*. Chambers was approached by Max Bedacht, chief of the party's underground arm, and instructed to enter underground work himself. He was told to leave the overt party and report directly to Bedacht. Chambers main function in the underground was as a courier, bringing material Soviet agents had procured to Soviet intelligence officers.

Chambers joined the party in 1924, left in 1929 after a factional dispute, and returned a year later. He left the party and its underground apparatus for good in 1938. For years he tried to alert the American public about the activities of Soviet intelligence and the CPUSA without success. Finally, in 1948 he was given a serious hearing when he testified before Congress about Soviet espionage and its use of CPUSA members as assets.

In 1938, the year Whittaker Chambers left his underground service to the Soviets, Elizabeth Bentley joined. Bentley had entered the Communist Party(CP) in 1935. She had joined a CP front group, the American League Against War and Fascism in New York, and was soon brought into the party proper. She was introduced to Jacob Golos, a high-level CPUSA official, who became both her lover and her supervisor in espionage activities. Bentley later testified that she served as a courier for two Soviet spy rings operating in the federal government in Washington and that she turned documents gathered by the agents over to Golos, who provided them to Soviet officers. Golos also was head of an organization called *World Tourists*, which while posing as a travel agency actually facilitated international travel to and from the United States by

Soviet agents and CPUSA members. World Tourists was also deeply involved in passport fraud. In 1940, Golos had specifically named for her the three branches of Soviet espionage operating in the United States as military intelligence, the Comintern, and the United State Political Directorate (OGPU).

In her testimony before Congress in 1948, Bentley named scores of Americans working for Soviet intelligence. She described two rings of spies of federal employees in Washington including penetrations of OSS, the State Department, and other agencies. She also indicated that most of the members of the rings were CPUSA members.

Hede Massing, an Austrian-born Soviet intelligence operative who served in the U.S. in the 1930s, provided another window into Soviet espionage in the United States at that time. Massing was a member of an OGPU apparatus and functioned under the direction of a Soviet illegal officer based in New York. Massing was assigned several duties, including that of a courier between the United States and Europe. However, her most important assignment was that of an agent recruiter, a task she apparently carried out with great skill. Massing was assigned targets for recruitment by her Soviet supervisor. She used appeals to ideology, especially preying on the strong anti-Nazi sentiments of New Deal liberals who dominated the Washington scene of the Roosevelt administration in the early 1930s. Massing left the Soviet intelligence apparatus in 1938 after a period of disillusionment with her Russian handlers. She provided a detailed resume of her activities to the FBI in the late 1940s.

As mentioned above, the FBI had virtually ceased investigations of subversive and "Communist" activity after 1924. Although J. Edgar Hoover never wavered in his distrust of American Communists or their Soviet comrades, he was aware that he had no political backing or support for launching a sustained campaign of investigation and scrutiny of the CPUSA or foreign communists and subversives in the United States.

This changed with the election of Franklin Roosevelt in 1932. With the international scene degrading, Roosevelt had become concerned with the threat of domestic subversion and fifth columnists in the United States Roosevelt made his first request for assistance on domestic subversion to Hoover in 1933. In 1936 the White House instructed the FBI to provide systematic intelligence about subversive activities in the United States, particularly Nazism and Communism. That request from Roosevelt to Hoover on August 25, 1936 was the basis for more than 40 years of investigative and proactive actions against the CPUSA and their Soviet allies. Hoover created in the mid-1930s a division for overseeing domestic intelligence that overshadowed any other peacetime effort in American history.

The United States now had a permanent, civilian investigative authority with responsibility for looking into treasonable actions by American citizens. This is significant, because prior to this a violation of law was necessary to trigger an FBI investigation. Now, under the new operating procedures, American citizens who had not violated any law could be subject to wiretapping, mail cover, and other investigative techniques by the FBI.

In a memorandum to then Attorney General Homer Cummings, Hoover wrote that the new General Intelligence Division was to "collect through investigative activity and other contact, and to correlate for ready reference information dealing with various forms of activities of either subversive or so-called intelligence type." The Bureau already had on file identities of some 2,500 persons suspected of communist or Nazi activities, including espionage. It is interesting to note that the financing of this expansion of the FBI's span of activities was not reported to Congress, but put under the "cover" of a continuation of a request from the Secretary of State to investigate foreign-based subversion.

In 1938, Germany annexed Austria, which heightened international tensions. In the United States, there arose demands from Congress and the public for increased vigilance against spies and saboteurs. In May of that year, Congressman Martin Dies called upon the house to organize a committee to investigate foreign "isms" which threatened America. The House Committee on un-American Activities (HUAC) was established. In October 1938, Hitler moved into Czechoslovakia, and the FBI established new facilities for "specialized training in general intelligence work." In June 1939 President Roosevelt issued a directive allocating intelligence responsibilities between the military services and the FBI, giving the FBI the Western Hemisphere.

After Hitler's invasion of Poland in September 1939, Roosevelt declared a state of emergency. Hoover appeared before the House appropriations committee and told the public what the FBI had been doing quietly since 1936. He revealed that what was now called the General Intelligence Division had compiled extensive dossiers on "individuals, groups and organizations engaged in subversive activities that are possibly detrimental to the internal security of the US."

This investigative mandate was somewhat ambiguous and could be interpreted broadly. In practice it meant the FBI could investigate groups who might come under subversive influence.

In 1940, Congress passed the Smith Act making the advocacy of overthrowing the US Government a federal crime. It also outlawed groups or organizations that advocated such an overthrow, and membership in such a group was also made a crime. However, officials in the Justice Department did not approve of the law, and little use was made of it until after WWII.

During the war years of 1941–45, the enemies were clearly Germany, Japan, and Italy. The focus of the FBI's domestic security program naturally was on the activities of those nations. The American Communist Party followed obediently its directions from Moscow and were kept in line by the Comintern representative in the United States Gerhart Eisler, former husband of Soviet spy Hede Massing.

After the invasion of the USSR by Germany in June 1941, the Soviets urged the CPUSA to agitate for US intervention in the war to save the USSR. This was a reversal of position for the American Communists, who had opposed any potential intervention after the 1939 Hitler-Stalin pact.

The Japanese attack on Pearl Harbor in December 1941 was greeted with joy by the CPUSA, which foresaw salvation for the USSR, by the US declaration of war against Germany and Japan. From this point on, the American Communist Party engaged in what was known as the "united front" effort.

This meant, at least publicly, dropping anti-American rhetoric and actions. Strikes in defense-related sectors were discouraged. However, Soviet espionage and the CPUSA's role in supporting those activities never was suspended, even though the American Communist Party went through the charade of disbanding and renaming itself the Communist Political Association. Now, the motivation for participating in espionage was "fighting fascism."

Since the resumption of the FBI's domestic security program in the mid-1930s, the CPUSA was an obvious target, and the Bureau had infiltrated a number of informers and agents into the party. As a result, the FBI obtained a good view of the party's internal structure and also its divisions and weaknesses, which could be exploited. With the advent of World War II and the FBI's attention primarily on the Axis targets in the United States and Latin America, the focus of counterintelligence shifted away from the CPUSA. However, even during the war, the FBI maintained a watch on the party and Soviet espionage.

Work begun on decryption of Soviet intelligence cable traffic during World War II and eventually led to the identification of Soviet espionage agents and activities after the war.[49] After the end of World War II, the alliance between the United States and USSR quickly faded.

The CPUSA reconstituted itself and resumed its strident pro-Moscow anti-US stance. The era of the united front was over. On Moscow's orders, the head of the CPUSA, Earl Browder, was dumped. His crime had been to follow Moscow's orders in 1941 and "disband" the party in a show of unity with the US Government. Now, that policy was in disrepute, and he had to go. The Soviet Union's actions in Eastern Europe in establishing subservient puppet regimes increased

Igor Gouzenko

tensions with the United States Communism was becoming a potent domestic political issue.

Public concern over the Communist threat to national security increased as a result of several high-profile incidents during the late 1940s. One was the defection in Ottawa of GRU cipher clerk Igor Gouzenko in 1945.[50] Gouzenko provided for the astonished Canadian Government proof of an extensive espionage operation directed from the Soviet embassy in the Canadian capital. He also provided the identities of Canadian citizens working for Soviet intelligence. His naming of the distinguished physicist Allan Nunn May as a Soviet spy had the greatest impact and not just in Canada.

Gouzenko had revealed that the Soviets had been engaged in a sustained effort, involving scores of agents from different nations, in obtaining information about the atomic bomb. Gouzenko's information led directly to the arrest and conviction of several Canadian and British citizens who had been working for the Soviets. But more importantly was the impact on public opinion of his revelations of Soviet spying and local communist party participation in that activity. Canadian public opinion was angered, particularly because Canada had been a close supportive ally of the USSR during the war, and a great deal of sympathy for the Soviet Union existed in Canada.

Now Gouzenko revealed that during the war years both the GRU and NKVD had been active in subverting Canadians. As naive as it seems now, Canadians were shocked that such intrigue had been practiced on their soil by a wartime ally. Overnight the popularity and prestige both of the USSR and the Canadian Communist party suffered. The information provided by Gouzenko was a windfall for the Canadian Royal Candian Mounted Police (RCMP) security service as well as MI5 and the FBI, with whom Gouzenko's information was shared. Gouzenko's information about Soviet atomic espionage dovetailed with other indications from different sources about soviet atomic syping.

Despite the publicity generated by Gouzenko's defection, and the HUAC testimony of Bentley-Chambers, by 1948 there had not been a conviction of an American for espionage on behalf of the USSR in any major spy case. This was especially frustrating for FBI agents working Soviet espionage, because they knew the identities of scores of Americans who had spied for the Russians. They simply lacked the evidence needed for prosecution.

All of that was to change dramatically when Soviet NKVD and GRU message traffic from the United States. to Moscow and back began to yield concrete results by 1948. FBI agent Robert Lamphere, working with Army Security Agency cryptologist Meredith Gardner, had made a major break in identifying members of what later became known as the Rosenberg ring.

The first major case to break from the decryption effort involved Judith Coplon. Coplon, an employee of the Department of Justice, had also been identified by the NKVD-GRU traffic. The Coplon case was tricky for the FBI, because Coplon, by virtue of her position at Justice, had access to many sensitive FBI investigative reports, many of which dealt with Soviet espionage. Intensive surveillance of Coplon revealed she was meeting with a Soviet attached to the United Nations in New York named Gubichev.

After observing her pattern of meeting with her Soviet controller during trips ostensibly to visit her mother in New York, a plan to catch her "in the act" was planned by SA Lamphere and approved by Attorney General Tom Clark. A phony document was prepared and allowed to pass across her desk dealing with Soviet espionage. The assumption was that she would attempt to pass the document to Gubichev on her next trip to New York.

When Coplon traveled to New York, shortly after receiving the bogus report, her meeting with the Soviet was observed by massive FBI coverage. She was

Allen Nunn May

arrested, along with Gubichev, and charged with espionage. However, only she went to trial in the spring of 1949. Coplon was convicted; the evidence against her based primarily on the FBI produced document. The Soviet cable traffic, which had identified her, was not mentioned in court. Coplon's attorneys successfully appealed for a second trial, and she was again convicted. However, the second conviction was thrown out on appeal based on the fact that a warrant had not been issued for Coplon's arrest and the use of wiretaps in the investigation. She was not retried, and went free.

The investigation into Coplon's background revealed a familiar trail. She had graduated from Barnard College, had been active in leftwing causes, and had joined the Young Communist League, a CPUSA front organization. She was a graduate student in international relations, writing a thesis on Soviet economic planning. The VENONA message traffic dealing with Coplon had also mentioned two other female acquaintances of hers that she had recommended for recruitment. One of the women, Flora Wovschin, graduated from Barnard with Coplon and also was a member of the Young Communist League. Wovschin had married a Soviet Amtorg employee and moved with him to Russia. Wovshin's parents then heard from her in 1949 that she had divorced. In cryptic language, she apparently hinted she was headed for China where the Communists had just triumphed. Later, the Wovshcins were informed that Flora had died. FBI agent Lamphere stated in his book, *The FBI-KGB War*, that he believed Flora Wovschin had died serving the communists in the Korean war.

On September 23, 1949, President Harry Truman announced that the USSR had exploded an atomic device. This was to have a drastic impact on US national security policy. US intelligence knew the Soviets were working on the bomb but believed the Russians were years behind the Americans. Immediately, the FBI attempted to determine to what extent had the Soviet's success been attributable to espionage. Following the Coplon case, the Army Security Agency, the forerunner of NSA, made major strides in decrypting Soviet messages. Newly decrypted material indicated the presence of a British spy in the Manhattan project. The FBI, working with MI5, identified a German expatriate physicist named Klaus Fuchs[51] as a suspect.

A look at Fuch's background indicated that he had been a member of the German Communist party and had fled Germany when the Nazis took over. Under questioning by MI5, Fuchs confessed to passing secrets of the Manhattan Project to Soviet intelligence while in the United States.

MI5, working with the FBI on the atom spy series, allowed FBI agents to interview Fuchs. Information Fuchs provided led to the arrest of Fuch's American courier, known as "Raymond," and later identified as Harry Gold.[52] It was the Gold arrest that led to a series of spy investigations, including the biggest FBI espionage case to date.

Under questioning, Gold cracked and named another American spy he had serviced as a courier at the US atomic center at Los Alamos, New Mexico. The FBI identified the second spy as David Greenglass,[53] who was also described in the VENONA message traffic. Greenglass was arrested and quickly confessed. He agreed to full cooperation with the FBI on the condition that his wife not be prosecuted. The Department of Justice agreed.

Greenglass implicated his brother-in-law, Julius Rosenberg,[54] as his accomplice. Greenglass's sister, Ethel, also was named as a witting member of the conspiracy. Other names were dragged in also, such as Morton Sobell, who fled to Mexico after the Rosenbergs were arrested. The backgrounds of the accused were remarkably similar. All were second-generation Americans of Jewish descent. All became active in left wing politics at an early age, and all had either joined the CPUSA or one of its front groups.

Several VENONA messages referred to the Rosenbergs but they were not used at their trial. Under interrogation, the Rosenbergs denied their involvement in espionage and their membership in the CPUSA. Greenglass described Julius Rosenberg as the hub of a wheel of Soviet espionage and his main contact and conduit to the Soviets other than Gold. It was through his brother-in-law, Julius, that Greenglass initiated his espionage.

The Rosenberg trial began in March 1951. Charged with espionage were Julius and Ethel Rosenberg and Morton Sobell. Testifying against them were David

Greenglass and Harry Gold. The Rosenbergs were unable to refute the detailed testimony of the defense witnesses and were found guilty. Sobell was sentenced to 30 years for being a coconspirator although his part in the conspiracy was never as clear as the Rosenbergs. Both Julius and Ethel Rosenberg were sentenced to death.

At the time of the Rosenberg trial, the United States was fighting a Communist army in Korea, Eastern Europe had fallen under Soviet domination, and the United States had lost its nuclear monopoly. The Rosenbergs were seen as willing agents of a sinister worldwide conspiracy to destroy the United States. After nearly two years of unsuccessful appeals, the Rosenbergs were executed in 1953. In the meantime, they had become a cause celebre for the Communist movement around the world. The Rosenbergs became martyr figures, victims of anti-Semitic and anti-Communist hysteria in the United States.

During the FBI's interrogation of Harry Gold, he provided insight into the communist espionage apparatus in the United States going back nearly 15 years. Gold, like the Rosenbergs and Sobell, was the offspring of Russian Jewish immigrants. Although young Gold did not join the Communist Party, he, like his parents, was a strong believer in Socialism. Gold thought that "progressive" Russia was the one place in the world where there was no anti-Semitism.

Gold stated that his supervisor at an industrial solvent plant had recruited him into espionage for the Soviet Union in 1935 where Gold worked as a chemist. The supervisor, named Black, provided industrial secrets to the Soviets. He had recruited Gold on ideological and ethnic grounds, appealing to Gold's Jewish identification, playing to an appeal that the USSR was the refuge for world Jewry. Black was a member of the CPUSA and pressured Gold to join.

Gold stated that the Soviets paid his tuition to study chemical engineering at Xavier and Cincinnati Universities in Ohio. He revealed the identities of several American spies and their Soviet handlers. One American named by Gold was Alford Dean Slack, also a chemist. Slack confessed to the FBI that he had provided military and industrial secrets to the Soviets. Slack was convicted of espionage and sentenced to 15 years in prison. However, Black was not prosecuted.

Another Soviet agent fingered by Gold was an industrial chemist named Abraham Brothman. Brothman had provided the Soviets with industrial secrets for years. Brothman and Gold had briefly been business associates and had fallen out. Gold had also been a courier for Brothman. Gold named others who were beyond the reach of the law having fled the United States when the arrests began. Names such as Barr[55] and Katz would haunt FBI investigators for years.

The Rosenberg executions brought to a close an era in US domestic security. The interlocking efforts of the Soviet intelligence services and the American Communist Party throughout the 1920s and 1930s had resulted in the establishment of significant penetrations into American Government and industry. The absence of a serious, sustained US counterintelligence presence from 1924–36 gave almost free reign to those forces. The total lack of public awareness of the problem exacerbated the situation.

This changed during the 1950s. The FBI's counterintelligence program, born in the mid-1930s, began to mature and by 1950 had a real effect on the opposition. The FBI's penetrations of the CPUSA, along with prosecutions under the Smith Act, inhibited the CPUSA. Finally, public awareness of the Soviet espionage threat increased dramatically with the Rosenberg and Coplon trials, the HUAC testimony of ex-Communists like Bentley and Chambers, and the trials of CPUSA members. The exposure of several Soviet espionage rings caused the Soviets to retrench and rethink their spy strategy in the United States.

In 1952 a directive was issued from KGB and GRU Headquarters in Moscow. Soviet intelligence services were directed to avoid utilization of local communist parties for espionage, unless specific permission was granted from Headquarters for such utilization. An era was over.

As the 1950s progressed, the CPUSA was battered by events. The revelations of Stalin's crimes by Khrushchev and the invasion of Hungary in 1956 stunned the Communist faithful. The ability of the Soviets to recruit capable, motivated spies in the United States to work on the basis of ideology decreased dramatically. From the mid-1950s on, spying by American citizens became almost exclusively a mercenary vocation.

This development, along with the FBI's increasing sophistication in countering Soviet intelligence, resulted in increased reliance on illegals in the United States. The capture of Rudolf Abel[56] in 1957 opened a window on these operations.

Whittaker Chambers and Alger Hiss

According to former KGB Col. Oleg Gordievsky, the KGB assigned a comparatively low priority to gathering intelligence within the United States until the late 1930s. At that time, however, several influential underground CPUSA cells maintained varying degrees of contact with Comintern and Soviet intelligence officers. Gordievsky stated that the first main link between the party underground and the Soviet Service was Whittaker Chambers.

Whittaker Chambers exemplified the success the communist movement had in the United States during the 1930s in recruiting some of the best minds in a generation to the task of ultimately serving the Soviet Union. Chambers was a remarkable intellectual, translating Felix Salten's novel, *Bambi*, from German. By his mid-twenties, Chambers was a committed Marxist and party member. Disillusionment with the Great Depression and the seeming inability of the democracies to remedy the situation, along with the rise of Nazism and Fascism in Europe, were among the factors driving Chambers and other like-minded idealists toward the Communist's corner. Revelations about the savage repression of the Kulaks and real and imaginary opponents of Stalin were in the future.

Because of Chamber's literary abilities, he was made editor of the party magazine, *New Masses*. Later, he was named to the editorial staff of the Party newspaper, *The Daily Worker*. At this time, 1930, Chambers was instructed by the party to cease all contacts with the overt party organization, including the newspaper where he was working. He was to join the party underground apparatus that existed parallel to the overt party.

Chambers then underwent an intensive tutorial in espionage tradecraft. In 1933, he was sent to Moscow for intelligence training and when he returned to the United States, his main controller was Sandor Goldberger, also known as "J. Peters," a former Comintern apparatchik who then worked for the Fourth Department. Starting in 1934, Chambers was assigned duty as a courier, servicing Communist party cells in Washington and New York, which were providing classified and sensitive information that was passed to Soviet intelligence. Harold Ware, a Communist official in the Department of Agriculture, who died in an automobile accident in 1935, founded the Washington cell.

One important source handled by Chambers was Alger Hiss. Hiss was then a rising young star in the FDR administration, and he not only was a source of information, but in the future would be in a position to influence US policy.

In April 1938, Chambers deserted the party and its underground machine and broke all contact with Soviet intelligence. Close observation of the CPUSA and its leadership had soured him on what had seemed earlier to be the solution to the nation's and the world's problems. For a time he feared assassination by Soviet intelligence and hid.

He tried to alert the authorities to Communist penetration of the government, but was brushed aside. His first attempt came on 2 September 1939 when he agreed to tell his story to Assistant Secretary of State Adolf Berle, who was also President Roosevelt's internal security advisor. Berle and others advised the President that his administration was penetrated by Soviet intelligence but Roosevelt appeared to dismiss the idea.

Even the FBI refused to take Chamber's allegations seriously. It was not until 1945, after revelations by others of Communist subversion of the US Government, that Chambers was given credence. In 1945 he was exhaustively debriefed by the FBI and in 1948 was asked

Whittaker Chambers

to testify before the House un-American Activities Committee (HUAC).

Chambers told HUAC that, when he made his first courier run to Washington in 1934, he discovered an underground spy apparatus already operating. Its leader was Nathan Witt, and the net had seven members, each of whom headed an underground cell of Communist agents. Ware had established this network, which was composed of persons who had first been recruited into Marxist study groups and then into the CPUSA. Each of these agents not only provided classified documents to Soviet intelligence, but was involved in political influence operations as well.

His testimony, along with that of Elizabeth Bentley, another ex- Soviet spy, created a sensation. Among the most explosive allegations was his naming of Alger Hiss as a member of a spy ring. Hiss by this time had been a high-ranking State Department officer and foreign policy advisor for President Truman, as he had been for FDR.

Chambers said that Hiss assisted in recruiting new people into the apparatus. One such successful recruitment, who worked in the State Department, was Noel Field. Hedda Massing recruited Field and his wife Herta. Knowing about the Fields' fear about the advance of Nazi Germany, Massing played on that fear as the basis for their recruitment. The Comintern apparatus ordered Field to leave his position at the Department of State and join the International Labor Organization in Geneva, Switzerland. During World War II, Field became affiliated with the Office of Strategic Services and was in direct contact with its Bern Chief, Allen Dulles.

Field remained loyal to the Soviets and maintained contact with Communist underground operatives in Nazi-occupied Europe on behalf of Soviet intelligence. He fled to Communist Hungary when his espionage activities became known to the West and spent years in Hungarian prison cells and torture chambers. He was freed from prison in 1961 but never lost his commitment to his Communist beliefs.[57]

During Chamber's extensive testimony before Congress, he had not accused any members of the group of espionage. He was attempting to protect Alger Hiss and other members of the ring, whom he hoped, had also broken with the Soviets. Chambers told the Committee that the purpose of the entire Communist network was initially not for espionage but to infiltrate the government and influence government policy by placing Communists in key positions.

Hiss denied all charges, and after Chambers repeated his allegations against Hiss on a network news interview, Hiss sued for libel. Before that could happen, Hiss was indicted for perjury by a New York federal grand jury, which charged that he had lied under oath while testifying in an inquiry involving Soviet espionage. In that testimony, Hiss had stated that he had never known Whittaker Chambers or had any relationship with him. Hiss was convicted after a second trial. The most damning evidence against him was an old typewriter that he had once owned. FBI forensic experts testified that Hiss's typewriter had produced classified documents, which had been in the possession of Chambers. These documents had been hidden on Chamber's farm in a hollowed out pumpkin, thus the name "pumpkin papers." Also damaging Hiss's credibility was the testimony of a former maid in his household who stated that Chambers had been a frequent visitor to the Hiss home, and the two appeared to have been friends.

Hiss had many defenders, including President Truman, who referred to the case against Hiss as a "red herring." Hiss never admitted his guilt and proclaimed

Alger Hiss

his innocence throughout his life. Hiss died at age 92 on 15 November 1996 at Lenox Hill Hospital in Manhattan.

Other Soviet agents in the apparatus named by Chambers included:

    John J. Abt–Department of Agriculture; Works Progress Administration; Senate Committee on Education and Labor; Justice Department.

    Henry H. Collins – National Recovery Administration; Department of Agriculture.

    Donald Hiss–State Department; Labor Department.

    Charles Kramer–National Labor Relations Board; Office of Price Administration; Senate Subcommittee of War Mobilization.

    Victor Perlo–Office of Price Administration; War Production Board; Treasury Department.

    Lee Pressman–Department of Agriculture; Works Progress Administration; General Counsel of the Congress of Industrial Organizations; a leading figure in Henry Wallace's presidential campaign.

    Harold Ware–Department of Agriculture.

    Nathan Witt–Department of Agriculture; National Labor Relations Board.[58]

Elizabeth Bentley

Elizabeth Bentley, like Whittaker Chambers and Alger Hiss, spied for the Soviet Union out of ideological conviction. Like Hiss and Chambers, Bentley was well educated (Vassar) and a native-born American. She became a convert to Communism during the heyday of Communist influence (and Soviet intelligence success) during the 1930s. A visit to Europe in the mid-1930s had filled Bentley with a dread of Nazism, and she became convinced, with the help of a Communist friend, that only the Soviet Union was standing up to the Nazis. She joined the party and in 1938 was assigned to the party underground. Also like Chambers, her primary duty was as a courier, servicing Soviet spy rings in Washington and New York.

Bentley's handler was Jacob Golos, (real name: Jacob Rasin). The Russian born Golos was a high-ranking member of the American Communist Party, a former Bolshevik revolutionary and Soviet secret police operative in the USSR. Golos illustrated the intimate relationship between Soviet intelligence and the American Communist party. The word intimate also describes the relationship between Golos and Bentley, for the two had become lovers.

By the mid-1940s, Bentley was becoming disillusioned with her new faith. This was accelerated by the death of Golos, in 1943, from a heart attack. His successors were a parade of boorish goons. She turned herself into the FBI in 1945 and gave up the names of scores of Americans who had spied for the Kremlin, including Alger Hiss. In 1948, Bentley appeared before the HUAC with her story of Communist penetration of the USG. Her testimony was a huge story, commanding wide interest, and contributed to the growing distrust of the USSR and their American adherents.

She provided testimony on two Soviet networks of government employees who had worked on behalf of the Soviets in the late 1930s and early 1940s. She identified over 30 high-level US Government officials that had worked for the two networks run by Nathan Silverman and Victor Perlo.

The Nathan Silverman Network consisted of the following members:

    Nathan Silverman: Director of the Labor Division, Farm Security Administration; Board of Economic Warfare.

    Solomon Adler: Treasury Department.

    Norman Bursler: Department of Justice.

    Frank Coe: Assistant Director, Division of Monetary Research, Treasury; Special Assistant to the United States Ambassador in London; Assistant to the Executive Director, Board of Economic Warfare; Assistant Administrator, Foreign Economic Administration.

Lauchlin Currie: Administrative Assistant to President Roosevelt; Deputy Administrator of Foreign Economic Administration.

Bela (William) Gold: Assistant Head of Program Surveys, Bureau of Agricultural Economics, Agriculture Department; Senate Subcommittee on War Mobilization; Office of Economic Programs in Foreign Economic Administration.

Mrs. Bela Gold: House Select Committee on Interstate Migration; Bureau of Employment Security; Division of Monetary Research, Treasury.

Abraham Silverman: Director, Bureau of Research and Information Services, US Railroad Retirement Board; Economic Adviser and Chief of Analysis and Plans, Assistant Chief of Air Staff, Material and Services.

William Taylor: Treasury Department.

William L. Ullmann: Division of Monetary Research, Treasury; Material and Services Division, Air Corps Headquarters, Pentagon.

The following were members of the Victor Perlo Network:

Victor Perlo: Head of branch in Research Section, Office of Price Administration; War Production Board; Monetary Research, Treasury.

Edward J. Fitzgerald: War Production Board (WPD).

Harold Glasser: Treasury Department; War Production Board; Advisor on North African Affairs Committee in Algiers, North Africa.

Charles Kramer (aka: Charles Krevitsky): National Labor Relations Board; Office of Price Administration; Economist with Senate Subcommittee on War Mobilization.

Harry Magdoff: Statistical Division of WPB and Office of Emergency Management; Bureau of Research and Statistics, WTB; Tools Division, War Production Board; Bureau of Foreign and Domestic Commerce, Commerce Department.

Alan Rosenberg: Foreign Economic Administration.

Donald Niven Wheeler: Office of Strategic Services.[59]

Bentley also identified seven members of the headquarters staff of the OSS who were working for Soviet intelligence. The most important of these may have been Duncan Chaplin Lee, a Rhodes scholar at Oxford who joined the law firm of William J. Donovan. When Donovan became the head of OSS in 1942, he chose Lee as his personal assistant.

On 3 December 1963, Bentley died. During the last five years of her life she taught English at an all-girls school in Middletown, Connecticut.

Indictment of Communists January 1949

In the 1920s, the US and state governments attempted to penalize Communists for alleged subversive activities. Many states enacted laws denying the Communists the right to hold public office or to obtain public jobs. In the 1940s, another attempt was made using the same arguments, but several Supreme Court decisions decided that simple membership in or an affiliation with the party was not, in itself, evidence of an intent to overthrow the US Government by force. To clarify the vague state of affairs, Attorney General Clark resolved, in 1949, to indict the Communist Party leaders for conspiracy under the Alien Registration Act of 1940. Following is the text of the indictment.

The grand jury charges:

1. That from on or about April 1, 1945, and continuously thereafter up to and including the date of the filing of this indictment, in the Southern District of New York, and elsewhere, William Z. Foster, Eugene Dennis, also known as Francis X. Waldron Jr., John B. Williamson, Jacob Stachel, Robert G. Thompson, Benjamin J. Davis Jr., Henry

Winston, John Gates, also known as Israel Regenstreif, Irving Potash, Gilbert Green, Carl Winter, and Gus Hall, also known as Arno Gust Halberg, the defendants herein, unlawfully, willingly, and knowingly did conspire with each other, and with divers other persons to the grand jurors unknown, to organize as the Communist Party of the United States of America a society, group, and assembly of persons who teach and advocate the overthrow and destruction of the Government of the United States by force and violence, and knowingly and willfully to advocate and teach the duty and necessity of overthrowing and destroying the Government by force and violence, which said acts are prohibited by Section 2 of the Act of June 28, 1940 (Section 10, Title 18, United States Code, commonly known as the Smith Act.

2. It was part of said conspiracy that said defendants would convene, in the Southern District of New York, a meeting of the National Board of the Communist Political Association on or about June 2, 1945, to adopt a draft resolution for the purpose of bringing about the dissolution of the Communist Political Association, and for the purpose of organizing as the Communist party of the United States of America a society, group, and assembly of persons dedicated to the Marxist-Leninist principles of the overthrow and destruction of the United States by force and violence.

3. It was further a part of said conspiracy that said defendants would thereafter convene in the Southern district of New York, a meeting of the National Committee of the Communist Political Association on or about June 18, 1945, to amend and adopt said draft resolution.

4. It was further a part of said conspiracy that said defendants would thereafter cause to be convened, in the Southern district of New York, a special national convention of the Communist Political Association on or about July 26, 1945, for the purpose of considering and acting upon said resolution as amended.

5. It was further a part of said conspiracy that said defendants would induce the delegates to said national convention to dissolve the Communist Political Association.

6. It was further a part of said conspiracy that said defendants would bring about the organization of the Communist Party of the United States as a society, group, and assembly of persons to teach and advocate the overthrow and destruction of the Government of the United States by force and violence, and would cause said convention to adopt a constitution basing said party upon the principles of Marxism-Leninism.

7. It was further a part of said conspiracy that said defendants would bring about the election of officers and the election of a National Committee of said party, and be elected as officers and as members of said National Committee and the National Board of said committee, and in such capacities said defendants would assume leadership of said party and responsibility for its polices and activities, and would meet from time to time to formulate, supervise, and carry out the policies and activities of said party.

8. It was further a part of said conspiracy that said defendants would cause to be organized clubs, and district and state units of said party, and would recruit and encourage the recruitment of members of said party.

9. It was further a part of said conspiracy that said defendants would publish and circulate, and cause to be published and circulated, books, articles, magazines, and newspapers advocating the principles of Marxism-Leninism.

10. It was further a part of said conspiracy that said defendants would conduct, and cause to be conducted, schools and classes for the study of the principles of Marxism-Leninism, in which would be taught and advocated the duty and necessity of overthrowing and destroying the Government of the United States by force and violence.

In violation of Sections 3 and 5 of the Act of June 28, 1940 (Sections 11 and 13, Title 18, United States Code), commonly known as the Smith Act.

The White House

Washington, D.C., July 24, 1950

INFORMATION RELATING TO DOMESTIC ESPIONAGE, SABOTAGE, SUBVERSIVE ACTIVITIES AND RELATED MATTERS

On September 6, 1939 and January 8, 1943 a Presidential Directive was issued providing that the Federal Bureau of Investigation of the Department of Justice should take charge of investigative work in matters relating to espionage, sabotage, subversive activities and related matters. It was pointed out that the investigations must be conducted in a comprehensive manner on a National basis and all information carefully sifted out and correlated in order to avoid confusion. I should like to again call the attention of all Enforcement Officers, both Federal and State, to the request that they report all information in the above enumerated fields promptly to the nearest Field Representative of the Federal Bureau of Investigation, which is charged with the responsibility of correlating this material and referring matters which are under the jurisdiction of any other Federal Agency with responsibilities in this field to the appropriate agency.

I suggest that all patriotic organizations and individuals likewise report all such information relating to espionage, sabotage and subversive activities to the Federal Bureau of Investigation in this same manner.

Harry Truman

Klaus Fuchs

Dr. Klaus Fuchs, a German-born nuclear physicist was a major contributor to the atom-bomb research programs of both Britain and the United States during and after World War II. Simultaneously he was an invaluable asset to the Soviet Union's atomic research program because he secretly communicated to the Soviet Union all the sensitive data on the work of US and British atomic establishments to which he had access. Interned by the British as an enemy alien at the beginning of the war, his abilities became known to the administrators of Britain's secret atomic research program, and he was recruited to work on the atomic bomb. By the end of 1943, his work was so outstanding that he was made one of a small team of British atomic scientists assigned to work in the United States with American physicists in developing the gaseous diffusion U-235 separation process, in making the earliest atom bombs, in planning atomic weapons, and in developing the theory underlying the development of the hydrogen bomb.

Although the security surrounding Western work in atomic energy had supposedly made the development and production of the atomic bomb one of world's best-kept secrets prior to the first explosions in the summer of 1945, it was discovered in 1949 that through the combined efforts of Dr. Klaus Fuchs, "a mild, unobtrusive, pleasant little man who never like politics," and his fellow agents, Julius and Ethel Rosenberg, David Greenglass, Theodore Hall, and Harry Gold, the Russians had obtained the final drawings of the atomic bomb before the first test bomb was exploded at Los Alamos in July 1945.

According to Klaus Fuchs' own statement, when he was first brought into the British program during the early 1940s and learned the purpose of the work, he decided to inform the USSR. He contacted the office of the Soviet Military Attaché in London and embarked upon his career of professional espionage agent for the Soviet Union. With all the classic trappings of clandestine activity, Fuchs collected the information at his disposal, passed it on to secret couriers, and met his Soviet principals in Britain and in various parts of the United States. He gave the Soviet Union extensive data

Klaus Fuchs, a German-born nuclear physicist.

regarding the Oak Ridge diffusion process, weapons work at Los Alamos, British activities at Harwell, and other projects located in the United States, Britain, and Canada.

After serving 10 years in prison in the United Kingdom for espionage, Dr. Fuchs flew to East Germany, where he was appointed deputy director of the East German nuclear research station near Dresden. When asked by the press there if he would repeat his acts of espionage if given a second chance he replied, "Whatever helps the Soviet Union is right."

Klaus Fuchs died in 1988.

The Rosenbergs

The only Americans ever to be executed for espionage were the husband and wife couple, Julius and Ethel Rosenberg. Julius was the son of first-generation Russian-Jewish immigrants and grew up in the lower east side of New York. As many of his generation and background, Rosenberg gravitated to the left at an early age and was a member of Communist youth organizations before joining the American Communist Party. He also had a technical and scientific bent, graduating from the City College of New York with a BS degree in engineering.

From 1940 to March 1945, Julius Rosenberg worked on classified projects for the Army Signal Corps in New York City, Philadelphia, and Newark, New Jersey. The Army learned of his membership in the Communist Party, and he was dismissed from the Signal Corps. He worked briefly for Emerson Radio and then had his own business in New York City.

David Greenglass

Rosenberg first came to the attention of the FBI regarding Soviet espionage when David Greenglass named him as a coconspirator in passing atom bomb information to the Soviets. Greenglass himself was identified by longtime Soviet spy and courier Harry Gold, who had also been part of the atom bomb spy ring. According to Greenglass, Rosenberg, who was his brother-in-law, persuaded him to provide information in the form of drawings and descriptions of his work at the Los Alamos lab where the Manhattan Project, the development of the atomic bomb, was under way. Greenglass, an Army NCO, was stationed at the Los Alamos lab and worked as a machinist on bomb components. According to Greenglass, Ethel Rosenberg was not only aware of her husband's activities, but helped type material procured by Greenglass.

The Rosenbergs were both charged with conspiracy to commit espionage, based on 1917 espionage statute. Their trial began March 6, 1951 and lasted until March 29, when they were found guilty after one day of jury deliberation. The prosecution's case relied heavily on Greenglass's testimony. The testimony of Greenglass revealed the following information.

Greenglass entered the US Army in April 1943, and, in July, 1944, he was assigned to the Manhattan Project, Oak Ridge, Tennessee. He did not know at the time what the project was but received security lectures about his duties and was told it was a secret project. Two weeks later, after being told his work was secret, he was assigned to Los Alamos, New Mexico, and reported there in August 1944.

In a VENONA transcript of a KGB New York to Moscow message, No. 1340 on 21 September 1944 states:

> *LIBERAL[60] recommended the wife of his wife's brother, Ruth Greenglass, with a safe flat in view. She is 21 years old, an American citizen, a GYMNAST[61] since 1942. She lives on Stanton Street. LIBERAL and his wife recommend her as an intelligent and clever girl.*
>
> *(15 groups unrecoverable)*
>
> *(Ruth) learned that her husband was called up by the army but he was not sent to the front. He is a mechanical engineer and is now working at the ENORMOZ[62] plant at Santa Fe, New Mexico.*

Greenglass went on to say that in November, 1944, Ruth Greenglass, who came to Albuquerque to visit him, told him that Julius Rosenberg advised her that her husband was working on the atom bomb. Greenglass stated he did not know that he was working on such a project. He stated that he worked in a group at Los Alamos under a professor of a New England university and described to the court the duties of his shop at Los Alamos. He stated that while at Los Alamos, he learned the identify of various noted physicists and their cover names.

Greenglass testified that his sister, Ethel, and Julius Rosenberg used to speak to him about the merits of the Russian Government. Greenglass stated that when his wife, Ruth, came to visit him at Los Alamos on November 29, 1944, she told David that Julius Rosenberg had invited her to dinner at the Rosenberg home in New York City. At this dinner, Ethel told Ruth that she must have noticed that Ethel had not been engaging in Communist activities and that they were not buying the *Daily Worker* any more or attending club meetings because Julius finally was doing what he always wanted to do, namely, giving information to the Soviet Union.

After Ethel informed Ruth that David was working on the atom bomb project at Los Alamos and said that she and Julius wanted him to give information concerning the bomb, Ruth told the Rosenbergs that she didn't think it was a good idea and declined to convey their requests to David but Ethel and Julius remarked that she should at least tell David about it and see if he would help. In this conversation Julius pointed out to Ruth that Russia was an ally and deserved the information and that Russia was not getting all the information that was due her.

From a VENONA transcript of a KGB New York to Moscow message, number 1600 on 14 November 1944:

OSA[63] has agreed to cooperate with us in drawing in ShMEL[64] (henceforth KALIBR–see your no 5258) with a view to ENORMOZ. On summons from KALIBR she is leaving on 22 November for the Camp 2 area. KALIBR will have a week's leave. Before OSA's departure LIBERAL will carry out two briefings.

David said at first he refused to have anything to do with the request of the Rosenbergs but on the next day agreed to furnish any available data. Ruth then asked David specific questions about the Manhattan Project, and David supplied her that information.

From a VENONA transcript of a KGB New York to Moscow message, number 1773, on 16 December 1944:

OSA has returned from a trip to see KALIBR. KALIBR expressed his readiness to help in throwing light on the work being carried out at Camp-2 and stated that he had already given thought to this question earlier. KALIBR said that the authorities of the Camp were openly taking all precautionary measures to prevent information about ENORMOZ falling into Russian hands. This is causing serious discontent among the progressive (workers)

17 groups unrecoverable

The middle of January KALIBR will be in TYRE.[65] LIBERAL referring to his ignorance of the problem, expresses the wish that our man should meet KALIBR and interrogate him personally. He asserts that KALIBR would be very glad of such a meeting. Do you consider such a meeting advisable? If not, I shall be obliged to draw up a questionnaire and pass it to LIBERAL. Report whether you have any questions of priority to us. KALIBR also reports: OPPENHEIMER[66] from California and KISTIAKOWSKI[67] (MLAD's[68] report mentioned the latter) are at present working at the Camp. The latter is doing research on the thermodynamic process. Advise whether you have any information on these two professors.

In January, 1945, David arrived in New York City on furlough, and about two days later Julius Rosenberg came to David's apartment to ask him for information on the A-bomb. He requested David to write up the information and stated that he would pick it up the following morning.

That evening Greenglass wrote up the information he had. The next morning he gave this material to Rosenberg, together with a list of the scientists at Los Alamos and the names of possible recruits working there who might be sympathetic to Communism and possibly furnish information to Russia.

Greenglass further stated that at the time he turned this material over to Rosenberg, Ruth Greenglass remarked that David's handwriting was bad and would need interpretation. Rosenberg answered that it was nothing to worry about because Ethel, his wife, would retype the information.

A day or two later, David and his wife went to the Rosenberg apartment for dinner where they were introduced to a woman friend of the Rosenbergs. After she left, Julius told the Greenglasses that he thought this person would come to see David to receive information on the atom bomb. They discussed a tentative plan to the effect that Ruth Greenglass would move to Albuquerque, where this woman would come to see her and meet Ruth in a movie theater in Denver, Colorado, where they would exchange purses. Ruth's purse would contain the information from David concerning Los Alamos.

During this discussion the point was raised as to how an identification might be effected. It was agreed that Ruth would use a sidepiece of a Jell-O box to identify the person who would come to see her. Julius held the matching piece of the Jell-O box. David made the suggestion that the meeting be held in front of a certain grocery store in Albuquerque. The date of the meeting was left in abeyance depending upon the time that Ruth would depart for Albuquerque.

Also during this visit, Julius said he would like to have David meet a Russian with whom he could discuss the project on which David was working. A few nights later, an appointment was made by Julius for David to meet a Russian on First Avenue between 42nd and 59th Streets, New York City. David drove up to the appointed meeting place and parked the car near a saloon in a dark street. Julius came up to the car, looked in, and went away, and came back with a man who got into David's car. Julius stayed on the street, and David drove away with the unknown man. The man asked David about some scientific information and, after driving around for a while, David returned to the original meeting place and let the man out. Rosenberg who was standing on the street then joined this man, and David observed them leaving together.

In the spring of 1945, Ruth Greenglass came to Albuquerque to live, and David would visit her apartment on weekends. On the first Sunday of June 1945, a man, subsequently identified by David as Harry Gold, came to visit him and asked if David's name was Greenglass. David said, "Yes." Gold then said, "Julius sent me." David went to his wife's wallet and took out the piece of Jell-O box and compared it with a piece offered by Gold. They matched.

When Gold asked David if he had any information, Greenglass said he did but would have to write it up. Gold then left, stating he would be back. David immediately started to work on a report, made sketches of experiments, wrote up descriptive material regarding them, and prepared a list of possible recruits for espionage. Later that day, Gold returned and David gave him the reports. In return, Gold gave David an envelope containing $500 that he turned over to Ruth.

In September 1945, David Greenglass returned to New York City with his wife, Ruth, on furlough. The next morning Julius Rosenberg came to the Greenglass apartment and asked what David had for him. David informed Julius that he had obtained a pretty good description of the atom bomb.

At Julius' request, he drew up a sketch of the atom bomb, prepared descriptive material on it, drew up a list of scientists and possible recruits for Soviet espionage, and thereafter delivered this material to the Rosenberg apartment. He stated that at the time he turned this material over to Rosenberg, Ethel and Ruth were present. Rosenberg remarked that the information was very good, and it should be typed immediately. The information was then prepared on a portable typewriter in the Rosenberg apartment by Ethel.

While Ethel was typing the report, Julius mentioned to David that he (Julius) had stolen a proximity fuse while working at a radio corporation and turned it over to the Russians.

After the report was typed, the handwritten notes were burned in a frying pan by Julius, flushed down a drain, and Julius gave David $200. Julius discussed with David the idea of David staying at Los Alamos after he was discharged from the Army so that he could continue to get information, but David declined.

From 1946 to 1949, David was in business with Julius, and during this period, Julius told David that he had people going to school and that he had people in upstate

New York and Ohio giving him information for the Russians.

Late in 1947, Julius told David about a sky platform project and mentioned he had received this information from "one of the boys." Rosenberg described the sky platform as a large vessel, which could be suspended at a point in space where the gravity was low and that the vessel would travel around the earth like a satellite. Rosenberg also advised David that he had a way of communicating with the Russians by putting material or messages in the alcove of a theater and that he had received from one of his contacts the mathematics relating to atomic energy for airplanes.

Greenglass testified that Rosenberg claimed to have received a citation and a watch from the Russians. Greenglass also testified that Rosenberg claimed to have received a console table from the Russians, which he used for photographic purposes.

In late February 1950, a few days after the news of the arrest of Dr. Fuchs in England was published, Julius came to David's home and asked David to go for a walk. During this walk Rosenberg spoke of Fuchs and mentioned that the man who had come to see David in Albuquerque was also a contact of Fuchs.

From the VENONA transcripts, a KGB New York to Moscow message, number 195, on 9 February 1944 describes the first meeting between Harry Gold and Klaus Fuchs.

> *On 5th February a meeting took place between GUS[69] and REST.[70] Beforehand GUS was given a detailed briefing by us. REST greeted him pleasantly but was rather cautious at first (1 group unrecovered) the discussion GUS satisfied himself that REST was aware of whom he was working with. R. arrived in the COUNTRY[71] in September as a member of the ISLAND[72] mission on ENORMOZ. According to him the work on ENORMOZ in the COUNTRY is being carried out under the direct control of the COUNTRY's army represented by General Somerville and Stimson; at the head of the group of ISLANDERS is a Labor member of Parliament, Ben Smith.[73]*
>
> *The whole operation amounts to the working out of the process for the separation of isotopes of ENORMOZ. The work is proceeding in two directions: the electron method developed by Lawrence (71 groups unrecoverable) separation of isotopes by the combined method, using the diffusion method for preliminary and the electron for final separation. The work (46 groups unrecoverable) 18th February, we shall report the results.*

Julius stated that David would have to leave the country. When David answered that he needed money, Rosenberg said he would get the money from the Russians.

In April 1950, Rosenberg again told David he would have to leave the country, and, about May 23, 1950, Rosenberg came to the Greenglass apartment with a newspaper containing a picture of Harry Gold and the story of Gold's arrest. Rosenberg said, "This is the man who saw you in Albuquerque." Julius gave David $1,000 and stated he would come back later with $6,000 more for him to use in leaving the country; also that Greenglass would have to get a Mexican tourist card. Rosenberg said he went to see a doctor who told him that a doctor's letter stating David was inoculated for smallpox would also be needed, as well as passport photos. He then gave Greenglass a form letter and instructions to memorize for use in Mexico City.

Upon David's arrival in Mexico City, he was to send this letter to the Soviet embassy and sign it "I. Jackson." Three days after he sent this letter, David was to go to the Plaza de la Colon at 5 p.m. and look at the Statue of Columbus there, carrying in his hand a guide to the city with his middle finger between the pages of the guide, and wait until some man came to him. David would then state, "That is a magnificent statue" and advise the man that he (David) was from Oklahoma. The man would then answer, "Oh there are more beautiful statues in Paris," and would give Greenglass a passport and additional money. David was to go to Vera Cruz and then go to Sweden or Switzerland. If he went to Sweden, he was to send the same type of letter to the Soviet ambassador or his secretary and sign the letter "I. Jackson." Three days later, David was to go to the statue of Linnaeus in Stockholm at 5 p.m., where a man would approach him. Greenglass would mention that the statue was beautiful and the man would answer, "There are much more beautiful ones in Paris." The man would then give David the means of transportation to Czechoslovakia, where upon arrival he was to write to the Soviet ambassador advising him of his presence.

Julius further advised Greenglass that he himself would have to leave the country because he had known Jacob Golos[74] and that Elizabeth Bentley probably knew him also.

Elizabeth Bentley was a member of the Communist underground, who served as a courier to collect information from Russian agents in the United States. Bentley stated that during her association with Golos, she became aware of the fact that Golos knew an engineer named "Julius." In the fall of 1942, she accompanied Golos to Knickerbocker Village but remained in his automobile. She saw Golos conferring with "Julius" on the street but at some distance. From conversations with Golos, she learned that Julius lived in Knickerbocker Village. She also stated that she had telephone conversations with "Julius" from the fall of 1942 to November 1943.

Bentley, in interviews with FBI agents, had described Julius as being 5'10" or 11" tall, slim, and wearing glasses. She had also advised that he was the leader of a Communist cell of engineers, which was turned over to Golos for Soviet espionage purposes and that Julius was to be the contact between Golos and the group. Golos believed this cell of engineers was capable of development.

Investigation by the FBI disclosed that Julius Rosenberg resided in a development known as Knickerbocker Village, was 5'10" tall, slim, and wore glasses. Bentley was unable to make a positive identification of Julius.

Sometime later David and his family went to a photography shop and had six sets of passport photos taken. On Memorial Day, Greenglass gave Rosenberg five sets of these photos. Later Rosenberg again visited David, whom he gave $4,000 in $10 and $20 bills wrapped in brown paper, requesting Greenglass to go for a walk with him and repeat the memorized instructions. David gave the $4,000 to his brother-in-law for safekeeping.

Also testifying was Harry Gold, who stated that Soviet intelligence was the ultimate recipient of the material. The Rosenbergs denied all charges, but were hurt by having to plead the fifth amendment when questioned about their membership in the Communist Party. The two were sentenced to death and executed June 19, 1953.

Based on the information supplied by Gold, Greenglass was arrested on June 16, 1950, and arraigned on the same date in New York. He was remanded to the custody of a US Marshal in default of $100,000 bail. On October 10, 1950, a superseding indictment was returned by a Federal Grand jury in the Southern District of New York charging Morton Sobell, Ethel Rosenberg, Julius Rosenberg, David Greenglass and Anatoli Yakovlev[75] with conspiracy to violate the Espionage Statutes. On October 18, 1950, he pleaded guilty to the superseding indictment. The presiding judge accepted the plea of Greenglass and bail of $100,000 was continued.

On January 31, 1951, a Federal Grand jury in the Southern District of New York, handed down a second superseding indictment charging Julius Rosenberg, Ethel Rosenberg, Anatoli Yakovlev, Morton Sobell, and David Greenglass with conspiracy to commit espionage between June 6, 1944, and June 16, 1950. The indictment was similar in all respects to the previous superseding indictment with the exception that it changed the beginning of the conspiracy from November 1944 to June 1944.

David Greenglass received a 15-year prison sentence after his guilty plea. He was released from Federal prison on November 16, 1960 and had to report periodically to a parole officer until November, 1965.

Gen. Mikhail Dokuchayev, who was a KGB officer from 1951 to 1989, confirms in his new book that Julius and Ethel Rosenberg worked for the KGB. The general gives the Rosenbergs credit for averting a nuclear disaster. "The Rosenbergs were a New York couple convicted in 1951 of conspiracy to commit espionage and executed in 1953. They were integral parts of a Soviet spying effort directed towards obtaining the secrets of the atomic bomb from the United States."

The Rosenberg Spy Apparatus

Morton Sobell
Morton Sobell was born April 11, 1917, in New York City, the son of Russian-born immigrants. He married

Helen Levitov Gurewitz at Arlington, Virginia, on March 10, 1945.

Sobell was a classmate of Julius Rosenberg and Max Elitcher in college and graduated from this college in June, 1933, with a bachelor's degree in electrical engineering. Subsequently, he attended a graduate school at a university in Michigan in 1941 and 1942 and received a master's degree in electrical engineering.

Sobell was employed during the summers of 1934 through 1938 as a maintenance man at Camp Unity, Wingdale, New York, reportedly a Communist-controlled camp. On January 27, 1939, he secured the position of junior electrical engineer with the Bureau of Naval Ordnance, Washington, DC, and was promoted to the position of assistant electrical engineer. He resigned from this position in October 1940 to further his studies. While employed at an electric company in New York State, he had access to classified material, including that on fire control radar. After resigning from this company, he secured employment as an electrical engineer with an instrument company in New York City where he had access to secret data. He remained in this position until June 16, 1950, when he failed to appear for work. It is noted that on this date the FBI arrested David Greenglass. On June 22, 1950, Sobell and his family fled to Mexico. He was thereafter located in Mexico City and on August 18, 1950, was taken into custody by FBI agents in Laredo, Texas, after his deportation from Mexico by the Mexican authorities.

Max Elitcher, an admitted Communist, advised that during the period he roomed with Morton Sobell in Washington, DC, he was induced by Sobell to join the Communist party. He stated that this occurred in 1939 and that Sobell had informed him that he, Sobell, was a member of the Communist Party.

During the same period, Sobell was reported to have been active in the American Peace Mobilization and the American Youth Congress, both of which organizations have been cited by the Attorney General as coming within the purview of Executive Order 10450. It was ascertained that Sobell appeared on the active indices of the American Peace Mobilization and was listed in the indices of the American Youth Congress as a delegate to that body from the Washington Committee for Democratic Action.

A resident at an apartment building located in Washington, DC, reported that Sobell and Max Elitcher were among the tenants of the building who attended meetings in the apartment of one of the tenants during 1940 and 1941. This individual was of the opinion that these were Communist meetings.

The New York Office of the FBI located a Communist Party nominating petition, which was filed in the name of one Morton Sobell, and the signature on this petition was identified by the FBI Laboratory as being in the handwriting of Morton Sobell.

A check at the instrument company where Sobell was employed reflected that Sobell failed to report for work after June 16, 1950. The company received a letter from Sobell on or about July 3, 1950, wherein he advised that he needed a rest and was going to take a few weeks off to recuperate. A neighborhood investigation by the FBI developed that Sobell, his wife, and their two children were last seen at their home on June 22, 1950, and that they had left hurriedly without advising anyone of their intended departure.

Through an airlines company at LaGuardia Field, it was determined that Sobell and his family had departed for Mexico City on June 22, 1950. It was further determined that roundtrip excursion tickets for transportation from New York City to Mexico and return were purchased on June 21, 1950, in the name of Morton Sobell.

Further investigation of Sobell's flight to Mexico reflected that he had communicated through the mail with relatives through the utilization of a certain man as a mail drop. This man was interviewed and reluctantly admitted receiving letters from Sobell with instructions to forward these letters to Sobell's relatives. This admission was made after the individual was advised that the FBI Laboratory had identified handwriting on the envelopes used in forwarding letters to Sobell's relatives as being in his handwriting.

In August, 1950, the Mexican authorities took Sobell into custody and deported him as an undesirable alien. On the early morning of August 18, 1950, FBI agents apprehended Sobell at the International Bridge, Laredo, Texas.

On 10 October 1950, a superseding indictment was returned by a Federal Grand jury in the Southern District of New York charging Morton Sobell, Ethel Rosenberg, Julius Rosenberg, David Greenglass, and Anatoli Yakovlev[76] with conspiracy to violate the Espionage Statutes. On 18 October 1950, he pleaded guilty to the superseding indictment. The presiding judge accepted the plea of Greenglass and bail of $100,000 was continued.

On 31 January 1951, a Federal Grand jury in the Southern District of New York handed down a second superseding indictment charging Julius Rosenberg, Ethel Rosenberg, Anatoli Yakovlev, Morton Sobell, and David Greenglass with conspiracy to commit espionage between 6 June 1944 and 16 June 1950. The indictment was similar in all respects to the previous superseding indictment with the exception that it changed the beginning of the conspiracy from November 1944, to June 1944.

On 5 February 1951, Morton Sobell made an application to a US District Judge, Southern District of New York, for a writ of habeas corpus based on the allegation that the indictment of 31 January 1951, was vague and that the incrimination of Sobell was a violation of his constitutional rights. The application was denied.

On 28 March 1951, counsel for both sides summed up their case to the jury, and, on 29 March 1951, the jury rendered a verdict of guilty against Morton Sobell. On 5 April 1951, Morton Sobell was sentenced to 30 years in prison.

Theodore Alvin Hall

The Washington Post identified Theodore Alvin Hall as an atomic bomb spy codenamed, "Mlad," in an article in its 25 February 1996 edition. The article used information from deciphered KGB messages released by the National Security Agency (NSA). The NSA program, actually started by the US Army's Signal Intelligence Service on 1 February 1943, was a small, highly secret program, codenamed VENONA. The object of the VENONA program was to examine, and possibly exploit, encrypted Soviet diplomatic communications.

In one of the encrypted messages, dated 12 November 1944, Hall is identified by name and says that a KGB officer visited Hall, who provided information on Los Alamos and its key personnel to the officer. The message read:

> BEK[77] visited Theodore Hall, 19 years old, the son of a furrier. He is a graduate of Harvard University. As a talented physicists he was taken for government work. He was a (member of the Young Communist League) and conducted work in the Steel Founders Union. According to BEK's account HALL has an exceptionally keen mind and a broad outlook, and is politically developed. At the present time, H. is in charge of a group at "CAMP-2".[78] H. handed over to BEK a report about the CAMP and named key personnel employed on ENORMOZ.[79] He decided to do this on the advice of his colleague Saville SAX, a GYMNAST[80] living in TYRE.[81] SAX's mother is a FELLOWCOUNTRYMAN[82] and works for RUSSIAN WAR RELIEF. With the aim of hastening a meeting with a competent person, H. on them following day sent a copy of the report to S. to the PLANT.[83] ALEKSEJ[84] received it. H had to leave for CAMP-2 in two days time. ALEKSEJ was compelled to make a decision quickly. Jointly with MAJ[85] he gave BEK consent to feel out H., to assure him that everything was in order and to arrange liaison with him. BEK met S (1 group garbled) our automobile. We consider it expedient to maintain liaison with H. (1 group unidentified) through S. and not bring in anybody else. MAJ has no objections to this. We shall send the details by post.

In another VENONA message, from KGB New York to Moscow, number 94, on 23 January 1945, it appears the KGB is running an investigative check on Hall and Sax:

> The checking of STAR[86] and MLAD we entrusted to ECHO[87] a month ago, the result of the check we have not yet had. We're checking STAR's mother also....

> BEK is extremely displeased over the handing over of STAR to ALEKSEJ. He gives a favorable report of him. Aleksej has met STAR twice but cannot yet give a final judgement. MLAD has been seen by no one except BEK. (On the 8th of January) MLAD sent a letter but never (made arrangements) for calling to a meeting. He has been called into the army and left to work in the camp.[88]

> STAR intends to renew his studies at Harvard University at the end of February.

Hall was subsequently investigated in the early 1950s for espionage by the FBI but was not prosecuted. He left the United States in 1962 and currently resides in Cambridge, England. A *Washington Post* reporter contacted Hall on several occasions but Hall declined to comment on the story that he is Mlad or to answer any questions about his possible involvement with Soviet intelligence.

A new book, *Bombshell: The Secret Story of America's Unknown Atomic Spy Conspiracy*, published on 1 October 1997, quoted Hall as saying that he passed nuclear secrets to the Soviets. According to Hall, he was concerned about the US monopoly of atomic weapons so in 1944, "to help prevent the monopoly I contemplated a brief encounter with a Soviet agent, just to inform them of the existence of the A-bomb project."

Hall anticipated only limited contact with the Soviets but things did not go as he planned. He notes that at the time of his espionage activities, the Soviet Union "was not the enemy but the ally of the United States; the Soviet people fought the Nazis heroically at tremendous human cost, and this may well have saved the Western Allies from defeat."

Hall wrote two statements to the authors. In one of them he said that his "decision about contacting the Soviets was a gradual one, and it was entirely my own. It was entirely voluntary, not influenced by any other individual or by any organization.... I was never recruited by anyone."

Hall's acknowledgment of his spying activities further confirms the VENONA transcripts, which identified him as a Soviet spy.

Joel Barr and Al Sarrant

Joel Barr, his close friend Al Sarant, and Sarant's lover Carol Dayton, the wife of a neighbor, fled the United States to Czechoslovakia. After living there for five years, they went to the Soviet Union, settling in Leningrad. To hide their identities, they each were given an alias. Joel Barr became Joe Berg, and Al Sarant became Filipp Staros.

Barr has denied that he spied for the Soviets, saying that he fled the United States because of his close, political ties to Julius Rosenberg. In a VENONA message from KGB New York to Moscow, No. 1600, dated 14 November 1944:

> LIBERAL[89] has safely carried through the contracting of HUGHES.[90] HUGHES is a good pal of METR's.[91] We propose to pair them off and get them to photograph their own materials having (been) given a camera for this purpose. HUGHES is a good photographer, has a large darkroom and all the equipment but he does not have a Leica. LIBERAL will receive the films from METR for passing on. Direction of the probationers will be continued through LIBERAL, this will ease the load on him. Details about the contracting are in letter no. 8

As for Al Sarant, who died in 1979 in Vladivostok, a VENONA message from KGB New York to Moscow, No. 628, dated 5 May 1944:

> Please carry out a check and sanction the recruitment of Alfred SARANT, a lead of ANTENNA's.[92] He is 25 years old, a Greek, an American citizen and lives in TYRE.[93] He completed the engineering course at Cooper Union in 1940. He worked for two years in the Signal Corps Laboratory at Fort Monmouth. He was discharged for past union activity. He has been working for two years at Western Electric.
>
> (45 groups unrecoverable)
>
> Entry in the FELLOWCOUNTRYMAN,[94] SARANT lives apart from his family. Answer without delay.

Rosenberg in fact recruited Sarant.

Barr worked in the Soviet defense industry, where he was recognized as a "father of Soviet micro-electronics."

Joel Barr

Barr and Sarant, in effect, began what can be called the Silicon Valley in the Soviet Union.

In 1992, Barr returned to the United States where he regained his US citizenship. He rented an apartment in New York and claimed to have voted in the 1992 primary in the state. Barr died on 1August 1998.

Other Spies in the Rosenberg Net

Max Elitcher

Elitcher testified that he first met Sobell while both were attending a high school in New York City. He further stated that he and Sobell also attended college together in New York from 1934 to 1938. Elitcher graduated with a bachelor's degree in electrical engineering and pointed out that Julius Rosenberg also studied engineering at the same college during this same period. Elitcher saw Sobell daily at school but saw Rosenberg less frequently. After graduating, Elitcher was employed with the Bureau of Ordnance, Navy Department, Washington, DC from November, 1938, until October, 1948.

In December 1938, Elitcher resided at Washington, DC. During December of that year, Sobell came to Washington and stayed at a house next to Elitcher's place of residence. In April or May of 1939, Elitcher and Sobell took up residence in a private home, and in May of 1940, they moved into an apartment. During the period they lived together, Sobell was also employed at the Bureau of Ordnance. In September 1941, Sobell left his employment to go to a university in Michigan in order to continue his studies.

Elitcher further advised that during the period he lived with Sobell they had conversations concerning the Communist Party and that at Sobell's request, Elitcher joined the Young Communist League. About September 1939, Elitcher attended a meeting with Sobell at which there was a discussion about forming a branch of the Communist Party. This branch was formed, and Elitcher joined the Communist Party at the end of 1939. Meetings of this group were held at the homes of various members and dues were paid to the chairman of the group. Elitcher stated that Sobell was the first chairman of the group. At meetings discussions were conducted of news events based on the *Daily Worker* and literature such as *The Communist*. The group also discussed Marxist and Leninist theory. Suggestions were made to the members to join the American Peace Mobilization and to assist the American Youth Congress convention. Discussions were also held concerning the Hitler-Stalin Pact, and members were instructed to strive to get support of other people for the Russian position. Elitcher continued to go to these meetings until September 1941. In 1942, Communist Party branches were formed, which contained groups of employees from particular government agencies, and Elitcher joined the Navy branch of the Communist Party.

Elitcher testified that around June 1944, he received a telephone call from Julius Rosenberg, who identified himself as a former college classmate of Elitcher. At Elitcher's invitation, Rosenberg visited the Elitcher home the same evening. Rosenberg told Elitcher what the Soviet Union was doing in the war effort and stated that some war information was being denied to the Soviet Union. Rosenberg pointed out, however, that some people were providing military information to assist the Soviet Union and that Sobell was helping in this way. Rosenberg asked Elitcher if he would turn over information of that type to him in order to the aid the Soviet Union. Rosenberg asked Elitcher to supply him with plans, reports, or books regarding new military equipment and anything Elitcher might think would be of value to the Soviet Union, pointing out that the final choice of the value of the information would not be up to Elitcher but that the information would be evaluated by someone else.

The VENONA transcripts show a message from the KGB New York to Moscow, No. 1053, on 26 July 1944 that states:

In July Antenna[95] was sent by his firm for ten days to work in Carthage.[96] There he visited his school friend Max Elitcher, who works in the Bureau of Standards as head of the fire control section for warships (comment: which mount guns) of over five-inch calibre. He has access to extremely valuable material on guns.

Five years ago, Max Elitcher graduated from the Electro-Technical Department of the City College of New York. He has a Master of Science degree. Since finishing college he has been working at the Bureau of Standards. He is a Fellow Countryman. He entered the Fellow Countrymen's organization after finishing his studies.

By Antenna he is characterized as a loyal, reliable, level-headed and able man. Married, his wife is a Fellow Countrywoman. She is a psychologist by profession, she works at the War Department.

Max Elitcher is an excellent amateur photographer and has all the necessary equipment for taking photographs.

Please check Elitcher and communicate your consent to his clearance.

In September 1944, Elitcher went on a one-week vacation in a state park in West Virginia with Morton Sobell and his future wife. During this vacation, Elitcher told Sobell about Rosenberg's visit and request for information to be given to the Soviet Union. When he remarked that Rosenberg had said Sobell was helping in this, Sobell became angry and said that Rosenberg should not have mentioned his name.

In the summer of 1945, Elitcher was in New York on vacation and stayed at the apartment of Julius Rosenberg. Rosenberg mentioned to Elitcher that he, Rosenberg, had been dismissed from his employment for security reasons and that his membership in the Communist Party seemed to be the basis of the case against him; he had been worried about this matter because he thought his dismissal might have had some connection with his espionage activity but that he had been relieved when he found out that it concerned only his party activity.

Elitcher also testified that, in September 1945, Rosenberg came to Elitcher's home and told him that even though the war was over, Russia's need for military information continued. Rosenberg asked Elitcher about the type of work he was going, and Elitcher told him he was working on sonar and anti-submarine fire-control devices.

In early 1946, Elitcher visited an electric company in connection with official business and stayed at the home of Sobell in Schenectady. At the time, Sobell was working at this electric company. On this occasion Sobell and Elitcher discussed their work.

Later that year Elitcher again saw Sobell, and Sobell asked about an ordnance pamphlet, but Elitcher said it was not yet ready. Sobell suggested that Elitcher see Rosenberg again.

At the end of 1946 or 1947, Elitcher telephoned Rosenberg and said he would like to see him. At this time Rosenberg advised Elitcher that there had been some changes in the espionage work; that he felt there was a leak; and that Elitcher should not come to see him until further notice. He advised Elitcher to discontinue his Communist activities.

Elitcher testified that in 1947, Sobell had secured employment at an instrument company in New York City doing classified work for the armed forces. Elitcher saw Sobell there several times and on one occasion had lunch with him at a restaurant in New York City. Sobell asked Elitcher on this occasion if Elitcher knew of any progressive students or graduates and if so, would he put Sobell in touch with them, but Elitcher said he did not know any.

In October 1948, Elitcher left the Bureau of Ordnance and went to work for the instrument company in New York City where Sobell was employed. He lived in a house in Flushing, New York, and Sobell lived on a street behind him. They went to work together in a car pool and, during a trip home from work one evening, Sobell again asked Elitcher about individuals Elitcher might know who would be progressive. Sobell pointed out to Elitcher that because of security measures being taken by the government, it was necessary to find students to provide information that no one would suspect.

Elitcher further testified that prior to leaving the Bureau of Ordnance, he had discussed with Sobell his desire to secure new employment during a visit Elitcher made to New York City in the summer of 1948. Sobell told Elitcher not to leave the Bureau of Ordnance until Elitcher had talked to Rosenberg.

Thereafter, Sobell made an appointment for Elitcher to meet with Rosenberg. They met on the street in New York, and Rosenberg told Elitcher that it was too bad Elitcher had decided to leave because he, Rosenberg, needed someone to work at the Bureau of Ordnance for espionage purposes. Sobell was present at this meeting and also urged Elitcher to stay at the Bureau of Ordnance. Thereafter, Rosenberg and Elitcher had dinner together at a restaurant in New York City where they continued to talk about Elitcher's desire to leave his job. Rosenberg wanted to know where important defense work was being done, and Elitcher mentioned laboratories in Whippany, New Jersey. Rosenberg suggested that possibly Elitcher could take courses at college to improve his status.

Elitcher also testified that in July 1948, he took a trip to New York City by car during which he believed he was being followed. He proceeded to Sobell's home and told Sobell of his suspicion. Sobell became angry and told Elitcher he should not have come to his home if he felt he was being followed. Sobell told Elitcher to leave the house and stay somewhere else but later agreed to allow Elitcher to stay with him. A little later that evening, Sobell mentioned to Elitcher that he had some information for Rosenberg that was too valuable to destroy, and he wanted to get it to Rosenberg that night. He requested Elitcher to accompany him.

Elitcher observed Sobell take a 35-mm film can with him and place it in the glove compartment of Sobell's car. He and Sobell then drove to a building in New York City and parked on Catherine Street. Sobell then took the can out of the glove compartment and left. When he returned, Elitcher asked him what Rosenberg thought of Elitcher's suspicion that he was being followed, and Sobell answered that Rosenberg thought it was nothing to worry about.

Elitcher testified that Sobell possessed a camera, some 35-mm film, and an enlarger and that all of the material Sobell worked on in his various places of employment was classified. He stated he last saw Sobell in June 1950.

On cross-examination, Elitcher recalled that during Rosenberg's visit to his house in June 1944, which was after D-day, Rosenberg mentioned that he had had a drink with a Russian in celebration of this event. Elitcher testified that Rosenberg contacted him at least nine times from 1944 to 1948 in an attempt to persuade him to obtain information for him, but that he always put Rosenberg off. In 1948, Elitcher told Rosenberg that he definitely would not cooperate with him.

Harry Gold

Harry Gold testified that he was engaged in Soviet espionage from 1935 up to the time of his arrest in May 1950 and that from 1944 to 1946 his espionage superior was a Russian known to him as "John." He identified a picture of Anatoliy A. Yakovlev, former Soviet vice consul in New York, as John.

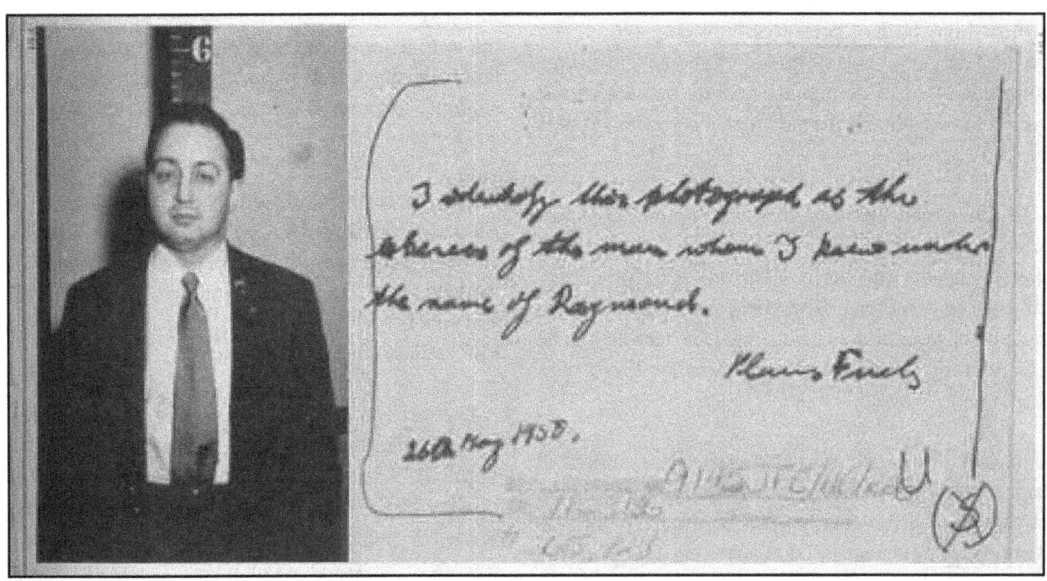

Photograph of Harry Gold shown to Klaus Fuchs who identified him as his American contact in May 1950.

In the middle of June 1944, Gold had an espionage meeting with Dr. Klaus Fuchs in Woodside, New York. As a result of this meeting, Gold wrote a report for Yakovlev. He also informed Yakovlev that at the next meeting, Fuchs would give Gold information relating to the application of nuclear fission to the production of military weapons.

In the latter part of June 1944, Gold met Fuchs in the vicinity of Borough Hall, Brooklyn, and received a package from Fuchs, which Gold later turned over to Yakovlev.

Gold's next meeting with Fuchs was in the middle of July 1944, in the vicinity of 90th Street and Central Park West, New York. About a week or two later, Gold turned over to Yakovlev a report he had written concerning this conversation and told Yakovlev that Fuchs had given further information concerning the work of a joint American and British project to produce an atom bomb. Subsequently, Gold had a regularly scheduled series of meetings with Yakovlev, who instructed Gold how to continue his contacts with Fuchs. In this connection, Gold stated that it was his duty to obtain information from a number of American espionage agents and to pass the information to Yakovlev. He pointed out that he effected his meetings with these sources by using recognition signals such as an object or a piece of paper and a code phrase in the form of a greeting, always using a pseudonym. He also stated that his sources lived in cities other than Philadelphia and that he paid money to these sources, which he had in turn received from Yakovlev.

Early in January 1945, Gold met Fuchs in Cambridge, Massachusetts, and received a package of papers which he later turned over to Yakovlev in New York City. He told Yakovlev that Fuchs had mentioned that a lens was being worked on in connection with the atom bomb. His next meeting with Fuchs was to be in Santa Fe on the first Saturday of June 1945.

Early in February 1945, Gold met Yakovlev on 23rd Street between Ninth and Tenth Avenues in New York. At this meeting, Yakovlev indicated the interests of the Russians in the plans mentioned by Fuchs.

On the last Saturday in May 1945, Gold met Yakovlev inside a restaurant on Third Avenue in New York, to discuss Gold's next meeting with Fuchs in Santa Fe. Yakovlev instructed Gold to take on an additional mission in Albuquerque, New Mexico. Gold protested, but Yakovlev said it was vital, pointing out that a woman was supposed to go but was unable to. Yakovlev gave Gold an onionskin paper on which was typed the name Greenglass, an address on High Street, Albuquerque, New Mexico, and the recognition signal, " I come from Julius." Yakovlev also gave Gold a piece of cardboard cut from a food package. He stated that Greenglass would have the matching piece and that if Greenglass was not in his wife would pass him the information. Yakovlev then gave Gold $500 in an envelope to turn over to Greenglass.

Gold arrived in Santa Fe on Saturday, June 2, 1945, and met Fuchs, who gave him a package of papers. Gold left Santa Fe on the afternoon of June 2 by bus and arrived in Albuquerque that evening. He went to the High Street address, found that Greenglass and his wife were not in, and stayed at a rooming house overnight. The next day he went to the High Street address and found David Greenglass.

Greenglass told Gold that the visit was a surprise and that it would take several hours to prepare the A-bomb material for Gold. He started to tell Gold about possible recruits at Los Alamos but Gold cut him short and pointed out that recruitment was very hazardous, and he should be more circumspect in his behavior. Gold left and returned later that afternoon, when Greenglass gave him material, which he said contained information on the atomic bomb. Gold turned over to Greenglass the envelope containing the $500. Greenglass mentioned to Gold that he expected to get a furlough sometime around Christmas and gave Gold the phone number of Julius in New York.

Gold returned to New York by train on June 5, 1945. While on route by train, he examined the material Greenglass had given him and put it in a manila envelope. He put the material he had received from Fuchs in another manila envelope. On the evening of June 5, 1945, Gold met Yakovlev along Metropolitan Avenue in Brooklyn and turned over to him both envelopes.

About two weeks later, Gold met Yakovlev on Main Street, Flushing, New York. Yakovlev told Gold that the information he had received from him on June 5 had been sent immediately to the Soviet Union and that the information provided by Greenglass had been considered "extremely excellent and valuable." At this meeting, Gold related the details of his conversation with Fuchs and Greenglass. Fuchs had stated that tremendous progress had been made on the atom bomb, and the first test was set for July 1945.

In early July 1945, Gold met Yakovlev in a seafood restaurant. Yakovlev said it was necessary to make arrangements for another Soviet agent to get in touch with Gold. At Yakovlev's instructions, Gold took a sheet of paper from his pocket that had the heading of a company in Philadelphia. Gold tore off the top portion containing the name and on the reverse side of the sheet wrote in diagonal fashion, "directions to Paul Street." Yakovlev then tore the paper in an irregular fashion. He kept one portion and Gold kept the other. Yakovlev said that if Gold received two tickets in the mail without a letter, it would mean that on a definite number of days after the date on the ticket Gold was to go to the Broadway stop of the Astoria line for a meeting, which would take place in a restaurant-bar. Gold's Soviet contact would be standing at the bar and approach Gold and ask to be directed to Paul Street. They would then match the torn pieces of paper.

In August 1945, Gold again met Yakovlev in Brooklyn and was told by Yakovlev that Gold was to take a trip in September 1945, to see Fuchs. Gold suggested to Yakovlev that since he was going to see Fuchs, he might as well go to Albuquerque to see David Greenglass also. Yakovlev answered that it was inadvisable because it might endanger Gold to have further contact with Greenglass.

In September 1945, Gold met Fuchs in Santa Fe, New Mexico. On his return to New York on September 22, 1945, Gold went to a prearranged meeting place to see Yakovlev who failed to appear. About ten days later, Gold met Yakovlev on Main Street, Flushing, and turned over to him the package he had received from Fuchs. He told Yakovlev that Fuchs had said there was no longer the open and free cooperation between the Americans and the British and that many departments were closed to Fuchs. Fuchs also stated he would have to return to England and that he was worried because the British had gotten to Kiel, Germany, ahead of the Russians and might discover a Gestapo dossier on Fuchs that would reveal his strong Communist ties and background. Fuchs and Gold also discussed the details of a plan whereby Fuchs could be contacted in England.

In November 1945, Gold had another meeting with Yakovlev at which Gold mentioned that Greenglass would probably be coming home for a furlough at Christmas and that plans should be made to get in touch with Rosenberg in an effort to obtain more information from Greenglass.

In January 1945, Gold again met with Yakovlev, who told Gold about a man Yakovlev had tried to contact and found out that the man was under continuous surveillance. Yakovlev used this story to illustrate that it was better to give up the contact than endanger their work.

Early in December 1946, Gold received two tickets to a boxing match in New York through the mail. The tickets were addressed to Gold's Philadelphia home incorrectly and too late for Gold to keep the appointment. At 5 p.m. on December 26, 1946, Gold received a telephone call at his place of employment. The voice said "This is John." Gold then arranged with John to meet an unidentified man in a certain movie theater that night. The man identified himself by handing Gold the torn piece of paper containing the heading, which Gold and Yakovlev had previously prepared. Gold was requested by this man to proceed to 42nd Street and Third Avenue to meet Yakovlev.

Gold met Yakovlev, who asked if Gold had anything further from Fuchs, apologized for his 10-month absence, and explained that he had to lie low. He stated that he was glad Gold was working in New York and told Gold that he should begin planning for a mission to Paris, in March 1947, where Gold would meet a physicist. He gave Gold an onionskin paper setting forth information for his proposed meeting in Paris. During the conversation with Yakovlev, Gold mentioned the name of his employer, and upon hearing this, Yakovlev became very excited. He told Gold that he had ruined 11 years of work by working with this individual because the FBI had investigated him in 1945. Yakovlev rushed away stating that Gold would never see him again.

William Perl

William Perl, born in New York City in 1918, was a classmate of both Julius Rosenberg and Morton Sobell at college. He worked for the National Advisory Committee for Aeronautics at Langley Field, Virginia, and Cleveland, Ohio, after his graduation. It was learned that Sobell maintained close contact with Perl through correspondence after their college graduation.

Perl admitted that in July 1950, a girl he recognized to be a former girl friend of a close friend of his visited him in Cleveland. He said that she explained in writing that a stranger instructed her to proceed from New York City to Cleveland to deliver a message to an aeronautical engineer. She wrote out the instructions for him to leave the United States and flee to Mexico. She mentioned the name "Rosenberg." This girl was located, and an interview verified the above information and stated that Perl refused to accept the sum of $2,000 that she offered to him.

Perl was called to testify before a Federal Grand Jury and denied that he had been acquainted and associated with Julius Rosenberg and Morton Sobell. He was found guilty on two counts of perjury concerning his denial of knowledge of Rosenberg and Sobell. On June 5, 1953, he was sentenced to serve five years on each count to run concurrently.

US Senator Joseph R. McCarthy[97]

Joseph McCarthy was born to a middle-class Wisconsin farm family in 1908. He attended a one-room public school in his small hometown and left after completing the ninth grade. After starting a poultry business that failed after disease destroyed his animals, young McCarthy moved to a neighboring city to manage a grocery store. He was very successful at this venture, and his innovations in marketing in this small city attracted considerable attention. McCarthy was by now nearly 20 years old, and he realized his lack of formal education would hinder his future. McCarthy decided to return to school. Like everything he did, he did it with a vengeance, completing four years worth of credits in one year with a nearly straight A average. McCarthy then enrolled at Marquette University in Milwaukee, eventually finishing with a law degree. During his student days, he worked full-time and was a member of the college boxing team.

In 1935 at age 27, McCarthy hung out his shingle as a smalltown lawyer, but his real interest was politics. In 1936 he made his first run for public office, losing a race for circuit court judge. He tried again two years later, switching from the Democratic to the Republican Party and won. McCarthy's trademark style was an aggressive backslapping, baby kissing campaign in which he kept his opponent off balance with a barrage of charges and allegations, most of which were of dubious validity.

When war broke out in 1941, McCarthy, although exempt from military service as a sitting judge, volunteered for duty. He was commissioned in the Marine Corps and was sent to the South Pacific as an air intelligence officer. In 1944, McCarthy left active duty and ran unsuccessfully for the US Senate seat from Wisconsin. In 1946 he tried again, this time taking on Democrat "Young Bob" LaFollette, the son of legendary progressive Robert LaFollette, and defeated him in a remarkable upset.

McCarthy attracted little attention during his early years in the Senate. It was not until 1950 that his star rose and that was virtually overnight as a result of his Wheeling, West Virginia, speech in which he claimed to have in his possession a list of 205 Communists working in the State Department. That speech, delivered in February 1950, created an uproar, which over the next four years centered nationwide attention on Senator McCarthy. Realizing that he had an issue that captured the imagination of millions of Americans, McCarthy became the center of a nationwide drama played out on the floor of the US Senate.

As chair of the Senate Permanent Subcommittee on Investigations, McCarthy was positioned to exploit his newfound fame to the hilt. From 1950–54, McCarthy initiated a series of hearings in which he named persons and organizations as Soviet agents or spies. The basis of McCarthy's charges were his access to raw, frequently unevaluated investigative files from various federal agencies, including the FBI and Department of State security.

One of the most notorious and misused source documents used by McCarthy was the so-called Lee list. This was a 1946 State Department security study conducted by a former FBI agent named Robert Lee.

This document purported to list all known or suspected security risks in the State Department after several wartime agencies were absorbed into the Department at the close of the War. Undoubtedly there were disloyal persons named. However, many were apparently listed on the basis of unsubstantiated allegations or associations. The Lee list was the source of McCarthy's original claim that the State Department was harboring hundreds of Communists.

McCarthy had a staff of investigators who in the main received leaked information from federal agencies and the military. McCarthy actively encouraged such unofficial reporting by "patriotic" citizens. McCarthy himself did not reveal in his hearings the nature of his sources, leading many to believe that he had in fact uncovered new facts as a result of his staff's investigative activities.

Initially, McCarthy's efforts won a great deal of public support. From the late 1940s into the early 1950s Americans were battered by a series of spy scandals and revelations of Soviet and Communist penetrations into the US Government and society. That, coupled with Communist advances in Eastern Europe and China led to an anxiety on the part of millions of Americans that some kind of action needed to be taken to retake the offensive, and Senator McCarthy seemed to be at least one public official doing just that. Polls taken at the time reveal that a majority of Americans believed that Communism at home and abroad was a serious threat to US security.

However, McCarthy had enemies, and as time went on, and his sloppy shotgun methods splattered more targets, an active opposition to the Senator began to build. McCarthy finally overreached himself in 1953 and 1954. With a Republican war hero, General Dwight Eisenhower as President, McCarthy made the mistake of taking on the US Army.

McCarthy's staff had received from leakers specific allegations of poor security and the presence of "subversives" at various Army installations. One of these installations was Fort Monmouth, home of the US Army's Signal Corps. To add to that, a small scandal ensued when it was learned that an Army dentist, Dr. Irving Peress, refused to answer a standard loyalty question regarding membership in the CPUSA. Due to bureaucratic inertia, Peress was promoted to major despite the flap over his alleged party membership. McCarthy was infuriated to learn of the promotion and planned hearings to excoriate the Army hierarchy on the issues of security at Fort Monmouth and Peress.

In the ensuing hearings, McCarthy subjected DoD officials and Army general officers to savage attacks in which he questioned their intelligence, patriotism, and fitness to wear the uniform. McCarthy's browbeating of defense officials turned those who should have been his allies against him. President Eisenhower was outraged at the treatment meted out by McCarthy to the military brass and finally moved to disassociate himself from the Senator's efforts.

The stage was now set for McCarthy's dramatic fall. Television, now becoming commonplace in American homes, was to be a factor. Hearings were scheduled, to be televised live, on the subject of the treatment of a former McCarthy staffer, David Schine, by the Army. The Army charged that McCarthy, through his staff, tried to influence Schine's conditions of service while he was stationed at Fort Dix, New Jersey. However, the real Army agenda was to expose McCarthy as a fraud and a bully before the nation through the television cameras.

The so-called Army-McCarthy hearings lasted for 36 days in 1954. During that time, the Army's general counsel, Robert Welch, clashed with McCarthy over several issues. McCarthy's usual tactics of bullying, insulting, and hectoring witnesses exposed for the first time to a wide live television audience, led to a tide of revulsion against him. Army counsel Welch expertly played a foil to McCarthy and at least once humiliated the Senator in debate over the alleged Communist past of a young attorney on Welch's staff. The actual results of the hearings were ambiguous except for one thing; McCarthy's reputation was virtually destroyed.

McCarthy's trajectory was straight down after the hearings. The following year, 1955, the Senate censured him for his actions over the previous four years. McCarthy, always a heavy drinker, responded by lapsing into alcoholism. In 1957, Joseph McCarthy died from complications of liver failure.

Without a doubt, most American security and CI officials would evaluate the result of McCarthy's efforts in a highly negative light. No Soviet spy or penetration of the US Government was exposed, or any significant legitimate security or CI issue settled, or even raised, by either McCarthy's hearings or his "investigative" activities. For at least the next 20 years, McCarthy's excesses permitted opponents of security or CI efforts to dismiss all such initiatives as symptoms of "McCarthyism."

The point could be raised in McCarthy's defense that he was, along with the other legislative investigative committees such as the HUAC, exposing to public view elements of a national problem that had for too long been the exclusive domain of highly secretive government agencies. The judgement of contemporary historians, however, is clear. They condemn McCarthy as the 1950s version of a witch hunter, without any socially redeeming qualities. And historians always have the last word.

William August Fisher[100]
"Rudolph Ivanovich Abel"

William August Fisher, a.k.a. William Genrykhovich Fisher, was a KGB illegal who operated an espionage network out of New York City under the name of "Abel" and other aliases from the late 1940s until his arrest by the FBI in June 1957.

There are actually several biographies of Fisher. There is the true one that is based on available information developed from official documents and defectors' statements. There is also the KGB operational legend to which Fisher/ "Abel" tried to adhere at the time of his arrest, trial, and imprisonment. Finally, there is the laudatory version, which the KGB fostered after his return to the USSR, to glorify its exploits and one of its greatest heroes who operated under the name of "Rudolph Ivanovich Abel."

"Abel" was actually born William August Fisher on 11 July 1903 in Newcastle-on-Tyne, England. He was the son of Henry Matthew Fisher (a.k.a. Genrykh Matveyevich Fisher), born 9 April 1871 in Russia and Lubov Vasilyevna Fisher, born Gidova, circa 1881 in Russia. Fisher had an older brother, Henry Fisher, born 18 April 1902 at Newcastle-on-Tyne.

The senior Fisher was a Communist. He apparently had been active in workers' circles in St. Petersburg in the 1890s and knew Lenin. He immigrated into England around the turn of the century and settled in Newcastle-on-Tyne where he worked as a fitter, metalworker, and engineer. In 1914 the senior Fisher applied for and received British nationality.

During his years in England, the senior Fisher did come to the attention of the British Special Branch for suspected Leftist activity. In May 1920 the senior Fisher applied for British passports for himself and his family to return to Rybinsk, Yaroslavl Oblast, USSR to visit his own and his wife's relatives. In July 1920 the British issued him a passport, replacing one obtained in July 1914, and the family apparently left the United Kingdom shortly thereafter. After his return to the USSR, the elder Fisher joined the CPSU and worked on economic matters. A book entitled, *In Russian and In England, Observations and Reminiscences of a Petersburg Worker, 1890-1921,* by the senior Fisher, was published in Moscow in 1922.

In 1922, William August Fisher reported to the British Mission in Moscow that he had lost his passport and applied for a new one. He left the Moscow area for the North, however, before formalities were completed.

The Fishers then dropped out of sight for about 10 years in the postcivil war in Russia. Over the years, however, the story of William August Fisher's odyssey in espionage gradually emerges. Much of the biographic

Rudolph Ivanovich Abel

data is based on a variety of sources, including defector and liaison reports, and much of it is fragmentary and incomplete. There is nevertheless a general outline revealing some of Fisher's activities over the years. Reports in KGB circles indicated that the Fishers had taken a longer name, something like "Shpigelglas" after their return to the USSR. There were rumors that the two Fisher sons, William August and Henry, both eventually worked for the KGB. There was another report indicating that William August Fisher had served in the Red Army during the 1920s and became a communications specialist. Then in 1930 there was a report that intercepted official documents from the Near East were translated at KGB Center in Moscow by a certain English Jew named Fisher, who was also in training at the time to go abroad as an illegal.

In April 1931, William August Fisher appeared at the British Consulate General in Moscow and applied for another passport. He claimed that he had trained as a draftsman in the United Kingdom and came to the USSR hoping to get work in shipbuilding. He found nothing in that line and therefore worked mainly as an electrician. It was noted that Fisher spoke English with an extreme North-country accent.

Fisher arrived in Oslo in August 1931 with his wife, Yelena Fisher, born Lebedeva, 29 September 1906 in Russia and their daughter Evelina, born 8 October 1929 in Russia. He stayed in Norway until January 1935, with occasional trips to Sweden and a voyage to England in February 1932. Reports indicate that during the time Fisher was in Norway he was suspected of running an illegal wire/telegraph station. While there, he was known as a first-class mechanic but he never had regular employment. He did a certain amount of work at home in repairs for a local radio agency and occasionally did some repair work for private individuals. During their Norwegian stay the Fishers lived mostly in rented private homes.

Fisher and his family left Norway in mid-January 1935, allegedly for the United Kingdom. The Norwegian Police refused Fisher permission to remain longer in Norway.

In August 1935, the Fishers arrived in Dover from Ostend. The family went on to London where they lived first in a hotel and then in a private home. In November 1935, Fisher went to Denmark for a week.

In May 1936, the Fishers left England for Denmark and again dropped out of sight. The family had apparently returned to the USSR. Reports from various sources over the years have referred to Fisher as a wireless operator for an illegal network in the United Kingdom in 1936, as an electrician who was working for the Kremlin in the mid-1930s, and as an intelligence instructor in the USSR during World War II.

In 1948, Fisher appeared in the West again. He traveled from LeHavre, France via Quebec, Canada, to New York as Andrew Kayotis, a US citizen of Lithuanian background, who was a bachelor and an electrician, in November 1948. He settled in New York City, frequently using the alias Emil H. Goldfus or Martin Collins. From the fall of 1948, he engaged in operational activity, mostly in the eastern part of the United States. In August or September 1954, he made his contact with his assistant Reino Hayhanen, to whom he was known as "Mark." In the summer of 1955, Fisher returned to the USSR for a vacation with his family. He came back to the United States shortly after 1956.

In June or July 1956, Fisher recontacted Hayhanen. The last operational meeting between them occurred in February 1957. Fisher ordered Hayhanen to return to the USSR because his assistant's performance was poor. Hayhanen sensed what was at stake, and he defected to CIA in Paris on 6 May 1957 while en route to Moscow. As a result of Hayhanen's defection and the information he supplied to US intelligence, the FBI arrested Fisher in Brooklyn on 21 June 1957. Apparently he was making preparations to leave the United States, probably for a return to Moscow. He admitted to being "Rudolph Ivanovich Abel." Fisher/ "Abel" was tried for conspiring to transmit US defense secrets to the USSR, gathering such information, and failure to register with the US Government as a foreign agent. Fisher/ "Abel" was fortunate in obtaining the services of James B. Donovan as his court-appointed defense counsel. Donovan represented Fisher/ "Abel" well, both in court during the trial and afterwards. The trial lasted from mid-to-late October 1957. Fisher/ "Abel" was found guilty as charged and was sentenced to 30 years and fined $3,000.

Fisher/ "Abel" apparently did not reveal much during his interrogation, trial, and imprisonment. He claimed that he was born "Abel" on 2 July 1902 in Moscow. He admitted to being a Soviet citizen and explained that the name "Abel" originally came from the German. The scanty information that he divulged or revealed to Hayhanen indicated that he had completed secondary school and then specialized in the electronics phase of engineering. He knew English, French, German, Russian, Polish, Yiddish, and Hebrew. He was also a skilled photographer and an artist. He reportedly joined the KGB in 1927. His wife and daughter had remained in the USSR during his long stay in the United States. Interestingly enough, several of his acquaintances in the New York area thought that he spoke English with a Scottish brogue or a New England "twang," which would seem to indicate that Fisher/ "Abel" had never quite lost his English North-country Tyneside accent.

In 1961 and early 1962, Attorney Donovan became involved in negotiations with the Soviets regarding an exchange of Fisher/ "Abel" for the ill-fated U-2 pilot, Francis Gary Powers, who was shot down over the Soviet Union in May 1960. Finally, on 10 February 1962, Fisher/ "Abel" was released and exchanged for Powers on the Glienicker Bridge in Berlin.

After his return to the USSR, Fisher/ "Abel" reportedly served for a time as a KGB instructor. Then, in the middle 1960s, the KGB began a propaganda campaign to glorify the exploits of their dedicated officers. Konon Molody, in his book, *Spy: Twenty Years in the Soviet Secret Service*, boasted that he had served with Fisher/ "Abel" during World War II in a series of daring operations behind enemy lines. Molody then went on to claim that he was Fisher/ "Abel's" radio man in the United States during the late 1940s and early 1950s, during which time they successfully carried out a series of successful operations under the noses of the FBI. Fisher/ "Abel" himself contributed to the KGB frolic in self-praise. He was the hero in a number of articles, which appeared in the Soviet press regarding his success as a KGB officer abroad. He also made a number of public statements about his career and in general did his bit for the KGB image.

"Abel's" death after "a grave illness" (probably lung cancer) was announced in the Soviet press on 16/17 November 1971. The *Tass* release praised the long and devoted service of this dedicated Chekist to the Soviet cause and the KGB. Interestingly enough his grave marker in a Moscow cemetery finally reveals a glimpse into his background. The marker refers to him as "Fisher, William Genrykhovich-Abel, Rudolf Ivanovich born July 11, 1903 and died November 15, 1971." At last in death the truth emerged.

Fisher was perhaps typical of the turn-of-the-century Russian-Jewish immigration to the textile and industrial belt in the north of England (Tyneside, Cheetham Hill, Manchester). Only in this case the Fishers returned to the Soviet Union and one or perhaps both sons served the Soviet cause effectively and well, using their knowledge of Western languages and lifestyles.

Fisher/ "Abel's" lawyer, James B. Donovan, presented an interesting study of this case in his book, *Strangers on a Bridge*, based on the diaries that he started to keep when he agreed to act as counsel for the defense in August 1957.

Reino Hayhanen

The key to the arrest of Abel was a 36-year-old lieutenant colonel of the KGB. Early in May 1957, he telephoned the US Embassy in Paris and subsequently arrived at the Embassy to be interviewed. To an Embassy official, the Russian espionage agent explained, "I'm an officer in the Soviet intelligence service. For the past five years, I have been operating in the United States. Now I need your help."

This spy, Reino Hayhanen, stated that he had just been ordered to return to Moscow. After five years in the

Reino Hayhanen

United States, he dreaded the thought of going back to his Communist-ruled homeland. He wanted to defect.

Hayhanen was born near Leningrad on May 14, 1920. His parents were peasants. Despite his modest background, Hayhanen was an honor student and, in 1939, obtained the equivalent of a certificate to teach high school.

In September 1939, he was appointed to the primary school faculty in the village of Lipitzi. Two months later, however, the NKVD conscripted him. Since he had studied the Finnish language and was very proficient in its use, he was assigned as an interpreter to a NKVD group and sent to the combat zone to translate captured documents and interrogate prisoners during the Finnish-Soviet war.

With the end of this war in 1940, Hayhanen was assigned to check the loyalty and reliability of Soviet workers in Finland and to develop informants and sources of information in their midst. His primary objective was to identify anti-Soviet elements among the intelligentsia.

Hayhanen became a respected expert in Finnish intelligence matters and in May 1943, was accepted into membership in the Soviet Communist Party. Following World War II, he rose to the rank of senior operative authorized representative of the Segozerski district section of the NKGB and, with headquarters in the Village of Padani, set about the task of identifying dissident elements among the local citizens.

In the summer of 1948, Hayhanen was called to Moscow by the MGB. The Soviet intelligence service had a new assignment for Hayhanen, one which would require him to sever relations with his family, to study the English language, and to receive special training in photographing documents as well as to encode and decode messages.

While his Ministry of State Security (MGB) training continued, Hayhanen worked as a mechanic in the City of Valga, Estonia. Then, in the summer of 1949, he entered Finland as Eugene Nicolai Maki, an American-born laborer.

The real Eugene Nicolai Maki was born in Enaville, Idaho, on May 30, 1919. His mother also was American born; but his father had immigrated into the United States from Finland in 1905. In the mid-1920s, Eugene Maki's parents became deeply depressed by glowing reports of conditions in "the new" Russia. They sold their belongings and left their Idaho farm for New York to book passages on a ship to Europe.

After leaving the United States, the Maki family settled in Estonia. From the outset, it was obvious that they had found no "Utopia" on the border of the Soviet Union. Letters that they wrote their former neighbors showed that Mr. and Mrs. Maki were very unhappy and sorely missed America.

As the years passed, memories of the Maki family gradually began to fade, and all but possibly two or three oldtime residents of Enaville, Idaho, forgot that there had ever been a Maki family in that area. In Moscow, however, plans were being made for a "new" Eugene Maki, one thoroughly ground in Soviet intelligence techniques, to enter the scene.

From July 1949 to October 1952, Hayhanen resided in Finland and established his identity as the American-born Eugene Maki. During this period, he was most cautious to avoid suspicion or attract attention to himself his Soviet superiors wanting him to become established as an ordinary, hard-working citizen. This false "build up," of course, was merely part of his preparation for a new espionage assignment.

While in Finland, Hayhanen met and married Hanna Kurikka. She was to join him in the United States on February 20, 1953, four months after his arrival here. Even his wife knew him only as Eugene Maki, so carefully did he cover his previous life.

On July 3, 1951, Hayhanen then living in Turku, Finland, visited the US Legation in Helsinki. He displayed his birth certificate from the State of Idaho, which showed that he was born in Enaville on May 30, 1919, and, in the presence of a Vice Consul, he executed an affidavit in which he explained that his family had left the United States in 1927: "I accompanied my mother to Estonia when I was eight years of age and resided with her until her death in 1941. I left Estonia for Finland in June 1943, and have resided there for the reason that I have no funds with which to pay my transportation to the United States.

One year later, July 28, 1952, a passport was issued to Hayhanen as Eugene Maki at Helsinki. Using this passport, he sailed October 16, 1952, from Southampton, England, aboard the Queen Mary and arrived at New York City on October 21, 1952.

Several weeks before he departed for America, Hayhanen was recalled to Moscow and introduced to a Soviet agent, "Mikhail," who was to serve as his espionage superior in this country. In order to establish contact with "Mikhail" in the United States, Hayhanen was instructed that after arriving in New York he should go to the Tavern on the Green in Central Park. Near the tavern, he was told, he would find a signpost marked "Horse Carts."

"You will let Mikhail know of your arrival by placing a red thumb tack in this signpost," a Soviet official told him. "If you suspect that you are under surveillance, place a white thumb tack on the board."

The information, which Hayhanen furnished to US officials in Paris, France, in May 1957, was immediately checked. There was no question of its accuracy. Accordingly, passage was secured for Hayhanen on an airliner, and he was permitted to return to the United States.

Following his arrival in New York on May 10, 1957, Hayhanen was given a thorough physical examination, suitable quarters were found for him, and arrangements were made for him to be interviewed by FBI agents.

From the fall of 1952 until early in 1954, he said, "Mikhail" served as his espionage superior in New York. They met only when necessary, the meeting place being the Prospect Park subway station. To exchange messages and intelligence data, they used "dead drops" in the New York area. One of the drops was an iron picket fence at the end of 7th Avenue near Macombs Bridge. Another was the base of a lamppost in Fort Tryon Park.

In one of the dead drops identified by Hayhanen, a hole in a set of cement steps in Prospect Park, FBI agents found a hollowed-out bolt. The bolt was about two inches long and one-fourth inch in diameter. It contained the following typewritten message:

"Nobody came to meeting either 8 or 9th...as I was advised he should. Why? Should he be inside or outside? Is time wrong? Place seems right. Please check."

The bolt was found on May 15, 1957. It had been placed in the dead drop about two years previously, but, by a trick of fate, a repair crew had filled the hole in the stairs with cement, entombing the bolt and the message it contained.

Questioned about the hollow bolt, Hayhanen said that the espionage apparatus that he served often used "trick" containers such as this. Among the items he had been supplied by the Soviets were hollow pens, pencils, screws, batteries, and coins; in some instances magnetized so they could adhere to metal objects.

The FBI wanted to identify "Mikhail," the Soviet with whom Hayhanen maintained contact from the fall of 1952 until early 1954, and "Mark," "Mikhail's" replacement. Hayhanen obtained the impression that "Mikhail" was a Soviet diplomat, possibly attached to the Embassy or the United Nations. He described "Mikhail" as probably between the ages of 40 and 50; medium build, long, thin nose, dark hair, and about five feet nine inches tall. This description was matched against the descriptions of Soviet representatives who had been in the United States between 1952 and 1954. From the long list of possible suspects, the most logical candidate appeared to be Mikhail Nikolaevich Svirin.

Svirin had been in and out of the United States on several occasions between 1939 and 1956. From the latter part of August 1952, until April 1954, he had served as First Secretary of the Soviet United Nations delegation in New York.

On May 16, 1957 FBI agents showed a group of photographs to Hayhanen. The moment his eyes fell upon a picture of Svirin, Hayhanen straightened up in his chair and announced, "That's the one. There is absolutely no doubt about it. That's Mikhail." Unfortunately, Svirin had returned to Moscow.

The FBI turned its attention to "Mark." Hayhanen did not know where "Mark" lived or what name he was using. He did provide other details.

According to Hayhanen, "Mark" was a colonel in the Soviet State Security Service and had been engaged in espionage work since approximately 1927. He had come to the United States in 1948 or 1949, entering by illegally crossing the Canadian border.

In keeping with instructions contained in a message he received from Soviet officials, Hayhanen was met by "Mark" at a movie theater in Flushing, Long Island, during the late summer of 1954. As identification symbols, Hayhanen wore a blue and red striped tie and smoked a pipe.

After their introduction, Hayhanen and "Mark" held frequent meetings in Prospect Park, on crowded streets, and in other inconspicuous places in the area of greater New York. They also made several short trips together to Atlantic City, Philadelphia, Albany, Greenwich, and other communities in the eastern part of the United States.

"Mark" also sent Hayhanen on trips alone. For example, in 1954, Hayhanen was instructed to locate an American army sergeant, one formerly assigned to the US Embassy in Moscow. At the time he related this information to FBI agents in May 1957, Hayhanen could not remember the Army sergeant's name. "I do recall, however, that we used the codename 'Quebec' in referring to him and that he was recruited for Soviet intelligence work while in Moscow."

An intensive investigation was launched to identify and locate "Quebec." In examining a hollow piece of steel from Hayhanen's home, the FBI laboratory discovered a piece of microfilm less that one-inch square. The microfilm bore a typewritten message that identified "Quebec" as Army Sergeant Roy Rhodes and stated that Soviet agents had recruited him in January 1952. Full information concerning Rhodes' involvement in Russian espionage was disseminated to the Army; and following a court-martial, he was sentenced to serve five years at hard labor.

Hayhanen described "Mark" as about 50 years old or possibly older; approximately five feet ten inches tall; thin gray hair; and medium build. The unidentified Soviet agent was an accomplished photographer, and Hayhanen recalled that on one occasion in 1955, "Mark" took him to a storage room where he kept photo supplies on the fourth or fifth floor of a building located near Clark and Fulton Streets in Brooklyn.

The search for this storage room led FBI agents to a building at 252 Fulton Street. Among the tenants was one Emil R. Goldfus, a photographer who had operated a studio on the fifth floor since January 1954 and who also had formerly rented a fifth-floor storage room there.

In April 1957 (the same month Hayhanen boarded a ship for Europe under instructions to return to Moscow), Goldfus had told a few persons in the Fulton Street building that he was going South on a seven-month vacation. "It's doctor's orders," he explained. "I have a sinus condition."

Goldfus disappeared about April 26, 1957. Less than three weeks later, FBI agents arrived at 252 Fulton Street in quest of the mysterious "Mark." Since Goldfus appeared to answer the description of Hayhanen's espionage superior, surveillance was established near his photo studio.

On May 28, 1957, Agents observed a man resembling "Mark" on a bench in a park directly opposite the entrance to 252 Fulton Street. This man occasionally walked about the park; he appeared to be nervous and created the impression that he was looking for someone, possibly attempting to determine any unusual activity in the neighborhood. At 6:50 p.m., this man departed on foot, the Agents certain their presence had not been detected chose to wait rather than take a chance of trailing the wrong man. "If that's 'Mark,' he'll return," they correctly surmised.

While the surveillance continued at 252 Fulton Street, other FBI agents made daily checks on the dead drops, which Hayhanen stated he and "Mark" used. The Agents' long hours of patience were rewarded on the night of June 13, 1957. At 10:00 p.m., they saw the lights go on in Goldfus's studio and observed a man moving in the room.

The lights went out at 11:52 p.m., and a man, who appeared to generally fit the description of "Mark" stepped into the darkness outside the building. This man was followed down Fulton Street to a nearby subway station. Moments later, FBI agents saw him take a subway to 28th street, and they stood by unnoticed as he emerged from the subway and walked to the Hotel Latham on East 28th Street.

On June 15, a photograph of Goldfus, which the FBI took with a hidden camera, was shown to Hayhanen. "You found him," the former Soviet agent exclaimed. "That's 'Mark.'"

Goldfus, registered at the Hotel Latham under the name of Martin Collins, was kept under surveillance from the night of June 13 until the morning of June 21, 1957. During this period, FBI agents discreetly tied together the loose ends of the investigation, matters which had to be resolved before he could be taken into custody.

Arrested by the Immigration and Naturalization Service on an alien warrant, based upon his illegal entry into the United States and failure to register as an alien. "Mark" displayed a defiant attitude. He refused to cooperate in any manner.

Following his arrest, "Mark" was found to possess many false papers, including not one American birth certificate, but two. The first showed that he was Emil R. Goldfus, born August 2, 1902, in New York City. According to the second one, he was Martin Collins, born July 2, 1897, also in New York City. Investigation was to establish that the Emil Goldfus, whose birth certificate "Mark" displayed, had died in infancy. The certificate in the name of Collins was a forgery.

But during his career as a Soviet spy, "Mark" also had used many other names in addition to the ones cited above. For example, during the fall of 1948, while en route to the United States from the Soviet Union, he had adopted the identity of Andrew Kayotis. The real Kayotis, believed to have died in a Lithuanian hospital, was born in Lithuania on October 10, 1895. He had arrived in the United States in October 1916 and became a naturalized American citizen at Grand Rapids, Michigan, on December 30, 1930.

On July 15, 1947, Andrew Kayotis, then residing in Detroit, was issued a passport so that he could visit relatives in Europe. Investigation in Detroit disclosed that several persons there considered Kayotis to be in poor physical condition at the time of his departure from the United States. Letters subsequently received from him indicated that he was in a Lithuanian hospital.

When Kayotis' friends in Michigan heard no more from him, they assumed that he had passed away.

Nearly 10 years later, "Mark" was to admit that he had used Kayotis' passport during the fall of 1948 in booking passage abroad an ocean liner from LeHarve, France, to Canada. On November 14, 1948, he disembarked from the ship at Quebec and quickly dropped out of sight.

"Mark" made one final admission— that he was a Russian citizen, Rudolph Ivanovich Abel.

The Case of the Substitute Colonel

The following is an example of a "legal" operation concerning the actives of Maksim Grigorlevich Martynov, born 17 February 1915 at Leningradskaya Oblast, USSR, who held the rank of colonel in the Soviet Military Establishment.

In August 1954, a Soviet officer invited a US Army Colonel, whom he knew through official contacts, to lunch with him in East Berlin. The Soviet, who knew the American planned to retire from the Army, indicated he wanted to have a private conversation with him. On the designated date, the two met by prearrangement and drove to a house that was unoccupied. There they met a newcomer, dressed in civilian clothes. He acknowledged the introduction by saying, "Hello, Colonel, how are you?" in perfect English. This Soviet stated he had been in New York during the war and inferred that he had worked at Amtorg (The Soviet Government's Purchasing Commission in the United States).

After the meal, the American colonel indicated that he must leave, but the Soviet officer insisted that he stay at least for a cup of coffee. The Soviet officer then left the room and was gone about 30 minutes. During his absence, the Soviet civilian talked about inconsequential things, then asked the colonel if he planned to live in Leavenworth, Kansas, (location of the Army Command and General Staff School) upon his return to the United States. The colonel replied that he did. (The colonel had not mentioned his place of retirement to the Soviet civilian, though he recalled he had previously mentioned it to another Soviet officer at an official function).

The Soviet civilian then asked, "colonel, if I come to the States, could I come and see you there"? The colonel's reply was "Why certainly." The Soviet then remarked that he was a man with a wife and child and wanted security for them. He asked the colonel if he would help him if he (the Soviet) came to the States, thereby implying that he might be seeking asylum or financial assistance by working as a double agent. Again the colonel replied that he would. The Soviet then made a chart of downtown Manhattan. He marked the northeast corner of 86th Street and Madison Avenue with a dot. The Soviet then asked if the colonel could come to New York, and the colonel replied that he might do so in the fall. The Soviet then indicated that if the colonel would come to the above mentioned spot he would meet him there in New York City at 4 p.m. on any of the following alternate dates: October 15, 25; or November 5, 15, or 25; January 1; February 1; or March 1.

The Soviet then contradicted his earlier comments by stating that although he himself would probably not meet the American in New York, someone would do so and would make the following statement, "Seems to me that I have met you at Spechstrasse, Colonel. What is the number of your house there?" The Soviet continued, "You should reply: "Oh yes, I have lived there at Spechstrasse 19."

The Soviet then asked if the colonel could bring some books, pamphlets, and maps from the school in Leavenworth with him. The colonel replied that since he would be retired, he would have nothing to do with the Leavenworth school. The Soviet suggested that he could perhaps get some material anyhow. The American, now realizing that he was definitely being approached for espionage purposes, stalled by replying: "I'll have to think it over." The Soviet then asked the colonel if he needed any money, and he replied in the negative. With that, the colonel left the house and returned to West Berlin.

The American Army Colonel immediately reported this meeting and approach to appropriate authorities and indicated his willingness to cooperate in any way with the proper intelligence agencies in connection with any future meetings with the Soviet. Shortly thereafter, the colonel returned to the United States and full details were made available to the FBI. On October 15, 1954—the first meeting date set by the Soviet civilian—FBI agents took inconspicuous positions near the intersection of 86th and Madison, in New York. At the same approximate time as the colonel's appointment, these agents observed Soviet officers attached to the Soviet representation at the United Nations obviously looking over the contemplated rendezvous point. They seemed to be expecting another party to appear.

The FBI made arrangements to effect a meeting on the next scheduled date of October 25, 1954. Plans were made for a Special Agent of the FBI to act as a substitute for the Army Colonel and accordingly, a Bureau agent who came closest to resembling the colonel was selected for the assignment. The agent also had to familiarize himself to a considerable extent with the background of the colonel, his family, activities and whereabouts, the colonel's previous assignments in Germany, and many other details that might be necessary to deceive the Soviets.

On October 25, the Special Agent posing as the Colonel arrived at the intersection. Two Soviet nationals were observed in the area closely scrutinizing the agent posing as the Colonel, but they made no attempt to contact him. Again on November 5, 1954, the Special Agent was present at the meeting place; however no Soviets were seen in the area.

On November 15, the Special Agent arrived at the designated intersection by taxicab. He noticed a man standing on the corner who was obviously watching him. He wore a dark blue overcoat, blue suit, and dark gray hat. For five minutes the stranger studied the Agent intensely, then after a series of passings by and general uninterested glances, he walked up to him and mumbled something. The substitute Colonel didn't hear him and queried: "Pardon me?" The Soviet national then gave the prearranged code phrase: "Seems to me that I have met you at Spechstrasse colonel, what is the number of your house there?" The Agent replied: "Oh yes, I have lived there at Spechstrasse 19." The Soviet then introduced himself as "Schultz" and suggested they go for a ride. The agent declined, suggesting a walk to Central Park instead. The Soviet accepted this proposal. "Schultz" was immediately recognized by FBI agents concealed in the area as one Martynov attached to the Soviet delegation at the UN.

As they walked, the "colonel" asked whether he would meet the Russian to whom he had been introduced in August in East Berlin. "Schultz" replied in the negative indicating that he was his friend and was carrying out the mission for him. The "colonel" then showed his identification card, which the Soviet examined.

Being unable to find an available bench upon their arrival in Central Park, the "colonel" and "Schultz" continued walking with the latter posing questions concerning Fort Leavenworth and the substitute colonel furnishing innocuous answers and unclassified data. The Soviet indicated he needed specific information about the Army school, which the "colonel" said he might be able to obtain. The Soviet then handed the "Colonel" 25 $10 bills after commenting on his heavy expenses in coming to New York for this meeting.

"Schultz" asked the "colonel" to meet him again the same hour at 86th and Madison Avenue on 15 January 1955. If "Schultz" did not appear on that date, he requested the "colonel' to come on the 1st Saturday of each succeeding month for 4 months to a Fifth Avenue book store, the address of which he furnished.

"Schultz" then indicated that if he did not appear, another Soviet would take his place and would carry in his left hand a red and blue pencil, sharpened at both ends with a street guide of Manhattan and the Bronx in his right coat pocket. The type of greeting was also agreed upon.

On 15 January 1955 "Schultz" himself was waiting at the appointed time and place when the substitute "colonel" arrived by taxicab and suggested they take a walk. When the "colonel" mentioned Central Park, "Schultz" refused and insisted on walking up Madison Avenue. They agreed to go to a hotel bar. As they walked along, the "colonel" told "Schultz" that he had been successful in getting some of the desired material and that he had it in his briefcase.

As the entered the bar, they sat down and the "colonel" placed the briefcase on the seat next to him. "Schultz" cautioned the "colonel" to speak in a low voice. The "colonel" then indicated he had in the briefcase all the material the Soviet desired. "Schultz" whispered, "I don't like this place" and appeared extremely anxious to leave the bar and get possession of the briefcase.

At this point the "colonel" placed the briefcase on the table in front of him. This was the signal for the other Special agents secreted in the area to approach. As they identified themselves to "Schultz," he appeared shaken but upon request displayed credentials identifying himself as Martynov, a member of the Soviet delegation to the UN. As such, he enjoyed diplomatic immunity. He was confronted with the knowledge of his act of espionage.

Martynov refused to talk further with the agents. He paid for the drinks, left the bar at 4:13 p.m., and proceeded by bus to the Soviet UN delegation headquarters. On 21 February 1955, Martynov was declared *persona non grata* and departed the United States on 25 February 1955.

Other Spies

Giuseppe E. Cascio

Giuseppe E. Cascio was a bombardier in World War II, who twice won the Distinguished Flying Cross. In 1952, Casio was assigned to Korea as a photo laboratory technician and occasional photographer with the 9th Air Base Group. On 21 September 1952, the US Air Force staff sergeant was arrested following a 6-week investigation and charged with 16 counts of accepting military payment certificates from a Korean civilian. He tried to sell the classified flight test data about the

Giuseppe E. Cascio

F-86E Sabre jet aircraft to North Korean Intelligence officers. The 9-year service veteran had obtained the classified information from US Air Force Sergeant John P. Jones.

Subsequent to his arrest, Cascio's wife revealed that her husband was "goofy at times." She is further quoted as saying, "That man is a psychopathic case and is not responsible for what he is doing." Additionally, the chief medical officer at the Veterans Administration Hospital in Houston, Texas stated that Sergeant Cascio had been diagnosed as "a dangerous paranoid."

On 8 June 1953, the 34-year-old Cascio was convicted by general court-martial and sentenced to 20 years at hard labor on charges of conspiracy to pass "secrets of the Sabre jet fighter to the Communists." Jones was not prosecuted because he suffered a nervous breakdown and was deemed incompetent to stand trial.

Jack Edward Dunlap

Jack Edward Dunlap was a high school dropout who served in the merchant marines for eight years before transferring to the US Army. On 23 April 1958, after 6 years of Army duty, including a combat tour in Korea, Dunlap was assigned to the National Security Agency (NSA). In June 1960, the married sergeant purchased a cabin cruiser for cash. Following this initial purchase, Dunlap, who also had a girlfriend, bought a hydroplane skimmer, joined a boat club, and bought two Cadillacs and a Jaguar automobile.

Although his lifestyle did attract some attention, it was not until Sergeant Dunlap sought to leave the military service and join NSA as a civilian that suspicions were aroused sufficiently to initiate an investigation into Dunlap's activities. The NSA routinely polygraphs civilian job applicants and as a result of these polygraph tests an intense investigation was conducted on Dunlap. Within days, in July 1963, the 38-year-old sergeant first class was found dead, an apparent suicide. Because his death occurred prior to questioning, or an admission of guilt, the exact nature and extent of his activities remain unknown.

Approximately one month following his death, Dunlap's widow discovered a cache of highly classified documents in their home. This discovery, along with additional investigations, confirmed that Dunlap had been involved in espionage rather than petty thievery or other immoral conduct. It is believed that Dunlap volunteered his services to the Soviets by walking into the Soviet Embassy in Washington DC, on or before June 1960.

Dunlap's espionage activity is thought to have netted him between $30,000 and $40,000 during his first year of spying. It is suspected that Dunlap removed documents from NSA, turned them over to the Soviets for microfilming, and then returned the originals to the NSA. He had access to classified material including Central Intelligence Agency estimates concerning Soviet missile forces and locations and Soviet troop dispositions in Eastern Europe, particularly East Germany.

George H. French

On April 5, 1957, an individual attempted to personally deliver a letter to the Soviet Embassy in Washington, DC, by placing the letter in a newspaper and leaving it on the Embassy grounds. The newspaper was recovered by the FBI and was found to contain a note with information identifying a hotel room in New York City (room 1877, Hotel New Yorker); instructions on how to make contact with the individual; and an offer to commit espionage.[101] The note included an offer to sell "valuable military information, including diagrams of weapons for $27,500. A check of the hotel disclosed that Cap. George H. French, from Mount Vernon, New York, and a bombardier-navigator assigned

George H. French

to the 60th Bombardment Squadron, Ramey Air Force Base, Puerto Rico, was registered in the room described in the note.

Air Force Office of Special Investigations (AFOSI) and FBI agents, posing as Soviet intelligence officers, followed the instructions provided by French in the note and met him in his hotel room in New York City. Believing the AFOSI and FBI agents to be Soviet intelligence, French offered to sell classified drawings, but indicated that they were in Puerto Rico. The agents identified themselves and arrested French.

A search of his room revealed a key to a train station locker, and French led agents to the locker that contained classified notes and diagrams pertaining to special weapons research and development. The sketches and notes concerned special weapons fuse and control systems, along with circuit wiring diagrams of the weapons. A search of his residence in Puerto Rico disclosed 60 classified documents, which French had collected and intended to provide at a later date to Soviet intelligence.

French had served in both World War II and the Korean war and had received several decorations during a career to include the American Defense Service Medal and the Air Medal with five oak leaf clusters. In Europe, he flew 35 combat missions as a B-17 bombardier and navigator, and during the Korean war he flew five combat missions in B-29s.[102]

His wife attributed her husband's espionage attempt to financial difficulties. He was supporting a family of five on $803.38 a month.[103] Captain French was addicted to gambling and could not afford the stakes he lost. His gambling losses apparently resulted in a debt of over $8,000 or almost one year of pay.[104]

On September 20, 1957, after a five-month investigation, French pled guilty and was convicted of espionage at a court-martial. He received a life sentence; however, although the conviction was upheld, the sentence was reduced to 10 years.[105]

Valentin Alekseyevich Gubichev
On March 1949, with the arrest in New York of Valentin Gubichev, a Soviet engineer employed by the United Nations and engaged in working on the construction of the United Nations headquarters building, the FBI ended a lengthy search for an individual known to have been channeling to Moscow confidential investigative material originating in the Bureau itself. Arrested as coconspirator and the source of Gubichev's reports to Moscow was a US citizen, Judith Coplon, an employee in the Department of Justice's Foreign Agent's Registration Section.

At the time of his arrest, associates of Gubichev at the UN described him as a good man who did his work in the planning office and "worked both inside and outside," a statement which cannot be considered inaccurate.

Although Gubichev claimed diplomatic immunity, and diplomatic immunity was claimed for him by Soviet officials (despite the fact that he was not a Soviet but a UN employee), he faced indictment, conviction of espionage, and eventual expulsion (in preference to a 15-year prison sentence) as the holder of an expired diplomatic visa.

Upon the arrest of the pair, whom Miss Coplon described in her later testimony as trysting lovers, Miss Coplon's purse was found to contain secret lists taken from the files of the Justice Department and containing the names of counterespionage agents and also of Communists engaged in espionage in the United States.

Although the true origin and history of the Gubichev-Coplon association is unknown, the Soviets are believed to have selected Gubichev to be Miss Coplon's contact and handler under the belief that official Soviet personnel in the United States at the time were more liable to close scrutiny than would be a member of the United Nations group.

Gubichev did not testify during his trial, claiming the whole situation an "illegal" one, but nonetheless was convicted on both counts of conspiring (with Miss Coplon) and espionage.

The Soviet had originally come to the United States in 1946 as an engineer/architect and had reportedly previously worked in the Soviet Ministry of Foreign Affairs, prior to which he was a construction engineer. He was recommended by the Soviets to the United Nations as an engineer and as part of the Soviet quota of employees on the United Nations headquarters project.

Following his conviction 10 March 1950, Gubichev departed the United States on the Polish ship *Batory*.

John P. Jones

On September 21, 1952, AFOSI apprehended Staff Sergeant John P. Jones, assigned to the Headquarters Squadron, Taegu, Korea, and a resident of Manchester, Massachusetts, for conspiring to "give intelligence to the enemy." Apprehended along with Jones was Staff Sergeant Giuseppe E. Casio.

Jones provided classified information to Casio, which Casio in turn provided to a Korean national. Casio was tried and convicted, receiving a 20-year prison sentence. Jones was not charged and returned to the United States after a medical board declared him to be insane and incompetent to stand trial.

Hans Kessler

Hans Kessler, a West German businessman, was arrested for espionage. He was recruited in 1953 by the foreign intelligence component of Polish State Security (UB) when he went to East Berlin to seek new business. The UB officer who spotted and recruited him was stationed in East Berlin under the cover of the Polish Trade Delegation. Kessler agreed to provide the UB with information if the Poles would provide him with business. Meetings were held in East Berlin and Warsaw.

During 1957, Kessler told his UB case officer that he was able to deliver valuable information on the American bomber "HUSTLER" as well as actual parts of the bomber. The UB notified Soviet Intelligence (KGB) of this development, and the KGB showed considerable interest. Kessler claimed to be able to subvert an American friend as his source on the bomber and said he would bring this American with him to a meeting with the UB in East Berlin. The KGB asked the UB if one of their officers could attend this meeting, and the UB agreed. Later, Kessler said that he could not bring the American with him, but would come alone.

The meeting took place finally in May 1957, in a Polish safehouse in East Berlin. At this meeting Kessler stated that he would be willing to introduce his friend, the American, to the Poles on the condition that he was paid his and the American's expenses and a bonus of $100,000 if it was possible to procure the necessary components of the "HUSTLER" bomber. The Soviets agreed to these demands despite their believing that the American was notional. During this meeting with the KGB officers in Berlin, Kessler mentioned that he had excellent contacts in Teheran, which he might be able to use to transship the necessary components of the "HUSTLER" bomber where he was able to procure them.

Further negotiations on this matter were carried on between the Russians and Kessler without Polish involvement. The Russians never discussed the outcome of this matter with the Poles, and it might be conjectured that the deal was actually consummated between Kessler and the KGB.

Kessler received a total of 10,000 West German marks from the Poles, as well as $1000 for expenses from the KGB. He also made profitable business deals with Poland, arranged by the UB.

Kessler's son, Hans, was also recruited by the UB, and Kessler was instrumental in arranging meetings between his technical advisor, Herbert Schweitzer, and the UB, which led to recruitment of Schweitzer. Kessler had excellent contacts in the West German munitions and chemical industries and would have been in a position to supply good information on them. He and his son ran Kesko GmbH and were well known for obtaining strategic materials for the Soviet bloc. An investigative procedure was brought against them in 1959 on charges of suspected treasonous contacts with Col. Eugeniusz Jajko (Z-II officer stationed at the Polish Military Mission, West Berlin) and Alexei Nikolayevich Ktorov, KGB officer stationed in Karlshorst.

The "American" mentioned was undoubtedly John Diess, German-born Canadian citizen who was arrested ca. March 1958, on charges of violating the US export laws, by shipping critical equipment to Kesko in Frankfurt. No mention was made of the "HUSTLER" in that account. However, in December 1959, there was a report from Vienna that a business contact had discovered in Kessler's briefcase complete blueprints on the jet fighter "BLASTER" (probably garble for HUSTLER) and other information pertaining to West

German mine detectors. Soviet Air Force General Romanov of the Soviet Embassy, Vienna, was overheard telling Kessler that $100,000 had been deposited for him in the Paris Bank du Nord.

The West German police again arrested the Kesslers. Kessler, Jr., was released for lack of evidence, but Kessler, Sr., was still in jail. Neither confessed.

Gustav Adolph Mueller

Gustav Adolph Muller was born in Rangoon, Burma, of an English mother and a Swiss father. His mother became a naturalized US citizen while Mueller was still less than 18 years of age. Mueller enlisted in the US Air Force in 1947 in St. Paul, Minnesota, after having attended the University of Minnesota.

Corporal Muller was assigned as a student in the European Command Intelligence School, Oberammergau, West Germany, when he sent a telegram to the Soviet Consulate in Bern, Switzerland. In the telegram, Mueller suggested that the Soviets would find it beneficial to contact him. Another student, who was with Mueller at the time he sent the telegram under the pseudonym John S. Watson, became suspicious and reported the incident to authorities.

On 7 October 1949, Mueller was arrested as he attempted to hand over two SECRET documents to the US Army investigators who were posing as his Soviet contacts. Mueller admitted to having stolen the documents from the school library where he was a student. He claimed in his defense that he was attempting to entice the Soviets into thinking he would serve as their agent. He said that it was easy to steal classified material because Americans were so careless. He further claimed that he hated Communism and that he sent the telegram on a juvenile impulse to see what would happen.

The medical examination conducted on Mueller showed the 19-year-old to be immature and emotionally unstable. Mueller is believed to be the first US active-duty serviceman to have attempted to pass classified information to the Soviets following World War II.

On 15 April 1950, Mueller was found guilty of attempting to deliver US classified information to the Soviets. He was sentenced by court-martial to five years in prison, received a dishonorable discharge, and forfeited all pay and allowances.

Joseph Sidney Petersen, Jr.

Joseph Sidney Petersen, Jr. was born on 30 September 1914. He attended Loyola University in his hometown of New Orleans, Louisiana, and received a Master of Science degree from St. Louis University in 1938. Prior to his government employment, Petersen taught physics courses at Loyola and Ursuline College in New Orleans.

In 1941, Petersen began work as a DoD civilian in communications analysis. During World War II, he established a close liaison relationship with the Dutch military and regularly exchanged information with his Dutch contacts. His friendship with a Dutch expert cryptologist, Col. J. A. Verkuyl, resulted in an introduction to Giacomo Stuyt, an official of the Dutch Embassy in Washington, DC. Petersen gave Stuyt information on movements of North Korean intelligence personnel, documents dealing with a Chinese telegraphic code, and a Hagelin cryptographic machine. Petersen removed the classified documents from his office and provided them to Stuyt who made photocopies and returned the original copies to Petersen.

Petersen was arrested on 9 October 1954 and charged with three counts, including two counts of violating espionage statutes. Petersen's espionage activity may have been discovered as a result of a routine updating

Gustav Adolph Mueller

of his security clearances when it was determined he was corresponding with Verkuyl. The complaint issued against Petersen charged that he obtained classified documents for illegal purposes from March 1948 to 31 December 1952. He was allowed to plead guilty on the lesser of three counts in order to avoid the need to disclose classified information at a public trial. There appeared to be no rationale for Petersen's actions beyond that of friendship. The Dutch Embassy stated that it was under the impression that Petersen had been authorized to provide the information to the Dutch Government.

On 4 January 1955, Petersen was sentenced to seven years in prison because he "knowingly and willfully used in a manner prejudicial to the safety and interest of the United States classified information concerning communications intelligence activities of the United States and foreign governments."

Roy Adair Rhodes

In 1951, US Army Master Sergeant Roy Adair Rhodes was assigned as a mechanic in the US Embassy garage, Moscow, USSR. Rhodes was on an unaccompanied tour, having left his wife and daughter in the United States.

In December 1951, Rhodes participated in a drinking party with his two Russian mechanics and two Russian girls. He awakened the next day in the presence of one of the girls and was subsequently accosted in the street by the other girl, her brother, and another man. Rhodes was then blackmailed into revealing information about himself to include his earlier training in code work. He also related information concerning the habits of other US personnel assigned to the US Embassy in Moscow. In return for the information he provided, Rhodes was paid between $2,500 and $3,000 in five or six payments.

Following his transfer from the USSR to the United States, Rhodes never tried to recontact the Soviets. His espionage activities in Moscow were not discovered until 1957 when Reino Hayhanen, a defector and confessed former Soviet spy, testified that he had been ordered to locate Sergeant Rhodes.

On 21 February 1958, Sergeant Rhodes was convicted by court-martial for conspiracy to spy for the USSR and falsifying a loyalty certificate. He was sentenced to five years in prison, received a dishonorable discharge, and forfeited all pay and allowances.

James Sattler

James Sattler was a well-known scholar and consultant to a private foreign policy study foundation. As such, he had access to US Department of State and Defense Department officials. In 1967 he was recruited by the East German Ministry of State Security and trained in microphotography.

He reported on US foreign policy via a witting letterdrop in West Germany until the FBI confronted him. In 1975 he confessed to his spying activities. He did not have access to classified documents; however, the insights he provided to the East Germans were undoubtedly useful.

Otto Verber

Otto Verber and Kurt Leopold Ponger, both born in Vienna, Austria, became naturalized US citizens in 1943. Verber served in the US Army during Word War II and was commissioned as a second lieutenant on 8 December 1944. He served as a military intelligence officer until 8 February 1945 and later as a civilian interrogator for the War Crimes Commission that conducted the trials of German war criminals at Nueremberg, Germany. Ponger joined the US Army on 11 June 1943 and subsequently was also employed as a civilian by the War Crimes Commission. Ponger married Verber's sister, and, in 1948, both men went to Vienna, where they were registered as correspondents for the Central European Press Agency. They also had attended school in Vienna under the GI Bill.

In 1949, a US Government employee in Vienna reported to US military intelligence that Verber had approached him for espionage purposes. US Army intelligence kept a 4-year watch on the activities of the two until they were arrested in Vienna on 14 January 1953 and returned to the U.S. for trial. Verber and Ponger, both married, were 31 and 49 years old, respectively, at the time of their arrest. The 14-count indictment against the brothers-in-law listed specific acts of conspiracy dating from mid-June 1949 until 4 January 1951. Named in the conspiracy charges was Yuri V. Novikov, Second Secretary of the Soviet Embassy, Washington, DC. Ponger and Verber were specifically charged with attempting "... to violate the espionage statutes by obtaining information relating to the intelligence and counterintelligence work of the US Army and Air Force, and data relating to aircraft, defense works, and other military installations and operations."

Motivations, not specifically mentioned, were alluded to by their attorney who claimed that the two had turned to Communism after Hitler's invasion of Austria.

In April 1953, both men pleaded guilty to several counts of the indictment and were sentenced in June; Verber from $3^{1}/_{3}$ to 10 years in prison and Ponger from 5 to 10 years in prison. In 1957, it was reported that a Federal judge revoked Ponger's citizenship and directed that Ponger be deported upon his release from prison.

Sybille Wambach

A defector from the principal East German foreign espionage organization, Central Intelligence Administration (HVA) reported on an operation directed against the American Consulate General in Munich and the American Embassy in Bonn from East Berlin.

Early in 1957 this defector was given a lead to a possible agent by one Kotek, a staff officer of the East German intelligence service. Kotek had recruited one Sybille Wambach, a kindergarten teacher in Spindlersfeld, to work against West German visitors to East German Mass Organizations (i.e., Free German Youth (FDJ)), but she had been unsuccessful in that assignment. Checks showed that Wambach was a loyal Socialist Unity Party (SED) member, and she was contacted and recruited for the East German intelligence service after a meeting with an officer of that service in a Spindlersfeld restaurant. She agreed to move to West Germany and eventually emigrated to the United States.

Until late in the summer of 1957, Wambach went once a week to a clandestine meeting place where she was trained in tradecraft, cover, surveillance, and communications and was briefed on West German security organizations. Her communications training included secret writing, microdots, and cryptography.

In September 1957, she was sent to Tuebingen, West Germany to live with her aunt and uncle, the latter, a philosophy professor at the University of Tuebingen, for a period long enough to acquire West German documentation and find a job as a domestic servant in an American home in the Munich area. By October, Wambach had found work in the home of a USAF major. She remained there until July 1958, when the officer was transferred to the States; she then returned to East Berlin for a meeting with her East German superiors.

At this meeting she reported on the morale of the American troops in the Munich area, training exercises she had seen or heard about, and the preparedness of the 7th Army. All reports were based on her observations. Wambach also gave the East German service a one-page list of the telephone numbers of her employer's unit. After the meeting in Berlin, Wambach returned to Munich and found employment at the home of another USAF officer, who was assigned to the same unit as her former employer. She was given the additional assignment of spotting and assessing other maids in American households for possible recruitment.

In spring 1958, at the time of the Lebanon crisis, she reported that paratroops had been alerted and the 7th Army was on an alert basis. This information was highly prized by the HVA and was passed immediately to the Soviets.

After her employer was transferred in December 1958, Wambach again met with the East German officer in East Berlin, this time reporting that she had found a new job with an unidentified Department of Army civilian in Munich, who was in the habit of bringing home work from the office and holding political discussions with his friends in his home. The East German Service trained Wambach to use a Minox camera and instructed her in the photographing of documents and how to reconnoiter the house of her employer for the possible installation of a microphone.

Before Wambach reported on the above mission, Horst Jaennicke, Chief of Department 3 of the HVA, decided to turn her over to the branch of the HVA that had as its major target the American Consulate General in Munich. Jaennicke was so impressed by Wambach's intelligence and her experience with children that he was certain she would have no problem finding a job with a family in the Consulate.

In the spring of 1959, Wambach was turned over to Gotthard Schramm, an officer of the HVA branch working the American Embassy in Bonn, and moved to Bonn. Between 1959 and 1961, Wambach was employed by several Americans in Bonn, including two officials in the American Embassy.

In June 1961, she received a telephone message that her mother, who lives in East Germany, was very ill and that she should come home immediately. She departed immediately.

Subsequently, Wambach telephoned and said that she was obliged to remain in Berlin because her mother had had a severe heart attack, but that she planned to return in a few days. Her employer received a second call from Wambach stating that she would not be able to return as expected.

Wambach telephoned a third time to apologize for her delayed return, and when her employer offered to forward her mail, she said this was not necessary since she would be returning soon.

A fourth telephone call was received from an unidentified female who asked for Wambach. When the caller was told that Wambach was not available, she requested that Wambach be told she was urgently expected. An attempt was made to obtain more details as to where Wambach was expected but the caller hung up.

The Soble Spy Ring

Jacob Albam

On August 9, 1957 Albam, like Mrs. Soble, was sentenced to five and a half years in prison after pleading guilty to, and being convicted of espionage in behalf of the Soviet Union as a member of the Soble spy ring.

On October 8, 1957, the sentences of Mrs. Soble and Albam were reduced, respectively, to four and five years. In lightening the sentences, the judge stated that he was taking into account the remorse of both people for what they had done and the valuable assistance they had given to the US Government since their arrest.

Jack Soble

On October 8, 1957, Soble was sentenced to seven years in prison after pleading guilty in his trial to spying for the Soviet Union.

A Lithuanian refuge who had come to the United States in 1941 and used a brush importing business as a cover for his activities as head of a Soviet spy ring, Soble was arrested in 1957 under an indictment, which might have brought the death penalty had he been convicted under it.

Soble at first claimed innocence but later had a change of heart, expressed remorse for what he had done, and cooperated with the US Government by giving it further information on Soviet espionage activities in the United States. At the time of his trial, he pleaded guilty to the second count of his indictment, conspiring to obtain information vital to the United States while knowing that it would be turned over to the Soviet Union. As a result, the first count of the indictment, which charged him with actually transmitting defense secrets to Moscow and carried a possible death penalty, was dropped. The chief government witness against Soble was US counterspy Boris Morros.

Myra Soble

On August 9, 1957, Myra Soble, wife of Jack, was sentenced to five and a half years in prison after pleading guilty, with him, to charges of espionage.

Jack Soble

Myra Soble

Mr. and Mrs. George M. Zlatovski

On July 8, 1957, the Zlatovskis were indicted as members of the global Soviet spy ring run by Soble. In all, 38 overt acts of espionage were charged against them. The indictment stated that they had been members of the Soble spy ring as early as 1945, that they had turned over information to Boris Morros, and that Soble had paid them for their work with funds supplied by the Soviet Union.

Zlatovski was a Russian-born engineer and a former US Army intelligence officer, who had left military service in 1948. His wife, the former Jane Foster, was an artist and an 11th-generation American, a former employee of the Office of Strategic Services, and the daughter of a prominent San Francisco family.

At the time of indictment, the Zlatovskis were in Paris where they had lived since 1949. They denied the charges made against them in the indictment, but refused to return to the United States to face trial.

One of the important elements in the Zlatovski case was that in 1955, when Mrs. Zlatovski's passport expired, Secretary of State Allen Dulles tried to have its renewal blocked on the basis of information concerning Communist activities on her part over a period of years up to and including 1948. She then sued for renewal of her passport, and Judge Burnita S. Matthews of the Federal district court in Washington, DC, ruled that the State Department had to renew her passport unless it could present more recent and damaging evidence against her.

Faced with the choice of revealing information that would have led to the disclosure of Boris Morros to the Soviets as a counterspy for the United States or renewing Mrs. Zlatovski's passport, the State Department took the latter course as the lesser of two evils. Mrs. Zlatovski was thus able to evade trial for the acts she had committed against her country in behalf of the international Communist conspiracy.

Mr. and Mrs. Alfred K. Stern

On June 16, 1958, a Federal grand jury returned a three-count indictment against Mr. and Mrs. Alfred Stern, which could have brought them the death penalty, if they were ever brought to trial. They were charged with being members of the Soviet spy ring that included Boris Morros and Vassili Zubilin, former second secretary of the Soviet Embassy in Washington.

The Sterns had been subpoenaed on March 14, 1958, to appear before the same grand jury that indicted the Sobles, Albam, and the Zlatovskis. Both were in Mexico at the time, having moved there in 1953. Following their refusal to appear before the grand jury, they were convicted of contempt and fined $25,000 cash.

Early in July 1958, they left Mexico City by plane for Zurich, renounced their US citizenship, and took refuge behind the Iron Curtain. Like the Zlatovskis, Mr. and Mrs. Stern had both been very active in Communist fronts in earlier years. Stern was a wealthy New York investment broker. In their contempt trial, the government prosecutor claimed that they were worth $1,250,000, that they had an annual income of $50,000 from securities, and that in February and March of 1957, they had liquidated in the United States securities worth $532,000 and also sold a large estate in Ridgefield, Connecticut. Mrs. Stern, the former Martha Dodd, was the daughter of US Ambassador, William Dodd, to Germany in the 1930s.

Boris Morros revealed that it was Mrs. Stern who placed him under suspicion with his Soviet espionage

Jane Zlatovski, a former employee of the OSS and the daughter of a prominent San Francisco family.

George M. Zlatovski, a Russian-born engineer and a former US Army intelligence officer.

bosses—and thus endangered his life—by writing a report to Moscow saying that she suspected his loyalty to the Soviet Union.

On September 9, 1957, the Sterns were indicted in absentia on espionage charges. The indictment charged them with conspiring to act as Soviet agents; receiving American military, commercial, and industrial information; and transmitting it to the Soviet Union. In 1979 the charges against them were dropped when the Department of Justice said witnesses considered crucial to the case had died.

From Mexico, they went to Prague, Czechoslovakia, and then to Moscow, where they resided for a year. In 1958 they returned to Prague where they lived until 1963, when they went to Cuba and lived there until 1970 before returning to Prague. In June 1986, Alfred Stern died of cancer.

Mark Zborowski

On November 20, 1958, Zborowski, a Russian-born anthropologist and former Harvard research assistant, was convicted of perjury in denying to a Federal grand jury investigating espionage that he had known Jack Soble.

Zborowski had come to the United States as a refuge in 1941. He had admitted that he had been an agent of the Soviet secret police in France in the early 1930s and that he had infiltrated the Trotskyite movement there to report to Moscow on its activities. He denied, however, that he had ever committed espionage while in the United States.

Jack Soble testified in the trial of Zborowski that he had met him 40 to 50 times and that Zborowski had given him information for transmission to the Soviet Union.

On December 8, 1958, Zborowski was sentenced to five years in prison, the maximum penalty for perjury.

Defectors

Yuriy Aleksandrovich Rastvorov

Yuriy Aleksandrovich Rastvorov, born 11 July 1921, Dmitriyev, Kurskaya Oblast, USSR, is a former Soviet State Security officer who defected to the West in 1954 while stationed in Japan.

Rastvorov's father was a colonel in the People's Commissariat of Internal Affairs (NKVD) who retired at the end of World War II. His mother was a physician who died in 1946. As a youth, Rastvorov was a member of the Young Pioneers and then the Komsomol.

After completing his secondary education, Rastvorov was drafted into the Soviet Army in 1939. Initially he was an enlisted man in the First Proletarian Division that participated in the occupation of Latvia and Lithuania. In December 1940 he was assigned to study Japanese at the Far Eastern Language Institute in Moscow. At that institute he automatically became a member of Soviet Military Intelligence (Chief Intelligence Directorate of the General Staff of the Ministry of Defense-GRU), and in 1941 he was commissioned as a junior lieutenant while serving on temporary duty in Mongolia. After graduating from this institute in March 1943 he was transferred to Soviet State Security (then the People's Commissariat of State Security-NKGB) and assigned to the Far East where he was involved in deciphering Japanese, British and German codes. In 1944 he was assigned to the Soviet State Security Intelligence School in Moscow. Upon completion of this school in 1946, he was assigned to the Soviet Mission in Tokyo under Foreign Ministry cover as an interpreter/translator.

In 1946, Rastvorov was recalled to the Soviet Union for security reasons primarily concerning his grandfather whom he had failed to identify as a kulak on his personal history statement. After successfully defending himself, he was assigned to the Japanese section of State Security in Moscow. A year later he became a member of the Communist Party, and in 1950 he was assigned to Japan as the senior political advisor at the Soviet Mission. His wife and daughter remained in Moscow because he believed that his assignment to Japan could be jeopardized if he attempted to obtain the necessary security clearances on them. At that time he was promoted to lieutenant colonel in the Soviet State Security (then the Ministry of Internal Affairs-MVD).

In January 1954, Rastvorov received a cable again recalling him to Moscow. He believed that this recall might have been in connection with the purge of Lavrenti

Beria and others in the intelligence community that was in progress at that time. He therefore questioned whether he too might not be in serious difficulty. After initially attempting to defect to the British in Tokyo, he sought out an officer of American Intelligence and defected to him on 24 January 1954. At that time he was a lieutenant colonel in Soviet State Security.

The debriefing of Rastvorov began in February 1954, soon after his arrival in the United States and continued for several years. He proved to have extensive information on the organization and personnel of the Soviet intelligence services, on active Soviet penetration of the Japanese Government, and on Soviet operations aimed at Americans in Japan. In all, he produced over 1,000 positive and operational intelligence reports, including the identification of about 600 Soviet intelligence officers and agents. The information that he provided was considered to be very important and useful.

Rastvorov also participated in operational activities and suggestions for covert action programs. He met with representatives of several US and foreign liaison services and he appeared as a witness before the Senate Subcommittee on Internal Security. He lectured at the Naval Intelligence School and at the Counterintelligence Corps School at Fort Holabird. Finally, he published a number of articles on Soviet intelligence in *Life* magazine.

Beginning in 1957, efforts were made to resettle Rastvorov, and he became involved in several unsuccessful business ventures. In 1960 he obtained US citizenship. Three years later he resumed work for American Intelligence as an analyst and consultant primarily in the counterintelligence field. Since that date he was employed to prepare analyses of selected Soviet cases and to provide photo identifications of Soviet intelligence personnel.

According to the KGB *Alphabetical List of Agents of Foreign Intelligence Service, Defectors, Members of Anti-Soviet Organizations, Members of Punitive Units and Other Criminals Under Search Warrant* published in 1969, Rastvorov was sentenced to death in absentia in September 1954 by the Military Collegium of the USSR Supreme Court.

Ivan Vasilyevich Ovchinnikov

Ivan Vasilyevich Ovchinnikov (born 28 January 1929, Selo Tochilnoye, Smolenskiy Rayon, Altayskiy Kray USSR) was a GRU officer who defected to the West in Berlin in December 1955. Three years later he redefected to the Soviets in Germany.

Ovchinnikov, the son of Siberian peasants, joined the Komsomol in 1944. That same year he also entered the Soviet Army. During his army service, he attended the Military Institute of Foreign Languages in Moscow from September 1949 to September 1954 and later served as a military translator with the rank of lieutenant in the 28th Special Purpose (Intercept) regiment in Stahnsdorf, East Germany.

On the night of 4 December 1955, Ovchinnikov made his move to defect to the West. While trying to cross the border between the American sector of West Berlin and the Soviet zone of Germany on foot, he became lost several times. However, he finally succeeded in riding an electric train across to the American sector. Once there, he contacted the police who turned him over to US Intelligence.

Ovchinnikov professed hatred for the Soviet regime, which he claimed had imprisoned his father for 13 years and, in effect, killed him. Ovchinnikov also stated that he had deep affection for his wife and son whom he had left behind in his flight.

At the time of this defection, Ovchinnikov seemed to be an almost fanatical anti-Communist who had defected for ideological reasons. On the other hand, there were various discrepancies in his story. His professed motivation did not appear wholly genuine to some US intelligence officials who interviewed him at length. Furthermore, his statements about his family ties were puzzling because he had scarcely known his father, and there were indications that he was not truly deeply attached to his wife.

Ovchinnikov, however, was cooperative during his debriefings by US Intelligence. He provided useful information on the Soviet military and Group of Soviet Forces Germany (GSFG); GRU intercept operations and activities; and the mission of the KGB signal battalion in Stanhnsdorf, which monitored official radio traffic of the Allied military and foreign diplomatic transmissions. Ovchinnikov also had access to Soviet intelligence bulletins and publications.

The defection of Ovchinnikov to the West precipitated a series of reactions by the KGB and GSFG components. KGB Third (Military Counterintelligence) Chief Directorate units investigated the case with the cooperation of the Soviet garrison in Berlin; GSFG GRU Headquarters, to which unit Ovchinnikov was subordinated; and the East German Volkspolizei.

In February 1957 Ovchinnikov was reinterviewed by US Intelligence and admitted that he defected because he believed opportunities for personal advancement were better in the West. He confessed that in order to gain acceptance and approval in the West, he felt he must appear to have an ideological motivation. His statements about his family ties, he claimed, were deliberately misleading.

After his redebriefing Ovchinnikov associated with various Russian émigré groups in West Germany. In December 1957 he joined Radio Liberty. He also became active in a small circle of émigrés that had a markedly anti-American, anti-Masonic, anti-Semitic, and pro Great Russian bias. Shortly thereafter he began to undermine the morale of other Radio Liberty personnel through constant office intrigues.

In August 1958, Ovchinnikov contacted the Soviet Embassy in Bonn to discuss repatriation. He redefected in East Germany two months later. During a "Return to the Homeland" radio broadcast on 31 October 1958, he confessed the folly of his ways.

Ovchinnikov, a highly unstable person, was often subject to fits of depression. His period of defection was characterized as one of strong enthusiasm and unrealized expectations followed by disappointments, which lead to denunciations of people and activities familiar to him.

According to a mid–1974 report, one Ivan Vasilyevich Ovchinnikov had become editor of *Veche*, a samizdat publication in the USSR. This new editor was reportedly of peasant stock and born in 1929. He allegedly had spent 10 years in a political concentration camp. It is probable that the editor of this magazine, which has an anti-Semitic and chauvinistic Great Russian bias, was identical with the defector.

Ismail Gusseynovich Akhmedov

Ismail Gusseynovich Akhmedov, born 17 June 1904, Orak, Orenburg Oblast (now Chkalov), Russia, was a GRU officer with the rank of colonel and one of the early Soviet defectors.

Akhmedov was the eldest of several children of a Tartar schoolteacher and Moslem mullah. He received his early education first in a Koranic school and then in a Russian school. During the confusion of the post Revolution and Civil War era, Akhmedov, who had joined both the Komsomol and the Communist Party, held various jobs in Central Asia. From 1925 until 1929, he attended the Leningrad Military School of Signal Communications from which he graduated as a junior lieutenant in the Red Army Signals Corps. He went to various Red Army communications schools and advanced in rank to major in the 1930s. While a language student in Tiffs in 1930, he met and married Tamara Yefimovna Perskaya. Although of Georgian-Jewish ancestry, Tamara was born in Germany and had a western outlook on life.

In 1940 after graduation from the General Staff Academy, Akhmedov joined the GRU and soon was named chief of the Technical Intelligence Section. A year later he was posted to Berlin using the alias Georgiy Petrovich Nikolayev and under the cover of assistant chief of *Tass*. After the German invasion of the USSR, the Germans interned Akhmedov. In July 1941, he was released and dispatched by train to the USSR via neutral Turkey. Akhmedov learned on arrival in Istanbul that the GRU had ordered him to remain there as a Soviet Embassy Press Attaché and organize an intelligence network to work against Germany.

While in Turkey, Akhmedov learned that his wife had died in the USSR in the fall of 1941. In June 1942, Akhmedov received orders to return to Moscow. Fearing that he would be arrested if he went home, he defected 3 June 1942, to the Turks, who accepted him as a political refugee and allowed him to change his name to Ismail Ege.

During World War II, Akhmedov tried unsuccessfully to contact US Intelligence. His failure to make contact was at least partly due to a KGB inspired story that he was a German agent. Finally in 1948, US Intelligence contacted him and began to use him operationally.

However, in 1951, it was discovered that the KGB was trying to ascertain Akhmedov's location in Turkey. US Intelligence then decided, for security reasons, to move him to Germany where he served as an interpreter. (It may be significant that the British SIS representative in Istanbul who debriefed Akhmedov after World War II in conjunction with US Intelligence personnel was Kim Philby.) Akhmedov subsequently moved to the United States where he testified before Congressional com-mittees and remained available to US Intelligence for debriefing on the Soviet intelligence services.

Akhmedov provided information on GRU scientific and technical operations in the United States during World War II, Soviet activities in Turkey in World War II, and Soviet communications school and research institutes prior to World War II. He also provided material on the GRU's modus operandi and aided in the compilation of a glossary of terms used in the KGB and GRU.

According to the *Alphabetical List of Agents of Foreign Intelligence Services, Defectors, Members of Anti-Soviet Organizations, Members of Punitive Units and Other Criminals Under Search Warrant* published in 1969, Akhmedov was condemned to death in August 1958 by the Military Collegium of the Supreme court of the USSR.

During Akhmedov's career, he used the following aliases: Georgiy Petrovich Nikolayev, Ismail Ege, Roger N. Witthof, and Hans Zuayter.

Anatoliy Mikhaylovich Granovskiy

Anatoliy Mikhaylovich Granovskiy, born 25 January 1922 or 25 June 1922, Chernigov, USSR, was a KGB agent who defected to the West in Sweden after World War II.

Granovskiy was recruited by the Soviet State Security service during World War II. He served as a partisan and a counterintelligence agent principally in the Ukraine and Czechoslovakia. He was demobilized at the end of the war and entered the Soviet maritime service. As a sailor aboard a Soviet ship, he defected in Sweden on 21 September 1946, thus becoming one of the first important post–World War II Soviet defectors.

Granovskiy's defection occurred at the very time that Swedish authorities were forcibly repatriating scores of Baltic refugees who had fled to Sweden when the USSR invaded and annexed their homelands. Also, the Swedish cabinet was involved in delicate commercial negotiations with the USSR when it received Granovskiy's request for asylum. Despite these factors, the request was granted.

US intelligence subsequently debriefed Granovskiy and from 1946 to 1947 he worked as a US Army translator in West Germany. He immigrated into Bolivia in October 1947 and in April 1948, he entered Brazil illegally. Later he was employed by Brazilian intelligence as a consultant. He also wrote for the press exposing the brutalities of the Soviet regime and the KGB. In 1955 he published his autobiography, *Choke*, (London, William Kimber & Co., Ltd).

Through his writings, Granovskiy attracted the attention of several prominent and influential Americans, principally Charles Edison, former Governor of New Jersey, who assisted him in settling in the United States in 1958. Supported by his friends, Granovskiy continued his efforts to publicize the plight of the Soviet people and the inhumanity of the regime. He appeared on several TV shows and had his book republished in the United States in 1962 under the title *I Was An NKVD Agent*, (New York, Devin-Adair Company). After settling in the United States, he again worked as a consultant for US Intelligence. He died of heart and lung disease complications during the night of 4 September 1974 at his home in the Washington, DC area.

Granovskiy used the following aliases during his career: Mikhail Jan Kulovic, Mikhail Vanov, Gheorghe Alex Filipas, Gradov and Shishkia.

Petr Sergeyevich Deryabin

Petr Sergeyevich Deryabin, born 1921, Lokot, Siberia, USSR, was a Soviet State Security officer who defected to the West in 1954, while stationed in Vienna.

Deryabin's peasant family was forced into a collective farm while he was quite young. At the age of nine he joined the Pioneers and the Komsomol at age 15. After graduating from secondary school in 1936, he completed a two-year course at a Teacher's Institute and then taught history until he was drafted into the Red Army in the fall of 1939. In the Army he became a political instructor and was commissioned. He participated in a number of battles, including Stalingrad, and was wounded four times.

In mid-1944, Deryabin transferred from line duty to military counterintelligence (Chief Directorate for Counterintelligence Ministry of State Security-GUKR/MGB). Later he worked as a senior case officer for State Security in Barnaul, the capital of Altay province. Following this assignment, he served for four years in the Guards directorate (Okhrana) of State Security where his duties included conducting security investigations of directorate personnel. This directorate was responsible for guarding high-level Soviet officials. After the Guards Directorate experienced a personnel cutback in the summer of 1951, Deryabin moved to the Foreign Intelligence directorate and was assigned to the Austro-German Section of the directorate. In the fall of 1953, he was posted to the Soviet Embassy in Vienna, Austria, as a major in the MVD running counterespionage agents and checking on other Soviet nationals in Austria. In February 1954, he defected.

A major factor in bringing about Deryabin's defection was his disillusionment with the difference between Soviet theory and reality, especially the corruption and ruthless power struggle among the Soviet elite. In addition, he was dissatisfied with his work and worried about his future career. The final impetus to his defection, however, was provided by the infidelity of his second wife.

Deryabin was brought to the United States in 1954 and obtained citizenship in 1960. After his defection he was employed by US Intelligence as a contract agent and later as a career agent.

The operational debriefing of Deryabin produced a vast amount of information on Soviet State Security organization and personalities. He had been used extensively as an operational consultant and planner, as an instructor in training courses, and as a lecturer. In addition, he published four books: *The Secret World; Watchdogs of Terror, The KGB: Masters of the Soviet Union* (with T.H. Bagley), and *The Spy who Saved the World: How a Soviet Colonel Changed the Course of the Cold War* (with Jerrold L. Schecter), and a number of magazine articles.

Deryabin was condemned to death in the USSR according to the KGB's *Alphabetical List of Agents of Foreign Intelligence Service, Defectors, Members of Anti-Soviet Organizations, Members of Punitive Units and Other Criminals Under Search Warrant* published in 1969. Deryabin died in 1992.

KGB Headquarters

Grigoriy Stepanovich Burlutskiy

In June 1953, Soviet State Security Lt. Col. Grigoriy Stepanovich Burlutskiy, defected to the West by crossing the Soviet-Afghan border.

Burlutskiy, born 30 January 1918, in Orenburg Oblast, USSR, was the son of a "poor Cossack peasant." In 1934 he began studying animal husbandry but after completing his studies in 1938, he switched to a military career. He was accepted by State Security as an officer candidate at its school for Border Troops in Saratov in 1938. He graduated two years later with an excellent record and was commissioned as a lieutenant.

He began his Border Troop career as the commanding officer of a Border Post but subsequently became assistant company commander of a border detachment, serving along the Western Ukrainian and Bessarabian border.

From 1942 to 1949, Burlutskiy was a member of the 95th Special Purpose Border Regiment. He joined the Communist Party of the Soviet Union in 1943 and one year later became assistant chief of staff of the regiment. He participated in the forced resettlement of the Chechan-Ingush, Kalmyk, Karachay, and Crimean Tartar minority groups. Between 1944 and 1945, he also participated in the liquidation of partisans and resistance leaders in Lithuania.

When World War II ended, he became chief of the 4th Komendatura on the East Prussian border. In 1949 he was again promoted, this time as head of the 2nd Komendatura of the 94th detachment in Lithuania where his unit was responsible for the Soviet-Polish border. In November 1950, he was promoted to lieutenant-colonel. The next year, Burlutskiy attended a course for State Security officers at the Moscow Border School. After completing this school, he was named commanding officer of the 4th Komendatura of the 68th Border Detachment in Turkmen, SSR.

According to Burlutskiy, he became disillusioned by the harsh treatment of minorities by the Soviets and said he thought about defecting during World War II. After being sent to the Soviet-Afghan border, he claimed he planned his escape by first studying the conditions at the border, looking for a place to cross. His opportunity to defect occurred on 3 June 1953, when his chief assistants were on duty elsewhere. He told his driver that he wanted to inspect the border. When he reached the point he had selected to cross, he told his driver to walk to the nearest telephone. When the driver disappeared from sight, Burlutskiy drove the jeep across the border. He asked the Afghan authorities for political asylum. He later was taken to Western Europe by US Intelligence.

Burlutskiy stated his reasons for defection at a June 1954 press conference in which he provided the media with firsthand information about the realities of Soviet life. Accounts of defection appeared in *Life* and other western publications during the spring and summer of 1954. Information provided by Burlutskiy served as source material for chapters in Robert Conquest's *The Nation Killers* as well as Simon Wolin's and Robert M. Slusser's *The Soviet Secret Police*.

The KGB's *Alphabetical List of Agents of Foreign Intelligence Services, Defectors, members of Anti-Soviet Organizations, Members of Punitive Units and Other Criminals Under Search Warrant*, published in 1969, stated that Burlutskiy was sentenced to death in absentia.

Cold War Counterintelligence Bibliography

Joseph Albright. *Bombshell: The Secret Story of America's Unknown Atomic Spy Conspiracy*, New York: Random House, 1997.

Ambrose, Stephen E. *Ike's Spies: Eisenhower and the Espionage Establishment*. Garden City, NY: Doubleday, 1981.

Anders, Roger M. "The Rosenberg Case Revisited: The Greenglass Testimony and the Protection of Atomic Secrets." *American Historical Review 83 (1978): 338-400.*

Athol, Justin. *How Stalin Knows: The Story of the Great Atomic Spy Conspiracy*. Norwich, UK: Jarrold, 1951.

Bentley, Elizabeth. *Out of Bondage: The Story of Elizabeth Bentley*. New York: Ivy Books, 1988. Reprint of 1951 book.

Borovik, Genriky. *The Philby Files: The Secret Life of Master Spy Kim Philby*. New York: Little, Brown and Company, 1994.

Boyle, Andrew. *The Climate of Treason: Five Who Spied for Russia*. London: Hutchinson, 1979.

Broadwater, Jeff. *Eisenhower and the Anti-Communist Crusade*. Chapel Hill, NC: The University of North Carolina Press, 1992.

Burnham, James. *Web of Subversion: Underground Networks in the U.S. Government*. New York: Day, 1954.

Chambers, Whittaker. *Witness*. Chicago: Regnery, 1952.

Costello, John. *Mask of Treachery*. New York: Morrow, 1988.

Dallin, David. *Soviet Espionage*. New Haven, CT: Yale University Press, 1955.

Deriabin, Peter and Frank Gibney. The Secret World. Garden City, New York: Doubleday, 1959.

Donovan, James B. *Strangers on a Bridge: The Case of Colonel Abel*. New York: Atheneum, 1964.

Fried, Richard M. *Nightmare in Red: The McCarthy Era in Perspective*. New York: Oxford University Press, 1990.

Gaddis, John Lewis. "Intelligence, Espionage and Cold War Origins," *Diplomatic History 13:2 (Spring 1989): 191-212.*

Hohne, Heinz and Hermann Zolling. *The General Was a Spy: The Truth About Gehlen-20th Century Superspy, Who Served Hitler, the CIA and West Germany*. New York: Coward, McCann & Geoghegan, 1971.

Hood, William J. *Mole: The True Story of the First Russian Intelligence Officer Recruited by the CIA*. London: Weidenfeld and Nicolson, 1982.

Hoover, J. Edgar. *Masters of Deceit: The Story of Communism in the America and How to Fight It*. New York: Holt, Reinhart & Winston, 1958.

Hyde, H. Montgomery. *The Atom Bomb Spies*. London: Hamish Hamilton, 1980.

Kehr, Harvey, John Earl Haynes and Fridrikh Igorevich Firsov. *The Secret World of American Communism*. New Haven, CT: Yale University Press, 1995.

Kirschner, Don S. *Cold War Exile: The Unclosed Case of Maurice Halperin*. Columbia, MO: University of Missouri Press, 1995.

Khokhlov, Nikolai. "Cold-Blooded Murder is Part of Russia's Cold War in the West." *American Mercury 79. (Sept. 1954): 144-157.*

_____. *In the Name of Conscience: The Testament of a Soviet Secret Agent.* New York: David McKay, 1959.

Knightly, Philip. T*he Master Spy: The Story of Kim Philby.* New York: Knopf, 1989.

Lamphere, Robert J. and Tom Shachtman. *The FBI-KGB War: A Special Agent's Story.* New York: Random House, 1986.

Lewis, Flora. *Red Pawn: The Story of Noel Field.* Garden City, NY: Doubleday, 1965.

Massing, Hede. *This Deception.* New York: Duell, Sloan and Pearce, 1951.

Morros, Boris. *My Ten Years as a Counterspy.* New York: Viking Press, 1959.

Moss, Norman. *Klaus Fuchs: The Man Who Stole the Atomic Bomb.* New York: St. Martin's, 1987.

Murphy, David E., Sergei A. Kondrashev and George Bailey. *Battleground Berlin: CIA vs KGB in the Cold War.* New Haven, CT: Yale University Press, 1997.

Noel-Baker, Francis E. *The Spy Web.* New York: Vanguard, 1955.

Radosh, Ronald and Joyce Milton. *The Rosenberg File: A Search for Truth.* New York: Holt, Rinehart & Winston, 1983.

Rastvorov, Yuri A. "How Red Titans Fought for Supreme Power." *Life* (29 Nov. 1954).

Rees, David. *Harry Dexter White: A Study in Paradox.* New York: Coward, McCann & Geoghegan, 1973.

Reese, Mary Ellen. *General Reinhard Gehlen: The CIA Connection.* Fairfax, VA: George Mason University Press, 1990.

Seth, Ronald. *The Sleeping Truth: The Hiss-Chambers Affair Reappraised.* New York: Hart, 1968.

Straight, Michael. *After Long Silence.* New York: Norton, 1983.

Stripling, Robert E. *The Red Plot Against America.* Drexel Hill, PA: Bell, 1949.

Tanenhaus, Sam. *Whittaker Chambers.* New York: Random House, 1997.

U.S. Congress. House. Committee on Un-American Activities. *Report on Soviet Espionage Activities in Connection with the Atom Bomb.* Sept. 28, 1948. 80th Cong., 2nd sess. Washington, DC: GPO, 1948.

_____. *The March of Treason.* Feb. 19, 1951. 82nd Cong., 1st sess. Washington, DC: GPO, 1951.

_____. *Attempts at Subversion and Espionage by Diplomatic Personnel: Hearings.* June 1956-June 1958. 9 pts. 84th and 85th Cong. Washington, DC: GPO, 1956.

U.S. Congress. Joint Committee on Atomic Energy. *Soviet Atomic Espionage.* 82nd Cong., 1st sess. Washington, DC: GPO, 1951. (Review of Fuchs, May, Greenglass and Gold cases.)

U.S. Congress. Senate. Committee on the Judiciary. Subcommittee to Investigate the Administration of the Internal Security Act and Other Internal Security Laws. *Espionage Activities of Personnel Attached to Embassies and Consulates Under Soviet Domination in the U.S. Hearings.* 82nd Cong., 1st and 2nd sess. Washington, DC: GPO, 1951-1952.

Weinstein, Allen. *Perjury: The Hiss-Chambers Case.* New York: Knopf, 1978.

Williams, Robert Chadwell. *Klaus Fuchs, Atom Spy.* Cambridge, MA: Harvard University Press, 1987.

Willoughby, Charles A. "Espionage and the American Communist Party." *American Mercury 88 (Jan. 1959): 117-123.*

Yarnell, Allen. "Eisenhower and McCarthy: An Appraisal of Presidential Strategy." *Presidential Studies Quarterly 10 (1980): 90-98.*

Cold War Counterintelligence

IMPORTANT DATES AND COUNTERINTELLIGENCE EVENTS
THE ATOMIC BOMB SPIES AND POST WORLD WAR II
1948-1959

1948		
	12 February	National Security Council Intelligence Directive (NSCID) 7 authorizes CIA to collect foreign intelligence from American citizens with overseas contacts.
	25 February	Communist coup in Czechoslovakia.
	1 May	The Soviet Union defies the United Nations and establishes a people's republic in North Korea.
	20 June	USSR initiates Berlin Blockade; lifted 11 May 1949.
	25 June	First IAC interdepartmental committee established.
	1 July	NSCID-9 put USCIB under the NSC and increases civilian control of signals intelligence.
	20 July	General Secretary Eugene Dennis and 11 other CPUSA leaders are arrested and indicted under the Smith Act of conspiring to advocate violent overthrow of the US Government.
	31 July	Elizabeth Bentley testifies before the House Committee on Un-American Activities (HCUA), publicly accusing Harry Dexter White and Lauchlin Currie of being Soviet agents.
	August	UK-USA Security Agreement signed, codifying cooperation on signals intelligence collections and sharing among the US, UK, Canada, Australia and New Zealand.
	August	The VENONA secret and techniques to decrypt Soviet messages leaked to the Soviets by Army Signals cipher clerk William Weisband.
	3 August	Whittaker Chambers publicly identifies Alger Hiss as a Communist agent. Chambers had provided information previously to the State Department and the FBI nine years earlier but three separate investigations of Hiss gave him a clean bill of health.
	September	British cryptanalysts join the VENONA project full-time.
	1 September	Donald Maclean, having been promoted to First Secretary of the British Embassy, is transferred out of the US to Cairo, Egypt.
	27 September	Alger Hiss unsuccessfully sues Whittaker Chambers for $75,000 for libel when Chambers accuses him of Communist party membership from 1934-1938.

Cold War Counterintelligence

IMPORTANT DATES AND COUNTERINTELLIGENCE EVENTS

THE ATOMIC BOMB SPIES AND POST WORLD WAR II
1948-1959

1948	October	The House Un-American Affairs Committee began an investigation of Dr. Edward U. Condon, Director of the Bureau of Standards and the first American labeled by the committee as an "atom spy."
	19 October	Meredith Gardner and Robert Lamphere meet at Arlington Hall and formally inaugurate full-time FBI-ASA liaison on the Soviet messages.
	November	The US Attorney General issues a list of 78 subversive organizations in the United States.
	10 November	The FBI recommends that Communist leadership be prosecuted under the Smith Act to set a constitutional precedent for legally arresting party members as "substanive violators" of the Act.
	17 November	Chambers produces the "Pumpkin Papers," and five rolls of microfilm of Secret state papers he hid in a pumpkin to substantiate his new charge that Hiss and White spied for Moscow during the 1930's.
	9 December	Army Intelligence Division and Security Group work out specific plan covering the exact duties that each will undertake in the production of domestic intelligence.
	16 December	A federal grand jury indicts Alger Hiss for perjury.
	29 December	FBI identifies covername SIMA as Justice Department analyst Judith Coplon.
1949	3 January	British government notified that VENONA intercepts show that information had been transmitted to the Soviets from the British Embassy in 1944 and 1945 from a spy codenamed HOMER (later identified as Maclean).
	17 January	11 Communist Party members are tried for violating the Smith Act violation. Convicted 14 October and sentenced to prison.
	22 January	Beijing, the capital of China, falls to the Communists.
	23 February	Inter-Departmental Intelligence Conference (IIC) members sign a new Delimitations Agreement to govern investigative activities by Army ID, ONI, FBI and AFOSI.
	4 March	FBI arrests Coplon and Soviet UN employee Valentin A. Gubitchev in New York. They are found guilty on 7 March 1950. Gubitchev is expelled from the U.S.

IMPORTANT DATES AND COUNTERINTELLIGENCE EVENTS
THE ATOMIC BOMB SPIES AND POST WORLD WAR II
1948-1959

1949

23 March		Truman approves NSC 17/4, which reconstitutes the secret Interdepartmental Intelligence Conference to coordinate jurisdiction of FBI and military counterintelligence.
28 March		Defense Department approval given for Army ID Censorship Plan which would become immediately effective in case of an emergency.
4 April		The North Atlantic Treaty is signed.
20 May		Defense Secretary Louis Johnson directs a quasi-merger of service signals intelligence in a new Armed Forces Security Agency (AFSA), subordinate to the JCS.
23 May		Federal Republic of Germany established.
31 May		Alger Hiss is tried the first time for perjury but it ends with a hung jury. The 3 year statute of limitations had run out on any possible espionage charges.
18 July		NSC authorizes a regular charter for the IIC and creates a new Inter-Departmental Committee on Internal Security (ICIS), composed of representatives from Departments of State, Treasury, and Justice and the National Military establishment to function within the security field but outside that of IIC.
21 July		The Senate ratifies the North Atlantic Treaty, creating the North Atlantic Treaty Organization.
3 August		Office of Provost Marshal given operational function of clearing civilian industrial facilities for work on classified Army projects.
10 August		National Military Establishment becomes Department of Defense.
14 August		FBI agent Robert Lamphere informs the British that the US concluded that Klaus Fuchs had transmitted information about the atomic bomb to the Soviets.
23 September		President Truman discloses that Soviet Union exploded its first atomic weapon.
1 October		The People's Republic of China is proclaimed in Beijing.
7 October		German Democratic Republic established.

Cold War Counterintelligence

IMPORTANT DATES AND COUNTERINTELLIGENCE EVENTS

THE ATOMIC BOMB SPIES AND POST WORLD WAR II
1948-1959

1949	7 October	Gustav Adolph Mueller, US Air Force, arrested for attempting to deliver classified information to the Soviets.
	10 October	Kim Philby arrives in Washington as the British intelligence liaison to the US intelligence community. Part of his responsibilities involves US/UK exchanges of VENONA material.
1950	19 January	Intelligence Community agrees on defector handling.
	21 January	Alger Hiss is found guilty of perjury.
	24 January	British Scientist Klaus Fuchs is arrested by British authorities and confesses his involvment in Soviet atomic espionage.
	31 January	President Harry Truman gives his approval to build the hydrogen bomb.
	9 February	Senator Joseph McCarthy comes to national attention when he charges that 205 (later changed to 57) State Department employees are Communist Party members. Without any evidence, he names State's Owen Lattimore as the "top Russian espionage agent."
	20 February	East Germany establishes Ministry for State Security (MSS).
	7 April	A Central Personality Index established at Camp Holabird, MD., in order to speed up security clearance procedures.
	15 April	Gustav Adolph, an Air Force enlisted student, is convicted of espionage and sentenced to five years in prison.
	22 May	FBI arrests Harry Gold for espionage.
	16 June	David Greenglass, a member of the Rosenberg Atomic Spy Ring, arrested for spying on behalf of the Soviet Union.
	25 June	North Korean Troops invade South Korea.
	17 July	Julius Rosenberg arrested on charges of espionage on behalf of the Soviet Union.
	24 July	President Truman issues statement that FBI should take charge of investigative work in matters relating to espionage, sabotage, subversive activities and related matters.

Cold War Counterintelligence

IMPORTANT DATES AND COUNTERINTELLIGENCE EVENTS
THE ATOMIC BOMB SPIES AND POST WORLD WAR II
1948-1959

1950	11 August	Ethel Rosenberg arrested for espionage on behalf of the Soviet Union.
	18 August	Morton Sobell, a member of the Rosenberg Atomic Spy Ring, was taken into custody by the FBI after his deportation from Mexico.
	24 August	AFSA assigns Soviet intercept material a restricted codeword BRIDE and special handling procedures.
	14 September	Alfred Dean Stark sentenced to 15 years in prison for conspiracy to commit espionage.
	23 September	Congress passes the Internal Security Act (the "McCarran Act"), which it would soon pass again over President Truman's veto. The Act requires Communist-linked organizations to register and allows emergency detention of potentially dangerous persons.
	6 October	Donald Maclean returns to London to head the British Foreign Office's American Department.
	5 December	U.S. Circuit Court of Appeals overturns Judith Coplon's conviction.
	9 December	Harry Gold is sentenced to 30 years imprisonment for conspiracy to commit espionage.
	27 December	Congress passes legislation giving federal agents the power to make warrantless arrests in cases involving espionage, sabotage and other major crimes.
1951	4 January	Deputy Directorate for Plans established in CIA; Allen Dulles named chief.
	6 March	Ethen and Julius Rosenberg go on trial for treason.
	29 March	The Rosenbergs are found guilty of treason and sentenced to death. Morton Soboll is sentenced to 30 years imprisonment for conspiracy to commit espionage.
	April	The British narrow the search for Homer to two persons, one of whom is Maclean.
	6 April	David Greenglass is sentenced to 15 years imprisonment for conspiracy to commit espionage.
	9 April	The Rosenbergs are sentenced to death by Judge Irving Kaufman.

THE ATOMIC BOMB SPIES AND POST WORLD WAR II
1948-1959

1951	14 April	A decoded VENONA message provides conclusive evidence that Maclean is HOMER. Surveillance of Maclean begins in order to gather evidence that can be used in court as the US and UK do not want to reveal the existence of the VENONA intercepts.
	21 May	British Foreign Office officials Donald Maclean and Guy Burgess flee Great Britain and defect to the Soviet Union. Kim Philby recalled from US.
	12 June	The CIA's counterintelligence chief William Harvey writes a memo to DCI Walter Bedell Smith making the case that Philby is a Soviet agent; a letter is sent to the British stating that Philby is no longer welcome in the US.
	10 July	Philby is asked to resign from British intelligence.
	11 July	CPUSA announces that the Party will operate as a "cadre organization," with many of its leaders underground.
	17 August	Army G-2 Central Records Facility at Fort Holabird, Md., established to provide centralized repository and master index for all personal security information available from closed investigative cases.
	4 November	A Gallup poll finds that 51 percent of Americans favor using the atomic bomb on military targets.
	10 December	Philby is subjected to a judicial inquiry in the UK.
1952	24 February	Attorney General J. Howard McGrath orders an end to FBI black bag jobs that involved trespass.
	1 May	Department of State bans US travel to Communist countries.
	13 June	Brownell Report on SIGINT completed; led to creation of the National Security Agency.
	21 September	Giuseppe Cascio, US Air Force, arrested in South Korea on charges of conspiring to pass secrets to the Communists.
	1 November	First US hydrogen bomb test.
	4 November	President Truman creates the National Security Agency (NSA) to supersede AFSA and further centralize control of signals intelligence under the Secretary of Defense and a reconstituted USCIB.

IMPORTANT DATES AND COUNTERINTELLIGENCE EVENTS
THE ATOMIC BOMB SPIES AND POST WORLD WAR II
1948-1959

1953	5 March	Stalin dies.
	6 April	KGB defector Alexander Orlov's story appears in Life magazine; finally alerting the FBI to his residence in the United States.
	1 June	President Eisenhower issues Executive Order 10459 establishing a new International Organizations Employees Loyalty Board.
	8 June	Kurt L. Ponger sentenced to 5-15 years imprisonment and Otto Verber sentenced to 3 1/2 years on charges of conspriracy to commit espionage.
	19 June	Ethel and Julius Rosenberg are executed at Sing Sing Prison in New York after President Eisenhower denies excutive clemency. First convicted spies ever executed in the U.S. on order of a civil court.
	10 July	Ouster of Beriya, Soviet Internal Security Minister; subsequent upheavel in Soviet intelligence services.
	26 July	Armistice signed in Korea.
	3 August	Senator McCarthy announces his intention to investigate the U.S. Army Signal Corps Engineering Laboratories at Ft. Monmouth, New Jersey.
	6 November	Attorney General Herbert Brownell sparks controversy by claiming in a Chicago speech that former President Truman had appointed Harry Dexter White to head the International Monetary Fund despite FBI warnings that White was a Soviet agent. Truman ridicules the charge.
1954	30 January	McCarthy probe of Army begins.
	13 March	KGB established.
	22 April	Senate hearings on Army-McCarthy dispute begin.
	20 May	Attorney General Brownell lifts former AG McGrath's ban on black bag jobs by FBI.
	24 August	Communist Control Act deprives Communist Party of rights, privileges and immunities.

THE ATOMIC BOMB SPIES AND POST WORLD WAR II
1948-1959

1954	6 September	Herbert Hoover's Commission on Government Organization report on CIA asserts that "no rules" existed in the struggle between the Free World and the international Communist conspiracy.
	9 October	Joseph Sidney Petersen Jr., DoD civilian, arrested and charged with violating espionage statutes.
	2 December	Senate votes to condemn McCarthy for contempt of Senate.
	20 December	CIA's Directorate of Plans creates the Counterintelligence Staff with James J. Angleton as its chief.
1955	11 May	The Berlin Tunnel becomes operational.
	14 May	Warsaw Pact created.
	25 July	First U-2 delivered to test site.
1956	8 March	NSC approves the FBI's proposed COINTELPRO operation against the CPUSA.
	1 April	Gehlen Organization turned over to West Germany as BND.
	17 April	Cominform dissolved.
	21 April	Berlin Tunnel "discovered" by East Germans. In reality, Soviet spy George Blake had previously informed the Soviets about the tunnel.
	4 June	CIA facilitates publication in the West of Khrushchev's "secret speech" to the Twentieth Party Congress, in which he denounced Stalin's crimes.
	5 August	FBI Director begins COINTELPRO (Counterintelligence Program) against the Communist Party USA.
	10 October	Soviet troops suppress a popular uprising in Hungary.
1957	4 May	KGB officer Reino Hayhanen, en route from the United States, defects at the US Embassy in Paris.
	17 June	Supreme Court in Yates vs. US rules the government had enforced the Smith Act too broadly by targeting protected speech instead of actual action to overthrow the political system; this ruling makes the Act almost useless for prosecuting Communists.

Cold War Counterintelligence

IMPORTANT DATES AND COUNTERINTELLIGENCE EVENTS

THE ATOMIC BOMB SPIES AND POST WORLD WAR II
1948-1959

1957	21 June	Federal authorities detain Hayhanen's superior, KGB illegal Colonel Rudolf Abel, in New York.
	9 September	Alfred Stern and Martha Dodd are indicted in absentia on charges of espionage. In 1979 the charges are dropped when witness considered key to the case had died.
	20 September	George H. French, a US Air Force Captain, is convicted of espionage and is sentenced to life in prison.
	15 November	Soviet illegal Rudolph Abel found guilty and sentenced to 30 years in prison for conspiring to commit espionage.
1958	21 February	M/Sgt. Roy Adair Rhodes was sentenced to five years of imprisonment at hard labor, dishonorable discharge from US Army, and forfeited all pay and allowances, for conspiring to deliver US secrets to the Soviet Union and falsifying loyalty certificates.
	29 July	NASA established.
	15 September	US Intelligence Board created.
	10 November	The Berlin crisis begins.
1959	1 January	Fidel Castro takes over Cuba.
	4 October	Soviet GRU officer Popov arrested for working for CIA.

CHAPTER 2

Counterintelligence in the Turbulent 1960s and 1970s

Introduction

The early 1960s was a golden period for American counterintelligence. The FBI and CIA recruited several valuable Soviet intelligence officers, and the CI community benefited from a small number of Soviet defectors. This utopia would not last long.

Among the defectors were Anatoliy Golitsyn and Yuriy Nosenko, both of who would eventually be the cause of tremendous embarrassment to the CIA and adversely affect the CI community. Except for one espionage arrest between 1966 and 1975, counterintelligence falls from the American scene. The year 1966 also marked an almost total break in FBI-CIA relations that lasted until 1972.

In the mid-to-late 1960s, Vietnam became the dominant intelligence issue and also the rallying call for dissent against the government by young Americans. Widespread violence and civil disorder arose in many cities and on many campuses across the country.

President Lyndon Johnson and later President Richard Nixon acted on a number of fronts, including the counterintelligence elements within the intelligence community, to determine who was to blame for the turbulence. Both Presidents believed that foreign influences caused the domestic strife confronting the nation, and each directed the CI Community to determine if America's enemies were behind the violence.

In 1967, the Department of Justice instituted the first in a series of secret units designed to collate and evaluate information concerning the growing domestic disorder. After Nixon's election, the Justice Department created new units but the President remained dissatisfied. The FBI's response was to continue to conduct COINTELPRO (Counterintelligence Program) operations against the New Left, the Black Nationalists, and the Right Wing, which were established in the late 1950s and 1960s. Army intelligence conducted its own domestic program, and CIA took action by creating the MHCHAOS (cryptonym used for CIA's collection of information on American dissidents) operation. All these efforts resulted from a realization by the Johnson and Nixon Administrations that the CI Community had no effective ability to evaluate intelligence on domestic incidents.

In the end, the CI community found no evidence of foreign control of American radical groups, and, by the early 1970s each of the agencies began phasing out its programs. The issue, however, stayed alive. DCI James Schlesinger, who was blindsided by not knowing about CIA's involvement in the break-in of Daniel Ellsberg's psychiatrist office in Los Angeles, was leery of being caught offguard again. To forestall such an event, he ordered all CIA employees to report on any CIA activities that they believed violated the Agency's charter.

On 9 May 1973, the CIA's Office of the Inspector General gave Schlesinger a list of "potential" activities that could cause embarrassment to the CIA. The list included the Agency's CI Staff's participation in the MHCHAOS operation, mail-openings, and the Huston Plan. Two days later, President Nixon named Schlesinger to be Secretary of Defense. The new DCI, William Colby, had to wait until September 1973 to take office and immediately had to resolve other pressing matters. The CI staff's questionable activities remained dormant.

This changed following a December 1974 *New York Times* article on alleged CIA spying on American citizens. The news article led to the appointment of a presidential commission (the Rockefeller Commission) and two Congressional committees to investigate the charges. Besides CIA, the investigation also looked at the FBI, DoD, and several other agencies. Almost coinciding with the news article was the firing of CIA's legendary CI Chief, James Jesus Angleton, who served in this position for 20 years.

On 18 February 1976, President Gerald Ford issued Executive Order 11905. The new policy guidelines, restrictions on individual agencies, and clarification of intelligence authorities and responsibilities were the result of the Rockefeller Commission's report. In announcing his order, the President wanted to sidestep any Congressional initiative to regulate the intelligence and counterintelligence communities. The president gave the new DCI, George Bush, only 90 days to implement the new order.

The Senate Committee, known as the Church Committee, published its six-volume report on the investigation on 23 April 1976. The House Committee, known as the Pike Committee, also wrote a classified report, which was leaked to and printed by the *Village Voice* on 12 February 1976.

The next crisis to strike US counterintelligence was the discovery of the illegal imprisonment of Soviet defector Nosenko by CIA. The Nosenko case had been a continuous point of contention between the Agency's CI Staff and the people responsible for recruiting and running operations against the Soviet Union. The case also clouded the bona fides of other Soviet defectors and in-place sources and contributed to the internal questioning by the FBI of the validity of their sources.

The revelations of these activities convinced Congress that they needed closer oversight and accountability over the intelligence community. The House of Representatives established the House Permanent Select Committee on Intelligence, and the Senate created the Senate Select Committee on Intelligence.

On 20 January 1977, Presidential Directive/NSC-2 reorganized the National Security Council System. A review of this reorganization shows no committees or group focusing on counterintelligence. Another Executive Order corrected this oversight. The order created the Special Coordination Committee for Counterintelligence, under the revised National Security Council structure.

Early in DCI Stansfield Turner's term, he also believed individual agencies ignored CI community interests. To remedy this, he wanted a new office to handle counterintelligence issues so that they would not fall into the proverbial black hole. He established such an office, Special Assistant to the DCI for Counterintelligence, in 1978.

Administratively Confidential

The WHITE HOUSE
June 30, 1965

Memorandum for the Heads of Executive Departments and Agencies

I am strongly opposed to the interception of telephone conversations as a general investigative technique. I recognize that mechanical and electronic devices may sometimes be essential in protecting our national security. Nevertheless, it is clear that indiscriminate use of those investigative devices to overhear telephone conversations, without the knowledge or consent of any of the persons involved, could result in serious abuses and invasions of privacy. In my view, the invasion of privacy of communications is a highly offensive practice which should be engaged in only where the national security is at stake. To avoid an misunderstanding on this subject in the Federal Government, I am establishing the following basic guidelines to be followed by all government agencies:

(1) No federal personnel is to intercept telephone conversations within the United States by any mechanical or electronic device, without the consent of one of the parties involved, (except in connection with investigations related to the national security)

(2) No interception shall be undertaken or continued without first obtaining the approval of the Attorney General.

(3) All federal agencies shall immediately conform their practices and procedures to the provisions of this order.

Utilization of mechanical or electronic devices to overhear non-telephone conversations is an even more difficult problem, which raises substantial and unresolved questions of Constitutional interpretation. I desire that each agency conducting such investigations consult with the Attorney General to ascertain whether the agency's practices are fully in accord with the law and with a decent regard for the rights of others.

Every agency head shall submit to the Attorney General within 30 days a complete inventory of all mechanical and electronic equipment and devices used for or capable of intercepting telephone conversations. In addition, such reports shall contain a list of any interceptions currently authorized and the reasons for them.

(S) Lyndon B. Johnson

US Double Agent Thwarts State Department Bugging

An effort by Communist agents to plant an electronic listening device in the State Department building in Washington was overcome by the FBI with the assistance and cooperation of a State Department employee of Czechoslovak heritage, Frank John Mrkva, who acted as a double agent for more than four years. The details of the case as released by the State Department in July 1966, have many of the trappings of a James Bond or Le Carre spy novel.

Two members of the Czechoslovak Embassy in Washington were directly implicated in this espionage operation. The first, Zdenek Pisk, served as Third Secretary and later as Second Secretary of the Czechoslovak Embassy. Pisk departed the United States on May 8, 1963, but had returned and occupied the post of First Secretary at the Czechoslovak United Nations Mission in New York City. The second agent, Jiri Opatrny, assigned as an Attaché of the Czechoslovak Embassy in Washington, took over the spy operation from Pisk upon his departure from Washington, DC, in May 1963.

In 1961, Pisk became acquainted with Frank John Mrkva, whose official US State Department duties included messenger runs to the Czechoslovak Embassy. At Pisk's invitation, Frank Mrkva attended social functions at the Czechoslovak Embassy. The first overt act on the part of Pisk to enlist Mrkva into Czechoslovak espionage activities was on November 30, 1961. Pisk invited Mrkva to dinner at a metropolitan restaurant, where he asked him numerous questions about his family, background, relatives in Czechoslovakia, and his duties at the State Department. In the course of subsequent meetings of this nature, Pisk revealed the fact they were aware of Mrkva's financial position... that he had a sizable mortgage on his home, his daughter needed an operation, and so on, and the Czechoslovak diplomat held out promises of money if Mrkva would cooperate in conducting espionage activities in their behalf. Immediately, Frank Mrkva notified the FBI.

There followed over a period from November 1961 up to July 1966, a series of 48 meetings. Eleven with Pisk and later 37 with Opatrny, during which the two Czechoslovak spies paid Mrkva a total of $3,440. Most of the meetings were held in the Maryland suburbs, on park benches in Northwest Washington, one in front of a theater in Northeast Washington, one in Southeast Washington, and another in a Virginia suburban shopping center.

From time to time, Frank Mrkva supplied the Czechoslovak spies with unclassified papers such as a State Department telephone book, press releases, and administrative reports, which had been cleared for transmittal. During the entire period of his contact with the Czechoslovak espionage agents, Mr. Mrkva acted with the full knowledge and guidance of the FBI and appropriate officials of the Department of State.

As the relationship between Frank Mrkva and the Czechoslovak agents matured, the latter's interests became more specific. Could he provide more information concerning the rooms and locations of the officers of the Department dealing with Czechoslovak affairs—particularly concerning the Director of the Office of Eastern European Affairs and the conference room for his staff meetings?

About May 1965, Opatrny revealed his interest in placing clandestine listening devices (CLDs) in various offices in the State Department. Mrkva subsequently provided Opatrny with a General Services Administration catalog of government furniture in December of 1965. This was to be used in designing a CLD in such a fashion that it could be introduced into an office of the State Department building.

On May 29, 1966, Opatrny delivered a CLD to Mrkva, which could be activated and deactivated by remote control and asked him to place it in the base of a bookcase in the office of Mr. Raymond Lisle, Director of the Office of Eastern European Affairs. Opatrny promised Mrkva $1,000 for this particular operation. Upon receipt of the device, Mrkva immediately turned it over to the FBI agents.

On June 9, 1966, Opatrny contacted Mr. Mrkva reporting that the CLD was not working, and he could not understand the reason, as it had operated successfully for 20 minutes after supposedly being planted in the State Department. When told by Frank Mrkva that he had accidentally dropped the device, presumably making it inoperative, Opatrny then instructed him to return it so that it could be sent to Prague for inspection and repair. There then followed a series of disputes over bad faith on the part of Opatrny in connection with payments due for past services. Frank Mrkva used this approach in stalling for time to preclude carrying out the instruction to return the CLD.

At their last meeting on July 6, 1966, Opatrny told Mrkva that they should work more closely together. There were other offices like that of Under Secretary of State Ball's in which they would want to place a device. "We want to bring this first device to a conclusion. Everyone wants to know what is wrong with it," Opatrny said.

The "roof fell" in on the Czechoslovak spy operation on July 13, 1966, when Walter J. Stoessel, Jr., Acting Assistant Secretary for European Affairs, called into the State Department the highest available ranking Czechoslovak Diplomat, the Second Secretary of the Czechoslovak Embassy, Miloslav Chrobok. He was informed that Mr. Opatrny had engaged in activities incompatible with the accepted norms of official conduct. " We find his continued presence in the US no longer agreeable to the Government of the US and request therefore, that he depart from the US as soon as possible and in any case within three days."

An interesting note was added to this case when Frank Mrkva revealed that Jiri Opatrny, the accused Czechoslovak spy, did not live up to his name. According to Mr. Mrkva, Opatrny's name can be translated as "George Careful."

MILITARY SURVEILLANCE

House Judiciary Committee,
Subcommittee on Constitutional Rights,
93rd Congress, Hearings April, 1974, p. 134

THE ASSOCIATION OF THE BAR
OF THE CITY OF NEW YORK

MILITARY SURVEILLANCE OF CIVILIAN
POLITICAL ACTIVITIES: REPORT AND
RECOMMENDATIONS FOR
CONGRESSIONAL ACTION (1973)

BY THE COMMITTEE ON CIVIL RIGHTS

INTRODUCTION

Domestic intelligence operations conducted by elements of the United States armed forces have raised serious problems involving rights of privacy, speech and association. Such problems have long been of concern to lawyers and to members of this Association in particular.

In January 1970, charges were made that the United States Army was engaged in widespread surveillance within the United States of the political activities of civilians. Publication of the charges received considerable coverage in the press, and provoked inquiries from a number of Senators and Congressmen about the scope of the Army's domestic intelligence operations. During 1971, the Senate's Subcommittee on Constitutional Rights held hearings on the subject, and since that time a number of bills aimed at limiting the scope of military surveillance have been introduced in Congress. To date, however, none of the bills has been reported out of committee.

High Defense Department officials have acknowledged that the charges of widespread domestic intelligence data gathering and storage were indeed accurate, and the Department has issued detailed regulations which sharply limit the scope of such operations. Significant legal and practical questions remain, however, for the official Department of Defense position appears to be that widespread information collection activities undertaken during the 1967-70 period, even if not "appropriate," were nonetheless "lawful." Manifestly, implicit in this position is a reservation by the Department of Defense of its alleged right to resume these activities whenever the Department deems it "appropriate" to do so.

The purpose of this report is threefold: (1) to review the historical background and current status of the controversy regarding military surveillance of civilian political activities; (2) to outline the principal legal considerations involved; and (3) to set forth our views with respect to possible Congressional action. Our principal conclusion is that Congress should enact legislation to prohibit all military surveillance of civilian political activities, except perhaps in certain well-defined circumstances where limited data gathering may be justifiable.

I. THE NATURE AND EXTENT OF THE PROBLEM

A. Military Surveillance Prior to 1967

Although military surveillance of civilian political activities reached a peak during the three years following the riots in Newark and Detroit in 1967, such surveillance is by no means a recent phenomenon. The modern origins of the problem can be found in the expansion of military intelligence work at the outbreak of World War I, in response to German efforts at espionage and propaganda within the United States. By the end of the war, military intelligence had established a nationwide network of agents and civilian informers, who reported to the Army not only on suspected German spies and sympathizers, but also on pacifists, labor organizers, socialists, communists, and other "radicals." The network remained in existence for several years after World War I, continuing to infiltrate civilian groups, monitor the activities of labor unions, radical groups and "left wing" political organizations, and occasionally harassing persons regarded as "potential troublemakers." It was finally disbanded in 1924, and until the outbreak of World War II the military's domestic intelligence activities were conducted on a much reduced basis.

The Federal Bureau of Investigations was the principal agency involved in domestic intelligence operations during the period between 1924 and 1940. With the outbreak of World War II, military intelligence operations were, of course, greatly expanded. Some elements of military intelligence again became involved in reporting on civilian political activities, mainly in an effort to counter suspected Axis "fifth column" attempts at subversion and sabotage. The monitoring continued, on a much reduced scale and in a haphazard and sporadic fashion, during the Cold War period of the 1940's and 1950's. The primary domestic responsibility of military intelligence units during this period was the conduct of loyalty and security investigations involving persons working in the defense establishment, but the carrying out of these responsibilities sometimes spilled over into fairly extensive surveillance of civilians.

During the early 1960's, the scope of domestic intelligence operations by the armed forces gradually began to expand. A number of factors were responsible for the expansion, including the general build-up of the defense establishment as the United States became increasingly involved in the war in Vietnam, the beginnings of the anti-war movement at home, repeated crisis over desegregation (which actually led to the deployment of troops in Alabama and Mississippi in 1962 and 1963), and instances of protest against racial discrimination in cities in both the North and the South. Officials charged with responsibility for deployment of federal troops during these years expressed a need for better knowledge of the problems that might have to be faced. Thus, for example, following the crisis in Birmingham, Alabama in May 1963, then Major General Creighton Abrams (now Chairman of the Joint Chiefs of Staff), wrote that:

"We in the Army should launch a major intelligence project without delay, to identify personalities, both black and white, develop analysis of the various civil rights situations in which they may become involved, and establish a civil rights intelligence center to operate on a continuing basis and keep abreast of the current situation throughout the United States, directing collecting activities and collating and evaluating the product. Based upon this Army intelligence effort, the Army can more precisely determine the organization and forces and operations techniques ideal for each."

The extent of the actual collection of information on individuals and groups during the early and mid–1960's seems to have varied considerably from one military unit to another, depending upon how broadly the unit commanders interpreted vague directives to keep track of "subversive activities." It was not until 1967, after large scale riots had taken place in ghetto areas of Newark and Detroit, that truly extensive, systematic, domestic intelligence operations independent of the loyalty-security programs began to get underway.

B. Formulation of the 1967–70 Surveillance Program

In July 1967, Federal troops were alerted for possible duty in connection with the riots which broke out in Newark and were actually committed to action in helping to quell the Detroit riots. In September 1967, Cyrus Vance, who had been a special representative of the President in Detroit at the time of the riots there, filed an extensive "after-action report." Mr. Vance's report recounted the events which had taken place and summarized his conclusions with respect to planning for situations of domestic violence requiring the use of Federal troops which might arise in the future. Among other things, he recommended the reconnoitering of major American cities in order to prepare folders listing bivouac sites, possible headquarters locations, and similar items of information needed for optimum deployment of Federal troops when committed. He particularly noted the utility of police department logs of incidents requiring police action, as indicators for determining whether a riot situation was beyond the control of local and state law enforcement agencies, and suggested that it would be helpful to develop a "normal incident level" curve as a base of reference. He also thought it would be useful to assemble and analyze data showing activity patterns during the riots in places such as Watts, Newark, and Detroit, in order to ascertain whether there were any typical "indicator" incidents or patterns spread. The Vance report did not suggest that the Army should collect data on personalities or organizations, but that is nevertheless what Army intelligence proceeded to do.

Extensive plans for expanding the Army's domestic intelligence operations and computerizing many of the files on civilian political activity were formulated during the fall and winter of 1967–68. A comprehensive Army civil disturbance plan was distributed to Army units in January 1968, and was followed the next month by issuance of an "intelligence annex" to the plan which contained a list of elements of information to be collected and reported to the U. S. Army Intelligence Command. The annex singled out "civil rights movements" and "anti-Vietnam/anti-draft movements" as "dissident elements," and authorized military intelligence units to collect a far wider range of information than had been recommended in the Vance report of the preceding September.

In May 1968, following the riots touched off in a number of cities by the assassination of Dr. Martin Luther King, the Army issued an even broader "Civil Disturbance Information Collection Plan." The Plan described this mission of Army Intelligence in very broad terms:

" To procure, evaluate, interpret and disseminate as expeditiously as possible information and intelligence relating to any actual, potential or planned demonstration or other activities related to civil disturbances, within the Continental United States (CONUS) which threaten civil order or military security or which may adversely affect the capability of the Department of the Army to perform its mission."

The Plan contained a detailed listing of various kinds of information to be obtained and accorded different priorities to particular kinds of information. Some examples of kinds of information on "predistribution activities" in local communities given high priority by the Plan are the following:

-presence of "militant outside agitators";

-increase in charges of police brutality, resentment of law enforcement;

-known leaders, overt and behind the scenes;

-plans, activities, and organization prepared by leaders;

-friends and sympathizers of participants, including newspapers, radio, television stations, and prominent leaders;

-efforts by minority groups to upset balance of power and political system;

-purposes and objectives of dissident groups (including estimates of plans and objectives, capabilities, resources to be employed, coordination with other minority groups and dissident organizations);

-source and extent of funds, how funds are distributed, and general purposes for which funds are used;

-organization of dissident groups (including location of functions and responsibilities, lines of authority, organizational charts, and rosters of key personnel, for both the "high command" and the "subordinate elements" of the group; and

-personnel (including the number of active members, a breakdown of membership by ethnic groups, age, economic status, and criminal record, and biographic data on key members.

C. The Scope of the Data Collection, 1967-70

Assistant Secretary of Defense for Administration Robert Froehlke later testified that the requirements of the civil disturbance information collection plan issued in May 1968, reflected an "all-encompassing and uninhibited demand for information" which Army was expected to meet. As he pointed out, it was "highly improbable" that many of the requirements listed could be obtained by other than covert collection means.

The Army's May 1968, plan was distributed to numerous Federal agencies and to top officials in each State government. The Army itself, through its Intelligence Command, vigorously sought to implement the plan. The massive sweep of its surveillance activities has been extensively documented and need not be reviewed in detail here. However, some particularly salient features may be noted to help illustrate the nature and extent of the program:

1. A great number of widely disparate groups were subject to Army surveillance. They covered the full range of the political spectrum and included, for example:

-The American Civil Liberties Union
-The American Nazi Party
-The John Birch Society
-The Socialist Workers Party
-CORE

- The NAACP
- The National Urban League
- The Southern Christian Leadership Conference
- The Mississippi Freedom Democratic Party
- The Revolutionary Action Movement
- Women's Strike for Peace
- The League of Women Voters
- Students for a Democratic Society

2. Files were also kept on a large number of private citizens and public officials. These dossiers often included data on the private and personnel affairs of citizens as well as on their activities in connection with political organizations. Computer print-outs and other publications generated by the Army in the course of the 1968-70 operations included, among other things, comments about the financial affairs, sex lives, and psychiatric histories of many persons wholly affiliated with the armed forces. Much of the information appears to have been unverified, sometimes consisting of nothing more than rumor or gossip.

3. Most of the data collected on groups and organizations consisted of matters of public record—a great deal of it simply clipped from newspapers. However, information also was obtained from private institutions and, in some cases, through covert operations. Thus, for example, former members of Army intelligence testified at the 1971 Senate hearings that the Army's domestic intelligence activities had included:

-infiltration of undercover agents into Resurrection City during the Poor People's Campaign in 1968;

-having agents pose as press photographers, newspaper reporters and television newsmen, sometimes with bogus press credentials, during the 1968 Democratic National Convention in Chicago;

-sending agents, enrolled as students, to monitor classes in the Black Studies program at New York University;

-keeping card files, dossiers, and photographs on students and faculty at the University of Minnesota; and

-infiltrating a coalition of church youth groups in Colorado Springs, Colorado.

4. An enormous amount of information was collected and stored. Some of it dated to as far back as World War I but most of it was collected during the 1967-70 period. The Army appears to have had more than 350 separate records storage centers containing files on civilian political activities. One such center, the Fourth Army Headquarters at Fort Sam Houston, Texas, reported the equivalent of over 120,000 file cards on "personalities of interest." Considerable duplication of files on individuals doubtless existed, but the staff of the Senate Subcommittee on Constitutional Rights is probably conservative in estimating that in 1970 Army intelligence had reasonable current files on the political activities of at least 100,000 individuals unaffiliated with the armed forces.

5. At least two of the Army's data banks had the capacity for cross-reference among "organizational," "incident" and "personality" files. The system thus had the technical capacity to produce correlation among persons, organizations and activities—e.g., list of citizens by name, address, ideology and political affiliation—virtually instantaneously.

6. The surveillance program seems to have developed a bureaucratic momentum of its own, and to have rapidly expanded without the knowledge or approval of civilian officials in the Department of Defense. Senator Ervin has cogently described the process:

"In the midst of crisis, Pentagon civilians issued vague, mission-type orders which essentially gave intelligence officers a free hand in collecting whatever information they deemed necessary to the efficient conduct of civil disturbance operations. Subsequently, neither the Pentagon's civilian hierarchy nor the Congress had any routine means by which to review the appropriateness of those decisions until former agents came forward and blew the whistle in 1970.

Meanwhile, the surveillance grew, as most governmental programs grow, by the quiet processes of bureaucratic accretion...(E)each subordinate element in the chain of command expanded on the orders it received from above, while the traditional secrecy we have granted our intelligence agencies immunized each echelon from effective review by its superiors."

Central Intelligence Agency Testimony on Domestic Spying

Mr. Vice President, Members of the President's Commission:

I appreciate this opportunity to appear before you to clarify the activities conducted by the Central Intelligence Agency within the United States. I would like to assure you at the outset that the Agency has not conducted a "massive illegal domestic intelligence operation" as alleged in *The New York Times* of December 22, 1974.

The agency and I shall be entirely forthcoming with this Commission's work in full confidence that a thorough understanding of the intelligence apparatus of the United States and the role of CIA will:

(1) demonstrate the high value and great importance of the intelligence work of the Agency,

(2) reassure you as to the legality and general propriety of the Agency's activities over the years, and

(3) lead you to constructive recommendations to improve the procedures and arrangements that govern Agency activities.

In short, we welcome the opportunity this inquiry brings to increase public confidence in the Agency and to make its work more effective in the future.

I shall start with a brief description of the CIA—its authority under the law, its mission, and the intelligence process itself.

This will include two Agency activities of special relevance to this inquiry—security and counterintelligence.

I shall then describe those activities of the Agency that take place within the United States to demonstrate the relationship between them and the collection of foreign intelligence.

I shall follow this with a discussion of the allegations raised in *The New York Times* of 22 December and several subsequent publications.

I shall conclude with some ideas which might be useful to the Commission in formulating its recommendations.

Mr. Vice President, in addition to this statement, I am submitting for the record a set of detailed appendixes discussing in greater depth some topics germane to the Commission's work. Most of these documents are classified and in their present form should remain so. We would, however, be glad to work with the Commission to make parts of them appropriate for public release if the Commission desires. In addition, of course, I am prepared to answer your questions in any detail you request, as will other current Agency employees you may wish to question, but on these matters also I respectfully request that you consult with the Agency to delete sensitive material prior to release.

The CIA, Authority and Background

CIA's existence and authority rests upon the National Security Act of 1947. The Act provides that the Agency will "correlate and evaluate intelligence relating to the national security, and provide for the appropriate dissemination of such intelligence within the Government...."

The Act calls for the Agency to perform certain services of "common concern as the National Security Council determines can be more efficiently accomplished centrally" and "to perform such other functions and duties related to intelligence affecting the national security as the National Security Council may from time to time effect."

The Act provides that "the Agency shall have no police, subpoena, law enforcement powers or internal security functions." I emphasize the latter phrase. The law is explicit that the Agency shall have no internal security functions—those are the responsibility of the FBI and other law-enforcement authorities. In its use of the term "intelligence" in connection with CIA activities, thus, the Act implicitly restricts CIA to the field of foreign intelligence.

Another proviso is that "the Director of Central Intelligence shall be responsible for protecting intelligence sources and methods from unauthorized disclosure." Incidentally, the Director is the only Government official specifically charged by statute to protect intelligence sources and methods.

The CIA Act of 1949 provides that, in order to implement the above proviso and in the interests of the security of the foreign intelligence activities of the United States, the Agency is exempted from the provisions of any "law which requires the publication or disclosure of the organization, functions, names, official titles, salaries, or numbers of personnel employed by the Agency."

In the intervening years since 1947, as the international role and responsibilities of the United States have grown, so has the importance of intelligence to its decision-making processes. The duties of the Director of Central Intelligence have also grown, and particularly his role as coordinator of all the intelligence efforts of the US Government.

Intelligence today is no simple, single-dimensional activity. It is primarily as intellectual process involving:

(1) the collection and processing of raw information,

(2) analysis of the information and development of reasoned judgments about its significance, and

(3) the dissociation and presentation of these findings to those needing them.

The process involves a number of different Departments and Agencies, which, together, we call the Intelligence Community.

Our overt collection includes, for example, monitoring public foreign radio broadcasts, press, and other publications, excerpts of which are produced by CIA as a service of common concern for the other members of the Community.

Other overt collection is done by State Department Foreign Service Officers, Treasury Department representatives, and Defense Attachés abroad.

Great technological advances have revolutionized intelligence over these years. The advent of sophisticated technical collection systems has enabled us to know with certainty many things which a decade ago we were debating on the basis of bits of circumstantial evidence.

This technology has been introduced at high cost. Collection systems being employed today have required hundreds of millions of dollars and substantial numbers of people to analyze and make sense of the information they deliver.

But overt and technical collection cannot collect the plans and intentions of a hostile general staff, sense the political dynamics of closed authoritarian societies, or enable us to anticipate new weapons systems during the research phase before they are completed and visible. For this, clandestine collection is needed, especially by human sources.

The immense flow of data from these collection systems must be correlated, evaluated, and analyzed to understand its true significance. Since the responsibilities of our policy-makers cover such a wide range of international subjects these days, intelligence must employ the analytical services of professionals with specialized backgrounds in politics, economics, the sciences, military strategy, geography, and other disciplines. CIA alone, for example, employs enough expertise in these fields to staff the faculty of a university.

Other Agencies play essential roles in intelligence work, but CIA is the only statutory Agency of the US Government with responsibilities exclusively in the field of intelligence.

It has three major functions:

(1) to produce intelligence judgments, based on information from all sources, for the benefit of policy-makers. The product is in the form of publications and bulletins on current develop-ments, estimates of future international situations, and in-depth studies on various topics—for

example, a study on the origins and growth—over time—of the Soviet strategic weapons systems;

(2) to develop advanced technical equipment to improve the collection and processing of US intelligence; and

(3) to conduct clandestine operations to collect foreign intelligence, carry out counterintelligence responsibilities abroad, and undertake—when directed—covert foreign political or paramilitary operations.

The production of intelligence judgments and analysis concerning foreign affairs is vested in the Directorate for Intelligence (DDI). Offices below the Deputy Director level specialize in economic, political, and military topics. DDI analysts often confer with a range of experts in the United States outside the Intelligence Community to benefit from the views of recognized authorities on topics of interest.

The Directorate for Science and Technology (DDS&T) is the unit responsible for research, development, and operation of advanced collection systems. These range from small technical devices concealed by agents abroad to complex and costly "black-box" collection systems involving electronics, photography, and the like. In the DDS&T also, our analysts keep under study scientific and technical developments abroad, including weapons and space systems.

The Directorate for Operations (DDO) is the unit responsible for covert collection, primarily through clandestine collection by human sources. The Directorate is organized along geographic lines. It has some special staffs which focus on problems that cut across regional boundaries (for example, international terrorism).

The Directorate for Administration (DDA) provides support to other Agency components. It is responsible for personnel programs, security, administration, training, logistics, communications, medical services, and the like.

Security and Counterintelligence

I have already mentioned my responsibility for protecting intelligence sources and methods. It is out of this responsibility, and because of the need to protect the nation's vital intelligence secrets, that CIA has built over the years a capability, using security and counterintelligence techniques, to protect those secrets and guard against penetration of our intelligence activities.

A degree of secrecy, and an ability to protect some secrets, is essential to our work. This literally can be a matter of life and death for agents operating abroad, whether they be our own employees whose identification with CIA would make them obvious targets for terrorists, or citizens of totalitarian regimes who have agreed to report to us on their own governments. Many of the American businessmen and professors who voluntarily share their foreign experiences with us want to protect the relationship to remain confidential, and we must protect their proprietary information which sometimes comes our way in the course of such exchanges.

Disclosure of the details of sophisticated (and costly) technical collection operations would tell a target country, for instance, just how to change its procedures in order to deny us reliable assessments of its military threat. Finally, no foreign government can be expected to continue intelligence cooperation and exchange with us unless it is confident that we can keep its secrets.

There is an obvious potential conflict here with the right of citizens in a democracy to know what their government is doing in their name (and with their money). I am trying to reconcile this dilemma by making as much as possible of the substantive product of intelligence activities available to the general public as well as to Government officials. I am also trying to make public as many as possible of the general categories of intelligence activities conducted by the US Government. But I cannot relax, and indeed am intensifying, efforts to preserve the secrecy of operational details. Our efforts on these lines concentrate on assuring us of the integrity of those we employ or work with, providing indoctrination in and monitoring our procedures to keep our secrets, and investigating weaknesses or leaks in our security machinery. We have requested some improvements in our legislative tools for this purpose, and during the course of this investigation, I shall be asking your support for some of these efforts.

Counterintelligence is an essential element of the intelligence process, assigned to CIA by the National Security Council.

The counterintelligence function was the subject of scrutiny back in 1954 by a special committee established by President Eisenhower and headed by General James Doolittle to examine the covert activities of CIA.

In his report, General Doolittle wrote:

'We cannot emphasize too strongly the importance of the continuation and intensification of CIA's counterintelligence efforts to prevent or detect and eliminate penetrations of CIA."

Findings such as this served to underscore the importance of our counterintelligence work.

Activities Within the United States

It is, of course, a fact that the CIA has a presence in and carries out certain activities within the United States. About three-fourths of its employees live and work in this country. Most are in the Metropolitan Washington Headquarters Area, performing analysis, staff direction, or administrative support. About 10 percent of CIA's employees work in the United States outside the Headquarters Area. These perform functions supporting our organization which must be done here, such as personnel recruitment and screening or contracting for technical intelligence devices, and they collect foreign intelligence here. Clearly much information on the world is available here from private American citizens and from foreigners, and it would be foolish indeed to spend large sums and take great risks abroad to obtain what could be acquired cheaply and safely here.

CIA's Domestic Collection Division (DCD) has representatives in 36 American cities. These representatives contact residents of the United States who are willing to share with their Government information they possess on foreign areas and developments. These American sources provide their information voluntarily, in full awareness they are contributing information to the Government.

The DCD assures them their relationship with CIA will be kept confidential and that proprietary interests (say, on the part of a businessman) will not be compromised.

Since 1947, the DCD has contacted many thousands of individuals and organizations representing American businesses, industry, and the scientific and academic communities. DCD of course maintains records on its relationships with the individuals and organizations it has contacted.

The information obtained by DCD is made available to other agencies in the Intelligence Community as a service of common concern. Army, Navy, and Air Force officers are assigned to some DCD offices to assist CIA personnel so that there is one coordinated program, rather than separate duplicating efforts.

I want to emphasize that this collection program focuses exclusively on the collection of information about foreign areas and developments.

In addition to their information collection responsibilities, DCD offices also assist in other CIA activities in the United States, such as the identification of individuals who might be of assistance to Agency intelligence operations abroad. DCD is also responsible for the resettlement of foreign defectors who take up residence in the United States.

Information is sometimes received by DCD representatives which more properly falls within the jurisdiction of other US Government agencies. Such information is always passed to the appropriate agency. When possible, the possessors of the information are referred to the appropriate local agency. In few cases, Domestic Collection Division offices have accepted and passed to CIA Headquarters, for forwarding to the appropriate agency, information about foreign involvement in US narcotics traffic, dissident activities, and terrorism which they learned while conducting their normal collection activity.

The Foreign Resources Division was known until 1972 as the Domestic Operations Division. The principal mission of this Division is to develop relationships with foreigners in the United States who might be of assistance in the clandestine collection of intelligence abroad. In this process, it also collects foreign intelligence from foreigners in the United States. It has offices in eight US cities, which operate under some cover other than CIA.

The work of this Division is closely coordinated with the FBI, which has the responsibility for identifying and countering foreign intelligence officers working within the US against our internal security.

The Cover and Commercial Staff exercises both staff and operating responsibilities in the conduct of the Agency cover programs, in commercial activities and funding necessary to support our other operations, and in arranging the cooperation of US business firms for cover purposes. It conducts negotiations with other US Government Departments and Agencies on official cover arrangements and with cooperating US business firms on non-official cover arrangements for Agency personnel, installations, and activities. It develops and maintains a variety of proprietary commercial mechanism to provide non-official cover and operational support to Agency operations against foreign targets. An example of the work of this Staff in the commercial area is the arrangement with a corporation, either an independent firm or a wholly-owned proprietary, to provide the ostensible source of income and rationale for a CIA officer to reside and work in a foreign country.

The Agency's Office of Security has eight field offices in the United States primarily engaged in conducting security investigations of Americans with whom the CIA anticipates some relationship—employment, contractual, informational, or operational. The investigators do not normally identify themselves as CIA.

The Office of Security investigates all applicants for employment with the Agency, actual or potential contacts of the Agency, and consultants and independent contractors to determine their reliability prior to their exposure to sensitive matters dealing with the Agency. We also conduct investigations of individuals employed by contractors to the Agency, such as the employees of Lockheed who worked on the U-2 program. Numerous files are, of course, built up in this activity, but are kept segregated from the Agency's operational and counterintelligence files.

Another responsibility of the Office of Security is the investigation of unauthorized disclosures of classified intelligence. This function stems from the Director's statutory responsibility to protect intelligence sources and methods. Thus, the CIA Office of Security would prepare a damage assessment and endeavor to determine the source of a leak so that we could take corrective action. The National Security Act of 1947 gives the Director authority to terminate the employment of an individual when he deems it "necessary or advisable in the interests of the United States.".

Research and development are necessary activities if we are to have the technical intelligence capabilities I discussed earlier. Nearly all such work is done for the CIA through contracts with US industrial firms of research institutes. In many such contracts, CIA sponsorship of the project is not concealed. But in some cases, the fact that the work is being done for the CIA—or even for the Government—must be hidden from many of the individuals working on the program. This was the case in the development of the U-2 aircraft, for example.

In such cases, a separate organization within an existing company may be established by the company to conduct the necessary R&D under a cover story of commercial justification. Management of the entire program is organized in a fashion which isolates it from any association with the CIA or the Government. In order that such operations can take place, special cover mechanism must be established to handle such problems as funding and security investigations of personnel being assigned to the job. Because of the Agency's ability to operate with greater flexibility than most other agencies of Government and because of its experience in such activities, it has also undertaken such activities on the basis of funding made available from the Department of Defense from appropriations for the purpose. Indeed, though the CIA's own R&D program is a vigorous one, it is very small when compared with the several large programs conducted in conjunction with the Department of Defense. All such activity is subject to regular and systematic review and audit. This activity represents another category of our domestic activities, bringing the Agency into contact directly or indirectly with large numbers of US citizens and requiring it to keep a large number of records involving US citizens and organizations.

The complexity of modern intelligence analysis requires the development and application of increasingly sophisticated methodology for treating the enormous quantity of data collected by the Intelligence

Community. Although the Agency has actively pursued such development using its own highly qualified staff, it has increasingly been forced to call on the capabilities of the American scientific and technical community for assistance.

This assistance is provided via contractual arrangement. It may be for the purpose of defining and developing the methodology, e.g., how to process poor quality foreign radar signal intercepts in order to be able to evaluate the emitting radar. Alternatively, it may require a continuous effort to apply a methodology, e.g., to provide assessments of foreign missile performance from intercepted signals. In either case, it both supplements and complements analogous efforts in the Agency itself. Such programs have been a standard means of carrying out the Agency's role for many years.

These sorts of research projects or studies can be misunderstood, as recently occurred with respect to one on foreign transportation technology. One critic has confused CIA's solicitation of bids for a study with a program to spy. This confusion steams from a lack of appreciation of the modern intelligence process in which "spying" plays only a small role. In fact, however, this project, and others similar to it, are purely analytical in character and expect no espionage or active intelligence collection by the contractor beyond research among open sources. Some such contracts do include analysis of information provided by CIA from its secret technical or clandestine sources, but only when the information is not available otherwise.

The Agency's Office of Personnel has a Recruitment Division to hire Americans with the required skills and expertise for Agency employment.

Agency recruiters identify themselves as CIA Personnel Representatives and carry CIA credentials. We maintain 12 domestic field offices (whose telephone numbers can be obtained from the public telephone directory). In addition, Agency representatives enter into confidential arrangements with some US residents who agree to assist us abroad in the conduct of our foreign intelligence responsibilities.

Here in the Headquarters area, we have an office in Rosslyn, Virginia, open to the general public. Since most of our professional applicants come from college campuses, primarily at the graduate level, our recruiters maintain close contact with college placement officials and faculty advisors. To round out our recruitment effort they also maintain contact with personnel representatives of private industry, professional and scientific associations, minority organizations, and the like. Our recruiters are authorized to place advertisements in newspapers, periodicals, and college publications for recruitment purposes.

The Agency must look to itself to provide training of its employees in those disciplines which are unique to its mission, ranging from clandestine operations and agent handling to intelligence analysis and technical skills. We also offer an extensive program in language training, communications, and the normal administrative and management courses associated with the Government operations. To this end we operate several training sites and occasionally take advantage of a large US city environment to expose a trainee to the difficulties of foot surveillance. In such instances, of course, the subject would be another Agency employees participating in the training exercise.

The four units I have just described carry out the major programs of the Agency which call for the operation of field offices in the United States. They all are proper under the Act which governs us.

Mr. Vice President, the foregoing provides you with a view of the extent of CIA activities in the United States. The classified appendixes I have submitted to the Commission provide additional detail.

Allegations and Some Details

The article of December 22, 1974, charged that CIA has engaged in a "massive illegal domestic intelligence operation." The article referred in particular to files concerning American dissident groups.

The factors are these (as outlined in my report to President Ford, a copy of which you have):

In mid–1967, the US Government was concerned about domestic dissidence. The obvious question was raised as to whether foreign stimulation or support was being provided to this dissident activity.

On August 15, 1967, the Director established within the CIA Counterintelligence Office a unit to look into the possibility of foreign links to American dissident elements.

And then, you will recall that President Johnson on July 27, 1967, appointed a National Advisory Commission on Civil Disorders. Mr. David Ginsburg, the Executive Director of that Commission, wrote to the Director on August 29, 1967, asking what the Agency might do to assist in that inquiry with "information, personnel, or resources."

The Director responded on September 1, offering to be helpful, but pointing out that the Agency had no involvement in domestic security. Some limited material from abroad, the Director wrote, might be of interest.

Later the same year, the CIA activity became part of an interagency program, in support of the National Commission, among others.

In October 1967, a report issued by the new CIA unit concluded that, although information was limited,

> "There is no evidence that anti-war demonstrations and related activities in the United States are controlled by Communist forces abroad. There are indications, however, that anti-war activity is partially responsive to North Vietnamese "inspiration.""

Periodically thereafter, various reports were drawn up on the international aspects of the anti-war, youth and similar movements, and their possible links to American counterparts. Specific information was also disseminated to responsible US agencies.

In September 1969, the Director reviewed this Agency program and stated his belief that it was proper "while strictly observing the statutory and de facto proscriptions on Agency domestic involvement."

In 1970, in the so-called Huston Plan, the Directors of the FBI, DIA, NSA, and CIA recommended to the President an integrated approach to the coverage of domestic unrest. While not explicit in the plan, CIA's role therein was to contribute foreign intelligence and counterintelligence to the joint effort.

The Huston Plan was not implemented, but an Interagency Evaluation Committee, coordinated by Mr. John Dean, the Counsel to the President, was established. The Committee was chaired by a representative of the Department of Justice and included representatives from CIA, FBI, DoD, State, Treasury, and NSA. Its purpose was to provide coordinated intelligence estimates and evaluations of civil disorders with CIA supplying information on the foreign aspects thereof.

Pursuant to this, CIA continued its counterintelligence interest in possible foreign links with American dissidents. The program was conducted on a highly compartmented basis. As is necessary in counterintelligence work, the details were known to few in the Agency.

We often queried our overseas stations for information on foreign connections with Americans in response to FBI requests or as a result of our own analyses. Most of these requests were for information from friendly foreign services, although there were instances where CIA collection was directed. In most cases the product of these queries was passed to the FBI.

In the course of the program, the Agency worked closely with the FBI. For example, the FBI asked the Agency about possible foreign links with domestic organizations or requested coverage of foreign travel of FBI suspects. The Agency passed to the FBI information about Americans it learned from its intelligence or counterintelligence work abroad. The FBI turned over to the Agency certain of its sources or informants who could travel abroad, for handling while there. In order to obtain access to foreign circles, the Agency also recruited or inserted about a dozen individuals into American dissident circles in order to establish their credentials for operations abroad. In the course of the preparatory work or on completion of a foreign mission, some of these individuals submitted reports on the activities of the American dissidents with whom they were in contact. Information thereby derived was reported to the FBI, and in the process the information was also placed in CIA files.

In 1973 this program was reviewed and specific direction given limiting it to collection abroad, emphasizing that its targets were the foreign links to

American dissidents rather than the dissidents themselves and that the results would be provided to the FBI.

In March 1974, the Director terminated the program and issued specific guidance that any collection of counterintelligence information on Americans would only take place abroad and would be initiated only in response to requests from the FBI or in coordination with the FBI, and that any such information obtained as a by-product of foreign intelligence activities would be reported to the FBI.

In the course of this program, files were established on about 10,000 American citizens in the counterintelligence unit.

About two-thirds of these were originated because of specific requests from the FBI for information on the activities of Americans abroad, or by the filing of reports received from the FBI.

The remaining third was opened on the basis of CIA foreign intelligence or counterintelligence information known to be of interest to the FBI.

For the past several months, we have been eliminating material from those files not justified by CIA's counterintelligence responsibilities, and about 1,000 such files have been removed from the active index but not destroyed.

In May 1970, the Department of Justice provided us with a machine-tape listing of about 10,000 Americans. The listing could not be integrated in CIA's files and was destroyed in March 1974.

Mr. Vice President, let me digress here for a moment to comment on this word "files" which has been bandied about widely and can mean many different things to different people.

The backbone of an intelligence operation, particularly a counterintelligence case, is detailed information—through which one can begin to discern patterns, associations, and connections.

In this sphere, therefore, any professional intelligence organization tries to systematically record all scraps of information on people who may be of interest to it or may provide avenues to persons of interest. Thus whenever a name—anyone's name—a date, place, a physical description, appears anywhere in any operational report, it is usually put into a cross-referenced master index.

Whenever there are one or more pieces of paper dealing primarily with a single individual—for whatever reason— there is probably, somewhere, a "file" on that individual; whether he is an applicant, an employee, a contractor, a consultant, a reporting source, a foreign target of intelligence interest, a foreign intelligence officer, or simply a person on whom someone else (such as the FBI) has asked us to obtain information overseas.

The fact that there is a "file" somewhere in one of our various record systems with a person's name on it does not mean that that "file" is the type of dossier that police would use in the course of monitoring that person's activities.

In this context, it is clear that CIA does have listings of large numbers of Americans, as applicants, current and ex-employees, sources and other contacts, contractors, Government and contractor personnel cleared for access to sensitive categories of intelligence, individuals corresponding with us, etc. I am sure you will find that most of these are unexceptional and necessary to run an institution of the size and complexity of CIA, and that these records are maintained in ways which do not suggest that the names are in any way suspect.

Our operational files also include people who were originally foreign intelligence targets but who later became US citizens, such as Cuban or other emigree groups.

There have been lists developed at various times in the past, however, which did appear questionable; for example, caused by an excessive effort to identify possible "threats" to the Agency's security from dissident elements, or from a belief that such lists could identify later applicants or contacts which might be dangerous to the Agency's security. They did not result from CIA collection efforts, but were compilations of names passed to us from other Government agencies such as the FBI, some police forces, or the House Un-

American Activities Committee. A number of these dubious listings have been eliminated in the past three years, and the Agency's current directives clearly require that no such listings be kept.

The New York Times article of December 22, 1974, made certain other charges:

> *that at least one member of Congress had been under CIA surveillance and that other Congressmen were in our "dossier" on dissident Americans, and that break-ins, wire-taps, and surreptitious inspection of mail were features of CIA activities.*

Let me provide background on these allegations.

On May 9, 1973, the Director issued a notice to all CIA employees requesting them to report any indication of any Agency activity any of them might feel to be questionable or beyond the Agency's authority.

The responses led to an internal review of the counterintelligence program and other Agency activity—a review, Mr. Vice President, that is continuing.

The initial responses and our review of them culminated in fresh policy determinations and guidance issued in August 1973. This guidance is a matter of detail in the classified appendices I will provide to this Commission.

As I have said, Mr. Vice President, this review continues in order to insure that our activities remain proper.

Let me discuss our findings with respect to the press allegations.

(1) *The New York Times* article of December 22, 1974, declared:

> "At least one avowedly anti-war member of congress was among those placed under surveillance by the CIA, the sources said."

Mr. Vice President, our findings are that there is no—and to my knowledge never has been—surveillance, technical or otherwise, directed against any sitting member of Congress.

The New York Times article also indicated that "Other members of Congress were said to be included in the CIA's dossier on dissident Americans."

No current Congressmen are included in the files of the counterintelligence program described above, although we do have lists and files of current Congressmen.

Some (about 14) were opened prior to the Congressmen's election as a step toward possible operational cooperating with the Agency. Some (about 2) because the names arose in the course of coverage of foreign targets. Some are files on ex-employees (2) or applicants. Some (about 17) are on contacts or sources of our Domestic Collection Division. And, of course, our Congressional liaison staff keeps working files on its contact with Congressmen.

(2) *The New York Times* article also referred to "break-ins," and said no "specific information about domestic CIA break-ins" could be obtained.

Our investigations to date have turned up a total of three instances, which could have been the basis for these allegations. Each of the three involved premises related to Agency employees or ex-employees.

In 1966, a new Agency employee, inspecting a Washington apartment he was thinking of renting, saw classified documents in the apartment, which was the residence of an ex-employee. The new employee advised CIA security officers who promptly went to the apartment, were admitted without stating their intentions, and removed the documents.

The second instance occurred in 1969. A junior Agency employee with sensitive clearances caused security concern by appearing to be living well beyond his means. Surreptitious entry was made into his apartment in the Washington area. No grounds for special concern were found.

The third instance occurred in 1971 in the Washington area. An ex-employee became involved with a person believed to be a Cuban intelligence agent. Security suspicions were that the two were engaged in trying to elicit information from Agency employees. A surreptitious entry was made into the place of business of the suspect Cuban agent. Results were negative. An attempt to enter the suspect agent's apartment were unsuccessful.

(3) *The New York Times* article also referred to wiretaps and said no specific information could be obtained.

Our findings show that there were telephone taps directed against twenty-one residents of the United States between 1951 and 1965, and none thereafter. In each case the purpose was to check on leaks of classified information. Nineteen of the individuals concerned were Agency employees or former Agency employees, including three defector contract agents (not US citizens) and one contract employee who was the wife of a staff agent. The two private citizens whose phones were tapped in 1963 were thought to be receiving sensitive intelligence information, and the effort was aimed at determining their sources. Our records show that these two taps were approved by the Attorney General.

In 1965, President Johnson issued an order that there be no wire-taps in national security cases without approval by the Attorney General. Only one of the operations mentioned above took place in 1965, against a CIA employee suspected of foreign connections. This operation was approved by the Attorney General.

Since World War II, successive Presidents have authorized the Attorney General to approve electronic surveillance in national security situations. The Omnibus Crime Act of 1968 prohibits interception and disclosure of wire or oral communications but further provides that nothing in such law:

> "...shall limit the constitutional power of the President to take such measures as he deems necessary to protect the Nation against actual or potential attack or other hostile acts of a foreign power, <u>to obtain foreign intelligence information deemed essential to the security of the United States, or to protect national security information against foreign intelligence.</u>" (Emphasis supplied.)

While this statute does not purport to convey a new power to the President, it is a recognition by the Congress that such measures are within the constitutional power of the President.

(4) *The New York Times* article also alleges physical surveillance of American citizens.

The Agency has conducted physical surveillance on our employees when there was reason to believe that they might be passing information to hostile intelligence services. this was done on rare occasions, and in recent years only three times—in 1968, 1971, and 1972. In 1971 and 1972, physical surveillance was also employed against five Americans who were not CIA employees. We had clear indications that they were receiving classified information without authorization, and the surveillance effort was designed to identify the sources of the leaks.

Also, in 1971 and 1972, a long-standing CIA source—a foreigner visiting in the US—told of a plot to kill the Vice President and kidnap the CIA Director. We alerted the Secret Service and the FBI and we carried out physical surveillance in two American cities. The surveillance came to involve Americans who were thought to be part of the plot— and the mail of one suspect was opened and read.

(5) *The New York Times* article also refers to "surreptitious inspection of mail."

As part of its foreign intelligence program, CIA has conducted at various places in the world a survey of mail to and from certain Communist countries. This provides technical information on Communist mail procedures and censorship. It provides addresses that might be used for various intelligence programs and, in those instances in which selected mail is opened, it sometimes provides information on conditions in the country as well as operational leads for agent recruitment.

From 1953 until February 1973, CIA conducted programs at three sites in the United States to survey mail between the United States and two Communist countries. Some of this mail was opened to determine Communist censorship techniques or to report the contents of the messages. The main product of this activity was material of an internal security nature, which was disseminated to the FBI.

The activities discussed above were reported as a result of the Director's 9 May 1973 notice and were reported to the Chairman of the Senate and House Armed Services Committees—the Congressional bodies responsible for oversight of CIA—on 21 May 1973.

CIA Relationships With Other Government Agencies

In August 1973, in connection with the review of all activities of the Agency which might be considered questionable under the terms of its charter, I ordered a review of assistance to other Federal, state, and local government components. Each of the Agency's Deputy Director was required to terminate all activities he considered inappropriate.

Based upon this review, I asked the CIA Inspector General and General Counsel to review and make recommendations on all activities not terminated by the Deputy Directors. On this basis, I made an individual determination to continue, modify, or terminate each such activity. Most assistance to other agencies was continued, but a substantial number of such activities were modified or terminated.

Assistance to agencies with foreign operations and not involved in domestic law enforcement was generally continued, while assistance which could involve the Agency even indirectly in law enforcement activities was appropriately modified or terminated.

In addition, some assistance activities not warranted on the basis of economy or necessity were discovered and terminated. This program of review of assistance to other Government agencies has been made permanent and each new proposal for this kind of assistance must be reviewed and approved by the Deputy Director concerned, the Inspector General, and the General Counsel before it may be instituted. In case any one of them disagrees, I personally make the decision.

I believe this continuing program will assure that all assistance is carefully considered and kept within the bounds of legality, propriety, and economy.

In discussing allegations of improper CIA domestic activity, I wish to comment on "the Watergate affair." This topic has been the subject of extensive hearings by the Ervin Committee and the four CIA Subcommittees of the Congress as well as by other investigations by the Grand Jury, the Department of Justice, and the Special Prosecutor. So I will comment only briefly on it. The allegation was that CIA had prior knowledge of the Watergate break-in and was somehow otherwise knowingly involved. While I have admitted the CIA made mistakes in providing certain equipment to Howard Hunt and in preparing a psychological assessment on Daniel Ellsberg, both in response to directives from the White House, we have no evidence, and none was developed in any of the hearings or inquiries I have just mentioned, to support the other allegations concerning CIA. Aside from these two instances, the main CIA role in Watergate was to refuse to be used in the coverup, and to avoid being misunderstood as involved. Most recent evidence clearly demonstrates CIA's non-involvement rather than involvement in Watergate.

While Senator Baker's minority report suggests that the Agency was involved in domestic activities beyond its charter, the testimony of 24 Agency witnesses covering 2,000 pages, along with the production of some 700 sensitive Agency documents, failed to result in any concrete evidence to support these allegations.

Although we entered into that investigation in the spirit of cooperation and in the interest of providing information relevant to the investigation, eventually extremely broad requests, which would have exposed sensitive intelligence sources and methods having no relationship to the inquiry, forced me to request a more precise bill of particulars, and to suggest that they might be handled more appropriately through our normal oversight procedure with the Senate Armed Services Committee.

I think it is interesting in this connection that despite the fact that the profile and the provisioning were requested by the White House, questions as to the propriety of these actions were brought to the attention of senior officials of the Agency by Agency employees at the working level.

For the Commission's background, I would also like to mention the Agency's relationships with American student and other associations and foundations, revealed in 1967 by *Ramparts* magazine. The Agency had developed confidential relationships with some officials of these groups to assist their activities abroad in exposing and counteracting Communist-controlled efforts to subvert international student and labor groups.

State Department Under Secretary Katzenbach chaired an interagency group which investigated this matter. The group's recommendations resulted in a ban on CIA covert assistance to American educational or voluntary organizations, and these restrictions are reflected in internal Agency regulations and policy.

The activities I have described to you in this statement related to *The New York Times* allegations and were among those, as I have said, that were reported to the Director by our officials and employees in 1973 in response to his notice to all employees asking them to report any and all activities that they or others might deem questionable. These were reported to the Chairmen of the Senate and House Armed Services Committees— the Congressional bodies responsible for oversight of CIA—in May 1973.

These briefings were accompanied by my assurances that the Agency's activities would be conducted strictly within its proper charter, and specific instructions were issued within the Agency along these lines. Recently, I was advised by the Acting Attorney General that I was obliged to call certain of these to his attention for review, and I have done so, although it is my opinion that none would properly be the subject of adverse action against men who performed their duties in good faith.

The Commission will be interested in some of the CIA's internal checks and balances—its safeguards designed to ensure that its activities remain within proper bounds.

In the first place, strength is to be found in the simplicity of CIA's organization. The command line runs from the Director to four Deputies and thence to Office or Division Chiefs. The arrangement provides the Director with an uncomplicated and direct access to action officers within the separate components, whether they be Deputies, Office Chiefs, analysts, or operators.

The Agency relies on certain functions, as well as organization, to provide safeguards. The Inspector General, who reports directly to me, is vested with an independent authority to review the activities of all elements of the Agency.

The CIA General Counsel reports to the Director and oversees the legal aspects of Agency activity.

The CIA Comptroller, who reports directly to the director, reviews programs and the allocation of

CIA Headquarters

resources independent of the Deputies and makes his advice known to the Director and the Deputies.

The CIA Audit Staff is responsible for checking the use of funds by Agency components and for assuring that the funds are properly used and are consistent with appropriate internal approvals and the law.

The Office of Finance watches the integrity of the Agency's accounting structure, supervises internal financial audits, and assures compliance with the fiscal requirements of the Agency and the Government.

In addition to my dealings with each Deputy Director and Independent Office Chief, they together comprise the CIA Management Committee. As such, they meet regularly to advise me on a wide range of policy decisions. This practice also ensures communication among the leadership of all components of the Agency and provides for cross-fertilization of ideas and opinions.

One characteristic of the Agency is the need for compartmentation to enhance security and protect particularly sensitive sources and methods. This does not diminish my responsibility to know of and approve all sensitive operations, but it does limit the awareness of employees not directly involved in the operation and leads to limits on written records to which substantial numbers of people have access. As a result the written records immediately available to describe the background of some Agency activities conducted in earlier years are less complete than I—and I am sure the Commission—would like. There is no implication here of improper destruction of records, but the intelligence profession does limit the detail in which they exist and the degree to which they are circulated.

Finally, every year Agency employees are instructed to bring either to my attention or to that of the Inspector General any activity which they think may be beyond our charter.

Mr. Vice President, in this presentation I have endeavored to provide the Commission with a frank description of our intelligence activities. That description is intended to demonstrate the importance of the CIA and the rest of the Intelligence Community in assisting the Government in developing and implementing its foreign policy and alerting it to potential crisis or war. I would now like to summarize the situation and present some thoughts as to possible Commission recommendations.

First, as I said at the outset, I flatly deny the press allegation that CIA has been engaged in a "massive illegal domestic intelligence operation."

Whether we strayed over the edge of our authority on a few occasions over the past 25 years is a question for you gentlemen, and whatever investigative bodies Congress may designated, to judge.

Mr. Vice President, any institution—in or out of Government—that has been functioning for 25 years finds it hard put to avoid some missteps, but I submit that any such missteps in the CIA's history were few and far between, and unconnected with the thrust of the Agency's important and primary mission–the collection and production of intelligence pertaining to foreign areas and developments.

Certainly at this time it is my firm belief that no activity of the Agency exceeds the limits of its authority under law.

Mr. Vice President, the President's charge to this Commission requires that your review lead to recommendations, some to be made to me as well as to the President. I look forward to those recommendations, including any you may make with regard to internal CIA safeguards and organization.

I would like to offer for the Commission's consideration certain suggestions which the Commission may deem to be appropriate subjects for eventual recommendations.

There are several bills now in Congress recommending certain amendments to the National Security Act so as to clarify the extent of CIA's activities within the United States.

One of these is to add the word "foreign" before the word "intelligence" wherever it appears in the Act, to make crystal clear that the Agency's purpose and authority lie in the field of foreign intelligence.

Another amendment proposes that within the United States the Agency will not engage.

"in any police or police-type operation or activity, any law enforcement operation or activity, any internal security operation or activity, or any domestic intelligence operation or activity."

The Agency full accepts these amendments as a clear statement of prohibited activity and as a way to reassure any concerned that CIA has any such function. Last September, I wrote to the Chairman of the Senate Armed Services Committee assuring him that the Agency will abide by the letter and the spirit of this proposed amendment..

The prohibition in this amendment is supplemented by the following additional proviso:

"Provided, however, that nothing in this Act shall be construed to prohibit CIA from protecting its installations or conducting personnel investigations of Agency employees and applicants or other individuals granted access to sensitive Agency information; nor from carrying on within the United States activities in support of its foreign intelligence responsibilities; nor from providing information resulting from foreign intelligence activities to those agencies responsible for the matters involved."

Again, we welcome this text as a clear statement of what the Agency properly does in the United States in support of its foreign intelligence mission. As I described to you earlier and explained in my confirmation hearings, these include:

(1) Recruiting, screening, training, and investigating employees, applicants, and others granted access to sensitive Agency information;

(2) Contracting for supplies;

(3) Interviewing US citizens who voluntarily share with the Government their information on foreign topics;

(4) Collecting foreign intelligence from foreigners in the United States;

(5) Establishing and maintaining support structures essential to CIA's foreign intelligence operations; and

(6) Processing, evaluating, and disseminating foreign intelligence information to appropriate recipients within the United States.

I respectfully suggest that the Commission might indicate its support of these legislative amendments in its recommendations.

A separate matter of concern deals with the question of appropriate oversight of the Agency. Within the Executive Department, the Director is appointed by the President with the advice and consent of the Senate and serves "at the pleasure of the President of the United States ."

The President has appointed a Foreign Intelligence Advisory Board to assist him in supervising the foreign intelligence activities of the United States.

This Board has a long and excellent record of reviewing the Foreign intelligence activities of the United States—those in CIA as well as the other departments and agencies.

The board has made a number of very important recommendations to the President and has stimulated and supported major advances in our intelligence systems.

The activities of the CIA and the Intelligence Community are also reviewed by the Office of Management and Budget, to which the Agency reports fully and through whom the Director's recommendations for the total foreign intelligence program are routed to the President.

General guidance of the CIA and the Intelligence Community is provided by the National Security Council through the Assistant to the President for National Security Affairs and the National Security Council staff. The National Security Council is assisted by the National Security Council Intelligence Committee and by several other National Security Council committees, such as the Washington Special Action group for crisis situations, the 40 Committee for covert actions, and others.

Pursuant to a Presidential Directive of 5 November 1971, reaffirmed by President Ford on 9 October 1974, the Director of Central Intelligence is also assigned a special role with respect to the Intelligence Community as well as the Central Intelligence Agency. He is required to exercise positive leadership of the entire Community and to recommend to the President annually the appropriate composition of the entire intelligence budget of the United States. He is directed to accomplish these with the advice of and through the United States Intelligence Board and the Intelligence Resources Advisory Committee, which include the intelligence elements of the State, Defense, and Treasury Departments, and other agencies concerned with intelligence.

The National Security Council exerts its direction over the Intelligence Community through a series of National Security Council Intelligence Directives assigning responsibilities and providing authorization for actions. These Directives are in the process of consolidation and updating and are supplemented by Directives issued by the Director of Central Intelligence under the general authority provided by the National Security Council Intelligence Directives. One of particular relevance to this Commission's work specifically outlines how CIA will operate within the United States. It is in its final stages of coordination and is essentially agreed between the FBI and CIA.

In my view, Mr. Vice President, the arrangements for administrative supervision of the Central Intelligence Agency and the Intelligence Community by the Executive Branch appear sufficient at this time, but you will certainly want to reassure yourselves on this in detail.

Congressional oversight of CIA has long been handled with full recognition by Congressional leaders of the necessary secrecy of the Agency's activities. As a result, from its earliest days, small subcommittees were established in the Appropriations and Armed Services Committees of the Senate and House to which the Agency reported its activities, but outside of which no information was made available concerning its sensitive operations. There are no secrets from these oversight committees, and between our meetings with the Committees, we are in continuing contact with the Staffs.

The Agency has reported publicly to other committees about matters which can be disclosed publicly, and it has reported extensively in Executive Session to other committees, providing classified substantive intelligence appreciation of world situations. Over the years, a number of suggestions have been made within the Congress to revise the oversight responsibility, but to date none has been agreed. The Agency's position has always been that it will work with the Congress in any way the Congress chooses to organize itself to exercise its responsibilities for oversight and for appropriations.

Whatever arrangements the Congress adopts, we trust there will be a continuation of congressional protection of the secrecy of our intelligence activities.

This raises the final subject to which I invite the Commission's attention—the need for improvement in our legislation to strengthen our ability to protect those secrets necessary to successful intelligence operations.

It is plain that a number of damaging disclosures of our intelligence activities have occurred in recent years. One affect of this has been to raise questions among some of our foreign official and individual collaborators as to our ability to retain the secrecy on which their continued collaboration with us must rest.

We certainly are not so insensitive as to argue that our secrets are so deep and pervasive that we in CIA are beyond scrutiny and accountability.

We of course must provide sufficient information about ourselves and our activities to permit constructive oversight and direction.

I firmly believe we can be forthcoming for this purpose, but there are certain secrets that must be preserved.

We must protect the identities of people who work with us abroad.

We must protect the advanced and sophisticated technology that brings us such high-quality information today.

To disclose our source and methods is to invite foreign states (including potential enemies) to thwart our collection.

The problem is that current legislation does not adequately protect these secrets that are so essential to us.

Current legislation provides criminal penalties, in event of disclosure of intelligence sources or methods, only if the disclosure is made to a foreigner or is made with an intent to injure the United States. The irony is that criminal penalties exist for the unauthorized disclosure of an income tax return, patent information, or crop statistics.

To improve this situation, we have recommended changes in legislation, and I invite this Commission to support the strengthening of controls over intelligence secrets. These can be fully compatible with the constitution, with the lawful rights of intelligence employees and ex-employees, and with the independence of our judicial authorities.

I believe this matter to be as important as possible improvements in our oversight by the Executive and Legislative Departments. For effective supervision of intelligence activities and the need for effective secrecy must go hand in hand.

Mr. Vice President, I mentioned at the outset that I have submitted for the record classified appendixes to this statement. I trust they will be useful to the Commission in its examination.

I am prepared to respond to any questions the Commission may have and to make available appropriate employees of the Agency for questioning.

Bill Harvey, Chief of Staff D.

As for ex-employees, I respectfully request—should the Commission seek them as witnesses—that they be contacted directly by the Commission. The Agency no longer has authority over them, and I have directed that they not be contacted by the Agency at this time in order to avoid any possibility of misunderstanding of such contacts.

In the event of testimony by ex-employees or others, I respectfully request an opportunity to review with the Commission the details of the testimony before a decision is made to publish them and perhaps reveal sensitive intelligence sources and methods.

In conclusion, Mr. Vice President, I sincerely believe that this Commission will find with me that the Agency did not conduct a massive illegal domestic intelligence activity, that those cases over its history in which the Agency may have overstepped its bounds are few and far between and exceptions to the thrust of its activities and that the personnel of the Agency, and in particular my predecessors in this post, served the nation well and effectively in developing the best intelligence product and service in the world. Lastly, I hope that this Commission may help us to resolve the question of how, and consequently whether, we are to conduct an intelligence service in our free society, and recognize its needs for some secrecy so that it can help protect our freedoms and contribute to the maintenance of peace in the world.

The Angleton Era in CIA

Yale professor, Norman Holmes Pearson, recruited his former student into the Office of Strategic Service's (OSS) X-2 (counterintelligence). In 1943, OSS sent Angleton to London where he learned counterintelligence from the British. He lived at the Rose Garden Hotel on Ryder Street, which was headquarters for the combined counterintelligence operations of OSS and MI6. During his tour in London, the British gave Angleton access to their intercepts of the broken German Abwehr code (ICE).

In 1944, X-2 ordered Angleton to Italy to assume control of its counterintelligence operations as the Allied forces drove northward up the peninsula against the retreating German army (for additional information on

Angleton's operations in Italy, see the article "ARTIFICE" in Volume II). Shortly after the Germans surrendered in May 1945, President Truman disbanded the OSS. Angleton remained in Rome as commanding officer of a small caretaker organization called the 2677th Regiment of the Strategic Services Unit (SSU).

In 1947, Angleton returned to the United States and joined CIA's Office of Special Operations. In December 1949 he became chief of Staff A (Operations), responsible for clearances for all agent operations, double agent operations, provocation, and operational interrogation. With his background in counterintelligence, it was surprising that Angleton was not assigned to Staff D, which was created at the same time. Staff D was responsible for CI, and William Harvey was named chief. Later, Staff D became Staff C. It operated primarily in the field of records exploitation, analysis of information, control of CI information, and name checks. Both Staffs in effect performed counterintelligence functions.

Staff C also acquired several responsibilities from the Office of Special Operations (OSO), which was eliminated. It acquired the physical security of all the Agency's foreign installations, the operational security of agents, and protective and counterespionage chores. From the Soviet branch it acquired the external USSR section (International Communism) and the Russian Intelligence Section.

In 1952, Angleton, with the support of the Office of Security, started operation HTLINGUAL. It conducted international mail openings from the main postal facility in Jamaica, New York. In proposing the operation, Angleton argued that the mail opening operation was a necessary alternate to the CIA's foreign operations. In 1958 the FBI was informed of the mail openings after it requested permission from the postmaster general to mount a similar operation. The postmaster general informed the Bureau that the CIA had been opening mail for five years.

CIA's Office of Security actually opened the letters, and the Counterintelligence Staff processed the information. The operation ran smoothly until Deputy Director of Operations, William Colby, recommended to DCI William Schlesinger that HTLINGUAL be terminated. Angleton made a strong appeal for its continuation, saying the mail information was valuable. To legalize the operation, he urged Schlesinger to obtain the President's personal approval. Not wanting to take sides, Schlesinger suspended the operation, and it eventually died from neglect.

The Philby Connection

Before CIA established its Counterintelligence Staff, Angleton worked with Harvey's Staff C to track down Soviet spies in the United States. Afterwords, Kim Philby, from British intelligence, arrived in Washington in September 1949 to become liaison officer to the FBI and CIA. Angleton and Harvey also collaborated closely with him. Philby and Angleton became friends and often lunched together. An unidentified CIA officer stated that "Philby was Angleton's prime tutor in counterintelligence."

Donald Maclean, head of the British Foreign Office's American Department.

Kim Philby, Angleton's prime tutor in counterintelligence.

In 1950, the British Foreign Office assigned Guy Burgess to the British Embassy in Washington as a second secretary. He previously worked for MI6 but his indiscretions caused MI6 to fire him. After his firing, the British Broadcasting Corporation hired him but he soon left to join the Foreign Office where he was appointed as the confidential secretary to the minister of state.

Upon his arrival in the United States, Burgess moved into Philby's home. Although Philby attempted to be a stabilizing influence for Burgess, the task was impossible because Burgess was a flagrant drunkard and unabashed homosexual. In the Spring of 1951, the British Foreign Office considered recalling Burgess to London for abusing his diplomatic privileges but changed its mind. The issue resurfaced one afternoon when the Virginia State Police stopped him for speeding three times. Each time he berated the state troopers to such an extent that the Governor of Virginia reported the incident to the State Department. The Foreign Office had no choice but to recall Burgess to London to face a disciplinary board for his indiscretions in the United States.

After his return to London, British security noted Burgess having several lunches with Donald Maclean. Maclean, head of the British Foreign Office's American Department, was suspected of being a Soviet agent. Suspicion of Maclean surfaced after intercepted KGB coded cables were decrypted by American intelligence pointing to a spy in the British Foreign Office. Of particular interest was an intercept that indicated that "Homer" (codenamed for Maclean) met his Soviet handler twice a week in New York using the cover story of visiting his wife. This pattern matched that of Maclean's movements of twice-a-week visits to his pregnant wife, Melinda, who was residing with her American mother in New York City.

On Friday, May 25, 1951, the British Foreign Office authorized MI5 to interrogate MacLean the following Monday. Burgess simultaneously knew of this decision. He reportedly told a companion that they would have to postpone plans for a weekend in France because "a friend of mine in the Foreign Office is in trouble. I am the only one who can help him." Burgess and MacLean defected to Russia. On June 7th, the press reported the disappearance of the two men. On June 26, 1951, the Bureau informed the code breakers at Arlington Hall that "Homer" was possibly identical to Maclean.

By early 1951 the British apparently focused on Philby as a Soviet spy. Their suspicions grew after the defection of Burgess and Maclean and because of further decrypted KGB messages being read by American intelligence. Before anything could be done, however, Bill Harvey and Angleton, aroused by their own suspicions of Philby, began an independent investigation. This unilateral action on the part of the CIA forced the British to recall Philby and show their hand.

When Burgess and MacLean defected on May 25, 1951, the DCI, Gen. Bedell Smith, directed Harvey, Angleton, and everyone else in CIA to prepare a memo on what they knew about them. Harvey's five-page memo, dated June 13, 1951, stated categorically that Philby was a Soviet agent. Angleton's memo of June 18, 1951, did not suggest any suspicions of Philby, according to a CIA officer who studied the memo closely. "It related two or three incidents, the bottom line of which was that you couldn't blame Philby for what this nut Burgess had done." In his memo, Angleton wrote, "Philby has consistently sold (Burgess) as a most gifted individual. In this respect, he has served as subject's apologist on several occasions when subject's behavior has been a source of extreme embarrassment in the Philby household. Philby has explained away these idiosyncrasies caused by a brain concussion in an accident..". Another source said that Angleton's memo did conclude that Philby was a Soviet agent.

After Philby had been unmasked, Angleton would claim to have had his doubts about Philby all along.

Guy Burgess, assigned to the British Embassy in Washington as a Second Secretary in 1950.

Two of Angleton's closest friends would support that contention, but three CIA officers who reviewed the Philby file in depth insisted that Harvey was the first to point the accusing finger. Angleton explained the absence of documentary evidence to support his claim that he had his doubts about Philby all along by saying one did not put in writing something so sensitive as suspicions about the loyalty of a trusted member of a friendly intelligence service. Angleton had not unmasked Philby. Never again would he permit himself to be so badly duped. He would trust no one. Philby was the greatest blow Angleton ever suffered.

Smith forwarded Angleton's and Harvey's memos to MI6 in London with a cover letter stating that Philby was no longer welcome as the British liaison officer in Washington.

Angleton Named Chief of CI Staff
In September 1954, the new DCI Allen Dulles selected Angleton to be chief of an expanded Counterintelligence Staff "to prevent or detect and eliminate penetration of CIA." He previously served as the DCI's personal advisor on CI problems, sometimes to the exclusion of the more official Staff C, and played a leading part in negotiating this restructuring. Angleton's aim was to prevent the CI mission of the Clandestine Services from becoming subordinate to other divisions.

Dulles decided that the Israeli account was too important to be entrusted to the pro-Arab specialists in the Near East Division. His solution was to give it to the Counterintelligence Staff. One rationale for this move was that Angleton had a wide range of contacts with Israeli leaders, many of whom he had met in Italy after the war.

Another responsibility Dulles gave Angleton was handling all liaison with allied intelligence services. This allowed Angleton to boost his personal authority within the CIA because it delegated to him ready access to the Director. He became the central figure through whom the director would learn of important secrets volunteered by allied intelligence services and also allowed him to control what information CIA passed to these services.

British MI5 officer, Peter Wright, in 1957, stated: "I was struck by (Angleton's) intensity. He had a razor-sharp mind and a determination to win the Cold War, not just to enjoy the fighting of it. Every nuance and complexity of his profession fascinated him, and he had a prodigious appetite for intrigue. I liked him, and he gave enough hints to encourage me into thinking we could do business together."

The CI Staff's charter, published in March 1955 as Chapter V of the revised CSI No. 70-1 established four subunits:

Special Investigations (mainly operational approvals and support).

Liaison (with the FBI regarding US internal security).

Research and Analysis.

Special Projects (especially touchy matters and liaison with the Israeli Service).

Anatoliy Golitsyn, Angleton's Rasputin
Anatoliy Mikhaylovich Golitsyn, born 25 August 1926, Piryatin, Ukraine, was a KGB staff officer who defected to the United States while stationed in Helsinki on 15 December 1961. Golitsyn was the first KGB staff officer defector since 1954. The first nine months after his arrival in the United States were very productive. He provided insights into the operations and personnel of the KGB but only compromised one significant spy— Georges Paques, a French national, working in the NATO press office. Many of his leads were vague; a factor compounded by his refusal to be debriefed in Russian. CIA accepted Golitsyn's bona fides in March 1962. Some of his information was

George Blake

deemed important enough by CIA that DCI McCone and later Richard Helms briefed President Kennedy and the British and French Governments as well, about it.

Golitsyn elaborated on the espionage work of previously identified agents as Heinz Felfe and George Blake. He espoused the theory that the Soviets had penetrated all the Western intelligence services. Peter Wright, an MI5 officer, became one of the most devoted followers of the Golitsyn theories and played a major role in the MI5 investigations of the supposed penetrations of the British services.

In November 1964, Golitsyn identified Ingeborg Lygren as a Soviet agent. She had recently returned to Oslo from Moscow and was serving as secretary to the head of military intelligence, Col. Wilhelm Evang, Norway's chief liaison with CIA. Angleton flew to Oslo but, instead of contacting Evang about Golitsyn's allegation, he told the chief of Norway's internal security service, Asbjorn Bryhn. Bryhn and Evang were bitter enemies and their noncooperation with each other was legendary in Norway. To Bryhn, the arrest of the secretary to his archenemy would be a plum in his cap.

The result of the investigation was insufficient evidence to bring the case to trial. Despite the lack of hard facts, Bryhn had Lygren arrested on 14 September 1965. Evang was informed three days later that his secretary had been arrested and was being held in solitary confinement. During her confinement, Lygren did admit indiscretions in Moscow with persons she presumed were under KGB control but claimed that she was never recruited.

Gunvor Haavik, served as secretary to the Norwegian Ambassador in Moscow.

On 10 December 1965, Lygren was formally charged as a Soviet spy. Four days later, Norway's state prosecutor promptly threw out the case because of the lack of hard evidence. Lygren was freed but the case did not disappear. The Norwegian press began a hue and cry and an impartial Norwegian investigation followed. This investigation cleared Lygren and criticized severely Evang and Bryhn for their distrust of each other. Both men were reassigned.

The whole affair caused an enormous flap that damaged CIA's liaison with Norway for many years. Two years later, Oleg Gordievskiy, a senior KGB officer who was recruited by the British and worked inplace for them, advised the British that a KGB agent worked in the Norwegian Ministry of Foreign Affairs. After an investigation, the Norwegian intelligence service arrested Gunvor Haavik, who served as secretary to the Norwegian ambassador in Moscow before Lygren arrived in Moscow in 1956.

Golitsyn arrived at a time when CIA officers were in a state of alarm about the KGB. He convinced many of them of the existence of a successful Soviet conspiracy to push "misinformation." Golitsyn was treated in an unusual manner. For instance, when his original handler died, he was turned over exclusively to the CI Staff, which allowed him access to CI files to look for material to support his theories about the Soviet conspiracy. Golitsyn then went on to encourage suspicions that there were high-ranking spies planted in the West.

The Nosenko-Golitsyn Debate

It was Golitsyn who provided the first information about the KGB's "disinformation" department. When CIA picked up on this, it began to assume that many KGB operations had "disinformation" as their purpose and that most Soviet defectors were in fact "dispatched" agents. Golitsyn also predicted that Moscow would send out another defector with the specific mission of undermining him and his information.

Yuriy Ivanovich Nosenko, a Lieutenant Colonel in the KGB's Second Chief Directorate with considerable experience in operating against Americans, first approached US Intelligence in Geneva, Switzerland in June 1962. He provided information dealing with KGB operations against Americans and other foreigners inside the USSR. In early February 1964, Nosenko defected while accompanying the Soviet delegation to the Geneva disarmament talks.

The first CIA interviewers who met with Nosenko favored cooperation with him. He was accepted as a defector in February 1964 and began to undergo intensive debriefing. One key item in this was Nosenko's report on the story in the USSR of Oswald and his flat denial that Oswald had been under KGB direction.

Angleton soon converted Nosenko's designated handler Chief, Soviet Russia/Counterintelligence (C/SR/CI) Tennant Bagley, to the Golitsyn point of view. The original attempt to establish Nosenko's bona fides turned into a prolonged effort to break him and to learn from him the details of his mission and its relation to possible penetration of US Intelligence and security agencies. For the remainder of DCI McCone's tenure, CIA held Nosenko in close confinement and periodically subjected him to hostile interrogation. For 10 years, starting in 1964, James Angleton devoted a substantial part of the resources of the Counter-intelligence Staff to investigating the charges and countercharges surrounding Yuri Nosenko, suspecting that the CIA harbored a Soviet double agent.

Pressure from the Clandestine Services led to a reopening of the Nosenko case. Near the end of DCI's Raborn's tenure, a Soviet Division officer laid out his reasons for believing that Nosenko was a bona fide defector and his recommendations for an impartial review in a paper that he sent to the Chief, SB Division. When no action was taken, he sent it to the DDCI. Toward the end of 1966, interrogation of Nosenko resumed under more humane conditions.

Still dissatisfied at the lack of a solution, the officer finally took his case to the DCI in December 1966. In March 1967, Helms turned the Nosenko case over to DDCI Rufus Taylor. Taylor assigned responsibility for the case to the Office of Security, thus getting it off to a fresh start. Bruce Solie took over Nosenko's handling and interrogation, and in due course turned around the Agency's official position. Nosenko was released from detention in October 1968. In May 1977, CIA finally accepted Nosenko's bona fides as valid.

Paradoxically, while SB's efforts against the Soviet target were handicapped by charges of plots, moles, and disinformation campaigns, the Soviets themselves were evolving in the other direction. By the late 1960s, a new generation—less bound by the idealism of the revolutionary period and the suspicions of the Stalinist era—were emerging as the group most often in contact with Westerners. They proved somewhat more susceptible than their elders to recruitment offers and more willing to supply intelligence information.

The Angleton Legacy and Deception

From 1963 to 1965, the Soviet Division collided with Angleton and his theories that any reports and information acquired from Soviet sources was likely to be planted for the purposes of deceiving US intelligence. Such views negated any accomplishments of the Division, and the Division itself was split over the issue of whether the Division was a victim of Soviet provocation and penetrations.

The Trust Operation and Its Impact on the CI Staff's View of Deception

The Trust was an organization especially created by the GPU (forerunner of the KGB) for the purpose of demoralization of the émigrés, specifically its monarchist faction. In four years after its creation, the "Trust" not only became a powerful organization, which attracted to itself all the orthodox monarchist and anti-Bolshevik elements, but also obtained control over most of the Russian émigrés. It not only achieved penetration into the principal anti-Soviet intelligence services and acquired influence over the information about Soviet Russia going to a number of European capitals, but it became capable of conducting deep recon-naissance in Europe and of committing sabotage in the realm of international relations. One could pose the obvious question: were there no suspicions aroused during this period lasting several years. Did it not seem suspicious that this organization, so much talked about in all the European capitals and all the émigré caberets, had not been uncovered by the Bolsheviks?

When the Trust ended, it had inflicted great damage on the Russian emigre movements. Their political and military capabilities were undercut to such an extent that, from 1927 on, its role became insignificant. The damage to the European intelligence services was just as devastating, since for several years they were severed from their own potential real sources, were fed notional and deception material, and were demoralized as a result of the apparent easiness of the work. The Trust was the cause of numerous misunderstandings between the various services, which destroyed that mutual confidence which, at first, united them in their work against the Soviets.

The Monster Plan vs. The Master Plan

The CI Staff took up the doctrine of Soviet use of disinformation techniques and automatically suspected all defectors of being KGB provocateurs. By the time of Nosenko's arrival, it had become virtually impossible for any defector from the Soviet intelligence service to establish his bona fides to the satisfaction of the CI Staff or the Soviet Division.

The feud escalated into competing "plot" scenarios, with CI Staff seeing a Moscow-directed conspiracy to subvert CIA by controlling key officials within it and with certain Soviet Division officers seeing a CI plot to undermine confidence in Agency leaders and CIA's Soviet experts. Productive activities were inhibited for long periods of time while accusations and counteraccusations about a possible Soviet-controlled "mole" in the top echelons of CIA were checked out. The damage to morale lasted longer.

CI Staff's "Monster Plot" theories—developed and elaborated from 1962 to 1970—were based on closely reasoned arguments. They began with the assumption that the KGB would run a Nosenko-style provocation only if it had a deep penetration of the organization against which the provocation was directed. This was reinforced by a dictum CI Staff applied to its own operations—that a deception or disinformation case cannot be run without controlled channels of communications. CI also had a deep conviction that CIA could not have escaped the sort of penetrations that had been proved in other Western services.

One extreme aspect of the plot theory was a special, rigidly compartmented project that included CI Staff, the Office of Security, and the FBI but excluded the Soviet Division. Much of the work under the special project was done by junior officers, who sought to document given hypotheses they assumed to be valid. CI Staff did not reveal its suspicions to the rest of the Clandestine Service, which remained unaware that some quarters considered all their Soviet Bloc operations contaminated.

The Loginov Affair

Yuriy Loginov was a KGB illegal dispatched to Finland in 1961. Rather than establishing a fictitious, non-Soviet identity there as his KGB superiors had directed, he informed the American Embassy in Helsinki that he wished to defect. Agency officers persuaded him to return to the USSR instead, to serve as a CIA agent. He maintained contact with CIA as he traveled abroad on KGB missions over the next six years, although his production was minimal.

After Nosenko's 1964 detention by CIA, the poisons of that case contaminated the Soviet Division's handling of Loginov as well. In part because Loginov's information substantiated Nosenko's and in part because of Golitsyn's hold over Angleton and the Soviet Division, prevailing CIA opinion when Loginov appeared in South Africa in February 1967 was that he was a witting KGB deception agent. Told that the Agency did not trust him, he asked permission to defect, only to be refused. Tipped by CIA that Loginov was a KGB-controlled agent, South African police arrested him in July, after promising to keep CIA's past association with him a secret. Two years of imprisonment and interrogation followed.

Yuriy Loginvo

In July 1969, South African officials, working through the West Germans, exchanged Loginov with the KGB for 11 Westerners jailed in the East. According to several reports, Loginov resisted his forced return to the end. He died before a firing squad.

The Cold Warrior

Angleton was one of a few CIA officers who was granted special authority to report directly to the DCI, outside the normal chain of command. This special reporting authority had arisen both from the need for tight security for sensitive activities and from each DCI's interest in keeping close control of certain matters. To the new DCI William Colby, this special access posed a problem because he wanted to eliminate any possibility that previous loyalties did not transcend current ones. He solved this by firing one of the officers previously given this special access. Angleton presented a much bigger problem.

Colby had first tried to get rid of Angleton in early 1973, when as Director of the Directorate of Operations he urged DCI James Schlesinger to fire the counterintelligence chief on the ground that Angleton's ultraconspiratorial mind was more of a liability than an asset to CIA. Schlesinger refused. In September 1973, with Schlesinger appointed as Secretary of the Department of Defense, Colby was named DCI. As Colby noted in his book, however, by the time the decision was his to make, he thought the Clandestine Service had had about all the personnel turbulence it could take and that it would see a move against Angleton as an omen of much more to come.

Reprieved from dismissal, Angleton faced a reduction of his virtual autonomy. In June 1973, Colby saw to it that the mission statement of the Counterintelligence Staff was revised and that Angleton was firmly told the CI Operations component would in the future report to and be directed by the Directorate of Operations. The private communications channels between the Chief of CI Staff and its representatives abroad were put on a case-by-case basis, and Angleton's control of counterterrorism liaison with the FBI was also taken away.

Colby has explained that he did not suspect that Angleton and his staff were engaging in improper activities, but that he just could not figure out what they were doing at all. He said he could not follow Angleton's tortuous arguments and could not find any tangible results from his activities. Colby's concern grew when he discovered that CI Staff's theories about Soviet deception and manipulation were distracting from CIA's efforts to gather positive intelligence information, damaging the careers of good CIA clandestine operations officers by casting doubt on their reputations, and, in the case of France, threatening the Station's relations with the host country by spreading accusations about the loyalty of the COS.

In another move, Colby stripped the Israeli account from Angleton. Colby hoped that Angleton would take the hint and retire. Angleton fought back but the publicity about illegal domestic surveillance, beginning with a long article by Seymour Hersh on December 22, 1974, tipped the scales.

Colby called Angleton to his office on Friday, December 20, 1974, and demanded his resignation. Colby offered Angleton another assignment, to spend the rest of his career writing an extensive study of the doctrine of counterintelligence complete with case studies. Colby later explained that he had assumed that Angleton would be outraged and quit. Three of Angleton's closest associates resigned at the time he was dismissed. All four were given short-term contracts or granted consultant status in order to provide for an orderly transfer of counterintelligence responsibilities.

The CI Staff was rebuilt with new people, with many of the positions filled on a rotational basis to ensure a continuing infusion of fresh personnel. Angleton's immediate successor was George Kalaris, who was brought in to become Acting Chief, CI.

Seymour Hersh in a *New York Times* article, dated June 25, 1978, stated, "The political struggles that, to one degree or another, were provoked by the Soviet Union after WWII left the West with a legacy of fear of Soviet expansionism. As in any political conflict, there were extremists on both sides, and over the years Angleton came to symbolize one end of the spectrum, his apprehension of the Communist threat affecting all things Russian."

FBI Counterintelligence Programs

House Judiciary Committee, Subcommittee On Civil and Constitutional Rights, Hearings November, 1975

Statement of the Honorable William B. Saxbe, Attorney General of the United States

In January of this year during the course of my initial briefing on current issues facing the Department of Justice, I was informed of the existence of an FBI "Counterintelligence Program."

After ascertaining the general thrust of the counterintelligence programs, I directed Assistant Attorney General Henry Peterson to form a committee charged with the responsibility of conducting a complete study and preparing a report for me which would document the Bureau's activities in each of the separate counterintelligence programs. That study committee consisted of four Criminal Division representatives and three representatives from the Federal Bureau of Investigation, selected by Director Kelley.

The Committee's report to me stated that there were seven separate programs—five directed at domestic organizations and individuals, and two programs directed at foreign intelligence services, foreign organizations and individuals connected with them. These programs were implemented at various times during the period from 1956 to 1971 when all programs were discontinued. The Committee further found that 3,247 counterintelligence proposals were submitted of which 2,370 were approved. In 527 instances, known results were ascertained.

It is not my intention at this time to detail for you the particulars of the seven programs inasmuch as you have been provided with a copy of the committee's report which has been edited to delete national security information. That document describes fully the activities involved in each of the programs.

The materials released today disclose that, in a small number of instances, some of these programs involved what we consider today to be improper activities. I am disturbed about those improper activities. However, I want to stress two things: first, most of the activities conducted under theses counterintelligence programs were legitimate—indeed, the programs were in response to numerous public and even Congressional demands for stronger action by the Federal Government. second, to the extent that there were, nevertheless, isolated excesses, we have taken steps to prevent them from ever happening again. In this connection, Director Kelly last December sent a memorandum to FBI personnel strongly reaffirming the Bureau policy that: "FBI employees must not engage in any investigative activity which could abridge in any way the rights guaranteed to a citizen of the United States by the Constitution and under no circumstances shall employees of the FBI engage in any conduct which may result in defaming the character, reputation, integrity, or dignity of any citizen or organization of citizens of the United States."

Attorney General William B. Saxbe and Federal Bureau of Investigation Director Clarence M. Kelley released today the details of certain counterintelligence programs conducted by the FBI from 1956 to 1971 against several domestic and foreign-based subversive or disruptive groups, organizations, and individuals.

These efforts, which carried the designation "COINTELPRO," were targeted against the Communist Party U.S.A., the Socialist Workers Party, the New Left, White House groups, and Black Extremist organizations, as well as certain espionage operations and hostile foreign-based intelligence services.

The materials released today significantly expand upon material released in December, 1973, by Director Kelley concerning the counterintelligence program conducted against radical and violent elements as part of the COINTELPRO—New Left.

Counterintelligence Program–Background Material

The FBI's Counterintelligence Program
I. Introduction

The FBI's counterintelligence program was developed in response to needs at the time to quickly neutralize organizations and individuals who were advocating and fomenting urban violence and campus disorder. The riots, which swept America's urban centers beginning in 1965, were quickly followed by violent disorders which paralyzed college campuses. Both situations led to calls for action by alarmed Government leaders and a frightened citizenry.

II. Tenor of the Times

An Associated Press survey noted that, during the first nine months of 1967, racial violence in 67 cities resulted in 85 deaths, injuries to 3,200 people and property damage of over $100,000,000. The February 1970 issue of *Security World* stated that during the period January 1 to August 31, 1969, losses specifically traced to campus disorders amounted to $8,946,972.

In March 1965, then Senator Robert F. Kennedy predicted more violence in the South and North after Congress passed voting rights legislation. Kennedy said, "I don't care what legislation is passed—we are going to have problems...violence."

A United Press International release on December 5, 1967, quoted Pennsylvania Governor Raymond P. Shafer as warning that "urban disaster" in the form of "total urban warfare" is waiting in the wings to strike if the race problem is not solved in the Nation's cities.

Attorney General Ramsey Clark reported to President Johnson on January 12, 1968, according to the *Washington Star*, that extremist activity to foment "rebellion in urban ghettos" has put a severe strain on the FBI and other Justice Department resources. Clark called this "the most difficult intelligence problem" in the Justice Department.

A United Press International release on February 13, 1968, stated that President Johnson expected further turmoil in the cities and "several bad summers" before the Nation's urban problems are solved.

III. Calls to Action

President Lyndon Johnson said in a television address to the Nation on July 24, 1967, in describing events that led to sending troops to Detroit during that city's riot, "We will not tolerate lawlessness. We will not endure violence. It matters not by whom it is done, or under what slogan or banner. It will not be tolerated." He called upon "all of our people in all of our cities" to "show by word and by deed that rioting, looting and public disorder will just not be tolerated."

In a second address to the Nation in just three days, President Johnson announced the appointment of a special Advisory Commission on Civil Disorder to investigate origins of urban riots. The President said that this country had "endured a week such that no Nation should live through; a time of violence and tragedy." He declared that "the looting and arson and plunder and pillage which have occurred are not part of a civil rights protest." "It is no American right," said the President, to loot or burn or "fire rifles from the rooftops." Those in public responsibility have "an immediate" obligation "to end disorder," the President told the American people, by using "every means at our command...."

The President warned public officials that "if your response to these tragic events is only business-as-usual, you invite not only disaster but dishonor," President Johnson declared that "violence must be stopped— quickly, finally and permanently" and he pledged "we will stop it."

House Speaker John W. McCormick said on July 24, 1967, after conferring with President Johnson, that the President had told party leaders that "public order is the first business of Government." The next day Senator Robert C. Byrd advocated "brutal force" to contain urban rioting and said adult looters should be "shot on the spot."

On April 12, 1968, Representative Clarence D. Long of Maryland urged J. Edgar Hoover in a letter and in a public statement to infiltrate extremist groups to head off future riots and said FBI Agents "could take people like Negro militants Stokely Carmichael and H. Rap Brown out of circulation."

The *St. Louis Globe–Democrat* in a February 14, 1969 editorial entitled, "Throw the Book at Campus Rioters," described campus disorders then sweeping the Nation as "a threat to the entire university educational system." This newspaper called on the Attorney General to "move now to stop these anti-American anarchists and Communist stooges in their tracks. He should hit them with every weapon at his command. The American people are fed up with such bearded, anarchist creeps and would applaud a strong drive against them. They have been coddled and given license to run roughshod over the rights of the majority of college students far too long. It is time it hit them hard with everything in the book."

On October 2, 1969, Senator Byrd said that "events in the news in the fast few days concerning activities by militant radical groups should alert us to the new trouble that is brewing on the Nation's college campuses and elsewhere." Senator Byrd said that "all of us would do well to pay heed now, and law enforcement authorities should plan a course of action before the situation gets completely out of hand."

Attorney General William B. Saxbe today has released a report regarding FBI counterintelligence programs. The report was prepared by a Justice Department committee which included FBI representatives that was specially appointed early this year to study and report on those programs.

Since taking the oath of office as Director on July 9, 1973, I also have made a detailed study of these same FBI counterintelligence programs.

The first of them—one directed at the Communist Party, USA—was instituted in September, 1956. None of the programs was continued beyond April, 1971.

The purpose of these counterintelligence programs was to prevent dangerous, and even potentially deadly, acts against individuals, organizations, and institutions—both public and private—across the United Sates.

They were designed to counter the conspiratorial efforts of revolutionary elements in this country, as well as to neutralize extremists of both the Left and the Right, who were threatening and in many instances fomenting acts of violence.

The study which I have made convinces me that the FBI employees involved in these programs acted entirely in good faith and within the bounds of what was expected of them by the President, the Attorney General, the Congress, and the American people.

Each of these counterintelligence programs bore the approval of the then Director J. Edgar Hoover.

Proposals for courses of action to be taken under these programs were subject to approval in advance, as well as to constant review, by FBI Field Office and Headquarters officials.

Throughout the tenure of these programs, efforts admittedly were made to disrupt the anarchistic plans and activities of violence-prone groups whose publicly announced goal was to bring America to its knees. For the FBI to have done less under the circumstances would have been an abdication of its responsibilities to the American people.

Let me remind those who would now criticize the FBI's actions that the United States Capitol was bombed; that other explosions rocked public and private offices and buildings; that rioters led by revolutionary extremists laid siege to military, industrial, and educational facilities; and that killings, maiming, and other atrocities accompanied such acts of violence from New England to California.

The victims of these acts of violence were human beings-men, women, and children who looked to the FBI and other law enforcement agencies to protect their lives, rights, and property. An important part of the FBI's response was to devise counterintelligence programs to minimize the threats and the fears confronting these citizens.

In carrying out its counterintelligence programs, the FBI received the personnel encouragement of myriad citizens both within and without the Government. Many Americans feared for their own safety and of their Government. Others were revolted by the rhetoric of violence and the acts of violence that were being preached and practiced across our country by hard-core extremists.

I invite attention to the gravity of the problems then existed, as well as the need for decisive and effective counteraction by the criminal justice and intelligence communities.

I want to assure you that Director Hoover did not conceal from superior authorities the fact that the FBI was engaging in neutralizing and disruptive tactics against revolutionary and violence-prone groups. For example, in a communication concerning a revolutionary organization that he sent to the then-Attorney General and the White House on May 8, 1958, Mr. Hoover furnished details of techniques utilized by the FBI to promote disruption of that organization.

A second communication calling attention to measures being employed as an adjunct to the FBI's regular investigative operations concerning this same revolutionary organization was sent to the Attorney General designate and the Deputy Attorney General-designate by Mr. Hoover on January 10, 1961.

Mr. Hoover also sent communications to the then-Attorneys General in 1965, 1967, and 1969 furnishing them information regarding disruptive actions the FBI was employing to neutralize activities of certain Rightist hate groups.

I have previously expressed my feeling that the FBI's counterintelligence programs had an impact on the crises of the time and, therefore, that they helped to bring about a favorable change in this country.

As I said in December, 1973:

> "Now, in the context of a different era where peace has returned to the college campuses and revolutionary forces no longer pose a major threat to peace and tranquility of our cities, some may deplore and condemn the FBI's use of a counterintelligence program—even against hostile and arrogant forces which openly sought to destroy this nation.
>
> "I share the public's deep concern about the citizen's right to privacy and the preservation of all rights guaranteed under the Constitution and Bill of Right."

My position remains unchanged.

After the August 24, 1970, bombing at the University of Wisconsin, Madison, a group of faculty members called for disciplinary action against students involved in disruption and violence. In a statement delivered to the Chancellor, 867 faculty members said "the rising tide of intimidation and violence on the campuses in the last few years has made normal educational and scholarly activities increasingly difficult. There has been a steady escalation of destructiveness that has culminated in an act of homicide. Academic freedom, meaning freedom of expression for all ideas and viewpoints, has been steadily eroded until now many are questioning whether it exists on the Madison campus." The faculty members said that "the acts of a few must not be allowed to endanger the rights and privileges of all members of the academic community."

The New York Times reported on October 11, 1970, on "The Urban Guerrillas—A New Phenomenon in the United States" and noted that the Senate Subcommittee on Internal Security recently heard four days of testimony on four bills aimed at "crushing the urban guerillas" including one "that would make it a crime to belong to or aid organizations advocating terrorism, and would prohibit the publication of periodicals that advocate violence against police and the overthrow of the Government."

The President's Commission on Campus Unrest in detailing "the law enforcement response" noted that "it is an undoubted fact that on some campuses there are men and women who plot, all too often successfully to burn and bomb, and sometimes to maim and kill. The police must attempt to determine whether or not such a plot is in progress, and, if it is, they must attempt to thwart it."

Finally, Allan C. Brownfeld, a faculty member at the University of Maryland, writing in *Christian Economics*, February 11, 1970, on "The New Left and the Politics of Confrontation" noted that "in many instances, those extremists who have fomented disorder have been in violation of state and Federal Statutes." But, Mr. Brownfeld noted. "What is often missing is the will to prosecute and to bring such individuals before the bar of justice." Mr. Brownfeld's article was subcaptioned "A Society Which Will Not Defend Itself Against Anarchists Cannot Long Survive."

IV. Appropriations Testimony

On February 10, 1966, FBI Director J. Edgar Hoover testified regarding the Ku Klux Klan, saying that "the Bureau continues its program of penetrating the Klan at all levels and, I may say, has been quite successful in doing so. The Bureau's role in penetrating the Klan has received public attention due to the solution of the brutal murders of Viola Luizzo in Alabama, Lieutenant Colonel Lemuel A. Penn in Georgia and the three civil rights workers in Mississippi. We have achieved a number of other tangible accomplishments in this field, most of which are not publicly known but are most significant." Discussion off the record to follow.

V. Public Support of the Counterintelligence Program

Following acknowledgement that the FBI had a counterintelligence program, syndicated columnist Victor Riesal wrote on June 15, 1973, "no apologies are due from those in the highest authority for secretly developing a domestic counterrevolutionary intelligence strategem in early 1970." Mr. Riesel detailed the record of "dead students," "university libraries on flames," and "insensate murdering of cops," and concluded "it would have been wrong not to have attempted to counter the sheer off-the-wall terrorism of the 1969-70 bomb seasons. And it would be wrong today. No one need apologize for counterrevolutionary action."

"Our reaction is that we are exceedingly glad he ordered it," wrote the *St. Louis Globe–Democrat* in a December 11, 1973, editorial on the counterintelligence program. This newspaper noted that "the Federal Bureau of Investigation under the late J. Edgar Hoover conducted a three-year campaign of counterintelligence 'to expose, disrupt, and neutralize' the New Left movement..." and that "many of these New Left groups were doing everything they could to undermine the Government and some of them resorted to bombings, street riots, and other gangster tactics. Others waged war on police across the Nation and on our system of justice. Still others disrupted the Nation's campuses. The Nation can be thankful it has a courageous and strong leader of the FBI to deal with the serious threats posed by New Left groups during this period."

On June 18, 1974, Eugene H. Methvin, Senior Editor, *The Readers Digest*, testified before the House Committee on Foreign Affairs regarding terrorism and noted, "...the FBI's counterintelligence program against the extremist core of the New Left was a model of sophisticated, effective counter-terrorist law enforcement action first developed and applied with devastating effect against the Ku Klux Klan in the mid-1960's. In that context the strategy won great publicity and praise; yet now we have the Attorney General condemning it. In the current climate of justifiable revulsion over Watergate, we are in danger of crippling law enforcement intelligence in a hysteria of reverse McCarthyism in which we close our eyes to evidence and some compelling necessities of domestic and international security."

Central Intelligence Agency Mail openings[98]

Inspector General's Survey of the Office of Security Annex II

Project SGPOINTER/HTLINGUAL[99]

1. This project is a sensitive mail intercept program started by the Office of Security in 1952 in response to a request from the SR Division. Under the original project, named SGPOINTER, representatives of the Office of Security obtained access to mail to and from the USSR and copied the names and addresses and addressers. In 1955 the DD/P transferred the responsibilities in his area for this program from SR Division to the CI Staff, the program was gradually expanded, and its name was changed to HGLINGUAL. Since then the program has included not only copying information from the exteriors of the envelope, but also opening and copying selected items.

2. The activity cannot be called a "project" in the usual sense, because it was never processed through the approval system and has no separate funds. The various components involved have been carrying out their responsibilities as a part of their normal staff functions. Specific DD/P approval was obtained for certain budgetary practices in 1956 and for the establishment of a TSD lab in 1960, but the normal programming procedures have not been followed for the project as a whole. However, the DCI, the DD/P, and the DD/S have been aware of the project since its inception and their approvals may thus be inferred.

3. The mechanics of the project can be summarized as follows. Mail to and from the USSR and other countries are processed through the branch office at LaGuardia Airport in New York City. The postal authorities agreed to a screening of mail by Agency representatives at this central point, and office space has been established there for three Agency officers and one representative of the postal service. As mail is

received it is screened by the Agency team and the exteriors of the envelopes are photographed on the site. The volume being photographed at the time of the inspection was approximately 1,800 items per day. From this total the Agency team selects approximately 60 items a day which are set aside and covertly removed from the post office at the end of the day. These are carried to the Manhattan Field Office (MFO) and during the evening they are steamed open, reproduced and then resealed. The letters are replaced in the mails the following morning. The films are forwarded to the Office of Security at headquarters and thence to the CI Staff, where dissemination is controlled.

4. The total flow of mail through the LaGuardia post office is not screened. The intercept team can work there only when the postal representative is on duty, which is usually the normal five-day, 40-hour week. Mail, of course, is received and processed at the post office 24 hours a day, seven days a week. Thus much of the overseas mail is simply not available for screening. Registered mail also is not screened because it is numbered and carefully controlled; however, on occasion, it has been possible to remove and process individually items on a priority basis. In such cases it has been necessary to hold up the entire pouch until the letter is replaced.

5. Three Security officers at the MFO work full-time on the project, and one clerical employee helps. Most of the officers' time is spent at the LaGuardia post office screening and photographing the exteriors of envelopes and supervising the actual openings during the evening. Several of the regular investigators of MFO have been cleared to work on the project, and overtime has been authorized up to eight hours per pay period for each employee involved. The normal evening sessions are from 5:00 to 9:00 PM. This is a highly efficient way to get the job done and the investigators enjoy the work and appreciate the opportunity to earn overtime pay. There is some question, however, concerning the administration of overtime pay. The Office of Security has ruled that overtime will not be paid to any person who takes leave, sick or annual, during the week within which the overtime is worked. This means that an officer who is ill after having worked his evening tour must nevertheless come to the office or forfeit his overtime pay. It also means that an officer who is sick in the week cannot afterward work his scheduled evening shift and be paid for it. The Office of Security should review its policy in this regard.

6. The principal guidance furnished to the interception team is the "watch list" of names compiled by the CI Staff. Names may be submitted by the SR Division, the FBI, the CI Staff, or the Office of Security. The list is revised quarterly to remove names, no longer of interest, and it ranges between 300 or 400 names. The list itself is not taken to the LaGuardia post office, and the three team members have to memorize it. Headquarters has compared the actual watch list intercepts with the photographs of all exteriors, and there has not been a case of a watch list item having been missed by the interceptors. Of the total items opened, about one-third are on the watch list and the others are selected at random. Over the years, however, the interceptors have developed a sixth sense or intuition, and many of the names on the watch list were placed there as a result of interest created by the random openings. A limited amount of guidance is given in specific area or topical requirements, but this is not very satisfactory. The interception team has to rely largely on its own judgment in the selection of two-thirds of the openings, and it should have more first-hand knowledge of the objectives and plans of operational components, which levy the requirements. Information is now filtered through several echelons and is more or less sterile by the time it is received in New York.

7. One of the uncertainties of the project is lack of specific knowledge concerning early agreements with postal authorities and any commitments, which the Agency may have made. Senior postal authorities in Washington approved the earlier phases of the activity. There are no documents to support this, however. After the initial acceptance of the project by postal authorities, liaison responsibilities were transferred to the Office of Security and have since been handled by the chief of MFO. The designated liaison officer for the postal service is the head of its Inspection Service in New York. The Agency has been fortunate in that the same persons have been associated with the project since its inception. Details of agreements and conversations have not been reduced to writing, however, and there is now some uncertainty as to what the postal authorities may have been told or what they might reasonably be expected to have surmised. This is important because the New York facility is being expanded in the expectation that we

will continue to have access to the mail. The very nature of the activity, however, makes it impossible at this point to try and have a firm understanding with postal authorities. There thus seems to be no alternative except to continue relying on the discretion and judgment of the persons involved.

8. The postal representative designated to work with the interceptor team at LaGuardia is a relatively junior but highly intelligent mail clerk. He probably suspects but has not been informed that the Agency is sponsoring the program. He is not a member of the postal Inspection Service, but reports to it on matters concerned with the project. This has placed him in a very unusual position in the post office, since he is on the T/O of the LaGuardia office. The chief of MFO unsuccessfully suggested to the local chief of the Inspection Service that the cover of this individual would be improved if he could be made a part of the service to which he reports. Because of the mail clerk's long association with the activity it should be assumed that he knows our basic objective. On the other hand, there is no evidence that he has ever communicated this knowledge to his New York supervisors. It is possible, of course, that key postal officials in New York and Washington suspect the true nature of the activity and have decided not to make an issue of it so long as they are not required officially to sanction it. In any event, the success of the project depends upon the cooperation of the mail clerk because mail cannot be removed without his knowledge. If he should be replaced it would probably be necessary to withdraw from the operation until his successor could be evaluated.

9. For the past four years processing of open letters has been limited to reproduction of the contents and analysis at headquarters. In February 1960, however, the Chief of Operations, DD/P, approved the establishment of a TSD laboratory to make technical examinations of the correspondence. The T/O for the unit is one GS-14 chemist, one GS-11 assistant and one GS-5 clerk/secretary with flaps and seals experience. A GS-11 has been hired and trained for the senior position, and a GS-9 is being sought for the other slot. The T/O and annual costs of the lab will be charged to TSD. Lab premises in New York were in the process of being leased during the inspection, and probably will be in the same building as MFO. The objectives of the lab group will be (a) examination of correspondence for secret messages, (b) detection of USSR censorship techniques and development of better operational methods to avoid such techniques, and (c) an increase in the quantity and quality of the present operations. TSD has shown considerable enthusiasm for the activity, not only because of the obvious contributions which, might be made to the intelligence effort, but also because it offers a workshop to test some of the equipment which TSD has developed.

10. Although an inspection of participating DD/P components is beyond the scope of this survey, the activity cannot be viewed from the Office of Security

FBI Headquarters.

alone. DD/P responsibilities for the activity now rest with the CI Staff and are discharged by the Projects Branch, a unit with 15 positions devoted full time to processing the film and reproduced correspondence. The T/O includes four senior analysts who have broad language capabilities, and a group of junior analysts who handle material in English. Also included is an IBM key punch operator who makes the IBM index cards for CI files. The clerical staff has had limited language training to facilitate the transliteration of Russian for indexing. As the reproduced letters are received by the Projects Branch, they are analyzed and dissemination proposed. This dissemination is subject to review by the Acting Chief, CI Staff, and extreme care is given to protecting the source.

11. The SR Division is the project's largest customer in the Agency. Information from the CI Staff flows to the SR Support Branch and from there to the operational branches. It may include items...of interest on conditions inside the country. In our interviews we received the impression that few of the operational leads have ever been converted into operations, and that no tangible operational benefit had accrued to SR Division as a result of this project. We have noted elsewhere that the project should be carefully evaluated, and the value of the project to SR Division should be one of primary consideration.

12. Dissemination to the FBI are approximately equal to those made to SR Division. Since the information is largely domestic CI/CE, it is not difficult to conclude that the FBI is receiving the major benefit from this project.

13. The annual cost of this activity cannot be estimated accurately because both administration and operations have always been decentralized. The costs are budgeted by the contributing components as a part of their regular operating program. The expenses of the New York facility are absorbed by the Office of Security as a part of the Manhattan Field Office budget. The cost of the new lab, including personnel and equipment, will be borne by TSD. The Project Branch of the CI Staff, the largest unit involved, is budgeted as a regular staff component of the CI Staff. Administrative costs within the headquarters component of SR Division and the Office of Security are included in their regular budgets. This dispersal of costs throughout the budgets of other components is an effective security device and should be continued, but we believe that it is nevertheless necessary that exact cost figures be developed to permit Agency management to evaluate the activity.

14. There is no coordinated procedure for presenting information received through the program; each component has its own system. The Office of Security indexes selected portions of the information in its Security Records Division. The CI Staff indexes the opened mail as well as a large percentage of the photographed exteriors. The SR Division maintains its own file system, and the information sent to SR Division by the CI Staff is frequently indexed by the Records Integration Division while it is in transit. The FBI is one of the largest customers and it is assumed that it also indexes the material it receives. The same material could thus be recorded in several indices, but there is no assurance that specific items would be caught in ordinary name traces. The CI Staff uses its IBM index cards to make fan-folds which are distributed monthly, quarterly, and semi-annually on a need-to-know basis.

15. The general security of the project has always been maintained at a very high level. When intelligence information is disseminated the source is concealed and no actions can be taken until a collateral source is found. The Office of Security has not obtained full clearances on post office personnel with whom it is dealing. This should be done in the case of the mail clerk who can be presumed to know much of what is going on. Another oversight is the absence of any emergency plan for use if the project should be exposed and time prevented consultation with headquarters. On the whole, security has been exceptionally good.

16. Probably the most obvious characteristic of the project is the diffusion of authority. Each unit is responsible for its own interests and in some areas there is little coordination. The Office of Security has full responsibility for the operation of the New York facility, for liaison and coordination with postal authorities, and for related matters. The CI Staff is the focal point of the DD/P interests. TSD will be responsible for the personnel and equipment in the new lab, although the lab will be under the administrative jurisdiction of MFO. SR Division requirements are forwarded through CI

Staff to the Office of Security, but SR Division has little knowledge of the capabilities of the interceptor group; interceptors have even less knowledge of the over-all aims and objectives of the SR Division. There is no single point in the Agency to which one might look for policy and operational guidance on the project as a whole. Contributing to this situation is the fact that all of the units involved are basically staff rather than command units, and they are accustomed to working in environments somewhat detached from the operational front lines. Because each of the units accustomed to this type of limited participation, there has been no friction and cooperation has been good. The greatest disadvantages of this diffusion of authority are (a) there can be no effective evaluation of the project if no officer is concerned with all its aspects, and (b) there is no central source of policy guidance in a potentially embarrassing situation.

17. We do not advocate a change in the methods of operation, nor do we believe that the responsibilities of the participating components should be diluted, but we feel that the activity has now developed to the point that clear command and administrative channels for the over-all project are essential. We also believe that a formal evaluation of the project is required.

18. Operational evaluation should include an assessment of overall potential. It is improbable that anyone inside Russia would wittingly send or receive mail containing anything of obvious intelligence or political significance. It should also be assumed that Russian tradecraft is as good as our own and that Russian agents communicating with their headquarters would have more secure channels than the open mails. On the other hand, many seemingly innocent statements can have intelligence significance. Comments concerning prices, crop conditions, the weather, travel plans, or general living conditions can be important. No intercept program can cover the entire flow of mail, and the best that can be done is to develop techniques which will provide a highly selective examination of a small portion. With the limitations imposed by budgetary and personnel ceilings, as well as by policy considerations, it must be recognized that the full potential of this project is not likely to be developed. However, it does provide a basic apparatus which could be expanded if the need arose.

Recommendation No. 41:

a. The DD/P and the DD/S direct a coordinated evaluation of this project, with particular emphasis on costs, potential and substantive contribution to the Agency's mission.

b. An emergency plan and cover story be prepared for the possibility that the operation might be blown.

FBI Mail opening

Introduction and Major Facts
The FBI, like the CIA, conducted several mail opening programs of its own within the United States. Eight programs were conducted in as many cities between the years 1940 and 1966; the longest was operated, with one period of suspension, throughout this entire twenty-six-year period; the shortest ran for less than six weeks. FBI use of this technique was initially directed against the Axis powers immediately before and during World War II, but during the decade of the 1950s and the first half of the 1960s all of the programs responded to the Bureau's concern with Communism.

At least three more limited instances of FBI mail opening also occurred in relation to particular espionage cases in the early 1960s.

Significant differences may be found between the FBI mail opening programs and those of the CIA. First, the stated purposes of the two sets of program generally reflects the agencies' differing intelligence jurisdiction: the FBI programs were, in the main, fairly narrowly directed at the detection and identification of foreign illegal agents rather than the collection of foreign positive intelligence. Thus, no premium was placed on the large-scale collection of foreign intelligence information per se; in theory (if not always in practice), only information that might reasonably be expected to provide leads in counterespionage cases was sought. Because of this, the total volume of mail opened in Bureau programs was less than that in the CIA programs. An equally important factor contributing to the smaller volume of opened mail lay in the selection criteria used in several of the FBI's programs. These criteria were more sophisticated than the random and

Watch List methods used by the CIA; they enabled trained Bureau agents to make more reasoned determinations, on the basis of exterior examinations of the envelopes, as to whether or not the communications might be in some sense "suspect." Third, the FBI mail opening programs were much more centralized and tightly administered than the CIA programs. All but one (which resulted in a reprimand from the Director) received prior approval at the highest levels of the Bureau. They were evaluated and had to be reapproved at least annually. Several of them—unlike the CIA's New York project—were discontinued on the basis of unfavorable internal evaluations. This high degree of central control clearly mirrored the organizational differences between the FBI and the CIA, and is not limited to mail opening operations alone. Finally, there is less evidence that FBI officials considered their programs to be illegal or attempted to fabricate "cover stories" in the event of exposure. Bureau officials, for the most part, apparently did not focus on questions of legality or "flap potential" strategies; they did not necessarily consider them to be legal or without the potential for adverse public reaction, they simply did not dwell on legal issues or alternative strategies at all.

In some respects, the Bureau's mail opening programs were even more intrusive than the CIA's. At least three of them, for example, involved the interception and opening of entirely domestic mail—that is, mail sent from one point within the United States to another point within the United States. All of the CIA programs, by contrast, involved at least one foreign "terminal." The Bureau programs also highlight the problems inherent in combining criminal and intelligence functions within a single agency: the irony of the nation's chief law enforcement agency conducting systematic campaigns of mail opening is readily apparent.

Despite their differences, however, the FBI mail opening programs illustrate many of the same themes of the CIA programs. Like the CIA, the FBI did not secure the approval of any senior official outside its own organization prior to the implementation of its programs. While these programs, like the CIA's, involved the cooperation of the Post Office Department and the United States Customs Service, there is no evidence that any ranking official of either agency was ever aware that mail was actually opened by the FBI.

Similarly, there is no substantial evidence that any President or Attorney General, under whose office the FBI operates, was contemporaneously informed of the programs' existence. As in the case of the CIA, efforts were also made to prevent word of the programs from reaching the ears of Congressmen investigating possible privacy violations by federal agencies. The record, therefore, again suggests that these programs were operated covertly, by virtue of deception, or, at a minimum, lack of candor on the part of intelligence officials.

Although the FBI relied on more sophisticated selection criteria in some of their programs, moreover, one again sees the same type of "overkill," which is inherent in any mail opening operation. These criteria, while more precise than the methods used by the CIA, were never sufficiently accurate to result in the opening of correspondence to or from illegal agents alone. Indeed, even by the Bureau's own accounting of its most successful program, the mail of hundreds of American citizens was opened for every one communication that led to an illegal agent. And several of the FBI programs did not employ these refined criteria: mail in these programs was opened on the basis of methods much more reminiscent of the CIA's random and Watch List criteria.

In the FBI programs one again sees the tendency of this technique, once in place, to be used for purposes outside the agency's institutional jurisdiction. While the Bureau has no mandate to collect foreign positive intelligence, for example, several of the programs did in fact result in the gathering of this type of information. More seriously, the record reveals for a second time the ease with which these programs can be directed inward against American citizens: the Bureau programs, despite their counterespionage purpose, generated at least some information of a strictly domestic nature, about criminal activity outside the national security area, and, significantly, about antiwar organizations and their leaders.

Perhaps the most fundamental theme illustrated by both the FBI's and the CIA's programs is this: that trained intelligence officers in both agencies, honestly perceiving a foreign and domestic threat to the security of the country, believed that this threat sanctioned—even necessitated—their use of a technique that was not authorized by any president and was contrary to law. They acted to protect a country whose law and traditions gave every indication that it was not to be "protected" in such a fashion.

The most pertinent facts regarding FBI mail opening may be summarized as follows:

(a) The FBI conducted eight mail opening programs in a total of eight cities in the United States for varying lengths of time between 1940 and 1966.

(b) The primary purpose of most of the FBI mail opening programs was the identification of foreign illegal agents; all of the programs were established to gather foreign counterintelligence information deemed by FBI officials to be important to the security of the United States.

(c) Several of these programs were successful in the identification of illegal agents and were considered by FBI officials to be one of the most effective means of locating such agents. Several of the programs also generated other types of useful counterintelligence information.

(d) In general, the administrative controls were tight. The programs were all subject to review by Headquarters semiannually or annually and some of the programs were terminated because they were not achieving the desired results in the counterintelligence field.

(e) Despite the internal FBI policy which required prior approval by Headquarters for the institution of these programs, however, at least one of them was initiated by a field office without such approval.

(f) Some of the fruits of mail openings were used for other than legitimate foreign counter-intelligence purposes. For example, information about individuals who received pornographic material and about drug addicts was forwarded to appropriate FBI field offices and possibly to other federal agencies.

(g) Although on the whole these programs did not stray far from their counterespionage goals, they also generated substantial positive foreign intelligence and some essentially domestic intelligence about United States citizens. For example, information was obtained regarding two domestic anti-war organizations and government employees and other American citizens who expressed "pro-communist" sympathies.

(h) A significant proportion of the mail that was opened was entirely domestic mail, i.e., the points of origin and destination were both within the United States.

(i) Some of the mail that was intercepted was entirely foreign mail, i.e., it originated in a foreign country and was destined to a foreign country, and was simply routed through the United States.

(j) FBI agents opened mail in regard to particular espionage cases (as opposed to general programs) in at least three instances in the early 1960s.

(k) The legal issues raised by the use of mail opening as an investigative technique were apparently not seriously considered by FBI officials while the programs continue. In 1970, however, after the FBI mail opening programs had been terminated, J. Edgar Hoover wrote that mail opening was "clearly illegal."

(l) At least as recently as 1972, senior officials recommended the reinstitution of mail opening as an investigative technique.

(m) No attempt was made to inform any Postmaster General of the mail openings.

(n) The Post Office officials who were contacted about these programs, including the Chief Postal Inspector, were not informed of the true nature of the FBI mail surveys, i.e., they were not told that the Bureau contemplated the actual opening of mail.

(o) The FBI neither sought nor received the approval of the Attorney General or the President of the United States for its mail opening programs or for the use of this technique generally.

(p) Although FBI officials might have informed Justice Department attorneys that mail was opened in two or three particular espionage cases and might have informed an Attorney General of some mail screening operations by the Bureau, no attempt was made to inform the Justice Department, including the Attorney General, of the full extent or true nature of these operations.

(q) There is no evidence that any President of the United States ever knew of any ongoing FBI mail opening program.

Description of FBI Mail Opening Programs

The eight FBI mail opening programs are summarized below.

A. Z-Coverage

Z-Coverage, the first and the longest-running FBI mail opening program, originally involved the opening of mail addressed to the diplomatic establishments of Axis powers in Washington, D.C.; in later years, mail coming to similar establishments of several Communist nations was targeted. The stated purpose of the program was "to detect individuals in contact with these establishments who might be attempting to make contact for espionage reasons, for purposes of defecting or who might be illegal agents."[1]

This program was initiated in 1940, before the United States entry into World War II, with FBI agents who had been trained in the technique of "chamfering" (mail opening by representatives of an allied country's censorship agency.)[2] It was suspended after the war but reinstituted in Washington, D.C. in the early or mid-1950's on the recommendation of the local FBI field office.[3] For more than a decade, mail from both foreign and domestic points of origin was intercepted at the Main Post Office, brought to the FBI Laboratory for opening and photographing, and returned to the Post Office prior to delivery. In 1959, Z-Coverage was extended to New York City as well. As implemented in New York, about 30 to 60 letters addressed to Grand Central and Lenox Hill Post Offices each day for opening and photographing at the New York Field Office.[4] Some registered mail sent to these establishments was opened as well.[5]

Despite its perceived success at both locations, Z-Coverage was terminated in July 1966.

B. Survey No. 1

Survey No. 1 operated in a total of six cities for varying lengths of time between 1959 and 1966. It involved the opening of certain outgoing mail to selected cities in Europe, Asia, and the Americas, and was considered to be the most successful of all the FBI mail opening programs. Its purposes, as summarized in a 1961 FBI memorandum, were two: "(1) to identify persons corresponding with known espionage mail drops in Europe, and (2) to identify persons in the United States who are directing letters to possible mail drops in Europe and whose letters appear to be the product of an illegal agent."[6]

Survey No. 1 was first instituted in New York City on October 1, 1959, as a direct result of knowledge the FBI had recently acquired about the means by which foreign illegal agents communicated to their principals abroad. Once in operation, Bureau agents, in a secure room at Idlewile Airport's Airmail Facility screened more than 425,000 letters from the United States to points in Western Europe each week.[7] Selected items—a total of 1,011 in seven years[8]—were returned to the New York Field Office for opening and photographing prior to reinsertion into the mailstream. In August 1961, after nearly two years of operation in New York, FBI officials believed that Survey No. 1 was so successful that it was extended to four additional cities—Boston, Los Angeles, Seattle, and Washington, D.C.[9]—where coverage included mail not only to European cities but to Asia and the Americas as well. Survey No. 1 was also extended to Detroit on a sixty-day trial basis in April 1962.[10]

The expanded coverage in all cities but Washington did not prove to be as successful as the original effort in New York, however. After thirteen months of operation in Los Angeles, seventeen months in Seattle, one year in Boston, and four months in Detroit, a decision was made at Headquarters to terminate the program in these cities because of "unproductivity and manpower needs."[11] After February 1963, therefore, Survey No. 1 operated only in New York and Washington. In these two cities the annual evaluations[12] continued to praise the effectiveness of Survey No. 1 and it was continued to operate at both locations until all of the mail opening programs were terminated in mid–1966.

C. Survey No. 2

Survey No. 2 operated in New York City, Detroit, and San Francisco for varying lengths of time between March 1961 and March 1962; its purpose was again the location and identification of illegal agents.[13] No. 2 was, in essence, an inverse No. 1: incoming mail to urban postal zones in which illegal agents were believed likely to reside was screened and opened, on the basis of the same criteria used in Survey No. 1, in an attempt to intercept the other half of the communication link between illegal agents and their principals. Since mail coming into these postal zones was screened irrespective of the point of origin much of the mail that was opened was entirely domestic mail.[14]

Survey No. 2 originated as an outgrowth of No. 1. It was first implemented on March 8, 1961, in postal zones 23, 24, and 25 in New York City, with Post Office employees rather than Bureau agents screening the incoming mail.[15] The Post Office personnel were briefed by the FBI as to the selection criteria but were not informed of the true nature of the program. When they discovered a suspect communication, it was turned over to the FBI and, without their knowledge, opened and photographed at the field office before being returned to the mailstream. On the basis of "test" letters sent by the Bureau, however, their performance was judged inadequate and, in September 1961, FBI agents replaced the postal workers in screening the mail.[16]

In October 1961, the program was also extended to both Detroit (zone 31 and the Hamtramck area)[17] and San Francisco (all mail sent to that city from New York and Washington) on a trial basis.[18]

Survey No. 2 was considered unsuccessful in all of these cities and was consequently discontinued in Detroit and San Francisco in February 1962, and in New York—after a total of approximately 2,350 letters had been opened[19]—on March 9, 1962.[20]

D. Survey No. 3

Survey No. 3 was conducted in New York City from June 1963 to June 1964, and involved the opening of mail (irrespective of point of origin) addressed to known or suspected intelligence agents employed at a diplomatic establishment. The purpose of Survey No. 3 was to detect contacts of an intelligence nature with these agents, who, FBI officials believed, received such mail using the secure cover of their diplomatic employment.[21]

This program was apparently an outgrowth of the Bureau's coverage of mail to various other diplomatic establishments in New York (Z-Coverage). Although its precise genesis is undocumented, one of the participants in the program recalled that the idea originated with another agent, then involved with Z-Coverage, who felt that existing coverage was inadequate and should be expanded.[22] Headquarters subsequently approved the idea, and, on June 25, 1963 Survey No. 3 was instituted in New York.

Each working day for the next year, a single agent from the New York office went to the Grand Central Post Office where a postal clerk brought him all the mail that was addressed to the Post Office box of the targeted diplomatic establishment—approximately 200 letters per day, according to the agent who was assigned to this task.[23] On the basis of a list of about thirty diplomatic officials, which was compiled from public source information, the agent segregated the mail addressed to these officials and carried the letters—estimated by him to average five or six per day[24]—to the New York office for opening and photographing.

Survey No. 3 was not considered to be successful by the Bureau and was discontinued on June 26, 1964.

E. Survey No. 4

Survey No. 4 was conduced in Miami, Florida, between January 1963 and July 1966. It involved the screening and opening of certain airmail from Miami and San Juan, Puerto Rico, to two Latin American countries for the purpose of locating clandestine communications in particular espionage cases.[25]

Survey No. 4 developed from an espionage case in which the Bureau had learned that a Latin American intelligence agent who operated in the United States but whose true identity was unknown, was under instructions to transmit material to his country's intelligence service by mail. In order to intercept this agent's written communications, Bureau officials at Headquarters formulated a plan to screen and selectively open mail from San Juan and Miami to that country utilizing their knowledge of its intelligence correspondence, and on December 21, 1962, they authorized the Miami Field Office to implement the program.[26]

While the program was initially instituted as a response to a single espionage case, it soon developed into a more generalized survey to detect clandestine communications from any suspected espionage agent working for the same country. Its scope was further broadened on December 9, 1963, when the Miami office was instructed to cover mail from that city to another Latin American country as well.[27]

Bureau agents in Survey No. 4 screened between 12,000 and 20,000 letters per day at the Biscayne Annex Post Office in Miami.[28] A total of 400 letters were opened,[29] either in the Post Office itself, or, when secret writing or microdots were suspected, in the FBI Laboratory in Washington, to which they were flown for more sophisticated examination before reinsertion into the mailstream.[30]

Survey No. 4 was considered to be successful but was terminated along with other FBI mail opening programs, in July 1966.

F. Survey No. 5

Survey No. 5 was the first of three FBI mail opening programs which were conducted in San Francisco and directed against Asian communists and their sympathizers. It began in September 1954 and continued until January 1966. This survey originally involved the physical inspection of third and fourth class propaganda from a Far East Asian country; after August 1956, incoming first class letter mail was selectively opened and photographed as well. The stated purpose of this program was to identify individuals in the United States who, because of the nature of their foreign contacts, were believed to constitute a threat to the internal security of the Untied States.[31]

Like the CIA's New Orleans and Hawaiian mail intercept projects, Survey No. 5 was initially an extension of the Customs Service examination of propaganda material entering the United States from abroad. Customs Service cooperation ceased, however, on May 26, 1965, as a result of the Supreme Court's decision in Lamont v. Postmaster General of the United States, 381 U.S. 301 (1965), which invalidated the statutory authority under which Customs conducted its propaganda inspection.[32] Contact was subsequently made with officials of the Post Office and, with their assistance, No. 5 Survey recommenced at the Rincon Annex Post Office on July 7, 1965.

Approximately 13,500 items of mail were screened in two hour periods each day by Bureau agents who participated in this program.[33] A daily average of 50 to 100 of these letters were returned to the San Francisco Field Office for opening and photographing prior to their reinsertion into the mailstream.[34]

Survey No. 5 was terminated on January 24, 1966, "for security reasons involving local changes in postal personnel."[35]

G. Survey No. 6

Survey No. 6 was also conducted in San Francisco, operating from January 1964 until January 1966. This program involved the screening and opening of outgoing mail from the United States to the same Far East Asian country; it was essentially an inverse Survey No. 5. The stated purposes of Survey No. 6 were to obtain foreign counterintelligence information concerning Americans residing in the Far East Asian country; to detect efforts to persuade scientists and other persons of Asian descent residing in the United States to return to that country; to develop information concerning economic and social conditions there; and to secure information concerning subjects in the United States of a security interest to the Bureau who were corresponding with individuals in that Asian country.[36]

In June 1963, the New York Field Office had extended its Survey No. 1 coverage to include airmail destined for Asia, which was then handled at the same location where European mail was processed. When Post Office procedures changed a few months later, and the Asian mail was routed through San Francisco rather than New York, Headquarters instructed the San Francisco office to assume responsibility for this coverage. The program operated, with one period of suspension, for two years until January 24, 1966, when it was terminated for the same security reasons as the Survey No. 5.[37] Figures as to the volume of mail screened and opened cannot be reconstructed.

H. Survey No. 7

Survey No. 7 was conducted in San Francisco from January to November 1961. It involved the screening and opening of mail between North Americans of Asian descent for the purpose of detecting Communist intelligence efforts directed against this country.[38]

Survey No. 7 evolved from the Survey No. 5 and particular espionage cases handled by the San Francisco Field Office. Without instructions from Headquarters, that office initiated a survey of mail between North Americans of Asian descent in January 1961, and informed Headquarters of the program shortly after it was implemented. On February 28, 1961, Headquarters officials instructed San Francisco to terminate the program because the expected benefits were not believed to justify the additional manpower required by the FBI Laboratory to translate the intercepted letters.[39] The San Francisco Field Office was permitted to use this source when it was deemed necessary in connection with particular espionage cases, but even this limited use proved unproductive. It was terminated on November 20, 1961, after a total of 83 letters had been opened.[40]

I. Typical Operational Details

The specific operational details of the eight programs described above obviously varied from program to program. The New York Field Office's conduct of Survey No. 1 represented a pattern that typified these programs, however, in terms of mechanical aspects such as the physical handling of the mail itself. In August 1961, before the extension of Survey No. 1 to Boston, Los Angeles, Seattle, and Washington, D.C., the New York Office was instructed to describe the operation details of this survey as implemented in that city for the benefit of field officers in the four additional cities. A memorandum was subsequently prepared for distribution to these cities, pertinent portions of which are reproduced below:

> [Survey No. 1] in New York is located in a secure room at the U.S. Post Office Airmail Facility, New York International Airport, Idlewild, New York.... This room...measures approximately 9 feet wide by 12 feet long and...is locked at all times, whether or not the room is in use...Postal employees have no access to this room which is known to them as the Inspector's Room.
>
> Seven Special Agents are assigned to [Survey No. 1] on a full-time basis. The survey operates 7 days a week and personnel work on rotating 8-hour shifts.... Personnel assigned to the survey work under the guise of Postal Inspectors and are known to Post Office personnel as Postal Inspectors working on a special assignment....
>
> ...[B]y arrangement with the postal officials, [mail] pouches to destinations in which we have indicated interest are not sealed but are placed in front of the [Survey No. 1] room. The [Survey No. 1] personnel then take the bag into the room, open the pouch, untie the bundles, and review the mail. Any suspect letters are held aside and the rest are rebundled and returned to the pouch. The pouch is then closed and placed outside the door to the room on a mail skid. Postal employees then take that pouch, seal it with a lead seal and place it aside for, or turn it over to, the carrier....
>
> It should be noted that the mail must be turned over by the Post Office Department to the carrier one hour before departure time....
>
> ...Each day, one of the Agents is selected as a courier, and when the opportunity presents itself, he returns to the Field Office with the suspected communications. At the Field Office, he or another Agent who has been trained by the Bureau in certain techniques opens the communications. The envelope and its contents are photographed.... There will be instances where the Field Office, upon opening the communication, may deem it advisable to immediately notify the Bureau and possibly fly it by courier to the Bureau for examination by the Laboratory. Before making any arrangements to fly the communication to the Bureau, the Field Office should consider the time the examination will take and the time the suspected communication may be placed back in the mail without arousing any suspicion on the part of the addressee.
>
> After the communication has been photographed and resealed, the courier returns to the airport and places the suspected communication in the next appropriate outgoing pouch examined in the [Survey No. 1] Room. If time permits, the

pouch is held in the room until the suspected communication is returned.[41]

A device developed by the FBI Laboratory and maintained at participating field offices facilitated the opening process. While this device was relatively simple, it was not as primitive as the kettle and stick method utilized by the CIA agents who opened mail in the New York project and allowed for greater efficiency: The FBI's opening process was reported to take only a second or two for a single letter,[42] in contrast to five to fifteen seconds for the CIA. According to one of the agents involved, special training in the use of this device was given at the field office rather than at Headquarters, and only on one or two days duration,[43] in contrast to the week-long training sessions required of CIA mail openers.

Filing and internal dissemination procedures also varied somewhat from program to program. In Z-Coverage, the negatives of the photographic copies were filed at the field offices in New York and Washington for approximately one year after interception, after which time they were destroyed.[44] If the developed prints were believed to contain valuable counterintelligence information, they would be disseminated to appropriate supervisors within the field office for placement in a confidential central file or a particular case file. In the latter case, the true source would be disguised by an informant symbol, although, as one supervisor in the New York office noted, the nature of the source would be clear to those familiar with Bureau operations.[45]

No index was maintained of the names of all senders and/or addressees whose mail was intercepted, as was maintained by the CIA in the New York project. In rare cases when a letter was considered to be of exceptional counterintelligence value, a photograph would be sent to Headquarters as well. As a general rule, however, there was no dissemination, either of the photographs themselves or of abstracts of the letters to other field offices.[46]

These procedures generally applied to Survey No. 1 and Survey No. 2 as well, but in these two surveys the photographs of intercepted letters were dated and numbered, and one copy or abstract was placed in a control file maintained by each participating field office.

In Surveys No. 5 and No. 6, the San Francisco Field Office was responsible for conducting "name checks" on all individuals sending or receiving mail that had been opened. If, on the basis of the name check or the text of the letter itself, it was determined that the intercepted letter had intelligence value, a copy of the letter (if written in English) or of the translation (if written in a foreign language) was placed in the main files of the San Francisco office. That office was also responsible for paraphrasing the contents of letters in which other field offices may have had an intelligence interest, and disseminating the information to them in a manner which would not reveal the true source of the information. Except for letters written in a foreign language, photographs of which were sent to Washington for translation, copies were not sent to Headquarters unless the letter was of particularly great intelligence value.

J. Other Instances of FBI Mail opening

In addition to the eight mail surveys described in sections A through H above, it has also been alleged that a Bureau agent actively participated in the CIA's Hawaiian mail intercept project during the mid-1950's. The CIA representative in Honolulu who conducted this operation stated that an FBI agent assisted him in opening and photographing incoming mail from Asia for a period of two months in early 1955.[47] No supporting Bureau documents could be located to confirm this participation, however.

Aside from generalized surveys of mail, several isolated instances of mail opening by FBI agents occurred in connection with particular espionage cases. It was, in fact, a standard practice to attempt to open the mail of any known illegal agent. As stated by one former Bureau intelligence officer: "... anytime...we identified an illegal agent...we would try to obtain their mail."[48] FBI agents were successful in this endeavor in at least three cases, described below.

1. Washington, D.C. (1961)

One isolated instance of mail opening by FBI agents occurred in Washington, D.C., in 1961, preceding the local implementation of Survey No. 1. This case involved the opening of several items or correspondence from a known illegal agent residing in the Washington area to a mail drop in Europe. The letters, which were returned to the FBI Laboratory for opening, were intercepted over a period in excess of six months.[49]

2. Washington, D.C. (1963-64)

A second mail opening project in regard to a particular espionage case occurred for approximately one and one-half years in Washington, D.C., in 1963 and 1964, in connection with the FBI's investigation of known Soviet illegal agents Robert and Joy Ann Baltch. This case was subsequently prosecuted, but the prosecution was ultimately dropped in part, according to FBI officials because some of the evidence was tainted by use of this technique.[50]

3. Southern California

A third isolated instance of mail opening occurred in a southern California city for a one to two-month period in 1962. This project involved the opening of approximately one to six letters received each day by a suspected illegal agent who resided nearby. The suspected agent's mail was delivered on a daily basis to three FBI agents who worked out of the local resident FBI office, and was opened in a back room in that office.[51]

Nature and Value of the Product

A. Selection Criteria

Those FBI mail opening programs which were designed to cover mail to or from foreign illegal agents utilized selection criteria that were more refined than the "shotgun" method[52] used by the CIA in the New York intercept project. Mail was opened on the basis of certain "indicators" on the outside of the envelopes that suggested that the communication might be to or from an illegal agent. The record reveals, however, that despite the claimed success of these "indicators" in locating such agents, they were not so precise as to eliminate individual discretion on the part of the agents who opened the mail, nor could they prevent the opening of significant volumes of mail to or from entirely innocent American citizens. Mail in those programs which were designed for purposes other than locating illegal agents, moreover, was generally opened on the basis of criteria far less narrow and even more intrusive than these "indicators."

1. The Programs Based on Indicators

Before 1959, the FBI had developed no effective means to intercept the communication link between illegal agents and their principals. In Z-Coverage, selection was originally left to the complete discretion of the agents who screened the mail based on their knowledge and training in the espionage field. The focus was apparently on mail from individuals rather than organizations, and typewritten letters were considered more likely to be from foreign agents than handwritten letters.[53] In March 1959, however, the FBI was able to develop much more precise selection criteria through the identification and subsequent incommunicado interrogation of an illegal agent. During the course of his interrogation by Bureau agents, he informed the FBI of the instructions and he and other illegal agents were given when corresponding with their principals.[54] Particular characteristics on the outside of the envelope, he advised them, indicated that the letter may be from such an agent.

Armed with a knowledge of these "indicators," the FBI agents involved in Z-Coverage were capable of a more selective and accurate means of identifying suspect communications. Survey No. 1 and Survey No. 2 were expressly developed to exploit this knowledge.[55] While Survey No. 1 also utilized a Watch List which consisted of the addresses of known or suspected mail drops abroad, as well as the (generally fictitious) names of known or suspected foreign intelligence agents,[56] the primary selection criteria in both Surveys No. 1 and No. 2 were the "indicators" about which the Bureau learned in early 1959.[57]

By means of the "indicators," the Bureau did, in fact, identify three illegal agents through these programs.[58] But even by the Bureau's own accounting of the number of letters that were opened in the programs, it is clear that the mail of hundreds of innocent American citizens was opened and read for every successful lead obtained.[59] The random element in the selection process was never eliminated: although FBI officials at Headquarters instructed agents in the field to select only letters with multiple "indicators" on their face,[60] the field agents frequently opened letters with but one "indicator," which could often be of such a common nature that it could be found on most letters mailed in the United States.[61]

One of the FBI agents who opened mail stated that he was trained in counterespionage work generally, and in the identification of the indicators specifically, but he conceded that in the final analysis "it was strictly my own judgment" as to which items would be selected for opening.[62] Perhaps as a result of such personal discretion on the part of participating agents, Survey No. 1 generated essentially domestic intelligence on at least two American antiwar organizations as well as genuine counterespionage information.[63]

In short, knowledge of the indicators did not enable the Bureau to be more precise in the selection of mail than was previously possible, but this knowledge was not so precise as to totally eliminate the discretion—or bias—of the agents involved.

2. The Latin American-Oriented Program

In Survey No. 4, which involved the interception of mail to two Latin American nations, letters were selected for opening on the basis of lists of (a) known fictitious names used by illegal agents to address correspondence to their principals, and (b) accommodation addresses used by a foreign intelligence service for receiving clandestine communications.[64] The "indicators" discussed above were not utilized in this or the Asian-oriented mail opening programs.

3. The Asian-Oriented Programs

Survey No. 5 and Survey No. 6 both employed seven general categories as selection criteria:

(a) Letters to or from a university, scientific, or technical facility;

(b) Letters to or from a doctor;

(c) Letters to or from selected Security Index subjects residing in the United States;

(d) Letters to or from an Asian country where certain scientific activities were reportedly taking place;

(e) Letters to or from individuals who were known to be "turncoats" from the Korean conflict;

(f) Letters believed to emanate from an Asian Communist intelligence service based on covers of which the FBI was aware; and

(g) Letters indicating illegal travel of Americans to denied areas in Asia.[65]

Even if one assumes that these guidelines were strictly observed by the agents opening the mail, (which, given some of the results of these programs as set forth below,[66] is not necessarily an accurate assumption) there was obviously ample room for the capture of large numbers of entirely personal communications with no counterintelligence value at all.

The selection criteria utilized in Survey No. 7 cannot be reconstructed.

B. Requests by Other Intelligence Agencies

No large-scale requirements were levied upon the FBI's mail opening programs by any other intelligence agency. Bureau officials, in fact, severely restricted knowledge of their programs within the intelligence community; only the CIA knew of any of the bureau's programs, and officers of that agency were formally advised about the existence of only one of the eight, Survey No. 1.

In July 1960, Bureau Headquarters originally rejected the recommendation of the New York Field Office to inform the CIA of Survey No. 1 in order to obtain from it a list of known mail drops in Europe for use in the program.[67] Headquarters then wrote: "Due to the extremely sensitive nature of the source…, the Bureau is very reluctant to make any contacts which could possibly jeopardize that source. Therefore, the Bureau will not make any contact with CIA to request from it [such a]… The Bureau will, however, continue to exert every effort to obtain from CIA the identities of all such mail drops in the normal course of operations."[68]

Within six months of this rejection, however, Headquarters officers changed their minds: Donald Moore, head of the Espionage Research Branch and Sam Papich, FBI liaison to the CIA, met with CIA representatives in January 1961, to inform them of Survey No. 1 and to exchange lists of known or suspected mail drops.[69] CIA provided the Bureau with a list of 16 mail drops and accommodation addresses and the name and address of one Communist Party member in Western Europe,[70] all of which were subsequently furnished the New York office for inclusion in Survey No. 1 coverage. The exchange of this information did not evolve into a reverse Project Hunter, however. While the Agency may have contributed a small number of additional addresses or names during the next five years, no large-scale levy of general categories or specific names was ever made by the CIA or solicited by the FBI. According to Donald Moore, the particularized nature and objectives of Survey No. 1, especially when contrasted with the CIA's New York project, precluded active CIA participation in the program.[71]

While there is no other evidence that any members of the intelligence community knew of or ever levied requests on the Bureau's mail opening programs, they did receive sanitized information from these programs when deemed relevant to their respective needs by the Bureau.[72]

C. Results of the Programs

In terms of their counterespionage and counterintelligence raison d'etre, several of the Bureau's programs were considered to be successful by FBI officials; others were concededly ineffective and were consequently discontinued before the termination of all remaining FBI surveys in 1966. Significantly, some of the surveys also generated large amounts of "positive" foreign intelligence—the collection of which is outside the Bureau's mandate—and information regarding the domestic activities and personal beliefs of American citizens, at least some of which was disseminated within and outside the FBI. The Bureau surveys did remain more focused on their original goal than did the CIA programs. But in them—whether because the selection criteria were overbroad, or because these criteria were not scrupulously adhered to, or both—one again sees the tendency of mail opening programs to produce information well beyond the type originally sought.

1. Counterintelligence Results

Five of the eight FBI mail opening programs—Z-Coverage, Surveys 1, 4, 5, and 6—were clearly seen to have contributed to the FBI's efforts in the area of counterintelligence. The relative success of these programs, in fact, led many Bureau officials to conclude that mail opening—despite its legal status—was one of the most effective counterespionage weapons in their arsenal.[73] The primary value of these five programs to the Bureau is summarized below:

Z-Coverage.—A lack of pertinent documentary and testimonal evidence prevents a meaningful evaluation of Z-Coverage during World War II, but a 1951 memorandum reflecting the Washington Field Office's recommendation for its reinstitution noted that "while Z-Coverage was utilized valuable information of an intelligence nature was obtained.".. [74]

In evaluating the program during the 1950s and 1960s, Bureau officials have rated it highly in terms of the counterintelligence results it produced. W. Raymond Wannall, former Assistant Director in charge of the Domestic Intelligence Division, testified about two specific examples of mail intercepted in Z-Coverage which revealed attempts on the part of individuals in this country to offer military secrets to foreign governments.[75] In the first case, the FBI intercepted a letter in July 1964, which was sent by an employee of an American intelligence agency to a foreign diplomatic establishment in the United States. In the letter, the employee offered to sell information relating to weapons systems to the foreign government and also expressed an interest in defecting. The Defense Department was notified, conducted a potential damage evaluation, and concluded that the potential damage could represent a cost to the United States Government of tens of millions of dollars. In the second case, which occurred in mid-1964, an individual on the West Coast offered to sell a foreign government tactical military information for $60,000.

Survey No. 1.—Survey No. 1 was considered to be one of the most successful of all the Bureau mail opening programs. In New York and Washington, a total of three illegal agents—the identification of which has been described by one senior FBI official as the most difficult task in counterintelligence work[76]—were located through No. 1.[77] In addition, numerous letters were discovered which contained secret writing and/or were addressed to mail drops in Western Europe. Survey No. 1 in Boston, Los Angeles, Seattle, and Detroit was not successful, however, and as noted above, was discontinued in those cities on the basis of "unproductivity and manpower needs."[78]

Survey No. 4.—Survey No. 4 resulted in the identification of the illegal agent whose presence in the United States had originally motivated development of the survey. In addition, this program led to the detection of a second intelligence agent operating in this country and to the discovery of approximately 60 items of correspondence which contained secret writing either on the letter itself or on the envelope containing the letter.[79]

Survey No. 5.—FBI officials have testified that Survey No. 5 was a very valuable source of counterintelligence (and interrelated positive intelligence) information about an Asian country. W. Raymond Wannall stated that its "principal value probably related to the identification of U.S. trained scientists of [Asian] descent who were recalled or who went voluntarily back to [an Asian country]."[80] Because of this, he continued, the FBI was able to learn vital information about the progress of weapons research abroad.[81]

Survey No. 6.—Survey No. 6 was also believed to be a valuable program from the perspective of counterintelligence, although it was suspended for a nine-month period because the manpower requirements were not considered to outweigh the benefits it produced. Through this survey the FBI identified numerous American subscribers to Asian communist publications; determined instances of the collection of scientific and technical information form the United States by a foreign country; and recorded contacts between approximately fifteen Security Index subjects in the United States and Communists abroad.[82]

The Other Programs.—Three of the FBI's programs were not believed to have produced any significant amount of counterintelligence information. Bureau officials testified that they "had very little success in connection with [Survey No. 3],"[83] and it was consequently discontinued after one year of operation. Similarly, no positive results were obtained through Survey No. 2 in any of the three cities in which it operated. Although the San Francisco office, for example, opened approximately 85 new cases as a result of Survey No. 2, all of these cases were resolved without the identification of any illegal agents, which was the goal of the program.[84] As one Bureau official stated in regard to Survey No. 2: "The indicators were good, but the results were not that good."[85] It, too, was terminated after approximately one year of operation.

Finally, the results of Survey No. 7, which was initiated without prior approval by Headquarters, were also considered to be valueless. Of the 83 letters intercepted in the program, 79 were merely exchanges of personal news between North Americans of Asian descent. The other four were letters from individuals in Asia to individuals in the United States, routed through contacts in North America, but were solely devoted to personal information.[86] As noted above, Headquarters did not believe that this coverage justified the additional manpower necessary to translate the items and the San Francisco Field Office was so advised.

2. "Positive" Foreign Intelligence Results

Although the FBI has no statutory mandate to gather positive foreign intelligence, a great deal of this type of intelligence is generated as a byproduct of several of the mail opening programs and disseminated in sanitized form to interested government agencies. In an annual evaluation of Survey No. 5, for example, it was written:

> This source furnishes a magnitude of vital information pertaining to activities with [an Asian country]; including its economical [sic] and industrial achievements.... A true picture of life in that country today is also related by the information which this source furnished reflecting life in general to be horrible due to the lack of proper food, housing, clothes, equipment, and the complete disregard for a human person's individual rights.[87]

Another evaluation stated that this program had developed information about such matters as the "plans and progress made in construction in railways, locations of oil deposits, as well as the location of chemical plants and hydraulic works."[88] It continued: "While this is of no interest to the Bureau, the information has been disseminated to interested agencies." Survey No. 6 even identified, through the interception of South American mail routed through San Francisco to an Asian country, numerous "[Asian] Communist sympathizers" in Latin America.[89]

Wannall explained that "as a member of the intelligence community, the FBI [was aware] of the positive intelligence requirements [which were] secularized within the community in the form of what was known as a current requirements list, delineating specific areas with regard to such countries that were needed, or information concerning which was needed by the community. So we contributed to the overall community need."[90] He conceded, however, that the FBI itself had no independent need for or requirement to collect such positive intelligence.[91] Just as the CIA mail opening programs infringed on the intelligence jurisdiction of the FBI, therefore, so the FBI programs gathered information which was without value to the Bureau itself and of a variety that was properly within the CIA's mandate.

3. Domestic Intelligence Results

In addition to counterespionage information and positive foreign intelligence, the FBI mail opening programs also developed at least some information of an essentially domestic nature. The collection of this type of information was on a smaller scale and less direct than was the case in the CIA's New York project, for none of the FBI programs involved the wholesale targeting of large numbers of domestic political activists or the purposefully indiscriminate interception of mail. Nonetheless, the Bureau programs did produce domestic intelligence. An April 1966 evaluation of Survey No. 1, for example, noted that "organizations in the United States concerning whom informant [the survey] has furnished information include...[the] Lawyers Committee on American Policy towards Vietnam, Youth Against War and Fascism...and others."[92]

An evaluation of the Survey No. 5 stated that the program had developed "considerable data" about government employees and other American citizens who expressed pro-Communists sympathies, as well as information about individuals, including American citizens, who were specifically targeted as a consequence of their being on the FBI's Security Index.[93] Examples of the latter type of information include their current residence and employment and "anti-U.S. statements which they have made."[94]

Another evaluation of a Bureau program noted that that program had identified American recipients of pornographic material and an American citizen abroad who was a drug addict in correspondence with other addicts in the New York City area;[95] it indicated that information about the recipients of pornographic material was transmitted to other field offices and stated that "pertinent" information was also forwarded to other Federal agencies.[96]

Given the ready access which Bureau agents had to the mail for a period of years, it is hardly surprising that some domestic intelligence was collected. Indeed, both logic and the evidence support the conclusion that if any intelligence agency undertakes a program of mail opening within the United States for whatever purpose, the gathering of such information cannot be avoided.

Internal Authorization and Controls

While the FBI and the CIA mail opening programs were similar in many respects, the issues of authorization and control within these agencies highlight their differences. The pattern of internal approval for the CIA mail opening programs was inconsistent at best: the New York project began without the approval of the Director of Central Intelligence; at least two Directors were apparently not even advised of its existence; and it is unclear whether any Director knew the details of the other mail opening programs.[97] Administrative controls in most of the CIA projects, especially the twenty-year New York operation, were clearly lax: periodic reevaluation was non-existent and operational responsibility was diffused.[98] Probably as a function of the FBI's contrasting organizational structure, the mail opening programs conducted by the Bureau were far more centrally controlled by senior officials at Headquarters. With one significant exception, the FBI mail programs all received prior approval from the highest levels of the Bureau, up to and including J. Edgar Hoover, and the major aspects of their subsequent operation were strictly regulated by officials at or near the top of an integrated chain of command.

A. Internal Authorization

While the documentary record of FBI mail opening programs is incomplete, that evidence which does exist reveals J. Edgar Hoover's explicit authorization for the following surveys:

—The extension of Survey No. 1 to Los Angeles, Boston, Seattle, and Washington, D.C., on August 4, 1961;[99]

—The re-authorization of Survey No. 1 in New York, on December 22, 1961;[100]

—The re-authorization of Survey No. 1 in New York and Washington, D.C., on April 15, 1966;[101]

—The extension of Survey No. 2 to three additional postal zones in New York and its implementation with FBI rather than Post Office employees, on August 31, 1961;[102] and

—The institution of Survey No. 6 in San Francisco, on November 20, 1963.[103]

The documentary evidence also reveals authorizations from former Associate Director Tolson and/or the former Assistant Director in charge of the Domestic Intelligence Division, Sullivan, for the following surveys:

—The extension of Survey No. 1 to Detroit on April 13, 1962;[104]

—The extension of Survey No. 2 to Detroit on October 4, 1961;[105]

—The re-authorization of Survey No. 2 in New York on December 26, 1961;[106] and

—Administrative changes in the filing procedures for the Survey No. 5 on June 28, 1963.[107]

Further, unsigned memoranda and airtels from Headquarters, "Director, FBI," authorized the extension of Survey No. 2 to San Francisco on October 18, 1961,[108] and the institution of Survey No. 4 on December 21, 1962.[109] Bureau procedures normally require that such memoranda and airtels must be seen and approved by at least an Assistant Director, and there is no reason to assume that this did not occur in these instances.

Despite the absence of some authorizing documents, witness testimony is consistent—and often emphatic—on the point that unwritten Bureau policy required J. Edgar Hoover's personal approval before the institution of a new mail opening program or even the initial use of mail opening as a technique in specific espionage cases.[110] The approval of at least the Assistant Director for the Domestic Intelligence Division, moreover, was required for the periodic re-authorization or the extensions of existing mail surveys to additional cities, as well as for their termination, upon the recommendation of the field office involved. The only surveys for which this policy was apparently violated were Survey No. 7 and possibly—though this is unclear—Survey No. 1.

The testimony of senior FBI officials conflicts on whether Hoover actually authorized the formal institution of Survey No. 1 in New York in 1959, or whether he merely approved the general concept of a mail opening program utilizing the recently acquired knowledge of the "indicators," but not Survey No. 1 in particular. The former heads of the Espionage Research Branch at Headquarters and of the Espionage Division at the New York Field Office both believe the former to be the case;[111] the Section Chief of the section at Headquarters out of which the program was run testified to the latter.[112] Even if Hoover only approved the general concept of such a project, however, he was soon aware of the program, and, as noted above, authorized its extension to four additional cities in August 1961.

Survey No. 7 was initiated by the San Francisco Field Office on its own motion without prior approval from Washington. When Headquarters was advised of the implementation of this program,[113] ranking FBI officials immediately demanded justification for it from the Field Office,[114] subsequently determined the justification to be inadequate, and ordered its termination as a generalized survey.[115] The last sentence of the instruction to end the program warns: "Do not initiate such general coverage without first obtaining specific Bureau authority."[116]

Unlike most of their CIA counterparts, then, it appears that the Bureau's mail opening programs were—with one clear exception—personally approved by the Director before their implementation, and at the highest levels of the organization before major changes in their operation. In the one certain case where prior Headquarters approval was not secured, the field office which implemented the programs was reprimanded.

B. Administrative Controls by Headquarters

FBI Headquarters exerted tight, centralized control over the mail opening programs in other ways as well. One manifestation of this control was found in the periodic evaluations of each program required of every participating field office for the benefit of Headquarters. In general, written evaluations were submitted semiannually for the first few years of the operation of a program in a city; and annually thereafter.[117] These evaluations frequently contained such headings as: "Origin;" "Purpose;" "Scope;" "Cost;" "Overall Value;" and "Operation of Source." Every field office was also obligated to determine whether the counterintelligence benefits from each program justified its continuation in light of manpower and security considerations; on the basis of this recommendation and other information supplied, Headquarters then decided whether to re-authorize the program until the next evaluation period or order its termination. The net effect of this system of periodic reexamination was that FBI officials were far better informed than were CIA officials of the true value of the programs to their organization. It was difficult for a program to continue unproductively without the knowledge of the highest ranking officials of the Bureau: as noted above, several programs—Surveys No. 2, 3, and 7—were in fact discontinued by Headquarters before 1966 because the results as set forth in the evaluations were felt to be outweighted by other factors.

Also in contrast to the CIA mail opening programs, the Bureau programs were conducted at the field level with Special Agents who were experienced in intelligence work and given detailed instructions regarding the "indicators" and other selection criteria.[118] No control procedure could ever eliminate the individual discretion of these agents—ultimately, selection was based on their personal judgment. But Headquarters ensured through the training of these agents that their judgment was at least more informed than that of the Office of Security "interceptors" in the CIA's New York project, who were neither foreign intelligence experts nor given guidance beyond the Watch List itself as to which items to select.[119] At both the Field Office and the Headquarters levels, moreover, responsibility for the operation of the programs was not diffused, as it was in the CIA's New York project but was centralized in the hands of experienced senor officials within a single chain of command.

C. Knowledge of the Mail opening Programs

Wiliam Sullivan

Within the FBI

Officials of the Domestic Intelligence Division at Headquarters carefully controlled knowledge and dissemination procedures of their mail opening programs within the FBI itself. Knowledge of the operations was strictly limited to the Domestic Intelligence Division. The Criminal Division, for example, was never advised of the existence of (and so never levied requests on) any of these programs, but an internal memorandum indicates that it may have received information generated by the programs without being advised of the true source.[120] Some FBI witnesses assigned to espionage squads which were engaged in mail opening even testified that they were unaware of other mail opening programs being conducted simultaneously by other espionage squads in the same field office.[121]

The direct dissemination of the photographic copies of letters or abstracts between field offices was prohibited, but Headquarters avoided some of the problems caused by restricted knowledge in the CIA programs by requiring the offices to paraphrase the contents of letters in which other field offices might have an intelligence interest and disseminate the information to them in sanitized form.

Thus, control over the major aspects of the programs was concentrated at the top of the FBI hierarchy to a degree far greater than that which characterized the CIA programs. With few exceptions, senior officials at Headquarters initially authorized the programs, maximized central influence over their actual operation, restricted knowledge of their existence within the Bureau, and regulated the form in which information from them should be disseminated.

External Authorizations

Despite the differences between the FBI's and the CIA's mail opening programs with regard to internal authorization, the respective patterns of authorization outside the agencies were clearly parallel. There is no direct evidence that any President or Postmaster General was ever informed about any of the FBI mail opening programs until four years after they ceased. While two Attorneys General may have known about some aspect of the Bureau's mail interceptions—and the record is not even clear on this point—it does not appear that any Attorney General was ever briefed on the full scope of the programs. Thus, like the CIA mail opening programs, the Bureau programs were isolated even within the executive department. They were initiated and operated by Bureau officials alone, without the knowledge, approval, or control of the President or his cabinet.

A. *Post Office Department*

The FBI mail opening programs, like those of the CIA, necessitated the cooperation of the Post Office Department. But the record shows that the Bureau officials who secured this cooperation intended to and did in fact accomplish their task without revealing the FBI's true interest in obtaining access to the mail; no high ranking Postal official was apparently made aware that the FBI actually opened first class mail.

1. Postmasters General

There is no evidence that any Postmaster General was ever briefed about any of the FBI mail opening programs, either by the FBI directly or by a Chief Postal Inspector. Henry Montague, who as Chief Postal Inspector was aware of the mail cover (as opposed to the mail opening) aspect of several Bureau programs, stated that he never informed the Postmaster General because he "thought it was our duty to cooperate in this interest, and really, I did not see any reason to run to the Postmaster General with the problem. It was not through design that I kept it away from... the Postmaster General.... It was just that I did not see any reason to run to [him] because he had so many other problems."[122]

2. Chief Postal Inspectors

It is certain that at least one and probably two Chief Postal Inspectors were aware of the fact that Bureau agents received direct access to mail, and in one case permission may have been given to physically remove letters from the mailstream as well, but there is no direct evidence that any Chief Postal Inspector was ever informed that FBI agents actually opened any mail.

Clifton Garner.—Clifton Garner was Chief Postal Inspector under the Truman administration during the period when Z-Coverage may have been reinstituted in Washington, D.C. No FBI testimony or documents, however, suggest that his approval was sought prior to this reinstitution, nor can he recall being contacted by Bureau officials about such a program.[123]

David Stephens.—Henry Montague testified that prior to the 1959 implementation of Z-Coverage in New York, when he was Postal Inspector in Charge of that region, he was instructed by Chief Postal Inspector David Stephens to cooperate with Bureau agents in their proposed program of special "mail covers."[124] As Montague recalls, Stephens approved the "mail cover" operation and left the mechanical arrangements up to him. Donald Moore has also testified that Stephens must have been contacted by Bureau officials in Washington prior to the implementation of Survey No. 1 in the same year,[125] although he did not participate in any such meeting himself, and no other FBI official who testified could shed any light on who might have made such contact. there is no evidence, however, that Stephens was ever informed that mail would actually be opened by Bureau agents in either program.

Henry Montague.—Postal Inspector in Charge of the New York Region, Montague followed David Stephens' instructions to cooperate with the FBI regarding Z-Coverage and made the necessary mechanical arrangements within his office. He stated, however, that he was told by the Bureau representatives who came to see him, including Donald Moore (whose testimony is consistent),[126] that this was a mail cover rather than a mail opening operation.[127] He was simply informed that the Bureau had an interest in obtaining direct access to particular mail for national security reasons and that his cooperation would be appreciated. While he realized that even this type of access was highly unusual, he agreed because "... they knew what they were looking for; we did not.... [T]hey could not give any names to the Postal Service, as far as I knew, for mail to look for.... [P]erhaps they knew who the agent might be, or something of this sort, which knowledge was not ours and which, at that time, I did not feel was in our province to question."[128] Montague also acknowledged that during his tenure as Postal Inspector in Charge of the New York Region, he may have known of an FBI operation at Idlewild Airport (Survey No. 1) as well, but stated that he had no "positive recollection" of it.[129]

As Chief Postal Inspector from 1961 to 1969, Montague personally authorized Postal Service cooperation with the Bureau's programs in at least two instances, and in one case possibly approved the removal of selected letters by Bureau agents to a point outside the postal facility in which they worked. According to a 1961 FBI memorandum, it was recommended by Bureau officials and approved by Director Hoover that Postal officials in Washington should be contacted "to explore the possibility of instituting" Survey No. 2.[130] In February of that year, Donald Moore met with Montague about this matter, explaining only—according to both Moore and Montague—that the program would involve screening the mail and that it was vital to the security of the country.[131] The fact that the FBI intended to open selected items was apparently not mentioned. Because he "felt it was our duty to cooperate with the Agency which was responsible for the national security in espionage cases,"[132] Montague agreed to assist the Bureau. On this occasion, however, he indicated that he would prefer to have postal employees rather than FBI agents conduct the "cover" since "it was our position that whenever possible...the mail should remain in the possession of the Postal Service."[133]

Less than two years later, Montague did allow Bureau agents to screen mail directly in Survey No. 4. A 1962 FBI memorandum noted that the FBI liaison to the Post Office approached him on December 19 to secure his approval for the Bureau's plan to cover mail from Miami to a Latin American country.[134] According to this memorandum, Montague did approve and authorized the removal of selected letters to the FBI laboratory as well. The former chief Postal Inspector remembers approving the screening aspects of the project and knowing that mail left the custody of postal employees,[135] but cannot recall whether or not he specifically granted his permission for flying certain letters to Washington.[136] He testified, in any event, that he was not informed that mail would be opened.[137]

In June 1965, Montague reconsidered his original approval of the project, possibly in light of Senator Edward Long's investigation into the use of mail covers and other techniques by federal agencies. A June 25, 1965 FBI airtel from the Miami office to Headquarters reads in part: "[The Assistant Postal Inspector in Charge of the Atlanta Region] said that due to investigations by Senate and Congressional committees, Mr. Montague requested he be advised of the procedures used in this operation."[138] Montague had appeared before the Long Subcommittee and had testified on the subject of mail covers several times earlier that year, but he recalls that his concern in determining the procedures used in Survey No. 4 in June focused more on the new Postal regulations regarding mail covers that were issued about that time than on the Senate hearings.[139] Regardless of his motivation, Montague asked the Assistant Postal Inspector in charge to ascertain the details of the Miami operation; the procedures were described to this postal official by representatives of the Miami Field Office, apparently without mention of the fact that mail was actually opened; and the Assistant Postal Inspector reported back to Montague, who found them to be acceptable and did not withdraw his support for the survey.[140]

Montague has stated that he was never informed that FBI agents in Survey No. 4 or in any of the other Bureau programs intended to or actually did open first class mail. This testimony is supported by that of Donald Moore, who on at least two occasions was the Bureau representative who sought Montague's cooperation for the programs. Moore does not believe that he ever told Montague that mail would be opened;[141] he said, moreover, that it was "understood" within the Bureau that Postal officials should not be informed.[142] Of his meeting with Montague about Z-Coverage, for example, Moore stated: "I am sure I didn't volunteer it to him and, in fact, would not volunteer it to him" because of the belief that such information should be closely held within the Bureau.[143] He added that it was a general, though unwritten, policy that whenever Bureau agents contacted Postal officials concerning the mail programs "it was understood that they would not be told [that mail opening was contemplated]."[144]

Montague, for his part, did not specifically warn FBI agents against tampering with the mail because they were Federal officers and he trusted them not to do so. He stated:

> I do not recall that I ask [if they intended to open mail], because I never thought that would be necessary. I knew that we never opened mail in connection with a mail cover. I knew that we could not approve it, that we would not approve any opening of any mail by anybody else. Both the CIA and the FBI were Government employees the same as we were, had taken the same oath of office, so that question was really not discussed by me....

With regard to the CIA when they first started [in 1953], we did put more emphasis on that point that mail could not be tampered with, that it could not be delayed, because, according to my recollection, this was the first time that we had any working relationship with the CIA at all. With the FBI, I just did not consider that it was necessary to emphasize that point. I trusted them the same as I would have to tell a Postal person that you cannot open mail. By the same token, I would not consider it necessary to emphasize it to any great degree with the FBI.[145]

In short, it does not appear that any senior postal official knew that the FBI opened mail. Postal officials did cooperate extensively with the Bureau, but out of trust did not ask whether mail would be opened and because of a concern for security they were not told.

B. Department of Justice

The record presents no conclusive evidence that any Attorney General ever knew of any of the FBI mail opening programs. The evidence summarized below, does suggest that one and possibly two Attorneys General may have been informed of selected aspects of the Bureau's mail operations, but generally supports the view that no Attorney General was ever briefed on their full scope.

1. Robert F. Kennedy

New York Field Office Briefings.—On April 5, 1962, and again on November 4, 1963, Attorney General Robert F. Kennedy visited the FBI's New York field office and was briefed in foreign espionage matters. The person who briefed him on these occasions, the Assistant Special Agent in Charge for the Espionage Division, testified that he may have mentioned the mail intercept projects then being conducted by the New York field office to the Attorney General, but has no definite recollection whether he did or not.[146] Other participants at these briefings could not recall the technique of mail opening being discussed,[147] nor do the internal FBI memoranda relating to the briefings indicate that the topic arose.[148]

The Baltch Case.—It is also possible, though again the evidence is far from conclusive, that Robert Kennedy learned that mail opening was utilized in the Baltch investigation. On July 2, 1963, FBI agents arrested two alleged Soviet illegal agents who used the names Robert and Joy Ann Baltch; they were indicted for espionage on July 15. Several conferences were held between FBI representatives and Assistant Attorney General for Internal Security, J. Walter Yeagley, regarding this case and the possibility that some of the evidence was tainted.[149] Yeagley subsequently briefed Kennedy on the problems involved in prosecuting the Baltchs.[150] Donald E. Moore, who was one of the FBI representatives who discussed the Baltch case with Yeagley, testified that he believed, though he had no direct knowledge, that the fact of mail opening did come to the attention of the Attorney General in this context.[151] Yeagley, however, cannot recall being specifically advised that mail was opened (although he knew that a "mail intercept or cover" had occurred) and stated that he did not inform Kennedy about any mail openings.[152]

Other Espionage Cases.—Internal FBI memoranda concerning at least two other espionage cases that were considered for prosecution while Kennedy was Attorney General, also raise the possibility that Justice Department attorneys, including Yeagley, may have been advised of mail openings that occurred.[153] Yeagley cannot recall being so advised, however, and, as noted above, stated that he never informed the Attorney General of any mail openings.[154] There is no indication in the memoranda, moreover, that these matters were ever raised with Kennedy.

2. Nicholas deB. Katzenbach

The Baltch Case.—The Baltch case did not come to trial until early October, 1964, when Nicholas deB. Katzenbach was Acting Attorney General. At the time the trial commenced, FBI representatives including Donald Moore, conferred with Thomas K. Hall, a Justice Department attorney who was assigned to the case, again on the subject of tainted evidence.[155] Hall then discussed the case with Katzenbach and, according to an FBI internal memorandum, "Katzenbach recognized the problems, but felt in view of the value of the case, an effort should be made to go ahead with the trial even if it might be necessary to drop the overt act where our tainted source is involved...."[156] Because he subsequently determined that the case "could not be further prosecuted without revealing national security information,"[157] however, Katzenbach ordered the prosecution to be dropped entirely.

In fact, there were at least two sources of tainted evidence other than mail opening involved in the Baltch case—a surreptitious entry and a microphone installation—and it is only these which Katzenbach recalls.[158] He testified that although he did discuss the tainted issues with both Hall and Joseph Hoey, the United States Attorney who originally presented the government's case, neither of them brought to his attention the fact of mail opening.[159] Hoey's recollection supports this contention: a Bureau memorandum suggests that Hoey may have learned of a "mail intercept" in the case,[160] but he recalls neither being informed of an actual opening nor conferring with the Acting Attorney General about any issue related to mail.[161] Assistant Attorney General Yeagley recalls discussing the case generally with Katzenbach also, and "may have informed him of the mail intercept or cover which had occurred." but Yeagley stated that he had no definite knowledge himself that the "intercept or cover" involved the actual opening of mail and so would not have been in a position to advise him that it did.[162]

Katzenbach has testified that he was never aware of the Bureau's use of mail opening in any espionage investigation.[163] He added:

> Even if one were to conclude that the Bureau did in fact reveal that mail had been opened and that this fact was relayed by lawyers in the [Baltch] case to me, I am certain that that fact would have been revealed by the FBI—and I would have accepted it—as an unfortunate aberration, just then discovered in the context of a Soviet espionage investigation, not a massive mail opening program. In that event, nothing would have led me to deduce that the Bureau was, as a matter of policy and practice, opening letters.[164]

The Long Subcommittee Hearings. —According to Donald Moore, he and Assistant Director Belmont did inform Katzenbach at the time of the 1965 Long Subcommittee hearings that Bureau agents screened mail both inside and outside postal facilities as a matter of practice, although he does not claim that the subject of actual opening arose.

In February of that year, the Long Subcommittee directed chief Postal Inspector Montague to provide it with a list of all mail covers, including those in the areas of organized crime and national security, by federal agencies within the previous two years. As a result of this and other inquiries by the Subcommittee, especially regarding electronic surveillance practices, President Johnson requested Katzenbach to coordinate all executive department matters under his investigation.[165]

In executing this responsibility, Katzenbach met with Moore, Belmont, and Courtney Evans, a former FBI Assistant Director who had retired from the Bureau but was then working as a special assistant to the Attorney General, on February 27, 1965, to discuss problems raised by the subcommittee which affected the FBI.[166] One of the subjects discussed at that meeting was the question of Bureau access to the mail. Four days earlier, the chief Postal Inspector had testified before the Subcommittee that he had no knowledge of any case in which mail left the custody of Postal employees during the course of a mail cover.[167] At the time, Montague did know that this practice had occurred[168]—indeed, as Chief Postal Inspector he had approved the direct screening of mail by FBI agents in Survey No. 4[169]—but he believed that "there was an understanding...that national security cases were not included within this particular part of the hearing."[170] According to Moore, Katzenbach had been made aware of the possible inaccuracy of Montague's testimony, and the Bureau officials consequently "pointed out [to the Attorney General] that we do receive mail from the Post Office in certain sensitive areas.".[171] Moore believes moreover, that they informed him that this custody was granted in on-going projects rather than isolated instances.[172]

Katzenbach acknowledged that he was aware, while Attorney General, that "in some cases the outside of mail might have been examined or even photographed by persons other than Post Office employees,"[173] but he stated that he never knew the FBI gained custody to mail on a regular basis in large-scale operations.[174] He also testified that the time of the February meeting he considered Montague's testimony to be "essentially truthful,"[175] while the record shows that he spoke to Senator Long less than a week after this meeting,[176] Katzenbach stated that this was in regard to the requested list of all mail covers by federal agencies rather than the issue of mail custody.[177] The testimony of Courtney Evans, who was also present at the February 27 meeting, supports that of Katzenbach: at no time, Evans said, was he personally ever made aware that FBI agents received direct access to mail on an on-going basis.[178]

Moore does not claim that he told Katzenbach that mail was actually opened by Bureau agents. According to him, this information was volunteered by neither Belmont nor himself and Katzenbach did not inquire whether opening was involved.[179] When asked if he felt any need to hold back from Katzenbach the fact of mail openings as opposed to the fact that Bureau agents received direct access to the mail, Moore replied: "It is perhaps difficult to answer. Perhaps I could liken it to…a defector in place in the KGB. You don't want to tell anybody his name, the location, the title, or anything like that. Not that you don't trust them completely, but the fact is that anytime one additional person becomes aware of it, there is a potential for the information to …go further."[180]

Probably the strongest suggestion in the documentary evidence that Katzenbach may have been made aware of actual FBI mail openings at the time of the Long Subcommittee hearings is found in a memorandum from Hoover to ranking Bureau officials, dated March 2, 1965. This memorandum reads, in part:

> The Attorney General called and advised that he had talked to Senator Long last night. Senator Long's committee is looking into mail covers, et cetera. The Attorney General stated he thought somebody had already spoken to Senator Long as he said he did not want to get into any national security area and was willing to take steps not to do this. The Attorney General stated that Mr. Fensterwald [Chief counsel to the Subcommittee] was present for part of the meeting and Fensterwald had said that he had some possible witnesses who are former Bureau agents and if they were asked if mail was opened, they would take the Fifth Amendment. The Attorney General stated that before they are called, he would like to know who they are and whether they were ever involved in any program touching on national security and if not, it is their own business, but if they were, we would want to know. The Attorney General stated the Senator promised that he would have a chance to look at the names if he wanted to, personally and confidentially, and the list would have any names involving national security deleted and he would tell the Senator how many but no more.[181]

Katzenbach testified as follows concerning this passage:

> [Even] assuming the accuracy of the memo, it is not consistent with my being aware of the Bureau's mail opening program. Had I been aware of that program, I naturally would have assumed that the agents had been involved in that program, and I would scarcely have been content to leave them to their own devices before Senator Long's committee. Moreover, it would have been extremely unusual for ex-FBI agents to be interviewed by the Senate committee staff without revealing that fact to the Bureau. In those circumstances both the Director and I would have been concerned as to the scope of their knowledge with respect to the very information about mail covers which the Senator was demanding and which we were refusing, as well as about any other matters of a national security nature. If the witnesses in fact existed (which I doubted strongly), then both the Director and I wanted to know the extent of their knowledge about Bureau programs, and the extent of their hostility toward the FBI. That is a normal concern that we would have had anytime any ex-FBI agent testified before any Congressional committee on any subject.[182]

The most that can reasonably be inferred from the record on possible knowledge of FBI mail openings by Attorney Generals may have known that mail was opened with regard to particular espionage investigations, and one Attorney General may have learned that the FBI regularly received mail from the Post Office and that five former FBI agents possibly opened mail. Evidence exists which casts doubt on the reasonableness of even these inferences, however. More significantly, there is no indication in either the documents or the testimony that the approval of any Attorney General was ever sought prior to the institution of any Bureau program, and despite a clear opportunity to inform Attorney General Katzenbach of the full scope and true nature of these operations in 1965, he was intentionally not told. In the name of security, the Bureau neither sought the approval of nor even shared knowledge of its programs with the Cabinet officer who was charged with the responsibility of controlling and regulating the FBI's conduct.

The first uncontroverted evidence that any Attorney General knew of the FBI mail opening programs is not found until 1970, four years after the programs were terminated. John Mitchell, upon reading the 1970 "Huston Report," learned that the Bureau had engaged in "covert mail coverage" in the past, but that this practice had "been discontinued."[183] While the report itself stated that mail opening was unlawful,[184] however, Mitchell did not initiate any investigation, nor did he show much interest in the matter. He testified:

> I had no consideration of that subject matter at the time. I did not focus on it and I was very happy that the plan was thrown out the window, without pursuing any of its provisions further.... I think if I had focused on it I might have considered [an investigation into these acts] more than I did.[185]

C. Presidents

There is no evidence that any President was ever contemporaneously informed about any of the FBI mail opening programs. In 1970, Bureau officials who were involved in the preparation of the "Huston Report" apparently advised Tom Charles Huston that mail opening as an investigative technique had been utilized in the past, for this fact was reflected in the report which was sent to President Nixon.[186]

Termination of the FBI Mail opening Programs

A. *Hoover's Decision to Terminate the Programs in 1966*

1. Timing

By mid-1966 only three FBI mail opening programs continued to operate: Z-Coverage in New York and Washington, Survey No. 1 in those same cities, and Survey No. 4 in Miami. Three of the programs—No. 2, No. 3, and No.7—and the extensions of Survey No. 1 to four cities other than New York and Washington had all been terminated prior to 1966 because they had produced no valuable counterintelligence information while tying up manpower needed in other areas.[187] Two of the programs—Surveys No. 5 and 6—had been suspended in January 1966 for security reasons involving changes in local postal personnel and never re-instituted. As the San Francisco Field office informed Headquarters in May of that year in regard to both programs: "While it is realized that these sources furnished valuable information to the Federal Government, it is not believed the value justifies the risk involved. It is not recommended that contact with sources be re-instituted."[188]

The remaining three programs were all terminated in July 1966 at the direct instruction of J. Edgar Hoover. Apparently this instruction was delivered telephonically to the field offices;[189] no memoranda explicitly reflect the order to terminate the programs. There is no evidence that the FBI has employed the technique of mail opening in any of its investigations since that time, although the FBI continued to receive the fruits of the CIA's mail opening program until 1973.

2. Reasons

Given the perceived success of these three programs the reasons for their termination are not entirely clear. While all FBI officials who testified on the subject were unanimous in their conclusion that the decision was Hoover's alone, none could testify as to the precise reasons for his decision.

At least three possible reasons are presented by the record. First, the Director may have believed that the benefits derived from mail opening were outweighed by the need to present espionage cases for prosecution which were untainted by use of this technique. Regardless of whether or not the mail opening in the Baltch case was actually a factor in Acting Attorney General Katzenbach's decision to drop the prosecution, for example, Bureau officials believed that their use of the technique in that case did in fact preclude prosecution.[190] On a memorandum dealing with the evidentiary issues in the Baltch case, Hoover wrote the following notation: "We must immediately and materially reduce the use of techniques which 'taint' cases."[191]

Second, Hoover may have believed that the Attorney General and other high government officials would not support him in the FBI's use of questionable investigative practices. It is known that Hoover cut back on a number of other techniques in the mid-1960's; the use of mail covers by the FBI was suspended in 1964,[192] and in July 1966—the same month which saw the end of the mail opening programs—Hoover terminated the technique of surreptitious entries by Bureau agents.[193] In a revealing comment on a 1965 memorandum regarding the Long Subcommittee's investigation of such techniques as mail covers and electronic surveillance, Hoover wrote:

> "I don't see what all the excitement is about. I would have no hesitation in discontinuing all techniques—technical coverage [i.e. wiretapping], microphones, trash covers, mail covers, etc. While it might handicap us I doubt they are as valuable as some believe and none warrant FBI being used to justify them."[194]

His lack of support from above had been tentatively suggested by some witnesses as a reason for this general retrenchment. Donald Moore, for example, surmised that:

> There had been several questions raised on various techniques, and some procedures had changed, and I feel that Mr. Hoover in conversation with other people of which I am not aware, decided that he did not or would not receive backing in these procedures and he did not want them to continue until the policy question was decided at a higher level.[195]

While former Attorney General Katzenbach testified that he was unaware of the FBI mail openings, his views on this subject tend to support Moore's. He speculated that the reason the programs were terminated in 1966 may have related to the then-strained relations between Mr. Hoover and the Justice Department stemming from the case of Black v. United States [196] and the issue of warrantless electronic surveillance.[197] Hoover had wanted the Justice Department to inform the Supreme Court, in response to an order by the Court that in that case electronic surveillance had been authorized by every Attorney General since Herbert Brownell. Katzenbach, not believing this to be so, approved a Supplemental Memorandum to the Court which simply stated that microphone installations had been authorized by long-standing "practice." According to Katzenbach, "this infuriated Hoover.... He was very angry, [and] that may have caused him to stop everything of this kind."[198]

A third related reason was suggested by Wannall, former Assistant Director in charge of the FBI's Domestic Intelligence Division. Wannall believed that there was a genuine "question in [Hoover's] mind about the legality" of mail opening, and noted that by at least 1970, as expressed in one of the Director's footnotes in the Huston Report, Hoover clearly considered mail opening to be outside the framework of the law.[199] This footnote also suggests that, like CIA officials, Hoover was concerned that the perceived illegality of the technique would lead to an adverse public reaction damaging to the FBI and other intelligence agencies if its use were made known. His note to President Nixon read:

> The FBI is opposed to implementing any covert mail coverage [i.e., mail opening] because it is clearly illegal and it is likely that, if done, information would leak out of the Post office to the press and serious damage would be done to the intelligence community.[200]

B. *Recommended Re-institution*
1. Within the Bureau

Whatever the reasons for it, the FBI Director's decision to terminate all mail opening programs in 1966 was not favorably received by many of the participating agents in the field. As one official of the New York Field Office at the time of the termination testified:

> ...the inability of the government to pursue this type of investigative technique meant that we would no longer be able to achieve the results that I felt were necessary to protect the national security, and I did not feel that I wanted to continue in any job where you are unable to achieve the results that really your job calls for.... That was a big influence on my taking retirement from the FBI.[201]

Several recommendations came in from the field to consider the re-institution of the mail opening programs between 1966 and the time of Hoover's death in 1972.[202] None of them was successful. A 1970 internal FBI memorandum, for example, reflects the recommendation of the New York office that the programs be re-instituted,[203] but Headquarters suggested that this course was "not advisable at this time."[204] Underlining the words "not advisable," Hoover noted: "Absolutely right."

There is no evidence that any recommendation to re-institute these programs ever reached the desk of an

Acting Director or Director of the Bureau after Hoover's death.

2. Huston Plan

The only known attempt to recommend re-institution of FBI mail opening by officials outside the FBI is found in the Huston Report in 1970.[205] The Report itself stated that mail opening did not have the "sanction of law,"[206] but proceeded to note several advantages of relaxing restrictions on this technique, among them:

> 1. High-level postal authorities have, in the past, provided complete cooperation and have maintained full security of this program.
>
> 2. This technique involves negligible risk of compromise. Only high echelon postal authorities know of its existence, and personnel involved are highly trained, trustworthy, and under complete control of the intelligence agency.
>
> 3. This coverage has been extremely successful in producing hard-core and authentic intelligence which is not obtainable from any other source....[207]

Primarily because of the objection Hoover expressed in the footnote he added, which are discussed above, this aspect of the Huston Plan was never implemented, however.

Legal and Security Considerations within the FBI

During the years that the FBI mail opening programs operated, Bureau officials attempted only once, in 1951, to formulate a legal theory to justify warrantless mail opening, and the evidence suggests that they never relied upon even this theory. At the same time, there is little in the record (until Hoover's comment in the 1970 Huston Report) to indicate that Bureau officials perceived mail opening to be illegal, as many CIA officials did. The FBI officials who directed the programs apparently gave little consideration to factors of law at all; ironically, it appears that of the two agencies which opened first class mail without warrants, that agency with law enforcement responsibilities and which was a part of the Justice Department gave less thought to the legal ramifications of the technique. Despite its inattentive attitude toward legal issues, the Bureau was at least as concerned as the CIA that disclosure of their programs outside the FBI—even to its own overseer, the Attorney General, and especially to Congress—would, as Hoover wrote in 1970, "leak...to the press and serious[ly] damage" the FBI.[208] To avoid such exposure, the Bureau, like the CIA, took measures to prevent knowledge of their programs from reaching this country's elected leadership.

A. Consideration of Legal Factors by the FBI

1. Prior to the commencement of Mail opening Programs In the Post-War Period.

In June 1951, when the Washington Field Office recommended to Headquarters that consideration should be given to the reinstitution of Z-Coverage, it was specifically suggested that Bureau officials determine whether or not Postal Inspectors have the authority to order the opening of first class mail in espionage cases.[209] Headquarters conducted research on this possible legal predicate to the peacetime re-institution of the program, and the results were summarized in a second memorandum on Z-Coverage in September 1951.[210] The basic conclusion was that Postal Inspectors had no authority to open mail; only employees of the Dead Letter Office and other persons with legal search warrants had such power. It was argued, however, that Postal Inspectors may have sufficient legal authority to open even first class mail whose contents were legally non-mailable under 18 U.S.C. Section 1717. This class of non-mailable items included, and includes today, "[e]very letter...in violation of sections...793, 794 [the espionage statutes]...of this title...." Since it was a crime to mail letters whose contents violated the espionage statutes, it was reasoned, it may not be unlawful to intercept and open such letters, despite the general prohibition against mail opening found in 18 U.S.C. Sections 1701, 1702, and 1703. The study concluded:

> ...it is believed that appropriate arrangements might be worked out on a high level between the Department and the Postmaster General or between the Bureau and the appropriate Post Office officials whereby the mail of interest to the Bureau could be checked for items in violation of the espionage and other security statutes which are itemized in Title 18, U.S. Code Section.... It

is respectfully suggested that appropriate discussions be held on this matter.[211]

This theory ignores the fact that the warrant procedure itself responds to the problem of non-mailable items. If, on the basis of an exterior examination of the envelope or on the basis of facts surrounding its mailing, there exists probable cause for a court to believe that the espionage statutes have been violated, a warrant may be obtained to open the correspondence. If the evidence does not rise to the level of probable cause, the law does not permit the mail to be opened. There is no indication, in any event, that discussions were ever held with any Postmaster General or Attorney General in an attempt to either test or implement this theory. While Z-Coverage was in fact re-instituted after this study was made, it was conducted with FBI personnel rather than Postal Inspectors, and its mail opening aspect was apparently unknown to any high-ranking Postal officials. In regard to the recommendation that "appropriate discussions be held on this matter," Assistant to the Director Belmont penned the notation, "No action at this time. File for future reference."[212]

2. Post-1951

After the mail opening programs were underway, there was apparently no further consideration by FBI officials of the legal factors involved in the operations. Unlike that regarding CIA mail opening, the documentary record on the FBI program does not contain references (until 1970, four years after the programs ceased) to the illegality of mail opening; nor does it suggest that mail opening was considered legal. At most, the record reveals the recognition by the Bureau officials that evidence obtained from their surveys was tainted and, hence, inadmissible in court,[213] but not the recognition that the technique was invalid per se. Indeed, after the Supreme Court decisions in Nardone v. United States, 302 U.S. 379 (1937) and 308 U.S. 338 (1939), this distinction was explicitly made in the area of electronic surveillance: while the Nardone decisions prohibited the admission in court of evidence obtained from wiretapping, the cases were not interpreted by the Bureau to preclude use of the technique itself, and the practice continued.[214]

The testimonial record, moreover, clearly suggests that legal considerations were simply not raised in contemporaneous policy decisions affecting the various mail surveys: Wannall, William Branigan, and others have all so testified.[215] None of these officials has any knowledge that any legal theory—either the one which was filed for "future reference" in 1951 or one based on a possible "national security" exception to the general prohibition against mail opening—was ever developed by Bureau officials after 1951 to justify their programs legally, or that a legal opinion from the Attorney General was ever sought. To these officials, such justification as existed stemmed not from legal reasoning but from the end they sought to achieve and an amorphous, albeit honestly held, concept of the "greater good." As Branigan stated: "It was my assumption that what we were doing was justified by what we had to do."[216] He added that he believed "the national security" impelled reliance on such techniques:

> The greater good, the national security, this is correct. This is what I believed in. Why I thought these programs were good, it was that the national security required this, this is correct.[217]

At least some of the agents who participated in the mail opening program have testified that they believed the surveys were legal because they assumed (without being told) that the programs had been authorized by the President or Attorney General, or because they assumed (again without being told) that there was a "national security" exception to the laws prohibiting mail opening.[218] Those officials in a policy-making position, however, apparently did not focus on the legal questions sufficiently to state an opinion regarding the legality or illegality of the programs. Nor did they advise the field offices or participating agents about these matters.

Only in the 1970's, at least four years after the FBI mail opening programs ceased, is there any clear indication that Bureau officials, like those of the CIA, believed their programs to be illegal. As noted above, Hoover's footnote to the 1970 Huston Report described the technique as "clearly illegal"; and in the recent public hearings on FBI mail opening, Wannall testified that, as of 1975, "I cannot justify what happened...."[219]

In light of the Bureau's major responsibilities in the area of law enforcement and the likelihood that some of the espionage cases in which mail opening was utilized would be prosecuted, it is ironic that FBI officials focused on these legal issues to a lesser degree than did their CIA counterparts. But the Bureau's Domestic Intelligence Division made a clear distinction between law enforcement and counterintelligence matters; what was appropriate in one area was not necessarily appropriate in the other. As Branigan again testified:

> In consideration of prosecuting a case, quite obviously [legal factors] would be of vital concern. In discharging counterintelligence responsibilities, namely to identify agents in the United States to determine the extent of damage that they are causing to the United States...we would not necessarily go into the legality or illegality.... We were trying to identify agents and we were trying to find out how this country was being hurt, and [mail opening] was a means of doing it, and it was a successful means.[220]

B. Concern with Exposure

Although Bureau officials apparently did not articulate the view prior to 1970 that mail opening was necessarily illegal, they did believe that their use of this technique was so sensitive that its exposure to other officials within the executive branch, the courts, Congress, and the American public generally should be effectively prevented. This fear of exposure may have resulted from a perceived though unexpressed sense that its legality was at least questionable; it was almost certainly a consequence of a very restricted, even arrogant, view of who had a "need to know" about the Bureau's operations. But whatever its source, this concern with security clearly paralleled the CIA's concern with the "flap potential" of their projects and resulted in similar efforts to block knowledge of their use of this technique from reaching the general public and its leaders.

The reluctance of FBI officials to disclose the details of their programs to other officials within the executive branch itself has been described above: there is no clear evidence that any Bureau official ever revealed the complete nature and scope of the mail surveys to any officer of the Post Office Department or Justice Department, or to any President of the United States. It was apparently a Bureau policy not to inform the Postal officials with whom they dealt of the actual intention of FBI agents in receiving the mail, and there is no indication that this policy was ever violated.[221] When Attorney General Katzenbach met with Moore and Belmont on the subject of Bureau custody of mail, Moore testified that he did not inform the Attorney General about the mail opening aspect of the projects because of security reasons: "anytime one additional person becomes aware of it, there is a potential for the information to...go further."[222] One Bureau agent at Headquarters who was familiar with the mail programs (but not in a policy-making position) also speculated that the questionable legal status of this technique may have been an additional reason for not seeking the Attorney General's legal advise. He testified as follows:

> Q. Do you know why the opinion of the Attorney General was apparently or probably not sought?
>
> A. Because of the security of the operation. I would imagine that would be the main reason. It was a program we were operating. We wanted to keep it within the Bureau itself—and the fact that it involved opening mail.
>
> Q. What do you mean by the last statement, "...the fact that it involved opening mail"?
>
> A. That was not legal, as far as I knew.[223]

With respect to the Justice Department generally, only the minimum knowledge necessary to resolve a specific prosecutive problem was imparted. Donald Moore said of his meeting with Assistant Attorney General Yeagley about the Baltch case, for example, that he did not disclose to him the FBI's general use of this technique: "I am sure it was confined to the issue at hand, which was anything at all which involved the prosecution of Baltch."[224] Even the term "mail opening" was avoided, and the more ambiguous term "mail intercept" was used:[225] while susceptible of only one meaning within the FBI, the latter term was apparently misinterpreted by Yeagley and other Justice Department officials with different assumptions about Bureau operations.[226]

The FBI's concern with exposure extended to the courts as well. In an internal memorandum regarding the Baltch case, it was written that "under no circumstances is the Bureau willing to admit [to the court] that a mail intercept was utilized...."[227]

Similarly, FBI officials, like their counterparts in the CIA, did not want their use of this technique known to Congress. One senior Bureau official testified that the FBI feared that the Long Subcommittee's 1965 investigation could publicly expose the mail programs;[228] another that such Congressional exposure could "wrack up" the Bureau.[229] Attorney General Katzenbach had been requested by the President to coordinate executive branch responses to inquires by the Subcommittee, but the FBI was apparently not content with his efforts in preventing the disclosure of "national security" information generally. To ensure that their mail surveys, as well as certain practices in the area of electronic surveillance, remained unstudied, Bureau officials themselves directly attempted to steer the Subcommittee away from probing these subjects.

Belmont's February 27, 1965, memorandum reflecting his meeting with the Attorney General about Montague's testimony on mail custody, reads in part: "I told Mr. Katzenbach that I certainly agree that this matter should be controlled at the committee level but that I felt pressure would have to be applied so that the personal interest of Senator [Edward} Long became involved rather than on any ideological basis."[230] The memorandum continues: "I called Mr. DeLoach [an Assistant Director of the FBI] and briefed him on this problem in order that he might contact Senator [James O.] Eastland in an effort to warn the Long committee away from those areas which would be injurious to the national defense. (Of course, I made no mention of such a contact to the Attorney General.)" According to an FBI memorandum, Hoover himself subsequently contacted Senator Eastland, who, he reported, "is going to see Senator Long not later than Wednesday morning to caution him that the chief counsel must not go into the kind of questioning he made of Chief Inspector Montague of the Post Office Department."[231]

The strategy worked. The Subcommittee never learned of the FBI's use of mail opening as an investigative technique. Despite the fact that in 1965 the FBI conducted a total of five mail opening programs in the United States—and despite the fact that in that year alone more than 13,300 letters were opened by CIA agents in New York—the Subcommittee, the general public, the Attorney General, and apparently even Montague himself accepted as true Montague's testimony that year that:

> The seal on a first-class piece of mail is sacred. When a person puts first-class postage on a piece of mail and seals it, he can be sure that the contents of that piece of mail are secure against illegal search and seizure.[232]

Warrantless National Security Electronic Surveillance

Historical Perspective

The following is taken from a prepared statement by Hon. Edward H. Levi, Attorney General of the United States. It has been slightly edited by NACIC Community Training Branch by inserting graphics where AG Levi cited specific figures. Edited wording appears in bold letters in the text.

As I read the history, going back to 1931 and undoubtedly prior to that time, except for the interlude between 1928 and 1931, and for two months in 1940, the policy of the Department of Justice has been that electronic surveillance could be employed without a warrant in certain circumstances.

In 1928 the Supreme Court in *Olmstead v. United States* held that wiretapping was not within the coverage of the Fourth Amendment. Attorney General Sargent had issued an order earlier in the same year prohibiting what was then known as the Bureau of Investigation from engaging in any telephone wiretapping for any reason. Soon after the order was issued, the Prohibition Unit was transferred to the Department as a new bureau. Because of the nature of its work and the fact that the Unit had previously engaged in telephone wiretapping in January 1931, Attorney General William D. Mitchell directed that a study be made to determine whether telephone tapping should be permitted and, if so, under what circumstances. The Attorney General determined that in the meantime the bureaus within the Department could engaged in telephone wiretapping upon the personal approval of the bureau chief after consultation with the Assistant Attorney General in charge of the case. The policy during this period was to allow wiretapping only with respect to the telephones of syndicated bootleggers, where the agent had probable cause to believe the telephone was being used for liquor operations. The bureaus were instructed not to tap telephones of public officials and other persons not directly engaged in the liquor business. In December 1931, Attorney General William Mitchell expanded the previous authority to include "exceptional cases where the crimes are substantial and serious, and the necessity is great and (the bureau chief and the Assistant Attorney General) are satisfied that the persons whose wires are to be taped are of the criminal type."

During the rest of the thirties it appears that the Department's policy concerning telephone wiretapping generally conformed to the guidelines adopted by Attorney General William Mitchell. Telephone wiretapping was limited to cases involving the safety of the victim (as in kidnapping), location and apprehension of "desperate" criminals, and other cases considered to be major law enforcement importance, such as espionage and sabotage.

In December 1937, however, in the first *Nardone* case the United States Supreme Court reversed the Court of Appeals for the Second Circuit, and applied Section 605 of the Federal Communications Act of 1934 to law enforcement officers, thus rejecting the Department's argument that it did not so apply. Although the Court read the Act to cover only wire interceptions where there had also been disclosure in court or to the public, the decision undoubtedly had its impact upon the Department's estimation of the value of telephone wiretapping as an investigative technique. In the second *Nardone* case in December 1939, the Act was read to bar the use in court not only of the overheard evidence, but also of the fruits of that evidence. Possibly for this reason, and also because of public concern over telephone wiretapping, on March 15, 1940, Attorney General Robert Jackson imposed a total ban on its use by the Department. This ban lasted about two months.

On May 21, 1940, President Franklin Roosevelt issued a memorandum to the Attorney General stating his view that electronic surveillance would be proper under the Constitution where "grave matters involving defense of the nation" were involved. The President authorized and directed the Attorney General "to secure information by listening devices (directed at) the conversations or other communications of persons suspected of subversive activities against the Government of the United States, including suspected spies." The Attorney General was requested "to limit these investigations so conducted to a minimum and to limit them insofar as possible as to aliens." Although the President's memorandum did not use the term "trespassory microphone surveillance," the language was sufficiently broad to include that practice and the Department construed it as an authorization to conduct trespassory microphone surveillance as well as telephone wiretapping in national security cases. The authority for the President's action was later confirmed by an opinion by Assistant Solicitor General Charles Fahy who advised the Attorney General that electronic surveillance could be conducted where matters affected the security of the nation.

On July 17, 1946, Attorney General Tom C. Clark sent President Truman a letter reminding him that President Roosevelt had authorized and directed Attorney General Jackson to approve "listening devices (directed at) the conversation of other communications of persons suspected of subversive activities against the Government of the United States, including suspected spies" and that the directive had been followed by Attorneys General Robert Jackson and Francis Biddle. Attorney General Clark recommended that the directive "be continued in force" in view of the "increase in subversive activities" and "a very substantial increase in crime." He stated that it was imperative to use such techniques "in cases vitally affecting the domestic security, or where human life is in jeopardy" and that Department files indicated that his two most recent predecessors as Attorney General would concur in this view. President Truman signed his concurrence on the Attorney General's letter.

According to the Department's records, the annual total of telephone wiretaps and microphones installed by the Bureau between 1940 and 1951 was **4,068 wiretaps and 753 microphones** (See figures 1 and 2). It should be understood that these figures, as in the case for the figures I have given before, are cumulative for each year and also duplicative to some extent, since a telephone wiretap or microphone which was installed, then discontinued, but later reinstated would be counted as a new action upon reinstatement.

In 1952, there were 285 telephone wiretaps, 300 in 1953, and 322 in 1954. Between February 1952 and May 1954, the Department's position was not to authorize trespassory microphone surveillance. This was the position taken by Attorney General McGrath, who informed the FBI that he would not approve the installation of trespassory microphone surveillance because of his concern over a possible violation of the Fourth Amendment. FBI records indicate there were 63 microphones installed in 1952, there were 52 installed in 1953, and there were 99 installed in 1954. The policy against Attorney General approval, at least in general, of trespassory microphone surveillance was reversed by Attorney General Herbert Brownell on May 20, 1954, in a memorandum to Director Hoover instructing him that the Bureau was authorized to conduct trespassory microphone surveillances. The Attorney General stated that "considerations of internal security and the national safety are paramount and, therefore, may compel the unrestricted use of this technique in the national interest."

A memorandum from Director Hoover to the Deputy Attorney General on May 4, 1961, described the Bureau's practice since 1954 as follows: (I)n the internal security field, we are utilizing microphone surveillances on a restricted basis even though trespass is necessary to assist in uncovering the activities of Soviet intelligence agents and Communist Party leaders. In the interests of national security, microphone surveillances are also utilized on a restricted basis, even though trespass is necessary in uncovering major criminal activities. We are using such coverage in connection with our investigations of the clandestine activities of top hoodlums and organized crime. From an intelligence standpoint, this investigative technique has produced results unobtainable through other means. The information so obtained is treated in the same manner as information obtained from wiretaps, that is, not from the standpoint of evidentiary value but for intelligence purposes."

The number of telephone wiretaps and microphones from 1955 through 1964 was **1794 wiretaps and 839 microphones.** (see figures 2 and 3)

It appears that there was a change in the authorization procedure for microphone surveillance in 1965. A memorandum of March 30, 1965, from Director Hoover to the Attorney General states that "(i)n line with your suggestion this morning, I have already set up the procedure similar to requesting of authority for phone taps to be utilized in requesting authority for the placement of microphones."

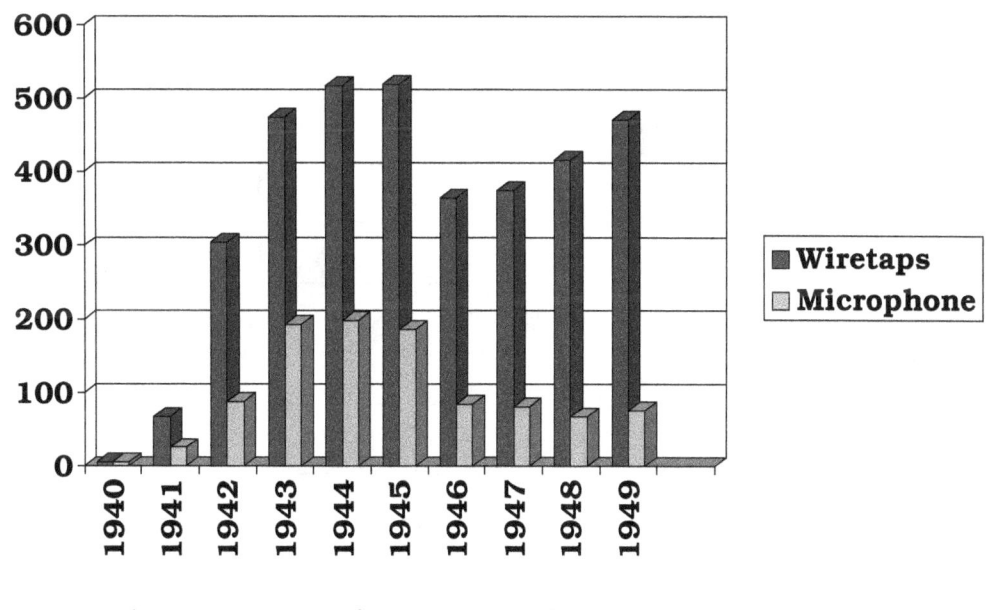

Figure 1.   FBI Electronic Surveillance 1940–1949

President Johnson announced a policy for federal agencies in June 1965, which required that the interception of telephone conversations without the consent of one of the parties be limited to investigations relating to national security and that the consent of the Attorney General be obtained in each instance. The memorandum went on to state that use of mechanical or electronic devices to overhear conversations not communicated by wire is an even more difficult problem "which raises substantial and unresolved questions of Constitutional interpretation." The memorandum instructed each agency conducting such an investigation to consult with the Attorney General to ascertain whether the agency's practices were fully in accord with the law. Subsequently, in September 1965, the Director of the FBI wrote the Attorney General and referred to the "present atmosphere, brought about by the unrestrained and injudicious use of special investigative techniques by other agencies and departments, resulting in Congressional and public alarm and opposition to any activity which could in any way be termed an invasion of privacy." "As a consequence," the Director wrote, "we have discontinued completely the use of microphones." The Attorney General responded in part as follows: "The use of wiretaps and microphones involving trespass present more difficult problems because of the inadmissibility of any evidence obtained in court cases and because of current judicial and public attitude regarding their use. It is my understanding that such devices will not be used without my authorization, although in emergency circumstances they may be used subject to my later ratification. At this time I believe it desirable that all such techniques be confined to the gathering of intelligence in national security matters, and I will continue to approve all such requests in the future as I have in the past. I see no need to curtail any such activities in the national security field."

The policy of the Department was stated publicly by the Solicitor General in a supplemental brief in the Supreme Court in *Black v. United States* in 1966. Speaking of the general delegation of authority by Attorneys General to the Director of the Bureau, the Solicitor General stated in his brief:

"An exception to the general delegation of authority has been prescribed, since 1940, for the interception of wire communications, which (in addition to being limited to matters involving national security or danger to human life) has required the specific authorization of the Attorney General in each instance. No similar procedure existed until 1965 with respect to the use of

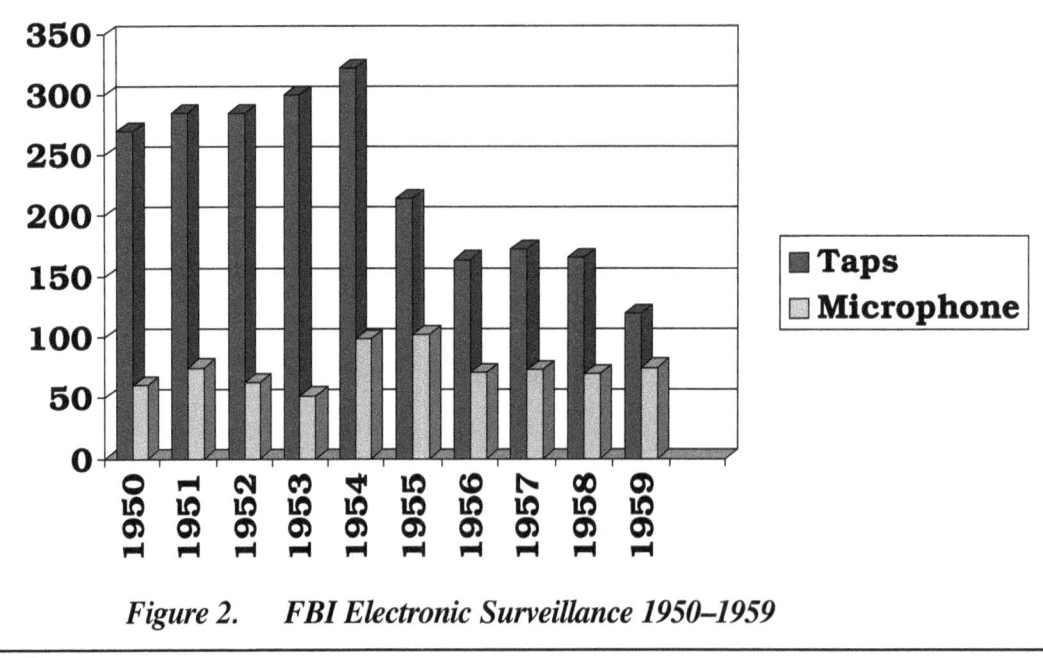

Figure 2.   FBI Electronic Surveillance 1950–1959

devices such as those involved in the instant case, although records of oral and written communications within the Department of Justice reflect concern by Attorneys General and the Director of the Federal Bureau of Investigation that the use of listening devices by agents of the government should be confined to a strictly limited category of situations. Under Department practice in effect for a period of years prior to 1963, and continuing until 1965, the Director of the Federal Bureau of Investigation was given authority to approve the installation of devices such as that in question for intelligence (and not evidentiary) purposes when required in the interests of national security or national safety, including organized crime, kidnappings and matters wherein human life might be at stake....

Present Department practice, adopted in July 1965 in conformity with the policies declared by the President on June 30, 1965, for the entire federal establishment, prohibits the use of such listening devices (as well as the interception of telephone and other wire communications) in all instances other than those involving the collection of intelligence affecting the national security. The specific authorization of the Attorney General must be obtained in each instance when this exception is invoked."

The Solicitor General made a similar statement in another brief filed that same term (*Schipani v U.S.*) again emphasizing that the data would not be made available for prosecutorial purposes, and that the specific authorization of the Attorney General must be obtained in each instance when the national security is sought to be invoked. The number of telephone wiretaps and microphones installed since 1965 **(through 1974) is 1,349 wiretaps and 249 microphones** (see figures 3 and 4).

Comparable figures for the year 1975 up to October 29 are: telephone wiretaps: 121; microphones: 24.

In 1968 Congress passed the Omnibus Crime Control and Safe Streets Act. Title III of the Act set up a detailed procedure for the interception of wire or oral communications. The procedure requires the issuance of a judicial warrant, prescribes the information to be set forth in the petition to the judge so that, among other things, he may find probably cause that a crime has been or is about to be committed. It requires notification to the parties subject to the intended surveillance within a period not more than ninety days after the application of the order of approval has been denied or after the termination of the period of the order or the period of

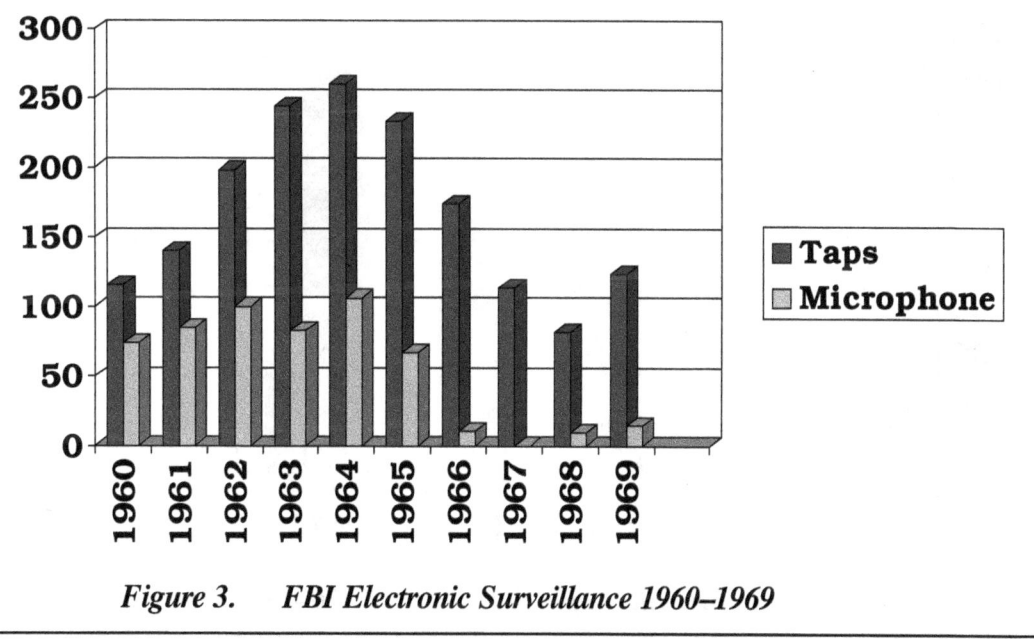

Figure 3.   FBI Electronic Surveillance 1960–1969

the extension of the order. Upon a showing of good cause the judge may postpone the notification. The Act contains a saving clause to the effect that it does not limit the constitutional power of the President to take such measures as he deems necessary to protect the nation against actual or potential attack or other hostile acts of a foreign power, to obtain foreign intelligence information deemed essential to the security of the United States, or to protect national security information against foreign intelligence activities. Then in a separate sentence the proviso goes on to say, "Nor shall anything contained in this chapter be deemed to limit the constitutional power of the President to take such measures as he deems necessary to protect the United States against the overthrow of the government by force or other unlawful means, or against any other clear and present danger to the structure or existence of the government."

The Act specifies the conditions under which information obtained through a presidentially authorized interception might be received into evidence. In speaking of this saving clause, Justice Powell in the *Keith* case in 1972 wrote: "Congress simply left presidential powers where it found them." In the case the Supreme Court held that in the field of internal security, if there was no foreign involvement, a judicial warrant was required for the Fourth Amendment.

Fifteen months after the *Keith* case, Attorney General Richardson, in a letter to Senator Fulbright which was publicly released by the Department, stated: "In general, I must be convinced that it is necessary (1) to protect the nation against actual or potential attack or other hostile acts of a foreign power; (2) to obtain foreign intelligence information deemed essential to the security of the United States; or (3) to protect national security information against foreign intelligence activities."

I have read the debates and the reports of the Senate Judiciary Committee with respect to Title III and particularly the proviso. It may be relevant to point out that Senator Philip Hart questioned and opposed the form of the proviso reserving presidential power. But I believe it is fair to say that his concern was primarily, perhaps exclusively, with the language which dealt with presidential power to take such measures as the President deemed necessary to protect the United States "against any other clear and present danger to the structure or existence of the Government."

I now come to the Department of Justice's present position on electronic surveillance conducted without a warrant. Under the standards and procedures established by the President, the personal approval of the Attorney General is required before any non-consensual electronic surveillance may be instituted

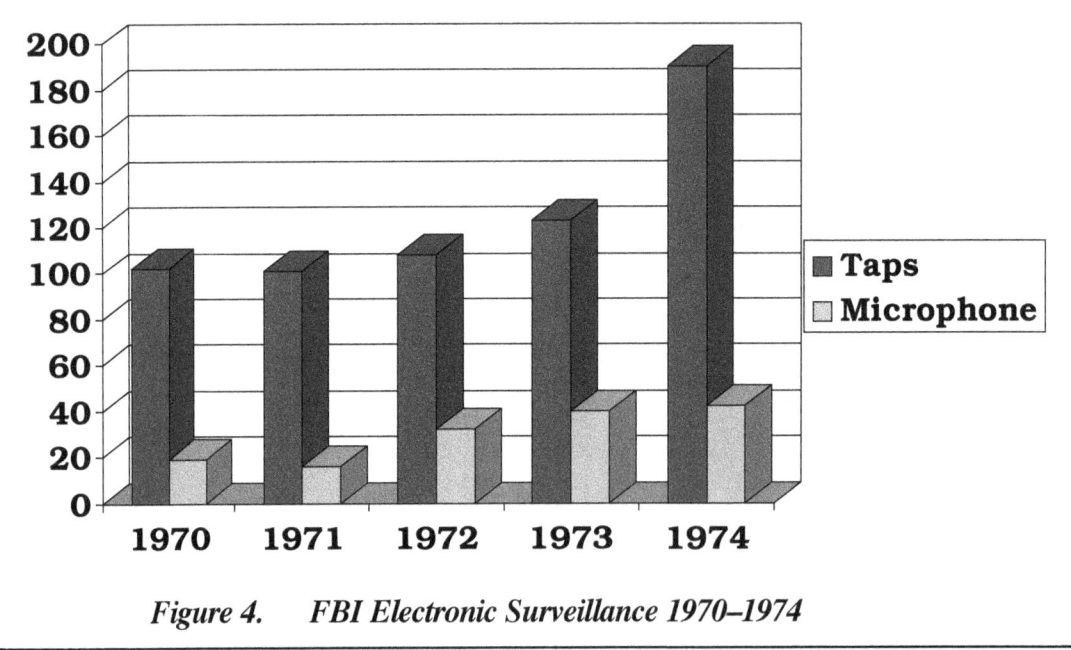

Figure 4. FBI Electronic Surveillance 1970–1974

within the United States without a judicial warrant. All requests for surveillance must be made in writing by the Director of the Federal Bureau of Investigation and must set forth the relevant circumstances that justify the proposed surveillance. Both the agency and the Presidential appointee initiating the request must be identified. These requests come to the Attorney General after they have gone through the review procedures within the Federal Bureau of Investigation. At my request, they are then reviewed in the Criminal Division of the Department. Before they come to the Attorney General, they are then examined by a special review group which I have established within the Office of the Attorney General. Each request, before authorization or denial, receives my personal attention. Requests are only authorized when the requested electronic surveillance is necessary to protect the nation against actual or potential attack or other hostile acts of a foreign power; to obtain foreign intelligence deemed essential to the security of the nation; to protect national security information against foreign intelligence activities; or to obtain information certified as necessary for the conduct of foreign affairs matters important to the national security of the United States. In addition the subject of the electronic surveillance must be consciously assisting a foreign power or foreign-based political group, and there must be assurance that the minimum physical intrusion necessary to obtain the information sought will be used. As these criteria will show and as I will indicate at greater length later in discussing current guidelines the Department of Justice follows, our concern is with respect to foreign powers or their agents. In a public statement made last July 9th, speaking of the warrantless surveillance then authorized by the Department, I said "it can be said that there are no outstanding instances of warrantless wiretaps or electronic surveillances directed against American citizens and none will be authorized by me except in cases where the target of surveillance is an agent or collaborator of a foreign power." This statement accurately reflects the situation today as well.

What, then, is the shape of the present law? To begin with, several statues appear to recognize that the Government does intercept certain messages for foreign intelligence purpose and that this activity must be, and can be, carried out. Section 952 of Title 18, which I mentioned earlier is one example; section 798 of the same title is another. In addition, Title III's proviso, which I have quoted earlier, explicitly disclaimed any intent to limit the authority of the Executive to conduct electronic surveillance for national security and foreign intelligence purposes. In an apparent recognition that the power would be exercised, Title III specifies the conditions under which information obtained through Presidentially authorized surveillance may be received into evidence. It seems clear, therefore, that in 1968 Congress was not prepared to come to a judgment that the Executive should discontinue its activities in this area nor was it prepared to regulate how those activities were to be conducted. Yet it cannot be said that Congress has been entirely silent on this matter. Its express statutory references to the existence of the activity must be taken into account.

The case law, although unsatisfactory in some respects, has supported or left untouched the policy of the Executive in the foreign intelligence area whenever the issue has been squarely confronted. The Supreme Court's decision in the *Keith* case in 1972 concerned the legality of warrantless surveillance directed against a domestic organization with no connection to a foreign power and the Government's attempt to introduce the product of the surveillance as evidence in the criminal trial of a person charged with bombing a CIA office in Ann Arbor, Michigan. In part because of the danger that uncontrolled discretion might result in use of electronic surveillance to deter domestic organizations from exercising First Amendment rights, the Supreme Court held that in cases of internal security, when there is no foreign involvement, a judicial warrant is required. Speaking for the Court, Justice Powell emphasized that "this case involves only the domestic aspects of national security. We have expressed no opinion as to the issues which may be involved with respect to activities of foreign powers or their agents.

As I observed in my remarks at the ABA convention, the Supreme Court surely realized, "in view of the importance the Government has placed on the need for warrantless electronic surveillance, that, after the holding in *Keith*, the Government would proceed with the procedures it had developed to conduct those surveillances not prohibited—that is, in the foreign intelligence area or, as Justice Powell said, "with respect to activities of foreign powers and their agents."

The two federal circuit court decisions after *Keith* that have expressly addressed the problem have both held that the Fourth Amendment does not require a warrant for electronic surveillance instituted to obtain foreign intelligence. In the first *United States v. Brown* the defendant, an American citizen, was incidentally overheard as a result of a warrantless wiretap authorized by the Attorney General for foreign intelligence purposes. In upholding the legally of the surveillance, the Court of Appeals for the Fifth Circuit declared that on the basis of "the President's constitutional duty to act for the United States in the field of foreign affairs, and his inherent power to protect national security in the conduct of foreign affairs...the President may constitutionally authorize warrantless wiretaps for the purpose of gathering foreign intelligence." The court added that "(r)estrictions on the President's power which are appropriate in cases of domestic security become inappropriate in the context of the international sphere."

In *United States v. Butenko*, the Third Circuit reached the same conclusion-that the warrant requirement of the Fourth Amendment does not apply to electronic surveillance undertaken for foreign intelligence purposes. Although the surveillance in that case was directed at a foreign agent, the court held broadly that the warrantless surveillance would be lawful so long as the primary purpose was to obtain foreign intelligence information. The court stated that such surveillance would be reasonable without a warrant even though it might involve the overhearing of conversations of "alien officials and agents, and perhaps of American citizens." I should note that although the United States prevailed in the Butenko case, the Department acquiesced in the petitioner's application for *certiori* in order to obtain the Supreme Court's ruling on the question. The Supreme Court denied review— this left the Third Circuit's decision undisturbed as the prevailing law.

Most recently, in *Zweibon v. Mitchell*, decided in June of this year, the District of Columbia Circuit dealt with warrantless electronic surveillance directed against a domestic organization allegedly engaged in activities affecting this country's relations with a foreign power. Judge Skelly Wright's opinion for four of the nine judges makes many statements questioning any national security exception to the warrant requirement. The court's actual holding made clear in Judge Wright's opinion was far narrower and, in fact, is consistent with holdings in *Brown* and *Butenko*. The court held only that "a warrant must be obtained before a wiretap is installed on a domestic organization that is neither the agent of nor acting in collaboration with a foreign power." This holding, I should add, was fully consistent with the Department of Justice's policy prior to the time of the *Zweibon* decision.

With these cases in mind, it is fair to say electronic surveillance conducted for foreign intelligence purposes, essential to the national security, is lawful under the Fourth Amendment, even in the absence of a warrant, at least where the subject of the surveillance is a foreign power or an agent or collaborator of a foreign power. Moreover, the opinions of two circuit courts stress the purpose for which the surveillance is undertaken, rather than the identity of the subject. This suggests that in their view such surveillance without a warrant is lawful so long as its purpose is to obtain foreign intelligence.

But the legality of the activity does not remove from the Executive or from Congress the responsibility to take steps, within their power, to seek an accommodation between the vital public and private interests involved. In our effort to seek such an accommodation, the Department has adopted standards and procedures designed to ensure the reasonableness under the Fourth Amendment of electronic surveillance and to minimize to the extent practical the intrusion on individual interests. As I have stated, it is the Department's policy to authorize electronic surveillance for foreign intelligence purposes only when the subject is a foreign power or an agent of a foreign power. By the term "agent" I mean a conscious agent; the agency must be of a special kind and must relate to activities of great concern to the United States for foreign intelligence or counterintelligence reasons. In addition, at present, there is no warrantless electronic surveillance directed against any American citizen, and although it is conceivable that circumstances justifying such surveillance may arise in the future, I will not authorize any warrantless surveillance against domestic persons or organizations such as those involved in the *Keith* case. Surveillance without a warrant will not be conducted for purposes of security against domestic or internal threats. It is our policy, moreover, to use the Title III procedure whenever it is possible and appropriate to do so, although the statutory provisions regarding probable cause, notification, and prosecutive purpose make it unworkable in all foreign intelligence and many counterintelligence cases.

The standards and procedures that the Department has established within the United States seek to ensure that every request for surveillance receives thorough and impartial consideration before a decision is made whether to institute it. The process is elaborate and time-consuming but it is necessary if the public interest is to be served and individual rights safeguarded.

I have just been speaking about telephone wiretapping and microphone surveillances which are reviewed by the Attorney General. In the course of its investigation, the committee has become familiar with the more technologically sophisticated and complex electronic surveillance activities of other agencies. These surveillance activities present somewhat different legal questions. The communications conceivably might take place entirely outside the United States. That fact alone, of course, would not automatically remove the agencies' activities from scrutiny under the Fourth Amendment since at times even communications abroad may involve a legitimate privacy interest of American citizens. Other communications conceivably might be exclusively between foreign powers and their agents and involve no American terminal. In such a case, even though American citizens may be discussed, this may raise less significant, or perhaps no significant, questions under the Fourth Amendment. But the primary concern, I suppose, is whether reasonable minimization procedures are employed with respect to use and dissemination.

With respect to all electronic surveillance, whether conducted within the United States or abroad, it is essential that efforts be made to minimize as much as possible the extent of the intrusion. Much in this regard can be done by modern technology. Standards and procedures can be developed and effectively deployed to limit the scope of the intrusion and the use to which its product is put. Various mechanisms can provide a needed assurance to the American people that the activity is undertaken for legitimate foreign intelligence purposes, and not for political or other improper purposes. The procedures used should not be ones which by indirection in fact target American citizens and resident aliens where these individuals would not themselves be appropriate targets. The proper minimization criteria can limit the activity to its justifiable and necessary scope.

Another factor must be recognized. It is the importance or potential importance of the information to be secured. The activity may be undertaken to obtain information deemed necessary to protect the nation against actual or potential attack or other hostile acts of a foreign power, to obtain intelligence information deemed essential to the security of the United States, or to protect national security information against foreign intelligence activities.

Need is itself a matter of degree. It may be that the importance of some information is slight, but that may be impossible to gauge in advance; the significance of a single bit of information may become apparent only when joined to intelligence from other sources. In short, it is necessary to deal in probabilities. The importance of information gathered from foreign establishments and agents must be regarded generally as high-although even here there may be wide variations. At the same time, the effect on individual liberty and security-at least of American citizens-caused by methods directed exclusively to foreign agents, particularly with minimization procedures, would be very slight.

Agreement Governing the Conduct of Defense Department Counterintelligence Activities in Conjunction with the Federal Bureau of Investigation

SECTION 1

Purpose

The purpose of this memorandum is to establish jurisdictional boundaries and operational procedures to govern the conduct of counterintelligence activities by the military counterintelligence services of the Department of Defense in conjunction with the Federal Bureau of Investigation. It implements Section 1-104 of Executive Order 12036, requiring procedures to govern the coordination of military counterintelligence activities within the United States, and supersedes the Delimitation's Agreement of 1949, as amended.

SECTION 2

Defense Components Authorized to Conduct Counterintelligence Activities

Within the Department of Defense, each of the military departments is authorized by Executive Order 12036 to conduct counterintelligence activities within the United States in coordination with the FBI and abroad in coordination with the Central Intelligence Agency. Within the military departments, the United States Army Intelligence and Security Command, the Naval Investigative Service, and the Air Force Office of Special Investigations, are authorized by departmental regulation to conduct such activities. The term "military counterintelligence service" or "military CI service," as used herein, refers to these components.

SECTION 3

Federal Bureau of Investigation Coordination with the Department of Defense

A. Policy matters affecting Defense counterintelligence components will be coordinated with the Office of the Under Secretary of Defense for Policy.

B. When a counterintelligence activity of the Federal Bureau of Investigation involves military or civilian personnel of the Department of Defense, the Federal Bureau of Investigation shall coordinate with the Department of Defense. (Section 1 - 1401 of Executive Order 12036). For military and civilian personnel of a military department, the military CI Service has coordination authority for the Department of Defense. For other civilian personnel of the Department of Defense, coordination shall be effected with the Office of the Under Secretary of Defense for Policy.

C. It is contemplated that representatives of field elements of the FBI and military counterintelligence services will maintain close personal liaison, and will meet frequently and routinely for the purpose of ensuring close operation in carrying out their counterintelligence activities.

SECTION 4

Definitions

For the purpose of this memorandum, the following definitions shall apply:

A. The term "coordination" means the process of eliciting objections and comments prior to undertaking a proposed action. As used here, the term implies that no such action will be taken so long as the party with whom the action in question is raised continues to have objections which cannot be resolved.

B. The term "counterintelligence investigation" is included in the term "counterintelligence," as defined in Section–202 of the Executive Order 12036, and refers to the systematic collection of information regarding a person or group which is, or may be, engaged in espionage or other clandestine intelligence activity, sabotage, international terrorist activities, or assassinations, conducted for, or on behalf of, foreign powers, organizations, or persons.

C. The term "counterintelligence operations" is included in the term "counterintelligence," as defined in Section 4-202 of Executive Order 12036, and refers to actions taken against hostile intelligence services to counter espionage and other clandestine intelligence activities damaging to the national security.

D. The term "DOD civilian personnel" includes all U.S. citizen officers and employees of the Department of Defense not on active duty and all foreign nationals employed by the Department of Defense.

E. The term "security service" refers to that entity or component of a foreign government charged with responsibility for counterespionage or internal security functions of such government.

F. The term "United States" includes the 50 States, the District of Columbia, the Commonwealth of Puerto Rico, and all territories, possessions, or protectorates under U.S. sovereignty or control; but does not include occupied territory governed under the President's authority as Commander-in-Chief.

SECTION 5

Policy

A. The responsibilities of each military counterintelligence service and the Federal Bureau of Investigation for the conduct of counterintelligence investigations and operations shall be governed by relevant statutes, Executive Order 12036, and this agreement.

B. Each military department is responsible for protecting its personnel and installations from physical threats and for ensuring that its programs and activities which involve the national security are not compromised to hostile intelligence agencies.

C. Within the United States, the Federal Bureau of Investigation conducts counterintelligence and coordinates the counterintelligence activities of other agencies.

D. Under combat conditions or other circumstances wherein a military commander is assigned responsibility by the President for U.S. Government operations in a particular geographic area, he shall have the authority to coordinate all counterintelligence activities within such area, notwithstanding the provisions of this memorandum, subject to such direction as he may receive from the Secretary of Defense.

E. The military CI Services and the Federal Bureau of Investigation are mutually responsible to ensure that there is a continuing and complete exchange of all counterintelligence information and operational data relevant to the particular concerns of each operating agency.

F. Policy issues arising in the course of counterintelligence activities which cannot be resolved at the FBI/military CI Service local or headquarters level, shall be jointly referred to the Attorney General and the Secretary of Defense for resolution, or referred to the Special Coordination Committee (Counterintelligence) of the National Security Council in accordance with SCC guidelines.

SECTION 6

Delineation of Responsibility for Counterintelligence Investigations

Responsibility for counterintelligence shall be apportioned between the Federal Bureau of Investigation (FBI) and the military counterintelligence services of the Department of Defense (DOD) as follows:

A. All investigations of violations of the Atomic Energy Act of 1946, which might constitute a counterintelligence investigation as defined herein, shall be the responsibility of the FBI, regardless of the status or location of the subjects of such investigations.

B. Except as provided by paragraph C (2) herein, all counterintelligence investigations of foreign nationals undertaken within the United States shall be the responsibility of the FBI.

C. Counterintelligence investigations within the United States shall be conducted in accordance with the following jurisdictional guidelines:

1. Except as provided herein, investigations of all civilians, including DOD civilian personnel, shall be the responsibility of the FBI;

2. Investigations of U.S. military personnel on active duty shall be the responsibility of the counterintelligence service of the appropriate military department;

3. Investigations of retired military personnel, active and inactive reservists, and National Guard members shall be the responsibility of the FBI; provided, however, that investigations of actions which took place while the subject of the investigation was, or is, on active military duty shall be conducted by the counterintelligence service of the appropriate military department; and

4. Investigations of private contractors of the Department of Defense, and their employees, shall be the responsibility of the FBI.

Provided, however, that nothing contained in this paragraph shall prevent the military counterintelligence services of the Department of Defense, in a manner consistent with applicable law and Executive Branch policy, from undertaking:

(a) In those cases where the FBI chooses to waive investigative jurisdiction, investigative actions which are necessary to establish or refute the factual basis required for an authorized administrative action to protect the security of its personnel, information, activities, and installations; or

(b) To provide assistance to the FBI in support of any counterintelligence investigation for which the FBI is herein assigned responsibility.

D. Counterintelligence investigations outside the United States shall be conducted in accordance with the following guidelines:

1. Investigations of military personnel on active duty shall be the responsibility of the military counterintelligence services of the Department of Defense.

2. Investigations of current civilian employees, their dependents, and the civilian dependents of active duty military personnel shall be the responsibilities of the military counterintelligence services, unless such responsibility is otherwise assigned pursuant to agreement with the host government, U.S. law, or Executive directive.

3. Investigations of retired military personnel, active and inactive reservists, National Guard members, private contractors and their employees, and other U.S. persons, who permanently reside in such locations, shall be undertaken in consultation with the FBI, CIA, and host government as appropriate.

Provided, however that nothing contained in this paragraph shall prevent the military counterintelligence services of the Department of Defense, in a manner consistent with applicable law and Executive Branch policy from undertaking:

(a) Investigative actions which are necessary to establish or refute the factual basis required for an authorized administrative action, to protect the security of its personnel, information, activities, and installations; or
(b) To provide assistance to the FBI or security service of a host government in support of counterintelligence investigations outside the United States for which DOD is not herein assigned investigative responsibility.

SECTION 7

Coordination of Counterintelligence Operations
(The procedures governing the coordination of counterintelligence operations within the United States by the military counterintelligence services with the FBI are contained in the classified annex to the memorandum.)

SECTION 8

Implementation
A. The policy and procedures set forth herein shall be implemented in the regulations of the affected agencies.

B. The provisions of this memorandum, and the classified annex made a part hereof, shall be effective immediately upon execution by the Attorney General and the Secretary of Defense.

GRIFFIN B. BELL
ATTORNEY GENERAL OF THE U.S.
Date: 4/5/79

C. W. DUNCAN, JR.
ACTING SecretARY OF DEFENSE
Date: 2/9/79

Executive Order No. 12139, Exercise of Certain Authority Respecting Electronic Surveillance

(MAY 23, 1979, 44 F.R. 30311, 50 U.S.C. 1803 NOTE)

By the authority vested in me as President by Section 102 and 104 of the Foreign Intelligence Surveillance Act of 1978 (50 U.S.C. 1802 and 1804), in order to provide as set forth in that Act for the authorization of electronic surveillance for foreign intelligence purposes, it is hereby ordered as follows:

1-101. Pursuant to Section 102 (a)(1) of the Foreign Intelligence Surveillance Act of 1978 (50 U.S.C. 1802(a)), the Attorney General is authorized to approve electronic surveillance to acquire foreign intelligence information without a court order, but only if the Attorney General makes the certificates required by that Section.

1-102. Pursuant to Section 102(b) of the Foreign Intelligence Act of 1978 (50 U.S.C. 1802 (b)), the Attorney General is authorized to approve applications to the court having jurisdiction under section 103 of that Act to obtain orders for electronic surveillance for the purpose of obtaining foreign intelligence information.

1-103. Pursuant to Section 104(a)(7) of the Foreign Intelligence Surveillance Act of 1978 (50 U.S.C. 1804(a)(7)), the following officials, each of whom is employed in the area of national security or defense, is designated to make the certifications required by Section 104(a)(7) of the Act in support of applications to conduct electronic surveillance:

- (a) Secretary of State.
- (b) Secretary of Defense.
- (c) Director of Central Intelligence.
- (d) Director of the Federal Bureau of Investigations.
- (e) Deputy Secretary of State.
- (f) Deputy Secretary of Defense.
- (g) Deputy Director of Central Intelligence.

None of the above officials, nor anyone officially acting in that capacity, may exercise the authority to make the above certifications, unless that official has been appointed by the President with the advice and consent of the Senate.

1-104. (Section 1-104 consisted of an amendment to section 2-202 of Executive Order No. 12036.)

1-105. (Section 1-105 consisted of an amendment to section 2-203 of Executive Order No. 12036.)

Jimmy Carter

Jimmy Carter

Congressional Committees and Executive Commissions 1934-1975

Special Committee To Investigate Un–American Activities

Congress established this committee in 1934 and appointed Representative John W. McCormack from Massachusetts as its chairman. It charged the committee with investigating activities by Communists, Nazis, and Fascists. After conducting its investigation, the committee concluded that Communism was not sufficiently strong enough to harm the United States but its continued growth did represent a future danger to the country.

The committee cited attempts made from abroad and by diplomatic or consular officials in the United States to influence Americans. They also found that some efforts were being made to organize some American citizens and resident aliens and said that constitutional rights of Americans had to be preserved from these "isms." The committee found Nazism, Fascism, and Communism all to be equally dangerous and unacceptable to American interests.

To solve the problem, the Committee recommended that a law be enacted:

that required the registration of all publicity, propaganda, or public relations agents, or other agents who represent any foreign country;

that the Secretary of Labor have authority to shorten or terminate any visit to the United States by an foreign visitor traveling on a temporary visa if that person engaged in propaganda activities;

that the Department of State and Department of Labor negotiate treaties with other nations to take back their citizens who are deported;

that Congress make it unlawful to advise, counsel or urge any military or naval member, including the reserves, to disobey the laws and regulations governing such forces;

that Congress enact legislation so the U.S. Attorneys outside the District of Columbia can proceed against witnesses who refuse to answer questions, produce documents or records or refuse to appear or hold in contempt the authority of any Congressional investigating committee; and

that Congress make it unlawful for any person to advocate the overthrow or destruction of the United States Government or the form of government guaranteed to the States by Article IV of the fourth section of the Constitution.

On the basis of the Committee's recommendation, Congress enacted the McCormack Foreign Agents Registration Act in 1938.

Special House Committee for the Investigation of Un-American Activities

On 21 July 1937, a Texas Congressman, Martin Dies, introduced a resolution in the House of Representatives to create a special committee to investigate subversion in the United States. After prolonged debate in the House, the resolution passed on 26 May 1938. Congress established the Dies Committee, named after its new chairman, on 6 June. Formal hearings of the committee opened on 12 August 1938.

The major target of the committee was organized labor groups, particularly the Congress of Industrial Organizations. A major tactic employed by Dies, and one that set a pattern for how the committee functioned, was his meeting alone and covertly with sympathetic witnesses who accused hundreds of individuals of supporting Communist activities. The American press dramatically reported the accusations but only a handful of the named individuals were provided an opportunity to defend themselves.

The Dies Committee was a special committee under House Rules, and its mandate had to be renewed by Congress every two years. It did so until 1945 when Congress replaced it with a permanent standing body called the Committee on Un-American Activities or HUAC. During the next five years, the Committee began investigations into the American film industry, hunting for Communists. This investigation resulted in Hollywood blacklisting various producers, writers, and actors.

The Committee's greatest distinction was its investigation of Alger Hiss, which led to his eventual perjury conviction. The Hiss case also defined Communism as the foremost political issue in the nation. The Committee became a major political force and used contempt citations as a primary weapon against individuals who refused to testify by taking the Fifth Amendment against self-incrimination. In 1950, for example, the Committee issued 56 citations out of the 59 citations voted by the House of Representatives.

In the 1950s, the Republican Senator from Wisconsin, Joseph McCarthy, began his probe for Communists in the US Government. McCarthy's inquisition overshadowed the Committee's own inquiries into Communism. Since McCarthy was in the background, his downfall had no effect on the Committee. It continued to pursue Communists and others engaged in un-American activities until the beginning of 1960.

In 1960 and for the next 15 years, the Committee's attention concentrated on the domestic unrest within the nation. They investigated the black militant and antiwar movements, other radical youth groups, and terrorism.

In 1968, the House of Representatives changed the committee's name to the Committee on Internal Security. In 1975, Congress abolished the Committee.

Commission on the Organization of the Executive Branch of the Government

In 1954, Congress revived the Commission on the Organization of the Executive Branch of the Government. Previously established in 1944, the commission's head was former President Herbert Hoover. The reinstituted commission came at a time when Senator McCarthy alleged that the Central Intelligence Agency (CIA) was infiltrated by Communists. McCarthy was ready to launch an investigation into the CIA but agreed to postpone it if the commission included the CIA in its study.

To appease the Senator, on 4 July 1954, the President appointed General Mark Clark, USA (Ret.) to chair a six-member committee under the commission to evaluate the intelligence community and report back to Congress. To accomplish this task, Clark divided the committee into groups. Clark and another committee member, Admiral Richard Conolly, USN (Ret.), inspected the CIA. After several months of discussions in 1955 with CIA officials, in particular with Director Allen Dulles, the two men completed their review. In May 1955, the commission completed its report and submitted it to Congress.

The report was divided between an unclassified and classified section. The main report covered the six agencies or departments having intelligence responsibilities. In its long descriptive narrative, the report did not make any extensive recommendations. It did say that the Cold War distracted the intelligence community from other tasks. As for the CIA, the commission found no valid information that organized subversives or Communists had penetrated the Agency. This conclusion discharged the commitment to Senator McCarthy.

The Doolittle Review

President Dwight Eisenhower wanted to avoid any investigation of the CIA's clandestine service by the Commission on the Organization of the Executive Branch of the Government. To do this, on 8 July 1954, he appointed General James Doolittle, USAF, to chair a four-member committee to do a comprehensive study of CIA's covert activities. The committee's report was submitted to the President on 30 September, less than three months after it was commissioned.

The White House released a press statement, which stated that General Doolittle found the CIA to be doing a good job and gradually improving its capabilities. To demonstrate his cooperation with the Congressional Commission, President Eisenhower provided a copy of the report to General Clark.

The Doolittle Review indicated several major concerns involving personnel, security, coordination and operations, organization and administration, and costs. It faulted the Agency for accepting additional tasking than its personnel could properly handle. The committee said the CIA had to be more aggressive in its covert action programs. In the committee's view, as long as the Cold War remained a national policy, the CIA needed to be more effective, clever, and, if necessary, more ruthless than the enemy.

Doolittle downplayed attempts to infiltrate agents in the Soviet Union and recommended inducing defections of Soviet and East European officials abroad. The committee also recommended greater use of technical means to collect intelligence.

The Rockefeller Commission

On 22 December 1974, the *New York Times* published an article by Seymour Hersh that accused the CIA of violating its charter by spying on Americans in the United States. Additional media coverage followed with new stories of CIA's unlawful activities. Congress made plans to investigate these charges and President Gerald Ford also decided to appoint a commission to look into the allegations.

On 4 January 1975, the President signed an executive order creating the Commission on CIA Activities, referred to as the Rockefeller Commission, named after its chairman, Vice President Nelson Rockefeller. The President tasked the commission to determine if the CIA exceeded its statutory authority and if existing safeguards were adequate to preclude CIA from engaging in activities outside its authority. During the next five months, the Commission investigated the charges and found that CIA indeed conducted illegal and improper activities and made 30 recommendations to prevent future abuses.

The Commission delivered its report to the President on 6 June 1975. On 11 June, the President released the report to the public. In the report, the Commission said that previous presidents requested, either directly or indirectly, that the CIA conduct some of the activities. The Commission did not recommend any changes in the law governing the CIA but recommended that the law be clarified and that a greater stress had to be made on external oversight and internal controls.

The report covered in some detail 11 "significant areas of investigation." They were:

CIA's intercepted mail operation between 1952 and 1973.

The activities of the Special Operations Group in the Counterintelligence Staff that from August 1967 to March 1972 ran Operation Chaos.

The five instances, from 1959 to 1972, CIA conducted wiretaps or physical surveillance of American newsmen.

Domestic operations of the Directorate of Operations.

The program of illegal drug testing from the late 1940s until 1967.

Turning over in 1971 of highly classified information to President Nixon, which, unknown to the CIA, was to serve Nixon's own personal ends.

CIA's relationships with other federal, state, and local agencies.

Domestic investigations by the Office of Security.

The unlawful holding of a Soviet defector for three years in solitary confinement.

Keeping indices and files on US persons.

Allegations concerning the assassination of President John F. Kennedy.

Select Committee To Study Government Operations With Respect to Intelligence Activities

On 27 January 1975, the US Senate voted to establish the Select Committee to Study Government Operations With Respect to Intelligence Activities with Senator Frank Church from Idaho as its chairman. Known as the Church Committee, the Senate assigned the committee with the task of determining:

If the CIA, FBI, or any of the 58 other US law enforcement and intelligence agencies conducted "illegal, improper or unethical activities.

If existing laws governing intelligence and law enforcement operations were adequate.

If present congressional oversight of the agencies was satisfactory.

The extent to which overt and covert intelligence activities in the United States and abroad were necessary.

The Senate gave the committee until 1 September 1975 to complete its investigation but the committee failed to meet the deadline. The committee released its final report on 23 and 26 August 1976. The committee first met in secret on 9 April 1975 and continued to meet secretly until 16 September when it began public hearings and issued reports on CIA activities.

The secret meetings concentrated on CIA's assassination schemes against foreign leaders. The Rockefeller Commission, with President Ford's approval, examined this question but did not complete its inquiry because time ran out. The Church Committee asked for the information gathered by the Commission and then proceeded to conduct its own investigation. The Committee published its report in November 1975, despite a last minute request by President Ford not to do so.

The public hearings started in September with the discovery by CIA that the Agency failed to destroy some deadly shellfish toxins as previously ordered by President Nixon. In late September the Committee focused on the FBI's and NSA's domestic intelligence collections and operations. During this phase of the hearing, the CIA's Counterintelligence Staff's mail opening operation, codenamed HTLINGUAL, surfaced.

In October, the Committee held closed hearings on covert action operations. Because the hearings continued to drag on, there were pressures on the Committee to complete its business. The White House wanted to announce its reorganization of the intelligence community but was delaying it while the Committee still met. The parallel House of Representative's investigation into the same subject area also compelled the Committee to soon end its review. Adding to the sense that any further prolong hearing was becoming futile was the lost of interest by the American public and Senator's Church's own presidential ambitions.

The House Select Committee on Intelligence

The House of Representatives was late getting started in its own investigation into the domestic intelligence scene and the role of the White House. Democratic Representative from Michigan, Lucien Nedzi, headed the House probe. One member of Congress, Michael Harrington (D-MA) chastised the committee for failing to move rapidly to investigate the CIA. He introduced a bill in Congress to create a new committee on intelligence. Harrington also wanted to chair the new committee but CIA and several supportive members of the House fought the bill because they did not want to see Harrington in such a position as he had earlier leaked classified House testimony to the press.

Nedzi also fought against the bill. He informed his colleagues that he would chair any House investigation of the CIA. On 6 January 1975, he restated his position that any investigation of the alleged abuses by the CIA was his subcommittee's prerogative. In addition, Nedzi worked behind the scenes to keep Harrington off any investigative committee.

On 19 February, the House voted 286 to 120, almost along party lines, to establish the House Select Committee on Intelligence and named Nedzi its chairman. Nedzi lost his battle to keep Harrington off the committee when House Speaker Carl Albert named him as a member.

For the next several weeks, Nedzi accomplished nothing but the appointment of a security director for the committee. His delay in getting started angered several representatives who wanted to push the investigation quickly. Harrington again led the charge. They accused Nedzi of neglecting to act although he knew for more than one year of CIA assassination planning and illegal domestic activities.

On 12 June, the DCI, William Colby, arrived on Capital Hill to testify in front of the committee. Upon his arrival he discovered there was no meeting because Nedzi had just resigned his chairmanship. The Speaker of the House, Carl Albert had placed the question of Nedzi's chairmanship on hold as pressure mounted from the Harrington-led group and the boycott by the Republican members of the committee.

On 17 July the House abolished Nedzi's committee and established a new select committee. Otis Pike (D-New York) was named chairman. Although the committee's size increased from 10 to 13, Harrington was not named to the committee.

Under Pike's leadership, the Committee began its investigation using preconceived notions and looking for a fight. Instead of compromising with the White House on information it sought, the Committee issued subpoenas. This confrontational attitude led to acrimonious relations with both the White House and CIA. After Pike leaked sensitive intelligence to the press, the White House sought reassurance from the committee that there would be no further leaks. The committee agreed but on 19-20 December abandoned its commitment to protect sensitive intelligence by voting to unilaterally declassify and publish documents revealing sensitive US covert operations in Angola and Italy.

The assassination of CIA's Chief of Station in Athens, Greece on 23 December further strained the relationship between the committee and the White House. The President informed the committee that they had enough information to write their report without revealing any additional sources and methods.

The committee provided the CIA the first draft of its final report on 19 January 1976. The committee wanted an immediate review and concurrence. The next day, parts of the report appeared in *The New York Times*. Despite further efforts by the White House and the DCI to get the committee to postpone its rush to publish, the committee proceeded on its own self-imposed agenda. On 23 January, members of the committee voted 9 to 7 to release the report to the public.

On 28 January, the House of Representatives, in a rare move, killed the committee's report.

In the United States District Court For the District of Maryland

UNITED STATES OF AMERICA
v.
DAVID HENRY BARNETT

RULE 11 STATEMENT OF FACTS

This case comes before the Court on a one-count indictment charging David Henry Barnett with espionage, for selling sensitive American intelligence information to the Union of Soviet Socialist Republics.

The indictment charges Barnett with a violation of 18 U.S.C. Sec. 794. The charge carries a maximum penalty of life imprisonment.

Section 794(a) requires that the Government prove beyond a reasonable doubt that Barnett knowingly and willfully communicated information relating to the national defense to the Soviet Union and that he did so with intent to injure the United States or give advantage to the Soviet Union.

The Government will establish this offense by showing that in 1976 and 1977 in Vienna, Austria and Jakarta, Indonesia, David Henry Barnett, a former Central Intelligence Agency employee, communicated national defense information including information about a CIA operation known as HABRINK to agents of the Soviet Committee for State Security, the KGB.

An overview of the case to be detailed is as follows: Barnett was employed by the CIA in the late 1950s and 1960s as a contract employee and staff officer. His primary responsibility involved the conduct of clandestine intelligence operations, including operations designed to collect information on the Soviet Union. Because of his position, he was given clearances up to and including Top Secret as well as several special compartmented clearances and had access to sensitive classified information, particularly concerning the CIA's clandestine intelligence collection operations. During this period he was an undercover employee.

Barnett, however, decided in 1970 that his employment with the CIA was not sufficiently remunerative and left his employment to go into business on his own. After a few years, however, Barnett encountered significant financial difficulties in the business world and incurred substantial debts. To solve his financial difficulties, he approached the KGB in 1976 to sell them classified information that he had garnered as a CIA employee. Over the course of the next few years, Barnett received approximately $92,600 in exchange for telling the KGB about CIA operations with which he was familiar, and the identities of numerous foreign nationals who at personal risk cooperated with the CIA by providing information of value to our nation's security. In addition, he furnished the true identities of CIA covert employees, and the identities of persons in the employ of the Soviet Union who had been targeted by the CIA for possible recruitment. He also agreed to seek re-employment in the intelligence field at the behest of the Soviet Union to collect further national defense information.

Among the items relating to the national defense that Barnett sold the Russians was a description of a covert operation known as HABRINK, a CIA effort that procured substantial technical information concerning Soviet weaponry. It is that operation which is specified in this indictment. The operation took place in a foreign country without that country's knowledge.

Information, other than HABRINK, that Barnett sold would have formed the basis for additional counts had the case gone to trial, and his communication of still other information would have been the subject of testimony as other acts evidencing intent. Because the Government can adequately establish the factual basis for a plea without extensive reference to these leads, the Government will submit to Court and counsel, under a protective order, an in camera sentencing memorandum detailing these items, so that the Court will be fully informed for sentencing. The defendant claims that he did not transmit certain classified information to the Soviets. The details of that claim will also be submitted to the Court in camera by his counsel.

With respect to the value of information Barnett sold, the Government does not take the position that the KGB paid $92,600 solely for the value of the information passed by Barnett. Undoubtedly, the KGB was motivated to pay this amount not only for the information obtained but also in anticipation of Barnett's becoming re-employed in the U.S. intelligence community, or with Congressional or White House oversight committees, a re-employment that would have been of great value to the KGB.

David Henry Barnett

The Government's proof of intent would rest principally on four items: First, Barnett's monetary motivation; second, the range of information Barnett sold—he passed a significant portion of his knowledge to the Soviet Union without regard to its significance to our national defense; third, his own intelligence training and background that should have made him fully aware of the significance of the information he sold; and fourth, his clandestine manner of communicating with the KGB.

The Government's proof includes a lengthy confession given by Barnett to the FBI during the course of twelve interviews over an eighteen day period in March and April 1980. The Government would also offer independent evidence establishing the trustworthiness of and corroborating the confession and expert testimony regarding the national defense character of the information passed.

With respect to proof of venue, it should be noted that 18 U.S.C. Section 3238 provides that if, as here, the offense is committed out of the jurisdiction of a particular State or District, the indictment may be brought in the district of the defendant's last known residence; in this case, Maryland.

If this case were to proceed to trial, the Government would provide as follows:

The defendant was employed by the CIA as a contract employee from November 1958 through May 1960 when his contract expired. He was rehired as a contract employee in June 1961 and remained in that capacity until March 1963 when he became a staff officer of the CIA. He remained in that position until January 1970. He was again employed as a contract employee from January 1979 to March 1980.

From March 1963 until December 1965, he served as an intelligence officer in a covert capacity in a foreign country. He then returned to CIA Headquarters where he stayed until November 1967.

In November 1967, he was sent to another foreign country where he was Chief of Base, a position he held until he left the CIA in January 1970 to enter private business for family reasons and to increase his income. As Barnett later admitted, and the FBI has corroborated, after Barnett left the CIA in 1970, he business ventures proved unsuccessful and as a consequence, he became substantially indebted.

During the fall of 1972, Barnett, together with his family, established residence in Indonesia for the purpose of working in private industry and starting a number of businesses. By 1976, however, Barnett's financial situation had become quite precarious. The Government would introduce the testimony of Lee Lok-Khoen and Jacob Vendra Syahrail, two employees of P.T. Trifoods, an Indonesian seafood processing corporation managed by Barnett in the mid-1970's. They would testify that Barnett was authorized to and did in fact take advances at will from this corporation, in excess of $100,000, for his own personal use or for the use of C.V. Kemiri Gading, one of his then personally owned companies.

Records kept by the two employees in the ordinary course of P.T. Trifoods business reflect that during 1977, after Barnett had been paid money by the KGB, the defendant repaid approximately $100,000 in advances that he or his personal companies had received. The Government is able to link $12,500 of the repayment to moneys paid Barnett by the KGB.

Barnett admits that in mid–1976, however, while he was still in the midst of these financial difficulties, he typed an unsigned note that he intended to give the Soviets when the occasion arose, setting forth his difficult financial situation, his CIA experience and training, and his willingness to sell his services to the KGB for approximately $70,000.

In the fall of 1976, Barnett went to the home of a Soviet Cultural Attaché in Jakarta, Indonesia with whom Barnett had met frequently while he had been with the Agency. As CIA records show, there had been extensive earlier contacts between this Soviet and Barnett during Barnett's tenure with the CIA—at a time when the CIA had been assessing the possibility of recruiting this Soviet. Moreover, CIA employees would testify that this Cultural Attaché is quite accessible to American diplomatic personnel and has had frequent contact with them. Barnett gave the Soviet Attaché the note and offered to provide information relating to his former CIA employment. The Soviet requested Barnett to return the following Sunday.

That Sunday at the Soviet's residence, Barnett was introduced to someone identified only as Dmitriy. During this meeting, Barnett outlined his financial situation, requested $70,000 and for the first time discussed CIA operations he had learned of while operating covertly for the CIA.

On a subsequent Sunday in late November 1976, Barnett again met with Dmitriy inside the Soviet compound in Jakarta and communicated more information that he had acquired during his CIA employment. For this, Dmitriy paid Barnett $25,000 in United States currency in $100, $50, and $20 bills and arranged a meeting between the defendant and the KGB in Vienna, Austria on February 27-28, 1977.

Once more before February 25, 1977, Barnett met with Dmitriy and was given an additional $3,000 for the travel expenses he would incur during his upcoming trip to Vienna.

On Friday, February 25, 1977, Barnett left Jakarta for Brussels, Belgium, where he took a commuter train to Antwerp. On the 26th he had a brief unrelated meeting in Antwerp with a business associate. After the meeting, Barnett took the train first to Brussels and then to Vienna. He arrived in Vienna on the morning of the 27th. During his trip from Antwerp to Vienna, Barnett's passport was not stamped.

Shortly after he arrived in Vienna, Barnett was met at the contact point by a man who exchanged the prearranged verbal code, known as a parole, and identified himself as Pavel. Barnett was then taken to a KGB safehouse on the outskirts of Vienna.

Barnett's meeting with the KGB in Vienna lasted eight to ten hours. He related his knowledge of national defense information to Pavel, and two other KGB agents identified only as Mike and Aleksey. Barnett also convinced the three that he could get a job in the United States which would give him access to classified information. The KGB told Barnett that their primary targets were the CIA, the Intelligence and Research Bureau at the State Department (INR) and the Defense Intelligence Agency (DIA). At the conclusion of the meeting, the defendant was paid $15,000.

On Tuesday, March 1, Barnett left Vienna by train for Brussels. Again, his passport was not stamped. After another meeting with his business associate in Antwerp, Barnett flew back to Jakarta from Brussels, arriving there on March 3 or 4, 1977.

In late March 1977, Barnett met again with Dmitriy in Jakarta. Dmitriy paid him an additional $30,000 and again instructed him to obtain a job in the United States with access to national defense information. As business records show, Barnett repaid P.T. Trifoods, the company he managed, $5,000 on March 29 and $7,500 on March 31. Barnett admits this money came from the KGB.

Barnett also admits that before flying to the United States on June 16, 1977, he met with Dmitriy and was paid $3,000 for expenses for his upcoming trip to the United States to search for a job.

Barnett was in the United States from June 16 to July 3. While in Washington, Barnett called David Kenny, a State Department employee, about obtaining a job on the White House Intelligence Oversight Board. Barnett subsequently reported his effort to Dmitriy.

Approximately July 10, 1977, after his return to Indonesia, Barnett met with Dmitriy and Pavel. Barnett falsely told Pavel that during his last trip to Washington, he had met with a senior CIA official. However, Barnett mentioned that he was afraid to become reemployed with the CIA because he felt that he could not pass the polygraph examination required for staff employment with the Agency. Nonetheless, the KGB instructed him to obtain a position in the CIA, INR or DIA. Barnett was given $3,000 for travel expenses to return to Washington for another attempt to find a job.

On August 11, 1977, Barnett traveled to Washington, D.C. While in Washington, he met with Joseph Dennin, General Counsel of the White House Intelligence Oversight Board, and with William Miller, Staff Director, Senate Select Committee on Intelligence, and applied for jobs on those committees. The Government would call Mr. Dennin and Mr. Miller to confirm that Barnett unsuccessfully sought employment in those sensitive organizations.

Barnett returned to Jakarta on September 5, 1977. On Wednesday following his arrival, he met with Dmitriy. During this meeting, Barnett claims he falsely told Dmitriy that he had obtained a job on the "White

House Oversight Committee." He also met with Dmitriy sometime between late September and early November and received approximately $3,600 for packing and moving expenses back to the United States.

Barnett's travels to meet with members of the KGB during 1977 are corroborated in large part by an examination of the defendant's passports. Robert G. Lockard, Chief of the Forensic Document Laboratory in the Immigration and Naturalization Service, would testify that Barnett's passports show either an entry or exit on February 25, 1977 from Indonesia and another entry into that country on March 4, 1977, the dates coinciding accurately with the dates on which he admits he traveled from that country to Vienna and returned.

The absence of European entries reflected on his passport also corroborates Barnett's statements that no European passport entries had been made during his trip to Vienna. The passport also reflects two departures from and entries into Indonesia during the summer of 1977, the time when Barnett states that he traveled to the United States to obtain a job with access to intelligence information.

In November 1977, in Jakarta, Barnett was introduced by Dmitriy to a Soviet who identified himself only as Igor. Igor claimed to be stationed in America and explained that he would be working with Barnett in Washington. Igor also mentioned that he lived in a Virginia apartment complex owned by Shannon and Luchs. During that meeting, Igor gave Barnett the location of two public telephones near an Exxon station at 7336 Little River Turnpike, Annandale, Virginia, which were to be used for contact purposes at 3:00 p.m. on the last Saturday of every month.

Igor also arranged a dead drop site near Lock 11 along the C&O Canal. Barnett was instructed to place a piece of red tape on the side of a nearby telephone booth to signal the KGB that the drop site had been serviced. Neither the two phone booths in Annandale nor the dead drop site, however, was ever used by Barnett.

During one of the FBI interviews, Barnett was shown a photograph of Vladimir V. Popov, a former Third Secretary at the Soviet Embassy, Washington, D.C., and identified Igor as Popov. The Government would offer further evidence establishing that the "Igor" Barnett met in November was, in fact, Vladimir V. Popov, former Third Secretary at the Soviet Embassy, Washington, D.C. As noted, Igor mentioned that he lived in a Shannon and Luchs apartment in northern Virginia in 1977. A copy of the lease for apartment 830, 1200 South Courthouse Road, Arlington, Virginia, an apartment managed by Shannon & Luchs, shows the lessee to be Vladimir Popov. To corroborate the fact that Popov met with the defendant in Jakarta in November 1977, the Government would also introduce two I-94 forms from the Immigration and Naturalization Service showing that Popov departed Dulles Airport on November 22, 1977 for Moscow and returned on December 6, 1977. Testimony from the CIA would establish that Barnett would not have had any reason to know Popov or his whereabouts from Barnett's employment with the CIA.

On April 21, 1978, Barnett returned to the United States and established residence in Bethesda, Maryland, where he resides today. Between April 1978, and January 1979, Barnett sought jobs both in the intelligence field and in the private sector. Barnett, for example, admits meeting with Richard Anderson, an employee of the House Permanent Select Committee on Intelligence (HPSCI), in Washington to discuss employment possibilities.

Mr. Richard D. Anderson, Jr., Professional Staff Member on the House Permanent Select Committee on Intelligence (HPSCI), would testify that Barnett called him in September 1978, regarding the possibility of obtaining a position on the HPSCI. The two met on September 27, 1978, and Barnett told Anderson that he "was well fixed for funds" and that his interest in the committee was a matter of personal interest rather than salary. Mr. Anderson, however, informed Barnett that there were no vacancies on the committee. Anderson would also testify that had Barnett obtained a position on the committee, he probably would have had access to information relating to CIA covert operations. Despite this job-seeking effort, Barnett did not contact the KGB during this time.

In January 1979, Barnett was rehired by the CIA as a contract employee to train CIA employees in operational tradecraft, on a part-time basis at a wage of $200 a day. This position, which did not provide him with access to CIA records and files, did provide him with access to some classified information. Because Barnett was still in dire financial straits, he traveled on March 31 from Maryland back to Indonesia. On his arrival, he went to the residence of the Soviet Attaché in Jakarta to re-establish contacts with the KGB. He told the Soviet that if the KGB wanted to contact him, they should meet him at 9:00 p.m. at the same place where Barnett first met Dmitriy. When no one appeared, Barnett returned to the attaché's residence where he met for an hour with another Soviet identified to Barnett only as Bob. According to Barnett, he told Bob of his experiences since his return to the United States and provided a general description of his new position with the CIA.

Two days later, Barnett says that he met with Bob again. During this session, Bob reiterated Igor's instructions given during the November 1977, meeting, by urging the defendant to use the emergency contact plan on the last Saturday of each month if a need arose. Barnett, however, told Bob that he did not feel that Igor's contact plan was secure and provided the number to a public telephone located at the Bethesda Medical Building on Wisconsin Avenue, Bethesda, Maryland. He later discovered, however, that he had transposed the first two numbers to this telephone number. As a result, Barnett was never able to use the emergency contact procedure. Arrangements were also made with Bob for another meeting with the KGB at the same location for June 30, 1979. At the conclusion of the meeting, Bob paid Barnett $4,000 for expenses. Barnett returned to the United States on April 14, 1979.

On June 30, 1979, as instructed by the KGB, Barnett traveled back to Jakarta, and met with another Soviet, identified only as George, in the Soviet compound. During this meeting, which lasted approximately two days, Barnett described his new position with the CIA, offered to photograph the training manual and to use the deaddrop site to transfer the information, and gave the correct number to the public telephone booth at the Bethesda Medical Building. The Government is not taking the position that these manuals had substantial significance.

George, the Soviet contact, told Barnett that if no contact were established on the last Saturday of each month, Barnett should go to the Annandale Bowling Alley on the following Sunday to meet Igor. George stressed that Barnett should attempt to obtain a permanent position with the CIA which would give him access to more sensitive information. Barnett, however, was reluctant, feeling that he would not pass the polygraph that the CIA gives to staff employees. Barnett arranged to meet again with the KGB in late November. George paid Barnett $3,000 for expenses.

As Barnett details in his confession, on the last Saturdays in September and October at 3:00 p.m., Barnett received calls at the Bethesda Medical Building from an individual whose voice he later positively identified to the FBI as belonging to Igor, the Soviet that he had met in November 1977. The exchanges between Barnett and Igor were brief, no classified information was exchanged, and the defendant told Igor that he was still looking for another job. During the October telephone contact, Barnett specified other days in December 1979, on which he could meet with the KGB should he not be able to meet at the scheduled date in November.

In his interviews with the FBI, Barnett admits traveling again to meet with the KGB in late November 1979 in Jakarta. On the day of his arrival, Barnett was picked up and taken to the Soviet compound where he met George. During the meeting, which lasted into the night and the following day, George told Barnett his present position with the CIA was of no interest to the KGB and urged Barnett to pursue actively a full time position with the CIA. The defendant also provided George with a number of a second public telephone which was to be used for future contacts and which was located at the corner of Wilson Lane and Cordell Avenue in Bethesda, Maryland.

George gave Barnett $3,000 for travel and expenses, for Barnett to meet with him in Vienna on April 25, 1980. The two were to meet at 64 Taberstrausse in front of the KOCH Radio Shop in the second district. To corroborate this fact, Leonard H. Ralston, FBI Legal Attaché, from Berne would testify that he traveled to 64 Taberstrausse in the second district. At that address is the KOCH Radio Shop.

The Government would further corroborate Barnett's dealings with the KGB in 1979, as they have been described here. His passport accurately reflects his 1979 journeys to Indonesia. Also, an American Express card slip shows his purchase of an airline ticket on November

31, 1979 from Dupont International Travel, Inc., a Washington, D.C. travel agency for one of these trips. Moreover, records of Barnett's bank account at Riggs National Bank shows a $2,600 cash deposit on December 5, 1979, only a few days after the KGB paid him $3,000 in late November.

When Barnett returned to the United States, he was called by Igor on the first Saturday in January at the public telephone in the Bethesda Medical Building. Barnett told Igor that he was still trying to obtain a full-time job with the CIA. Barnett also suggested that he be called at the second telephone number.

The defendant also states that he was again contacted by Igor at 3:00 p.m. on the first and third Saturdays in February. The first telephone call was received at the public telephone at the corner of Cordell Avenue and Wilson Lane; the second at the Bethesda Medical Building. According to Barnett, he told Igor in the first call that he would traveling abroad in connection with his CIA employment and gave his itinerary during the second call. During the second conversation, the defendant gave Igor the number of a telephone at the Bradley Shopping Center on Arlington Road in Bethesda which was to be used for the contact on the following Saturday, March 1, 1980.

On March 1, Barnett received a telephone call at the Bradley shopping Center from Igor. During the conversation, Igor told the defendant that the KGB would not meet with Barnett during Barnett's upcoming overseas trip for the CIA, but would meet with him in Europe as previously scheduled.

In his confession, Barnett also told the FBI that on April 5, 1980, Igor was to call him at the Bradley Shopping Center at 3:00 p.m. If the call was not completed at 3:00, Igor was to call again at 4:00 p.m. By April 5, 1980, of course, Barnett had been confronted by the FBI. However, Special Agent Michael Waguespack would testify that he went to the phone booth described on the fifth of April and heard it ring three different times between 2:58 p.m. and 3:03 p.m.

In fairness to Barnett, it should be noted that after his initial sale of information in 1976 and 1977, he did not do everything that the KGB wished. He claims that he failed to communicate with the KGB as directed between April 1978, and January 1979, in the United States. Barnett told the FBI he was fearful of detection if he operated in this country. He also failed to regain staff officer status with CIA and thus had not attained access to the type of intelligence information that the KGB primarily sought or would consider of major importance. It could well be that these failures could have caused some skepticism in the KGB about his bona fides and, retrospectively, the value of the information that he had previously sold.

In March 1980, Barnett was interviewed by the FBI about his suspected espionage activities involving the KGB, and confessed his involvement as has been described here. Special Agents Michael J. Waguespack, R. Dion Rankin, Charles T. McComas and Paul K. Minor of the FBI would testify that they interviewed the defendant either singly or in pairs on twelve occasions during the period between March 18 and April 4, 1980. They would also present testimony and FBI Advice of Rights forms establishing that Barnett's statements were given voluntarily and that his rights under the <u>Miranda</u> decision and its progeny were not violated.

Barnett was first interviewed by the FBI on the morning of March 18, 1980 at his place of work. Special Agents Waguespack and Rankin would testify that they told Barnett that they wished to speak with him regarding his involvement with the KGB and that they knew he had been in contact with the KGB. At no time did the agents indicate that the defendant was under arrest or that his freedom of movement had been deprived in any way. In fact, Barnett was told that the FBI's function was only to investigate the facts and that the Attorney General would decide whether a prosecution was warranted. After a short discussion with the agents, Barnett began his confession. He was read his rights and signed the standard waiver form prior to his drafting and signing a written statement outlining briefly his activities with the representatives of the Soviet Union. He left his office for home after the interview. Prior to each of the subsequent eleven interviews which all occurred in motel rooms, Barnett was read his <u>Miranda</u> rights and signed a standard waiver form.

Barnett admitted that during his meeting with Dmitriy in the Fall of 1976 and early 1977 and his meeting with the KGB in Vienna, he communicated information relating to (1) the details of the CIA's collection of personality data on seven Soviet consular officials in the late 1960s, where Barnett had been Chief of Base; (2) the identities of thirty covert CIA employees as well as personality data on some of them; and (3) numerous CIA operations with which the defendant was familiar from his employment with the CIA, including HABRINK, the operation that forms the basis for the indictment. Again, the details and significance of the remaining information will be discussed in an in camera sentencing memorandum.

Barnett's access to the classified information which he confessed to having communicated to the Soviets can be proved through both CIA documents and the testimony of Barnett's former colleagues within the CIA. Personnel records maintained at the CIA indicate that Barnett had security clearances while he was employed by the CIA and had access to the information which he confessed to having communicated to the KGB. In particular, the CIA has documents, authored by Barnett during his employment, detailing his involvement in studies of the recruitment potential of the seven Soviets and his participation in some of those operations, the details of which he confessed to having transmitted. Moreover, testimony from one of the defendant's former colleagues within the CIA would establish that Barnett worked closely on the HABRINK operation, which is the subject matter of the indictment.

HABRINK was a clandestine intelligence collection operation designed to obtain information on Soviet weaponry. The information was collected by utilizing a net of agents with access to information concerning sophisticated weaponry which the Soviets were, during that period, supplying to a foreign nation, whose relationships, however, at the time were very close to the Soviet Union. Recently, however, that country has enjoyed good relations with the United States.

In the early 1960's that country had begun to receive current conventional Soviet army, navy and air force weapons systems. The purpose of the HABRINK operation was to secure, without the knowledge of the government of that country or the Soviet Union, the weaponry itself or parts thereof and classified Soviet documents providing the operational characteristics and technical description of these weapons systems. The operation was very successful and provided a large volume of Soviet documentary data and a limited amount of Soviet hardware on a large variety of weapons systems deployed in that country.

The operation collected detailed information concerning the Soviet SA-2 surface-to-air missile system, the Russian Styx naval cruise missile, and the Soviet W-class submarine. The information regarding that weaponry has never been available from any other source. Information pertaining to the KOMAR-class guided missile patrol boats, the RIGA-class destroyer, the SVERDLOV-class cruiser, the TU-16 (BADGER) bomber aircraft an the associated KENNEL air-to-surface missile systems as well as other weaponry information of lesser significance was also obtained.

One example of the importance of this operation to the national defense of this country during the late 60's and early 70's was the securing by HABRINK of the guidance system from an SA-2, familiarly known as a SAM missile. That missile had been used very effectively by the North Vietnamese to shoot down many U.S. aircraft. As a result of HABRINK's obtaining the guidance system, it became possible to determine the radio frequencies used to direct the missile and jam those frequencies, resulting in the saving of the lives of many bomber crews engaged in action in Vietnam. This example is cited to demonstrate the utility of the HABRINK operation and its relationship to the national defense. The Government, however, is not attempting to argue that Barnett's disclosure of HABRINK in 1976 had a deleterious impact on the United States with respect to that particular item of Soviet weaponry and American countermeasures.

As indicated above, this operation was run without the knowledge and consent of this foreign nation, has not been publicly disclosed and—so far as can be determined—was not known by the Soviet Union until Barnett revealed it to the KGB.

The operation was run by the CIA through an individual assigned to cryptonym HABRINK/1 who had wide access to the information sought and utilized an extensive network of sub-agents who supplied him with the information desired by the United States. This agent is alive, though no longer active as a source.

Barnett told the KGB HABRINK/1's true name. The CIA has confirmed that the name Barnett admits giving to the KGB is, in fact, the agent's true name. As a result of Barnett's actions, HABRINK/1 is exposed to retribution if the Soviets find it to their advantage.

Clearly, Barnett knew, when he told the Soviets about HABRINK, that the operation related to the national defense and that there was a continued need to keep the operation secret. When Barnett was asked by the FBI in March 1980, if there was one event or operation that was big and that stood out in his mind, he promptly identified HABRINK. Barnett's acknowledgment of HABRINK's importance is further evidence of his intent.

Barnett also admits telling the Soviets that HABRINK obtained Soviet training manuals and hardware from all over the country and from air force, army and navy bases and received $300,000 for the material, being paid approximately $175 per manual. He claims not to have any recollection of which manuals were secured. However, experts from the CIA would testify that Barnett's disclosures sufficed to alert the KGB that the compromise to the United States of the weapons supplied to that country was total. Barnett also admits that the KGB was interested in knowing where the manuals came from, when the operation started, when it ended, which agents and subagents were still in the country and the circumstances behind the termination of the operation. Finally, he accurately revealed to the KGB that HABRINK had secured the antenna guidance system and gyroscope from the Soviet Styx missile, but the KGB for its own reasons, falsely denied that the missiles supplied had that equipment. In short, Barnett fully and accurately described his knowledge of the HABRINK operation.

Barnett claims, however, that when he disclosed information about HABRINK at the Vienna meeting, Dmitriy did not question him extensively concerning the operation. Barnett told the KGB that he had been afraid to tell them about this operation for fear they would be angered by his involvement. Dmitriy, according to Barnett, shrugged the operation off, claiming that the KGB assumed that when hardware gets out of their hands, it is compromised. According to Barnett, Dmitriy said that "the Americans got the information so they are happy, and the Soviets got the benefits from supplying the hardware in the first place, so everybody's happy."

To the contrary, expert testimony from the Government would establish that the decision to supply sophisticated weaponry to this nation involved was the subject of an intense internal debate within the Soviet Union. The Soviet faction opposing the supplying of these weapons argued this supplying would lead to the compromise of detailed Soviet defense information. The decision to supply the weapons was eventually made on purely political grounds. In short, the Government's position would be that while debriefing Barnett, the KGB gave short shrift to HABRINK because it did not want to acquaint him with the value of the HABRINK operation or the value to them of learning that such an operation had taken place.

At the height of its productivity in the late 1960s, HABRINK was considered by the CIA as one of its highest priority operations. It should be noted that Barnett's compromise of HABRINK in 1976 and 1977 was far less damaging then if it had been compromised while it was ongoing in the late 1960's or soon after its termination in 1969. Nonetheless, Barnett's disclosure of HABRINK to the KGB in 1976 and 1977 has military, operational and diplomatic implications for the United States.

To address the military significance of Barnett having revealed the HABRINK operation, the Government would call among its expert witnesses Rear Admiral John L. Butts of the Office of Naval Intelligence, Mr. Jerry Sydow, Program Director of the Navy Foreign Material Program, and Mr. Jay Dewing, Intelligence Officer, Physical Sciences, of the Central Intelligence Agency, as well as other military and technical witnesses. Collectively, they would testify that among the items received by the HABRINK operation were the components of a Styx cruise missile, including the seeker and autopilot, and its wiring manuals and associated diagrams. The Styx missile is a patrol boat missile that has the demonstrated capacity of sinking a destroyer at a range of at least 15 miles. Although developed in the later 1950s and in the early 1960s, the Soviet Union still supplies the Styx to a number of third-world countries. The Soviet Union makes extensive use of updated and modified versions of the Styx in their own fleet. Unlike most military programs of the

United States that develop new weapons systems to replace old ones, the Soviet Union frequently updates its arsenal by piecemeal modification of existing weapons. For this reason, information about the Styx missile has continuing use to the United States, even after the Soviet Union replaced it with successor weapons.

The United States benefited from HABRINK's obtaining the Styx and related information. As a result of this information, the military refined and developed offensive and defensive countermeasures, including electronic, design, tactical and other countermeasures to a high degree of effectiveness. According to these experts, some of these countermeasures can be expected to be useful in combating the successors of the Styx. Moreover, the HABRINK information enabled the United States to identify as ineffective other costly countermeasures previously underway and to cease those efforts.

Barnett's disclosure to the KGB that the United States got the guidance system for the Styx missile signals the Soviets that the United States has likely developed effective electronic counter measures just as it did with the SA-2 missile. As a result of Barnett's actions, the Soviet Union may make design changes on its successor missiles intended to nullify the electronic and other countermeasures that the United States has developed. This could make the United States more vulnerable to these weapons systems.

Limitations on resources require the Soviet Union, like the United States, to select priorities in weapons development. Government experts would say, confirmation of HABRINK's success in obtaining the Styx would make the Soviet Union's choices more informed, since it would now definitely know that the United States possessed this information and would have developed countermeasures.

In other words, should the United States become engaged in an armed confrontation with the Soviet Union or it allies who have Styx missiles or their successors, Barnett's transmission of the information concerning HABRINK's success may allow the Soviet Union to use those missiles more effectively against our ships where, before Barnett's revelation, those ships might well have been able to take appropriate countermeasures.

HABRINK obtained the battery discharge curves for the Soviet W-class submarines. The W-class submarines are diesel submarines, still in use because they have certain advantages over nuclear powered submarines in certain tactical situations. The Soviet Union uses these submarines in its own arsenal. Indeed, it has continued manufacturing diesel submarines that use either the same or similar batteries. The battery discharge curves could not then have been predicted without this information.

The United States learned from the discharge curves how long Soviet submarines may stay submerged. That period of time was longer than the United States had previously thought and that information was disseminated, under classification, within the American fleet.

In an engagement, a Soviet submarine commander might well make some tactical decisions if he believed the United States did not know how long he could stay submerged. The United States, in fact, having that knowledge would not be misled by those decisions and therefore could have a distinct tactical advantage in such an engagement.

However, as a result of Barnett's revelations, Soviet submarine commanders have undoubtedly been notified that the United States is aware of the discharge curves and will thus forego engaging in strategies that would erroneously attempt to take advantage of our supposed ignorance. In short, Barnett's compromise of the information garnered by HABRINK eliminates the tactical advantage the information originally provided.

An expert witness from the Soviet East Europe Division of the Directorate of Operations of the CIA would testify concerning the operational damage done by Barnett's transmission of this information. According to this expert, Barnett's compromise is the first definite indication to the Soviets that the CIA has been able to obtain successfully technical information in such quantity and detail regarding Soviet military equipment supplied by the Soviets to foreign countries by means of clandestine intelligence operations conducted without the knowledge or cooperation of the government of the country involved. As I mentioned above, the Soviets made the decision to supply this foreign nation with the sophisticated weapons for political reasons and over the objections of those factions within the Soviet Union who felt that such action could compromise sensitive weaponry information. This expert would testify that, in his judgment, the Soviets, having learned through Barnett's revelations that CIA has such capability, may now further restrict the dissemination of technical information when it exports equipment to nonaligned nations. If this were to happen, continued access to such information by clandestine means would become exceedingly difficult.

Barnett's revelation of this information to the Soviet Union has serious implication for our diplomatic relationship with this country. The country where this operation was carried out has definite geopolitical significance to the United States and which is one with whom this country currently enjoys a good relationship. It is also a country with natural resources important to the United States. The Soviets could use this information to the disadvantage of the United States' relationships with the country involved. If the Soviets were to reveal to the government of the country involved that CIA had conducted clandestine intelligence collection operations, without that country's government's knowledge, the country involved may well take steps to monitor and restrict essential activities there.

The Soviet Union has the option of attempting to use its knowledge of this operation to damage our relationship with that country, by conveying to that country's government the fact of, the nature of, and the extent of the HABRINK operation. The Soviets can withhold disclosure until conditions prevail that maximize the impact of disclosure.

If the Soviet Union chooses to reveal this information, diplomatic relations may be soured for some period of time and the CIA's capability in that country could be substantially curtailed. The Government, had the case gone to trial, would have called as experts persons from the Department of State and the Central Intelligence Agency to describe the use that the Soviet Union could make to damage our diplomatic relations with that country.

Mr. Barnett's awareness that the Soviet Union could make use of the HABRINK operation to the damage of the United States' diplomatic interests is demonstrated by Barnett's admission to the FBI that during the HABRINK operation the CIA was concerned about political implications, should the operation be exposed. Thus, Barnett must have been aware that he was giving the Soviet Union an opportunity to do exactly what had been a concern of the United States all along, and that was to avoid the diplomatic damage that would flow from its exposure.

Your honor, if the case were to go trial, the Government would present ample proof—beyond a reasonable doubt—that David Henry Barnett communicated information to the Soviet Union relating to the national defense of the United States with intent and reason to believe that the information would aid the Soviet Union and injure the United States.

Operation Lemonaid

"Operation Lemonaid" took place in New York in the late 1970s and utilized a Navy Lt. Cdr. Art Lindberg as a double agent.

Lt. Cmdr. Lindberg was approached by the Naval Investigative Service (NIS) (now the Naval Criminal Investigative Service) in April 1977. After some meetings and interviews, NIS Special Agent Terry Tate asked Lt. Cmdr. Lindberg if he would be willing to consider performing a sensitive assignment for his country. Lt. Cmdr. Lindberg accepted the assignment and was later introduced to FBI agents from New York, who assisted in briefing him on the operation.

In August 1977, Lt. Cmdr. Lindberg took a trip on the Soviet cruise ship *Kazakhstan*. Upon the ship's return to New York, Lt. Cmdr. Lindberg passed a note to one of the Soviet officers containing an offer to sell

Rudolph Chernyayev

Valdik Enger

information. He was later contacted by telephone by a Soviet agent.

During subsequent telephone calls, Lt. Cmdr. Lindberg was given contact instructions on the type of information to get and the locations of drop sites where that information could be left and payment money could be found. NIS and FBI agents kept the drop zones under surveillance and later identified the Soviet agents.

On 20 May 1978, Lt. Cmdr Lindberg was asked to make another drop. This time, however, FBI agents moved into the drop zone and arrested three Soviets.

One of them was Vladimir Petrovich Zinyakin, who was a member of the Soviet Mission to the United Nations. Zinyakin, who had diplomatic immunity, was expelled from the United States. The other two, Rudolph Petrovich Chernyayev and Valdik Aleksandrovich Enger, did not have diplomatic immunity. They were subsequently convicted of espionage and later traded for five Soviet dissidents in a dramatic swap at Kennedy Airport in New York.

Other Spies

Joseph B. Attardi

Staff Sergeant Joseph B. Attardi joined the Army in 1963. He copied Top Secret plans from the document section of an Army unit in Heidelberg, West Germany, and gave an acquaintance a copy of a four-page document dealing with defense measures in Europe.

Based on information provided by the acquaintance, Attardi was arrested on 11 April 1969. On 27 August 1969, the 29-year-old staff sergeant was sentenced to three years in prison on charges of providing NATO defense plans to a fellow soldier.

Herbert W. Boeckenhaupt

On 25 May 1967, Air Force sergeant, Herbert W. Boeckenhaupt, was found guilty of conspiring to commit espionage on behalf of the Soviet Union. Federal District Court Judge Lewis, commenting on the fact that the evidence showed "this young man did give away some secrets involving the national security of his adopted country," sentenced the 24-year-old Boeckenhaupt on 7 June 1967 to serve 30 years on charges of conspiring to deliver US defense secrets to Russian agents.

Boeckenhaupt was born on 26 November 1942, in Mannheim, Germany. He first came to the United States with his mother in 1948. He lived with his stepfather and mother in Wisconsin, achieving derivative citizenship through his mother. He enlisted in the Air Force on 29 July 1960. He was assigned to Sidi Slimane AFB, Morocco, from May 1962, to July 1963; served at Andrews AFB from July 1963 through March 1964; and performed duties at the Pentagon Communications Command Center from April 1964 to August 1965. As a radio operator, he required and was granted a Secret clearance in October 1961, and a Top Secret clearance was issued on 20 March 1964.

To his associates, he was considered difficult to understand, arrogant, a "loner," yet capable at times of an outstanding performance of his duties. He never seemed completely satisfied with his assignments and kept requesting changes of duty hours and immediate supervisors. He enjoyed discussing politics and German culture and had revealed that his father had been a former Nazi during WWII. Although professing to be broke most of the time, he nevertheless seemed to possess money when needed and gained the reputation as a "big spender." He mentioned an inheritance, variously described to range from $1,500 to $10,000. He alleged that his stepfather was a Reynolds, and he spoke often

Herbert W. Boeckenhaupt, Air Force Sergeant found guilty of conspiring to commit espionage on behalf of the Soviet Union.

of the Reynolds Tobacco Company, implying a family tie but in truth there was no relationship. To substantiate his apparent affluence, perhaps, he made vague reference on occasions to holding choice electronic company stocks; yet when pressed for details he declined to reveal any amounts or sources.

Boeckenhaupt was arrested by the USAF, taken into custody, and questioned on 24 October 1966. He was initially charged with failure to report contact with a foreign government agent. He consented to a search of his residence, and certain items found therein were confiscated as material evidence. Finally, on 31 October 1966, he was formally charged with committing an espionage conspiracy. His coconspirator was the former Soviet Embassy official, Aleksey R. Malinin. Malinin was declared "persona non grata" by the State Department and ordered to leave the country within three days, thus becoming the twenty-first Soviet diplomat to be expelled for engaging in espionage activities since the end of W.W.II.

Boeckenhaupt told the FBI that sometime in June 1963, while working part-time in a Washington, DC, clothing store, he was approached by an individual who expressed interest in purchasing a raincoat. Boeckenhaupt claimed the latter introduced himself as "Robert," subsequently identified as Malinin, an Assistant Commercial Counselor at the Soviet Embassy. He addressed Boeckenhaupt by name and made reference to having knowledge of his natural father and suggested "they get together after work." "Robert" and Boeckenhaupt later drove to a park near Exit 13 (Virginia Route 193) off the Capital Beltway where Malinin allegedly talked about his father, who resided in Germany. According to Boeckenhaupt, Malinin implied that although the father's health was good at the present time, it might not continue to be that way. (Boeckenhaupt entered the plea during his trial that he had the definite impression that if he did not cooperate with the Russian agent, harm might befall his father!) During a subsequent meeting in July 1965, Malinin was informed of Boeckenhaupt's forthcoming transfer to the Air Force Crypto school at Lackland AFB, Texas. He requested that he be kept informed "about the type of thing" Boeckenhaupt would be studying.

Boeckenhaupt admitted to the FBI that he and Malinin met on some five or more occasions, during which he was given various instructions and espionage equipment. Included in the spy equipment and instructions were pressure sensitive paper for secret writing; a London address; hollowed-out flashlight battery containing a 35-mm slide on which were listed certain "deaddrop" locations, meeting dates and signal points within the Washington, DC, metropolitan area, and code words to interpret communications from the Soviets.

At the time of his trail, he admitted using the above furnished London address to communicate three times with Malinin, twice while assigned at Lackland AFB and again the following spring when he learned of his pending transfer to March AFB, California. Shortly after Boeckenhaupt's arrest, an Anglo-American businessman, Cecil Mulvena, was arrested in London on charges of obtaining an illegal passport. At the time, sources stated this was the same individual to whom Boeckenhaupt forwarded his secret communications in London. Mulvena later pleaded guilty to violating the British Official Secrets Act and was sentenced to a prison term.

The sensitized pressure paper, taken from his home at the time of his arrest, was analyzed by the FBI and several incriminating secret messages were lifted. One stated, "I'm going to California. I will meet you at the agreed place on April 20th. It is very important." Another read, "I need more paper to write with. Send some money. I can give you plans for power equipment plus copies of our code cards and I can start on these right away. There is a lot of copying…but photos are still possible if the camera is very, very small…I could use a lot of money to pay some bills and work on the car. Thank you, 'H.'" In still another revealed message, he asked his handler, "Are you interested in an airplane called 'Stepmother'?"…with an added reference to "Airborne Command Post." Other exhibits obtained by the FBI from his apartment included a letter signed "David" and postmarked September 4, 1966, from Alexandria, Virginia. This was revealed to be from Malinin and contained the code word "Barbara," which according to notations on the 35mm slide meant "Change the London address."

In 1963, Boeckenhaupt had picked up his first Avanti sports car, paying $5,000 cash for it. Prior to his transfer from Washington, DC, to Texas, he traded in the 1963

Avanti on a 1964 Avanti ($6,000), made a partial cash payment, and mortgaged the balance. Upon completing his schooling in Texas, he rented a U-Haul trailer, attached it to the Avanti and returned to Washington, DC, where he was married. The newlyweds then proceeded back across the country to his next assignment at March AFB, California. However, the U-Haul proved to be too much strain on the Avanti's gear system, and upon arrival Boeckenhaupt discovered he had burned out his engine. He then passed another secret message to his handler stating, "My car engine was ruined on the trip out. Ought to get a new one put in. Will you send me the money to fix it plus some money for added costs. The car is very important and must be fixed right away so I can keep driving. I must take it to Los Angeles to fix it."

Although Boeckenhaupt's initial defense was based on the plea that he was the victim of a hostage threat, evidence indicates that his real motives were money and fast cars, both of which disappeared in short order. Further, he was fully aware that his father resided in West Germany, an area under Western allied protection, where any alleged hostage threat would be remote. Following his arrest, his wife had to sell the heavily mortgaged Avanti in order to obtain funds to return home to her family in Washington, DC. Further, Boeckenhaupt was unable to hire his own defense lawyer, and both the Justice Department and the USAF appointed legal counsel to represent him after he was declared a pauper. His defense further attempted to prove that Boeckenhaupt had never passed any secrets to the Russians.

On 1 March 1968, the Fourth US Circuit Court of Appeals rejected these allegations and affirmed the earlier conviction. The court noted in its decision that Boeckenhaupt had been under surveillance by the FBI and the Air Force after he was seen with a Soviet Embassy official in northern Virginia in 1966...that the Air Force had probable cause to arrest Boeckenhaupt and had no obligation to take him before a US Commissioner before espionage charges were filed.

Harold N. Borger

Harold N. Borger worked in West Germany as a civilian in an import-export business in Nuremberg. During a visit to East Berlin, Borger allegedly was led to believe that a woman he met was a Jew working for Israeli intelligence. The woman convinced Borger to attempt to collect classified information from US servicemen in West Germany. His espionage attempts were identified by a defector, and Borger was arrested by West German authorities in March 1961. The US Air Force Reserve Major later admitted that he had fabricated the details of his recruitment. The West German authorities accused Borger of attempting to provide to East German intelligence an Army manual dealing with nuclear warfare, information on new protective masks, and details on plans for evacuating US dependents in the event of conflict.

The court determined that Borger, the first American to be tried in West Germany on espionage charges, was a very intelligent man who passionately served East Germany based on his admiration for Communism. Although the court did not establish that Borger actually passed military information to the East Germans, it stated that he greatly endangered American and West German defenses. In May 1962, the 42-year-old Borger was sentenced to two years and six months in prison with time spent in pretrial confinement subtracted from his sentence.

Christopher J. Boyce and Andrew Dalton Lee

Christopher J. Boyce, an employee of TRW Inc., a California-based Defense contractor, and his friend Andrew Dalton Lee, were arrested in January 1977, for selling classified information to the Soviets.

Over a period of several months, Boyce, employed in a vaulted communications center, removed classified code material. He gave this material to Lee who passed the information to the Soviets in Mexico City. The scheme, which netted the pair $70,000, was discovered only after Lee's arrest by the Mexico City security police as he attempted to deliver classified material at the Soviet embassy.

A search of the material Lee had in his possession revealed film strips marked Top Secret. These strips were turned over to American officials. Under questioning by Mexican security police and FBI representatives, Lee implicated Boyce. The FBI arrested Boyce on 16 January 1977 in California.

The pair are reported to have seriously compromised the Ryolite surveillance satellite system developed at

TRW. Lee was sentenced to life in prison, Boyce received 40 years.

In 1980, Boyce escaped from prison and spent 19 months as a fugitive. Following Boyce's second apprehension, his sentenced was increased by 28 years.

John William Butenko

John William Butenko was born in New Jersey of Soviet parents. Butenko's father was a naturalized US citizen. The younger Butenko had served for almost one year in the US Navy during World War II until his discharge for a medical disability. The medical disability was later described as being "emotional instability." He was an honors student at, and graduate of, Rutgers University.

In 1963, the 38-year-old bachelor worked as an electronics engineer at American Telephone and Telegraph Corporation, for a salary of $14,700 per year. He was described as quiet and nondescript, as well as a heavy drinker who liked high-stake card games. Butenko lived with and cared for his widowed father and was considered a dutiful son. He was also described as being given to violence and a defender of homosexuals.

On 29 October 1963, the FBI arrested Butenko on charges of conspiracy to commit espionage. Also arrested was Igor A. Ivanov, a chauffeur for Amtorg, a Soviet trading agency. The pair was apprehended in a parking lot in Englewood, New Jersey after Butenko had transferred a briefcase to the Soviet. In the briefcase were documents and data relating to a US Air Force contract dealing with a worldwide electronic control system for the Strategic Air command.

The complaint issued against Butenko charged that conspiratorial meetings were held, specifically on 21 April, 28 May, and 24 September 1963 with Ivanov and two other Soviets: Yuri A. Romashin and Vladimir I. Olenev, employees of the Soviet Mission. Also named in the complaint was Gleb A. Pavlov, a Soviet Mission attaché.

In his defense, Butenko testified that he had received a letter from George Lesnikov, whom he believed to be associated with the United Nations, with an offer to discuss his relatives in Russia. They met once and conferred once on the telephone for this purpose between April and October 1963. It was later determined that Lesnikov was Gleb A. Pavlov. Under cross-examination, Butenko admitted that he had visited the Soviet Embassy in Washington, DC, in 1953 or 1954 to ask about his relatives in the Soviet Union. Papers submitted for his security clearance indicated he had no known relatives living outside the United States.

On 2 December 1964, Butenko was found guilty of conspiring to commit espionage and of failing to register as an agent of a foreign government. The Russian chauffeur, Igor A. Ivanov, was found guilty on one count of conspiracy to commit espionage. Two weeks later, Butenko was sentenced to 30 years in a Federal penitentiary, while Ivanov received a prison term of 20 years.

Butenko was paroled in April 1974 after serving 10 years of his 30-year prison sentence.

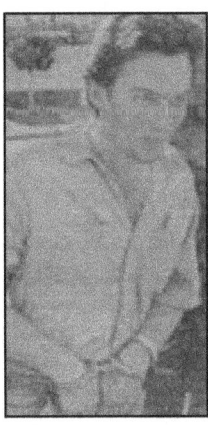

Christopher J. Boyce, arrested in 1977 for selling classified information to the Soviets.

Andrew Dalton Lee, arrested by the Mexico Security Police as he attempted to deliver classified material to the Soviet Embassy.

Morris and Lona Cohen
a.k.a. Peter and Helen Kroger

Morris and Lona Cohen were native-born Americans who had been absent from their native land since 1950. Morris Cohen fought in the Abraham Lincoln Brigade during the Spanish Civil War in 1937, and his involvement with Soviet intelligence may have begun at that time. He returned to the United States on a false passport obtained from unknown sources.

Following the Second World War, Cohen went through Teachers College at Columbia University and later obtained a teaching job with the Curtiss Summer Day High School in New York City. Cohen had been teaching only a short while when, in mid–1950, Julius and Ethel Rosenberg and David Greenglass were arrested on charges of having engaged in espionage on behalf of the Soviets. Coincident with these arrests, Cohen resigned his teaching position and suddenly left the United States with his wife. Four years later—as the "Krogers"— they appeared in England.

Sometime later, the names of the Cohens once again came to the attention of US authorities. This time it was in connection with the arrest of a key Soviet agent —Col. Rudolf Ivanovich Abel—in New York City in June 1957. Among Abel's effects were photographs of Morris and Lona Cohen. Subsequent investigation further indicated the involvement of the Cohens in Abel's espionage work in the United States.

Thus, the names of the Cohens were linked with two major Soviet espionage efforts against the United States

Peter and Helen Kroger, Alias Lona and Morris Cohen, who were arrested in London with GRU illegal Konon Molody, Alias Gordon Lonsdale.

In tracing the movement of the Cohens, it appears that they resided for a short period in Canada in 1950, but then remained in obscurity until they applied in Vienna in the spring 1954, for New Zealand passports in the name of Kroger.

The Kroger identities are completely false, and the supporting documents for the passport application were supplied by the KGB. Upon receipt of the New Zealand passports, the Krogers traveled through Europe and the Far East before returning to settle in the United Kingdom in the spring of 1955, arriving only two months after Gordon Lonsdale, a Soviet illegal.

Peter Kroger set himself up as a dealer in antiquarian books and a specialist in Americana. Although he originally opened an office in London, he gave it up in 1958 and conducted his business by mail from his home in Ruislip, which had been selected for its isolated location and corresponding security.

The Cohens were arrested by British intelligence in 1961 and sentenced to 20 years in prison. The couple was exchanged in 1969 for British teacher Gerald Brooke, arrested in Moscow by the KGB for distributing anti-Communist propaganda. Lona Cohen died in 1992. Morris Cohen died 23 June 1995 at the age of 84 in a Moscow hospital.

Raymond George DeChamplain

On 5 June 1971, it was learned that Viktor Vladimir Mizan, a Third Secretary at the Soviet Embassy, and a known KGB officer in Bangkok, Thailand, was in contact with a US serviceman for the purpose of committing espionage. The US serviceman had been previously in contact with Yuri Markin (another known KGB officer who had recently returned to the Soviet Union) and was in contact with Mizan to provide him with information Markin had requested. Mizan was observed meeting with an individual who was later identified as MSgt Raymond George DeChamplain, a direct descendant of Samuel DeChamplain, the famous French explorer and founder of the Canadian province of Quebec.

Surveillance coverage was initiated on DeChamplain, and a second contact with the Soviets was observed, which DeChamplain had failed to report as required by USAF Regulations. On 2 July, 1971, AFOSI detected

DeChamplain removing a Top Secret document from his duty section, along with three Secret and several unclassified documents. Later, DeChamplain was observed taking a taxi from his residence, heading for downtown Bangkok and was apprehended as he was about to deliver the package of classified material to Mizan. At the time of his arrest, DeChamplain was 40 years old and had over 20 years in the Air Force.

DeChamplain was born 6 August, 1931 in Hartford, Connecticut. He was raised in a white, lower middle-class neighborhood, along with his three sisters and two brothers. Without any civilian prospects, he enlisted in the USAF in 1951 at the age of 19, after dropping out of the University of Maryland. His assignments included tours in Japan, France, Germany, and Italy before being assigned to Thailand in November 1967. He was granted a Top Secret clearance in 1966.

He worked as an administrative specialist, and at the time of his apprehension he was assigned as the Non-Commissioned Officer in Charge (NCOIC) of J-1 (personnel) at the Joint US Military Advisory Group (JUSMAG) in Bangkok. He was inattentive, incompetent, and frequently absent from his duty station. He was disliked by his coworkers and often derided, although he tried hard to make friends by freely spending his money – even on those who mistreated him. Although not popular with his peers, he quickly acquired a good grasp of the Thai language (not an easy feat) and made several close friends within the Thai community. Although many coworkers knew of DeChamplain's homosexual relationships with young Thais, they did not report his activities to his commander. His coworkers and others who knew him described him as being "weak, vulnerable to persuasion, moody and a carouser." He enjoyed frequenting the many bars in Bangkok where military personnel spent their off-duty time, with his favorite bar being the Sea Hag, a known homosexual hangout.

While in Thailand, DeChamplain married a Thai woman; however, after a few weeks she moved out. There is strong evidence which indicates that he was having a homosexual relationship with his brother-in-law, a musician who, after his sister moved out, continued to live with DeChamplain.

DeChamplain did not appear to have any strong political convictions; however, he was chronically in debt. His landlady said he seemed poor to her compared with other GIs. He usually asked her if he could put off paying the rent for a few days. Later he admitted to investigators that he had always been bad at managing his money and frequently took out one loan to pay off another, resulting in debt exceeding $13,000.

DeChamplain alleged that he had been blackmailed by the Soviets into committing espionage, but this seems unlikely. Although a Soviet intelligence spotter seems to have introduced him to Markin at a party, Markin did not follow up on the introduction. It was DeChamplain who, four years later, approached the Soviets, and the evidence indicates he volunteered to betray his country in an effort to obtain money to repay some of his debts.

DeChamplain had approximately 10 personal meetings with the KGB in Thailand before being apprehended, he was provided with a codename, verbal recognition codes (parole), and safety signals. Because he was bringing out such large quantities of documents, the KGB feared that their operation would be detected and they would lose a valuable volunteer that was successfully being exploited. In order to overcome this problem, the KGB prepared to train him in the use of a camera, so that he could photograph the documents instead of removing them from the office. In July 1971, he was scheduled to receive training on the Minox camera and other methods of clandestine communication and operation, but was arrested beforehand.

Raymond George DeChamplain

Although he had only received $3,800, he had been promised additional payments ranging from between $10,000 and $25,000. He was also to be paid a retainer of $400 per month. During the few days of his treason, his duty performance improved tremendously. He suddenly volunteered for extra work, taking over duties processing and distributing all Top Secret documents. All he had to do was to briefly delay in-processing the documents and he could then remove them to show the KGB, or copy them if necessary. The destruction of Top Secret documents requires that a witness be present, but DeChamplain falsified the necessary signatures. He came to work early and volunteered to stay late to keep up the office work, but in reality, this provided him with uninterrupted access to the office copy machine. When questioned by investigators about which documents he passed to the KGB, he nonchalantly pointed to all the safes in the room indicating that he passed everything to which he had access.

In November 1971, DeChamplain was convicted at a court-martial and sentenced to 15 years confinement, reduction to the lowest grade, and forfeiture of all pay and allowances. This sentence was later reduced to seven years confinement at hard labor.

Nelson Cornelious Drummond

Yeoman First Class Nelson Cornelious Drummond, US Navy, first came to the attention of the Office of Naval Intelligence (ONI) in June 1962, when the FBI provided information that a particular classified document concerning guided missile systems, dated May 1961, has been compromised to the Soviets in New York. The document in question was traced to the Mobile Electronics Technical Unit No. 8 (METU-8) at Naval Base, Newport, Rhode Island. Drummond was responsible for receipt, filing, and disposition of classified material at METU-8. An investigation mounted by ONI and the FBI discovered that Drummond was removing documents from METU, he had a Minox camera, made frequent trips to New York City, and deposited large sums of cash in local banks upon his return from New York.

Drummond was arrested by the FBI on 19 September 1962, outside a diner in Larchmont, New York. He was in the company of two known GRU officers, Evgeni M. Prokhorov and Ivan Y. Vyrodov, and eight classified documents were recovered. During interrogation, Drummond confessed to have been recruited, while stationed in London, England, by the Soviets in 1958, to commit espionage. He said he was approached one day in London while on his way home from work. The man making the approach indicated that he was aware that Drummond had financial problems and gave him 250 British pounds (about $700). The individual asked for Drummond's Navy identification card and a receipt for the money.

At a later meeting, this individual told Drummond that he was a "colonel in the Russian Army." The Soviet also told Drummond that he knew Drummond was about to be investigated by the Office of Naval Intelligence and that the investigation had nothing to do with his relationship with the Soviet so he was not to be concerned. The Soviets were also aware of Drummond's transfer back to the United States before Drummond informed them of the transfer. Over the next five years, he had regular contact with Soviet handlers and provided sensitive communications information as well as other classified material.

Drummond had had financial problems and had been living well beyond his means. At the time of his arrest, he owned two automobiles and had recently purchased a bar and grill near his base in Newport, Rhode Island. At the base, Drummond was an administrative assistant to the officer-in-charge of a mobile electronics technical unit where he had access to classified defense information. A damage assessment estimated it would cost the United States 200 million dollars to recover from damage done by Drummond's activities.

Drummond was indicted for attemtping to obtain information relating to naval weapons systems, maintenance data relating to submarines, and electronic data. Drummond was suspected of having received a

Nelson Cornelious Drummond

total of $10,000 from the Soviets for his espionage activity. He was found guilty of espionage in Federal Court, and on 15 August 1963 he was sentenced to life imprisonment.

George John Gessner

George John Gessner, with an IQ of 142, enlisted in the US Air Force at age 17 and was assigned to Patrick Air Force Base, Florida. After serving his four-year listment, Gessner was discharged from the Air Force and worked on Titian and Atlas missile projects as a civilian.

In 1960, Gessner enlisted in the US Army and worked on nuclear weapons projects. Ten months later, on 7 December 1960, Private First Class Gessner deserted his post at Fort Bliss, Texas. He was subsequently apprehended and was given a one-year sentence for desertion. While still in custody for desertion, he was charged with passing classified information to Soviet Intelligence agents in Mexico City, Mexico.

The espionage indictment charged that Gessner provided information to the Soviets on the internal construction and firing systems of the Mark VII nuclear weapon as well as information on elements of design of the 280-millimeter cannon and 8-inch weapon. During the trial, witnesses stated that Gessner admitted passing classified information in December 1960, and January 1961. Gessner was quoted as saying, "I knew those weapons were going to be used on little children… just let all those things build up inside me."

Gessner had traveled to Mexico City and made contact with the Soviet Embassy. In meetings with two alleged Soviet colonels in two different public parks, he provided the information to the Soviets and received $200 in payment for the information. The Soviets instructed him to use the money to travel to Cuba. Gessner, lacking a passport, was unable to go to Cuba. He received another $800 from the Soviets and drifted to Panama City where he was picked up by Panamanian police for failure to have registration papers in his possession. The police turned Gessner over to US authorities who arrested him on desertion charges.

Initially Gessner would not admit to US authorities his reason for being in Mexico and Panama. Eventually he confessed his willful compromise of US classified information following a visit to the post chaplain. In 1962, Gessner underwent a month-long mental examination, and the US District Judge hearing the case ruled that he was mentally incapable of standing trial on the charges in the indictment. A psychiatrist stated that Gessner suffered from "delusions and hallucinations" and was "unable to assist his attorney" in preparing a defense.

In April 1964, Gessner was declared mentally competent to stand trial. The trial lasted only two weeks and on 9 June 1964 he was convicted of the charges of providing classified information to the Soviets. In a footnote to this case, the Federal Government dropped the espionage charges against Gessner on 9 March, 1966 and immediately set him free. The Federal Court of Appeals found that Gessner confessed only following a lengthy interrogation and under extreme pressure from the Army chaplain.

Oliver Everett Grunden

In September 1973, an AFOSI source reported that Airman First Class Oliver Grunden, a 20-year-old airman assigned to the 100th Organizational Maintenance Squadron, Davis Monthan Air Force Base, Arizona, was attempting to sell classified information concerning the U-2 aircraft. AFOSI's source informed Grunden that she might be able to introduce him to someone who would be willing to purchase the classified information.

Grunden provided the source with a tape recording containing classified information pertaining to U-2 tail numbers, performance data, overflight information, and Olympic Fire Missions. Later, Grunden met with two AFOSI special agents posing as Soviet intelligence officers and was paid $950 for two sheets of paper, which contained classified information concerning the U-2 aircraft. Grunden additionally offered to take the two "Soviet" intelligence officers on a tour of the base and flight line to observe the U-2 aircraft. Grunden was confronted and apprehended by AFOSI.

Grunden was born on July 27, 1953, in Mitchell, Indiana and raised in a white, middle-class family. After graduating from high school, he entered the United States Air Force in 1973 at age 19 and after basic and technical training was assigned as a maintenance specialist for the U-2. Grunden had been granted a Secret security clearance.

At the time of his attempted espionage, he was married, had one child, and his wife was pregnant with their second child; however, the couple had separated and his wife was living with her parents. He was described as being weak, naïve, immature, and a carouser. His motivation for committing espionage was strictly financial gain.

In March 1974, Grunden was tried by court-martial and convicted, receiving a five-year prison sentence, reduction in grade to Airman Basic, forfeiture of all pay and allowances in excess of $300 a month, and a dishonorable discharge. The US Court of Military Appeals overturned his conviction based on prosecution procedural errors and, in March 1977, Grunden was re-tried and again found guilty, with his sentence reduced to time already served.

Robert Lee Johnson

US Army Sergeant Robert Lee Johnson was a clerk in West Berlin when, in early 1953, he traveled to East Berlin with the intention of defecting to the Soviets. Johnson was disgruntled due to having been passed over for promotion and to other grievances he harbored against the US Army. While in East Berlin, two KGB agents convinced Johnson that he could do a better job of "getting even" with the US Army by remaining on active duty in West Berlin and acting as an agent for Soviet intelligence.

Several months after agreeing to work with the KGB, Johnson married his German mistress. Both Johnsons subsequently received intelligence training by the Soviets. Shortly thereafter Johnson recruited a friend, US Army Sergeant James Allen Mintkenbaugh, to work with him in his espionage endeavors. The Soviets were at first upset with Johnson for having recruited someone without proper approval. They soon learned however, that Mintkenbaugh was a homosexual, and this facet of his personality was of interest to Soviet intelligence. One of the first assignments the Soviets gave Mintkenbaugh was to spot other homosexuals in the American community in West Berlin. The Soviets regarded homosexuality as an exploitable trait since the homosexual frequently felt he was an outcast in his society and often felt compelled to retaliate against those who shunned him due to his homosexuality.

Johnson was voluntarily discharged from the service in 1956, but reenlisted in 1957 at the urging of Mintkenbaugh who had been tasked by the Soviets to reactivate Johnson. Mintkenbaugh had also been discharged from the service in 1956 and continued to work for the Soviets in various capacities. For a time, Mintkenbaugh was a real estate agent in northern Virginia.

Subsequent to his reenlistment, Johnson was moderately successful in providing classified defense information to his Soviet handlers. It was not until his assignments in France, however, that Johnson's espionage resulted in highly damaging compromises. In 1962, Johnson was assigned to the Armed Forces Courier Center at Orly Air Field near Paris, France. While on this assignment, he gained unauthorized access to sensitive US defense information contained in sealed pouches en route to various US Commands within Europe.

By use of sophisticated and finely honed surreptitious entry techniques and careful KGB control, Johnson was able to access sealed pouches, which were stored overnight in a triple-locked vault. Johnson, whenever on duty alone, would remove the pouches and deliver them to the Soviets and return to his post. The Soviets entered the pouches, copied the material, and resealed them so that no one knew that they had been opened. Johnson would then retrieve the pouches from the Soviets and replace them in the vault. It was not discovered until Johnson's arrest that the pouches had been opened and the information compromised.

Robert Lee Johnson

James Allen Mintkenbaugh

Johnson received approximately $300 per month for his espionage activities, plus bonuses totaling at least $2,800. Mrs. Johnson's constantly deteriorating mental condition caused her to confess to authorities that she, her husband, and Mintkenbaugh had been engaged in espionage. At the time of his arrest, the then 43-year-old Johnson was a courier at the Pentagon. He had been reduced to the rank of corporal in December 1964 for absence without authorized leave. Both Johnson and Mintkenbaugh admitted to their involvement in espionage for pay.

On 30 July 1965, both men were sentenced to 25 years each in prison, having pleaded guilty on 7 June to lesser charges of conspiracy to obtain defense secrets and acting as Soviet agents. Johnson's prison sentence came to an unexpected end on 18 May 1972 when he was stabbed to death in his prison cell in the Lewisburg Federal Penitentiary by his son, who had visited him that day.

William Kampiles

In August 1978, the FBI arrested William Kampiles, a lower echelon CIA employee from March to November 1977, on charges he stole a Top Secret technical manual on an intelligence surveillance system and later sold it to a Soviet intelligence officer in Athens, Greece for $3,000.

Kampiles had resigned from the CIA after being told he was not qualified to work as a field agent. He then proceeded to Greece where he contacted Soviet representatives. His detection followed receipt of a letter by a CIA employee from Kampiles in which he mentioned frequent meetings with a Soviet official in Athens.

Wiliam Kampiles

On returning to the United States, Kampiles was contacted by FBI special agents and confessed to an act of espionage. Kampiles maintained that his objective was to become a double agent for the CIA.

He was sentenced on 22 December 1978 to 40 years in prison.

Joseph Patrick Kauffman

Joseph Patrick Kauffman graduated from the University of Wyoming and enlisted in the Army Air Corps in 1942. He left the military service for several years following World War II, but returned to active duty during the Korean conflict. Beginning in September 1960, the then Captain Kauffman began collaboration with an East German intelligence officer, Guenter Maennel. Kauffman was on a holiday trip to Berlin en route from his assignment in Greenland to his new assignment in California when he first met Maennel. He had been picked up by East German Police for questioning and was held for three days in East Berlin for interrogation. This detention was followed by subsequent meetings in West Berlin with East German intelligence officers during which time Kauffman agreed to cooperate with the East Germans.

Following his arrival at his new assignment at Castle Air Force Base in California, the 43-year-old bachelor was revealed by Maennel, who had defected to the West, as having been an agent of East German intelligence. Kauffman was returned to the European Headquarters of the US Air Force in December 1961 for a preliminary hearing being specifically accused of turning over information to Maennel on 29 September 1960.

Charges against Kauffman included providing information to East Germany on US Air Force installations in Greenland and Japan and providing information on fellow officers from those two locations, including their identities, descriptions, shortcomings, and weaknesses. Maennel testified that he had introduced Kauffman to Soviet security agents and that Kauffman had signed a two-page statement in German and English that listed the information he provided to the Soviets.

On 18 April 1962, Kauffman was found guilty of the charges of passing US defense information to the East Germans. He was sentenced to 20 years' imprisonment at hard labor, dismissal from the service, and forfeiture of all pay and allowances. In a reversal of the earlier conviction and sentencing, on 13 December 1963, the US Court of Military Appeals dismissed an espionage conspiracy charge while affirming his conviction for failing to report attempts by enemy agents to recruit him. Kauffman had already served almost two years of a 10-year sentence. His original sentence of 20 years had been reduced by a review board. Successful appeals had been based principally on procedural matters connected with the US Air Force investigation.

Erich Englehardt and Karl Heinz Kiefer

During late July 1960, the West German police arrested Erich Englehardt and with him a woman, Lore Poehlmann, for espionage on behalf of the Soviet Military Intelligence (GRU). Investigations and confessions of the principals uncovered extensive GRU activity against US Army and Air Force installations since 1955.

Early in 1955, Englehardt recruited his half brother Erich Heinz Kiefer, to work for the GRU. Both men were used to collect order of battle data on US Army and Air force installations in West Germany, especially in the vicinity of Wiesbaden and Kaiserslautern. Between 1957 and 1959, both men were inactive, but during 1959 their intelligence activity increased. Kiefer made a number of trips to Erfurt to meet his case officer, Lt. Col. Petr Sokolov. He was furnished cipher pads and secret writing materials for purposes of communication. Kiefer's intelligence targets included US military maneuvers, atomic cannon, and missiles. He was ordered to set up a dead drop for the passage of bulky materials. Emergency communications, not used in this operation, involved a radio in the Soviet Military Liaison Mission in West Germany. Kiefer's dead drop was to be served by personnel of this Mission.

During 1959, Kiefer was introduced to Lore Poehlmann, who thereafter served as his support agent and courier. Surveillance of Poehlmann as she made her rounds uncovered Kiefer and scores of other agents. Several of their agents worked also for the East Germany state security (MfS) and even for the Poles. A large and complicated network was uncovered.

Kurt Kuehn

On 17 October 1960, Kurt Kuehn, section Chief of the Technical Publications Branch of the Adjutant General's Division, Northern Area Command, was arrested by West German security forces for acts of espionage. The exposure and arrest of Kuehn resulted from information supplied by an agent of the East German intelligence service, who had in his possession when arrested filmed copies of US Army documents, which were subsequently traced back directly to Kuehn.

After his arrest, Kuehn confessed that he had been recruited by the East Germany intelligence service during a visit to his mother in Gera, Germany, in 1957. He had transmitted official materials and information to his East German employers in East Berlin since that time. Kuehn received his instructions from East Berlin, either directly through radio communications or via a courier. He supplied his East Berlin employers with information in the same manner. In his position, he had access to various US Army Regulations and documents, some of which were classified. He furnished the East German intelligence officers in East Berlin, at their request, a copy of the index of official documents filed at the United States Technical Army Regulations Administration. Using this index, the MsF was then able to tell Kuehn, which documents were to be photographed and transmitted to East Berlin. Kuehn also made written and verbal reports regarding his coworkers in the US office, details regarding office operations, and information regarding agencies and military installations in the Frankfurt area.

Kuehn's East German intelligence superiors provided him with cryptographic material for the decoding of radio messages and trained him in its use. He was also provided with concealment devices (hollowed-out book ends) for the transmittal of material. These espionage materials were found in Kuehn's apartment after his arrest.

Joseph Werner Leben

On 11 July 1961, Joseph Werner Leben, a 29-year-old German immigrant, was arrested in Sao Paulo by Brazilian police for engaging in espionage activities on behalf of the Germany Democratic Republic. A search of his apartment revealed a large amount of correspondence to and from his East Germany superiors, codes and ciphers, chemically-treated stationary for use in secret writing, and photographic equipment. He confessed to being a spy and gave complete information about his intelligence career.

Leben said he was first brought to the attention of East German Intelligence at the 1956 Leipzig Fair by a West German Communist Party member. He was introduced to one Heinz Schwerdt, a Captain in the East German Intelligence Service, and later to Lt. Heinz Schmallfuss who was known to him as "Herr Hansen." Schmallfuss began a concentrated study of Leben aimed toward his eventual use as an agent, but at no time indicated that he himself was an intelligence officer. When Leben traveled to Brazil in May 1956, Schmallfuss corresponded with him, and finally offered to pay his expenses back to East Berlin for a visit. On this trip, Leben was recruited as an agent, assigned the cover name "ARMADO," and paid 6000 German Marks (approximately $1,500).

In December 1956, Leben again returned to Brazil at the direction of the East German Intelligence Service and commenced his intelligence activities against the Brazilian Government and United States interests there. By October 1958, Lt. Guenter Maennel of the East Germany Intelligence Service, had assumed control of Leben's case from East Berlin, and ordered Leben back to East Berlin for additional training.

Leben returned to Berlin and acquired a room in a West Berlin pension. He met his East German Intelligence Service superiors, however, in a private home located at Fontanastrasse 17A, in the East sector of the city. This address was frequently used by the East Germans for similar situations and the residents, Herr Otto Kilz and his wife, were in the employ of the East German Intelligence Service. At Fontanastrasse, Leben was instructed in secret writing using chemically treated stationary, microdots, and ciphers to be used in sending his reports to East Germany. Leben signed an agreement obligating himself to work actively against anti-Communist elements and US interests in Brazil. He was given a Praktika FX II camera to assist him in his work. For his past endeavors, Leben received 15,000 German Marks (approximately $3,750), a holding account in East Berlin amounting to US $75 per month, and was reimbursed for his operational expenses.

Upon the completion of his training subject was again dispatched to Sao Paulo where he obtained employment with a local firm composed mostly of Americans. He continued his espionage activity for the Communists until the time of his arrest.

Gary Lee Ledbetter

Gary Lee Ledbetter, Petty Officer Second Class, US Navy, was assigned as a ship fitter on the *Simon Lake* at the US submarine base, Holy Loch, Scotland. In April 1967 he was approached in a bar by two British civilians and asked to provide information. The 25-year-old Ledbetter subsequently passed a classified training booklet about the Polaris submarine piping systems to the two civilians. The British civilians involved with this case had been recruited by a former East German bartender named Peter Dorschel, who in turn, had been recruited by the Soviets. He was directed by the Soviets to settle near Holy Loch to spy on the base.

Ledbetter was court-martialed and on 26 August 1967 was sentenced to 6 months of imprisonment at hard labor, and was given a bad-conduct discharge. A British court sentenced Dorschel to 7 years in prison.

Lee Eugene Madsen

Lee Eugene Madsen was a 24-year-old Yeoman Third Class in the US Navy when assigned to the Strategic Warning Staff at the Pentagon in 1979. Madsen used his position at the Pentagon to obtain highly sensitive documents, including documents of the Drug Enforcement Agency (DEA) dealing with the worldwide movement of drugs and information on the location of DEA agents. He attempted to sell these documents to an individual who turned out to be an informer who told authorities of the offer to compromise classified defense documents.

An undercover agent of the FBI, along with the informer, set up a meeting with Madsen to receive the documents and pay Madsen $700 for the information. Madsen attended the meeting with 22 highly classified documents. He also offered to sell monthly narcotics intelligence reports for $10,000 a month. In addition to providing the documents to the undercover agent, Madsen brought the agent, under a false name, into the Pentagon and signed him into a restricted area.

On 14 August 1979, Madsen was arrested by the FBI when he turned over classified materials and accepted the $700 payment from the undercover agent. On 26 October 1979 he was sentenced to eight years in prison.

Edwin G. Moore II

Edwin Moore, a retired CIA employee, was arrested by the FBI in 1976 and charged with espionage after attempting to sell Soviet officials classified documents. A day earlier, an employee at a residence for Soviet personnel in Washington, DC had discovered a package on the grounds and turned it over to police, fearing it was a bomb.

The package was found to contain classified CIA documents and a note requesting that $3,000 be dropped at a specific location. The note offered more documents in exchange for $197,000. Moore was arrested after picking up what he thought to be payment at a drop site near his home.

A search of his residence yielded ten boxes of classified CIA documents. Moore retired from the CIA in 1973, and although financial gain was a strong motivational factor leading to espionage, it is known that he was disgruntled with his former employer due to lack of promotion.

Moore pleaded not guilty by reason of insanity, but was convicted and sentenced to 15 years in prison. He was granted parole in 1979.

Walter T. Perkins

Air Force MSgt Walter T. Perkins was the top-ranking noncommissioned officer in the Intelligence Division, Defense Weapons Center, Tyndall Air Force Base, Florida in 1971. His 19 years of service, beginning with his enlistment in December 1952, were spent in intelligence. His overseas assignments included Vietnam, Turkey, and multiple assignments in Japan.

Walter T. Perkins

On 21 October 1971, Perkins was apprehended at the Civil Air Terminal in Pensacola, Florida by AFOSI agents as he started to board a flight for Mexico City for a rendezvous with Soviet agents. In his briefcase, he carried one Air Force and four Defense Intelligence Agency (DIA) classified documents totaling over 600 pages. Also in his possession were operational instructions for meeting his Soviet intelligence contact in Mexico City, Mexico.

After being alerted by US authorities, the Mexican Federal Security Service detained Oleg A. Shevenko, a GRU officer working undercover at the Soviet embassy in Mexico City, who was waiting for Perkins at a prearranged meet location. He was later expelled from the country by Mexican authorities.

Charged with improper possession and use of documents dealing with national security, Perkins entered a plea of not guilty to all charges by reason of temporary insanity caused by acute alcoholism.

On 11 August 1972, Sergeant Perkins was convicted and sentenced to three years in prison. He also received a dishonorable discharge, reduction in rank to airman-basic, and a fine of more than 50 percent of the monthly pay he would receive while in prison.

Leonard Jenkins Safford and Ulysses L. Harris

On 25 August 1967, the Department of Defense announced the arrest of two US Army sergeants on charges of conspiring to deliver to unauthorized individuals information pertaining to the national defense. Two Soviet diplomats were named as conspirators and were declared *persona non grata*. Sergeant First Class Ulysses L. Harris, 38 years old, and Staff Sergeant Leonard Jenkins Safford, 31 years old, received a rollover camera from the Soviets. On two occasions, Sergeant Safford delivered documents to the diplomats. The Soviets involved were identified as Nikolai F. Popov, First Secretary, Soviet Embassy, Washington, DC, and Anatoloy T. Koreyev, a counselor of the Soviet Mission to the United Nations.

Sergeant Safford was court-martialed on 5 December 1967 and sentenced to 25 years of hard labor after he pleaded guilty to charges of espionage and larceny. In addition to his conspiracy, Safford had stolen a $24,076 government check. A veteran of 12 years of military service, Safford became involved in espionage for monetary reasons. He admitted to receiving $1,000 from Popov. Safford served as an administrative supervisor in the Army Strategic Communications Command, Suitland, Maryland, at the time of his espionage activity.

On 15 December 1967, Sergeant Harris, who had 15 years of military service, was sentenced to seven years hard labor. Testimony revealed that an "undercover agent" worked with Harris and Safford. Harris had been transferred to Korea only a short time before his arrest. Charges against Harris and Safford established February to August 1967 as the time during which the two were involved in a conspiracy to commit espionage.

Irvin C. Scarbeck

On 14 June 1961, the FBI arrested Irvin C. Scarbeck, a State Department foreign service officer, for passing classified information to Polish intelligence.

Scarbeck, 41 years old at the time of his arrest, had a good record when he arrived in Warsaw as a second secretary in December 1958. His German-born second wife and their three children accompanied him. He was in charge of travel arrangements, embassy property, and procuring and maintaining the living quarters for Americans assigned to the Embassy. He also had access to coded messages exchanged between the Embassy and the State Department.

In Warsaw, Scarbeck met a beautiful Polish girl, blonde and 22 years old. She told him that she had previously worked at the US Embassy and still had friends working there. They began to date although Scarbeck was married. They became intimate. Soon afterwards, Polish intelligence officers confronted Scarbeck with tape recordings and photographs. They threatened to expose his illicit relationship to the American embassy if he did not cooperate with them. He agreed rather than face exposure. US Government officials said he did not pass any military secrets to the Polish service, but acted more as a listening post for the Poles on policy matters.

Scarbeck joined the State Department in 1949 and became a foreign service officer in 1956. He received a meritorious service award in 1959 for his work on exchange student programs in San Francisco, California. Prior to his employment with State, he was in the US Army from 1942 to 1946 where he obtained the rank of staff sergeant. After leaving the military, he worked for a time for the West German Government.

In March 1961, Scarbeck was to transfer from Warsaw to Naples, Italy, but his replacement developed a problem. The Department informed Scarbeck that he would have to extend his tour in Warsaw until August. However, on 22 May he received orders from the Department to return to Washington. Less than a month later, the FBI arrested him.

In November 1961 he received three concurrent 10-year prison terms for violation of the 1950 Internal Security Act for passing classified papers to Polish intelligence officials. On 1 April 1966 the Federal Board of Parole granted Scarbeck a paroled from prison. The Board cleared him for freedom under a section of the Penal Code permitting parole of federal prisoners after they have served a third of their sentences.

Robert Glenn Thompson

Born in Detroit, Michigan, on 30 January 1935, Robert Glenn Thompson dropped out of high school to enlist in the US Air Force in December 1952. His initial assignment as a mechanic came to an early termination as a result of back injury caused by a fall. Following his first three years of service, Thompson, described as a capable airman of average intelligence, was reassigned to West Berlin, Federal Republic of Germany.

Robert Glenn Thompson

Thompson's espionage activity began in Berlin where he was in charge of the investigative files room of the Air Force's Office of Special Investigation. He had access to information classified as high as Secret concerning activities of counterintelligence agents.

Prior to his involvement in espionage, Thompson married a West German girl. As a result of a court-martial, Thompson was demoted from Airman First Class to Airman Second Class and was forced to send his wife back to the United States. After his wife left for the United States, he became involved with another West German girl and concurrently was "... very lonely, and disgusted and bitter." After being chastised by his commander for inappropriate attire and need of a shave while on duty, Thompson went over to East Berlin. When he was later contacted by the Soviets, they threatened to expose him concerning his East Berlin visit and also threatened the well-being of his wife's grandparents and other relatives who resided in East Germany. Thompson stated that he was disillusioned with the methods used to lure East and West Germans into counterintelligence operations and was frightened by the threats toward him and agreed to cooperate with the Soviets.

Thompson was provided relatively sophisticated intelligence training in a short period of times along with intelligence paraphernalia for operational use. From June 1957 to July 1963, he engaged in espionage for the Soviets. During the six months that remained of his Berlin tour following his recruitment and training, Thompson admitted to providing 50 to 100 documents every two weeks for about three months. In return for the documents, he was paid $3,800. Thompson explained the paltry payments by stating, "Let's face it. I wasn't in this for the money. I was disgusted, and it was part of my plan to get revenge." One of his last actions for the Soviets prior to his departure from Berlin was to hide a radio transmitter in one wall of his office.

From Berlin, he was transferred to Malmstrom Air Force Base, Great Falls, Montana, from where he sent one letter using secret writing. At Malmstrom, Thompson volunteered for an assignment to Goose Bay, Labrador. In late 1958, he was discharged from the service. Upon his return home in Detroit, he found that someone had been to his home looking for him. He soon discovered that the Soviets were trying to recontact him. The Soviets eventually caught up with him and urged him to rejoin the Air Force or join the Army. At one point they asked him to get a job with the Federal Bureau of Investigation.

After moving to Long Island, New York, Thompson occasionally supplied information to his Soviet contact concerning water reservoirs on Long Island, gas lines between New York and Long Island, and power plants and gas storage tanks in those areas. He was also told to look up certain people and provide information on their whereabouts, their jobs, and their financial status. Thomspson claims to have received approximately $400 for the information provided during his civilian employment. He summed up his activities by saying, "If you need (a) motivation for what I did, just say I was alone, just a young guy, I was hurt by what I saw, I was disillusioned."

At his trial, Thompson's plea of not guilty was changed to guilty. On 13 May 1965, he was sentenced to 30 years in prison. Thompson was released from prison in late April 1978 as a part of a prisoner exchange, which included an Israeli pilot held in Mozambique.

William Henry Whalen

William Henry Whalen, a high school graduate, came to the attention of the Federal Bureau of Investigation (FBI) in early 1959 when he was observed meeting with two Soviet Embassy officials. Determining that there was no official reason for these meetings, the FBI decided to investigate further. Although not arrested until

William Henry Whalen

12 July 1966, Whalen had actively engaged in espionage from December 1959 to March 1961 during which time he was on active duty in the US Army as a lieutenant colonel.

Colonel Whalen began his military career in 1940 and held several sensitive posts including assignments in Army intelligence. His terminal position, when he retired in 1961 with a physical disability, was with the Joint Chiefs of Staff. During this last assignment, Whalen met with two Russians, Colonel Sergei Edemski and Mikhail A. Shumaev, and provided them with information concerning retaliation plans of the US Strategic Air Command, and information pertaining to troop movements. He obtained this information as a consequence of his own position but also through questioning of fellow officers on topics of interest to Soviet intelligence. Colonel Whalen would meet Colonel Edemski in various shopping centers in northern Virginia for the purpose of passing on his information.

It is not known how much information of value Colonel Whalen passed to the Soviets subsequent to his retirement from the military, although some information, obtained through his continued contacts with fellow officers, was undoubtedly provided to the Soviets. His conspiracy with the Soviets allegedly terminated in 1963 at about the time Shumaev returned to the Soviet Union. Whalen allegedly was paid $5,500 between December 1959 and March 1961 for the information he passed.

In December 1966, Whalen pleaded guilty to a charge of acting to promote the interests of a foreign government and removing classified information from its place of safekeeping. On 1 March 1967, the 51-year-old Whalen was sentenced to 15 years in prison.

Defectors

Michal Goleniewski

Michal Goleniewski was born on 16 August 1922 in Niewswierz, Poland. His father was a low-level Polish Government employee and/or wood cutter who was attracted to Communism. In 1938, Goleniewski's father left his family behind in western Poland and moved to Lvov in search of work. Michal, in the meantime, completed his high school studies just prior to the German occupation of Poland. At age 17, he was drafted into a forced labor unit and worked there until the German defeat in World War II. While working as a forced laborer, he learned to speak fluent German.

In 1940 his father returned to the German occupied area of Poland as a Soviet military counterintelligence collaborator and recruited Michal for operations with the Polish underground. After the end of hostilities in 1945, Goleniewski joined the newly established Polish intelligence and security service (commonly referred to as the SB) as a guard. By 1948 he was an operations officer with the rank of lieutenant. From 1948 until 1953, he served as director of counterintelligence units in provincial SB offices.

In 1953, Goleniewski was transferred to SB headquarters in Warsaw where he advanced rapidly due to Soviet behind-the-scenes influences. Goleniewski had a liaison/informant relationship with the KGB. During the next three years, he served first as chief of a section responsible for deception operations and then as deputy director of the counterintelligence department. In December 1955, he was named deputy chief of the military counterintelligence service (GZI) but was removed from this position a year later when the service was reorganized.

Through the intervention of the Soviet advisors and old friends in the SB, Goleniewski was reinstated in the SB, which had also undergone a reorganization. Goleniewski became chief of the Science and Technology branch in the foreign intelligence department. This was his post in 1958 when he made contact with the West.

The most important element of Goleniewski's intelligence career was his liaison/informant relationship with the KGB. The Soviets patterned the postwar Polish intelligence services after their own organizations and placed Poles with Soviet connections at the head of various departments. From his first indoctrination in counterintelligence by the Soviets during Worold War II, Goleniewski's career advancement was supported by the Soviets. His relationship with the KGB was always close, whether he was an acknowledged liaison officer or reporting to a Soviet advisor at night as an informant.

Goleniewski was married to a Ukranian woman and had a daughter. His wife began suffering from mental illness, which led to their divorce and his family's total disappearance from his life.

In 1948 a letter was received at the residence of a US ambassador in a West European capital, the outer envelope of which was addressed to the ambassador and contained another envelope on which was printed "Private" Sir Edgar Hoover." The ambassador opened the envelope addressed to Hoover and found in it a letter written in German and signed "Heckenschutze." He scanned the letter and then turned it over to the CIA Chief of Station. Thus began CIA's relationship with Goleniewski.

For almost three years, Goleniewski carried on an anonymous letterwriting contact with what he thought was the FBI. In all he sent 27 lengthy and detailed letters to the West. There were suspicions of a provocation or deception operation when the first letters arrived, but their gradual processing and exploitation convinced Western intelligence services of Goleniewski's bona fides.

Goleniewski defected with his mistress in January 1961 in West Berlin and continued to provide valuable information for another three years. He was able to make an unparalleled contribution to Western intelligence because of his almost total recall, his intimate association with SB and KGB officers, and his experience as an operational intelligence officer. While still in place in Warsaw, he provided 1,000 pages of classified documents and cached 750 Minox film frames of documents, which were retrieved after his defection. Goleniewski provided details on over 1,500 intelligenec personalities — SB, KGB, and GRU officers and agents. Because of his relationship with the KGB, he was able to provide extensive information on and valuable leads to KGB operations. His leads exposed the KGB illegals network in London headed by Molody Lonsdale; George Blake, who was a KGB penetration of MI6; and KGB penetrations of the BND, Heinz Felfe and Hans Clemens. He identified Polish intelligence officers stationed in the United States to the FBI. He also made an important contribution in the field of US State Department security by providing information on SB and KGB recruitment methods against diplomatic personnel and penetration of Western diplomatic installations.

As early as 1962, it was evident that Goleniewski's mental health had begun to deteriorate. By 1963 he surfaced a list of grievances and criticism of the CIA. He also began to claim that he was the son of the last Russian Tsar and stated his claim to the Romanov fortune; all of which was publicized and exploited by television, books, and the press. Goleniewski's marriage to his German mistress immediately after their defection produced a daughter in 1964. His emotional and psychological problems were compounded by his wife's assimilation of his fantasies and irrational anxieties. The "Romanov" fantasy intensified to the point where it consumed his entire existence. By the end of August 1964 all substantive debriefing had ceased.

Frantisek August

Frantisek August (DPOB: 1928, Prague, Czechoslovakia) was a Czechoslovak foreign intelligence staff officer who defected to the West in Lebanon in 1969.

August's early service was in the counterintelligence element of the Czechoslovak security service. After a tour in Belgrade in the early 1960s, he was assigned to the Czechoslovak embassy in London under the cover of attaché in charge of the Consular Department. In the mid-1960's, while at headquarters in Prague, he was transferred to the unit, which directed operations in the Near and Middle East. Subsequently, he was posted to Beirut, Lebanon as a Commercial Attaché.

In the summer of 1969, August contacted US Intelligence officials in Beirut. After a short period of time "in place," he defected and was brought to the USA for debriefing and resettlement.

August provided useful information on Czechoslovak intelligence operations in the near and mid-East, especially against American targets. He also gave the British an insight into Czechoslovak intelligence and KGB operations against the British establishment, including Parliament. He supplied data on a Czechoslovak operation directed against William Owen, an elderly British Member of Parliament, whom the Czechs planned to develop into an intelligence asset and agent of influence. The British arrested Owen in 1970 on espionage charges. He confessed that he had accepted payments of some $6,000 over a period of nine years from Czechoslovak intelligence officers. He was acquitted by a jury, however, after denying that he had ever transmitted anything important to the Czechs.

During his career, August used aliases Frantisek Benda and "Adam."

Ladislav Bittman

Ladislav Bittman (DPOB: 12 January 1931, Prague, Czechoslovakia) was a Czechoslovak foreign intelligence staff officer who defected to the West in Germany in 1968.

In 1954, Bittman joined the Czechoslovak foreign intelligence service where he specialized in covert action and deception operations. He served in East Germany from 1961 to 1963 under the cover of the Cultural Attaché at the Czechoslovak Embassy in East Berlin. As Deputy Chief of "Active Measures" (CA Operations) from 1964 to 1966, Bittman frequently visited Berlin and Vienna on operational missions. He also traveled throughout Eastern and Western Europe, but he never visited the USSR. On one occasion he made a courier run to Latin America. From 1966 to 1968, he was a case officer in Vienna, Austria, under the cover of Press Attaché at the Czechoslovak Embassy.

Bittman left his intelligence post in Vienna in early September 1968, after the Soviet invasion of Czechoslovakia and traveled to West Germany, where he defected. The West Germans debriefed him extensively for two months and then turned him over to US intelligence, which brought him to the United States for more debriefing and resettlement. Bittman taught international journalism at American University.

During this career, Bittman used the following aliases: "Brychta," Vladimir Baumann, Lawrence Martin, and Lawrence Britt.

Joseph Frolik

Josef Frolik (AKA "Florian" DPOB: 22 September 1928, Libusin, Czechoslovakia) was an intelligence officer with the rank of major in the Czechoslovak Intelligence Service. He came over the West in 1969.

Frolik's specialty was counterintelligence, but in the mid-1960s he became a case officer for Western European operations. He served one tour in the United Kingdom under cover of Labor Attaché in the Czechoslovak Embassy, London, from 1965 to 1967.

In the summer of 1969, while on a vacation at a Ministry of Interior resort in Bulgaria, Frolik traveled to Belgrade and "walked in" to the US Embassy and defected. US Intelligence exfiltrated him to the United States for debriefing. The British also debriefed Frolik.

Frolik provided useful information on the CIS, including a list identifying approximately 200 staff officers. He also revealed much helpful background on CIS operations in the UK. He wrote a book, *The Frolik Defection*, (London, Leo Cooper, 1975), which provided a good insight into CIS and KGB operations in Western Europe and KGB domination of the CIS.

Vaclav Marous

Vaclav Marous (aka Mazourek), born 30 May 1929, Kelcanky, Czechoslovakia, was a Czechoslovak foreign intelligence staff officer who defected to the West in Switzerland in 1968.

From 1954 to 1963, Marous served first as a uniformed policeman and later worked on routine criminal matters. Subsequently, he was assigned to the counterintelligence department of Czechoslovak foreign intelligence as a senior referent for counterintelligence operations in North America. In this capacity he visited the USA and Mexico during the mid 1960s, under cover as a courier, to discuss operational matters.

While on leave in Bulgaria in August 1968, Marous learned of the Soviet invasion of Czechoslovakia and decided not to return to his homeland. From Bulgaria he traveled via Yugoslavia and Austria to Switzerland where he asked for asylum. In Switzerland, he applied for an American immigration visa. Shortly thereafter Marous was in contact with US Intelligence.

Marous, who was divorced, defected with his mistress Vlasta Semerakova and her fourteen-year-old son. He resettled in Australia.

Marous supplied much helpful information on MV CI operations in North America. He also revealed details on Operation VOLANT, an MV effort to identify US Intelligence personnel throughout North America.

Yuriy Vasilyevich Krotkov

Yuriy Vasilyevich Krotkov (DPOB: 11 November 1917, Kutaisi, Georgia, USSR) was a Soviet film script writer and coopted KGB agent who defected to the West while on a trip to England in the fall of 1963.

After a short period of service in the Soviet army during World War II, Krotkov became a *Tass* and Radio Moscow correspondent in Moscow. Krotkov's play, *John, Soldier of Peace*, based on the life of Paul Robeson, was first staged in 1949 and then ran for several years in Moscow and the provinces. In 1955, Krotkov became a script writer and entered the cultural and literary life of the Soviet capital.

In 1945, the Counterintelligence Directorate of the Soviet State Security Service recruited Krotkov to report on people in Moscow's drama circles. Soon thereafter, he was used in provocation operations against foreigners. From the late 1940s until the mid-1960s, he took part in many such operations in the USSR and East Germany. The most important of these was one directed against French Ambassador Maurice De Jean in 1956-58. Krotkov also traveled abroad as a tourist to Poland, Germany, and Czechoslovakia in 1959 and to India, Japan, and the Philippines in 1962.

In September 1963, while on a trip to England with a tour group, Krotkov defected to the British Security Service. He was debriefed by the British, Americans, and French. After his defection, Krotkov lived in England where he wrote *The Angry Exile*. He also visited Spain and worked for Radio Liberty. In 1969 he testified before the US Senate Internal Security Committee, under the name George Karlin, on KGB operations. In January 1970 he gained permanent resident status in the USA and worked as writer/consultant for the *Readers Digest*. In October 1974 he appeared as a witness against the Australian leftist writer, Wilfred Burchett, during his libel action against charges that he was a Communist agent.

Krotkov provided much information on KGB operations against western diplomats and visitors in the USSR and the Soviet Bloc. After his defection he took an active part in anti-Soviet activities through his writing and work as a consultant.

Krotkov is listed in the KGB *Alphabetical List of Agents of Foreign Intelligence Service, Defectors, Members of Anti-Soviet Organizations, Members of Punitive Units and Other Criminals Under Search Warrant* published in 1969 as being a criminal under search warrant.

During his career, Krotkov used the aliases George Moore, George Karlin, and Suliko.

Aleksandr Nikolayevich Cherepanov

Aleksandr Nikolayevich Cherepanov, born circa 1919, Siberia, USSR, was a retired KGB officer who desired to defect to the West.

As a Soviet State Security officer, Cherepanov parachuted behind German lines on a special mission, which resulted in the capture of a German general during World War II. From circa 1948 to circa April 1956, he was assigned to the Soviet embassy in Belgrade as Second Secretary, First Secretary, and Charge d'Affaires, respectively. In Yugoslavia he developed many contacts among students and workers. During October 1953 the American Embassy in Belgrade was informed that Cherepanov wished to defect to the West and was willing to bring valuable information with him. Fearing a provocation, the embassy was extremely reluctant to contact Cherepanov. Finally, in February 1954, an American officer talked with Cherepanov, who indicated complete adherence to the Soviet cause and no desire for further contact. Although the officer left the door open, Cherepanov did not recontact US Intelligence prior to his return to the Soviet Union.

Cherepanov, a lieutenant colonel in the KGB, served in the Foreign Intelligence directorate until circa 1958 when he was assigned to the first Department (American), Second chief directorate (Internal Counterintelligence) as a senior case officer to run operations against American Embassy personnel in Moscow. In August 1961, Cherepanov was retired from the KGB due to his incompetency.

After retiring from the KGB, Cherepanov began to work for Mezhdunarodnaya Kniga, the international book store, in Moscow. In November 1963, while employed at the store, he passed a package to an American business contact, asking him to deliver the package to the US Embassy. The American did so. The embassy, fearing a provocation, returned the package the following day to the Soviet Ministry of

Foreign Affairs (MFA) after first reproducing its contents. The MFA gave the documents to the KGB, which identified Cherepanov as the person who provided them to the Americans. In December 1963, Cherepanov was arrested in Baku, where he was attempting to flee across the Soviet border. After his arrest, he was detained and later executed.

The parcel that Cherepanov presented to the American consisted of documents, which have become known as "The Cherepanov Papers." All appear to have come from the files of the KGB First Department, Second Chief Directorate for the period 1958 to 1960. A number are handwritten drafts, probably made by Cherepanov. The reports contained information about operational plans against US Embassy personnel (expulsion actions, personality profiles, and surveillance records), as well as a list of Soviets who wrote to the US Embassy and a report, dated April 1959, on operational conditions in the USA.

Rupert Sigl

Rupert Sigl, born 12 April 1925, Rossatz, Bezirk Melk, Austria, was a KGB illegal who defected in West Berlin in 1969.

Sigl served in the German army during World War II. In 1947, the Soviet Security Service recruited him to inform on local personalities in Lower Austria where he was living at the time. After a period of inactivity, the KGB recontacted him in the early 1950s and asked him to report on the Volkspartei, the Austrian conservative Catholic political Party, and to assess persons of interest to the KGB.

After an abortive effort to steal some registered mail for the KGB from a local postmistress, Sigl went to Moscow in December 1952, where he received basic espionage training. In October 1953 he traveled to East Berlin and then to Leipzig, where he worked as a carpenter from early November 1953 to early 1955. From Leipzig Sigl handled a series of low-level KGB missions in West Berlin and West Germany. During this time he also studied English.

In early 1955 Sigl moved to East Berlin on KGB orders. During the next four years he carried out a variety of intelligence missions for the Soviets and continued his language studies. In 1958 he began preparations to go to Turkey under cover as a German businessman, but this effort was aborted in the winter of 1959–60 when a Munich periodical published a series of articles on espionage, one of which described Sigl's efforts to steal registered post office mail and intimated that he worked for the Soviets. Following this disclosure, Sigl worked exclusively for the KGB in the DDR until his defection in 1969.

Sigl defected to US intelligence authorities in West Berlin on 11 April 1969. Three months later he entered the United States for resettlement. After 1960, Sigl had concentrated on assessing and recruiting Germans and persons of other nationalities of interest to the KGB within the DDR. As a result, he was able to provide useful information on KGB facilities and modus operandi in the DDR. He also brought out documented lists of agents who worked for the KGB in the West.

During Sigl's career, he used the following aliases: Gerhard Reichl, Gerhard Reichelt, Heinz Bernd/Berndt, Peter Klein, Kurt Hager, and Gerhard Blum.

Yuriy Ivanovich Nosenko

Yuriy Vanovich Nosenko, born 30 October 1927, Nikolayev, Ukraine, USSR, was a KGB Second Chief Directorate (SCD) counterintelligence officer who defected in Switzerland on 4 February 1964.

As a child, Nosenko lived in Nikolayev in the Ukraine and Leningrad where his father, Ivan Isidorovich Nosenko, was a prominent Soviet shipbuilding engineer. At the time of his death in 1956, his father, Ivan Nosenko, was the Soviet Minister of Shipbuilding in Moscow.

As a teenager during World War II, Nosenko attended various naval training schools. At the end of the war he entered the Institute of International Relations in Moscow where he specialized in International Law and English. While attending this institute in 1947 he married the daughter of a Soviet lieutenant general. This marriage was subsequently dissolved when his father-in-law was arrested in connection with Stalin's purge of Marshal Georgiy Zhukov's associates. Upon completion of his studies at this Institute in 1950 Nosenko joined Naval Intelligence (GRU) and served in the Far East and in the Baltic area for about two years.

In early 1953, Nosenko arranged a transfer to the KGB SCD where he was assigned as a counterintelligence officer to the American Embassy Section of the American Department. As a member of the Embassy Section, he was targeted against American correspondents and US Army personnel residing in Moscow.

In June 1953, Nosenko married the daughter of the first deputy chief of the State Committee for Coordination of Scientific Research Work in the Soviet Union. His wife and children by this marriage were left in the Soviet Union when he defected in Switzerland in 1964.

In June 1955, Nosenko transferred to the Tourist Section of the Seventh Department of the SCD. While in this section he was primarily involved in operations designed to recruit American and British Commonwealth tourists in the Soviet Union. In 1957 he joined the Communist Party. In 1957 and again in 1958 he used the alias Yuriy Ivanovich Nikolayev to visit London as a security escort for a Soviet sports delegation. In 1958 he joined the newly created American-British Commonwealth Section of the Seventh Department, which was responsible for identifying and recruiting foreign intelligence agents visiting the Soviet Union as tourists. As deputy chief of this section, he engaged in many counterintelligence operations involving sexual entrapment of foreign tourists.

In January 1960, Nosenko transferred to the American Embassy Section of the American Department. Nosenko stated that this section was responsible for monitoring contact between US Embassy personnel and Soviet citizens and for the collection of information on American embassy personnel to facilitate their recruitment.

In March 1962, Nosenko accompanied the Soviet delegation to the Disarmament Conference in Geneva, Switzerland, as a security escort. He remained in Switzerland until 15 June 1962 at which time he returned to the Soviet Union and resumed his duties in the American-British Commonwealth Section. In January 1964 he again traveled to Switzerland as a security escort for the Soviet delegation to the Disarmament Conference in Geneva. He defected in Geneva on 4 February 1964 and was subsequently brought to the United States.

Olga Aleksandrovna Farmakovskaya

Olga Aleksandrovna Farmakovskaya, nee Mogulevskaya, born July 1921, Leningrad, USSR, was a Soviet English-language interpreter who defected to the West in Beirut in October 1966.

Olga, according to her own account, was a native of Leningrad and the daughter of Alexander Edward Henry, who was born in Italy of British parentage. Educated in Leningrad, she received a diploma qualifying her as a teacher and translator of English.

In 1946, Olga temporarily worked at the fur auction in Leningrad, escorting foreign fur buyers and reporting on them to the Soviet State Security Service. On the completion of that assignment, she applied for Security Service employment in Moscow, but she was not accepted. She believed that the reason she was not hired was because she had not joined the Komsomol.

As of 1950, Olga was employed at the Naval Engineering and Technical School in Leningrad, preparing English-language and testing materials. There she met and married Vadim Vadimovich Farmakovskiy, a student in the Naval School. She and her husband continued to live in Leningrad until 1956, during which period she worked first as an English teacher for a naval school in Pushkin, and, later from 1952 to 1956, for Inturist in Leningrad.

In 1956, Farmakovskiy was assigned to the Military Diplomatic Academy (MDA), the GRU strategic Intelligence School in Moscow, where he studied until 1959. During his last year at the Academy, Farmakovskiy obtained a job as a GRU officer assigned to the Committee for Coordination of Scientific Work (GKKNR), where Oleg Vadimirovich Penkovskiy was also employed. Farmakovskiy remained in this job until 1962, taking occasional business trips abroad during this period. In 1961, for example, Penkovskiy identified Farmakovskiy as one of the five GRU officers including himself assigned to the GKKNR in November 1960.

In September 1962, Farmakovskiy, accompanied by Olga, was posted to the Soviet Trade Delegation in

Stockholm, Sweden. Initially his task was to establish himself in his Trade Delegation cover job, but he did pick up two contacts. Farmakovskiy, who did not discuss his operational work with his wife, found this clandestine activity distasteful. In December 1962, however, Farmakovskiy was recalled to Moscow because of his associations with Penkovskiy, who was arrested according to the Soviet press on 22 October 1962.

Farmakovskiy and Olga agreed in late 1962 that she would take the first opportunity to defect to the West. In the spring of 1963, Farmakovskiy was discharged from the GRU because of his apparent unwillingness to engage in espionage. Subsequently, he worked as a civil engineer.

In 1963, Olga was again employed briefly at the Leningrad fur auction and again served as a KGB informant. Although she had reported nothing of value during this assignment, her Leningrad KGB case officer valued her refusal to engage in black marketeering or other disapproved behavior, and he referred her to a contact in the KGB Center in Moscow.

In January 1964, Olga was hired by UPDK (the department of the Foreign Ministry concerned with providing services for foreign diplomats in Moscow). UPDK placed her as a translator at the Nepalese embassy in Moscow. In this position, Olga was required to report to the KGB on all embassy personnel, especially the ambassador. She was also required to draw a detailed diagram of the embassy interior.

Because she disliked working with the Nepalese, Olga requested a transfer to another position. In March 1965, she was assigned to work as a translator for Peter Worthington, a Canadian journalist in Moscow. In this assignment she was also required to report to KGB on Worthington. Olga told Worthington early in 1966 of her desire to defect, and she continued to work for him.

In the fall of 1966 Olga took a Mediterranean cruise aboard the Soviet tourist ship SS *Litva*. On 16 October 1966, she left the ship, approached the US embassy in Beirut, and requested political asylum. US intelligence and Lebanese security officers debriefed her in Beirut where the local officials eventually fined her for illegal entry. In the meantime, on 7 November 1966, *Pravda* published an account of her defection. Eight days later, Olga traveled to Brussels through the efforts of Russian refugee channels. In the Belgian capital, US intelligence and Belgian Surete officials again debriefed her. US intelligence terminated interviews with Olga on 8 December 1966 in Brussels.

In mid-December 1966, Vidam Farmakovskiy lunched with Worthington in Moscow. The Soviet told the Canadian that he knew that the Canadian journalist was aware of Olga's defection plans and that he believed Worthington had encouraged her to defect and also added that he knew Worthington and Olga had an affair in Moscow. Farmakovskiy told Worthington that he planned to use this information to ruin him unless he agreed to go to Brussels and persuade Olga to return to the USSR where all would be forgiven. If Worthington would not agree to these terms, then Farmakovskiy would send letters with details on this affair to Worthington's family, his employers, and the Canadian Embassy in Moscow.

On 29 December 1966, Worthington left Moscow, passed through London, and went to Brussels where he rejoined Olga. On 26 December, Worthington flew to Canada and returned shortly to Brussels. On 6 January 1967, the US Consul in Brussels advised Olga and Worthington that her application for entry to the USA was denied. Olga eventually went to Canada and in the late 1960s was working for the University of Toronto. Worthington continued his career as a journalist with Canadian newspapers in Canada.

During the time that US intelligence had access to Olga in Beirut and Brussels, there was some question about her bona fides. The case is an interesting one, however, because Olga, her husband and Worthington all had contacts with or were involved with the KGB and GRU. As noted above, Olga's husband, worked at the GKKNR with Penkovskiy who was executed for spying on behalf of the United States. Olga herself proffered information from a variety of unspecified sources on Cherepanov, who was allegedly a classmate of her husband's and had been executed for supplying information to the US Embassy. She claimed that Cherepanov was not posted abroad after his graduation from the MDA in 1959 and became bitter and resentful. In revenge, he passed documents to the US Embassy which returned them to the Soviet Foreign Ministry.

Although her information differs in some respects from data developed by US intelligence (Cherepanov was reportedly KGB rather than GRU and had served in Belgrade), it is possible that she presented the information as she knew it. She also stated that she had heard about but did not know the defector Nosenko. Her information, especially about the KBG's Second Chief Directorate, tended to support in part his bona fides. Whether she was a dispatched KGB agent or a genuine, but troublesome, defector, she did provide some insight into developments in the Penkovskiy, Cherepanov and Nosenko cases. Most of the information was allegedly hearsay, and it is difficult to ascertain if that information was a deception. She did, however, give an accurate insight into the continuing operations of the KGB's Second Chief Directorate against foreigners in the USSR.

According to the *KGB Alphabetical List of Agents of Foreign Intelligence Services, Defectors, Members of Anti-Soviet Organizations, Members of {punitive units and Other Criminals Under Search Warrant* dated in 1969, the deputy Procurator general authorized Olga's arrest.

Oleg Vladimirovich Penkovskiy

Oleg Vladimirovich Penkovskiy was a Soviet military intelligence (GRU) officer who worked in place for the CIA and British intelligence from 1960 to 1962.

Oleg Vladimirovich Penkovskiy

A professional Red Army officer who had risen through the ranks, Penkovskiy served with distinction as a Soviet artillery officer throughout World War II. After the war, he attended the Frunze Academy for two years. He then joined the GRU and attended the Military-Diplomatic Academy for four years.

Following his training, he served as a GRU desk officer and subsequently as assistant military attaché in Turkey in 1955 and 1956. Subsequently, he was reassigned to the Near Eastern and Far Eastern desks in Moscow and attended the missile refresher course at the Dzerzhinskiy Artillery Academy. In 1960 he was assigned by the GRU in the State Scientific Technical Committee (GNTK) to perform intelligence collection functions. By the fall of 1962 he had risen to the position of Deputy Chief of the Foreign Liaison Department of the External Relations Directorate of the State Committee for Coordination of Scientific Research Work (GKKNR, predecessor organization to the GKNT).

After several unsuccessful attempts to make contact with the CIA via American tourists and a Canadian diplomat, Penkovskiy was finally able to make contact with MI6. After this contact, MI6 and CIA handled Penkovskiy jointly. Because he was a trusted senior GRU officer, Penkovskiy had unique access to Soviet military information need by the West. He often jeopardized his personal security by providing hugh amounts of material to CIA and MI6 officers, particularly during three visits he made to the West; two in London and one in Paris, France.

In Moscow, he was handled by MI6. He frequently had short meetings with the wife of a British Embassy official. The intelligence Penkovskiy passed to the West was highly valuable. The Cuban missile crisis in October 1962, demonstrated the unique value of Penkovskiy's contribution. He provided manuals and other detailed technical information on Soviet missiles that helped identify the devices Premier Khrushchev had secretly installed in Cuba. It was his intelligence that allowed President Kennedy to expertly handle the missile showdown with the Soviet Union.

Penkovskiy was arrested by the KGB. He was given a show trail after which he was executed.

Defection of Bernon F. Mitchell and William H. Martin

Bernon F. Mitchell was born on March 11, 1929, at San Francisco, California. He was interviewed by a National Security Agency recruiter on February 25, 1957, while a university student. He had gained field experience in cryptology during the course of Navy service from 1951 to 1954 (during which time he and William Martin became friends) and had acquired familiarization and experience with computers. Based on Mitchell's academic record, the recruiter's recommendation, the personal knowledge of an NSA supervisor as to Mitchell's work performance while in the Navy, and the fact that he had been previously cleared by the Navy for access to cryptologic information, he was offered, and accepted, employment as a mathematician, GS-7, reporting for duty on July 8, 1957.

On July 17, 1957, the Office of Security Services requested the Civil Service Commission to conduct a national security check on Mitchell. On July 23, 1957, Mitchell was given a polygraph interview. At that time he refused to answer any questions about sexual perversion or blackmail. Eleven days later, Mitchell submitted to another polygraph interview and admitted that, between the ages of 13 and 19, he had participated in sexual experimentation with dogs and chickens.

The Office of Security Services evaluator who reviewed the data on Mitchell—including the results of the polygraph interviews, a national agency check, and a background investigation conducted by the Navy in 1951—did not refer the case to another evaluator for a supporting or dissenting judgment before approving Mitchell for an interim security clearance, which was granted on August 7, 1957, five days after his second polygraph session. On September 4, 1957, Mitchell executed a Security Indoctrination Oath. On the same day he was issued a badge permitting access to information through Top Secret on a "need-to-know" basis. It was not until September 9, 1957—two months after he had been placed on the payroll—that NSA requested a full field investigation into his background. The Air Force agency, which conducted this investigation was not given the benefit of any of the information revealed during his polygraph interviews.

On January 3, 1958, the Air Force Office of Special Investigations submitted its report on Mitchell's background investigation to NSA. On January 23, 1958, he was given final clearance.

NSA's director of the Office of Security Services told the Committee on Un-American Activities at an executive session that the agency did not turn over information obtained from polygraph interviews to other investigative organizations because NSA employees had been promised by NSA that polygraph interviews would be kept confidential. The only exception to this policy, the committee was told, would be in cases where interviews turned up information about undetected crimes and subversive activities.

William H. Martin was born on May 27, 1931, at Columbus, Georgia. He was interviewed by an NSA recruiter on March 8, 1957, while a university student. He had become experienced as a cryptologist during a tour of duty in the Navy from 1951 to 1955 and continued the same type of work as a civilian for the Army in Japan for nearly a year after receiving his discharge from the Navy. As in the case of Mitchell, the recruiter detected no reason why Martin would have any difficulty in obtaining security clearance to work at NSA. Based on the recruiter's recommendation, Martin's academic record, and the recommendation of an NSA supervisor who had known both Martin and Mitchell in Japan, he was hired as a mathematician, GS-7, and reported for duty on July 8, 1957, with Mitchell.

The National Agency check on Martin and his polygraph interview disclosed no information that the NSA evaluator considered to be a bar to interim security clearance. During the background investigation on Martin, which included the results of the 1951 Navy investigation, it was revealed that acquaintances described him as (1) an insufferable egotist; (2) a little effeminate; (3) not wholly normal; (4) rather irresponsible; and (5) one who might be swayed by flattery. Former supervisors, both Navy and Army, were almost unanimous in expressing the opinion they would not want to have him work for them again. Nevertheless, with only one exception, persons interviewed recommended him as one who could have access to classified information.

The NSA security evaluator concerned saw nothing sufficiently derogatory about the above characterizations of Martin to recommend that he be denied a security clearance. The findings of the field investigation, of course, in accordance with the practice at that time were not turned over to NSA's personnel office or any other office having to do with Martin's employment. Martin was granted an interim clearance on August 14, 1957.

On August 28, 1957, more than a month and a half after he had been hired, NSA requested the Department of the Navy to conduct a full field investigation on Martin. On September 4, 1957, he executed a Security Indoctrination Oath, and on the same day he was issued a badge permitting access to information, classified Top Secret on a "need-to-know" basis. NSA received the Navy's report of investigation on April 22, 1958. On May 12, 1958, Martin was granted a final clearance.

The Martin-Mitchell case became a matter of immediate interest to the committee on August 1, 1960, when the Department of Defense made a public announcement that these two NSA employees had failed to return from a supposed vacation trip, which they had taken together. The committee had already begun a preliminary investigation when, on August 5, 1960, the Defense Department made a follow-up statement concluding that, as a result of its own investigation into why Mitchell and Martin had not returned from leave, "there is a likelihood that they have gone behind the Iron Curtain."

On September 6, 1960, at a press conference in Moscow, the Soviet Union presented Mitchell and Martin to the world in the role of traitors, willing to accuse the United States of acts about which they possessed no knowledge. Mitchell and Martin did possess much knowledge, however, about the organization and operation of NSA, and it was reasonable to presume that their disclosure to the USSR of information about the NSA adversely affected the security of the United States.

On September 7, 1960, the Committee on Un-American Activities authorized a formal investigation and hearings on the National Security Agency for the following legislative purposes:

1. Strengthening of security laws and regulations by amending those parts of H.R. 2232 referred to this Committee on January 12, 1959 relating to unauthorized disclosure of certain information affecting national defense and Section 349 of the Immigration and Nationality Act providing for loss of nationality in certain cases;

2. Consideration of legislation to amend the Act of August 26, 1950, relating to the suspension of employment of civilian personnel of the United States in the interest of national security in line with H.R. 1989, introduced by the Chairman on January 9, 1959;

3. Proposed legislation affixing procedures for investigative clearance of individuals prior to government employment with a view to eliminating employment of subversives and security risks;

4. Performance of the duties of legislative oversight.

CI in the Turbulent 1960s and 1970s
Bibliography

Anders, Karl. *Murder to Order*. New York: Devin-Adair, 1967.

Bamford, James. *The Puzzle Palace*. New York: Pengiun Books, 1983.

Barnett, Harvey. *Tales of the Scorpion*. Boston, MA: Allen and Unwin, 1988.

Bentley, Eric, ed. *Thirty Years of Treason: Excepts from Hearings before the House Committee on Un-American Activities, 1938-1968*. New York: Viking, 1971.

Bittman, Ladislav. *The Deception Game: Czechoslovak Intelligence in Soviet Political Warfare*. Syracuse, NY: Syracuse University Press, 1972.

Blackstock, Nelson. *COINTELPRO: The FBI's Secret War on Political Freedom*. New York: Vantage, 1975.

Buranelli, Vincent and Nan. *Spy/Counterspy: An Encyclopedia of Espionage*. New York: Simon & Schuster, 1974.

Cline, Ray. *Secrets, Spies and Scholars: Blueprint of the Essential CIA*. Washington, DC: Acropolis Books, 1976.

Colby, William with Peter Forbath. *Honorable Men: My Life in the CIA*. New York: Simon and Schuster, 1978.

Collins, Richard. "Army Counter-Intelligence Operations." *Army Information Digest* (Sept. 1964): 8-14.

Cookridge, E.H. *Gehlen: Spy of the Century*. New York: Pyramid Books, 1971.

———. *George Blake: Double Agent*. New York: Ballantine Books, 1982.

Copeland, Miles. *The Real Spy World*. London: Meidenfeld and Nicolson, 1974.

Elliff, John T. *The Reform of FBI Intelligence Operations, Written Under the Auspices of the Police Foundation*. Princeton, NJ: Princeton University Press, 1979.

———. "Attorney General's Guidelines for FBI Investigations." *Cornell Law Review* 69:4 (Apr. 1984) 785-815.

Epstein, Edward J. *Deception: The Invisible War Between the KGB and the CIA*. New York: Simon & Schuster, 1989.

———. *Legend: The Secret World of Lee Harvey Oswald*. New York: The Reader's Digest Press/McGraw-Hill Book Company, 1978.

Felt, W Mark. *The FBI Pyramid From the Inside*. New York: G.P. Putnam's Sons, 1979.

Frolik, Joseph. *The Frolik Defection: The Memoirs of an Agent*. London: Leo Cooper, 1975.

Granovsky, Anatoli. *I was a NKVD Agent: A Top Soviet Spy Tells His Story*. New York: Devin-Adair, 1962.

Grose, Peter. *Gentleman Spy: The Life of Allen Dulles*. New York: Houghton Mifflin Company, 1994.

Halpern, Samuel and Hayden Peake. "Did Angleton Jail Nosenko?" *International Journal of Intelligence and Counterintelligence* 3:4 (1989): 451-464.

Hart, John L. "Popov: A Man Who Was Faithful." *Intelligence and National Security*, vol. 10 (1995), no.1.

Haswell, Jock. *Spies and Spymasters: A Concise History of Intelligence*. London: Thomas and Hudson, 1977.

Huminik, John. *Double Agent*. New York: New American Library, 1967.

Hunt, E. Howard. *Undercover: Memoirs of an American Secret Agent*. New York: Holt, Rinehart and Winston, 1971.

Hunt, Henry. "CIA in Crisis: The Kampiles Case." *Reader's Digest* 114 (June 1979): 65-72.

Hurt, Henry. *Shadrin: The Spy Who Never Came Back*. New York: Reader's Digest Press, 1981.

Jensen, Joan M. *Military Surveillance of Civilians in America*. Morristown, NJ: General Learning Press, 1975.

Lindsey, Robert. *The Falcon and the Snowman: A True Story of Friendship and Espionage*. New York: Simon & Schuster, 1979.

Mangold, Thomas. *Cold Warrior; James Jesus Angleton: The CIA's Master Spy Hunter*. New York: Simon & Schuster, 1991.

Martin, David C. *Wilderness of Mirrors*. New York: Harper & Row, 1980.

Monat, Pawel, with John Dill. *Spy in the U.S.* New York: Harper & Row, 1962.

Morgan, Richard E. *Domestic Intelligence: Monitoring Dissent in America*. Austin, TX: University of Texas Press, 1980.

Mr. X, pseud., with Bruce E. Henderson, *Double Eagle: The Autobiography of a Polish Spy Who Defected to the West*. Indianapolis, IN: Bobbs Merrill, 1979.

Myagkov, Aleksei. *Inside the KGB: An Expose by an Officer of the Third Directorate*. New Rochelle, NY: Arlington House, 1977.

Ott, John. "Espionage Trial Highlights CIA Problems: The Case of William P. Kampiles." *Aviation Week and Space Technology* 109 (27 Nov. 1978): 21.23.

Penkovsky, Oleg. *The Penkovsky Papers*, London: Collins, 1965.

Pincher, Chapman. *Their Trade Is Treachery*. London: Sidgwick and Jackson, 1981.

Powers, Richard Gid. *Secrecy and Power: The Life of J. Edgar Hoover*. New York: Macmillan, 1986.

Powers, Thomas. *The Man Who Kept the Secrets*. London: Weidenfeld and Nicolson, 1979.

Pyle, Christopher H. "CONUS Intelligence: The Army Watches Civilian Politics" *Washington Monthly* 1 (Jan 1970): 4-16.

Richards, Guy. *Imperial Agent: The Goleniewski-Romanov Case*. New York: Devin-Adair, 1966.

Rositzke, Harry. *The CIA's Secret Operations: Espionage, Counterespionage and Covert Action*. New York: Reader's Digest Press, 1977.

Sawatsky, John. *For Services Rendered: Leslie James Bennett and the RCMP Security Service*. New York: Doubleday and Company, 1982.

Sayer, Ian and Douglas Botting. *America's Secret Army: The Untold Story of the Counter Intelligence Corps*. London: Grafton-Collins, 1989.

Schecheter, Jerrold L. and Peter Deriabin. *The Spy Who Changed the World: How a Soviet Colonel Changed the Course of the Cold War*. New York: Scribner's, 1992.

Sigl, Rupert. *In the Claws of the KGB: Memoirs of a Double Agent*. Philadelphia, PA: Dorrance, 1978.

Sullivan, William C. with Bill Brown. *The Bureau: My Thirty Years in Hoover's FBI*. New York: W.W. Norton & Company, 1979.

Theohoris, Athan. *Spying on Americans: Political Surveillance from Hoover to the Huston Plan.* Philadelphia, PA: Temple University Press, 1978.

Tully, Andrew. *White Tie and Dagger.* New York: William Morrow, 1967.

U.S. Congress. House. Committee on Un-American Activities. *Communist Espionage in the United States: Hearings and Testimony of Frantisek Tisler, Former Military and Air Attaché, Czechoslovak Embassy in Washington, DC*, 86th Cong. 2nd sess. Washington, DC: GPO, 1960.

———. *Amending the Internal Security Act of 1950 to Provide for Maximum Personnel Security in the National Security Agency.* H. Report 2120. Aug 2, 1962. 87th Cong., 2nd sess. Washington, DC: GPO, 1962.

West, Nigel. *Molehunt: The Full Story of the Soviet Spy in MI-5.* London: Weidenfeld and Nicholson, 1987.

Winks, Robin. *Cloak and Gown: Scholars in the Secret War, 1939-1961.* New York: Quill, 1987.

Wise, David. *Molehunt: The Secret Search for Traitors That Shattered the CIA.* New York: Random House, 1992.

Wright, Peter. *Spycatcher: The Candid Autobiography of a Senior Intelligence Officer.* New York: Viking Penquin, Inc., 1987.

CI IN THE TURBULENT 60s AND 70s
1960–1979

1960

3 January	United States breaks relations with Cuba.
1 May	Gary Francis Powers, a CIA U-2 pilot, shot down over the Soviet Union.
16 May	Khrushchev breaks up summit meeting over U-2 incident; Eisenhower promises not to resume overflights of USSR.
1 June	Sino-Soviet dispute surfaces.
20 August	GRU Officer Oleg Penskovskiy becomes agent-in-place for CIA and British intelligence.
10 November	President Kennedy announces retention of Dulles at CIA and Hoover at FBI.
10 November	David Greenglass released after serving only 9½ years for conspiracy to commit espionage.

1961

3 March	Harold N. Borger arrested by West German authorities. He was the first American tried in West Germany on espionage charges. Although it was not firmly established he passed information to East Germany, he received 2 years and 6 months in prison with time spent in pretrial confinement subtracted from his sentence.
17 April	Bay of Pigs landing and associated battles.
4 May	President's Board reactivated as President's Foreign Intelligence Advisory Board (PFIAB); Maxwell Taylor named Chairman.
13 June	Irvin C. Scarbeck, US diplomat, arrested for passing classified documents to Polish intelligence.
7 August	Dr. Robert A. Soblen was sentenced to ten years for conspiracy to steal national secrets and life imprisonment for transmitting the secrets to the Soviet Union.
13 August	Construction of the Berlin Wall begins.
10 September	Morris and Lona Cohen arrested by British Intelligence and sentenced to 20 years in prison. The couple was exchanged in 1969 for British teacher Gerald Brooke, who had been arrested in Moscow by the KGB for distributing anti-Communist propaganda.

CI in the Turbulent 1960s and 1970s

IMPORTANT DATES AND COUNTERINTELLIGENCE EVENTS

CI IN THE TURBULENT 60s AND 70s
1960-1979

1961	1 October	The Defense Intelligence Agency is established by Department of Defense Directive 5105.21.
	15 December	Anatoliy Golitsyn defects to CIA.
	18 December	Joseph Patrick Kauffman, U.S. Army Air Corps, was arrested for passing information to the East Germans.
1962	10 February	Soviet illegal Rudolph Abel exchanged for CIA U-2 pilot Gary Francis Powers.
	16 April	Office of the DCI reorganized and expanded; Executive Committee established.
	9 June	President Kennedy transfers Interdepartmental Intelligence Conference from National Security Council to the Attorney General.
	October	The Army Intelligence and Security Branch created in the Regular Army. (It was redesignated the Military Intelligence Branch in 1967).
	October	Oleg Penkovskiy, a GRU officer working for CIA and British intelligence, arrested by Soviets.
1963	16 May	Oleg Penskovskiy executed by Soviets for espionage.
	30 August	Washington/Moscow "hot line" activated.
	October	The Department of Defense issues a comprehensive directive establishing intelligence career programs to create a broad professional base of trained and experienced intelligence officers.
	29 October	John W. Butenko and Ivan Ivanov are arrested on charges of espionage for the USSR and failure to register as agents of a foreign power. Butenko received 30 years and Ivanov received 20 years of imprisonment.
	November	Robert D. Haguewood, who worked at the National Security Agency, defects to the Soviet Union.
	22 November	President John Kennedy assassinated.
1964	4 February	Yuri Nosenko, KGB Second Chief Directorate officer, defects to CIA.
	April	Soviet audio-surveillance of US Embassy in Moscow disclosed.

CI IN THE TURBULENT 60s AND 70s
1960-1979

1964	6 April	Yuri Nosenko confined by CIA; hostile interrogation begins.
	2 September	FBI begins COINTELPRO operations against the Ku Klux Klan.
1965	7 January	Robert Gordon Thompson was tried on charges of espionage for the USSR and failure to register as an agent of a foreign power. He was sentenced to 30 years in prison.
	1 April	Program of public exposure of Soviet intelligence officers abroad begins.
	6 April	Robert Lee Johnson was arrested and later tried in June for unauthorized transmission of classified information to the Soviet Union. He was sentenced to 25 years in prison.
	May	James Allen Mintkenbaugh, arrested with Johnson, was accused of unlawful possession of documents in aid of a foreign agent. He was also tried in June and sentenced to 25 years in prison.
	June	Fourteen thousand National Guardsmen are called out during a riot at Watts, a black ghetto in South Los Angeles; 34 die, 4,000 are arrested, and the area is in ashes after five days.
	November	The U.S. Army Intelligence Command (INSCOM) is established to handle counterintelligence functions in the U.S. (It was discontinued in 1974 and replaced with the U.S. Army Intelligence Agency)
1966	31 January	Students demonstrate nationwide against the Vietnam war.
	4 February	Naval Investigative Service established. Name is later changed to Naval Criminal Investigative Service.
	12 July	William Henry Whalen, US Army, arrested for espionage.
	14 July	Senate rejects proposal to permit Foreign Relations Committee members to participate in Senate oversight of US intelligence operations.
	24 October	Air Force Sergeant Herbert Boeckenhaupt is arrested and later charged with conspiracy to commit espionage on behalf of the Soviet Union. On 7 Jun 1967 he was sentenced to 30 years in prison.

CI in the Turbulent 1960s and 1970s

IMPORTANT DATES AND COUNTERINTELLIGENCE EVENTS
CI IN THE TURBULENT 60s AND 70s
1960-1979

1967	May	Gary Lee Ledbetter, U.S. Navy, arrested and court-martialed for passing information to two British civilians recruited by East Germany.
	June	Detroit black riots end after 8 days, 43 dead.
	July	Newark Black riots end after six days with 26 dead.
	4 July	Freedom of Information Act goes into effect.
	15 August	CIA develops Operation Chaos in response to President Johnson's persistent interest in the extent of foreign influence on domestic unrest.
	25 August	Leonard Jenkins Safford and Ulysses L. Harris, US Army, are arrested for espionage.
	25 August	FBI begins COINTELPRO operation Black nationalists.
	21 October	Antiwar protesters make night march on Pentagon.
1968	2 January	President Johnson signs measure to bring "new life" into the idle Subversive Activities Control Board.
	23 January	U.S. Navy intelligence gathering ship *Pueblo* captured by North Korea. Crew released on 22 Dec.
	April	Black militancy increases on campuses; the president of San Francisco University resigns as black instructors urge black students to bring guns on campus.
	26 April	Secretary of Defense Clark Clifford announces establishment of Riot Control Center at the Pentagon.
	9 May	FBI begins COINTELPRO operations against the New Left.
	26 August	Yuppies lead major riots at Democratic Convention in Chicago.
1969	18 February	House Committee on Un-American Activities changed to House Committee on Internal Security.
	11 April	Joseph B. Attardi, Army Staff Sergeant, arrested and sentenced on 27 August 1969 to 3 years in prison on charges of providing NATO defense plans to a fellow soldier.

IMPORTANT DATES AND COUNTERINTELLIGENCE EVENTS
CI IN THE TURBULENT 60s AND 70s
1960-1979

1969	20 April	A group of black students armed with machine guns take over a building on Cornell University; they leave after negotiations with the administration.
	22 July	Attorney General Mitchell establishes the Civil Disturbance Group to coordinate intelligence policy and actions within Justice concerning domestic civil disturbance.
	15 October	National Moratorium antiwar march.
	15 November	Second and larger National Moratorium antiwar march.
1970	20 January	Army domestic surveillance program is revealed.
	6 March	A Greenwich Village townhouse in New York is destroyed by an explosion in what is believed to be a "bomb factory" of a radical group known as the Weathermen; three bodies are found.
	19 March	Executive Protection Service established placing a heavier guard around embassies.
	9 May	Nearly 100,000 students demonstrate in Washington, D.C.; Nixon unable to sleep, goes to the Lincoln Memorial to address them.
	5 June	President Nixon holds meeting in White House to create Interagency Committee on Intelligence (ICI). FBI Director Hoover named chairman.
	8 June	Hoover convenes meeting of Intelligence principals to plan writing of a Special Report for the President; names William Sullivan work group chairman.
	9 June	First meeting of ICI work group at Langley. Each agency assigned task of preparing a list of restraints hampering intelligence collection.
	23 June	Hoover terminates all FBI formal liaison with NSA, DIA, Secret Service and the military services.
	25 June	Principals meet in Hoover's office to sign the Special Report.
	9 July	In a memo, Huston proclaims himself the "exclusive" contact point in the White House on matters of domestic intelligence or internal security.

IMPORTANT DATES AND COUNTERINTELLIGENCE EVENTS
CI IN THE TURBULENT 60s AND 70s
1960-1979

1970	23 July	Huston Plan for expanding domestic intelligence gathering approved; canceled 28 Jul.
	10 August	John Dean takes over Huston's intelligence responsibilities in the White House.
	10 September	Huston urges White House expansion of Subversive Activities Control Board via an Executive Order.
	17 September	Attorney General Mitchell tells Dean he approves of an Interagency Evaluation Committee (IEC) to improve intelligence coordination.
	3 December	IEC holds first meeting in Dean's office.
1971	3 February	Hoover refuses to provide FBI staff for IEC
	27 April	FBI's COINTELPRO operations terminated in response to disclosures about the program in the press.
	13 June	The New York Times publishes the first installment of "The Pentagon Papers," a secret (classified) history of American involvement in Vietnam since World War II.
	2 July	Erhlichman forms "Plumbers" Group at President Nixon's request.
	21 October	Walter T. Perkins, US Air Force, arrested for improper possession of and use of documents dealing with national security.
	15 November	Soviet illegal Rudolph Abel dies.
1972	2 May	FBI Director J. Edgar Hoover dies.
	19 May	CIA gets court injunction against Victor Marchetti's publication of classified information.
	19 May	Bomb explodes in the Pentagon Building.
	3 June	Berlin agreement recognized the existence of separate East and West German sectors.
	17 June	Watergate break-in; five men arrested had past CIA ties.
	12 August	Last U.S. combat troops leave South Vietnam. Heavy air raids conducted over North Vietnam.

IMPORTANT DATES AND COUNTERINTELLIGENCE EVENTS
CI IN THE TURBULENT 60s AND 70s
1960-1979

1973	June	IEC abolished
	July	CIA's mail opening program stopped.
	21 July	James D. Wood, US Air Force, arrested for espionage on behalf of the Soviet Union.
1974	3 March	Airman First Class Oliver Everett Grunden, US Air Force, is convicted of espionage. He is dishonorably discharged from the Air Force and receives a five-year prison sentence.
	19 March	CIA's Operation Chaos program terminated.
	4 September	U.S. and East Germany establish formal diplomatic relations.
	4 October	Philip Agee publishes list of American officials working overseas whom he claims work for CIA.
	14 October	U.S. Army Specialist Fifth Class Leslie J. Payne and his East-German born wife, Krista, were arrested by West German police for espionage on behalf of East Germany.
	22 December	New York Times publishes article on CIA's domestic activities.
	24 December	Dismissal of CIA's CI chief James J. Angleton announced.
	31 December	George T. Kalaris is appointed to replace James J. Angleton, the CIA's embattled Chief of Counterintelligence.
1975	4 January	President Ford signs Executive Order establishing a Presidential Commission to examine CIA operations within the US. It is chaired by Vice President Nelson Rockefeller and becomes known as the Rockefeller Commission.
	15 January	DCI William Colby testifies before Congress that provocative CIA domestic operations were discontinued after February 1973.
	27 January	The Senate passes Senate Resolution 21 (94th Congress), which establishes a Senate Select Committee to Study Government Operations with Respect to Intelligence Activities. It is chaired by Senator Frank Church and becomes known as the Church Committee.

CI in the Turbulent 1960s and 1970s

IMPORTANT DATES AND COUNTERINTELLIGENCE EVENTS
CI IN THE TURBULENT 60s AND 70s
1960-1979

1975	19 Febraury	The House of Representatives passes Resolution 139 (94th Congress), which establishes the House Select Committee on Intelligence. It is chaired by Representative Lucien Nedzi.
	5 Apr 1976:	Attorney General Edward Levi's guidelines for domestic security and intelligence investigations became the FBI's standard operating procedures.
	June	Sarkis Paskalian admits to FBI that he was a Soviet spy and names Sahag Dedyan as his accomplice.
	10 June	The Rockefeller Commission Report, which had been submitted to President Ford on 6 June is released. The report states that almost all of the CIA's domestic activities were lawful, but that some were clearly unlawful.
	27 June	Sahag K. Dedayan, John Hopkins Applied Physics Laboratory, is arrested for spying for the USSR.
	17 July	House Resolution 591 (94th Congress) is passed. It re-staffed the House Select Committee on Intelligence. Representative Otis Pike is named to chair the committee, and it becomes known as the Pike Committee.
	2 November	General shakeup of President Ford's national security officials. William Colby dismissed as Director of Central Intelligence.
	21 November	The Senate's Church Committee publishes report on assassinations.
	23 December	Richard Welch, CIA's Chief of Station in Athens, assassinated.
1976	29 January	The Pike Committee report is submitted to the House of Representatives. The House votes not to release the results of the report until President Ford states that its release will not damage US intelligence activities.
	30 January	George Bush becomes Director of Central Intelligence.
	16 February	A portion of the Pike Committee report, which was given to the *Village Voice* by CBS correspondent Daniel Schorr, appears in the *Village Voice*. Additional portions appear on 23 February 1976.

CI IN THE TURBULENT 60s AND 70s
1960-1979

1976	19 February	The House passes House Resolution 1042 (94th Congress). It authorizes the House Committee on Standards of Official Conduct to look into the publication of the classified Pike Committee report.
	1 March	The Senate Committee on Government Operations reports on Senate Resolution 400 (94th Congress). The resolution creates a standing Senate Committee on Intelligence.
	28 April	The Church Committee releases its Final Report, Intelligence Activities and the Rights of Americans. It maintains that poor oversight of intelligence activities had permitted violations of constitutional rights.
	8 May	FBI chief Clarence Kelly apologizes publicly for bureau excesses, such as the Martin Luther King and Black Panther surveillance.
	16 May	Senate Resolution 400 creates permanent Senate Select Committee on Intelligence (SSCI),
	18 May	New National Security Council Intelligence Directives (NSCIDs) and Director of Central Intelligence Directives (DCIDs) issued in conjunction with Executive Order 11905.
	19 May	Senate votes to establish a permanent Select Committee on Intelligence to monitor the activities of the CIA and other federal intelligence agencies.
	11 August	Clarence Kelley transferred domestic intelligence investigations to the General Investigative Division of the FBI.
	22 December	Edwin G. Moore, retired CIA, is arrested for attempting to spy for the USSR.
1977	1 January	The US Army Intelligence and Security Command is created.
	6 January	Andrew Dalton Lee is arrested in Mexico City. Police find microfilm containing highly secret American documents. He is returned to the United States.
	7 January	Ivan N. Rogalsky arrested on charges of conspiring to commit espionage.
	16 January	Christopher J. Boyce, TRW, arrested for spying for the USSR.

CI IN THE TURBULENT 60s AND 70s
1960-1979

1977	17 January	Andrew Dalton Lee was arrested by the FBI for spying for the USSR.
	18 May	The SSCI's first annual report is issued. It says that the intelligence agencies are now accounting properly to Congress and that Executive Oversight appears to be working.
	14 July	The House passes Resolution 658 (95th Congress), which creates a House Intelligence Committee. Representative Edward Boland is named as chairman.
	4 August	President Jimmy Carter announces reorganization of the Intelligence Community, creating a high-level committee chaired by the DCI to set priorities for collecting and producing intelligence, and giving the DCI full control of budget and operational tasking of intelligence collection.
1978	24 January	President Carter signs Executive Order 12036, which reshapes the intelligence structure and provides explicit guidance on all facets of intelligence activities.
	31 January	Ronald L. Humphrey, US Information Agency, arrested for spying for Vietnam.
	6 April	Arkadiy N. Schevchenko, Soviet official at the United Nations, defects to the United States.
	July	Ion Mihai Pacepa, Deputy Director of Romania's Department of Foreign Intelligence, defects to the U.S.
1979	15 November	British government publicly identifies Sir Anthony Blunt as the "fourth man" of a Soviet spy ring that included Guy Burgess, Donald Maclean, and Kim Philby.

CHAPTER 3

Decade of the Spy

Introduction

If 1985 is the year of the spy (although 1984 had 12 reported espionage cases to 11 for 1985) then the 1980s is the decade of the spy. US counterintelligence arrested or neutralized over 60 Americans who attempted to or actually committed espionage. Not since the beginning of the Cold War when the United States was rocked by the Julius Rosenberg, et. al. spy cases, did the nation experience the phenomenon of a rise in traitors in our midst.

Unlike the early Cold War spies, the new breed of American spies was motivated by money not ideology. Except for the Clyde Lee Conrad and John Walker spy rings, most of the new breed of American spies operated alone.

This chapter includes short summaries on all espionage cases reported in the public media or in unclassified sources, which have occurred in the United States during the 1980s or which have involved Americans abroad during this period.

Spy cases were not the only major counterintelligence events to take place during these 10 years. In December 1981, President Ronald Reagan signed Executive Order 12333, which defined counterintelligence as 'Information gathered and activities conducted to protect against espionage, other intelligence activities, sabotage, or assassinations conducted for or on behalf of foreign powers, organizations or persons, or international terrorist activities, but not including personnel, physical, document or communications security programs." This definition is still used by the CI community to this day.

This Executive Order also presented the mission requirements and authority for US Intelligence community agencies. It required that, before CIA could conduct any foreign intelligence collection or counterintelligence in the United States, the FBI had to coordinate. Likewise, before the FBI did any counterintelligence overseas, the CIA had to coordinate on the activity. The Department of Defense needed coordination from either the CIA or FBI depending on the location of its proposed counterintelligence activity.

On 13 January 1982, President Reagan signed National Security Decision Directive-2, which created a CI community body known as the Senior Interagency Group. This Group was to develop standards and doctrine for counterintelligence activities of the United States and resolve any interagency differences concerning the implementation of counterintelligence policy.

In April 1988, the Counterintelligence Center was created within CIA to improve the planning, coordination, management, and effectiveness of counterintelligence activities with the CIA and the Intelligence Community.

President George Bush signed National Security Directive 1 in January 1989, which reorganized the National Security Council structure. His Executive Order abolished the Senior Interagency Group but did not replace it with another body. It was not until several months later that another CI community body was established.

All the work of the CI community's interagency body is classified and unavailable for inclusion in this reader. The key to remember is that while the spy cases made the headlines, counterintelligence started its journey toward building CI community cooperation. Keep this in mind as you read this chapter.

Executive Order 12333
4 December 1981

TABLE OF CONTENTS

Preamble

Part 1. Goals, Direction, Duties, and Responsibilities With Respect to the National Intelligence Effort

Sec.
1.1 Goals
1.2 The National Security Council
1.3 National Foreign Intelligence Advisory Groups
1.4 The Intelligence Community
1.5 Director of Central Intelligence
1.6 Duties and Responsibilities of the Heads of Executive Branch Departments and Agencies
1.7 Senior Officials of the Intelligence Community
1.8 The Central Intelligence Agency
1.9 The Department of State
1.10 The Department of the Treasury
1.11 The Department of Defense
1.12 Intelligence Components Utilized by the Secretary of Defense
1.13 The Department of Energy
1.14 The Federal Bureau of Investigation

Part 2. Conduct of Intelligence Activities

2.1 Need
2.2 Purpose
2.3 Collection of Information
2.4 Collection Techniques
2.5 Attorney General Approval
2.6 Assistance to Law Enforcement Authorities
2.7 Contracting
2.8 Consistency With Other Laws
2.9 Undisclosed Participation in Organizations Within the United States
2.10 Human Experimentation
2.11 Prohibition on Assassination
2.12 Indirect Participation

Part 3. General Provisions
3.1 Congressional Oversight
3.2 Implementation
3.3 Procedures
3.4 Definitions
3.5 Purpose and Effect
3.6 Revocation

Timely and accurate information about the activities, capabilities, plans, and intentions of foreign powers, organizations, and persons, and their agents, is essential to the national security of the United States. All reasonable and lawful means must be used to ensure that the United States will receive the best intelligence available. For that purpose, by virtue of the authority vested in me by the Constitution and statutes of the United States of America, including the National Security Act of 1947, as amended (see Short Title note above), and as President of the United States of America, in order to provide for the effective conduct of United States intelligence activities and the protection of constitutional rights, it is hereby ordered as follows:

PART 1-Goals, Direction, Duties and Responsibilities With Respect To The National Intelligence Effort

1.1 GOALS

The United States intelligence effort shall provide the President and the National Security Council with the necessary information on which to base decisions concerning the conduct and development of foreign, defense and economic policy, and the protection of United States national interests from foreign security threats. All departments and agencies shall cooperate fully to fulfill this goal.

(a) Maximum emphasis should be given to fostering analytical competition among appropriate elements of the Intelligence Community.

(b) All means, consistent with applicable United States law and this Order, and with full consideration of the rights of United States persons, shall be used to develop intelligence information for the President and the National Security Council. A balanced approach between technical collection efforts and other means should be maintained and encouraged.

(c) Special emphasis should be given to detecting and countering espionage and other threats and activities directed by foreign intelligence services against the United States Government, or United States corporations, establishments, or persons.

(d) To the greatest extent possible consistent with applicable United States law and this Order, and with full consideration of the rights of United States persons, all agencies and departments should seek to ensure full and free exchange of information in order to derive maximum benefit from the United States intelligence effort.

1.2 THE NATIONAL SECURITY COUNCIL
(a) Purpose. The National Security Council (NSC) was established by the National Security Act of 1947 (see Short Title note above) to advise the President with respect to the integration of domestic, foreign and military policies relating to the national security. The NSC shall act as the highest Executive Branch entity that provides review of, guidance for and direction to the conduct of all national foreign intelligence, counterintelligence, and special activities, and attendant policies and programs.

(b) Committees. The NSC shall establish such committees as may be necessary to carry out its functions and responsibilities under this Order. The NSC, or a committee established by it, shall consider and submit to the President a policy recommendation, including all dissents, on each special activity and shall review proposals for other sensitive intelligence operations.

1.3 NATIONAL FOREIGN INTELLIGENCE ADVISORY GROUPS
(a) Establishment and Duties. The Director of Central Intelligence shall establish such boards, councils, or groups as required for the purpose of obtaining advice from within the Intelligence Community concerning:

(1) Production, review and coordination of national foreign intelligence;

(2) Priorities for the National Foreign Intelligence Program budget;

(3) Interagency exchanges of foreign intelligence information;

(4) Arrangements with foreign governments on intelligence matters;

(5) Protection of intelligence sources and methods;

(6) Activities of common concern; and

(7) Such other matters as may be referred by the Director of Central Intelligence.

(b) Membership. Advisory groups established pursuant to this section shall be chaired by the Director of Central Intelligence or his designated representative and shall consist of senior representatives from organizations within the Intelligence Community and from departments or agencies containing such organizations, as designated by the Director of Central Intelligence. Groups for consideration of substantive intelligence matters will include representatives of organizations involved in the collection, processing and analysis of intelligence. A senior representative of the Secretary of Commerce, the Attorney General, the Assistant to the President for National Security Affairs, and the Office of the Secretary of Defense shall be invited to participate in any group which deals with other than substantive intelligence matters.

President Ronald Reagan

1.4 THE INTELLIGENCE COMMUNITY

The agencies within the Intelligence Community shall, in accordance with applicable United States law and with the other provisions of this Order, conduct intelligence activities necessary for the conduct of foreign relations and the protection of the national security of the United States, including:

(a) Collection of information needed by the President, the National Security Council, the Secretaries of State and Defense, and other Executive Branch officials for the performance of their duties and responsibilities;

(b) Production and dissemination of intelligence;

(c) Collection of information concerning, and the conduct of activities to protect against, intelligence activities directed against the United States, international terrorist and international narcotics activities, and other hostile activities directed against the United States by foreign powers, organizations, persons, and their agents;

(d) Special activities;

(e) Administrative and support activities within the United States and abroad necessary for the performance of authorized activities; and

(f) Such other intelligence activities as the President may direct from time to time.

1.5 DIRECTOR OF CENTRAL INTELLIGENCE

In order to discharge the duties and responsibilities prescribed by law, the Director of Central Intelligence shall be responsible directly to the President and the NSC and shall:

(a) Act as the primary adviser to the President and the NSC on national foreign intelligence and provide the President and other officials in the Executive Branch with national foreign intelligence;

(b) Develop such objectives and guidance for the Intelligence Community as will enhance capabilities for responding to expected future needs for national foreign intelligence;

(c) Promote the development and maintenance of services of common concern by designated intelligence organizations on behalf of the Intelligence Community;

(d) Ensure implementation of special activities;

(e) Formulate policies concerning foreign intelligence and counterintelligence arrangements with foreign governments, coordinate foreign intelligence and counterintelligence relationships between agencies of the Intelligence Community and the intelligence or internal security services of foreign governments, and establish procedures governing the conduct of liaison by any department or agency with such services on narcotics activities;

(f) Participate in the development of procedures approved by the Attorney General governing criminal narcotics intelligence activities abroad to ensure that these activities are consistent with foreign intelligence programs;

(g) Ensure the establishment by the Intelligence Community of common security and access standards for managing and handling foreign intelligence systems, information, and products;

(h) Ensure that programs are developed which protect intelligence sources, methods, and analytical procedures;

(i) Establish uniform criteria for the determination of relative priorities for the transmission of critical national foreign intelligence, and advise the Secretary of Defense concerning the communications requirements of the Intelligence Community for the transmission of such intelligence;

(j) Establish appropriate staffs, committees, or other advisory groups to assist in the execution of the Director's responsibilities;

(k) Have full responsibility for production and dissemination of national foreign intelligence, and authority to levy analytic tasks on departmental intelligence production organizations, in consultation with those organizations, ensuring that appropriate mechanisms for competitive analysis are developed so that diverse points of view are considered fully and differences of judgment within the Intelligence Community are brought to the attention of national policymakers;

(l) Ensure the timely exploitation and dissemination of data gathered by national foreign intelligence collection means, and ensure that the resulting intelligence is disseminated immediately to appropriate government entities and military commands;

(m) Establish mechanisms which translate national foreign intelligence objectives and priorities approved by the NSC into specific guidance for the Intelligence Community, resolve conflicts in tasking priority, provide to departments and agencies having information collection capabilities that are not part of the National Foreign Intelligence Program advisory tasking concerning collection of national foreign intelligence, and provide for the development of plans and arrangements for transfer of required collection tasking authority to the Secretary of Defense when directed by the President;

(n) Develop, with the advice of the program managers and departments and agencies concerned, the consolidated National Foreign Intelligence Program budget, and present it to the President and the Congress;

(o) Review and approve all requests for reprogramming National Foreign Intelligence Program funds, in accordance with guidelines established by the Office of Management and Budget;

(p) Monitor National Foreign Intelligence Program implementation, and, as necessary, conduct program and performance audits and evaluations;

(q) Together with the Secretary of Defense, ensure that there is no unnecessary overlap between national foreign intelligence programs and Department of Defense intelligence programs consistent with the requirement to develop competitive analysis, and provide to and obtain from the Secretary of Defense all information necessary for this purpose;

(r) In accordance with law and relevant procedures approved by the Attorney General under this Order, give the heads of the departments and agencies access to all intelligence, developed by the CIA or the staff elements of the Director of Central Intelligence, relevant to the national intelligence needs of the departments and agencies; and,

(s) Facilitate the use of national foreign intelligence products by Congress in a secure manner.

1.6 DUTIES AND RESPONSIBILITIES OF THE HEADS OF EXECUTIVE BRANCH DEPARTMENTS AND AGENCIES

(a) The heads of all Executive Branch departments and agencies shall, in accordance with law and relevant procedures approved by the Attorney General under this Order, give the Director of Central Intelligence access to all information relevant to the national intelligence needs of the United States, and shall give due consideration to the requests from the Director of Central Intelligence for appropriate support for Intelligence Community activities.

(b) The heads of departments and agencies involved in the National Foreign Intelligence Program shall ensure timely development and submission to the Director of Central Intelligence by the program managers and heads of component activities of proposed national programs and budgets in the format designated by the Director of Central Intelligence, and shall also ensure that the Director of Central Intelligence is provided, in a timely and responsive manner, all information necessary to perform the Director's program and budget responsibilities.

c) The heads of departments and agencies involved in the National Foreign Intelligence Program may appeal to the President decisions by the Director of Central Intelligence on budget or reprogramming matters of the National Foreign Intelligence Program.

1.7 SENIOR OFFICIALS OF THE INTELLIGENCE COMMUNITY

The heads of departments and agencies with organizations in the Intelligence Community or the heads of such organizations, as appropriate, shall:

(a) Report to the Attorney General possible violations of federal criminal laws by employees and of specified federal criminal laws by any other person as provided in procedures agreed upon by the Attorney General and the head of the department or agency concerned, in a manner consistent with the protection of intelligence sources and methods, as specified in those procedures;

(b) In any case involving serious or continuing breaches of security, recommend to the Attorney General that the case be referred to the FBI for further investigation;

(c) Furnish the Director of Central Intelligence and the NSC, in accordance with applicable law and procedures approved by the Attorney General under this Order, the information required for the performance of their respective duties;

(d) Report to the Intelligence Oversight Board, and keep the Director of Central Intelligence appropriately informed, concerning any intelligence activities of their organizations that they have reason to believe may be unlawful or contrary to Executive order or Presidential directive;

(e) Protect intelligence and intelligence sources and methods from unauthorized disclosure consistent with guidance from the Director of Central Intelligence;

(f) Disseminate intelligence to cooperating foreign governments under arrangements established or agreed to by the Director of Central Intelligence;

(g) Participate in the development of procedures approved by the Attorney General governing production and dissemination of intelligence resulting from criminal narcotics intelligence activities abroad if their departments, agencies, or organizations have intelligence responsibilities for foreign or domestic narcotics production and trafficking;

(h) Instruct their employees to cooperate fully with the Intelligence Oversight Board; and

(i) Ensure that the Inspectors General and General Counsels for their organizations have access to any information necessary to perform their duties assigned by this Order.

1.8 THE CENTRAL INTELLIGENCE AGENCY

All duties and responsibilities of the CIA shall be related to the intelligence functions set out below. As authorized by this Order; the National Security Act of 1947, as amended (see Short Title note above); the CIA Act of 1949, as amended (see Short Title of 1949 Amendment note above); appropriate directives or other applicable law, the CIA shall:

(a) Collect, produce and disseminate foreign intelligence and counterintelligence, including information not otherwise obtainable. The collection of foreign intelligence or counterintelligence within the United States shall be coordinated with the FBI as required by procedures agreed upon by the Director of Central Intelligence and the Attorney General;

(b) Collect, produce and disseminate intelligence on foreign aspects of narcotics production and trafficking;

(c) Conduct counterintelligence activities outside the United States and, without assuming or performing any internal security functions, conduct counterintelligence activities within the United States in coordination with the FBI as required by procedures agreed upon (by) the Director of Central Intelligence and the Attorney General;

(d) Coordinate counterintelligence activities and the collection of information not otherwise obtainable when conducted outside the United States by other departments and agencies;

(e) Conduct special activities approved by the President. No agency except the CIA (or the Armed Forces of the United States in time of war declared by Congress or during any period covered by a report from the President to the Congress under the War Powers Resolution (87 Stat. 855) (50 U.S.C. 1541 et seq.)) may conduct any special activity unless the President determines that another agency is more likely to achieve a particular objective;

(f) Conduct services of common concern for the Intelligence Community as directed by the NSC;

(g) Carry out or contract for research, development and procurement of technical systems and devices relating to authorized functions;

(h) Protect the security of its installations, activities, information, property, and employees by appropriate means, including such investigations of applicants, employees, contractors, and other persons with similar associations with the CIA as are necessary; and

(i) Conduct such administrative and technical support activities within and outside the United States as are necessary to perform the functions described in sections (a) and (sic) through (h) above, including procurement and essential cover and proprietary arrangements.

1.9 THE DEPARTMENT OF STATE

The Secretary of State shall:

(a) Overtly collect information relevant to United States foreign policy concerns;

(b) Produce and disseminate foreign intelligence relating to United States foreign policy as required for the execution of the Secretary's responsibilities;

(c) Disseminate, as appropriate, reports received from United States diplomatic and consular posts;

(d) Transmit reporting requirements of the Intelligence Community to the Chiefs of United States Missions abroad; and

(e) Support Chiefs of Missions in discharging their statutory responsibilities for direction and coordination of mission activities.

1.10 THE DEPARTMENT OF THE TREASURY

The Secretary of the Treasury shall:

(a) Overtly collect foreign financial and monetary information;

(b) Participate with the Department of State in the overt collection of general foreign economic information;

(c) Produce and disseminate foreign intelligence relating to United States economic policy as required for the execution of the Secretary's responsibilities; and

(d) Conduct, through the United States Secret Service, activities to determine the existence and capability of surveillance equipment being used against the President of the United States, the Executive Office of the President, and, as authorized by the Secretary of the Treasury or the President, other Secret Service protectees and United States officials. No information shall be acquired intentionally through such activities except to protect against such surveillance, and those activities shall be conducted pursuant to procedures agreed upon by the Secretary of the Treasury and the Attorney General.

1.11 THE DEPARTMENT OF DEFENSE

The Secretary of Defense shall:

(a) Collect national foreign intelligence and be responsive to collection tasking by the Director of Central Intelligence;

(b) Collect, produce and disseminate military and military-related foreign intelligence and counterintelligence as required for execution of the Secretary's responsibilities;

(c) Conduct programs and missions necessary to fulfill national, departmental and tactical foreign intelligence requirements;

(d) Conduct counterintelligence activities in support of Department of Defense components outside the United States in coordination with the CIA, and within the United States in coordination with the FBI pursuant to procedures agreed upon by the Secretary of Defense and the Attorney General;

(e) Conduct, as the executive agent of the United States Government, signals intelligence and communications security activities, except as otherwise directed by the NSC;

(f) Provide for the timely transmission of critical intelligence, as defined by the Director of Central Intelligence, within the United States Government;

(g) Carry out or contract for research, development and procurement of technical systems and devices relating to authorized intelligence functions;

(h) Protect the security of Department of Defense installations, activities, property, information, and employees by appropriate means, including such investigations of applicants, employees, contractors, and other persons with similar associations with the Department of Defense as are necessary;

(i) Establish and maintain military intelligence relationships and military intelligence exchange programs with selected cooperative foreign defense establishments and international organizations, and ensure that such relationships and programs are in accordance with policies formulated by the Director of Central Intelligence;

(j) Direct, operate, control and provide fiscal management for the National Security Agency and for defense and military intelligence and national reconnaissance entities; and

(k) Conduct such administrative and technical support activities within and outside the United States as are necessary to perform the functions described in sections (a) through (j) above.

1.12 INTELLIGENCE COMPONENTS UTILIZED BY THE SECRETARY OF DEFENSE

In carrying out the responsibilities assigned in section 1.11, the Secretary of Defense is authorized to utilize the following:

(a) Defense Intelligence Agency, whose responsibilities shall include:

(1) Collection, production, or, through tasking and coordination, provision of military and military-related intelligence for the Secretary of Defense, the Joint Chiefs of Staff, other Defense components, and, as appropriate, non-Defense agencies;

(2) Collection and provision of military intelligence for national foreign intelligence and counterintelligence products;

(3) Coordination of all Department of Defense intelligence collection requirements;

(4) Management of the Defense Attaché system; and

(5) Provision of foreign intelligence and counterintelligence staff support as directed by the Joint Chiefs of Staff.

(b) National Security Agency, whose responsibilities shall include:

(1) Establishment and operation of an effective unified organization for signals intelligence activities, except for the delegation of operational control over certain operations that are conducted through other elements of the Intelligence Community. No other department or agency may engage in signals intelligence activities except pursuant to a delegation by the Secretary of Defense;

(2) Control of signals intelligence collection and processing activities, including assignment of resources to an appropriate agent for such periods and tasks as required for the direct support of military commanders;

(3) Collection of signals intelligence information for national foreign intelligence purposes in accordance with guidance from the Director of Central Intelligence;

(4) Processing of signals intelligence data for national foreign intelligence purposes in accordance with guidance from the Director of Central Intelligence;

(5) Dissemination of signals intelligence information for national foreign intelligence purposes to authorized elements of the Government, including the military services, in accordance with guidance from the Director of Central Intelligence;

(6) Collection, processing and dissemination of signals intelligence information for counterintelligence purposes;

(7) Provision of signals intelligence support for the conduct of military operations in accordance with tasking, priorities, and standards of timeliness assigned by the Secretary of Defense. If provision of such support requires use of national collection systems, these systems will be tasked within existing guidance from the Director of Central Intelligence;

(8) Executing the responsibilities of the Secretary of Defense as executive agent for the

communications security of the United States Government;

(9) Conduct of research and development to meet the needs of the United States for signals intelligence and communications security;

(10) Protection of the security of its installations, activities, property, information, and employees by appropriate means, including such investigations of applicants, employees, contractors, and other persons with similar associations with the NSA as are necessary;

(11) Prescribing, within its field of authorized operations, security regulations covering operating practices, including the transmission, handling and distribution of signals intelligence and communications security material within and among the elements under control of the Director of the NSA, and exercising the necessary supervisory control to ensure compliance with the regulations;

(12) Conduct of foreign cryptologic liaison relationships, with liaison for intelligence purposes conducted in accordance with policies formulated by the Director of Central Intelligence; and

(13) Conduct of such administrative and technical support activities within and outside the United States as are necessary to perform the functions described in sections (1) through (12) above, including procurement.

(c) Offices for the collection of specialized intelligence through reconnaissance programs, whose responsibilities shall include:

(1) Carrying out consolidated reconnaissance programs for specialized intelligence;

(2) Responding to tasking in accordance with procedures established by the Director of Central Intelligence; and

(3) Delegating authority to the various departments and agencies for research, development, procurement, and operation of designated means of collection.

(d) The foreign intelligence and counterintelligence elements of the Army, Navy, Air Force, and Marine Corps, whose responsibilities shall include:

(1) Collection, production and dissemination of military and military-related foreign intelligence and counterintelligence, and information on the foreign aspects of narcotics production and trafficking. When collection is conducted in response to national foreign intelligence requirements, it will be conducted in accordance with guidance from the Director of Central Intelligence. Collection of national foreign intelligence, not otherwise obtainable, outside the United States shall be coordinated with the CIA, and such collection within the United States shall be coordinated with the FBI;

(2) Conduct of counterintelligence activities outside the United States in coordination with the CIA, and within the United States in coordination with the FBI; and

(3) Monitoring of the development, procurement and management of tactical intelligence systems and equipment and conducting related research, development, and test and evaluation activities.

(e) Other offices within the Department of Defense appropriate for conduct of the intelligence missions and responsibilities assigned to the Secretary of Defense. If such other offices are used for intelligence purposes, the provisions of Part 2 of this Order shall apply to those offices when used for those purposes.

1.13 THE DEPARTMENT OF ENERGY
The Secretary of Energy shall:

(a) Participate with the Department of State in overtly collecting information with respect to foreign energy matters;

(b) Produce and disseminate foreign intelligence necessary for the Secretary's responsibilities;

(c) Participate in formulating intelligence collection and analysis requirements where the special expert capability of the Department can contribute; and

(d) Provide expert technical, analytical and research capability to other agencies within the Intelligence Community.

1.14 THE FEDERAL BUREAU OF INVESTIGATION

Under the supervision of the Attorney General and pursuant to such regulations as the Attorney General may establish, the Director of the FBI shall:

(a) Within the United States conduct counter-intelligence and coordinate counterintelligence activities of other agencies within the Intelligence Community. When a counterintelligence activity of the FBI involves military or civilian personnel of the Department of Defense, the FBI shall coordinate with the Department of Defense;

(b) Conduct counterintelligence activities outside the United States in coordination with the CIA as required by procedures agreed upon by the Director of Central Intelligence and the Attorney General;

(c) Conduct within the United States, when requested by officials of the Intelligence Community designated by the President, activities undertaken to collect foreign intelligence or support foreign intelligence collection requirements of other agencies within the Intelligence Community, or, when requested by the Director of the National Security Agency, to support the communications security activities of the United States Government;

(d) Produce and disseminate foreign intelligence and counterintelligence; and

(e) Carry out or contract for research, development and procurement of technical systems and devices relating to the functions authorized above.

PART 2–Conduct Of Intelligence Activities

2.1 NEED

Accurate and timely information about the capabilities, intentions and activities of foreign powers, organizations, or persons and their agents is essential to informed decision making in the areas of national defense and foreign relations. Collection of such information is a priority objective and will be pursued in a vigorous, innovative and responsible manner that is consistent with the Constitution and applicable law and respectful of the principles upon which the United States was founded.

2.2 PURPOSE

This Order is intended to enhance human and technical collection techniques, especially those undertaken abroad, and the acquisition of significant foreign intelligence, as well as the detection and countering of international terrorist activities and espionage conducted by foreign powers. Set forth below are certain general principles that, in addition to and consistent with applicable laws, are intended to achieve the proper balance between the acquisition of essential information and protection of individual interests. Nothing in this Order shall be construed to apply to or interfere with any authorized civil or criminal law enforcement responsibility of any department or agency.

2.3 COLLECTION OF INFORMATION

Agencies within the Intelligence Community are authorized to collect, retain or disseminate information concerning United States persons only in accordance with procedures established by the head of the agency concerned and approved by the Attorney General, consistent with the authorities provided by Part 1 of this Order. Those procedures shall permit collection, retention and dissemination of the following types of information:

(a) Information that is publicly available or collected with the consent of the person concerned;

(b) Information constituting foreign intelligence or counterintelligence, including such information concerning corporations or other commercial organizations. Collection within the United States of foreign intelligence not otherwise obtainable shall be undertaken by the FBI or, when significant foreign intelligence is sought, by other authorized agencies of the Intelligence Community, provided that no foreign intelligence collection by such agencies may be undertaken for the purpose of acquiring information concerning the domestic activities of United States persons;

(c) Information obtained in the course of a lawful foreign intelligence, counterintelligence, international narcotics or international terrorism investigation;

(d) Information needed to protect the safety of any persons or organizations, including those who are targets, victims or hostages of international terrorist organizations;

(e) Information needed to protect foreign intelligence or counterintelligence sources or methods from unauthorized disclosure. Collection within the United States shall be undertaken by the FBI except that other agencies of the Intelligence Community may also collect such information concerning present or former employees, present or former intelligence agency contractors or their present or former employees, or applicants for any such employment or contracting;

(f) Information concerning persons who are reasonably believed to be potential sources or contacts for the purpose of determining their suitability or credibility;

(g) Information arising out of a lawful personnel, physical or communications security investigation;

(h) Information acquired by overhead reconnaissance not directed at specific United States persons;

(i) Incidentally obtained information that may indicate involvement in activities that may violate federal, state, local or foreign laws; and

(j) Information necessary for administrative purposes.

In addition, agencies within the Intelligence Community may disseminate information, other than information derived from signals intelligence, to each appropriate agency within the Intelligence Community for purposes of allowing the recipient agency to determine whether the information is relevant to its responsibilities and can be retained by it.

2.4 COLLECTION TECHNIQUES

Agencies within the Intelligence Community shall use the least intrusive collection techniques feasible within the United States or directed against United States persons abroad. Agencies are not authorized to use such techniques as electronic surveillance, unconsented physical search, mail surveillance, physical surveillance, or monitoring devices unless they are in accordance with procedures established by the head of the agency concerned and approved by the Attorney General. Such procedures shall protect constitutional and other legal rights and limit use of such information to lawful governmental purposes. These procedures shall not authorize:

(a) The CIA to engage in electronic surveillance within the United States except for the purpose of training, testing, or conducting countermeasures to hostile electronic surveillance;

(b) Unconsented physical searches in the United States by agencies other than the FBI, except for:

(1) Searches by counterintelligence elements of the military services directed against military personnel within the United States or abroad for intelligence purposes, when authorized by a military commander empowered to approve physical searches for law enforcement purposes, based upon a finding of probable cause to believe that such persons are acting as agents of foreign powers; and

(2) Searches by CIA of personal property of non-United States persons lawfully in its possession.

(c) Physical surveillance of a United States person in the United States by agencies other than the FBI, except for:

(1) Physical surveillance of present or former employees, present or former intelligence agency contractors or their present or former employees, or applicants for any such employment or contracting; and

(2) Physical surveillance of a military person employed by a nonintelligence element of a military service.

(d) Physical surveillance of a United States person abroad to collect foreign intelligence, except to obtain significant information that cannot reasonably be acquired by other means.

2.5 ATTORNEY GENERAL APPROVAL

The Attorney General hereby is delegated the power to approve the use for intelligence purposes, within the United States or against a United States person abroad, of any technique for which a warrant would be required if undertaken for law enforcement purposes, provided that such techniques shall not be undertaken unless the Attorney General has determined in each case that there is probable cause to believe that the technique is directed against a foreign power or an agent of a foreign power. Electronic surveillance, as defined in the Foreign Intelligence Surveillance Act of 1978 (50 U.S.C. 1801 et seq.), shall be conducted in accordance with that Act, as well as this Order.

2.6 ASSISTANCE TO LAW ENFORCEMENT AUTHORITIES

Agencies within the Intelligence Community are authorized to:

(a) Cooperate with appropriate law enforcement agencies for the purpose of protecting the employees, information, property and facilities of any agency within the Intelligence Community;

(b) Unless otherwise precluded by law or this Order, participate in law enforcement activities to investigate or prevent clandestine intelligence activities by foreign powers, or international terrorist or narcotics activities;

(c) Provide specialized equipment, technical knowledge, or assistance of expert personnel for use by any department or agency, or, when lives are endangered, to support local law enforcement agencies. Provision of assistance by expert personnel shall be approved in each case by the General Counsel of the providing agency; and

(d) Render any other assistance and cooperation to law enforcement authorities not precluded by applicable law.

2.7 CONTRACTING

Agencies within the Intelligence Community are authorized to enter into contracts or arrangements for the provision of goods or services with private companies or institutions in the United States and need not reveal the sponsorship of such contracts or arrangements for authorized intelligence purposes. Contracts or arrangements with academic institutions may be undertaken only with the consent of appropriate officials of the institution.

2.8 CONSISTENCY WITH OTHER LAWS

Nothing in this Order shall be construed to authorize any activity in violation of the Constitution or statutes of the United States.

2.9 UNDISCLOSED PARTICIPATION IN ORGANIZATIONS WITHIN THE UNITED STATES

No one acting on behalf of agencies within the Intelligence Community may join or otherwise participate in any organization in the United States on behalf of any agency within the Intelligence Community without disclosing his intelligence affiliation to appropriate officials of the organization, except in accordance with procedures established by the head of the agency concerned and approved by the Attorney General. Such participation shall be authorized only if it is essential to achieving lawful purposes as determined by the agency head or designee. No such participation may be undertaken for the purpose of influencing the activity of the organization or its members except in cases where:

(a) The participation is undertaken on behalf of the FBI in the course of a lawful investigation; or

(b) The organization concerned is composed primarily of individuals who are not United States persons and is reasonably believed to be acting on behalf of a foreign power.

2.10 HUMAN EXPERIMENTATION

No agency within the Intelligence Community shall sponsor, contract for or conduct research on human subjects except in accordance with guidelines issued by the Department of Health and Human Services. The subject's informed consent shall be documented as required by those guidelines.

2.11 PROHIBITION ON ASSASSINATION

No person employed by or acting on behalf of the United States Government shall engage in, or conspire to engage in, assassination.

2.12 INDIRECT PARTICIPATION

No agency of the Intelligence Community shall participate in or request any person to undertake activities forbidden by this Order.

PART 3–General Provisions

3.1 CONGRESSIONAL OVERSIGHT

The duties and responsibilities of the Director of Central Intelligence and the heads of other departments, agencies, and entities engaged in intelligence activities to cooperate with the Congress in the conduct of its responsibilities for oversight of intelligence activities shall be as provided in title 50, United States Code, section 413. The requirements of section 662 of the Foreign Assistance Act of 1961, as amended (22 U.S.C. 2422), and section 501 of the National Security Act of 1947, as amended (50 U.S.C. 413), shall apply to all special activities as defined in this Order.

3.2 IMPLEMENTATION

The NSC, the Secretary of Defense, the Attorney General, and the Director of Central Intelligence shall issue such appropriate directives and procedures as are necessary to implement this Order. Heads of agencies within the Intelligence Community shall issue appropriate supplementary directives and procedures consistent with this Order. The Attorney General shall provide a statement of reasons for not approving any procedures established by the head of an agency in the Intelligence Community other than the FBI. The National Security Council may establish procedures in instances where the agency head and the Attorney General are unable to reach agreement on other than constitutional or other legal grounds.

3.3 PROCEDURES

Until the procedures required by this Order have been established, the activities herein authorized which require procedures shall be conducted in accordance with existing procedures or requirements established under Executive Order No. 12036 (formerly set out above). Procedures required by this Order shall be established as expeditiously as possible. All procedures promulgated pursuant to this Order shall be made available to the congressional intelligence committees.

3.4 DEFINITIONS

For the purposes of this Order, the following terms shall have these meanings:

(a) Counterintelligence means information gathered and activities conducted to protect against espionage, other intelligence activities, sabotage, or assassinations conducted for or on behalf of foreign powers, organizations or persons, or international terrorist activities, but not including personnel, physical, document or communications security programs.

(b) Electronic surveillance means acquisition of a nonpublic communication by electronic means without the consent of a person who is a party to an electronic communication or, in the case of a nonelectronic communication, without the consent of a person who is visably (sic) present at the place of communication, but not including the use of radio direction-finding equipment solely to determine the location of a transmitter.

(c) Employee means a person employed by, assigned to or acting for an agency within the Intelligence Community.

(d) Foreign intelligence means information relating to the capabilities, intentions and activities of foreign powers, organizations or persons, but not including counterintelligence except for information on international terrorist activities.

(e) Intelligence activities means all activities that agencies within the Intelligence Community are authorized to conduct pursuant to this Order.

(f) Intelligence Community and agencies within the Intelligence Community refer to the following agencies or organizations:

(1) The Central Intelligence Agency (CIA);

(2) The National Security Agency (NSA);

(3) The Defense Intelligence Agency (DIA);

(4) The offices within the Department of Defense for the collection of specialized national foreign intelligence through reconnaissance programs;

(5) The Bureau of Intelligence and Research of the Department of State;

(6) The intelligence elements of the Army, Navy, Air Force, and Marine Corps, the Federal Bureau of Investigation (FBI), the Department of the Treasury, and the Department of Energy; and

(7) The staff elements of the Director of Central Intelligence.

(g) The National Foreign Intelligence Program includes the programs listed below, but its composition shall be subject to review by the National Security Council and modification by the President:

(1) The programs of the CIA;

(2) The Consolidated Cryptologic Program, the General Defense Intelligence Program, and the programs of the offices within the Department of Defense for the collection of specialized national foreign intelligence through reconnaissance, except such elements as the Director of Central Intelligence and the Secretary of Defense agree should be excluded;

(3) Other programs of agencies within the Intelligence Community designated jointly by the Director of Central Intelligence and the head of the department or by the President as national foreign intelligence or counterintelligence activities;

(4) Activities of the staff elements of the Director of Central Intelligence;

(5) Activities to acquire the intelligence required for the planning and conduct of tactical operations by the United States military forces are not included in the National Foreign Intelligence Program.

(h) Special activities means activities conducted in support of national foreign policy objectives abroad which are planned and executed so that the role of the United States Government is not apparent or acknowledged publicly, and functions in support of such activities, but which are not intended to influence United States political processes, public opinion, policies, or media and do not include diplomatic activities or the collection and production of intelligence or related support functions.

(i) United States person means a United States citizen, an alien known by the intelligence agency concerned to be a permanent resident alien, an unincorporated association substantially composed of United States citizens or permanent resident aliens, or a corporation incorporated in the United States, except for a corporation directed and controlled by a foreign government or governments.

3.5 PURPOSE AND EFFECT
This Order is intended to control and provide direction and guidance to the Intelligence Community. Nothing contained herein or in any procedures promulgated hereunder is intended to confer any substantive or procedural right or privilege on any person or organization.

3.6 REVOCATION
Executive Order No. 12036 of January 24, 1978, as amended, entitled "United States Intelligence Activities," is revoked.

Ronald Reagan

National Security Decision Directive Number 84 – 11 March, 1983

Safeguarding National Security Information
As stated in Executive Order 12356, only that information whose disclosure would harm the national security interests of the United States may be classified. Every effort should be made to declassify information that no longer requires protection in the interest of national security.

At the same time, however, safeguarding against unlawful disclosures of properly classified information is a matter of grave concern and high priority for this Administration. In addition to the requirements set forth in Executive Order 12356, and based on the recommendations contained in the interdepartmental report forwarded by the Attorney General, I direct the following:

1. Each agency of the Executive Branch that originates or handles classified information. Such procedures shall at a minimum provide as follows:

a. All persons with authorized access to classified information shall be required to sign a nondisclosure agreement as a condition of access. This requirement may be implemented prospectively by agencies for which the administrative burden of compliance would otherwise be excessive.

b. All persons with authorized access to Sensitive Compartmented Information (SCI) shall be required to sign a nondisclosure agreement as a condition of access to SCI and other classified information. All such agreements must include a provision for prepublication review to assure deletion of SCI and other classified information.

c. All agreements required in paragraphs 1.a. and 1.b. must be in a form determined by the Department of Justice to be enforceable in a civil action brought by the United States. The Director, Information Security Oversight Office (ISOO), shall develop standardized forms that satisfy these requirements.

d. Appropriate policies shall be adopted to govern contacts between media representatives and agency personnel, so as to reduce the opportunity for negligent or deliberate disclosures of classified information. All persons with authorized access to classified information shall be clearly apprised of the agency's policies in this regard.

2. Each agency of the Executive branch that originates or handles classified information shall adopt internal procedures to govern the reporting and investigation of unauthorized disclosures of such information. Such procedures shall at a minimum provide that:

a. All such disclosures that the agency considers to be seriously damaging to its mission and responsibilities shall be evaluated to ascertain the nature of the information disclosed and the extent to which it had been disseminated.

b. The agency shall conduct a preliminary internal investigation prior to or concurrently with seeking investigative assistance from other agencies.

c. The agency shall maintain records of disclosures so evaluated and investigated.

d. Agencies in the possession of classified information originating with another agency shall cooperate with the originating agency by conducting internal investigations of the unauthorized disclosure of such information.

e. Persons determined by the agency to have knowingly made such disclosures or to have refused cooperation with investigations of such unauthorized disclosures will be denied further access to classified information and subjected to other administrative sanctions as appropriate.

3. Unauthorized disclosures of classified information shall be reported to the Department of Justice and the Information Security Oversight Office, as required by statute and Executive orders. The Department of Justice shall continue to review reported unauthorized disclosures of classified information to determine whether FBI involvement is warranted. Interested departments and agencies shall be consulted in developing criteria for evaluating such matters and in determining which cases should receive investigative priority. The FBI is authorized to investigate such matters as constitute potential violations of federal criminal law, even though administrative sanctions may be sought instead of criminal prosecution.

4. Nothing in this directive is intended to modify or preclude interagency agreements between FBI and other criminal investigative agencies regarding their responsibility for conducting investigations within their own agencies or departments.

5. The Office of Personnel Management and all departments and agencies with employees having access to classified information are directed to revise existing regulations and policies, as necessary, so that employees may be required to submit to polygraph examinations, when appropriate, in the course of investigations of unauthorized disclosures of classified information. As a minimum, such regulations shall permit an agency to decide that appropriate adverse consequences will follow an employee's refusal to cooperate with a polygraph examination that is limited in scope to the circumstances of the unauthorized disclosure under

investigation. Agency regulations may provide that only the head of the agency, or his delegate, is empowered to order an employee to submit to a polygraph examination. Results of polygraph examinations should not be relied upon to the exclusion of other information obtained during investigations.

6. The Attorney General, in consultation with the Director, Office of Personnel Management, is requested to establish an interdepartmental group to study the federal personnel security program and recommend appropriate revisions in existing Executive orders, regulations, and guidelines.

Ronald Reagan

The Walker Spy Ring

John Anthony Walker Jr. and his son, Michael Lance Walker, were indicted 28 May 1985, by a Federal grand jury in Baltimore, Maryland, on six counts of espionage. The elder Walker, a retired Navy warrant officer who had held a Top Secret Crypto clearance, was charged with having sold classified material to Soviet agents for the past 18 years.

John Walker Jr. was raised in Scranton, Pennsylvania. He had an unhappy childhood with alcoholic and separated parents. Walker left high school while in the 11th grade and on 25 October 1955, he joined the US Navy. While serving in the Navy, Walker was considered highly competent and in the first half of his 21 years of active duty, he rose from the seaman grade to warrant officer. He also earned the Navy equivalency for a high school and college diploma. When he retired in July 1976, he was a Chief Warrant Officer. His active duty assignments included responsible positions in communications, including Communications Systems Officer for the Amphibious Force Atlantic Fleet and Communications Officer for the Naval Surface Force Atlanta Fleet.

During his military career, Walker made some investments in which he lost money. To make up for his losses, in late 1968 at the age of 30, Walker went to the Soviet Embassy in Washington, DC and offered his services for the purpose of espionage. He was paid $2,000 or $3,000 at this first meeting, although he stated he could not remember the exact amount. He compromised key cards used for enciphering messages and also provided information on the encryption devices themselves. The Soviets provided Walker with a rotor decryption device used for testing wiring circuitry for rotors used by the US Navy for encryption purposes.

During his more than 17 years of espionage performed on behalf of the Soviet KGB, Walker compromised at least a million classified messages of the military services and US intelligence agencies. In addition, Walker recognized that when he left active duty he would no longer have direct access to classified information. He therefore recruited a friend, Jerry Alfred Whitworth, who also held communications positions similar to those previously occupied by Walker.

Upon retirement and his opening of a private investigation firm, Walker attempted to expand his espionage net further by first recruiting his brother, Arthur James Walker, a retired US Navy officer, and urging him to find civilian employment with a Department of Defense contractor. Next he recruited his son, Michael Lance Walker, who had recently enlisted in the US Navy. Earlier he had attempted without success to recruit one of his daughters who was, at the time, serving in the US Army.

John Walker's arrest resulted from a tip to the FBI from his former wife. She knew from almost the beginning that her husband was involved in espionage. On numerous occasions she had threatened to turn him in to authorities. An unhappy marriage eventually led to divorce and finally, in 1985, Walker's former wife informed the FBI of Walker's espionage activities. The

John Walker, charged by a Federal grand jury in Baltimore, Maryland on six counts of espionage.

FBI initiated an investigation and surveillance of Walker. He was apprehended on 20 May 1985, at a Maryland motel after depositing a number of documents at a roadside drop. Soviet embassy official, Alexei Tkachenko, who was spotted in the area, returned to Moscow within days of Walker's arrest.

Vitaliy Yurchenko, Deputy Chief of the First Department of the First Chief Directorate of the KGB, defected to the United States by voluntarily walking into the US Embassy in Rome, Italy, in July 1985. Soon after Walker's arrest and the attendant publicity, Yurchenko was briefed and consulted about the Walker case. The KGB did not believe that the FBI had been tipped by Barbara Walker and suspected that one of the KGB officers directly involved with Walker had been compromised by Western intelligence agencies. Because of his expertise in internal security matters, Yurchenko's advice was sought with regard to the appropriate course of action for dealing with the suspected compromise. In his position in the First Department, it was also appropriate to brief him concerning the Walker and Whitworth case. Because of the high degree of compartmentalized protection given to a case like Walker-Whitworth, Yurchenko, despite his previous assignments involving internal security and at the Soviet's US Embassy, had not previously been aware of the Walker/Whitworth operation.

From his briefings, Yurchenko learned that the KGB regarded the Walker/Whitworth operation to be the most important operation in the KGB's history. Yurchenko stated that the information delivered by Walker enabled the KGB to decipher over one million messages. Early on, the operation was transferred to Department Sixteen of the KGB, which handled only the most sensitive and important clandestine KGB operations around the world.

The KGB officers who handled the operation received important promotions and decorations for their successes. One of these officers secretly received the "Hero of the Soviet Union" award after the Soviet Navy expressed its delight over the success of the operation. Two other KGB officers involved with the Walker/Whitworth operation were awarded the coveted "Order of the Red Banner." Certain KGB officers from Department Sixteen were, at various times, assigned to the Soviet Embassy in Washington solely to handle "drops" made in connection with Walker/Whitworth espionage.

Yurchenko was informed by a high KGB official that the information learned from the Walker/Whitworth operation would have been "devastating" to the United States in time of war.

On 28 October 1985, John Walker pleaded guilty to espionage charges under a plea agreement by which Walker agreed to testify in the trial of Jerry Whitworth and to provide full information on what was given to the Soviets in exchange for a lesser sentence for his son. On 6 November 1986, John Walker was sentenced to two life terms plus 10 years to be served concurrently. A federal grand jury was convened to pursue some of the unresolved questions including the location of up to $1 million possibly hidden by John Walker and the involvement of minor players in the espionage ring.

Jerry Alfred Whitworth

Jerry Alfred Whitworth was born in Muldrow, Oklahoma, on 10 August 1939. His parents separated shortly after he was born, and his grandparents and an uncle raised him. He was known as a good-natured youth who, in his senior year in high school, was voted class clown. In September 1956, Whitworth joined the US Navy. Following his four-year enlistment in the Navy, Whitworth left the service and enrolled in college. He was unsuccessful in his college classes and reenlisted in the Navy in 1962.

Jerry Alfred Whitworth, convicted on 24 July 1986 on seven counts of espionage.

During an assignment in 1970, when Whitworth and John Anthony Walker were stationed together, the two became acquainted, and Walker eventually started a conscious effort to assess Whitworth as a potential agent for expanding and continuing Walker's espionage efforts on behalf of the KGB. In 1974, Whitworth had decided to resign from active duty. During this same year, in a San Diego restaurant, Walker finally asked Whitworth to join him in a conspiracy that would allow them to receive significant payments for selling classified information. Walker asked Whitworth to provide him information which he, in turn, would sell to criminal elements where there was a known market. The two men would then split the profits. Whitworth agreed to cooperate with the knowledge that the information was being sold to the KGB coming only at a later date in their conspiracy.

Whitworth thereafter reenlisted in the Navy. He advanced to Senior Chief Radioman and received the highest ratings from his supervisors. Following his recruitment by Walker, Whitworth became a model service member and excelled in his specialty until his retirement on 31 October 1983.

Whitworth was secretly married in 1976. Between that year and 1985, Whitworth met with Walker on an average of two to four times a year at which time he would pass to Walker 25 to 50 rolls of Minox film containing classified information. Whitworth was originally paid $2,000 per month for the material he supplied; however, this was subsequently increased to $4,000 and then $6,000 per month later in the conspiracy. It is estimated that Whitworth received total pay of at least $332,000 for the documents he passed. The activities of Whitworth, continuing as the principal agent of collection for John Walker, permitted the Soviets to gauge the true capabilities and vulnerabilities of the US Navy.

Whitworth's trial began on 6 March 1986. He was convicted on 24 July 1986 on seven counts of espionage and one count of tax evasion. On 28 August 1986 Whitworth was sentenced to 365 years in prison and a $410,000 fine.

Arthur James Walker

Arthur James Walker is the eldest brother of John Walker Jr. Arthur grew up in West Scranton, Pennsylvania, where he attended parochial school and two years at the University of Scranton. He enlisted in the US Navy when he was 19 years old, was subsequently commissioned and reached the rank of lieutenant commander prior to his retirement in July 1973. According to court testimony of both Arthur and John Walker, Arthur was recruited by John to obtain employment with a Department of Defense contractor. At the time of his recruitment, Arthur was having serious financial problems. His active involvement in espionage was restricted to 1981 and 1982.

At VSE Corporation of Chesapeake, where he was hired in February 1980, as an engineer, Arthur had limited access to classified information. He provided John with two classified documents obtained from his employment with VSE for which he was paid a total of $12,000. One document was a repair manual for two command and control fleet vessels. The second document consisted of breakdown reports on amphibious landing craft. Arthur had rationalized that these documents were not significant and could do no serious damage to US security interests. John had also tasked Arthur to obtain US defense readiness plans.

On 20 May 1985, following the arrest of John Walker, Arthur was visited at his home by FBI agents. He was taken in for questioning and admitted to his cooperation with his brother in espionage activities. On 9 August 1985, the 51-year-old Arthur was found guilty on seven counts of espionage and on 12 November 1985 was

Arthur James Walker

sentenced to life in prison. His sentence included three life terms plus three 10-year terms as well as a fine of $250,000.

Michael Lance Walker

Michael, the only son of John Walker, dropped out of high school in 1980 due to problems associated with use of drugs and poor grades. Having left his divorced mother's house to live with his father in Norfolk, he reentered high school and graduated from Ryan Upper High School in June 1982. Although he wanted to go to college, his grades were inadequate for college acceptance. He enlisted in the US Navy on 13 December 1982. His father convinced Michael that he could make money by turning over classified documents to him. Michael agreed to the arrangement for monetary reasons as well as his desire to please his father.

Following his recruitment in approximately August 1983, Michael began turning over classified documents to his father for which he was paid $1,000. His access to classified material increased when he was assigned to Operations Administration as a seaman (E-3) aboard the aircraft carrier *Nimitz*. Following the arrest of John Walker, Michael was interviewed abroad the carrier. In his sleeping area, investigators found approximately 15 pounds of classified information, which had been destined for destruction but which Michael had hidden away to turn over to his father at the time of his next port call.

Michael was arrested on 22 May 1985 and during his admissions it was determined that he had passed so many documents to his father that he had no accurate count of the total. However, it was later determined that he had passed in excess of 1,500 documents since his initial agreement to cooperate with his father. On 28 October 1985, the 22-year old Michael pleaded guilty to five counts of espionage. On 6 November 1986 he was sentenced to two 25-year terms and three 10-year terms to run concurrently.

Meeting the Espionage Challenge: Review of United States Counterintelligence and Security Programs

*Report of the Select Committee on Intelligence
United States Senate
3 October 1986*

(Paragraphs not pertinent to counterintelligence omitted)

I. Introduction and Summary

As espionage is ancient, so is counterintelligence. The Chinese military theorist Sun Tzu stated the principle in the fourth century BC: "It is essential to seek out enemy agents who have come to conduct espionage against you..."[1] Today, over two millennia later, the battle is still being waged.

A. Background

At the beginning of the 99th Congress, the Select Committee on Intelligence initiated a comprehensive review of the capabilities of U.S. counterintelligence and security programs for dealing with the threat to the United States from Soviet espionage and other hostile intelligence activities. This decision was an outgrowth of eight years of Committee interest in these issues. The review is also consonant with the Committee's mission to "oversee and make continuing studies of the intelligence activities and programs of the United States Government, and to submit to the Senate appropriate proposals for legislation and report to the Senate appropriate proposals for legislation and report to the Senate concerning such intelligence activities and programs." Senate Resolution 400, which established the Committee ten years ago, specifies that intelligence activities include "activities taken to counter similar activities directed against the United States."

Michael Walker

The Committee's review had barely begun when the arrests of John Walker and two of his relatives began to make 1985 the "Year of the Spy." In June 1985, the Committee pledged that it would prepare a report to the full Senate at the earliest possible time. In light of this Committee's ongoing efforts, the Senate decided not to create a National Commission on Espionage and Security. On June 20, 1985, the Chairman of the Committee wrote to the President, saying, "You and we share an historic opportunity-both to dramatically improve U.S. counterintelligence and security and to demonstrate how Congress and the Executive can work together to achieve progress in sensitive intelligence areas."

The ensuing fifteen months have generated an amazingly sustained interest in counterintelligence and security on the part of both policymakers and the public. There have been over a dozen arrests for espionage, nearly all leading to guilty pleas or verdicts; Americans and West Germans with sensitive information have defected to the Soviet Union and East German; and Soviets with sensitive information have defected to the West, and in one major case then returned to the Soviet Union. Most recently, the Soviet arrest of an innocent American journalist in retaliation for the U.S. arrest of a Soviet U.N. employee has made it clear that counterintelligence, while seemingly a peripheral element in superpower relations, can even become the focus of U.S.-Soviet confrontation.

The "Year of the Spy" was characterized by intensive Executive branch attention of problems of counterintelligence and security. Of particular note were the efforts of the Department of Defense Security Review Commission, chaired by General Richard G. Stilwell, USA (retired) and the Secretary of State's Advisory Panel on Overseas Security, chaired by Admiral Bobby R. Inman, USN (retired) and Executive branch steps to implement their recommendations. The Stilwell Commission led to significant progress in Defense Department personnel and information security policies, and the Inman Panel led to restructuring of State Department security functions and a major embassy rebuilding program around the world.

The Committee's efforts have encouraged, and have greatly benefited from this sustained Executive branch attention to counterintelligence and security matters. The Committee received an unprecedented level of cooperation from the President, the National Security Council staff, the Intelligence Community Staff, and the many departments and agencies with counterintelligence or security functions. Executive branch experts and policymakers testified in sixteen closed hearings on specific counterintelligence cases and the current state of U.S. programs to counter hostile intelligence activities. Scores of staff briefings and the provision to the Committee of many sensitive Executive branch studies enabled the Committee to compile the very best ideas and recommendations of those in government, as well as suggestions from security experts in industry. The Committee, in turn, evaluated those ideas and submitted a comprehensive set of recommendations for Executive branch consideration.

The Intelligence Authorization Act for FY 1986 included a statutory requirement that the President submit to the House and Senate Intelligence Committees a report on the capabilities, programs and policies of the United States to protect against, detect, monitor, counter and limit intelligence activities by foreign powers, within and outside the United States, directed at the United States Government. The report was to

Awareness Brochures

include plans for improvements that the Executive branch has authority to effectuate on its own, and recommendations for improvements that would require legislation. To assist the Senate Intelligence Committee in its work, the conferees on the Act requested an interim report developed in consultation with the Intelligence Committees. This Committee, in turn, prepared its own interim report, which it shared with the Executive branch last winter.

The many good ideas and recommendations that the Committee obtained from Executive branch officials and studies had not yet been implemented for two basic reasons: counterintelligence and security had failed to receive substantial attention; and the ideas frequently challenged established ways of doing things, cut across bureaucratic lines of responsibility, or required substantial changes in resource allocation. External events provided substantial impetus for interagency attention to these issues. The Committee's efforts and the Executive branch's cooperation are producing the interagency decision-making that is required for progress.

The President began, responding to a request from the Committee, by designating the Director of Central Intelligence to represent the Administration at a series of Committee hearings on counterintelligence and security programs and selecting a counterintelligence expert on the NSC staff as liaison to the Committee. An interagency mechanism under the Senior Interdepartmental Group for Intelligence (SIG-I) supplied coordinated Executive branch reactions to the Committee's interim report recommendations. This not only helped the Committee, but also gave the Executive branch itself the opportunity to address and decide these important policy issues. The resulting positions were conveyed to the Committee in the President's interim report and transferred to an NSC staff committee for implementation.

The President's interim report and subsequent consultation between Executive branch officials and the Committee were thus of great value in the preparation of the present Report. The Committee looks forward to receipt of the President's final report, which will serve as an important benchmark of the progress achieved thus far to strengthen counterintelligence and security capabilities....

B. Organization of the U.S. Government to Meet the Hostile Intelligence Challenge

The Committee's findings underscore a fundamental challenge to the nation. The hostile intelligence threat is more serious than anyone in the Government has yet acknowledged publicly. The combination of human espionage and sophisticated technical collection has done immense damage to the national security. To respond to the threat, the United States must maintain effective counterintelligence efforts to detect and neutralize hostile intelligence operations directly, and defensive security countermeasures to protect sensitive information and activities.

The Committee believes that, as a result of significant improvements in recent years, the nation's counterintelligence structure is fundamentally sound, although particular elements need to be strengthened. The Executive branch and the Committee agree on the importance of developing and implementing a coherent national counterintelligence strategy that integrates the work of the FBI, the CIA and the Department of State, Defense, and Justice. Executive branch agencies are already drafting such a document. The Committee expects this strategy to play a major role in its oversight of Executive branch counterintelligence efforts in the years to come.

By contrast, defensive security programs lack the resources and national policy direction needed to cope with expanding hostile intelligence operations. Personnel security policies remain fragmented despite persistent attempts to develop national standards. Information security reforms are long overdue. America faces vulnerability to hostile intelligence activities in the areas of communications and computer security, where countermeasures must keep pace with increasing technological change. Consequently, in December 1985, the Committee called for the development of a National Strategic Security Program that would address these issues. The Committee believes that a new and permanent national policy mechanism is needed to create this program and then to coordinate and foster the protection of information and activities having the greatest strategic importance.

In recent months, the Executive branch has come to understand the sense of urgency with which the Committee views the need for an integrated strategic security program and an improved security policy structure. An effort to develop such a security program is now likely. The Director of Central intelligence, in his capacity as chairman of the Senior Interdepartmental Group for Intelligence, recently revamped the security committee structure under the SIG-I and called for greater participation in those committees by policymakers, so that decisions could be reached on interagency issues and policy initiatives.

The Committee believes that these changes are insufficient because they fail to bridge the gaps between the various security disciplines. Most Executive branch officials, although opposing further changes at this time, do not dispute the likely need for them in the future. The Committee will continue to push for more effective policy review and formulation, for it believes that the national security cannot afford much more delay. This is especially true if the current Administration is to leave as a legacy a workable security policy system that will not have to be reinvented by each succeeding administration. The Committee recommends that the eventual new security policy structure be one that transcends currently politics and policy and is codified in an Executive Order.

C. Counterintelligence: Learning the Lessons of Recent Cases

The Committee has examined in detail each of the espionage cases that have come to public attention in recent years, as well as the Yurchenko defection case and cases that remain classified. Although this report does not discuss individual cases in detail, many of the recommendations in sections III and IV reflect lessons learned through those cases.

The first lesson of these cases is the need for greater counterintelligence and security awareness. The Committee found insufficient tailoring of security awareness material to the needs of particular audiences-defense contractors, workers at government facilities, U.S. personnel stationed overseas, members of ethnic groups known to be targeted by foreign intelligence services, congressional staff and others. The usefulness of such material is illustrated by the fact that once the U.S. Navy began to improve its security awareness briefings after the Walker case, co-workers of Jonathan Pollard noted his unusual pattern of document requests and alerted authorities.

The second lesson is the need for earlier involvement of the FBI and the Department of Justice in cases of suspected espionage. When offices or agencies have held back from bringing in the FBI, events have often gotten out of control. When the FBI has been alerted in time, their investigative resources and interview skills have often led to confessions. When the Justice Department has been involved at an early stage, cases destined for prosecution have been built on more solid ground, resulting in numerous convictions.

The third lesson is the need for more attention and better access to information on the finances, foreign travel and foreign contacts of persons with sensitive information. The Committee found that the FBI sometimes lacked access to financial and telephone records in its counterintelligence investigations; that insufficient attention was given to signs of trouble regarding former employees with sensitive accesses; and that too few people were alerting office security personnel or the FBI when they were approached by possible foreign intelligence officers.

The Chin, Pollard and Scranage cases have taught the clear lesson that espionage services outside the Soviet bloc also engage in illegal activities targeted at the United States, which must not be tolerated. The Bell and Harper cases, among many, underscored the need for controls on the activities of certain Eastern European representatives and of U.S. companies controlled by the Soviet Union or its allies. And the Zakharov case, like the Enger and Chernyayev case eight years ago, reminds us that the KGB is willing to use the United Nations Secretariat for intelligence cover.

The Edward Lee Howard case led to investigations and corrective action in the CIA, just as the Walker case led to formation of the Stilwell Commission and to additional steps by the U.S. Navy. The FBI and the Justice Department are still absorbing the lessons of the Howard case. The Committee will continue to monitor how well all the agencies implement improvements in response to those lessons.

The defection and re-defection of Vitaliy Yurchenko, which highlighted both the counterintelligence value of defectors and apparent shortcomings in their handling and resettlement, also led to internal reviews and useful actions by the CIA to improve its handling of defectors.

The Committee believes that more must be done, however, to change the basic objectives with which the U.S. Government approaches defectors. We must accept the obligation to help defectors succeed in, and contribute to, American society. Executive branch efforts to analyze and learn from the Yurchenko case continue, and the Committee expects to see more progress in this area.

The CIA has taken significant steps to improve recruitment and career development programs for counterintelligence personnel. The Scranage and Howard cases suggest that there was, and is, substantial need for improvement in CIA counterintelligence, and the Committee will continue to monitor CIA efforts. The military services and the FBI are also beginning to improve their recruitment and career development programs for counterintelligence, but progress is uneven.

The Committee will continue to press Executive branch agencies to incorporate into their operations improved counterintelligence awareness procedures. While agencies have moved in the last year to remedy problems that were exposed in recent espionage cases, they have been much slower to accept the painful need to confront the implications of hostile intelligence successes. Attentiveness to possible hostile knowledge of classified U.S. operations must be increased, and analysis of the impact of known losses of classified information must extend to the unhappy possibility that operations or weapons systems will require modification. While there is always a need not to let worse case analyses paralyze our military and intelligence services, the greater current danger appears to be a wishing away of the consequences of hostile intelligence efforts....

G. Respect for Individual Rights

A free society cannot allow the fear of foreign adversaries to undermine the constitutionally protected rights that define the true character of our nation. This principle has guided the Committee in its review of counterintelligence and security programs. As President Reagan stated on June 29, 1985:

> *We can counter this hostile threat and still remain true to our values. We don't need to fight repression by becoming repressive ourselves....But we need to put our cleverness and determination to work and we need to deal severely with those who betray our country. We should begin by realizing that spying is a fact of life and that all of us need to be better informed about the unchanging realities of the Soviet system.... There is no quick fix to this problem. Without hysteria or finger point, let us move calmly and deliberately together to protect freedom.*

The Committee's recommendations seek to strengthen U.S. counterintelligence and security measures without violating constitutional rights or upsetting the delicate balance between security and freedom. A broad range of improvements can be made without adversely affecting the rights of individuals, and the additional tools needed for counterintelligence and security purposes can be made subject to reasonable safeguards that minimize intrusion into the privacy of American citizens....

III. Counterintelligence

An effective response to the foreign intelligence threat requires a combination of counterintelligence and security measures. The Committee believes it is important to distinguish between counterintelligence efforts and security programs, while ensuring that both are part of a national policy framework that takes account of all aspects of the threat. The best way to explain the difference is to say that counterintelligence measures deal directly with foreign intelligence service activities, while security programs are the indirect defensive actions that minimize vulnerabilities. The FBI, CIA, and the counterintelligence components of the Defense Department have primary responsibility for operations and analysis dealing directly with foreign intelligence services. In addition, the Committee and the Executive branch have included within the national counterintelligence policy structure those diplomatic and regulatory policies that control the numbers and movements of particular countries' foreign intelligence service officers and co-opted agents in the United States and at U.S. facilities abroad.

By statue and executive order, counterintelligence functions are divided among the FBI, CIA, and components of the Defense Department. The FBI has the lead within the United States, while CIA is in charge abroad. The Defense Department, which deals with threats to classified defense information worldwide, divides its counterintelligence functions among the military services, DIA, and NSA. No single official is responsible for the full range of counterintelligence activities below the level of the President and his National Security Adviser. Given these circumstances, there is a constant risk of fragmentation and conflict among organizations with different methods and priorities.

The Committee has found that communication and cooperation among U.S. counterintelligence agencies have improved greatly in recent years and are probably better today than at any time since World War II. Nevertheless, more needs to be done to ensure that agencies learn from each other's experiences and that progress achieved in one area can have benefits for others. The issue is not just communication and operational coordination to bridge jurisdictional boundaries, but better long-range planning is also needed to make optimal use of limited resources worldwide against well-organized and sophisticated adversaries.

Soviet bloc and PRC intelligence operations do not respect geographic boundaries. Thus, in many recent cases Americans who committed espionage in the United States met their foreign intelligence service contacts abroad. The targets and techniques needed for counterintelligence success transcend agency jurisdictions. For these and other reasons, the Chairman and Vice Chairman of the Committee stated in October, 1985, that the Executive branch should develop a national counterintelligence strategy that establishes national objectives and integrates the planning and resources of each agency to achieve these objectives. The President's interim report to the Intelligence Committees indicated agreement with this proposal, and in fact the Executive branch is now preparing such a document.

The organizational structure is already in place, fortunately, to develop a national counterintelligence strategy. Under the National Security Council there is a Senior Interdepartmental Group for Intelligence (SIG-I) chaired by the Director of Central Intelligence. Within that framework, an Interagency Group for Counterintelligence (IG-CI), chaired by the FBI Director, develops national policy recommendations and provides a forum for agreement on new initiatives. A small secretariat for the IG-CI has expert personnel drawn from the FBI, CIA, and Defense Department. This staff evaluates the threat and recommends policy initiatives for counterintelligence and countermeasures improvements.

The IG-CI, assisted by its secretariat, is the proper place to develop a national counterintelligence strategy. This structure ensures joint participation by the FBI, CIA, and Defense Department, and other interested departments and agencies (such as the State and Justice Departments) are also represented on the IG-CI. Ultimate responsibility for resolution of policy issues rests with the National Security Council, which has recently brought onto its staff an experienced FBI counterintelligence specialist.

The President's interim report to the Intelligence Committee indicates that the IG-CI has, in fact, been tasked to frame strategic guidance of the sort proposed by this Committee. As noted earlier, member agencies are now engaged in the drafting process.

Findings and Recommendations

1. Findings.–The IG-CI has been charted to frame national counterintelligence objectives and an associated strategy (or master plan) to further those objectives, and to submit the objectives and plan for consideration by the SIG-I and thence the NSC. The Committee is pleased to learn that Executive branch agencies are actively drafting this document. This is a positive response to proposals presented by the Chairman and Vice Chairman in testimony before the Permanent Subcommittee on Investigations in October 1985.

2. Recommendation.–The National Security Council should approve a statement of major counterintelligence objectives and a strategy, i.e., a time-phased master plan, to attain those objectives. The House and Senate Intelligence Committees should receive this document. An effective oversight mechanism should be established to ensure that major programs and associated budgets, legislative proposals, and other key actions are validated against the master plan, constitute judicious and operationally efficient allocation of resources, and achieve all feasible synergism. There should also be a process for continuing review and evaluation.

3. Recommendation.–The National Foreign Intelligence Program should provide for, and Congress should authorize, augmentation of the staff that assists the IG-CI to ensure effective performance of its expanded responsibilities regarding the development and implementation of the national counterintelligence strategy....

C. Counterintelligence Awareness Programs

One key to a successful counterintelligence strategy is thorough analysis of the hostile intelligence threat and communication of the results to those who need to take countermeasures. Current efforts range from the FBI's Development of Counterintelligence Awareness (DECA) program for briefing defense contractors to the improved assessment of Soviet deception, disinformation and active measures. Informing the public, industry and other government agencies can have a direct payoff, as in the case where a student at Columbia University contacted the FBI about a Bulgarian exchange visitor after seeing a TV documentary on espionage that described conduct similar to that of the Bulgarian. The student's report led to an FBI offensive double agent operation resulting in the arrest of a Bulgarian intelligence officer. At a classified level, U.S. counterintelligence agencies must work with a great variety of government programs and security officials to provide tailored information and analysis.

On November 1, 1985, the President issued NSDD-197 requiring each U.S. Government agency to establish a security awareness program for its employees, including periodic formal briefings on the threat posed by hostile intelligence services, and to provide for the reporting of employee contacts with nationals of certain foreign powers. These programs are to be tailored to the sensitivities of particular work and designed so as not to intrude into employees' privacy or freedom of association.

According to the NSC staff, department and agency heads have responded positively and have given high priority to this enterprise. The State Department contact reporting directive, which has been provided to the Committee, serves as a good model because it specifies reporting procedures clearly and identifies those countries that require the greatest attention. Civilian agencies without extensive national security responsibilities also appear to be taking this policy initiative seriously.

The Committee strongly supports this policy and is recommending that a similar security awareness program be established for the U.S. Senate. The Committee has used the State Department's new program as its model.

The Larry Wu-tai Chin case highlighted the threat posed by Chinese intelligence operations. As indicated in section II of this Report, however, the PRC intelligence threat differs greatly from the Soviet one. These differences require development of new counterintelligence approaches geared to the special characteristics of the PRC threat. In particular, the FBI should develop specialized threat awareness briefings geared to the unique problems posed by PRC operations. At the same time, FBI threat awareness programs do not-and should not-leave the implication that lawful association with or assistance to Chinese technical and scientific researchers is a sign of disloyalty to the United States.

Another aspect of counterintelligence awareness is the knowledge by agency security officials of when to bring a matter to the attention of a U.S. counterintelligence agency. In the Edward Lee Howard case, CIA security officials failed to alert and involve the FBI in a timely fashion. The CIA has taken steps recently to guard against a recurrence of this problem. The FBI should continue to work closely with security officials of all U.S. Government agencies to ensure that they understand its requirements and guidelines. A good example is the Pollard case, where the Naval Investigative Service Command brought in the FBI at an early stage. The Committee is pleased that the Navy has given a commendation and a monetary award to the official who was responsible for bringing the FBI into the Pollard case promptly when certain questionable behavior was observed.

The lessons of the Howard and Pollard cases should be extended to all departments and agencies that handle highly sensitive information. Interagency procedures for reporting suspicious conduct to the FBI should be strengthened. Moreover, the Howard and Pelton cases demonstrate that former employees with grievances or financial problems can compromise our most sensitive national security programs. Individuals who choose to work in positions as sensitive as those occupied by a Howard or a Pelton should expect to be held to a higher security obligation than personnel with access to less sensitive information. Therefore, the FBI should be informed when employees with access to extremely sensitive information resign or are dismissed under circumstances indicating potential motivations for espionage. The decision as to whether the circumstances justify investigation in varying degrees should be made by the FBI, in light of its counterintelligence experience, not by the employing agency. Interagency procedures should be established to address borderline cases.

Threat analysis functions are shared among U.S. counterintelligence, foreign intelligence and security agencies. Development of an effective national counterintelligence strategy, as well as a comprehensive and balanced set of security measures, requires centralized assessment of the threat posed by all forms of collection-technical as well as human. Since 1981, an interagency staff has compiled assessments of the hostile intelligence services threat and U.S. countermeasures, based on inputs from throughout the Government. The Committee has found these assessments to be increasingly valuable and is pleased that they continue to have high priority.

National assessments are no substitute, however, for high-quality threat assessments tailored to meet more specific needs. The Committee is pleased to learn that progress is being made regarding one such need for tailored material that was highlighted in the most recent interagency assessment.

DOD counterintelligence agencies have taken the lead in analyzing the threat to particular military installations and activities. The Committee supports increased efforts in this area, especially to assess the threat to highly sensitive research and development projects and to make the findings available to the officials responsible for security countermeasures. In recognition of the importance of this function, the Stilwell Commission has recommended, and the Secretary of Defense has directed, that the Defense Intelligence Agency establish a Multidisciplinary Counterintelligence Analysis Center as a service of common concern for DOD to meet the counterintelligence analytic requirements of the Defense Counterintelligence Board and the various DOD components. DIA should have the task of ensuring that other agencies' threat assessments are responsive to security and program management needs of DOD components. Efficient allocation of limited security resources depends on careful evaluation of the threat.

Special attention is required for two aspects of the hostile intelligence threat that directly relate to U.S. foreign intelligence analysis: deception; and "active measures," including disinformation, forgeries and other political influence operations. Hostile intelligence services conduct these operations in addition to their collection efforts.

An interagency committee and a community-wide intelligence analysis office are both active in the analysis of deception efforts. Pursuant to the Committee's classified reports accompanying the Intelligence Authorization Acts for FY 1985 and FY 1986, a small interagency staff has been assigned to the analysis office.

In recent years, with the help of the intelligence community, the State Department has stepped up efforts to expose Soviet "active measures," such as forgeries and Soviet control of political organizations and conferences abroad. The Committee supports recent initiatives to improve intelligence support for U.S. efforts to counter these Soviet activities.

The State Department and other appropriate agencies should do more to disseminate the results of such analyses to opinion leaders and policymakers worldwide. Recent steps to increase the effectiveness of the Active Measures Working Group, which is chaired by State/INR, are welcomed by the Committee. The Working Group has briefed U.S. Embassies on its role, encouraged the formation of embassy committees to monitor and combat Soviet active measures, and arranged for both classified and unclassified guidance to be provided to the field on specific cases. These efforts should be supported and fully staffed by the relevant agencies, especially the State Department. The Committee is pleased that a new office has been established recently in State/INR for this purpose.

The FBI prepares reports and testifies before Congress on efforts in the United States by the Soviets and other designated countries to influence public opinion and government policy through "front" organizations and other covert operations. For example, in 1986 the Committee received a classified FBI report on "Trends and Developments in Soviet Active Measures in the United States," which updated a previous study prepared in 1982. The FBI report reviews covert Soviet political influence operations directed at U.S. public opinion and policymakers. The Committee regularly requests further counterintelligence information from the FBI on such operations. The Bureau should continue to report these assessments in a manner that provides the necessary facts about hostile intelligence activities and that fully respects First Amendment rights.

Findings and Recommendations

11. Recommendation.–All elements of the U.S. Government should give high priority to implementation of the policy requiring security awareness briefings and the reporting of contacts with nationals of designated countries. A similar procedure should be adopted for U.S. Senate personnel.

12. Recommendation.–The Howard case demonstrates the need for strengthening interagency procedures for bringing possible espionage cases to the FBI's attention in a timely manner. The FBI should also be informed when employees with access to extremely sensitive information, such as Howard and Pelton, resign or are dismissed under circumstances indicating potential motivations for espionage.

13. Recommendation.–The FBI should develop threat awareness briefings tailored to the special characteristics of the PRC espionage threat. Such briefings should alert American citizens to the risks of giving assistance to PRC nationals who may have espionage assignments, while respecting the freedom to associate with lawful scientific and technical research.

14. Finding.–Significant efforts are underway to improve counterintelligence threat analysis, including publication of regular interagency assessments of the hostile intelligence services threat and U.S. countermeasures and the establishment in DIA of a multidisciplinary CI Analysis Center to meet DOD threat analysis requirements in conjunction with other DOD components. The Committee is also pleased to note that there has been progress in the effort to provide tailored analyses of the hostile intelligence threat.

15. Recommendation.–The relevant interagency intelligence analysis office should coordinate and sponsor analytic efforts on Soviet deception, disinformation and active measures. The State Department and other agencies should increase dissemination of information about Soviet active measures abroad. The FBI should continue to be responsible for reports on active measures in the United States by hostile intelligence services and should cooperate with interagency analytic efforts. Reports on active measures in the United States that are prepared by agencies other than the FBI should be prepared in coordination with the FBI and/or the Attorney General.

D. Domestic Operations

Counterintelligence operations in the United States differ from such operations abroad, because the environment is generally more favorable. U.S. counterintelligence has greater resources, easier access to the target, and public attitudes favorable to citizen cooperation. While legal requirements place constraints on surveillance techniques and investigative methods, those limits are vital for maintaining our free society and (with exceptions discussed below) do not inhibit necessary counterintelligence efforts.

Domestic operations can be divided into the following categories: surveillance coverage of foreign government establishments and officials; offensive operations to recruit agents-in-place and defectors or to control double agents; and espionage investigations and prosecutions. Many of the strategic requirements for domestic operations are unique, especially with respect to surveillance of establishments and officials and the investigation and prosecution of espionage cases. Other requirements have more in common with overseas operations, particularly with regard to penetration of hostile services, handling of defectors and double agents, and analysis of the *bona fides* of sources. Unique features of overseas operations, as well as personnel management and training programs that cross geographic divisions, are treated in later sections of this Report.

1. Coverage Of Establishments And Officers

The foundation for domestic counterintelligence is systematic collection on a foreign country's official representatives in the United States. Such collection may be technical or human.

Recent cases have shown the vital importance of comprehensive coverage of Soviet bloc embassies and consulates as a means of detecting offers to sell U.S. secrets. Pelton, Cavanagh, Jeffries and others made their initial contacts with the Soviets by contacting an establishment. Skilled counterintelligence work is required in such cases, and frustrations may be unavoidable. The Pelton case is an example in which it took years to achieve a positive identification.

The strategic importance of covering certain foreign establishments and their employees justifies continuing resource investments to upgrade the FBI's surveillance capabilities. The Committee has supported such investments over the years and continues to do so.

In this connection, the importance of the contact reports discussed earlier in this Report cannot be overemphasized. While government regulations can require federal employees to report contacts with possible foreign intelligence officers, a free society must rely on the voluntary cooperation of private citizens to advise the FBI of approaches and other contacts by such officials. Frequently the FBI requests citizens to report this information about particular individuals, based on surveillance of a contact. The FBI's DECA briefings, which are designed to encourage such contact reports from defense contractors and their employees, have now reached over 15,000 contractor employees. FBI and other intelligence community officials have used speeches and public appearances to emphasize the importance of public cooperation.

The American people have a legitimate concern that their government should not intrude upon their lawful associations with foreign officials and their First Amendment right to exchange ideas with visitors from abroad. For that reason, the FBI operates under guidelines established by the Attorney General and internal FBI policies overseen by the Committee that are designed to respect the free exercise of constitutional rights. As Director Webster stated in a recent speech:

We certainly don't have enough agents to keep track of every citizen of this country nor do we want to investigate the activities of lawful organizations without predication for doing so. Rather, our focus-indeed our strategy-must be on the intelligence operatives themselves and the identification of those who have come here with intelligence commissions. By building a spiderweb throughout the United States that focuses on them rather than our own citizens, we make it much more difficult for those who would betray our country by surreptitiously supplying national secrets to foreign intelligence officers. I believe that in a free society this is the only way we can function without turning ourselves into a police state.

The existence of those safeguards should give the public confidence that cooperation with FBI counterintelligence not only serves the national interest, but also is consistent with respect for constitutional rights.

Findings and Recommendations

Recommendation.–Congress should continue to fund increases in FBI surveillance capabilities.

Recommendation.– American citizens in all walks of life should be encouraged to assist counterintelligence efforts by providing information to the FBI, either upon request or when they are approached by possible foreign intelligence officers.

2. Offensive Operations

A major element in counterintelligence is offensive operations, especially efforts to recruit agents-in-place within hostile intelligence services and to induce defections from those services. The strategic payoff of agents and defectors can be immense, as demonstrated by the exposure of Edward Lee Howard and the successful prosecution of Ronald Pelton.

The greatest area of concern is the handling of defectors, as dramatized by the Yurchenko case. According to a CIA survey, most of the defectors resettled in the United States with CIA assistance are basically satisfied with their treatment. Nevertheless, a significant minority has problems that require special attention on a continuing basis.

In the aftermath of the Yurchenko re-defection, the CIA has undertaken a comprehensive review of its practices for handling defectors. Deputy Director of Central Intelligence Robert M. Gates summarized the CIA's conclusions and corrective actions at his confirmation hearing on April 10, 1986:

There were organizational deficiencies. We have made organizational changes so that a single individual and a single organization are accountable and are in charge of the entire process for defectors. Another element that we have changed ... is to ensure that the same person is basically the principal case officer for a defector with continuity, so that a defector isn't facing a while new set of people all the time and there is somebody there that he gets to know and that he can depend upon and that understands him and understands his concerns, and can identify when he is going through a particular psychological crisis....

Mr. Gates also called it "imperative" to assign individuals who speak the same language as a defector so that someone is available to talk in his or her own language; he did not know, however, whether the CIA has actually been able to implement this approach.

The actions taken and under consideration by the CIA reflect a constructive effort to upgrade the defector program and respond to the lessons of the Yurchenko case. They need continuing high-level support, both in the CIA and in other agencies. The Committee will continue to assess the CIA improvements along with other approaches.

The Executive branch continues to examine the broad question of how defectors might best be welcomed, assisted and utilized. A private organization formed to assist defectors, the Jamestown Foundation, has recommended major changes in the defector-handling program. The Committee intends to follow this issue closely in the coming year and looks forward with great interest to seeing the results of Executive branch deliberations.

The Committee considers it of the utmost importance that our nation's goals in welcoming and assisting defectors be more clearly enunciated and boldly implemented. Too often, the only operative goals have been the national security benefits that result from debriefing a defector; the defectors personal security against attacks by his or her country's security service; and enabling the defector to survive without continuing U.S. Government intervention. Other goals must be added to the list: to encourage achievement in American society consonant with the defector's talents and accomplishments; and to assist the defector in making a continuing contribution to the United States. While the Executive branch has taken steps to administer its current defector program more effectively, it must also effect this important change in attitude and commitment.

The Permanent Subcommittee on Investigations of the Senate Committee on Governmental Affairs has begun a major study of the U.S. Government's handling of defectors and other refugees from the Soviet Bloc. This study will focus particular attention on the contributions that defectors can and so make to American society and on the need to encourage that process. The Intelligence Committee supports this PSI study and is cooperating with the Subcommittee in its effort to inform the public regarding the needs of defectors and of the agencies that assist them.

Perhaps the greatest risk in a strategy of penetrating hostile services is that the agent-in-place or defector may be a double agent, pretending to be recruited by or escaping to the United States, but actually controlled by a hostile counterintelligence service. Disputes over the *bona fides* of sources have plagued the U.S. intelligence community in the past. Such differences are sometimes unavoidable, but they should not disrupt interagency cooperation. Counterintelligence is not an exact science. The important thing is not to rely on a single source without careful testing and corroboration of his information. In this regard, the Committee has sought and received assurances that intelligence officials are alert to the risk of over-reliance on the polygraph.

The FBI, CIA, and DoD counterintelligence components have made extensive use of double agents, as evidenced in the recent Izmaylov and Zakharov cases. Last June, the Soviet air attaché, Col. Vladimir Izmaylov, was expelled after being apprehended by the FBI. On August 23 Gennadiy Zakharov, a Soviet physicist working for the United Nations, was arrested and charged with espionage. Both Soviets had been maintaining clandestine contact with individuals who were cooperating with the FBI.

There is a clear need for these operations to be carefully managed. Counterintelligence managers must also review operations to ensure that they have not been compromised. The committee found Executive branch officials sensitive to these and other issues raised by double-agent operations.

The most difficult counterintelligence task is countering the use of "illegals," that is, hostile intelligence service officers who operate under deep cover than officials cover. Some "illegals" may be used primarily for performing espionage support functions (e.g., clearing drops). The FBI and the Justice Department should consider improved ways to prosecute "illegals" for such espionage support activity.

Findings and Recommendations

18. Finding.–In the aftermath of the Yurchenko re-defection, the CIA has made improvements in its procedures for handling defectors. The Committee will continue to review the implementation of those procedures to ensure that needed resources and personnel as well as continuing high-level support are provided. The Administration has commissioned an independent assessment of the CIA defector resettlement program, and the results will be provided to the Committee.

19. Recommendation.–Objectives for the defector resettlement program must include encouraging the fullest possible achievement in American society and assisting defectors to make a continuing contribution to the United States. The Committee strongly supports the efforts of the Permanent Subcommittee on Investigations of the Senate Governmental Affairs Committee to focus public attention on the contributions that defectors can make to American society and on the need to enhance their ability to make such contributions.

20. Finding.–The Executive branch has reassured the Committee regarding the risk of over-reliance on the polygraph in testing sources and defectors and has demonstrated sensitivity to issues concerning the management of U.S-controlled double-agent operations.

21. Recommendation.–The Justice Department and the FIB should work together to develop improved ways to prosecute "illegals" who perform espionage support functions. If further legislation is needed, the Justice Department should so inform the Congress.

3. Espionage Investigations and Prosecutions

Espionage investigations that may lead to criminal prosecution raise delicate issues of interagency cooperation and balancing of interests. Some senior officials support imposition of the most severe penalties on an individual found to have engaged in espionage or behalf of a hostile foreign power. Law enforcement objectives may conflict, however, with counterintelligence requirements and other national security interests.

Espionage cases involving non-Soviet bloc countries raise foreign policy issues, because of the desire of the United States to maintain good relations with particular governments. In the recent Pollard and Chin cases, however, the Executive branch has demonstrated its willingness and ability to investigate and prosecute espionage by agents acting on behalf of friendly countries—in these cases Israel and China. The Committee fully supports enforcement of the espionage laws, without regard to the foreign country involved. This policy does not necessarily conflict with other U.S. objectives requiring good relations with such countries, so long as it is applied even-handedly. The United States should make clear to every country that it will not tolerate violation of our espionage laws and that it will investigate the intelligence operations of countries that control or permit the commission of espionage in or against the United States on their behalf. The Committee is pleased with recent assurance of State Department cooperation with enforcement action whenever evidence of espionage is presented.

For many years U.S. counterintelligence officials assumed that information acquired by intelligence techniques could not be used for law enforcement purposes because of legal obstacles and the need to protect sources and methods. The Foreign Intelligence Surveillance Act and the Classified Information Procedures Act have made espionage prosecutions somewhat easier, although other difficulties still remain. These problems include the use of certain investigative techniques, the need for more expertise in handling sensitive espionage matters, and requirements for better cooperation among and within agencies.

One of the principal differences between espionage investigations and other criminal cases is the overriding need for secrecy to protect counterintelligence sources and methods. That is why Presidents have asserted claims of "inherent constitutional power" to authorize the use of intrusive techniques with Attorney General approval rather than a judicial warrant. That is also why Congress has established a special secure court order procedure under the Foreign Intelligence Surveillance Act and exempted counterintelligence from the law enforcement procedures for access to bank records in the Right to Financial Privacy Act. U.S. counterintelligence officials have consistently contended that ordinary judicial procedures do not provide adequate security in dealing with hostile intelligence services. In normal criminal cases the objective—either immediate or long-term—is always prosecution in open court. Counterintelligence operations have other objectives that may be more strategically important, such as learning the methods of the hostile service.

Federal law does not adequately take account of such differences in several areas. The FBI has found that the counterintelligence exemption in the Right to Financial Privacy Act is insufficient to obtain access to bank records when financial institutions refuse to cooperate on a voluntary basis. Consequently, the FBI is requesting legislation to give U.S. intelligence agencies the authority to require financial institutions to provide access to records. Unlike the law enforcement procedures under the Right to Financial Privacy Act, neither a court order nor notice to the subject of the records would be required. The FBI has a strong case for replacing the current voluntary system with a law that provides mandatory access for counterintelligence purposes within a framework of Attorney General guidelines and congressional oversight to provide safeguards against abuses. The Committee, therefore, has included legislation to address this need in the Intelligence Authorization Act for Fiscal Year 1987.

There is a similar problem with access to telephone and other telecommunications records. Paradoxically, it is easier in some states to wiretap an individual than to get the phone company to provide access to his or her bill records. For security reasons the law enforcement alternative of a grand jury subpoena is usually impractical; and the Foreign Intelligence Surveillance Act does not cover access to records. As with bank records, the FBI is tasking for legislation that provides mandatory access for counterintelligence purposes to such telecommunications records as telephone billing records. The Committee has incorporated such legislation in the Intelligence Authorization Act for Fiscal Year 1987.

A third gap in federal law concerns physical searches. The Foreign Intelligence Surveillance Act (FISA) authorizes a special court composed of Federal District Judges to grant orders for electronic surveillance to meet counterintelligence requirements, but the Act does not apply to physical search. The FBI supported broadening the Act to cover searches as part of the intelligence charter legislation considered by the Committee in 1980, but the only provision of the charter to be enacted were the congressional oversight authorities. Pursuant to Executive Order 12333, the Attorney General authorizes warrantless searches for counterintelligence purposes.

The absence of a statutory court order procedure creates at least two problems. First, as with bank and telephone records, there is no authority to require cooperation from private parties. Second, the Federal appeals court in the *Truong* case ruled that evidence derived from a warrantless counterintelligence search may not be used in court if the search occurs after the Government decides to prosecute. Neither problem exists for wiretaps and other forms of electronic surveillance under the Foreign Intelligence Surveillance Act, which provides a court order procedure to secure the cooperation of private parties and permits the use of information for law enforcement purposes with appropriate security.

In light of this situation, the Committee recommended in 1984 that legislation be developed to establish statutory procedures comparable to FISA for physical search. The Committee is prepared to develop and introduce such legislation in cooperation with the Executive Branch.

The President's interim report to the Intelligence Committees comments, "It is imperative that FISA be retained as it now exists." The Committee similarly endorsed FISA in 1984, finding that it has resulted in "enhancement of U.S. intelligence capabilities" and also "contributed directly to the protection of the constitutional rights and privacy interests of U.S. persons." The Committee believes that physical search legislation can be achieved, with Executive branch support, without endangering FISA.

Espionage investigations and prosecutions would also be more successful if greater expertise and resources were brought to bear in certain areas. Since 1985 the

Army has recognized its counterintelligence efforts and instituted a specialized training program to develop greater expertise at the field level in espionage investigations.

The espionage prosecutions in 1985 and 1986 demonstrated the importance of early consultation with Justice Department attorneys in developing tactics that reconcile intelligence and law enforcement interests. In the Pelton case, close cooperation between NSA, and the FBI, and the Justice Department resulted in a conviction with minimal disclosure of sensitive information. In the Sharon Scranage case, the combined efforts of the CIA, the FBI, the Justice Department, and the State Department produced a strategy that successfully led both to convictions and to the exchange of the Ghanaian official convicted in the case for several prisoners in Ghana and their families.

The Committee understands that such consultation is now being instituted in a more timely manner than often occurred in the past. This welcome coordination requires that the Justice Department, in turn, have a sufficient number of attorneys trained and experienced in handling the unique problems in these cases. The Committee is especially concerned that those attorneys learn how to maintain controls on the release of sensitive information. Department attorneys should also work with U.S. counterintelligence agencies in potential espionage cases to ensure that their methods are as consistent as possible with successful prosecution. In this regard, the Justice Department's Criminal Division has begun to build a cadre of experienced personnel and to provide additional training to United States Attorneys.

The Howard case, which is discussed in some details in the Committee's classified Report, revealed serious shortcomings in CIA performance relating to espionage investigations. The Committee is pleased to learn that the CIA has taken steps to correct problems pinpointed in investigations by its Inspector General and an interagency group. The Committee will monitor the implementation of those changes.

Issues relating to the handling of the Howard case by the FBI and the Justice Department have also been pinpointed and are the subject of continuing consideration. The Committee expects remedial actions to be taken, as appropriate, and will continue to follow this matter.

Findings and Recommendations

22. Recommendation.–The United States should not tolerate violation of our espionage laws by any country and should investigative the intelligence operations of countries that control or permit the commission of espionage in or against the United States on their behalf. The Committee is pleased to learn on their behalf. The Committee is pleased to learn that the State Department has pledged to cooperate with enforcement action whenever evidence of espionage is presented, and the Committee supports efforts to set up a mechanism for regular interagency consultation on cases that might warrant action.

23. Finding – The Foreign Intelligence Surveillance Act continues to be considered by U.S. counterintelligence agencies to be highly beneficial to their efforts. They strongly favor retention of FISA as it now exists.

24. Recommendation.–Congress should enact legislation to give the FBI the authority to require financial institutions and telecommunications carriers to provide access to records, with notice restrictions comparable to FISA. Any such authority should be limited to counterintelligence matters, governed by the current Attorney General's guidelines, and accompanied by improved provisions for congressional oversight.

25. Recommendation.–Congress should enact legislation comparable to FISA to authorize physical search for intelligence purposes, so as to reduce legal uncertainties in counterintelligence investigations that have prosecution as one of their objectives.

26. Recommendation.–U.S. counterintelligence agencies should continue to emphasize, as standard procedure, consultation with the Justice Department at an early stage in potential espionage cases. The Justice Department should provide increased training to Criminal Division attorneys and U.S. Attorneys concerning the prosecution of espionage cases, including the need to protect sensitive information relating to such cases.

27. *Finding.*–The CIA has taken some steps that are likely to improve counterintelligence investigations and prosecutions, in the wake of investigations of the Howard case. The Committee will monitor implementation of those improvements.

28. *Recommendation.*–The FBI and the Justice Department should take actions, as appropriate, to remedy shortcomings exposed by the Howard case.

E. Overseas Operations

Strategic counterintelligence objectives abroad differ from those in the United States not only because of the different environment, but also because of the added requirements for counterintelligence support in intelligence collection programs. The Committee welcomes recent CIA initiatives to improve both its counterintelligence efforts and its career opportunities in counterintelligence.

The Committee's classified Report discusses further issues regarding CIA and Department of Defense counterintelligence overseas.

The investigation of espionage by U.S. civilian and contractor personnel abroad raises jurisdictional questions. The Committee believes that the FBI should be called in and should work closely with agency security officials from the outset.

Finding and Recommendations

29. *Finding.*–The CIA has begun initiatives to improve its counterintelligence efforts.

30. *Recommendation.*–U.S. agencies abroad should continue to obtain the timely advice and assistance of the FBI in cases of possible espionage by civilian and contractor personnel.

F. Personnel Management and Training

Counterintelligence is not the main function of any of the organizations responsible for U.S. counterintelligence programs. The CIA's primary task is collection and analysis of political, economic and military intelligence; the FBI is a law enforcement organization; and each of the service counterintelligence organization is part of a larger criminal investigative or intelligence agency. This is one reason why there have been less specialized training and fewer incentives for careers in counterintelligence. Personnel are recruited for law enforcement or intelligence positions generally and are usually not assigned to counterintelligence until they have experience in other fields. The advantage of this practice is that personnel can develop their basic investigative or intelligence skills in less sensitive areas before taking on more important counterintelligence duties. The disadvantage is that specialization and career advancement in counterintelligence may be discouraged because of the organization's emphasis on other functions.

Every agency is taking steps to upgrade counterintelligence training, but the results thus far have been uneven. More should be done to encourage agencies to share their experience with successful methods. While each agency operates in a different environment and with different internal regulations, joint discussion of such topics as the nature of the threat from particular hostile services and the techniques for offensive operations and counterespionage investigations could be very useful. This would also make more efficient use of expert personnel to assist in other agencies' training. In the CIA and military services, better training in agency guidelines is also needed.

In the aftermath of the Miller case, the Committee has taken a close look at FBI personnel management policies for counterintelligence. At the Committee's request, the FBI prepared a study reviewing the impact of FBI personnel policies on the Foreign Counterintelligence (FCI) Program in order to determine how the FBI may more effectively recruit, select, assign, train, promote and retain Special Agents for counterintelligence matters. The FBI study indicated a need for improvements in several areas.

The FBI confronts unusual personnel management problems because of the large hostile intelligence presence in New York City, where the cost of living has discourage FBI agents from seeking assignments or pursuing careers. Unlike State Department personnel, FBI agents in New York do not have a special housing allowance to defray the cost of living in town. The Committee believes that action is needed to improve benefits and incentives in New York and is prepared to develop legislation that may be needed for this purpose.

Another manpower issue is the limited number of FBI senior grade positions in the counterintelligence field, as compared to positions as Special Agent in Charge of a field office and comparable headquarters positions with primarily law enforcement duties. The Committee supports efforts to change this situation, including funds requested in the FY 1987 budget to increase the number of senior grade counterintelligence positions at FBI Headquarters. The committee also supports the FBI policy requiring that all new Special Agents in Charge of field offices who have not previously served in a full-time counterintelligence position must receive FCI training.

The Committee intends to continue its review of FBI counterintelligence personnel policies as part of a broader ongoing study of intelligence community personnel issues.

DoD counterintelligence components have similar problems and should develop appropriate revisions in personnel policy to encourage specialized counterintelligence career development. In all the DoD counterintelligence units, as well as the FBI, greater efforts are needed to recruit and retain the best possible personnel.

Findings and Recommendations

31. Recommendation.–More should be done to encourage agencies to share their experience with successful CI methods and to make more efficient use of expert training personnel.

Stephen Joseph Ratkai, a Canadian-born son of a Hungarian emigre.

32. Recommendation.– Additional measures should be taken to improve benefits and incentives for FBI Agents in New York City, including any legislation needed to give the FBI comparable authority to the State Department.

33. Finding.–The FBI is planning to increase the number of senior grade counterintelligence positions at FBI Headquarters. The Committee supports these efforts.

34. Recommendation.–While each counterintelligence agency must recruit to satisfy its unique needs, grater attention should be given to determining specialized qualifications required for personnel to meet each agency's CI needs as distinct from law enforcement or foreign intelligence needs.

35. Recommendation.–DoD counterintelligence components should continue to develop appropriate revisions in personnel policy to encourage specialized counterintelligence career development.

Operation Station Zebra

On 2 December 1986, Donna Geiger walked onboard a Soviet scientific research vessel, the *Akademik Boris Petrov*, which was in the harbor of St. John's, Newfoundland, for a three-day rest and relaxation. Geiger, a Navy lieutenant who was later promoted to lieutenant commander, was a double agent who had been recruited by the Naval Investigative Service. She was the key figure in a highly successful double-agent operation involving the NIS, the Royal Canadian Mounted Police (RCMP) and the Canadian Security Intelligence Service (CSIS).

According to Cpl. Gary Bass, head of the RCMP National Crime Intelligence Section in St. John's, the operation was conducted to learn if Soviet ships visiting the city were involved in collecting intelligence, particularly against the US naval facility in Argentia.

Lt. Cmdr. Geiger had just been stationed at the US Naval Facility (NAVFAC) in Argentia, Newfoundland. When she went onboard the Soviet ship, she portrayed herself as a "disgruntled female naval officer…working in a world dominated by men…assigned to an isolated duty station." She brought classified material to prove her intentions. She met with the captain and chief mate of the Soviet ship and gave them the number of a post office box in St. John's where she could be contacted.

In February 1987, Lt. Cmdr. Geiger received the first letter indicating someone would meet with her. The letter was postmarked in Ottawa. The meeting was postponed in subsequent letters before a meeting was finally held.

On 17 May 1987, acting on directions she received by mail, Lt. Cmdr Geiger went to the entrance of the Hotel Newfoundland in St. John's where she met an individual identified as "Michael" at approximately 1600.

They went to her car in the parking lot of the hotel where she was given money and some tasking to collect information. No documents were passed at this time.

On 24 May 1987, another meeting was held. This time they met at a monument called the "War Memorial" about six blocks from the Hotel Newfoundland. After a brief meeting, they went to a restaurant where classified information was exchanged for money. During this meeting she was tasked to provide information on highly classified Sound Underwater Surveillance System (SOSUS) and NAVFAC Argentia's area of responsibility.

The two were scheduled to meet again in October but the meeting had to be postponed. Lt. Cmdr. Geiger, who was married with one child, gave birth to her second child in October.

In December 1987, at about 1600 they met again at the entrance of the Hotel Newfoundland. The meeting lasted about one and half hours. Lt. Cmdr. was given more money in exchange for eight documents, including classified material. During this meeting she was given additional tasking to find out what the United States knew about the acoustics of Soviet submarines and any US methods of tracking them. In addition, she was provided with a modified camera designed for document photography, secret writing materials, and an "accommodation address" in East Berlin where she could mail letters to signal for other meetings.

On 11 June 1988, Lt. Cmdr. Geiger and "Michael" met again. By this time "Michael" had been identified as Stephen Joseph Ratkai, a Canadian-born son of a Hungarian emigre. Ratkai held dual Canadian and Hungarian citizenship.

Unknown to Ratkai, the RCMP had been waiting for him. From the time he deplaned at St. John's airport on 8 June to the time of his arrest, the RCMP was carefully monitoring him. Cpl. Bass stated that the RCMP did not know if Soviet ships visiting St. John's intercepted radio communications while in port, but the RCMP refused to take any chances. They established a network of telephone communication without the use of radios. He also said the RCMP did not conduct any moving surveillance but had static surveillance around the city where they believed Ratkai would travel during his stay. The RCMP also placed audio coverage in several different hotels, including the one Ratkai checked into after his arrival. The RCMP and CSIS officers were occupying rooms across and adjacent to Ratkai's room.

When they met at the Hotel Newfoundland, Lt. Cmdr. Geiger steered Ratkai to a room, which had been outfitted with audio and video surveillance. The meeting lasted about one hour and 25 minutes. Lt. Cmdr. Geiger was given more money in exchange for one classified document and portions of another. When Ratkai left the room he was immediately arrested in the hallway.

Ratkai initially pleaded not guilty to three charges of espionage and one attempted espionage charge. But on 6 February 1989, Ratkai pleaded guilty to espionage in the Supreme Court of Newfoundland. The government then consolidated the three charges into one. It marked the first conviction under Section 3(1C) of the Canadian Official Secrets Act for Espionage.

Meeting between Lt. Cmdr. Geiger and "Michael," identified as Stephen Joeseph Ratkai.

On 9 March 1989 Ratkai was sentenced to two concurrent nine-year prison terms. Ratkai was subsequently paroled and, after the fall of Communism in Eastern Europe, he was allowed to return to Hungary.

Spies

Michael Hahn Allen

Michael Hahn Allen, from Ponchatoula, Louisiana, served for 22 years in the US Navy as a Radioman and retired in 1972, as a Senior Chief Petty Officer. Following his retirement, Allen ran a bar in Olongapo, the Philippines, until 1982, when he was hired as a photocopy clerk at the Naval Air Station, Cubi Point, in the Philippines. Allen also had an automobile dealership and ran a cock-fighting operation.

Coworkers at the communications center became suspicious of Allen's activities, and reported him to authorities. On 4 December 1986, the 53-year-old Allen, who had routine access to information classified CONFIDENTIAL and SECRET, was arrested by the Naval Investigative Service on suspicion of espionage.

He admitted he gave US classified information to unauthorized persons to foster his self-esteem and personal interests. The documents provided by Allen included summaries of rebel force movements and planned Philippine Government actions for most of 1986. Because of Allen's status as a US civilian employed in an overseas location, his case brought special concerns as to how it should be handled. After the US Justice Department indicated Allen would not be prosecuted in Federal Court, John Lehman, Secretary of the Navy, exercised his authority under Article of the Uniform Code of Military Justice to have Allen apprehended and prosecuted in the military justice system as a retired US Navy member.

On 14 August 1987, Allen was convicted at a Court Martial of compromising US classified documents and sentenced to eight years in prison, fined $10,000, and as a result forfeited his military retirement benefits.

Stephen Anthony Baba

Described as a brilliant student, Stephen Anthony Baba at age 18 graduated with honors from the University of Maryland with a degree in business finance. He received his commission in the US Navy in 1980 from the Officer Candidate School, Newport, Rhode Island. His first assignment was as an Electronics Material Officer aboard a San Diego based frigate, USS *Lang*.

On 30 September 1981, a source released to the Naval Investigative Service (NIS) a package containing US classified material consisting of a copy of the May 1980 document, "Electronic Warfare Evaluation and Education Quarterly," and two microfiche classified "SECRET."

A 12-page letter accompanied the package from an individual claiming to be an officer in the US Navy assigned to an unidentified ship. The writer advised he was willing to provide classified material in return for money and provided detailed instructions as to how the transaction would take place.

On 6 October, 1981, the executive officer of USS *Lang* contacted NIS Resident Agency Naval Station, San Diego, California, and advised that during the preceding weekend, an officer assigned to USS *Lang* had been arrested for attempted "unarmed" robbery of a local jewelry store.

Michael Hahn Allen

Stephen Anthony Baba

During interrogation, Baba indicated a desperate need for money and admitted to an unsuccessful attempt to extort money from the Navy Federal Credit Union. It was subsequently determined that the possibility existed that Baba was the individual involved in the forwarding of the classified material to a foreign embassy.

On 23 October 1981, Baba was placed in pretrial confinement at Metro Correction Center, San Diego, California. On 26 October 1981, Baba was transported to Chula Vista, California, to attend a pretrial hearing, during which time he attempted to escape from confinement. On 20 January 1982, Baba was sentenced to eight years imprisonment, forfeiture of all pay and allowances, and dismissal from the Navy.

William Holden Bell

William Holden Bell attended the University of California, Los Angeles campus and in 1952, went to work for Hughes Aircraft Company. Later in his career with Hughes Aircraft, he worked in Belgium and following a divorce from his first wife, married a Belgian citizen. His costly divorce and subsequent remarriage placed Bell under considerable financial strain as he resettled in a suburb of Los Angeles.

Bell became acquainted with Marian W. Zacharski, a Polish citizen who was vice president of the Polish American Machinery Corporation (Polamco), in Los Angeles, California, and a covert member of the Polish intelligence service. In the summer and autumn of 1977, Bell and Zacharski played tennis together, took their wives out to dinner on occasion, and generally enjoyed a friendly relationship. Gradually, Zacharski was able to learn some of the details of Bell's work, and Bell showed Zacharski a classified document on which he had worked. At the same time, the apartment project in which both families lived was being sold for condominium conversion. When Bell told Zacharski that he would have to move since he could not afford the downpayment on the condominium, Zacharski provided Bell with the cash necessary for the purchase.

Bell soon realized that he was caught in a compromising position, and the relationship rapidly developed into a conspiracy to commit espionage for money. The Poles provided Bell with a list of documents they desired, and he traveled to Innsbruck, Austria, and Geneva, Switzerland, to turn over classified information and receive payments for his services.

Arrested by the FBI in July 1981, the 61-year old Bell quickly confessed to his espionage activities and cooperated with the FBI in entrapping Zacharski. Bell admitted to receiving a grand total of $110,000, mostly in $100 bills and gold coins, from the Poles.

Documents compromised by Bell included reports on a so-called "quiet" radar system; a look-down, shoot-down radar system; an all-weather radar system for tanks; an experimental radar system for the US Navy; the Phoenix air-to-air missile for the F-14; a ship surveillance radar; a new air-to-air missile; the improved HAWK surface-to-air missile; the Patriot air defense missile; and a submarine sonar system.

Bell was sentenced to eight years in prison and was fined $10,00 for his role in compromising the classified Hughes' documents. This relatively light sentence was given as a result of Bell's full cooperation with investigative authorities. Zacharski was sentenced to life in prison. On 10 June 1985, Zacharski was released in a prisoner exchange between the United States, East Germany, and Poland.

Edward Owen Buchanan

Airman Edward Owen Buchanan, a student assigned to a munitions and weapons maintenance technical training school, Lowry AFB, Colorado telephoned the East German Embassy in Washington, DC, on 6 May 1985. He was attempting to learn if Embassy officials had received a letter he had sent in April 1985, containing an offer to commit espionage for the East German Government.

William Holden Bell

During the telephone conversation, an Embassy employee told Buchanan that the Embassy was closed, and he was instructed to telephone the next day. The next day he telephoned the Embassy again as he was instructed; however, an Embassy employee told him that he couldn't help him. An hour later he called again and requested to speak to the Ambassador, but was unsuccessful and hung up.

Irritated with being put off by the East Germans, Buchanan telephoned the Soviet Consulate located in San Francisco. He tried to tell the official his name, duty location, and that he was in the USAF, but, unable to understand the Soviet official who answered the telephone, he hung up. On 9 May 1985, he mailed a letter to the Soviet Embassy in Washington, DC fully identifying himself (name, military organization, duty station, and career specialty). The letter stated that he had information of a scientific and technological nature that he wanted to sell to the Russian Government. He indicated he would continue to conduct business with the Soviets if they liked his material.

At this point, AFOSI/FBI agents, posing as Soviet representatives, contacted Buchanan. Believing that he was doing business with Soviet Intelligence Officers, Buchanan offered to commit espionage and sell classified documents. He then provided documents to the undercover AFOSI/FBI agents, which he claimed were classified SECRET and he was paid $1,000. After taking the money, Buchanan was apprehended.

A later examination of the documents disclosed that they were copies of unclassified articles from an electronics magazine. During an interview following his arrest, Buchanan admitted contacting the East German Embassy and the Soviet Embassy for the purpose of committing espionage. Buchanan also admitted that, although he did not have access to classified information at that time (because of his student status), he planned to sell classified information once his clearance had been granted and he was assigned to a base in Germany.

Buchanan was born in Orlando, Florida, on 7 August 1963, and was raised in a white, middle-class family environment. After graduating from high school, his civilian job prospects were limited so he enlisted in the USAF on 16 January 1985. At the time of his apprehension, he was unmarried and had completed approximately one year of college. Investigative interviews disclosed that he was very naive and immature. Although he expressed an interest in defecting and living in the Soviet Union, financial gain was his primary motivating factor in committing espionage.

Buchanan was court-martialed on 26 August 1985 and sentenced to 30 months confinement, reduced to Airman Basic, forfeited of all pay and allowances, and given a dishonorable discharge.

Thomas Patrick Cavanagh

Thomas Patrick Cavanagh worked for Hughes Aircraft Corporation from 1969 to 1981. In November 1981, he secured employment with the Advanced Systems Division of Northrop Corporation in Pico Rivera, California. In late 1984, Cavanagh was living separately from his wife and two sons and was deeply in debt. At the same time, Cavanagh's security clearance was being reviewed for upgrading from Secret to Top Secret, and he was fearful that he would not receive the higher clearance when his indebtedness was disclosed.

With his financial plight in mind, Cavanagh attempted to establish contact with Soviet intelligence. He had secrets to sell and left no doubt that his motive was money. "Before our relationship ends, I want to be independently wealthy," he told the prospective buyers. He knew espionage was a serious crime. He also knew that the FBI arrested several people recently, and they were now in jail. In order to clear up mounting debts, and make himself rich, the Northrop engineer was still willing to take some chances.

Thomas Patrick Cavanagh

At the first meeting on 10 December 1984, Cavanagh introduced himself to his contacts as Mr. "Peters." Two topics dominated his conversation: his financial problems and worries about getting caught. "They're real security conscious (at Northrop)..." he remarked, "So somehow we have to come to an agreement on money." He added that he needed several thousand dollars, "Just to get the bill collectors off my back." He thought he could bypass the document controls and random searches at the plant.

He didn't want to talk about his contacts on the telephone "because it's constantly being bugged; they bug it with microwaves." His biggest source of anxiety, however, was the security program at Northrop. He was extremely concerned about his accountability for documents. He refused to turn them over to the "KGB" agents because he wanted to get them back to the plant as quickly as possible. "I can't give you the documents and have them back in time. They have audits. A guy just came by today and asked me how many secret documents I have." He was afraid that Security might open his safe and check his documents at any time. By sheer coincidence, Cavanagh had a surprise audit of his classified documents on the very day he first met with the "KGB." It was strictly a random check by a company security representative, who had no suspicion that the material he reviewed was about to be sold to the Soviets. The security officer found everything in order but Cavanagh was visibly shaken, according to coworkers interviewed after the arrest.

Reproduction controls at Northrop hampered Cavanagh. "You can't run your own copies in the plant. They got that regulated too." Northrop Advanced Systems Division controlled document reproduction through a system of "fully-controlled machines." There is no self-service as special operators handle all copying machines under the oversight of security. They guarantee that all requirements meet authorization, marking and accountability regulations. The "KGB agents" had to obtain a camera and a portable copier to make copies in the motel room.

Northrop employees were subject to random search of anything carried in or out of the plant. Cavanagh worried about that as well. "I had to stick it in my shirt and walk out with it." He couldn't always fit things under his shirt, but he thought he could get through exit searches without detection because they were sufficiently infrequent and predictable.

When he arrived for a second meeting on 12 December, his "friends" greeted him warmly. He again mentioned the difficulty of getting documents out. He pressed anxiously for quick payment and wanted several thousand dollars in two days, but the "Russians" wouldn't make any promises. Concerned because his background investigation was due to begin, Cavanagh wanted to cover his debts.

The third and final meeting with the "KGB agents" occurred on 18 December. When Cavanagh arrived, he asked about the money. Cavanagh showed them the documents he brought. He spoke of his financial bind and displayed bitterness that he could not get a business loan for his Amway distribution, while foreign immigrants easily got them.

The agents suggested that future meetings be held outside the United States. Cavanagh refused by saying that he did not want to keep his documents out that long. Besides, he said that unexplained foreign travel might flag his activities with security.

After copying the documents, the agents handed Cavanagh the payment in small bills. He counted it eagerly. He wanted to have monthly meetings with substantial payment each time. After they finished their business, there was a knock on the door. When they opened the door, FBI agents entered the room and arrested Cavanagh. Charged and convicted on two counts of espionage, he was sentenced on 23 May 1985 to concurrent life terms in prison.

The FBI caught Cavanagh before he reached the Soviets. Greed and indebtedness were the major motivations for Cavanagh, but he showed some traits seen before in other spy cases. Job and career dissatisfaction were big ones. Cavanagh, in addition, showed some tendency to violent or disruptive behavior, some instances of dishonesty, and a general lack of respect for authority and procedural process. Still, none of this rose to the level where supervisors considered reporting it for security purposes. Cavanagh was not a model citizen, but his behavior was well within tolerable limits. He went over the edge, quite suddenly by all indications, and tried to sell out the country to make himself rich.

Larry Wu-Tai Chin

Larry Wu-Tai Chin, retired CIA employee, was arrested 22 November 1985 and accused of having carried out a 33-year career of espionage on behalf of the People's Republic of China (PRC).

According to media reports, Chin, who retired in 1981 at age 63, had been an intelligence officer in the CIA's Foreign Broadcast Information Service. During his career, he held a Top Secret clearance and had access to a wide range of intelligence information.

Born in Beijing, Chin was recruited by Chinese intelligence while he was a college student in the early 1940s. Later, he became a naturalized US citizen and worked for the US Army Liaison Office in China in 1943. In 1952 he joined the CIA.

It is believed that he provided the PRC with many of the CIA's Top Secret reports on East Asia written over the past 20 years. Chin reportedly smuggled classified documents from his office and between 1976 and 1982, gave photographs of these materials to Chinese couriers at frequent meetings in Toronto, Canada, Hong Kong, and London. He met with Chinese agents in East Asia in March 1985. Chin may have received as much as one million dollars for his complicity.

He was indicted on 17 counts of espionage-related and income tax violations. At his trial, which began on 4 February 1986, Chin admitted providing the Chinese with information over a period of 11 years, but for the purpose of reconciliation between China and the United States.

Larry Wu-Tai Chin, retired CIA employee who was indicted on 17 counts of espionage-related and income tax violations.

On 8 February 1986, Chin was convicted by a Federal jury on all counts. Sentencing was set for 17 March; however, on 21 February the former CIA employee committed suicide in his cell. His death was ruled a suicide by medical authorities. A few days prior to his death, Chin had agreed to discuss his espionage activities with the CIA in exchange for immunity from future prosecution. The CIA's debriefing of Chin was to take place prior to Chin's sentencing.

Clyde Lee Conrad

Clyde Lee Conrad, retired US Army Sergeant First Class, was arrested on 23 August 1988 in West Germany and charged with copying and transmitting classified documents to the Hungarian intelligence service for nearly a decade.

He was recruited in 1974 by a Hungarian-born immigrant, Zoltan Szabo, a veteran of Vietnam, who served as an Army captain in Germany. Szabo began working for Hungarian intelligence in 1967. Szabo was convicted of espionage by an Austrian court in 1989, but served no jail time because of his cooperation with authorities in the prosecution of Conrad.

Two Hungarian-born doctors arrested at the same time in Sweden acted as couriers in the espionage operation. Conrad is believed to have hired at least a dozen people in the US Army to supply classified information. The Conrad ring was one of the biggest spy rings since World War II. Conrad's recruits continued to work for him after returning to the United States, illegally exporting hundreds of thousands of advanced computer chips to the East Bloc through a phony company in Canada.

Conrad was granted a Top Secret security clearance in 1978 when assigned to the US 8th Infantry Division headquarters in Bad Kreuznach, Germany. Despite his administrative specialist's job, which gave him access to extensive classified materials, Conrad had not been subject to a periodic reinvestigation before his retirement in 1985.

Documents provided to Hungarian agents concerned NATO's plans for fighting a war against the Warsaw Pact detailed descriptions of nuclear weapons, and plans for movement of troops, tanks, and aircraft. Conrad, in charge of a vault where all the 8th Infantry Division's secret documents were kept, took suitcases stuffed with classified papers out of the base. The former sergeant is reported to have received more than one million dollars for selling documents.

The two Hungarian couriers, Sandor and Imre Kercsik, were sentenced by a Swedish court on 18 October to 18 months in prison. In 1989, Conrad was charged with treason under West German law. It took more than a year to charge him formally due to the complexity of the case which initially was declared one of espionage and then broadened to include the more serious charge of treason.

Tried in a West German Court, Conrad was sentenced to life imprisonment on 6 June 1990. He died on 8 January 1998 in a German prison where he was serving his sentence.

Christopher M. Cooke

On 23 December 1980, it was learned that an unidentified American had placed a telephone call to Richmond, Virginia, from inside the Soviet Embassy in Washington, DC. Christopher M. Cooke, a second lieutenant, Titan missile launch officer, and deputy commander of an Air Force Titan missile crew assigned to McConnell AFB, Kansas, was on leave and had traveled home to Richmond, Virginia, for the holidays and could have been this caller.

On 2 May 1981, Lt. Cooke departed McConnell AFB, Kansas on leave, flying first to St. Louis and then to Washington National Airport. He checked his luggage in a locker and, empty handed, hailed a taxicab, returning shortly to the airport. The cabdriver said that he had dropped his passenger at the Soviet Embassy, but that the passenger had returned quickly because the Embassy was closed. Cooke then took a bus from the airport to his home in Richmond. He had failed to report his contacts with Soviet officials in violation of AFR 205-57, Reporting Espionage, Sabotage and Subversion, and was confronted and arrested on 21 May 1981 by the Air Force Office of Special Investigations.

Christopher Cooke was born on 14 July 1955, at Fort Lee, Virginia. His father was fatally shot when Cooke was a child, and as he grew older, Cooke developed a suspicion that his grandfather had murdered his father. Over the years, his family provided Cooke with little information about his father or the circumstances surrounding the shooting. After his arrest, a psychological examination disclosed an adolescent identity crisis that centered on the lack of information, he received as a child, concerning his father. Although he had a strong dislike for his stepfather, he was close to his mother.

Cooke graduated from Old Dominion University in May 1978 and later earned a master's degree from William and Mary College. His thesis, completed in 1979, centered on nuclear weaponry. He applied twice, although unsuccessfully, to join the CIA and was in the process of preparing a third application at the time of his arrest. Although he was raised Catholic, he espoused a belief in Hinduism (nonpracticing) and traveled to Bombay, India, during the summer of 1979 to visit an Indian woman he had met and fallen in love with while at William and Mary College.

On one occasion, his stepfather threw him out of the house when he came home one evening and expressed the view that socialism was better than capitalism. He entered the USAF in 1979, graduated from officers training school, were he was considered a "know it all," argumentative, intelligent, insecure, and not well liked by his peers.

After receiving a commission and completing missile launch officer training, he was granted a TOP SECRET security clearance and assigned to the 532 Strategic Missile Squadron at McConnell AFB, Kansas. At the time of his arrest, he was 25 years old and unmarried. He had ordered a book from Walden Books in Wichita

Christopher M. Cooke

Kansas entitled *Wilderness of Mirrors*, by David C. Martin, which had recently been published in paperback and concerned the CIA and counterintelligence matters. Cooke was fascinated with espionage, constantly talking to his friends and coworkers and even acting out some of his fantasies.

When first interviewed, Cooke claimed to have a serious interest in political science and explained that his contacts with the Soviets were to ensure future employment with the US Government. In effect, he hoped to make a name for himself as a great political scientist. Cooke claimed that his contacts with the Soviets were made to persuade them to let him publish "a breakthrough in Soviet foreign policy." He was vague when it came to explaining what this new "breakthrough" would be. He went on to describe various overt and quasi-secret attempts to engage the Soviets that he could be discreet and trusted as a political analyst if they wanted to announce their change in foreign policy through him.

Although he had been rebuffed by the Soviets, he remained keen on the idea that someday he would be able to persuade them to use him to announce a foreign policy breakthrough. According to Cooke, his first attempt to contact the Soviets was on 15 or 16 June 1980, from a hotel in St. Louis and again during 24 - 30 June 1980, from his apartment in Wichita. During the second telephone call, he offered to provide copies of Emergency War Orders, but was rebuffed. Cooke described these attempts as "spontaneous," although he noted that the "thought of committing espionage was ever present in my mind."

When Cooke became Deputy Commander of his missile crew, he seriously began to think about selling information to the Soviets, but could not explain why. He borrowed a friend's Kodak 110 instamatic camera to photograph documents at the missile site. He tried to develop this film himself but failed. The next time he took photographs of documents, but this time he had them processed into negatives only at a local photo store. Later he provided these negatives to the Soviets along with a note regarding his willingness to provide information concerning nuclear strike capabilities and added personal meet instructions at a Holiday Inn in Richmond, Virginia. Cooke used a pseudonym "Mark Johnson." Underneath the name "Johnson" he wrote "Scorpion." On 19 December he telephoned the Holiday Inn asking if "Sally Rogers" (a name he had specifically asked that the Soviets use for the woman he requested they send to the hotel to meet him) had registered and Cooke became frustrated when he discovered she had not. Although confused and extremely frustrated by the Soviets' lack of interest, Cooke was undaunted in his desire to commit espionage.

On 22 December 1980, he telephoned the Soviet Embassy, using the name Johnson, and on 23 December he drove his mother's car to Washington, but used a taxi to go to the Embassy after the car broke down. Cooke was paid $50 by the Soviets for handwritten notes he had copied from classified material. They allowed him to use the telephone to call home and tell his parents the car had broken down and that he would be late in returning. Cooke went back to Richmond and shortly after the holidays resumed duty at McConnell AFB, Kansas.

From February to April 1981, Cooke continued to gather classified information from his duty section. In May, Cooke returned to Washington, DC and Richmond on leave. He expected the Soviets to telephone him on 3 May 1981, and, when they did not, he telephoned them on 4 May, again extremely frustrated at being rebuffed. Cooke claimed that money was not his motivation (although he was going to ask the Soviets for $3,000) but that he was trying to live out his fantasies of espionage. He intended to ask them for 1,000 British pounds ($2,000) and a British passport. If the Soviets had asked, Cooke was prepared to travel abroad to meet with them.

During an interview, Cooke requested legal counsel and a grant of immunity before being interviewed further. Believing that Cooke was part of a larger spy ring, Air Force prosecutors and legal officials offered him an oral agreement of immunity for full disclosure so that a damage assessment could be accomplished. Later he was charged with violation of Article 92, Uniform Code of Military Justice, for failing to obey a lawful order or regulation (AFR 205-57).

On 22 February 1882, the Court of Military Appeals issued a decision, in which the majority held that prosecution of Cooke constituted a violation of due process of law. This was based on the court's opinion that "de facto" immunity had been granted and that Cooke held a reasonable expectation that if he satisfactorily cooperated with USAF officials in their damage assessment, there would be no court-martial. The Court of Military Appeals ordered his release, and Cooke resigned his commission.

Robert Ernest Cordrey

Robert E. Cordrey, a US Marine Corps private, was an instructor at the Camp LeJeune, North Carolina, warfare school. In April 1984, Cordrey began making numerous phone calls to foreign embassies in an attempt to sell documents and manuals relating to nuclear, biological and chemical warfare. After numerous futile attempts, Cordrey made contact with a Czechoslovak intelligence officer, and he drove to Washington, DC from Camp LeJeune for a clandestine meeting. Cordrey showed his contact the list of documents in his possession (all unclassified), and he was told that he would be contacted later.

On 12 April 1984, the FBI and the US Naval Investigative Service learned that Cordrey was attempting to sell information to agents of the USSR, Czechoslovakia, East Germany, and Poland. The 23-year-old Cordrey was convicted on 13 August 1984, on 18 counts of failing to report contacts with citizens of Communist countries. He was sentenced to 12 years at hard labor, forfeiture of all pay and allowances, and a dishonorable discharge. In according with Cordrey's pretrial agreement, his confinement was limited to two years inasmuch as Cordrey successfully underwent post-trial interrogation and polygraph examinations.

John Allen Davies

John Allen Davies, a 33-year-old San Jose, California resident at the time of his arrest and a former US Air Force Staff sergeant and a lab technician at a Silicon Valley defense contractor, was formally charged on 27 October, 1986 with trying to deliver classified US military information to agents of the Soviet Union. Davies a 10-year veteran, who was separated from active service for poor performance in 1984, had held a Secret clearance during his military service and worked as an avionics sensor system technician. According to the FBI, on 22 September 1986, Davies met with an FBI undercover agent posing as a Soviet official in San Francisco's Golden Gate Park. During the meeting, Davies provided detailed verbal information and a hand drawing concerning US reconnaissance technology. At a second meeting in October, he provided additional classified information.

According to Davies's recorded statement, he was motivated "out of revenge because of the unfair way he was treated by the Air Force." He was also quoted as saying that he wanted to do something to embarrass the United States and to interfere with the effectiveness of its reconnaissance activities. Asked why he waited two years before providing the information, Davies said he waited "just to make sure they couldn't link me with it if I told anybody, just sort of... hide my trail."

Davies, born in East Leigh, England in 1953, became a naturalized US citizen at the age of 11. Since October 1984, Ford Aerospace and Communications Corp. had employed him in Palo Alto, California. Federal officials stated that the former airman did not hold a clearance at the time and that no information from the contractor facility was involved in the case. Davies was released on $200,000 bail with the condition that he undergo psychological evaluation. But on 27 May 1987 he pleaded guilty to a reduced charge of attempting to communicate secrets to an unauthorized person and was sentenced to five years in prison.

Sahag K. Dedeyan

Sahag K. Dedeyan, a naturalized US citizen, was engaged in defense research with the Applied Physics Laboratory, John Hopkins University. The 41-year-old mathematician had been working at John's Hopkins for nine years until his arrest by the FBI on 2 June 1975. Arrested on the same date and also charged with conspiring to turn over classified US and NATO documents to the Soviets was a distant relative of Dedeyan, Sarkis O. Paskalian. Dedeyan allowed Paskalian to photograph classified documents in his home.

A document specifically identified in the charges was entitled *Vulnerability Analysis: U.S. Reinforcement of NATO*. Dedeyan allegedly was paid $1,000 for providing the document. Paskalian living in the US as a permanent resident alien had been recruited by Soviet intelligence for the purpose of coming to the United States on an espionage mission. He was ordered by the Soviets to develop a close relationship with his distant cousin for the purpose of obtaining classified information.

Also named in the case as coconspirators were Edward B. Charchyan and Adbulkhalik M. Gadzhiyev, both third secretaries at the Soviet Mission to the United Nations and Petros Petrosyan, a Soviet delegate to a United Nations conference on human rights. Dedeyan was specifically charged with having failed to report the illegal photographing of the defense documents in his home by Paskalian.

Hou Desheng

The FBI detained Hou Desheng, a military attaché of the Peoples Republic of China, on 21 December 1987 while Hou attempted to obtain secret National Security Agency (NSA) documents from a federal employee. Hou was taken into custody at a restaurant in Washington, DC's Chinatown section after accepting what he believed to be classified NSA documents.

The federal employee, a US citizen, had been working under FBI direction. Arrested at the same time was Zang Wei Chua, a PRC consular official in Chicago. Both diplomats were asked to leave the country as a result of "activities incompatible with their diplomatic status," the first Chinese diplomats expelled since formal relations were established with the PRC in 1979.

Thomas Joseph Dolce

Thomas Joseph Dolce, civilian research analyst at Aberdeen Proving Grounds, Maryland, admitted in Federal court on 11 October 1988 that he had supplied scores of Secret documents related to Soviet military equipment to the Republic of South Africa between 1979 and 1983.

Dolce, who had been under investigation by the FBI since April, resigned from his position on 30 September "for personal reasons." Dolce had held a Secret clearance at the US Army Material Systems Analysis Activity at Aberdeen where he was employed since 1973.

In pleading guilty to a single count of espionage, he acknowledged passing documents on 40 or more occasions by mail or in person to military attaches at the South African Embassy in Washington and at South African missions in London and Los Angeles, California. According to Dolce, he was motivated by ideological rather than financial reasons and had a long-term interest in the Republic of South Africa. He had in fact moved to South Africa in 1971, but had later returned to the United States because of better employment opportunities.

Prior to 1971, Dolce had been a US Army clandestine warfare specialist. His contacts with South African representatives began when he sent them an unclassified paper on clandestine warfare which he had written. There is no evidence that Dolce received money in exchange for documents.

On 20 April 1989, the former analyst was sentenced to 10 years in prison and fined $5,000.

Waldo H. Dubberstein

Waldo H. Dubberstein, a former senior intelligence analyst, was indicted by a Federal grand jury on 28 April 1983 on charges of having sold secret US military information to Libya through Edwin P. Wilson. The 75-year-old Dubberstein was charged with having received more than $32,000 from Wilson between 1977 and 1980 for summaries and analyses of Middle East security arrangements and military strength. Dubberstein was considered an expert on Middle East affairs with the Central Intelligence Agency from which he retired in 1982.

The grand jury charged that Dubberstein traveled under an alias in the spring of 1978 to meet with Libyan intelligence officers in Tripoli. He then discussed with them the deployment of Middle East military forces and passed to them several written assessments of Middle East military preparedness.

On 29 April 1983, Dubberstein was found dead, an apparent suicide from a shotgun wound.

Robert Wade Ellis

Robert Wade Ellis, a US Navy Petty Officer, stationed at the US Naval Air Station, Moffett Field, California, contacted the Soviet consulate in San Francisco with an offer to sell classified documents for $2,000. Ellis was arrested in February 1983 while attempting to sell documents to an undercover FBI agent. He was convicted at a general court-martial for unauthorized disclosure of classified information and was sentenced to three years confinement.

David Fleming

David Fleming, US Navy Chief Petty Officer, was convicted by a six-member military court on 4 October 1988 for the theft of 16 Secret photographs and four classified training manuals, which he had at his home.

At the time of his arrest in October 1987, Fleming was chief photographer aboard the submarine *La Jolla*, based at San Diego, California. At that time, Federal agents found classified material in Fleming's apartment. Fleming contended that cramped quarters aboard the ship led him to develop photographs at home.

Concluding that he knew that the materials, if kept at home, could result in damage to national security, the court convicted Fleming under statutes, which apply to acts of espionage. However, no evidence was presented to the court that the Chief Petty Officer had intended to provide classified materials to representatives of another country.

Fleming was sentenced to four years confinement and was given a bad conduct discharge from the Navy. In April 1989, a Navy parole board in San Diego recommended that the reminder of the four-year sentence be commuted. He was released on parole in 1990.

Ernst Forbrich

On 19 March 1984, Ernst Forbich, a West German automobile mechanic was arrested in Clearwater Beach, Florida, after paying $550 for a classified document supplied by an undercover agent posing as an Army intelligence officer.

Forbich was described as a conduit who passed US military secrets to East German intelligence and by his own admission had been selling documents to East Germany for a period of 17 years. Forbich traveled frequently to the United States, contacting former US military personnel who had served in West Germany.

Convicted in June on two counts of espionage, Forbich was sentenced to 15 years.

Wilfredo Garcia

In late 1985, the Naval Investigative Service (NIS) and FBI became aware of alleged espionage activity being conducted by a group of civilians in the Vallejo, California area. Utilizing information provided by a cooperating citizen, investigators determined that classified documents were being stolen from the nearby shipyard and sold to a civilian in Vallejo. The investigation revealed that documents were being held by the individuals who planned to take them to a foreign country to sell. Agents discovered that the source of the documents was an active duty Navy member at the shipyard. Later in the investigation, one of the criminal participants cooperated with investigators and identified Garcia as the source.

Agents learned the espionage scheme resulted in a number of classified documents being taken to the Philippines for the purpose of selling them to a foreign power there. Participants in the conspiracy carried the documents on commercial aircraft and had gathered the material at a residence in Manila. NIS agents in Manila entered the home with a search warrant and recovered the documents before the planned sale.

NIS and FBI agents conducted in-depth surveillance of Garcia that corroborated and supported the evidence against him. When agents confronted Garcia with investigative findings, he admitted to the criminal activity. At a General Court-Martial convened in January 1988, Garcia was found guilty of espionage, conspiracy to commit espionage, larceny, conspiracy to commit larceny, sale of government property, and violations of military regulations. He was sentenced to 12 years confinement, reduced in rank to E-1, forfeiture pay and allowances, and received a dishonorable discharge from the US Navy. Garcia had served in the Navy for 15 years.

Wilfredo Garcia

Otto Attila Gilbert

Otto Attila Gilbert, Hungarian-born US citizen, was arrested on 17 April 1982 after paying $4,000 for classified documents provided by a US Army officer who was working as a double agent under Army control.

The officer, CWO Janos Szmolka, had been approached in 1977 by agents of Hungarian military intelligence while on a visit to his mother in Hungary and had reported the contact to Army intelligence. While stationed in Europe, Szmolka agreed to work as a double agent. In 1981 he received $3,000 for 16 rolls of film of unclassified documents and was offered $100,000 for classified material on weapon and cryptographic systems.

Szmolka was assigned to Fort Gordon, Georgia, in 1980, but maintained his contacts with Hungarian intelligence, which led to the meeting with Gilbert. Gilbert was convicted of espionage and sentenced to 15 years in prison.

This case is considered to be a classic example of recruitment based on a hostage situation since implied threats were made against the Hungarian relations of a US service member.

Robert Dean Haguewood

Robert Dean Haguewood was a 24-year-old Petty Officer 3d Class, US Navy, assigned to the Pacific Missile Test Center, Point Mugu Naval Station, California. The Pacific Missile Test Center is a testing site for the cruise missile. Haguewood's assignment at Point Mugu from November 1984 to March 1986 ended abruptly on that date with his arrest on charges of attempting to sell half of an aircraft ordinance-loading manual to an undercover agent with the alleged intent that the document be transmitted to a foreign government.

The Springfield, Missouri, native was separated from his wife and in financial trouble at the time he attempted to sell the information, classified Confidential, for $400.

Haguewood admitted that he believed the document in question, a weapons-loading manual, was classified Confidential even though it had been declassified at the time he sold it to the undercover agent. He was paid $360 for the manual and a related document.

On 19 June 1986, Haguewood pleaded guilty to violating regulations governing the handling of classified documents as part of a plea-bargain agreement and was sentenced to two years in prison and received a dishonorable discharge from the US Navy.

James Hall III

James Hall III, US Army Warrant Officer, was arrested on 21 December 1988 in Savannah, Georgia, after bragging to an undercover FBI agent that over a period of six years he had sold Top Secret intelligence data to East Germany and the Soviet Union. At the time, Hall believed he was speaking to a Soviet intelligence officer.

During this conversation, he claimed that he had been motivated only by money. He told the FBI agent, posing as a KGB officer, "I wasn't terribly short of money. I just decided I didn't ever want to worry where my next dollar was coming from. I'm not anti-American. I wave the flag as much as anybody else."

Also arrested in Bellear, Florida, was Huseyin Yildirim, code named "the Meister," a Turkish-American. Yildirim served as a conduit between Hall and East German agents. He worked as a civilian mechanic at a US Army auto shop in Germany at the time.

According to FBI sources, Hall started passing documents to East German agents in 1982 while serving in West Berlin as a communications analyst monitoring Eastern Bloc traffic. Later, Hall was transferred to

James Hall III, sentenced to 40 years in prison for selling Top Secret intelligence data to East Germany and the Soviet Union.

Decade of the Spy

Frankfurt where he continued to pass "massive amounts" of highly classified data on communications intelligence. Hall is believed to have received over $100,000 from agents of two countries during this period of time.

In July 1987, he was reassigned to Ft. Stewart, near Savannah, Georgia. Hall had been under investigation by FBI and US Army counterintelligence officers for several months before his arrest. He had been observed meeting Yildirim three times in November and December. According to US officials, the operation appears to have inflicted serious damage on US electronic intelligence activities in Europe.

On 9 March 1989, Hall was sentenced to 40 years in prison, fined $50,000 and given a dishonorable discharge. Yildirim was convicted 20 July 1989 of scheming with Hall and sentenced to life. Prosecutors contended that from 1982 to 1988, Yildirim carried classified military intelligence from Hall to East Bloc agents and returned with money.

James Durward Harper, Jr. and Ruby Louise Schuler

James Durward Harper, Jr., a freelance consulting engineer and an ex-Marine, began working for Polish intelligence in 1975. He was introduced to the Poles by a longtime business associate, William Bell Hugle. Harper was given a list of high technology items desired by the Poles and paid $10,000 as advance money for his efforts in obtaining these items. Polish intelligence was so impressed with the information Harper provided that they made an early decision to bypass Hugle and deal directly with Harper.

Harper, who did not have direct access to classified information, initially obtained information from friends including Ruby Louise Schuler and business associates. In October 1980, Harper married Schuler, a secretary–book keeper at Systems Control Inc., which had defense contracts related to the Minuteman missile system. Schuler, a 36-year-old alcoholic, brought her husband into her office in the evenings and on weekends so he could photograph documents from the office safe. She also brought material home for photographing and would return the documents to the safe the following day.

Schuler agreed to help her husband commit espionage out of love and greed. She was also an alcoholic. She carried a bottle of vodka in her purse and drank during work hours. On one occasion, a coworker accompanied her as she made a large cash deposit to her bank account. Coworkers noticed but failed to report her unusual behavior.

Numerous overseas meetings were held in Vienna, Austria; Switzerland and Warsaw, Poland. At one meeting in Warsaw, on 5 June 1980, the documents Harper provided the Poles were determined to be so valuable that he was paid $100,000 in $100 bills. During the approximate eight years of his espionage activity, Harper received at least $250,000.

In 1981, Harper anonymously contacted a lawyer in an attempt to gain immunity from prosecution by turning State's evidence. Through a combination of information gained in what little Harper told his lawyer and bits and pieces of information passed by a Polish agent of the Central Intelligence Agency, the FBI was able to establish Harper's Identity.

James Durward Harper, Jr.

Ruby Louise Schuler

The 49-year-old Harper was arrested on 15 October 1983. His wife died of cirrhosis of the liver in June 1983. It was discovered that Harper had classified documents in his home as well as up to 200 pounds of classified documents hidden in other locations. These documents concerned lasers, satellites, and advanced weaponry. It was eventually determined that the Soviets, who had acquired Harper's information from the Poles, had gained access to over 100 highly sensitive documents dealing with the MX and Minuteman missiles and other US nuclear defense capabilities.

Harper was sentenced to life imprisonment on 14 May 1984. Expert testimony at Harper's trial stated that the secrets Harper sold could impair the nation's defense program into the 21st century. Harper had confessed that he sold the secrets for the "money and the thrill of it." The judge urged that Harper never be paroled, stating, "You are a traitor to your country who committed the crime not for any political reason but for greed."

Stephen Dwayne Hawkins

On 18 June 1985, a witness reported seeing a confidential message at the off base residence of Quartermaster Third Class Stephen Dwayne Hawkins in Naples, Italy. NIS special agents interviewed Hawkins, but he denied any knowledge of a classified message at his home. Later, he admitted to having mistakenly taken the message home and added that he did not know about the message until his neighbor pointed it out to him. Hawkins stated he then laced the message in his briefcase and returned it to his unit, COMSUBGRU-8. A search of Hawkins' home revealed two CIA originated Secret/Noforn/WNintel messages. Hawkins explained that the message must have accidentally been mixed in with some study materials he brought home from work.

During polygraph examinations on 7, 8, and 9 August 1985, Hawkins indicated deception. Upon interrogation, Hawkins admitted that he had taken the secret messages as "souvenirs" and also stated that he had taken five or six classified messages from COMSUBGRU-8 and thought about engaging in espionage. Hawkins further confessed to taking about 15 additional Secret messages with the idea of selling them to a hostile intelligence service.

Hawkins was charged with violation of Article 92, wrongful removal of classified material and wrongful destruction of a Top Secret message. A General Court-Martial was held 14-15 January 1986, and Hawkins was sentenced to a bad conduct discharge, one-year confinement at the US Navy Brig at Philadelphia, Pennsylvania, and reduction in grade to E-1.

Joseph George Helmich

Joseph George Helmich, Jr., was born on 13 July 1936 in Fort Lauderdale, Florida. His parents were divorced, and his mother remarried a career Army officer. Helmich was a high school dropout who enlisted in the US Army on 8 November 1954 at 17 years of age. He was trained in communications at the southeastern Signal School and served in Korea from October 1955 to February 1957. In 1958, he was granted a GED equivalency for high school, married a US citizen who had been married previously, and in April of that year was assigned to the Signal Company of the US Army Communications Zone, Orleans, France, where he served until April 1959.

From April 1959 to April 1960, he was assigned to the US Army Garrison, Paris, France, and from May 1960 to March 1963, he was assigned to the 275th Signal Company, Paris. While serving in Paris, he was appointed Warrant Officer (22 December 1961). After leaving Paris, he went to Fort Bragg, North Carolina, where he served in a signal battalion until July 1964. With US involvement in Vietnam, Helmich was sent there where he worked in two signal units between September 1964 to December 1965. He returned to the United States and from January to November 1966 he was at the school and training center at Fort Gordon, Georgia. He resigned from the US Army on

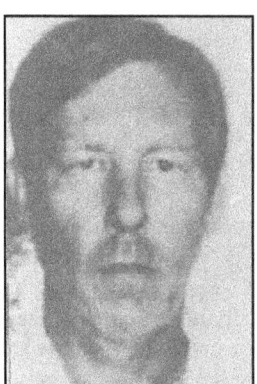
Joseph George Helmich

4 November 1966 rather than face termination after his clearance was revoked on 22 September 1966 because of financial instability.

Helmich was granted a TOP SECRET clearance by the US Army Signal Training Center, Fort Gordon, on 10 February 1958 based on a background investigation (BI) completed by Third Army on 30 January 1958. On 26 June 1958, Headquarters, US Army Communications Zone Europe based on the same BI, granted him a cryptologic clearance. Years later, in early 1974, the FBI furnished the Army an unknown subject profile of a Soviet intelligence service agent, who was an Army member during the mid-1960s. Later in 1974, Helmich was identified by the Special Operations Detachment, US Army INSCOM, as the only person meeting the FBI profile. The FBI began debriefing Helmich during the summer of 1980 and, although he initially claimed to have been recruited, he later admitted that he had contacted a member of Soviet intelligence in Paris and offered to sell classified information.

Helmich stated that in January 1963, he was several hundred dollars in debt and had written a number of worthless checks. His commanding officer in Paris called him in and gave him 24 hours to clear up his debts and redeem the worthless checks or face a court-martial and ejection from the service. Thereupon, he walked into the Soviet Embassy in Paris with classified teletype tape to establish his bona fides. The following day his Soviet GRU handler gave him enough money to settle all his debts and buy a miniature camera. During the next few weeks, until his rotation from France to Fort Bragg, Helmich met by his own count with his handler more than a dozen times about half of them at the Soviet Trade Mission. During these meetings, he furnished key lists, tapes, plain-text messages, portions of a maintenance manual, and access to a set of rotors; he was also trained in tradecraft.

While assigned to Fort Bragg, Helmich flew to Paris and met with his GRU handler on four occasions. Each time, he carried copies of key lists that he had photographed while on duty as Officer-of-the-Day. On the second trip, he stayed at the Soviet Trade Mission. On the next trip, his wife and sister accompanied him, and on the last trip, his wife may have gone with him. During the last trip, in February 1964, he told his handler that he had been alerted for transfer to Vietnam. In July 1964, he had one more meeting with Soviet intelligence, this time in Mexico City. He claimed that he passed no material then but he was given several thousand dollars. It was at this encounter that he probably told the Soviets all he knew about the new cryptographic system (KW26), which had just been introduced at Fort Bragg. After the 1964 meeting with Soviet intelligence in Mexico City, he had no contact with them except one letter and one visit to the Soviet Embassy in Ottawa, Canada. He admitted being paid in toto between $131,000 and $141,000 by Soviet intelligence.

In 1964 his purchase of expensive cars, a house, and other expensive items led to questions concerning his unexplained affluence and resulted in his being investigated. He explained his affluence as being the result of an inheritance from his grandmother and by returns from "investments" he made in France. He refused a polygraph examination, and the investigation was terminated. Shortly afterward, he was transferred to Vietnam.

After he returned from Vietnam, he had no access to classified material; his financial irresponsibility resulted in revocation of his clearance. On 4 November 1966, he resigned from the Army in lieu of being forced out. He drifted through a variety of menial jobs and even tried to reenlist in the Army. He also wrote a letter to the Soviets in an attempt to reestablish contact with them, but received a noncommittal answer suggesting he come to Paris. In 1980 he visited the Soviet Embassy in Ottawa to reestablish contact and to inquire about "matching funds," which he had been told were deposited in Switzerland each time he received payment from the Soviets. The visit was unsuccessful, and he was told again to travel to Paris.

During the latter half of 1980 and early 1981, the FBI debriefed Helmich, concluding with polygraph examinations in February 1981. During these examinations, deception by him was indicated concerning his passing information about one of the cryptographic systems during the Mexico City meeting and the involvement of another person in his activity with the Soviets. In July 1981, Helmich was arrested and indicted on four counts of espionage. In October he pleaded guilty to one count of espionage and was sentenced to life imprisonment; he would have to serve 10 years before being eligible to apply for parole.

The key to this case appears to be the handling of Helmich's financial situation in Paris in January 1963. He was in a desperate situation and was forced into desperate measures by insensitive management. This is not to excuse Helmich's actions. Although management cannot be held responsible for Helmich's financial irresponsibility, it placed him in an untenable position after the fact. Then, when Helmich miraculously paid all his debts and redeemed his checks in a matter of hours, there was no apparent curiosity on the part of management. Once the contact with the Soviets had been made and the initial payment accepted, Helmich belonged to them for as long as he was useful to them.

By 1964 his lifestyle and purchases of expensive cars and other items were obvious signs of unexplained affluence. The resultant investigation did not resolve the questions. He claimed to have inherited money from his grandmother—he had inherited a few thousand dollars in 1958—but had spent the sum in a short time-and he claimed to have made profitable investments in France. When asked to take a polygraph examination he refused. The investigation was then terminated without any apparent effort to verify his claims of investments in France, although US forces were still present there. At least one Army enlisted man, a subordinate of Helmich, and his wife knew of his flights to Paris, but did not report these facts. His wife knew that he was photographing classified material in his home, but never reported this until after his trial.

This case, in retrospect, is based on a series of fortuitous circumstances. If Helmich had worked in a "no lone" environment, there would have been little opportunity to remove or photograph classified material. If management has been more sensitive and helpful in assisting him to resolve his chronic financial problems, he might never have contacted Soviet intelligence. Had management been curious about his immediate repayment of his debts, there may not have been more than the initial loss of material. Had there been a requirement for a periodic polygraph examination, Helmich might not have contacted the Soviets. And, if Helmich had not been investigated in 1964, his records would have been destroyed and so he would not have been identified. One of the major factors in identifying him was that he refused to take a polygraph examination.

Rudolph Albert Herrmann

Rudolph Albert Herrmann, a KGB officer, entered the United States illegally with his family from Canada in 1968. He operated as a Soviet agent within the United States under the guise of a freelance photographer. His primary assignment was political information.

While Herrmann claimed not to have recruited Americans for espionage, he admitted to having transmitted sensitive information collected by other spies and to acting as a courier for the KGB. Apprehended by the FBI in 1977, he agreed to operate as a double agent until the operation was terminated in 1980.

Herrman and his family were granted asylum in the United States and were resettled under a new identity.

Brian Patrick Horton

Brian P. Horton enlisted in the US Navy in August 1979, completed basic training, and served aboard the US aircraft carrier *Enterprise* prior to being reassigned to the Nuclear Planning Branch, Fleet Intelligence Center, Norfolk, Virginia. While at the latter assignment, between April and October 1982, the 28-year-old married analyst placed four telephone calls and wrote one letter to the Soviet Embassy in Washington, DC. In his communications, he offered to sell classified military information to the Soviets. Specifically mentioned by him was his access to the Single Integrated Operations Plans, a classified master plan of how the United States would fight a war.

In June 1982, an extensive NIS/FBI investigation was initiated based on the above communications. The investigation subsequently identified the Navy man as Intelligence Specialist Second Class Brian Patrick

Brian Patrick Horton

Horton, assigned to the Nuclear Strike Planning Branch at the Fleet Intelligence Center, Europe and Atlantic, located in Norfolk, Virginia.

After documenting his activities through sophisticated investigative techniques, Horton was interrogated and admitted efforts to commit espionage. During prepolygraph interrogation on 2 and 3 October 1982, Horton additionally admitted that he had single integrated operations plans (SIOP) for sale. Based on evidence accumulated during the investigation, Horton chose to plead guilty under a pretrial agreement that included a posttrial grant of immunity. This allowed NIS to question Horton after his conviction and sentencing for a period of up to six months to determine any damage to national security caused by his actions.

This technique, now labeled the "Horton Clause" by the NIS, allows not only for prosecution but also for a determination as to any possible damage to national security. With the advent of the "Horton Clause," the damage assessment is considered after the prosecution phase, which entices the suspect to cooperate under a post trial grand-of-immunity in an effort to reduce his sentence.

Horton was convicted on five counts of failure to report contacts with hostile country nationals and one count of solicitation to commit espionage. He was sentenced to six years confinement at hard labor, forfeiture of all pay and allowances, a dishonorable discharge, and reduction in pay grade to E-1.

Edward Lee Howard

Edward Lee Howard, former CIA officer, was reportedly forced to resign in June 1983 after failing a polygraph examination, which indicated his involvement in petty theft and drug use. According to news reports, Howard was one of two former CIA employees identified by Soviet KGB defector Vitaliy Yurchenko who sold classified information to Soviet intelligence. Howard worked for the CIA from January 1981 until June 1983.

Although placed under surveillance by the FBI at his Santa Fe, New Mexico, home, Howard, who had been trained in surveillance and evasion tactics, eluded the FBI team and fled the United States. At the time, he was working as an economic analyst with the New Mexico Legislature.

Howard was born in Alamagordo, New Mexico in 1951. His father was a career Air Force sergeant. He graduated from the University of Texas in 1972. He served for four years with the Peace Corps in South America and the United States. From 1976 to 1979, he was in Peru working for the Agency for International Development. He returned to the United States and obtained a master's degree in business administration from American University. After his graduation, he went to work for the CIA.

He allegedly met with KGB officers in Austria on 20 September 1984 and received payment for classified information. He is reported to have revealed to the KGB the identity of a valuable US intelligence source in Moscow. It was also reported that five American diplomats were expelled from the Soviet Union as *persona non grata* as a result of information provided by Howard.

On 23 September 1985, espionage charges were filed in a federal arrest warrant issued in Albuquerque. He is charged with conspiracy to deliver national defense information to an unspecified foreign government.

On 7 August 1986, Howard was granted "The Right of Residence in the USSR" by the Soviet Union. According to an *Izvestia* article, Howard's request for political asylum was motivated by "the necessity to hide from the Special Services (Soviet term for CIA) of the USA, which groundlessly (without reason) are following him." The Presidium of the Supreme Soviet, "guided by humanitarian considerations," granted political asylum to Howard.

Edward Lee Howard

Ronald Louis Humphrey

Ronald Louis Humphrey was hired by the United States Information Agency (USIA) in 1966 as a civilian program evaluator. He held both a bachelor and master's degree from the University of Washington. Although married, Humphrey had a mistress in Vietnam and was attempting to get the mistress and her children out of Vietnam in the mid-1970s.

Beginning in 1976, Humphrey obtained State Department material for passage to a Vietnamese student in the United States, Truong Dinh Hung. Truong, in turn, passed the information to a courier for delivery to Vietnamese officials. The information passed included, but was not limed to, "... information concerning United States political, military, and diplomatic relations, efforts, and intelligence assessments" in Thailand, Singapore, Vietnam, China, and Ethiopia.

On 31 January 1978, both Humphrey and Truong were arrested on a seven-count indictment charging espionage on behalf of Vietnam. The 42-year-old Humphrey was charged with conspiring with Truong to deliver classified State Department communications "relating to the national defense of the United States" to Vietnamese officials. A search of his apartment revealed classified document as well as notes on how to recruit spies.

Humphrey and Truong were sentenced on 7 July to 15 years each in prison.

Vladimir Izmaylov

On 19 June 1986, GRU Colonel Vladimir Izmaylov, was apprehended by the FBI as he tried to dig up secret documents left as part of a joint FBI-Air Force double-agent operation. The documents had been buried next to a telephone pole in rural Maryland. Before he was arrested, Izmaylov buried a milk carton with the latest installment of the $41,000 he paid the US officer for military documents.

Izmaylov had been trying to obtain classified documents about the US program to develop a space-based defense system against missiles. He was also interested in details of the cruise missile program and the technology used to help military aircraft escape detection by radar and a hypersonic passenger jet known as the transatmospheric vehicle. According to the US officer, the Soviets evaluated him for nearly a year before asking him to photograph classified documents.

In written instructions to the Air Force officer, Izmaylov said he was only interested in current material concerning the advanced and prospective weapon's system such as being developed under the SDI program. All transactions and communications were to be carried out by the use of dead drops at remote locations.

Izmaylov was expelled from the United States for activities incompatible with his diplomatic role. He was the highest-ranking Air Force officer at the Soviet Embassy.

Randy Miles Jeffries

From 14 December to 20 December 1985, Randy Miles Jeffries was in contact with Soviet intelligence officers and subsequently with agents of the Federal Bureau of Investigation who were posing as Soviet intelligence officers. The 26-year-old Jeffries, married and the father of three children, requested $5,000 for Secret and Top Secret documents. Jeffries had taken 60 pages of classified documents, including transcripts from Department of Defense testimony before the House of Representatives Subcommittee on the Procurement of Military Nuclear Systems. Hired only six weeks previously as a $500-per-month messenger for the Acme Recording Company, Inc., Jeffries had worked from 1980 to 1982 for the Federal Bureau of In-vestigation. Jeffries was a known drug user; however, his background investigation did not reveal any causative factors for withholding a security clearance.

During the time Jeffries was employed by Acme, he set aside material intended for destruction and carried them out of his place of employment hidden under his coat. He contacted the Soviet Military Office in Washington, DC, in person in an attempt to sell the documents. In subsequent contacts he used a cover name of "Dano." The material he passed to the Soviets included transcripts of US nuclear war-fighting machines, vulnerabilities of US computer and telephone systems, and operating areas of the Trident submarine. He planned to also sell additional sensitive documents on command, control, communications, and intelligence (C31) as well as Top Secret data on US Navy communications systems used to signal nuclear submarines.

Decade of the Spy

On 13 March 1986, Jeffries was sentenced to three to nine years in prison.

Mikhail Katkov

Mikhail Katkov, a second secretary assigned to the Soviet Mission at the United Nations, was detained in New York City on 17 December 1987 as he was attempting to acquire defense-related technology. He was ordered to leave the United States on the following day.

Although few details about the case have been released, officials acknowledged that Katkov had been under surveillance for "some time" and that his activities amounted to "not a high deal, but nonetheless serious espionage." According to a State Department source, Katkov was the 42nd Soviet representative to have been expelled from the United States for espionage since 1950.

Bruce Leland Kearn

Bruce Leland Kearn, Navy operations specialist, assigned as command Secret control officer on board the USS *Tuscaloosa*, was arrested in March 1984 and convicted at a General Court Martial for dereliction of duty and willfully delivering, transmitting or communicating classified documents to unauthorized persons. No nation was named as having received any of the classified documents.

While absent without leave, Kearn left behind a briefcase, which was found to contain 147 classified microfiche (copies of 15,000 pages of Secret documents), seven Confidential crypto publications, and child pornographic photographs and literature. He was sentenced to four years confinement.

Karl F. Koecher

Karl F. Koecher, former CIA employee, and his wife, naturalized US citizens of Czechoslovak origin, were arrested 27 November 1984 as they were preparing to fly to Switzerland.

At the time, Karl Koecher was believed to be the first foreign agent to have penetrated the CIA for having operated successfully as an "illegal" for Czech intelligence for 19 years. In 1962, Czech intelligence trained Koecher to be a foreign agent. He and his wife staged a phony defection to the United States in 1965, and soon they became known as outspoken anti-Communist members of the academic community. In 1971 they became naturalized citizens.

Two years later, Karl obtained a translator's job with the CIA where he translated Top Secret materials until 1975. Koecher, who claimed that he was a double agent, was arrested after being observed making frequent contact with KGB operatives.

According to federal prosecutors, Mrs. Koecher operated as a paid courier for Czech intelligence until 1983. An FBI agent testified that from February 1973, to August 1983, Karl Koecher passed on to Czechoslovak intelligence highly classified materials including names of CIA personnel.

The case never came to trial. On 11 February 1985, the Koerchers were exchanged in Berlin for Soviet dissident Anatoliy Shcharansky.

Penyu B. Kostadinov

Penyu B. Kostadinov, a commercial counselor at the Bulgarian Commercial Office in New York, was arrested in December 1983 at a New York restaurant as he exchanged a sum of money for classified material. Kostadinov had attempted to recruit a graduate student who had access to documents related to nuclear energy. The American agreed to work under FBI control to apprehend Kostadinov.

One of Kostadinov's official functions was to arrange for exchange students between Bulgaria and the United

Karl F. Koecher

States. Although Kostadinov claimed diplomatic immunity at the time of his arrest, this was later denied by a Federal court. In June 1985, Kostadinov was "swapped" along with three other Soviet Bloc agents for 25 persons who had "been helpful" to the United States.

Craig Dee Kunkle

The FBI arrested Craig Dee Kunkle, former Chief Petty Officer who specialized in antisubmarine warfare, on 10 January 1989 as he attempted to sell classified information for $5,000 to FBI agents posing as Soviet diplomats. The arrest took place at a Williamsburg, Virginia motel.

On 9 December 1988, Kunkle mailed a packet of diagrams, photographs, and information related to antisubmarine warfare tactics to an Alexandria, Virginia, post office box he believed to be a Soviet drop point. The material was collected by Federal agents who had been in communication with Kunkle on six previous occasions.

An investigation by the Naval Investigative Service and FBI began in early December 1988, when Kunkle's attempt to contact the Soviet Embassy in Washington was intercepted. Kunkle had served for 12 years in the US Navy in antisubmarine squadrons in the Atlantic and Pacific fleets and was discharged in 1985 "under less than honorable conditions," reportedly for multiple incidents including indecent exposure. Kunkle also had a history of alcohol and drug abuse in addition to marital and financial problems. During his period of active duty, he held a Secret clearance.

Clayton John Lonetree, found guilty of espionage on 21 August 1987.

The former Chief Petty Officer was employed as a security guard at a local hospital. At the time of his arrest, Kunkle stated that he offered to sell classified information because he was short of cash and angry with the Navy.

Kunkle was indicted on one count of attempted espionage and ordered held without bond. He pleaded not guilty to the charge. On 4 May 1989, Kunkle changed his plea to guilty because, he said, he did not want to subject his family to a trial. He faced a maximum sentence of life in prison and a $250,000 fine. The judge imposed a 12-year sentence that was agreed upon by prosecutors and Kunkle's attorneys. The judge, noting Kunkle's money problems, fined him $550. He is not eligible for parole and was placed on three years probation in addition to the sentence.

Yuriy P. Leonov

On 18 August 1983, Yuriy P. Leonov, a lieutenant colonel in the GRU (Soviet military intelligence), under cover as a Soviet Air Force attaché, was apprehended after receiving 60 pounds of government documents from an editor working under FBI control. The following day Leonov, who had diplomatic immunity, was declared *persona non grata* and expelled from the United States.

This ended a two-year recruitment attempt by Leonov against Armand B. Weiss, an editor of technical publications and a former government consultant. Weiss had previously held a Top Secret clearance. In all, Leonov paid Weiss $1,800 for sensitive but unclassified publications on weapon systems. Ultimately, Leonov demanded a classified document. Under FBI direction, Weiss provided the item with a large number of highly technical publications for $500 cash. Leonov was arrested by FBI agents waiting outside the editor's office.

Clayton John Lonetree

Clayton J. Lonetree enlisted in the US Marine Corps and in 1984 was posted to Moscow, USSR, where he served as part of the Marine Corps Guard Detachment for the US Embassy. During his assignment in Moscow, Lonetree had an affair with a Soviet woman, Violetta Seina, who had previously been a telephone operator and translator at the US Embassy. Soon after their relationship began, Seina introduced Lonetree to her

"Uncle Sasha" who was later identified by US intelligence as being a KGB agent.

In December 1986, Lonetree turned himself in to authorities at the US Embassy in Vienna, Austria. Lonetree was tried on 13 counts, including espionage. Among these counts were charges that he conspired with Soviet agents to gather names and photographs of American intelligence agents, to provide personality data on American intelligence agents, and to provide information concerning the floor plans of the US Embassies in Moscow and Vienna. On 21 August 1987, the 26-year-old Lonetree was found guilty of espionage and 12 related charges.

On 24 August 1987, he was sentenced to 30 years in prison, fined $5,000, lost all pay and allowances, reduced to the rank of private, and given a dishonorable discharge. On 27 February 1996, Lonetree was released from prison.

John Raymond Maynard

John Raymond Maynard, a US Navy seaman, while on unauthorized absence, was found to have 51 Top Secret documents in his personal locker. Until the time of his arrest in August 1983, Maynard was assigned to the staff of the Commander-in-Chief Pacific Fleet in Hawaii as an intelligence specialist. He was convicted at a General Court Martial for wrongfully removing classified material and was sentenced to 10 years confinement.

Richard Miller, the first member of the FBI to be indicted for espionage.

Alice Michelson

The FBI arrested Alice Michelson on 1 October 1984 as she was boarding an airline flight in New York bound for Czechoslovakia. Michelson, an East German national, had in her possession tape recordings hidden in a cigarette pack.

Michelson was in the United States as a courier for Soviet intelligence. Her assignment was to meet with a US Army sergeant who was to provide her with classified material. Unknown to Michelson and her Soviet handlers was the fact that the sergeant was a double agent, posing as a KGB collaborator.

Michelson was indicted and held without bail; however, before coming to trial she was "swapped" in June 1985 along with three other Soviet Bloc agents for 25 persons who had "been helpful" to the United States. The FBI described the case as a classic spy operation.

Richard Miller

On 3 October 1984, Richard Miller, the first FBI special agent to be indicted for espionage, was arrested with two accomplices, Svetlana and Nikolai Ogorodnikov.

According to news reports, Miller provided classified documents to the Russians in exchange for a promise of $50,000 in gold and $15,000 in cash and the sexual favors of Svetlana, a Russian emigre who, as a KGB illegal agent, developed Miller for recruitment and introduced him to a KGB officer.

Miller, who was married and had eight children, had trouble keeping up with the mortgage payments on his home in San Diego county and had been moonlighting to keep afloat financially. Compounding his problems was a two-week suspension without pay in April 1984, because of what FBI officials described as a chronic problem of being overweight. Only a few weeks after his suspension, Miller was approached by Ogorodnikova and asked to become a Soviet spy. Miller, who was assigned to the counterintelligence squad, met Ogordnikova clandestinely.

On one occasion, Miller waited outside while Ogordnikova visited the Russian consulate general in San Francisco. Miller stated, but later denied, that he had let her take his FBI credentials into the consulate. After discussions between Ogorodnikova and a senior consulate official, Aleksandr Grishin, including a conversation that the government presented as wiretap evidence, the couple planned a trip to Vienna. There, prosecutors said Miller was to meet at a safehouse with KGB officials. Grishin was later named an unindicted coconspirator and left the United States. Miller did not go to Vienna. A week before the departure date, he went to his FBI supervisor and reported his dealings with Ogorodnikova. A search of Miller's residence uncovered several classified documents.

At the time of their trial, the Ogorodnikovs were accused of having been "utility agents" for the KGB since 1980. After a 10-week trial, and in an agreement with federal prosecutors, each pleaded guilty to one count of conspiracy. Nikolai Ogorodnikov was immediately sentenced to eight years imprisonment. His wife later received a sentence of 18 years.

Richard Miller pleaded innocent and after 11 weeks of testimony, a mistrial was declared. Following a second trial, which ended on 19 June 1986, Miller was convicted on six counts of espionage for the Soviet Union and bribery. His claimed that he was trying to infiltrate the KGB as a double agent was rejected by the jury.

On 14 July 1986, Miller was sentenced to two life prison terms plus another 50 years and fined $60,000. This conviction following his second trial was overturned in 1989 on the grounds that US District Judge David Kenyon erred in admitting polygraph evidence.

Miller was granted bail in October 1989, while awaiting a new trial on charges that he passed Top Secret FBI data to the Soviet woman who was his lover. Miller was forbidden to leave the Los Angeles area without special permission and underwent therapy as ordered by the Probation Department.

On 9 October 1990, he was convicted on all counts of espionage for the second time. On 4 February 1991, he was sentenced to 20 years in Federal prison. On 28 January 1993, a federal appeals court upheld his conviction. On 6 May 1994, Miller was released from prison following the reduction of his sentence to 13 years by a Federal judge.

Francisco de Asis Mira

Francisco de Asis Mira, a Spanish-born naturalized US citizen, entered the Air Force in May 1979. He was subsequently assigned to detachment 1, 601st Tactical Control Group, Birkenfeld, West Germany. Sergeant Mira had been disgruntled because he had been trained as a computer technician but was not being used in that capacity. Beginning in May 1982, while still assigned in West Germany, Mira initiated a method of passing classified defense information to the East German State Security Service.

Mira sneaked a 35-mm camera into the radar site where he worked and photographed the cover and random pages of code books and maintenance schedules of Air Defense Radar installations. He processed the photos, with the help of his girlfriend, and then used two local minor drug dealers to carry the material to East Germany and attempt to make contact with the KGB. Mira also sent a request for $30,000 to $50,000 for the film. The requested amount of money was not provided but the East Germany intelligence officer did express interest in a longer term relationship. The two drug dealers were told by the intelligence officer to stop their drug dealing and obtain steady employment.

The drug dealers made four trips between September 1982 and March 1983, each time passing information provided by Mira, and were paid between $1,136 and $1,515 per visit. Realizing he was "in over his head" and feeling used by his accomplices, Mira sought to extricate himself from a bad situation.

In March 1983, Mira went to the Air Force Office of Special Investigations (AFOSI) and related what he had done, not realizing how thorough the investigative process would be. Under questioning, Mira claimed that he wanted to become a double agent and that he "wanted to show the Air Force I could do more with my intelligence." But in subsequent interviews he admitted he had originated the idea to commit espionage to make some money and enlisted the two West Germans to assist him. He was disgruntled because he had not gotten the assignment he wanted.

In August 1984, Mira was dishonorably discharged and sentenced to 10 years confinement. Under a plea bargain he would serve only seven years of the sentence.

Samuel Loring Morison

Samuel Loring Morison was born in London, England, on 30 October 1944, where his father was stationed during World War II. Much of Morison's younger years were spent in New York and Maine. He attended Tabor Academy, a college preparatory school in Massachusetts and in 1967 graduated from the University of Louisville.

His family has a history of service to the US defense community, and his paternal grandfather was a Navy historian. His grandfather was also a Rear Admiral in the Naval Reserve and a professor at Harvard University. Morison served as an officer in the US Navy to include duty off the Vietnam coast in 1968. In 1974, Morison was employed as an analyst at the Naval Intelligence Support Center (NISC).

In 1976, Morison affiliated himself with *Jane's Defense Weekly* by doing part-time work as the American editor for the London-based firm. In the years that followed, Morison became increasingly dissatisfied with his position at NISC and more intent on obtaining a full-time position with *Jane's* where he was earning up to $5,000 per year for his part-time employment. As a GS-12 Soviet amphibious ship analyst with a Top Secret clearance, Morison provided *Jane's* with three Secret satellite photographs that he had taken in July 1984, from the desk of a coworker at NISC. The classified control markings were cut away by Morison before mailing them to *Jane's*.

Jane's, in turn, published the photographs, which depicted a nuclear-powered Soviet aircraft carrier under construction. The 11 August 1984 edition of *Jane's*, which included these still classified photographs was noted by authorities who instituted an investigation of the leaked information. The joint investigation by the Naval Investigative Service and the FBI led to Morison, resulting in his arrest on 1 October 1984. A search of Morison's apartment in Crofton, Maryland, revealed several hundred government documents. Many of the documents were classified.

Investigations of this incident never revealed any intent to provide information to a hostile intelligence service. Morison was charged with espionage and theft of government property and at his trial he testified that his only purpose in sending the photographs to *Jane's* was because the "public should be aware of what was going on on the other side." On 17 October 1985 and Morison was found guilty in Federal Court of the charges in Federal Court and on 4 December 1985, was sentenced to two years in prison.

Tommaso Mortati

Tommaso Mortati, former US Army paratrooper, was arrested in Vincenza, Italy, by Italian security authorities. He was charged with passing Top Secret documents to the Hungarian military intelligence service.

According to European news reports, the former army sergeant who was born in Italy, confessed to disclosing secrets about American and NATO bases in Italy, and claimed he belonged to a still-active espionage net. He is presumed to have been a member of the same network that included the Clyde Lee Conrad spy ring in Bad Kreuznach, Germany.

Mortati emigrated to the United States where he obtained US citizenship. He left the army in 1987 but remained in Italy as his American wife continued to work for the U.S. Army base in Vincenza.

Mortati's arrest followed that of Hungarian-born naturalized American Zolton Szabo who recruited Mortati in 1981, sent him for two weeks of training in Budapest, and continued to be his contact. Mortati confessed to Italian authorities that he attempted to bribe several Italian officers in 1984 and 1985, offering money for information.

Press reports state that Italy's military secret service was informed about Mortati's activities by German and Austrian counterintelligence authorities. A search of

Samuel Loring Morison

his home revealed a hidden two-way radio to transmit his reports in code. Up until the time of his arrest, he had received $500 a month from the Hungarian Intelligence Service plus a payment for every report filed based on its importance.

Michael R. Murphy

Michael R. Murphy, a US Navy Seaman assigned to the USS *James K. Polk*, reportedly made several calls to the Soviet Mission to the United Nations in June 1981. Murphy offered to make a deal, which he said "would benefit both the Soviets and himself." He was offered immunity from prosecution in exchange for cooperation. A polygraph examination indicate that he had contacted the Soviets three times, but had not passed any information. In August 1981, Murphy was discharged from the Navy.

Frank Arnold Nesbitt

Frank Arnold Nesbitt, a former Marine and Air Force communications officer was arrested by the FBI on 14 October 1989 and charged with delivering unauthorized information to the Soviet Government.

Nesbitt, a Memphis, Tennessee, resident, left behind family and bewildered colleagues in June 1989, appending a terse note to his weed trimmer ("I'm gone. Don't look for me.") and flew to Belize in Central America. Plans to settle there did not work out, so he moved on to Guatemala City where he enrolled in Spanish classes. In August while sightseeing in Sucre, Bolivia, he happened to board a bus full of Russian Ballet dancers. He attended the ballet that evening and the next day bumped into a Soviet official traveling with the group. This meeting set in motion his trip to Moscow.

Frank Arnold Nesbitt

From Sucre he went to La Paz where a Soviet Embassy official arranged for his flight to Moscow. Nesbitt claims he stayed 11 days in Moscow in a safe house, wrote from memory 32 pages detailing US defense communications, was polygraphed, toured the city, and met important KGB personnel. However, he grew upset over the Soviets' failure to grant him citizenship and provide him with an apartment and a job.

He returned, in a circuitous route, to Guatemala where he contacted US authorities who then accompanied him to Washington, DC. He was met by the FBI and arrested 11 days later. He offered his services as a double agent to the FBI claiming he did not give the Soviets any useful information. The National Security Agency, however, determined that information Nesbitt said he provided is still classified.

The former communications officer served in the military between 1963-66 and 1969-79. On 8 November 1989, he was indicted on a charge of conspiring with a Soviet agent to pass sensitive national defense information to the Soviet Union. Nesbitt initially pleaded innocent to espionage and conspiracy charges.

According to his lawyer, Nesbitt "wanted to have some excitement in his life." A Soviet foreign minister spokesman has said that Nesbitt was denied Soviet citizenship because a check of his autobiography he gave the Soviet parliament "led to suspicion of his possible connections with the criminal underworld."

On 1 February 1990, Nesbitt changed his plea to guilty in order to receive a substantially reduced sentence. On 27 April he was sentenced in US District Court to 10 years in a psychiatric treatment facility at a federal prison. His psychiatric evaluation states that he suffers from severe personality disorders.

Bruce Damian Ott

Bruce Ott originally from Erie, Pennsylvania, joined the US Air Force in December 1983, having first served four years in the US Army reserve. Ott was a high school honors student, who in April 1984 was assigned duties as an administrative clerk at the First Strategic Reconnaissance Wing, Beale AFB, California.

In early January 1986, Airman 1st Class Ott, then 25 years old, attempted to contact the Soviet Consulate General in San Francisco, California, for the purpose of providing sensitive material to the Soviets. An investigation was initiated, and Ott was arrested on 22 January 1986 by Air Force Office of Special Investigations and FBI agents at a Davis, California, motel as he attempted to sell classified information to undercover agents posing as Soviet representatives. One of the documents he tried to sell was "The Strategic Air Command Tactical Doctrine for SR-71 Crews" Regulation 55-2, Volume XI. At the time, Beale Air Force Base was the home base of the SR-71 "blackbird" reconnaissance aircraft.

A military prosecutor contended that Ott had told the "Soviet official" that he would like to be a "long-term mole." Ott was in serious financial difficulties, and his motivation to commit espionage was to extricate himself from debt. He had hoped to be paid up to $165,000 for his information. Several friends described Ott as being immature, quiet, naive, and friendly.

Following an eight-day General Court Martial proceeding, Ott was convicted and found guilty for failing to report unauthorized contacts, attempting to deliver a classified document to a foreign agent, and for unauthorized removal of classified information from his duty section. On 7 August he was sentenced to 25 years at hard labor in prison, reduced to the lowest rank, forfeited all pay and allowances, and a dishonorable discharge. According to his defense lawyer, Ott was a "damaged individual who desperately turned to spying in an attempt to release himself from pressures and to save his fading self-image."

Yuriy N. Pakhtusov

Yuriy N. Pakhtusov, a lieutenant colonel in the Soviet army, arrived in the United States in June 1988. He was assigned to the Soviet Military Mission as assistant military attaché.

Two months later, he began approaching an American employee of a defense contractor to obtain documents dealing with how the US government protects classified and other sensitive information contained in its computer systems. What he didn't know was that the American reported the approaches to US authorities.

Pakhtusov, 35-years-old, was caught as part of a sting operation after he received classified documents from the American employee working under FBI control. On 9 March 1989, he was ordered out of the country and declared *persona non grata* for engaging in activities incompatible with his diplomatic status.

Leslie J. Payne

Specialist Fifth Class Leslie J. Payne was stationed in the US Army in West Germany when he attempted to pass classified documents to an unnamed foreign government. The 27-year-old Payne gave the classified documents to his East German–born wife, 29-year-old Krista, who acted as the intermediary.

The West German police arrested the couple in October 1974, and a West German court tried Krista, who may have been working for the East German intelligence. Payne was tried by US Army court and found guilty of passing classified documents "for the benefit of a foreign government." On 15 January 1975, Payne was sentenced to four years hard labor and given a dishonorable discharge.

Ronald William Pelton

Ronald William Pelton grew up in Benton Harbor, Michigan, and graduated in 1960 in the upper 25 percent of his high school class. Following high school, he joined the US Air Force for a four-year tour. In November 1965, at the age of 24, Pelton was hired as a civilian employee communications specialist at the National Security Agency (NSA). At NSA, Pelton held

Bruce Damian Ott

a Top Secret security clearance. From 1966 to 1972, Pelton was assigned to Great Britain.

Pelton is married and has four children. During the 14 years he was employed at NSA, Pelton had serious monetary problems and he and his family lived in poverty in the Washington, DC area. Of the opinion that he could earn a greater income in the private sector, Pelton resigned from the NSA in July 1979, when he was earning a salary of approximately $24,000 (the approximate salary of a GS-12 in 1979). That year he filed for bankruptcy. He had a series of jobs between 1979 and 1985 unrelated to defense or communications intelligence.

In January 1980, Pelton went to the Soviet Embassy in Washington, DC, with an offer to sell information he had gained as a result of his NSA employment. Pelton had several meetings between 1980 and 1983 with Anatoly Slavonic, an officer of the KGB assigned to the Soviet Embassy. In October 1983, he made the first of several trips to Vienna for extensive debriefings concerning his knowledge of an US intelligence collection project targeting the Soviet Union. The debriefing routinely lasted three to four days, eight hours per day. In January 1983 during a trip to Vienna, Pelton was paid $15,000 and during his five years of providing US intelligence information to the Soviets he was paid a total of at least $35,000.

In the summer of 1985, Pelton and his wife separated but did not obtain a divorce. On 25 November 1985, he was arrested on charges of espionage. Authorities were led to Pelton as a result of information provided by Soviet defector Vitaliy Yurchenko.

Pelton was convicted on 5 June 1986 on one count of conspiracy, two counts of espionage, and one count of disclosing classified information to unauthorized persons. On 16 December 1986, he was sentenced to three concurrent life terms plus a 10-year concurrent term.

Michael A. Peri

Michael A. Peri, age 22 and an electronic warfare signals specialist for the US Army, fled on 20 February 1989 to East Germany with a laptop computer and military secrets. He voluntarily returned to the West on 4 March of that year to plead guilty to espionage. He was sentenced to 30 years in a military prison.

Even after his court-martial, authorities were at a loss to explain what happened. Peri said he made an impulsive mistake, that he felt overworked and unappreciated in his job for the 11th Armored Cavalry Regiment in Fulda, West Germany. His work involved operating equipment that detects enemy radar and other signals.

Peri had been described as a "a good, clean-cut soldier" with a "perfect record." During his tour of duty in Germany, he had been promoted and twice nominated for a soldier of the month award.

Ronald William Pelton

Michael A. Peri

Jeffrey Loring Pickering

On 7 June 1983, an individual using the name Christopher Eric Loring entered the Naval Regional Medical Clinic, Seattle, Washington, acting very erratic and stating that he possessed a large quantity of "secret documents vital to the security of our country." The individual was in possession of one plastic addressograph card imprinted with the address of the Soviet Embassy, Washington, DC. During permissive searches of Pickering's automobile and residence by NIS Special Agents, four Government marked envelopes containing classified microfiche and 147 microfiche cards containing a variety of classified defense publications were located.

Through investigation, the individual was identified as Jeffery Loring Pickering, who had previously served in the US Marine Corps. During his Marine enlistment, he was described as a thief, thrill seeker, and a perpetual liar. Pickering left the Marines in August 1973, but became dissatisfied with civilian life and began efforts to reenlist in the military. Pickering assumed an alias, Christopher Eric Loring, hid the facts of his prior USMC affiliation, and enlisted in the US Navy on 23 January 1979.

During interrogation, Pickering admitted stealing the classified material from the ship's office of the USS *Fanning* (FF-1076) between July and October 1982. Pickering likewise expressed an interest in the KGB and advised of fantasizing about espionage. He ultimately admitted mailing a five-page Secret document to the Soviet Embassy, Washington, DC, along with a typed letter offering additional classified material to the Soviet Union.

On 3 October 1983, Pickering pled guilty at a General Court-Martial to several violations of the UCMJ, including espionage. He was convicted and sentenced to five years at hard labor, forfeiture of $400 per month for 60 months, reduction to E-1 and a bad conduct discharge.

Jonathan Jay Pollard

On 21 November 1985, the FBI arrested Jonathan Jay Pollard, a 31-year-old Naval Investigative Service analyst (Antiterrorism Unit) and charged him with selling sensitive documents to the Israelis. He was turned in by a colleague at work who noticed that Pollard requested classified documents not needed in his work. Pollard used his position as an analyst to justify his requests for documents to the Navy Message Center rather than clandestinely acquire the documents. He also had courier orders, and the Navy Message Center wrapped the documents Pollard passed to the Israelis.

The FBI entered the case on November 15 and began a series of interviews with Pollard. After an interview with FBI agents on November 21, Pollard and his wife drove to the Israeli Embassy in Washington where they stayed for approximately 20 minutes. Inside the Embassy, Pollard requested political asylum with the hope of fleeing the United States. The Israelis refused to grant them asylum.

When they came out, the FBI arrested Pollard who then confessed he worked for the Israelis and that he sold sensitive documents to them since June 1984. The next day, the FBI arrested his wife, Anne Henderson Pollard. Both were charged under the espionage code for selling classified documents to an Israeli intelligence unit for $50,000.

Immediately after the arrest, the Israeli Government announced that this news came as a complete surprise and that the Government would cooperate in any with the US Government. The Israelis also promised to return any stolen classified documents. An Israeli Government postarrest investigation, codenamed Siren, was launched. A few days after the investigation began, the Israeli Government announced that the Pollard case was a rogue operation conducted by a few intelligence operatives. The United States was not satisfied with the Israeli explanation and pressed Prime Minister Simon Peres.

In response to Peres' agreement to cooperate fully, a delegation of high-ranking officials from the FBI and Departments of State and Justice traveled to Israel in December 1985 to pursue the Pollard investigation. The delegation included Abraham Sofaer, Legal Affairs Advisor at State and his assistant, Pat Schaubel; Joseph diGenova, US Attorney for the District of Columbia; Assistant Attorney General Edward S.G. Dennis Jr., head of the criminal division; Deputy Assistant Attorney General Mark M. Richard; and William J. Birney, the second-ranking prosecutor in the US attorney's office in Washington, DC; and FBI agents Joseph Johnson and Eugene Noltkamper.

The delegation remained in Israel for one week. The cooperation promised by Peres was not forthcoming. The Israelis finally relented and gave up their stonewalling after the delegation threatened to return to the United States. When the delegation returned to the United States, they believed that the Israelis had fully cooperated with them. The Department of State issued a statement to that effect. Later, the American Government learned that the Israelis had not been as honest as once thought.

When the United States learned that the Israelis withheld the role of Col. Aviem Sella, Israeli Air Force, who recruited and handled Pollard for several months, the United States protested again to Israel. The Americans threatened to withdraw its immunity from prosecution granted to Rafael Eitan, Yossi Yagur, and Irit Erb, all involved in the Pollard operation. The Israelis again agreed to fully cooperate but, to this day, it is believed they still did not come clean on the Pollard operation.

According to the Israelis, at their first meeting with Pollard, he identified himself as a civilian Navy intelligence officer and produced his ID card and his courier authorization. He said he wanted to give the Israelis certain information that was being withheld from them by the United States. At the first meeting, Pollard did not provide any classified information but did at a subsequent meeting. At a meeting in Paris, Pollard was introduced to his new handler, Rafael Eitan, who agreed to pay Pollard $1,500 each month.

Jonathan Jay Pollard

On 4 June 1986, Jonathan Jay Pollard pleaded guilty in US District Court to reduced charges of espionage in return for providing government prosecutors with details of what was described as a highly organized and well-financed Israeli spy operation of which he was a part. A negotiated plea avoided a trial that would have made it necessary to declassify some of the sensitive information and would have obviously strained relations between the United States and Israel. The Israeli Embassy in Washington released a statement labeling as "baseless" recent news reports, which suggested Pollard was part of a widespread Israeli espionage operation in the United States.

Pollard pleaded guilty to one count of conspiring to deliver national defense information to a foreign government. The usual sentence for espionage is life in prison but by Pollard's pleading guilty, the government, as part of its plea bargain, waived the right to ask for a life sentence. Anne Henderson Pollard also pleaded guilty to lesser charges: being an accessory after the fact to possession of national defense documents and conspiring to receive embezzled government property. Each of her offenses carried a maximum penalty of five years imprisonment and a $250,000 fine. The government agreed to recommend to the judge that Anne Pollard serve her sentences concurrently. As part of the plea-bargain agreements, the Pollards had to continue to cooperate with investigators and testify if necessary.

In February 1987 Wolf Blizter, a reporter for *The Jerusalem Post*, stated that "far from the small-time bungler portrayed in some news accounts," Pollard was "a master spy, who provided very important information to the Israelis." News wire reports stated that information provided by Pollard "included detailed information that expedited Israel's raid on Tunisia in 1985 and noted that a report in *The Jerusalem Post* described him as one of the most important spies in Israel's history."

On 4 March 1987, Pollard was sentenced to life in prison. His wife, Anne, received a five-year term. After Anne was released from prison, she went to Israel to reside. She is now divorced from her husband.

Pollard has continuously sought pardon for his activities but in 1997, for the second time, President

Clinton denied clemency to Pollard. The President cited Pollard's lack of remorse and said that to shorten his sentence after he had served only 10 years was unwarranted and would not serve the goal of deterrence. He previously denied clemency in March 1994, as did President Bush in January 1993.

Daniel Walter Richardson

Daniel Walter Richardson, a US Army sergeant stationed at the Aberdeen Proving Ground, Maryland, was arrested on 7 January 1988 and charged with attempting to spy for the Soviet Union.

Richardson intended to offer unspecified national defense information to Soviet representatives in exchange for money. No information is believed to have been compromised. Officials stated that Richardson was apprehended after electronic surveillance picked up his efforts to contact Soviet representatives. This led to his negotiation with an undercover government agent posing as a Soviet.

He was arrested at the Holiday Inn in Aberdeen, Maryland, (with an unclassified military manual and circuitry from the M-1 tank in his possession) as he attempted to meet with the undercover agent. An Army spokesman stated that Richardson had a Secret clearance but "no ready access to classified materials." Although trained as an instructor, his job was to issue tools to students at the Ordinance Center School at Aberdeen.

An administrative official identified "money and revenge against the military" as Richardson's chief motivations for espionage. Described as a mediocre soldier, Richardson was demoted in August 1987 for repeated tardiness. He was charged at the time of arrest with espionage, failure to report contacts with a foreign government, theft, and unauthorized disposition of government property.

On 26 August 1988, Richardson was sentenced by a military jury to 10 years in prison, fined $36,000, and discharged with a bad conduct record.

Ivan N. Rogalsky

Ivan N. Rogalsky, a Soviet alien living in New Jersey, entered the United States in December 1971. He had been a merchant sailor in the Soviet Union and while in the United States was employed as an electrician and mechanic.

In November 1975, Rogalsky met an Radio Corporation of America (RCA) engineer at a party in Palo Alto, California. Rogalsky asked the engineer, who was associated with the RCA Space Center, Princeton, New Jersey, for unclassified information concerning the space shuttle program. The engineer reported the request to the FBI and agreed to cooperate with the FBI counterintelligence operation directed against Rogalsky. On 7 January 1977, after accepting a classified document from the engineer, Rogalsky was arrested on charges of conspiring to commit espionage. The document concerned a highly classified and sensitive project under study at RCA for the Department of Defense. A ranking official assigned to the Soviet Mission of the United Nations, Yevgeniy Petrovic Karpov, was named coconspirator in the case.

In January 1981, Rogalsky, then 38 years old, was released from Federal custody without standing trial. The Federal District Court judge hearing the case ruled that Rogalsky was mentally incompetent to stand trial and ordered him to undergo periodic psychiatric counseling.

Sharon Marie Scranage

Sharon Marie Scranage was a CIA clerk stationed in Ghana. Shortly after her arrival there in May 1983, she began to date Michael Soussoudis, a cousin of the Ghanaian head of state. The two became intimate, and Scranage began to provide sensitive CIA information to him. Later, when Scranage hesitated to cooperate with him, he not only threatened her but other CIA employees if she did not continue with her espionage activities. Scranage provided the identity of several CIA

Sharon Scranage being led away from arraignment on 11 July 1985 at the US District Court in Alexandria, Virginia.

affiliates to Soussoudis and compromised intelligence on communications, radio, and military equipment.

In May 1985, Scranage returned to the United States and took a routine CIA polygraph examination. When her responses aroused concern, the FBI initiated an investigation. Scranage admitted providing information to Soussoudis, who had since relocated to the United States. Scranage cooperated with the FBI in apprehending him.

In November 1985, she was sentenced to five years' imprisonment, which was later reduced to two years. Soussoudis' 20-year prison sentence was suspended on the condition he leave the United States and that eight Ghanaians accused of working for the CIA be released from custody and allowed to leave Ghana.

Brian Everett Slavens

PFC Brian Everett Slavens, USMC, Marine Barracks, Adak, Alaska, advised his sister, while on leave, that he did not intend to return to the Marine Corps and that he had visited the Soviet Embassy in Washington, DC, during late August/early September 1982. Slavens' father alerted the Marine Corps of his son's intent to desert, and summarily, Slavens was arrested by Naval Investigative Service Special Agents on 4 September 1982.

During interrogation, Slavens admitted entering the Soviet Embassy and offering to provide information concerning the military installation where he worked on Adak. He denied transferring any classified material to the Soviets, but explained that his intent was to sell US military information for $500 to $1,000. According to Slavens, he was actually inside the Soviet Embassy less than 30 minutes, during which time he was asked to provide an autobiographical sketch and to reconsider his actions.

Slavens subsequently requested legal counsel, and his lawyer later agreed to have Slavens undergo a polygraph examination. Slavens was administered a polygraph examination on 5 September 1982, the results of which indicated that he did not disclose any classified information to the Soviets.

On 24 November 1982, Slavens pled guilty to a charge of attempted espionage at a General Court-Martial held at Marine Corps Base, Camp LeJeune, North Carolina. He was sentenced to two years confinement, a dishonorable discharge, and forfeiture of all pay and allowances.

Glenn Michael Souther

On 11 July 1988, the Soviet newspaper *Izvestia* announced that Glenn Michael Souther, a former US Navy photographic specialist, who disappeared in May 1986, had been granted political asylum in the Soviet Union.

Just before his disappearance, Souther, a recent graduate with a major in Russian Studies from Old Dominion University in Virginia, was questioned by FBI counterintelligence agents. According to one source, investigators were acting "on more than suspicions, but didn't catch him in the act of espionage, and thus couldn't hold Souther at the time he was questioned."

According to US Government officials, several years before Souther was granted access to highly classified satellite intelligence, his estranged wife warned Navy investigators that her husband was a Soviet spy. An investigation did take place but failed to turn up any evidence to support his wife's charges.

While attending Old Dominion University, Souther had been assigned as an active reservist to the Navy Intelligence Center in Norfolk where he had access to classified information. Souther's sudden disappearance was of considerable concern to FBI and Navy officials

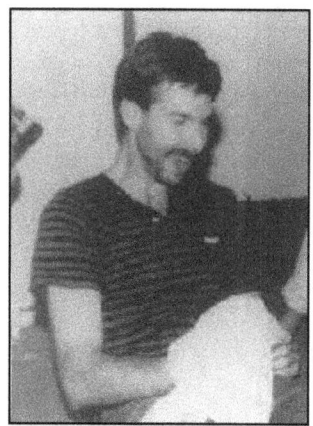

Glenn Michael Souther

since the former Navy enlisted man had held special security clearances while on active duty with the Sixth Fleet in the early 1980s. During that time he had access to highly classified photointelligence materials. Souther joined the Navy in 1975 and left active duty in 1982 with the position of photographer's mate.

According to the Soviets, the former Navy specialist had asked for asylum because "he had to hide from the US special services which were pursuing him groundlessly." Described as a bright but undisciplined young man by former teachers and acquaintances, Souther reportedly had wanted to become a US Naval officer, but had been turned down as a Navy officer candidate.

On 22 June 1989, at the age of 32, he reportedly committed suicide by asphyxiation after shutting himself in his garage and starting his Russian-made car. Russian newspapers suggested he had been disappointed by aspects of Soviet life after defecting in 1986 and was prone to depression.

Michael Timothy Tobias

On 29 July 1984, Radioman Seaman Michael T. Tobias, assigned aboard the landing ship USS *Peoria* (LST-183), secreted crypto cards from a shredder before their destruction. The theft occurred when a second radioman signed off the destruction report for 12 cards without witnessing their actual destruction.

In August 1984, Tobias and a friend, Francis Pizzo, Jr., drove to the Soviet Consulate in San Francisco, but arrived during the early morning before regular business hours. Having failed in their initial attempt to contact a "foreign power" and obviously having second thoughts about committing espionage, the pair drove back to San Diego and called the US Secret Service offering to sell the cards back to the Government for amnesty and money.

The price to the US Government was discounted from $100,000 to $1,000, a price that Tobias's younger brother, Bruce Edward, participated in setting. Several calls were placed to the Secret Service by Pizzo, one of which was traced by the FBI. The suspects were confronted by FBI agents and submitted to an interview to verify their identification. The interview concluded with insufficient evidence to detain the subjects. The following day, both Tobias and Pizzo fled with the help of an acquaintance, Dale Irene.

On 17 August 1984, Tobias and Pizzo were arrested in San Francisco. While confined, Tobias called Irene, suggesting he retrieve and destroy nine cards from behind a toilet in Tobias's apartment. On 22 August 1984, Irene was interviewed at his house at which time he produced the nine crypto cards that he had failed to destroy.

The Government withdrew plea-bargain arrangements with Pizzo, Irene, and Bruce Tobias when the three repeatedly failed lie detector tests, particularly on matters regarding the existence and disposition of two more crypto cards, which were never found.

On 22 January 1985, Bruce Tobias and Dale Irene pled guilty to two counts of theft of Government property. Bruce Tobias was sentenced to time served (159 days) and 10 years probation. Dale Irene was sentenced to two years confinement. On 7 August 1985, Pizzo pleaded guilty to four counts of conspiracy and one count of theft of Government property and was sentenced to 10 years confinement and five years probation. On 14 August 1985, Michael Tobias was convicted on four counts of conspiracy and three counts

Michael Timothy Tobias

Francis Pizzo, Jr.

of theft of Government property and sentenced to 20 years confinement and five years' probation.

Arne Treholt

Arne Treholt, head of the press section of the Norwegian Foreign Ministry, was arrested on 20 January 1984 by Norwegian authorities while boarding an airplane for Vienna, Austria. At the time of his arrest, he had a suitcase of classified documents in his possession.

A search of his apartment uncovered a collection of 6,000 pages of classified material. Treholt, charged with supplying secret NATO documents to the KGB, had come under suspicion as early as 1980 while he was serving as a member of the Norwegian delegation to the United Nations in New York. At that time he was placed under surveillance by the FBI.

Pretrial statements and testimony reveal that he received over $7,000 from Soviet intelligence and that he had been subject to blackmail. It is also believed that Treholt was motivated by pro-Soviet ideological beliefs. Treholt pleaded innocent to charges and underwent an 11-week trial by jury.

On 20 June 1985, the Norwegian court found Treholt guilty of seven counts of espionage. He was sentenced to 20 years' imprisonment.

Douglas Tsou

Douglas Tsou, Chinese-born former FBI employee, was indicted in 1988 on one count of espionage following his admission that in 1986 he had written a letter to a representative of the Government of Taiwan in which he revealed the identity of an intelligence officer of the Peoples Republic of China.

According to testimony at the trial, which was delayed until October 1991, the unidentified agent operating in Taiwan had unsuccessfully approached the FBI with an offer to work as a double agent. Although the information Tsou passed to a Taiwanese representative in Houston, Texas, was classified Secret, Tsou claimed that he considered the information to be declassified since the offer was not accepted.

Tsou fled to Taiwan when the Communists rose to power on the mainland in 1949 and moved to the United States 20 years later where he began a naturalized US citizen. He worked for the FBI from 1980 to 1986, first in San Francisco and later Houston.

On 4 October 1991, Tsou was found guilty as charged. However, prosecutors claimed that this represented only "the tip of the iceberg" of what Tsou gave to Taiwanese officials during his six years with the FBI.

On 2 January 1992, Tsou was sentenced to a 10-year federal prison term.

James R. Wilmoth and Russell Paul Brown

James R. Wilmoth, a US Navy Airman Recruit, was a food service worker aboard the aircraft carrier USS *Midway*. The Naval Investigative Service arrested him in Yokosuka, Japan, in July 1989, for attempting to sell classified information to a Soviet agent in Japan, where the *Midway* was based.

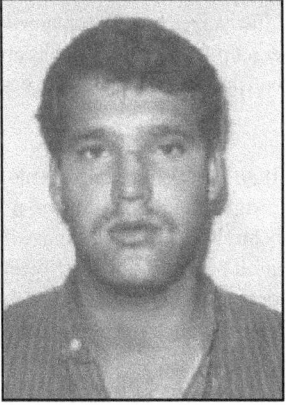

James R. Wilmoth

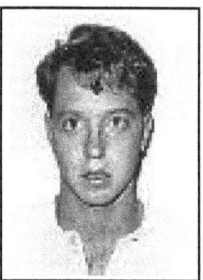

Russell Paul Brown

He was tried and convicted at a General Court-Martial on 24 September 1989. In addition to attempted espionage, Wilmoth was convicted of failure to report a contact with a citizen of the Soviet Union, conspiracy to unlawfully transfer classified material, and possession, use, and distribution of hashish.

He was sentenced to 35 years at hard labor; however, since he cooperated in the investigation, his sentence was reduced to 15 years. He also received a dishonorable discharge and was ordered to forfeit all his pay.

He had been in the US Navy for over two years and had a history of disciplinary problems, including unauthorized leave of absence. Wilmoth did not have a security clearance.

Classified information was procured by Petty Officer Third Class Russell Paul Brown, also stationed aboard the *Midway*. Brown held a Secret security clearance and took classified documents obtained from the burn bag in the electronic warfare center of the *Midway*. He passed the documents to Wilmoth, who planned to exchange the documents for cash in an arrangement with a KGB intelligence officer in Japan.

Brown was convicted in October 1989 of conspiracy to commit espionage and lying to Navy investigators. A military judge sentenced him to 10 years in prison, a dishonorable discharge, reduction in rank from E-3 to E-1, and forfeiture of all pay and allowances. Motivation for the attempted sale to the Soviets was "money and greed."

Edward Hilledon Wine

In August 1968, Sonar Technician First Class Edward Hilledon Wine, Jr., US Navy, arranged to provide classified US submarine information to a civilian associate for passage to representatives of the Soviet Union in New York City. Wine had been assigned to a nuclear submarine, USS *Skate* (SSN-578), home ported in New London, Connecticut. The civilian associate informed the FBI of Wine's intention, and the FBI contacted the Naval Investigative Service (NIS).

An investigation resulted in the arrest of Wine. A subsequent search resulted in the discovery of handwritten notes containing Secret data pertaining to submarine patrol schedules and a confidential technical publication. Wine was given a General Court-Martial, pled guilty to mishandling classified material, sentenced to three years in prison, reduced to E-1, and given a dishonorable discharge.

Hans Palmer Wold

Hans Palmer Wold was an Intelligence Specialist Third Class assigned to the Intelligence Division aboard USS *Ranger*, when he requested and was granted leave from 13 June through 2 July 1983. The leave was granted with the understanding that Wold could remain in the local San Diego area, but on or about 2 July, Wold's command received a message from the American Red Cross, Subic Bay, Republic of the Philippines, in which Wold requested an extension of leave. Wold's request was granted, and his leave extended to five additional days. But he failed to report for duty on 7 July 1983 and was listed as an unauthorized absentee.

Wold's command then requested Naval Investigative Service (NIS) assistance in locating him and ensuring his turnover to the Special Security Officer for the Commander of the US Naval Forces in the Philippines (COMUSNAVPHIL) at Subic Bay for appropriate debriefing. On 19 July 1983, NIS special agents apprehended Wold at his fiancée's residence in Olongapo City, in the Republic of the Philippines, for being an unauthorized absentee. During Wold's apprehension, an undeveloped roll of Kodak 110-color film was seized.

Wold was released to the Intelligence Officer at COMUSNAVPHIL to be debriefed. During his processing, Wold told a Chief Intelligence Specialist that the roll of film seized by NIS contained photographs from a Top Secret publication. NIS was apprised of the contents of the film and initiated an investigation into the matter.

Wold admitted to NIS special agents that he had covertly photographed portions of a Top Secret publication aboard USS *Ranger* during early June 1983, with the intention of contacting the Soviets. The film, processed under strict security measures, revealed that it did in fact contain images of pages from a Top Secret publication entitled "Navy Application of National Reconnaissance Systems." It was determined that a total of 12 out-of-focus images were on the roll of film.

On 5 October 1983, Wold pled guilty at a General Court-Martial to unauthorized absence; using marijuana aboard USS *Ranger*; false swearing; and, three specifications of violating title 18 US Code, Section 793, "making photographs with intent or reason to believe information was to be used to the injury of the U.S. or the advantage of a foreign nation."

Wold was sentenced to four years at hard labor; a dishonorable discharge; forfeiture of all pay and allowances; and reduction in rate to E-1.

Ronald Craig Wolf

Ronald Craig Wolf, a former Air Force pilot from 1974 to 1981, was arrested on 5 May 1989 in Dallas, Texas, for selling classified information to an FBI undercover officer posing as a Soviet agent. During his Air Force career, Wolf was trained as a Russian voice-processing specialist and flew intelligence missions on reconnaissance aircraft in the Far East. He held a TOP SECRET clearance.

Discharged from the military in 1981 because of his "unsuitability for service due to financial irresponsibility," he worked as an automobile salesman for a while, but was unemployed at the time of his arrest. The FBI's investigation began in March 1989 when information was obtained indicating Wolf's desire to sell sensitive information to the Soviet Union. Wolf talked with FBI undercover agent "Sergei Kitin" on a number of occasions thinking he was a representative of the Soviet Union assigned to the Soviet Embassy.

During these conversations Wolf talked about his military experience, and his desire to "defect" and provide Air Force secrets "for monetary gain and to get revenge for his treatment by the United States Government." He was directed to mail letters to a post office box in Maryland detailing the type of information he was capable of providing. Wolf passed along classified documents concerning Top Secret signal intelligence. The FBI says they are "confident there was no exchange of information (with foreign agents) in this case."

On 28 February 1990, Wolf pleaded guilty in federal court. In return for his guilty plea, the government reduced the severity of the charges against Wolf from life imprisonment to up to 10 years in prison. In June 1990, Wolf was sentenced to 10 years without parole.

Jay Clyde Wolff

On 17 December 1984, the FBI arrested Jay Clyde Wolff, a 24-year-old auto painter and former US Navy enlisted man, in Gallup, New Mexico, for offering to sell classified documents dealing with US weapons systems aboard a US Navy vessel.

Wolff, who was discharged from the Navy in 1983, met with an undercover agent and offered to sell classified material for $5,000 to $6,000. According to the FBI, a tip led to the meeting with Wolff at a convenience store where he was apprehended.

Wolff pleaded guilty to one count of attempting to sell classified documents. On 28 June 1985, a judge sentenced him to five years in prison.

James D. Wood

James D. Wood, a US Air Force technical sergeant with an unblemished military record was arrested in New York on 21 July 1973. Sergeant Wood was charged with committing espionage on behalf of the Soviet Union.

The 35-year-old had been with the US Air Force Office of Special Investigations for four years prior to his arrest. At the time of the arrest, Wood was discovered to have highly classified documents in the trunk of his rental car. The documents were described as containing counterintelligence procedures and data showing what the United States had learned about the Soviet Union.

James D. Wood

Included in the Confidential and Secret documents was a listing of names, possibly of Soviets supplying information to US intelligence.

Apparently motivated by money, Sergeant Wood was discovered by FBI agents when they followed a Soviet diplomat from Washington, DC, to New York. The Soviet was later identified as Victor Chernyshev, First Secretary, Soviet Embassy, Washington, DC. Wood would not reveal in court "for security reasons," why he had attempted to commit espionage. He received an initial payment of $1,000 in a dead drop in California. The Soviets provided him with elaborate written instructions for a meeting in New York in July, as well as a promise that his initial payment "would be greatly increased provided you supply us with valuable information."

The married veteran of 18 years' military service was sentenced to two years of hard labor and given a dishonorable discharge after pleading guilty to charges of trying to pass Secret documents to a Soviet diplomat.

Gennadiy F. Zakharov

Gennadiy F. Zakharov, a Soviet physicist employed at the United Nations Secretariat, was arrested on 23 August 1986, on a Queens New York subway platform as he gave $1,000 to an employee of a US defense contractor for three classified documents.

Zakharov, who did not have diplomatic immunity, had attempted to recruit the employee over a period of three years. At the time of Zakharov's first approach, a Guyanese national and resident alien of the United States, was in his junior year at Queens College, New York. Zakharov met with the student on numerous occasions and paid several thousand dollars for a wide range of technical but unclassified information about robotics, computers, and artificial intelligence.

At the time of Zakharov's first approach in April 1983, the recruitment target, identified only by the codename "Birg," informed the FBI and agreed to work under FBI control in order to apprehend the Soviet agent. Following his graduation in 1985, Birg obtained a position with a high-technology firm.

Under FBI direction, he agreed to sign a 10-year written contract with Zakharov to provide classified information. Money to be paid by the Soviets was to be determined by the quantity and quality of the information.

On 30 September 1986, Zakharov pleaded no contest to espionage charges and was ordered to leave the country within 24 hours. Zakjarov's expulsion came less that 24 hours after the release of American correspondent Nicholas Daniloff, who had been arrested in the Soviet Union for alleged espionage activities.

Alfred Zehe

Alfred Zehe, an East German physicist and operative for East German intelligence, was arrested on 3 November 1983, the result of a successful sting operation.

On 21 December 1981, Bill Tanner, a civilian engineer employed at the US Naval Electronic Systems Engineering Center in Charleston, South Carolina, walked into the East German Embassy in Washington, DC. Tanner offered to exchange classified information for money. Tanner was actually a double agent working under the control of the Naval Investigative Service and the FBI. The FBI's target was the East German intelligence service, the Ministerium fuer Staatssicherheit (MfS); how it worked and what type of information it was looking for.

Zehe was Tanner's primary contact. Zehe is reported to be the first East German operative apprehended in this country. In July 1984, Zehe was freed on $500,000 bail to await trial. He subsequently pleaded guilty and was sentenced on 4 April 1983 to eight years imprisonment with a fine of $5000.

Alfred Zehe

In June 1985, Zehe was traded with three other Eastern Bloc agents for 25 persons who had "been helpful" to the United States.

Defectors

Artush Sergeyevich Oganesyan

Artush Sergeyevich Oganesyan, born 21 May 1939, Leninakan, USSR, was a lieutenant in the Armenian KGB who defected in Turkey in July 1972 and later redefected to the USSR.

Oganesyan grew up in Leninakan and attended secondary schools there from 1947 until 1956. He was working as a tailor in 1959 when he was conscripted into the Soviet Army. Although he attended the Military Technical School for Rocket Troop Officers near Riga, Latvia he failed to qualify for a Commission. Subsequently, he served with an air defense rocket regiment as a corporal until his discharge on 9 December 1962. After returning home he worked as a merchandise inspector from January 1963 until April 1970. In 1969 he became a Communist Party member. A year later he joined the KGB in Leninakan and became a counterintelligence operations officer. Oganesyan married a local girl on 3 April 1971 without formally notifying the KGB. Later the KGB ordered him to divorce his wife. This development and a growing disillusionment led Oganesyan and his wife and infant son to flee from the USSR on foot, cross the border into Turkey, and defect to Turkish border guards on 10 July 1972.

Oganesyan underwent extensive interrogation by Turkish authorities in Istanbul for several weeks. He was then released to US Intelligence for appropriate processing and arrived in the United States in the fall of 1972. Oganesyan provided information on KGB internal security operations and personnel, as well as the local Armenian scene. He also brought out a KGB document entitled *Alphabetical List of Agents of Foreign Intelligence Service, Defectors, Members of Anti-Soviet Organizations, Members of Punitive Units and Other Criminals Under Search Warrant* published in 1969. This document gave a good insight into KGB counterintelligence operations and practices, especially concerning Soviet defectors and their backgrounds and status.

The Oganesyans were resettled in the United States in mid-March 1973. They could not, however, adjust to life here. On 20 September 1973, Mrs. Oganesyan, who was eight and a half months pregnant, insisted on an immediate return to the USSR to give birth in Armenia. On 27 September 1973, she was interviewed by a US State Department official who was satisfied that she was going of her own free will. The official turned her and her child over to the Soviets. During the meeting, Oganesyan also decided to return to the USSR.

During his career, Oganesyan used the aliases Atom Bagratuni, Arthur Zebum, and Artush Hohenesyan.

Nikolay Grigoryevich Petrov

Nikolay Grigoryevich Petrov, born 24 October 1939, Korov Oblast, USSR, was a GRU officer who defected to the West in Indonesia in June 1972. He redefected to the Soviet Embassy in Washington, DC, and returned to the USSR in November 1973.

Petrov came from a peasant family whose ethnic origin was Mari, a Finno-Ugrian group. From 1947 until 1957, he attended local primary and secondary schools. After completing secondary school, he entered a nearby technical school to become an electrician. Upon graduation in 1959 he obtained a job with a collective farm in the area, traveling from village to village to install and repair electrical equipment. Petrov claimed that on this job he had easy access to home-distilled liquor, and he soon found that he was drinking to excess. To escape from this situation, he persuaded the collective farm chairman to release him so that he could join the Soviet Army.

Petrov began his military service in November 1959, in a tank training regiment in the Urals. After basic training, he was assigned to an armored regiment in Hungary in 1960. By early 1961 he was a tank commander and senior sergeant.

In 1962, Petrov was admitted to the Military Institute of Foreign Languages. He returned to Moscow to begin a five-year course in Indonesian with English as his second language. In September 1965, while at the Institute, Petrov married Nina Alekseyevna Kotenina, an economist in the Central Statistical Directorate of the RSFSR. In 1966, Petrov became a member of the

CPSU. While at the Institute, he had a favorable Party and academic record.

Petrov graduated from the Institute with the rank of lieutenant and joined the Tenth Directorate of the Soviet Army General Staff, which controls Soviet military aid programs. In 1967, Petrov was assigned as an interpreter to a Soviet State Committee for Economic Relations project in Surabaya, Indonesia. The project was responsible for the delivery and maintenance of Soviet naval craft and equipment provided to the Indonesian navy. A year later, Petrov was reassigned to Jakarta.

Up until that time, Petrov had had no contact with Soviet intelligence. Shortly after his arrival in Jakarta, however, he was approached by the Soviet military attaché who offered Petrov a translator's job in the attaché's office. Petrov accepted the new job out of deference to the military attaché, with the proviso that he first be allowed home leave in the USSR. The approval for this transfer came through in July 1969, and, when Petrov returned to Moscow on leave, the Tenth Directorate personnel office sent him on to the GRU personnel office.

While still in the USSR, Petrov entered the Military Diplomatic Academy. He completed the basic eight-month course in intelligence operations and clandestine tradecraft in April 1970 and then joined the GRU Indonesian Desk.

In January 1971, Petrov with his wife and son arrived again in Jakarta, where he served as interpreter and driver for the Soviet naval attaché. Within the GRU residency, he had the title of referent and the rank of senior lieutenant. At first his duties consisted of translating reports and assisting the more experienced operations officers. In December 1971, he received one agent to handle. This agent was an Indonesian navy civilian employee, who supplied current information on naval forces and personnel. Petrov also handled all of the military attaché's administrative finances. His superiors were satisfied with his work, and he was promoted to captain in March 1972.

On 6 June 1972, Petrov's wife and son left Jakarta on home leave. His own departure was delayed because of an agent meeting that was scheduled for late June. By himself, Petrov began to play slot machines in Jakarta restaurants and drink heavily. On 12 June while gambling in a restaurant near the American Embassy he became slightly drunk. He also became exhilarated by an initial winning streak. When he began to lose, however, he went to the Soviet Embassy and took money from the military attaché's fund to which he had access as the accountable officer. He then went to dinner with a Soviet friend. During dinner Petrov had more to drink. After leaving his friend, Petrov returned to the restaurant in hopes of recouping his losses. However, at the end of the day he had lost all of his own money plus about $900 from the military attaché fund.

In a drunken state Petrov went to the US Embassy to sell information for money. After waiting half an hour to see the defense attaché, he left the Embassy. While driving away in his car he swerved too sharply and his car overturned. Petrov succeeded in righting the car with local help and drove back to the US Embassy. He had been slightly injured in the accident, and his car was battered. This time he met the US defense attaché and other US officials.

Petrov returned to the Soviets for about a day and a half. During this period he claimed that he tried to commit suicide by hanging but the cord broke. Then on the morning of 13 June, while in the home of a fellow GRU officer, Petrov became sick. He went to the bathroom, managed to slip out of the house, and made his way to the home of the US naval attaché. While there, he signed a request for political asylum. He was subsequently exfiltrated to the USA.

Despite Petrov's request for US assistance, after his defection he showed no basic change of heart from his past loyalty as a dedicated Communist. He admitted that there was no ideological motivation for his defection. He claimed instead that he defected due to circumstances only. Petrov had a strong attachment to his wife and young son. He also had a deep feeling for his village and his close relatives who continued to live there.

Due to the circumstances of his defection and his continued loyalty to the Soviet system, Petrov was considered a good candidate for redefection. He did, however, provide a good deal of information on counterintelligence and positive intelligence topics while being debriefed. The most detailed and useful data that he reported was on the training he received at the Military Institute of Foreign Languages and the Military Diplomatic Academy. Much of this was actually new information. Tight operational compartmentation substantially limited his knowledge about GRU headquarters and its operations. On the other hand, his reporting on GRU activities in Jakarta and on Soviet colony life there was more extensive and quite valuable. He was, for example, asked questions about which US intelligence had information just to test his reliability, and he in turn usually responded with accurate answers.

An attempt was made to resettle Petrov in a midwestern city, where he could have access to schools and job opportunities. This effort unfortunately failed. Petrov continued to be a "hot and cold" handling problem. During the summer of 1973, on several occasions when Petrov was under the influence of liquor, he started calling Soviet diplomatic installations in Washington and New York. Finally, he contacted the Soviet Embassy and turned himself in on the evening of 12 November 1973. At a meeting on 15 November 1973 with State Department officials, Petrov stated that it was his own decision to return to the USSR. On 18 November 1973, Petrov, accompanied by a flying squad of KGB and GRU officers from the Embassy and the UN delegation, boarded an Aeroflot flight enroute to Moscow.

Decade of the Spy
Bibliography

Andrew, Christopher and Oleg Gordievsky. *KGB: The Inside Story of its Operations From Lenin to Gorbachev*. New York: Harpers Collins Publishers, 1990.

Bamford, James. "The Walker Espionage Case." *U.S. Naval Institute Proceedings* 12:5 (1986): 110-119.

Barron, John. *Breaking the Ring: The Bizarre Case of the Walker Family*. New York: Houghton Mifflin, 1987.

———. *KGB Today: The Hidden Hand*. New York: Reader's Digest Press, 1983.

———. *Operation Solo: The FBI's Man in the Kremlin*. Washington, DC: Regnery Publishing Inc., 1996.

Blitzer, Wolf. *Territory of Lies, the Exclusive Story of Jonathan Jay Pollard: the American Who Spied on His Country for Israel and How He Was Betrayed*. New York: Harper & Row, 1989.

Blum, Howard. *I Pledge Allegiance...The True Story of the Walkers: An American Spy Family*. New York: Simon & Schuster, 1987.

Brook-Shepard, Gordon. *The Storm Birds: Soviet Postwar Defectors*. New York: Weidenfeld & Nicolson, 1989.

Corson, William R. and Robert T. Crowley. *The New KGB: Engine of Soviet Power*. New York: Morrow, 1985.

Crawford, David J. *Volunteers: The Betrayal of National Defense Secrets by Air Force Traitors*. Washington, DC: GPO, 1988.

DeForrest, Orrin and David Chanoff. *Slow Burn: The Rise and Bitter Fall of American Intelligence in Vietnam*. New York: Simon & Schuster, 1990.

DeGraffenreid, Kenneth E. ed. *Report on a Conference of Security, Counterintelligence, and Strategic Experts on Counterintelligence and Security Requirements for National Security*. Washington, DC: National Strategy Information Center, 1989.

Dillon, Francis R. "Counterintelligence: One Perspective." *American Intelligence Journal* 10:2 (1989): 37-42.

Early, Pete. *Family of Spies: Inside the John Walker Spy Ring*. New York: Bantam, 1988.

Eggert, David S. "Executive Order 12333: An Assessment of the Validity of Warrantless National Security Searches." *Duke Law Journal* (1983): 611.

Geimer, Bill. "The Handling of Defectors: Afterthoughts on the Yurchenko Case." *ABA Standing Committee Intelligence Report* 7:12 (1985): 3-4.

Goodson, Roy, ed. *Intelligence Requirements for the 1980s*, (Washington, DC) 6 vols. Vol: 3: *Counterintelligence*. National Strategic Information Center, Inc., 1980.

Headley, Lake, with William Hoffman. *The Court Martial of Clayton Lonetree*. New York: Henry Holt, 1989.

Kessler, Ronald. *Spy vs Spy: Stalking Soviet Spies in America*. New York: Scribner's, 1988.

———. *Moscow Station: How the KGB Pentrated the American Embassy*. New York: Scribner's, 1989.

———. *The Spy in the Russian Club: How Glenn Souther Stole America's Nuclear War Plans and Escaped to Moscow*. New York: Scribner's, 1990.

Kuzichkin, Vladimir. *Inside the KGB: My Life in Soviet Espionage*. New York: Pantheon, 1990.

Levchenko, Stanislav. *On the Wrong Side: My Life in the KGB*. Washington: Pergamon Brassey's, 1988.

Maldon Institute. *American's Espionage Epidemic*. Washington, DC: 1986.

McNamara, Francis J. *U.S. Counterintelligence Today*. Washington, DC: Nathan Hale Institute, 1985.

Pacepa, Ion Mihai. *Red Horizons: Chronicles of a Communist Spy Chief*. Washington, DC: Regnery Gateway, 1987.

Pincher, Chapman. *Traitors: The Labyrinths of Treason*. London: Sidgwick & Jackson, 1987.

Polgar, Tom. "Defection and Redefection." *International Journal of Intelligence and Counterintelligence* 1:2 (1986): 29-42.

Richelson, Jeffrey T. *Sword and Shield: The Soviet Intelligence and Security Apparatus*. Cambridge, MA: Ballinger, 1986.

Richelson, Jeffrey T. and Desmond Ball. *The Ties That Bind: Intelligence Cooperation Between the UKUSA Countries*. Boston, MA: Allen and Unwin, 1985.

Romerstein, Herbert and Stanislav Levchenko. *The KGB Against the "Main Enemy": How the Soviet Intelligence Service Operates Against the United States*. Lexington, MA: Heath, 1989.

Shevchenko, Arkady N. *Breaking With Moscow*. New York: Knopf, 1985.

Shvets, Yuri B. *Washington Station: My Life as a KGB Spy in America*. New York: Simon & Schuster, 1994.

Wise, David. *The Spy Who Got Away: The Inside Story of Edward Lee Howard, The CIA Agent Who Betrayed His Country's Secrets and Escaped to Moscow*. New York: Random House, 1988.

Decade of the Spy

THE DECADE OF THE SPY
1980-1989

1980	21 January	Christopher J. Boyce escapes from Federal Prison in Lompoc, California.
	29 October	David H. Barnett, former CIA employee, arrested for spying for the USSR.
1981	24 June	William H. Bell, Hughes Aircraft Corporation, arrested for spying for Poland.
	15 July	Joseph George Helmich Jr., US Army, arrested and charged with delivering classified information and equipment to Soviet agents.
	21 August	Christopher J. Boyce recaptured at Port Angeles, Washington.
	23 October	Stephen A. Baba, US Navy, arrested for providing classified documents to the South Africans. In Jan 1982 sentenced to eight years in prison.
	4 December	President Reagan signs Executive Order 12333, "United States Intelligence Activities."
1982	23 June	President Reagan signs Intelligence Identities Protection Act during a visit to CIA.
	22 September	Anatoliy Bogaty, KGB officer, defects in Athens, Greece.
1983	11 March	President Ronald Reagan signs National Security Decision Directive Number 84 "Safeguarding National Security Information" into law.
	6 June	Chinese Ministry of State Security established to collect foreign intelligence and conduct counterintelligence.
1984	12 April	Robert E. Cordrey, US Marine Corps, arrested for spying for the USSR and Czechoslovakia.
	22 August	Michael Timothy Tobias and Francis Xavier, US Navy, arrested for espionage in San Francisco, California.
	23 August	Bruce Edward Tobias, US Navy, arrested for espionage in San Diego, California. Convicted of non-espionage charges; theft of Government Statute. Dale Verne Irene, friend of Tobias also arrested.
	1 October	Alice Michelson, KGB cooptee, arrested for espionage.

Decade of the Spy

IMPORTANT DATES AND COUNTERINTELLIGENCE EVENTS
THE DECADE OF THE SPY
1980-1989

1984	1 October	Samuel Loring Morison, US Navy analyst, arrested for passing classified photographs to a publisher.
	3 October	Richard W. Miller, FBI, arrested for spying for the USSR.
	27 November	Karl Frantisek Koecher, CIA, and his wife Hanna are arrested for spying for the USSR and Czechoslovakia.
	15 December	Jay Clyde Wolff, former US Navy, arrested for espionage in Albuquerque, New Mexico.
	18 December	Thomas P. Cavanagh, Northrop Corporation, arrested for attempting to pass classified information to Soviet intelligence.
1985	22 January	Bruce Edward Tobias, US Navy, is convicted of espionage. Dale Verne Iren, a friend of Tobias, is also convicted.
	14 March	Thomas Patrick Cavanagh is convicted of espionage charges and is sentenced to life in prison.
	16 April	Rick Ames first walks into Soviet Embassy, gives classified information to KGB.
	17 May	Edward O. Buchanan, USAF, is arrested for spying for Soviets and East Germans.
	17 May	Jay Clyde Wolff, former US Navy, convicted of espionage.
	19 May	John Walker, former US Navy officer, is arrested on espionage charges. Later sentenced to two life terms plus 10 years.
	22 May	Michael Lance Walker, US Navy, arrested for espionage aboard the *USS Nimitz*, off Haifa, Israel.
	29 May	Arthur James Walker, former US Navy, arrested for espionage.
	31 May	Alice Michaelson is convicted of espionage.
	11 July	Sharon Marie Scranage, CIA employee, arrested for espionage.
	6 August	Francis Xavier Pizzo, US Navy, is convicted of espionage.
	9 August	Arthur James Walker of the Walker spy ring is convicted of espionage.

Decade of the Spy

IMPORTANT DATES AND COUNTERINTELLIGENCE EVENTS

THE DECADE OF THE SPY
1980-1989

1985	14 August	Michael Timothy Tobias, Radioman Third Class, US Navy, is convicted of espionage and sentenced to twenty years in prison.
	26 August	Edward O. Buchanan is convicted of espionage and is sentenced to prison.
	27 September	Sharon Marie Scranage, a CIA employee is convicted of espionage and is sentenced to five years in prison.
	17 October	Samuel Loring Morison, a naval analyst, is convicted of espionage and sentenced to two years in prison.
	28 October	Michael Walker, son of John Walker, is found guilty of espionage and is sentenced to 25 years in prison.
	2 November	KGB defector Vitali Yurchenko flees to KGB residence in Washington following dinner in Georgetown restaurant with his CIA handler.
	21 November	Jonathan J. Pollard, a naval intelligence analyst, arrested for spying for Israel.
	24 November	Ronald Pelton, a former NSA employee, is arrested on espionage charges. Sentenced to three concurrent life sentences.
	25 November	Lawrence W. Chin, a CIA analyst, is arrested for spying for Chinese Ministry of State Security.
	20 December	Randy Miles Jeffries, a congressional courier, arrested for espionage.
1986	22 January	Bruce D. Ott, US Air Force, arrested for espionage.
	23 January	Randy Miles Jeffries, a congressional courier, is convicted of espionage and sentenced to ten years in prison.
	7 February	Lawrence Wu-Tai Chin, a CIA analyst, is convicted of espionage. He commits suicide while awaiting sentencing.
	12 February	Karl and Hana Koecher are released in an East-West trade of prisoners.
	4 March	Robert Dean Haguewood, US Navy, arrested on charges of attempting to sell classified documents to a foreign government.

THE DECADE OF THE SPY
1980-1989

1986	7 March	U.S. orders Soviet Union to reduce its staff at the UN by 38%.
	14 March	Michael Sellers expelled for spying from the Soviet Union; first American expelled since June 1985.
	4 June	Johnathan Jay Pollard and his wife, Anne Louise Pollard, are convicted of espionage.
	5 June	Ronald William Pelton, formerly of the NSA, is found guilty of espionage and is sentenced to life in prison.
	19 June	Richard W. Miller, a FBI agent, is convicted of espionage and is sentenced to life in prison.
	19 June	KGB officer Oleg Agraniants defects in Tunis.
	24 July	Jerry Whitworth, US Navy, is convicted of espionage and sentenced to 365 years in prison for spying for the USSR.
	6 August	Bruce Damian Ott, an Air Force sergeant, is found guilty of espionage and is sentenced to 25 years at hard labor.
	7 August	Edward Lee Howard, former CIA employee, granted "The Right of Residence in the USSR" by the Soviet Union.
	23 August	Gennadiy Fedrovich Zakharov, KGB officer, arrested for espionage. Soviets retaliate by arresting US journalist Daniloff.
	22 October	Adolf Tolkachev, codenamed Farewell, executed for high treason by Soviet government.
	27 October	Allen Davies, a former Air Force staff sergeant, is arrested on espionage charges. He is then tried, convicted, and sentenced to five years in prison.
	18 November	The Intelligence Community argues against the Moscow Embassy staffing plan proposed by US Ambassador to Moscow Hartman on the grounds that it allows too many support personnel at the expense of intelligence and other substantive functions.

Decade of the Spy

IMPORTANT DATES AND COUNTERINTELLIGENCE EVENTS
THE DECADE OF THE SPY
1980-1989

1986	4 December	Michael H. Allen, US Navy, arrested for spying for the Philippine police. In August 1987 sentenced to eight years in prison.
	31 December	Clayton Lonetree, a US Marine Corps sergeant, is arrested on espionage charges.
1987	2 April	Moscow announces the defection of an American soldier, William E. Roberts, serving in West Germany.
	12 May	James Angleton, former CIA CI Chief, dies of lung cancer.
	28 May	John Allen Davies, formerly of the Air Force, is convicted of espionage.
	6 June	Maj. Florentino Azpillaga Lombard, from Cuban Ministry of Interior, defects to U.S. in Czechoslovakia.
	14 June	Former CIA employee Philip Agee returns to the US for the first time in 16 years.
	25 June	A State Department report describes Moscow's use of its Chamber of Commerce and Industry as a major front for KGB agents to collect western technology through trade promotion efforts.
1988	14 January	Daniel Walter Richardson, US Army, arrested for espionage.
	4 April	CIA's Counterintelligence Center established.
	16 April	Thomas J. Dolce, US Army, arrested for spying for South Africa.
	18 July	Former Navy enlisted man Glen Souther, who was the subject of an FBI espionage investigation, surfaces in Moscow and is granted political asylum.
	23 August	Imre Kercsik and Sandor Kercsik, arrested by Swedish authorities for espionage. Both acted as couriers for the Clyde Lee Conrad espionage ring.
	December	Randall S. Bush, US Navy, arrested for attempting to pass information to a foreign power.
	21 December	James W. Hall, US Army, arrested for spying for the USSR and East Germany. He is sentenced to 40 years in prison.

Decade of the Spy

IMPORTANT DATES AND COUNTERINTELLIGENCE EVENTS

THE DECADE OF THE SPY
1980-1989

1989	10 January	Craig D. Kunkle, former U.S. Navy technician, arrested and charged with espionage by two FBI agents posing as Soviet officials.
	7 February	Alan C. Thompson, executive director of New York-based National Council of American-Soviet Friendship, a Soviet front group used to promote propaganda and disinformation, arrested on currency charges.
	4 March	Donald Wayne King and Ronald Dean Graf, US Navy, arrested on charges of espionage and stealing $150,000 worth of classified military parts and electronic components.
	8 March	Soviet Army Lieutenant Colonel Yuri Pakhtusov, an assistant military attaché in the United States, is arrested for spying. He is declared persona non grata and is expelled from the US.
	21 May	Zoltan Szabo, U.S. Army, arrested by Austrian police for espionage as part of Clyde Lee Conrad ring.
	25 July	Russell P. Brown, US Navy, arrested for spying for the USSR.
	14 October	Frank Nesbitt, former Marine and Air Force officer, arrested and charged with delivering classified information to the Soviets.
	9 November	Berlin Wall's dismantling begins. On the same day, East Germany throws open its borders, allowing its citizens to travel freely to the West.
	1 December	Thomas Morati, former Administrative clerk, US Army, arrested in Italy as part of the Clyde Lee Conrad espionage ring. Sentenced on 21 December 1989 to 20 months in jail.

CHAPTER 4

CHAPTER 4

Counterintelligence at the End Of the 20th Century

Introduction

The breakup of the Soviet Union in 1991 and its ongoing volatile political environment, the liberation of Eastern Europe, and the reunification of Germany all led people in the United States to believe that espionage was out-of-date and the foreign intelligence war over. But the beginning of the post-Cold War did not signal the end of espionage.

In 1994 the nation was hit by a bombshell when the FBI arrested Hazen Aldrich Ames, a senior CIA officer, for spying for almost 10 years for the Russians. The deadly consequences of Ames' personal betrayal and the compromise of national security drastically altered US counterintelligence. Congress was furious about this "failure" and demanded change. To preclude any action by Congress to legislate changes in counterintelligence, President Clinton issued Presidential Decision Directive/NSC-24 on 3 May 1994, which reorganized counterintelligence.

Under the Executive Order, a National Counterintelligence Policy Board (NACIPB) was created to coordinate CI activities and resolve interagency disagreements. The NACIPB, unlike previous groups, reports to the National Security Council. In addition, the order created a National Counterintelligence Center (NACIC) to share and evaluate information regarding foreign intelligence threats.

In 1995, Congress recognized that countries that formerly had not been considered intelligence threats were stealing American technology and decided to take action. They enacted legislation, the Economic Espionage Act of 1996, which the President signed on 11 October 1996. In April 1997, the first conviction under the new law took place with the sentencing in Pennsylvania of Daniel Worthing.

The nation again was reminded in 1996 that traditional espionage did not take a holiday when Robert Chaegon Kim, a computer specialist in the Maritime Systems Directorate of the Office of Naval Intelligence, was arrested on 25 September 1996 on charges of passing classified information to South Korea. Almost two months later, Harold J. Nicholson, a 16-year CIA veteran and former station chief with access to "very damaging information," was arrested on 15 November 1996 and charged with passing Top Secret information to the Russians. A month later, on 17 December 1996, Earl E. Pitts, a Special Agent with the FBI since 1983, was arrested and charged with compromising FBI intelligence operations to the SVRR, successor to the Soviet KGB.

This chapter is not complete. There are two more years before the beginning of the 21st Century and, during this time, additional spies will undoubtedly be detected, arrested, or neutralized. Threats to our nation's national security will continue unabated as the rest of the world looks at the United States as the "great Satan," the technology store to be robbed, the "bullying big brother," or a target to knock down to size. New technological advances in communications and information sharing will also create new difficulties for American counterintelligence to resolve. All of these developments indicate that US counterintelligence will continue to face threats to the national security in the future.

The Jacobs Panel

On 23 May 1990, a blue-ribbon panel, called the Jacobs panel after its chairman Eli Jacobs, reported its recommendations to the Senate Intelligence Committee. The panel had been asked by the chairmen of the Committee, Senator David L. Boren, Democrat of Oklahoma and Senator William S. Cohen, Republican of Maine, to review espionage cases from the 1980s and to make recommendations to change the nation's espionage laws.

The eight-member panel suggested 13 legislative proposals. According to Jacobs, "The past 20 years of espionage indicate that the main threat is not the ideologically motivated spy but rather the voluntary spy- the insider who betrays his country not from belief, but for money or revenge."

The Senate Committee was told that the panel looked at 19 espionage cases from 1975 to the present day and found that most of the people studied had access to Top Secret or codeword information. They also visited the CIA, FBI, Pentagon, National Security Agency, and others. Both the CIA and FBI said they offered suggestions but did not identify them.

In making its recommendations, the panel was proposing to make it easier for counterintelligence and law enforcement entities to "deter, detect and prosecute" espionage cases through stiffer Top Secret clearance checks, polygraph tests and new penalties for "espionage-related activities."

The 13 ways to improve counterintelligence recommended by the panel were:

1. Require people with top secret clearances to grant investigators access to financial, consumer credit and commercial records.

2. Amend privacy laws to allow unlimited access to financial records of top secret clearance holders.

3. Require government code and communications specialists and manufacturers of code machines to undergo regular polygraph examinatons.

4. Permit the National Security Agency to help former employees financially so that they have no need to obtain money by spying.

5. Amend espionage laws to make it a crime to possess espionage equipment with intent to spy.

6. Amend espionage laws to make the sale of top secret documents a crime, without having to disclose the information contained in the documents.

7. Amend espionage laws to make it a crime to remove top secret documents from secure areas.

8. Expand laws requiring forfeiture of profits obtained from crime to include espionage.

9. Amend federal retirement laws to permit the government to deny retirement pay to people convicted of espionage in foreign courts when U.S. secrets are involved.

10. Amend consumer law to permit the FBI to obtain consumer reports on people suspected of being foreign agents.

11. Amend privacy laws to permit FBI access to unlisted telephone numbers of suspected foreign agents.

12. Amend law to permit offering up to $1 million rewards for information about espionage.

13. Amend surveillance law to create a process for obtaining court orders for physical searches in national security cases.

Senator Boren said espionage cases "continue to surface with disturbing frequency." Despite the changes occurring in the Soviet Union and Eastern Europe, Boren noted that the United States has not seen a decrease in hostile spying, instead, "we have seen an increase in espionage activities."

Both Senator Boren and Senator Cohen indicated that economic espionage will be the big problem in the future. Senator Boren stated that although the KGB was trying to improve its public image by showing a less aggressive intelligence service, the KGB Chairman Vladimir Kryuchkov indicated "in simple terms, espionage against commerical targets will become the great equalizer for the shortcomings of the Soviet economy."

Senator Cohen said, "The era of the cloak and dagger may be over, but the cloaks are likely to multiply and become even more pervasive in their effort to procure military, industrial, and commercial secrets."

THE WHITE HOUSE

Office of the Press Secretary

For Immediate Release   September 13, 1993

EXECUTIVE ORDER
12863

PRESIDENT'S FOREIGN INTELLIGENCE ADVISORY BOARD

By the authority vested in me as President by the Constitution and the laws of the United States of America, and in order to enhance the security of the United States by improving the quality and effectiveness of intelligence available to the United States, and to assure the legality of activities of the Intelligence Community, it is ordered as follows:

Part I. Assessment of Intelligence Activities

Section 1.1. There is hereby established, within the White House Office, Executive Office of the President, the President's Foreign Intelligence Advisory Board (PFIAB). The PFIAB shall consist of not more than 16 members, who shall serve at the pleasure of the President and shall be appointed by the President from among trustworthy and distinguished citizens outside the Government who are qualified on the basis of achievement, experience and independence. The President shall establish the terms of the members upon their appointment. To the extent practicable, one-third of the PFIAB at any one time shall be comprised of members whose term of service does not exceed 2 years. The President shall designate a Chairman and Vice Chairman from among the members. The PFIAB shall utilize full-time staff and consultants as authorized by the President. Such staff shall be headed by an Executive Director, appointed by the President.

Sec. 1.2. The PFIAB shall assess the quality, quantity, and adequacy of intelligence collection, of analysis and estimates, and of counterintelligence and other intelligence activities. The PFIAB shall have the authority to review continually the performance of all agencies of the Federal Government that are engaged in the collection, evaluation, or production of intelligence or the execution of intelligence policy. The PFIAB shall further be authorized to assess the adequacy of management, personnel and organization in the intelligence agencies. The heads of departments and

---

The Jacobs Panel

Eli Jacobs: Baltimore Orioles owner. He was a Reagan-era arms control advisor; and sat on Pentagon advisory panels.

Richard Helms: former Director of Central Intelligence.

Lloyd Cutler: former Carter White House counsel.

Arthur Culvahouse: former Reagan White House counsel.

Seymour Weiss: former ambassador and top Department of State official.

Sol Linowitz: former Xerox executive, ambassador and Mid-East negotiator.

Warren Christopher: former deputy Secretary of State.

Harold Edgar: Columbia University professor; espionage law expert.

agencies of the Federal Government, to the extent permitted by law, shall provide the PFIAB with access to all information that the PFIAB deems necessary to carry out its responsibilities.

Sec. 1.3. The PFIAB shall report directly to the President and advise him concerning the objectives, conduct, management and coordination of the various activities of the agencies of the Intelligence Community. The PFIAB shall report periodically, but at least semiannually, concerning its findings and appraisals and shall make appropriate recommendations for the improvement and enhancement of the intelligence efforts of the United States.

Sec. 1.4. The PFIAB shall consider and recommend appropriate action with respect to matters, identified to the PFIAB by the Director of Central Intelligence, and the Central Intelligence Agency, or other Government agencies engaged in intelligence or related activities, in which the advice of the PFIAB will further the effectiveness of the national intelligence effort. With respect to matters deemed appropriate by the President, the PFIAB shall advise and make recommendations to the Director of Central Intelligence, the Central Intelligence Agency, and other Government agencies engaged in intelligence related activities, concerning ways to achieve increased effectiveness in meeting national intelligence needs.

Part II. Oversight of Intelligence Activities

Sec. 2.1. The Intelligence Oversight Board (IOB) is hereby established as a standing committee of the PFIAB. The IOB shall consist of no more than four members appointed from among the membership of the PFIAB by the Chairman of the PFIAB. The Chairman of the IOB shall be appointed by the Chairman of the PFIAB. The Chairman of the PFIAB may also serve as Chairman of the IOB. The IOB shall utilize such full-time staff and consultants as authorized by the Chairman of the PFIAB.

Sec. 2.2. The IOB shall:

(a) prepare for the President reports of intelligence activities that the IOB believes may be unlawful or contrary to Executive order or Presidential directive;

(b) forward to the Attorney General reports received concerning intelligence activities that the IOB believes may be unlawful or contrary to Executive order or Presidential directive;

(c) review the internal guidelines of each agency within the Intelligence Community that concern the lawfulness of intelligence activities;

(d) review the practices and procedures of the Inspectors General and General Counsel of the Intelligence Community for discovering and reporting intelligence activities that may be unlawful or contrary to Executive order or Presidential directive; and

(e) conduct such investigations as the IOB deems necessary to carry out its functions under this order.

Sec. 2.3 . The IOB shall, when required by this order, report to the President through the Chairman of the PFIAB. The IOB shall consider and take appropriate action with respect to matters identified by the Director of Central Intelligence, the Central Intelligence Agency or other agencies of the Intelligence Community. With respect to matters deemed appropriate by the President, the IOB shall advise and take appropriate recommendations to the Director of Central Intelligence, the Central Intelligence Agency or other agencies of the Intelligence Community.

Sec. 2.4. The heads of departments and agencies of the Intelligence Community, to the extent permitted by law, shall provide the IOB with all information that the IOB deemed necessary to carry out its responsibilities. Inspectors General and General Counsel of the Intelligence Community, to the extent permitted by law, shall report to the IOB, at least on a quarterly basis and from time to time as necessary or appropriate, concerning intelligence activities that they have reason to believe may be unlawful or contrary to Executive order or Presidential directive.

Part III. General Provisions

Sec. 3.1. Information made available to the PFIAB, or members of the PFIAB acting in their IOB capacity, shall be given all necessary security protection in accordance with applicable laws and regulations. Each member of the PFIAB, each member of the PFIAB's staff and each of the PFIAB's consultants shall execute an agreement never to reveal any classified information obtained by virtue of his or her services with the PFIAB except to the President or to such persons as the President may designate.

Sec. 3.2. Members of the PFIAB shall serve without compensation but may receive transportation expenses and per diem allowances as authorized by law. Staff and consultants to the PFIAB shall receive pay and allowances as authorized by the President.

Sec. 3.3. Executive Order No. 12334 of December 4, 1981, as amended and Executive Order No. 12537 of October 28, 1985, as amended, are revoked.

WILLIAM J. CLINTON
THE WHITE HOUSE

September 13, 1993.

President, Bill Clinton

IN THE UNITED STATES DISTRICT COURT FOR THE EASTERN DISTRICT OF VIRGINIA

Alexandria Division

UNITED STATES OF AMERICA
v.   Criminal No. 94-64-A
ALDRICH HAZEN AMES,
A/K/A "Kolokol",
a/k/a "K"

STATEMENT OF FACTS

In the event that this matter were to proceed to trial, the government would prove the following beyond a reasonable doubt:

I. INTRODUCTION

ALDRICH HAZEN AMES is 52 years old, born on May 26, 1941. In June 1962, ALDRICH HAZEN AMES accepted employment with the Central Intelligence Agency (CIA) of the United States, and he has been a full-time CIA employee for more than 31 years. At the time of his arrest, AMES was a GS-14 Operations Officer in the Counternarcotics Center at CIA Headquarters in Langley, Virginia.

During his employment with CIA, AMES held a variety of positions including the following: from 1983 to 1985, AMES was the Chief, Soviet Operational Review Branch in the Operational Review and Production Group of the Soviet/East European (SE) Division of the Directorate of Operations (DO) of the CIA; from 1986 through 1989, AMES was assigned to the United States Embassy in Rome, Italy; from September 1989 through December 1989, AMES was Chief, Europe Branch, External Operations Group, SE Division; from December 1989 through August 1990, AMES was the Chief, Czechoslovak Operations Branch, East European Operations Group, SE Division; from September 1990 through August 1991, AMES was assigned to the USSR Branch, Analytical Group, Counterintelligence Center; from September 1991 through November 1991, AMES was Chief, KGB.[1] Working Group, Central Eurasia (CE) Division; from December 19091 through August 1993, AMES was a referant for CE Branch, regional Programs Branch, International Counternarcotics Group, Counternarcotics Center (ICG/CNC) and from August 1993 to February 1994, AMES was Chief, Europe and CE Branch, ICG/CNC. Throughout AMES' employment with the CIA, he held a TOP SECRET security clearance and had regular access to information and documents classified SECRET and TOP SECRET pursuant to Executive Order 12356.

On August 10, 1985, AMES married Maria del Rosario Casas Dupuy in the Commonwealth of Virginia. Prior to their arrests on February 21, 1994, ALDRICH and ROSARIO AMES resided at 2512 North Randolph Street, Arlington, Virginia, in the Eastern District of Virginia, with their minor son.

II. ESPIONAGE RELATED ACTIVITIES

In 1984, as part of his duties as a CIA Operations Officer, ALDRICH HAZEN AMES began meeting with officials of the Embassy of the Union of Soviet Socialist Republics ("U.S.S.R." or "Soviet Union." in Washington, D.C. These meeting were authorized by the Central Intelligence Agency and the Federal Bureau of Investigation, and were designed to allow AMES to assess Soviet officials as possible sources for intelligence information and recruitment. AMES was required to report each of his meetings with these Soviet officials to CIA officials.

In approximately April 1985, AMES agreed with Soviet officials to sell classified information from the Central Intelligence Agency and other branches of the United States government to the KGB, in return for large sums of money. In May and July 1985, AMES engaged in authorized meetings with Soviet officials, meetings he used as a cover to provide classified information to the KGB in exchange for money. Although AMES stopped regularly reporting these meetings to the CIA in July 1985, over the next year AMES continued to meet with the KGB in Washington, D.C. During many of these meetings, AMES provided classified information relating to the national defense of the United States to the KGB in return for cash payments.[2]

In July 1986, ALDRICH HAZEN AMES was assigned to the United States Embassy in Rome, Italy, where he served until July 1989. During this time, AMES met with his KGB handler, codenamed "SAM." AMES reported a few of these meetings to the CIA, claiming that he was obtaining information from "SAM," a Soviet Embassy official. During these meetings, AMES continued to disclose classified information relating to the national defense of the United States which AMES obtained through his work for the CIA in Rome.

In the Spring of 1989, as AMES was preparing to return to CIA Headquarters in Langley, Virginia, the KGB provided him with two written documents. The first document was a financial accounting which indicated that as of May 1, 1989, AMES had already receive approximately $1.8 million and that some $900,000 more had been appropriated for him. The

Aldrich Hazen Ames

second document was a nine-page letter which listed the types of classified information the KGB wanted AMES to obtain for them upon his return to CIA Headquarters,[3] discussed arrangements for cash payments to AMES upon his return to the United States, warned AMES to avoid traps set by the CIA, and detailed a communication plan governing further communications between AMES and the KGB. Pursuant to this communication plan, AMES would pass documents to and receive money from the KGB in the Washington, D.C. area at set times throughout the year using signal sites and dead drops. AMES would also meet personally with the KGB at least once yearly in meetings outside the United States. The fixed site for these meeting would be in Bogota, Colombia, on the first Tuesday every December, although additional meetings could be held in other cities, including Vienna, Austria, on an as needed basis.

In 1990, the KGB provided AMES with a communications plan for 1991 through a dead drop in the Washington, D.C. area. The 1991 communication plan provided for impersonal contacts through signal sites and dead drops, and for personal meetings between AMES and the KGB in Vienna, Austria, in April, and in Bogota, Colombia, in December. On December 17, 1990, AMES obtained valuable intelligence information regarding a KGB officer cooperating with the CIA. AMES prepared a letter for the KGB on his home computer advising the KGB of this information and the cryptonym of the KGB officer.

Pursuant to AMES' communication schedule with the KGB, on April 25, 1991, AMES traveled to Vienna, Austria, to meet with his KGB handlers. Although

One of Ames' dead drop sites.

AMES was present in Vienna and prepared to exchange classified information for money, the KGB failed to meet with AMES at that time. Later that year, in December 1991, AMES met personally with the KGB in Bogota, Colombia, where he exchanged classified information for a large amount of cash. At that meeting, the KGB provided AMES a communications plan for 1992, pursuant to which they would communicate through signal sites and dead drops in March and August, and meet personally in Caracas, Venezuela, in October of 1992.

In March 1992, defendant ALDRICH HAZEN AMES communicated with the KGB by placing a signal at signal site SMILE and leaving a message with a package of documents at dead drop BRIDGE. In this message to the KGB, AMES requested that they promptly transmit more money to him through a dead drop. Again in June, 1992, AMES prepared a message on his computer to the KGB in which he complained of their failure to provide him money in response to his previous message, indicated that he was forced to sell stocks and certificates of deposit in Zurich to meet pressing needs, and asked them to deliver to him up to $100,000 in cash through dead drop PIPE. This message was transmitted to the KGB by placing a signal at signal site SMILE and leaving the message at dead drop BRIDGE.

On August 18, 1992, AMES typed a letter to the KGB on his home computer, at his home in the Eastern District of Virginia, discussing dead drops and his access to classified information, stating: "My lack of access frustrates me, since I would need to work harder to get what I can to you. It was easier to simply hand over cables! Documents are enclosed in this package which should be of interest."

In discussing his possible transfer to a different position within the CIA, AMES stated that, "If this job offer becomes serious during the next week or so, I will surely take it. It would be more interesting and productive for us." In this letter, AMES agreed to a personal meeting with the KGB in Caracas, Venezuela and AMES also provided them with information on the level of CIA operations in Moscow, U.S. conclusions about Russian technical penetrations of our embassy in Moscow, and CIA recruitment plans for Russian officials. The letter also stated that, "My wife has accomodated (sic) herself to understanding what I am doing in a very supportive way."

AMES attempted to transmit this letter and accompanying classified documents to the KGB on August 19, 1992, by placing a pencil mark at signal site HILL in the morning and thereafter leaving the documents and letter at dead drop GROUND at 4 p.m. that day. Early the next day, however, AMES returned to the signal site and determined that his signal to the KGB had not been erased, signifying that they had not picked up his package from the dead drop. AMES thereafter retrieved his package, and on September 1, 1992, typed a second letter to the KGB on his home computer. This letter advised them that he had been forced to retrieve his earlier drop and would signal them again. This message, along with the earlier package, was retransmitted to the KGB in early September through dead drop GROUND.

On October 2, 1992, pursuant to his communications plan, AMES traveled to Bogota, Colombia, and then on to Caracas, Venezuela, to meet with officers of the KGB. During this meeting, AMES provided the KGB with classified information and received in return approximately $150,000 in cash. The KGB also provided AMES with a communications plan for 1993, pursuant to which AMES would transmit information and messages to them by dead drops in January, April, July, and October, receive money and messages from the KGB in March, June, and September, and would meet with them personally in Bogota, Colombia, in November or December 1993. Upon his return to the United States, AMES deposited more than $85,000 of the KGB money received in Caracas into accounts he controlled with his wife in banks in Northern Virginia, all deposits in amounts of less than $10,000.

On March 9, 1993, AMES typed a message to the KGB on his home computer discussing a variety of topics including the morale of the CIA division concerned with the former U.S.S.R and Russia, personnel changes and budgetary matters in the CIA, and the fact that he was transmitting to them a "variety" of documents. AMES opened this message telling the KGB, "All is well with me—I have no indications that anything is wrong or suspected." This message, along with a package of classified documents and information, was transmitted to the KGB through a dead drop in March 1993.

On May 26, 1993, AMES transmitted an "urgent" message to the KGB, asking for money to be delivered to him immediately through a dead drop in the Washington, D.C. area. Four days later, the KGB transmitted a package containing a substantial amount of cash to AMES through dead drop BRIDGE. In July 1993, the KGB transmitted to AMES additional money through a dead drop, as well as a message discussing an upcoming personal meeting, and their plan to test a dead drop to determine whether it was secure. In this message, the KGB advised AMES that they would provided additional money shortly, unless the money was postponed due to the "diplomatic pouch schedule."

In preparation for his trip to Bogota on September 8, 1993, AMES drafted a message to the KGB stating that he would be available to meet with them on October 1, 1993. On September 9, 1993, AMES left this message for the KGB, and that evening drove with his wife into the District of Columbia to determine whether the KGB had received the message. Later that month, the KGB signaled AMES through signal site NORTH, advising him they would be unavailable to meet with him on October 1, 1993, and transmitted a message to him through dead drop PIPE stating they would meet with him between November 1 and November 8, 1993. On October 18, 1993, AMES signaled his willingness to attend this meeting in Bogota by placing a chalk mark at signal site SMILE.

One of Ames' signal sites.

Thereafter, on October 30, 1993, AMES traveled to Bogota, Colombia, where he met with officers of the KGB. In Bogota, AMES provided the KGB with classified information in exchange for a substantial amount of cash. In Bogota, AMES also received a communications plan for 1994 which established new signal sites throughout the Washington metropolitan area and provided for dead drops in February, March, May, August, and September, face-to-face meetings in Caracas, Venezuela, or Quito, Ecuador, in November 1994, and a face-to-face meeting in 1995 in either Vienna, Austria, or Paris, France. During this meeting, the KGB also advised AMES that they were holding $1.9 million for him.

III. COMPROMISE OF CLASSIFIED INFORMATION

When ALDRICH HAZEN AMES began spying for the KGB in the Spring of 1985, his position within the CIA guaranteed him access to most information relating to penetrations of the Soviet military and intelligence services and intelligence operations against the Soviet Union. AMES disclosed substantial amounts of this information, including the identities of Russian military and intelligence officers who were cooperating with the CIA and friendly foreign intelligence services, including but not limited to, sources codenamed GTACCORD, GTCOWL, GTFITNESS, GTBLIZZARD, GTGENTILE, GTMILLION, GTPROLOGUE, GTWEIGH, GTTICKLE, and others.[4] AMES' disclosures included a substantial amount of TOP SECRET information including signals intelligence. AMES' compromise of these penetrations of the Soviet military and intelligence services deprived the United States of extremely valuable intelligence material for years to come.

During his assignment to the U.S. Embassy in Rome from 1986 to 1989, AMES provided the KGB with valuable intelligence information concerning CIA activities against the Soviet Union, including a large number of double agent operations launched against the Soviet Union. AMES compromised a substantial number of double agent operations organized by U.S. intelligence agencies, and also advised the KGB of our knowledge of Soviet double agent operations targeted against the U.S. AMES informed the KGB of important CIA strategies involving double agent operations and answered detailed inquiries regarding past penetrations of the Soviet intelligence services. During this period AMES also disclosed to the KGB the identities of an Eastern European security officer who had begun cooperating with the CIA, code named GMMOTORBOAT, and a soviet official cooperating with CIA, codenamed GTPYRRHIC.

Following his return in 1989 to CIA Headquarters, AMES continued to provide the KGB with valuable classified information related and unrelated to his specific CIA job assignments. AMES also provided the KGB with a substantial amount of information regarding CIA and other U.S. intelligence agencies, including information on budgets, staffing, personnel, morale, strategy, and other issues affecting the Soviet Union and Russia.

IV. THE FINANCES AND FALSE TAX RETURNS

During this conspiracy, defendant ALDRICH HAZEN AMES received approximately $2.5 million from the KGB for his espionage activities. AMES received this money primarily in face-to-face meetings overseas, but also through dead drops in the Washington, D.C. area. While AMES was stationed in Rome, he deposited the bulk of this cash into two accounts at Credit Suisse Bank in Zurich, Switzerland.[5] For example, on June 29, 1989, prior to departing Rome for the Untied States, AMES deposited a total of $450,00 in cash into two accounts he controlled at Credit Suisse.

AMES and his wife, Rosario Casas Ames, used the money received from the KGB to purchase a residence in Arlington, Virginia for $540,000, property in Colombia, expensive automobiles, extensive wardrobes, and to pay approximately one-half million dollars in credit card bills. A portion of the money was used to support Rosario Casas Ames' family in South America as well. Most of the money deposited in cash into United States banks was deposited in sums less than $10,000 to avoid having the financial institutions file a Currency Transaction Report.

Of the approximately $2.5 million paid to AMES by the KGB, none of the money was declared on AMES' United States income tax returns. ALDRICH HAZEN AMES subscribed and filed false Joint Income Tax Returns for tax years 1985, 1986, 1987, 1988, 1989, 1990, 1991, and 1992.

In committing the foregoing acts, ALDRICH HAZEN AMES acted knowingly, willfully, and unlawfully, not by accident or mistake.

Respectfully submitted,

HELEN F. FAHEY
UNITED STATES ATTORNEY

(NOTE: On 28 April 1994 Rick Ames was sentenced to life inprisonment.)

Central Intelligence Agency

Washington, D. C. 20505

Immediate Release   31 October 1995

DIRECTOR OF CENTRAL INTELLIGENCE JOHN DEUTCH STATEMENT TO THE PUBLIC ON THE AMES DAMAGE ASSESSMENT

For the past year and a half, an independent team of Intelligence Community analysts and operations officers has conducted a Damage Assessment of the actions of Aldrich Ames, who, while a CIA Directorate of Operations officer from 1985 to 1994, committed espionage for Soviet (and later Russian) intelligence. This Damage Assessment, commissioned by my predecessor, is now complete. I testified before the House and Senate Permanent Select Committees on Intelligence on October 31st and laid out the findings and actions that I have put in place to remedy the shortcomings it identified.

The Ames case is one of those landmark events which defines the course of an organization. It requires some public discussion because the American people need to know that the Central Intelligence Agency has drawn the right lessons from the incident, and is moving determinedly to make fundamental changes which will reduce the chance that something like this will happen again. Smart organizations use every experience — whether good or bad — as motivation to improve. I am determined to use the Ames case as the basis for bringing bold management changes to the CIA.

I have provided the congressional intelligence oversight committees with details concerning the damage caused by Aldrich Ames' treachery. But let me describe a basic outline of the damage that was done, the weaknesses in the CIA which the incident revealed, and the corrective actions which have been and are being taken.

The damage which Aldrich Ames did to his country can be summarized in three categories:

— By revealing to the Soviet Union the identities of many assets who were providing information to the United States, he not only caused their executions, but also made it much more difficult to understand what was going on in the Soviet Union at a crucial time in its history;

— By revealing to the Soviet Union the way in which the United States sought intelligence and handled assets, he made it much more difficult for this country to gather vital information in other countries as well;

— By revealing to the Soviet Union identities of assets and American methods of espionage, he put the Soviet Union in the position to pass carefully selected "feed" material to this country through controlled assets;

The damage done by Aldrich Ames is documented in the Damage Assessment Report which I have submitted to the intelligence committees. I endorse the Report. I have also made this painstaking work of many months available to other agencies of government so that damage control actions can be taken.

While Ames damaged our intelligence activities in a number of areas, his betrayal of our most important assets is particularly egregious. In a single disclosure, he revealed the identities of CIA's most valuable Soviet/Russian assets.

The Report also revisits deficiencies in the organization, procedures, and management of the Central Intelligence Agency. These deficiencies fall into two major categories:

— The counterintelligence function in the CIA had become neglected by management compared to other functions. It was poorly staffed and organized, and characterized by lax procedures. Its coordination with the Department of Justice was badly flawed by turf-tending and bureaucratic infighting.

— Most troubling of all was an important new finding of the Assessment, which is substantiated by a Special Inspector General Report I requested this summer, that consumers were not informed that some of the most sensitive human intelligence reporting they received came from assets that were known or suspected of being controlled by the KGB/SVR. This finding disturbs me greatly, and this deficiency is one of the first I have moved to correct.

These are the major issues underlying the damage done and the shortcomings that were revealed by Aldrich Ames' espionage activities, and are documented in the thorough report which has been submitted to the intelligence committees.

What is critically important in this incident is the future. What is the Central Intelligence Agency doing as a result of this incident, and its aftermath, to reduce the chance that this happens again?

My most urgent task is to re-establish credibility with our consumers. I will establish a new, independent Customer Review Process for sensitive human reporting that will be managed by the National Intelligence Council. Both the Directorate of Operations and our customers agree with this mechanism to improve customer knowledge without excessive intrusion into operations.

When I took office six months ago, I found that many corrective actions in the wake of the Ames case were underway, well documented in a strategic plan for change. I have taken additional actions in my time as Director of Central Intelligence, particularly in the areas of personnel, organization, and accountability.

DCI, John Deutch

The major categories of the corrective actions and improvement are these:

— A major changeover in the management of the Central Intelligence Agency, including the replacement of the top three levels of Agency management and much of the fourth level with new leadership committed to change. This new management team includes a new Deputy Director for Operations, as well as Associate Deputy Directors for Operations, Counterintelligence, and Human Resources, and seven Directorate of Operations component chiefs.

The Ames Notebook

Ames passed the names of two CIA officers, who were handling compromised CIA agents, to the KGB in an effort to throw suspicion on them for the loss of American intelligence penetrations of the Soviet Union.

In an endeavor to be promoted, Ames asked the KGB to provide a Russian spy for him to recruit but the KGB denied his request as too risky.

The KGB changed their dead drop modus operandi after Ames gave them an FBI report on Soviet intelligence dead drop methodology. For the first time, the KGB used public parks to clear dead drops and to communicate with Ames.

Despite missing three personal meetings because of drunkenness, Ames met with the KGB 11 times between 1985 and 1993. The KGB recorded the 40 hours Ames spent with them.

The KGB expressed interest in their former republics and asked Ames about CIA operations in these areas and if CIA communicated directly with agents there.

The KGB asked Ames about a suspected KGB officer in Vienna, Austria.

After the Soviets advised Ames that they had set aside $2 million for him, he attempted to have the money transferred to his bank account in the United States. The Soviets refused fearing he might stop spying for them.

Ames never considered living on the property the KGB arranged for him in Moscow; instead he thought about retiring in southern France or Colombia.

— The establishment of the National Counterintelligence Center at CIA, headed by a senior FBI officer;

— Significantly increasing the application of counterintelligence to operations, and emphasizing counterintelligence awareness and training in all activities;

— New guidelines for Agency managers on handling employee suitability issues and strengthening internal discipline procedures;

— Policies to ensure that new emphasis is placed on the quality of agent recruitment and agent handling, rather than on the quantity of recruitment. This includes a complete scrubbing of standards and criteria for personnel evaluation as well as a system of rewards that moves away from quantity to quality in asset recruitment as the prime measure of success;

— A revitalized system within the Directorate of Operations to validate assets, bringing in a team approach involving analysts and counterintelligence officers from the very beginning of cases;

— Clearly defined standards and expectations for the performance of Chiefs of Station along with a clearly defined policy for their selection;

— Initiatives aimed at improving the Agency's records management system and bolstering computer security; and,

— Perhaps most important, insistence from the top down on integrity and accountability in the Central Intelligence Agency. This includes the establishment of component-level accountability boards within the Directorate of Operations and a senior Directorate-level accountability board.

I also considered the accountability of certain CIA officers in connection with the Damage Assessment Team Report and the Inspector General Report on the same subject. In making my determinations I applied the following standards:

— That the performance deficiency at issue must be specific;

— That, unlike military practice, the individual being held accountable must have had a direct responsibility and role—that is, the individual, by virtue of his/her position, had the opportunity or responsibility to act; and,

— That high levels of professionalism are required.

The Inspector General, in the special report provided to me last month, recommended 12 CIA officers be held responsible for their roles in this matter. All but one of those individuals has retired, thereby restricting my options for disciplinary action. Based on the information in the Damage Assessment Team Report as well as the IG report, if these officers were still employed, I would have dismissed two individuals from CIA and taken no disciplinary action against five. I have reprimanded the one officer who is currently employed. As for the two I would have dismissed, both now are banned from future employment with the Agency. Four other former officers have been given reprimands or warnings.

I want to emphasize that the Ames Damage Assessment, in all of its detail, does nothing to shake my conviction that we need a clandestine service. Of all the intelligence disciplines, human intelligence is, indeed, the most subject to human frailty, but it also brings human intuition, ingenuity, and courage into play against the enemies of our country. Often there is no other way to penetrate a terrorist cell or a chemical weapons factory or the inner circle of a tyrant. At critical times human intelligence has allowed our leaders to deal with the plans and intentions—rather than the weapons—of our enemies.

I believe that the right actions are underway for the Ames incident to become the most powerful catalyst for change in the history of the Central Intelligence Agency. The key is drawing unflinchingly the right lessons and making the necessary changes. It will take time to implement all these reforms and accomplish required changes to some aspects of the CIA's habits, practices, and attitudes. The United States must have the best intelligence capability in the world, and that capability includes the Operations Directorate of the Central Intelligence Agency.

The Directorate of Operations must be staffed by top-notch people. This means that first-class people are hired, their careers are managed properly, and the promotion system rewards those who maintain the highest standards of integrity, but also who are prepared to take risks. By clearly defining the rules and management expectations, we will encourage these officers to take the risks necessary to produce the critical intelligence needed by our Nation.

It must have solid procedures which ensure a quality product for decision-makers throughout government. This means emphasizing quality and authenticity over numbers and volume. This also means that safeguards against false information are comprehensive and effective.

I believe that the changes which were taken before my watch, and the additional measures I have taken—coupled with the desire for fundamental, positive change by the overwhelming majority of CIA officers themselves— ensure that we are on the right track.

Statement of the Director of Central Intelligence on the Clandestine Services and the Damage Caused by Aldrich Ames

7 December 1995

Introduction and Overview

From the earliest days of the Republic, the United States has recognized the compelling need to collect intelligence by clandestine means. For much of our history, this collection could only be done by human agents. Recent technological developments have, of course, vastly increased our ability to collect intelligence. The capacity of these technical systems is awesome and our achievements are astonishing. However, these technical means can never eliminate the need for human sources of information. Often, the more difficult the target is, the greater is the need for human agents.

Throughout our history, the contribution of the clandestine service of the United States has frequently been the difference between victory and defeat, success and failure. It has saved countless American lives.

In recent years, human agents have provided vital information on military and political developments in the Soviet Union, terrorist groups, narcotics trafficking, development of weapons of mass destruction and other grave threats to the United States. These agents often provided the key piece of information that formed the United States' understanding of a critical international situation.

For decades, information from human agents inside the Soviet Union gave us vital insights into the intentions and capabilities of the Soviets. Ames clearly dealt a crushing blow to those efforts. Nonetheless, I am convinced that when the full history of the Cold War is written, American intelligence-and human intelligence in particular-will be recognized as having played an important role in winning that war.

It must be remembered that for over forty years the United States faced a hostile state with enormous nuclear power. A misstep by either side could have destroyed the world. That nuclear war did not occur and that the Soviet Union ultimately collapsed is in no small part attributable to the brave, tireless and too often thankless efforts of the clandestine intelligence service of the United States. The DCI has a great responsibility to preserve and nurture this vital capability.

That said, it must be pointed out that while human agent operations have the potential for high gain, they also entail high risk. Human agent operations are almost always in violation of another country's laws. It is therefore imperative that they be subject to tight policy control and carried out within the scope of American law. These operations must be carried out in secret, for secrecy is vital to success.

The American public is often troubled by activities that are done in secret. This is a natural and healthy instinct. It has served our democracy extremely well for over two hundred years. However, I believe the American people understand the need for secrecy in human agent operations. They agree with a letter written by George Washington when he was Commander-in-Chief of the Continental Army in the summer of 1977:

"The necessity of procuring good intelligence is apparent & need not be further urged-All that remains for me to add is, that you keep the whole matter as secret as possible. For upon Secrecy, Success depends in Most Enterprises of the kind, and for want of it, they are generally defeated, however well planned & promising a favorable issue."

The American people will accept secret intelligence activity only if four conditions are met. First the acts must be consistent with announced policy goals. Second, they must be carefully controlled under U.S. law. Third, the operations should be consistent with basic American values and beliefs. And fourth, when American intelligence services make mistakes—as we have and will surely do again—we learn from those mistakes.

Because much of what the intelligence services do is secret, Congressional oversight is the key to providing the American people the confidence that their intelligence services are meeting these four conditions. Indeed Congressional oversight is the best way this confidence can be assured.

We must not quit simply because we have made errors, even serious ones. The need for effective intelligence is too important. We must constantly learn from our mistakes, make the necessary changes, and continue to take the risks necessary to collect vital intelligence so urgently needed by the President, the Congress, and other senior policy-makers.

With this in mind, we have moved quickly to strengthen the capabilities of the clandestine service across a broad spectrum. Counterintelligence programs have been significantly enhanced, tradecraft techniques are being tailored for the world in which we now live, and the technologies needed for the future are being rapidly developed. Underpinning these efforts has been a renewed emphasis on quality management that pays attention not only to what we do, but how we do it. All these initiatives, imbedded in a strategic plan developed by the clandestine service this past year, position the clandestine service to meet our future challenges.

The Actual Damage

On the 31st of October, I appeared before the House and Senate Intelligence Committees in closed session to describe the results of the Ames damage assessment commissioned by my predecessor, Jim Woolsey. Following that testimony, we have continued to review the report of the Damage Assessment Team (DAT) and to consult with both Committees, the Department of Defense, the Department of State and other interested agencies. Accordingly, I believe it is appropriate to report to you on our continuing review and our consultation with other agencies. I also believe it is important that additional information be made available to the American public so that they can understand the nature and extent of the damage caused by Ames. (It should also be recalled that in the 1980's, the U.S. experienced a number of other espionage cases. Edward Lee Howard, an agency officer, like Ames, caused considerable damage to US HUMINT Operations against the USSR. John Walker and Ronald Pelton caused immense damage to US interests. (In Walker's case, vast amounts of information on our military capabilities and plans were exposed which could have had tragic consequences in the event of war.) I have attached a copy of the public statement that I issued on the 31st of October. Let me add some detail on the scope of the damage.

Aldrich Ames' espionage on behalf of the Soviet Union and Russian from April 1985 through February 1994 caused severe, wide-ranging and continuing damage to US national security interests. In addition to the points that I made in my public statement on 31 October, Ames did the following:

In June 1985, he disclosed the identity of numerous U.S. clandestine agents in the Soviet Union, at least nine of whom were executed. These agents were at the heart of our effort to collect intelligence and counterintelligence against the Soviet Union. As a result, we lost opportunities to better understand what was going on in the Soviet Union at a crucial time in history.

He disclosed, over the next decade, the identity of many US agents run against the Soviets, and later the Russians.

He disclosed the techniques and methods of double agent operations, details of our clandestine tradecraft, communications techniques and agent validation methods. He went to extraordinary length to learn about U.S. double agent operations and pass information on them to the Soviets.

He disclosed details about US counterintelligence activities that not only devastated our efforts at the time, but also made us more vulnerable to KGB operations against us.

He identified CIA and other intelligence community personnel. Ames contends that he disclosed personal information on, or the identities of, only a few American intelligence officials. We do not believe that assertion.

He provided details of US intelligence technical collection activities and analytic techniques.

He provided finished intelligence reports, current intelligence reporting, arms control papers, and selected Department of State and Department of Defense cables. For example, during one assignment, he gave the KGB a stack of documents estimated to be 15 to 20 feet high.

Taken as a whole, Ames' activities also, facilitated the Soviet, and later the Russian, effort to engage in "perception management operations" by feeding carefully selected information to the United States through agents whom they were controlling without our knowledge. Although the extent and success of this effort cannot now be determined with certainty, we know that some of this information did reach senior decision-makers of the United States.

As the Committee knows, one of the most disturbing findings of the DAT was that consumers of intelligence were not informed that some of the most sensitive human intelligence reporting they received came from agents known or suspected at the time to be under the control of the KGB, and later the SVR. This finding was substantiated by a detail audit done by the CIA's Inspector General. Because this aspect of the assessment is so important and has generated so much public interest, I would like to discuss it in some detail.

In response to requests from the DAT, some consumers of sensitive human reporting identified just over 900 reports from 1985 to 1994 that they considered particularly significant. These consumers included CIA's Directorate of Intelligence, the Defense Intelligence Agency, the National Security Agency, the Military Services and other agencies. The DAT then reviewed the case files of the agents who were the source of just over half of these reports and conclude that a disturbingly high percentage of these agent were controlled by the KGB, and later the SVR, or that evidence exists suggesting that they were controlled.

Although some of the reports from these sources were accompanied by warnings that the source might be suspect, many other reports did not include adequate warning. The IG was asked to review reporting from the sources that the DAT concluded were known or suspected to be controlled. They concluded that CIA did not provide adequate warning to consumers of 35 reports from agents whom we have good reason to believe at the time were controlled and 60 reports from agents about whom we had suspicions <u>at the time</u>. Of these 95 reports, at least three formed the basis of memoranda that went to the President: one of those reports was from a source who we had good reason to believe was controlled.

The DAT intended to review the source of each of these reports but, for a variety of reasons, was not able to do so. For example, the filing system of the DO was incomplete and the sources for some reports could not be identified. To expedite the review, the DAT did not review the files of sources who produced only one or two reports. In the end, the Team examined and thoroughly reviewed the sources who produced roughly 55% of the reports cited by consumers as significant suspicions. While these and other reports could well have been reflected in other such analytic products, we have not identified them.

The fact that we can identify only a relatively few significant reports that were disseminated with inadequate warning does not mitigate the impact of Ames' treachery or excuse CIA's failure to adequately warn consumers. We believe that, whatever the numbers of such reports, the provision of information from controlled sources without adequate warning was a major intelligence failure that calls into doubt the professionalism of the clandestine service and the credibility of its most sensitive reporting.

The situation requires us to take two steps. First, and most importantly, we must ensure that such information does not reach senior policy-makers in the future without adequate warning that the information comes from sources we know or suspect to be controlled. Second, we must examine certain important decisions taken by the United States to ensure that they were not influenced by these reports. If any decisions were influenced by faulty reports, we must determine what, if any, corrective measures should be taken.

With respect to the first step, I have established a new Customer Review Process under the National Intelligence Council. This process, which will include appropriately cleared representatives to our customer agencies, will work with the Directorate of Operations to ensure that recipients of extremely sensitive human intelligence reports are adequately advised about our knowledge of the source of the reports. This does not mean that these representatives of other agencies will be told the identity of the source of the information. Rather, our goal is that recipients of especially sensitive information can adequately understand and evaluate the intelligence.

With respect to the second step-reviewing decisions that might have been made using controlled information— it is important to understand that our knowledge of the details of a Soviet perception management effort is limited, as is what can be said publicly about the subject. Also, it is not the job of the DCI to review decisions made by other agencies. However, it is very likely that the KGB and later the SVR, sought to influence U.S. decision-makers by providing controlled information designed to affect R&D and procurement decisions of the Department of Defense. The DAT believes one of the primary purposes of the perception management program was to convince us that the Soviets remained a superpower and that their military R&D program was robust.

In an effort to understand the impact of this Soviet/Russian program, the DAT reviewed intelligence reporting relevant to a limited number of acquisition decisions taken by the Department of Defense to determine whether any reports from controlled or suspect agents had an impact on the decisions. The reporting covered eight categories of weapon systems, including aircraft and related systems, ground force weapons, naval force weapons, air defense missiles and cruise missiles. The DAT concluded, in coordination with DIA and the intelligence components of the military departments, that the impact varied from program to program. In some cases the impact was negligible. In other cases, the impact was measurable, but only on the margin.

The dissemination of reports on Soviet/Russian military R&D and procurement programs from questionable sources had the potential to influence U.S. military R&D and procurement programs costing billions of dollars. The DAT surveyed a number of intelligence consumers in the Department of Defense. They found that consumers were often reluctant to state that this reporting had any significant impact. Determining damage always involves much speculation, but the team concluded that "clear cut damage" to intelligence analysis may have been limited to a "few cases." They cited three in particular:

A report in the late 80's that would have influenced debates on U.S. general purpose forces,

Analyses of Soviet plans caused us to revise logistics support and basing plans in one overseas theater (see also above), and

Studies of certain Soviet/Russian cruise missile and fighter aircraft R&D programs may have overestimated the pace of those programs.

In addition, the team reviewed intelligence reporting that supported decisions in a number of defense policy areas, including U.S. military strategy. The team found that reporting from controlled or suspect agents had a substantial role in framing the debate. The overall effect was to sustain our view of the USSR as a credible military and technological opponent. The DAT found that the impact of such information on actual decisions, however, was not significant. In some cases, our military posture was altered slightly. In one example, changes already underway to enhance the survivability and readiness of the basing structure in an overseas theater was justified by information received from a controlled source. However, before the changes could be fully carried out, the Soviet Union collapsed, obviating the need for the change.

The DAT also reviewed a handful of national security issues that were the most likely to have been impacted by Ames' actions. For example, Ames passed U.S. all-source analysis of Soviet motives and positions in arms control negotiations. His espionage assisted their efforts to feed us information that supported the Soviet positions. The DAT interviewed a limited number of officials with respect to arms control issues and related programs. The DAT found no major instance where Soviets maneuvered U.S. or NATO arms control negotiators into giving up a current or future military capability or agreeing to monitoring or verification provisions that otherwise would not have been adopted. This conclusion is buttressed by the fact that the Soviet's bargaining position grew increasingly weak as its economy deteriorated and Gorbachev struggled to maintain control.

After reviewing the DAT report, I believe it is incorrect to maintain that this reporting was completely irrelevant or completely determinate in U.S. weapon system decisions. The process by which U.S. weapons system development and acquisition decisions are made is complex and involves many considerations. These include technical feasibility, force modernization, life cycle cost, and industrial base considerations, as well as estimates of the near and long term threat. No single strand of intelligence information ever serves as the full justification for undertaking a large program.

The kind of impact that intelligence does have is:

Influencing the pace and timing of a development program to meet an anticipated threat. This is an influence at the margin of system acquisition.

Shaping the thinking of the technical and contractor community on the threat envelope facing a system under development.

Creating an impression, in combination with other information, of the status and vitality of an adversary's military R&D and procurement activities.

All of this affects the context in which U.S. acquisition decisions are made. I believe the net effect of the Soviet/Russian "directed information" effort was that we overestimated their capability. Why the Soviet/Russian leadership thought this was desirable is speculative.

A DoD team, working at the direction of the Deputy Secretary of Defense, recently completed the Department's review of the impact of directed reporting on military policy, acquisition, and operations. That report has been briefed to the Secretary and Deputy Secretary of Defense and the Congress.

The combination of the loss of key human sources compromised by Ames, plus the directed information the KGB and SVR provided to the U.S. through controlled sources, had a serious impact on our ability to collect and analyze intelligence information. The DAT concluded that Ames' actions diminished our ability to understand:

> Internal Soviet development, particularly the views and actions of the hard liners with the respect to Gorbachev in the late 1980's;

> Soviet, and later Russian, foreign policy particularly Yeltsin's policies on non-proliferation and Russian involvement in the former CIS states; and

> The extent of the decline of Soviet and Russian military technology and procurement programs.

The Ames case—and the other espionage cases of the 80s—remind us that other issues must be addressed. These include the serious lack of adequate counterintelligence during much of the 80s and early 90s. My predecessors, the Attorney General and the Director of the FBI have made great progress in repairing this extremely important function. We have continued to make progress, but much works remains to be done. I detailed in my statement of 31 October a number of steps that are underway to correct these serious problems.

I look forward to working with the Committees to ensure the adequate implementation of these measures. I assure you that my colleagues in the Intelligence Community are fully committed to achieving these important reforms.

Conclusions

I regret that I cannot discuss in public more detail about the actual damage done by Aldrich Ames. To do so would compound that damage by confirming to the Russians the extent of the damage and permit them to evaluate the success and failures of their activities. That I cannot do.

However, it is extremely important that we not underestimate the terrible damage done by Ames' treachery. It is impossible to describe the anger and sense of betrayal felt by the Intelligence Community. It reverberates to this day and has given all of us renewed motivation to do our jobs. Across the board, in all areas of intelligence activitie—from collection, to counterintelligence, to security, to analysis and production, to the administrative activities that support the Community effort—we must renew our efforts to ensure that our activities are conducted with integrity, honesty, and the highest standards of professionalism. To do less is to fail.

I believe that the most important value the Intelligence Community must embrace is integrity—both personal and professional. We operate in a world of deception. It is our job to keep this nation's secrets safe and to obtain the secrets of other nations. We engage in deception to do our job and we confront deception undertaken by other nations.

But we must never let deception become a way of life. We must never deceive ourselves. Perhaps more than any other government agency, we in the CIA must have the highest standards of personal and professional integrity. We must be capable of engaging in deceptive activities directed toward other nations and groups while maintaining scrupulous honesty among ourselves and with our customers. We must not let the need for secrecy obscure the honest and accurate presentation of the intelligence we have collected or the analyses we have produced.

I believe we have approached the damage done by Ames with honesty and integrity. We have made the hard calls. We may have to make more. We have taken the steps necessary to discipline those responsible, to reduce the likelihood of such damage recurring and to begin to restore the confidence of our customers and the American people.

As I said at the beginning of this report, clandestine human operations remain vital to this country's security. They are often the most dangerous and difficult intelligence operations to conduct. But I want to assure the Congress and the American people that the American clandestine service will continue to conduct these operations and do so in the highest tradition of integrity, courage, independence and ingenuity that have made our service the best in the world.

Unclassified Abstract of the CIA Inspector Generals Report on the Aldrich H. Ames Case

Preface to the Report from the IG

Procedurally, this has been an unusual report for the CIA IG to write. In the first instance, our inquiry was directly requested by the Chairman and Vice-Chairman of the Select Committee on Intelligence of the U.S. Senate in late February 1994—shortly after Aldrich H. Ames was arrested. Normally, our congressional oversight committees ask the Director of Central Intelligence to request an IG investigation. On this occasion their request was directed to the IG.

Second, the DCI chose to ask us to look into the Ames matter in phases after Ames' arrest for fear of disrupting the Ames prosecution. We were requested to inquire into the circumstances surrounding the CI investigation of the Ames betrayal:

What procedures were in place respecting CIA counterespionage investigations at the time Ames volunteered to the Soviets in 1985;

How well did they work; and

What was the nature of CIA's cooperation with the FBI in this case.

On March 10, 1994, the DCI asked us to seek to determine if individuals in Ames' supervisory chain discharged their responsibilities in the manner expected of them and directed the Executive Director of CIA to prepare a list of Ames' supervisors during the relevant periods. The DCI also directed that awards and promotions for the individuals on the Executive Director's list be held in escrow pending the outcome of the IG investigation. I wish to state at this point that neither I nor any member of the team investigating the Ames case have viewed the DCI's escrow list. We wanted to be as completely unaffected by the names on the list as we could be in order to discharge our responsibility to advise the DCI objectively of possible disciplinary recommendations. As a precautionary measure, I did ask my Deputy for Inspections, who is otherwise uninvolved in the Ames investigation, to view the escrow list to advise of any individuals on it whom we might have failed to interview through inadvertence. That has been our only involvement with the escrow list.

Third, there was an unusual limitation placed on our inquiry at the outset caused by a desire on the part of the DCI, the Department of Justice and the U.S. Attorney in the Eastern District of Virginia to do nothing that would complicate the Ames trial. We willingly complied with these constraints, confining ourselves to background file reviews and interviews of non-witnesses until the Ameses pled guilty on April 28, 1994. The consequence has been that we have had to cover a great deal of ground in a short period of time to conduct this investigation in order to have a report ready for the DCI and the congressional oversight committees by September 1994. I am extremely proud of our 12-person investigative team.

Apart from the unusual procedures affecting this investigation, the Ames case presented several major substantive problems as well. This case raised so many issues of concern to the DCI, the oversight committees and the American people, that we have not chosen to tell the story in our normal chronological way. Instead, we have focused on themes: Ames' life, his career, his vulnerabilities. We have tried to discuss how counterespionage investigations have been conducted in CIA since the Edward Lee Howard betrayal and the Year of the Spy, 1985—in the context of this particular case. Necessarily, we have made analytical judgments about what we have learned—some of them quite harsh. We believe this is our job—not just to present the facts, but to tell the DCI, the oversight committees and other readers how it strikes us. We have the confidence to do this because we have lived with the guts of Ames's betrayal and his unearthing for countless hours and we owe our readers our reactions. In this sense our 12 investigators are like a jury—they find the facts and make recommendations to the DCI for his final determination. This investigative team, like a jury, represents the attitude of the intelligence professionals from whose ranks they are drawn and from whom they drew testimony—sometimes shocked and dismayed at what we've learned, often appreciative of the individual acts of competence and courage, and always intrigued by the complexity of the Ames story.

In the end, the Ames case is about accountability, both individual and managerial. The DCI and the congressional oversight committees have made this the issue, but if they had not, we would have. As a postscript to my opening sentences, let me note that the CIA IG had begun to look into the Ames case on its own, even before the SSCI or the DCI had requested it, because we believe that the statute setting up our office requires it. The issue of managerial accountability has been one of this office's principal points of focus since its inception in 1990—and we have enjoyed mixed success in our reviews and recommendations to promote it.

Seeking to determine managerial accountability in the Ames case has not been an easy task. On the individual level, we have uncovered a vast quantity of information about Ames' professional sloppiness, his failure to file accountings, contact reports and requests for foreign travel on time or at all. We have found that Ames was oblivious to issues of personal security both professionally—he left classified files on a subway train—and in his espionage—he carried incriminating documents and large amounts of cash in his airline luggage; he carried classified documents out of CIA facilities in shopping bags; and he openly walked into the Soviet Embassy in the United States and a Soviet compound in Rome. We have noted that Ames' abuse of alcohol, while not constant throughout his career, was chronic and interfered with his judgment and the performance of his duties. By and large his professional weaknesses were observed by Ames' colleagues and supervisors and were tolerated by many who did not consider them highly unusual for Directorate of Operations officers on the "not going anywhere" promotion track. That an officer with these observed vulnerabilities should have been given counterintelligence responsibilities in Soviet operations where he was in a prime position to learn of the intimate details of the Agency's most sensitive operations, contact Soviet officials openly and then massively betray his trust is difficult to justify. The IG investigative team has been dismayed at this tolerant view of Ames' professional deficiencies and the random indifference given to his assignments, and our recommendations reflect that fact.

Finally, on the grander scale of how the reaction to the major loss of Soviet cases in 1985-86 was managed, our team has been equally strict, demanding and greatly disturbed by what we saw. If Soviet operations—the effort to achieve human penetrations of the USSR for foreign intelligence and counterintelligence information—was the highest priority mission of the clandestine service of CIA in 1985-86, then the loss of most of our assets in this crucial area of operations should have had a devastating effect on the thinking of the leaders of the DO and CIA. The effort to probe the reasons for these losses should have been of the most vital significance to U.S. intelligence, but particularly to the CIA, and should have been pursued with the utmost vigor and all necessary resources until an explanation—a technical or human penetration—was found.

It is true that the spy was found, but the course to that conclusion could have been much more rapid and direct. While those few who were engaged in the search may have done the best they could with what they had, in this investigation we have concluded that the intelligence losses of 1985-86 were not pursued to the fullest extent of the capabilities of the CIA, which prides itself on being the best intelligence service in the world. The analytical judgments and recommendations in this Report reflect that conclusion. We wish it could have been otherwise.

Frederick P. Hitz
Inspector General

Aldrich Hazen Ames

Summary

1. In the spring and summer of 1985, Aldrich H. Ames began his espionage activities on behalf of the Soviet Union. In 1985 and 1986, it became increasingly clear to officials within CIA that the Agency was faced with a major CI problem. A significant number of CIA Soviet sources began to be compromised, recalled to the Soviet Union and, in many cases, executed. A number of these cases were believed to have been exposed by Edward Lee Howard, who fled the United States in September 1985 to avoid prosecution for disclosures he made earlier that year. However, it was evident by fall of 1985 that not all of the compromised sources could be attributed to him.

2. Later in 1985, the first Agency efforts were initiated to ascertain whether the unexplained compromises could be the result of:

    a. faulty practices by the sources or the CIA officers who were assigned to handle them (i.e., whether the cases each contained "seeds of their own destruction");

    b. a physical or electronic intrusion into the Agency's Moscow Station or Agency communications; or

    c. a human penetration within the Agency (a "mole").

Although they were never discounted altogether, the first two theories diminished in favor over the years as possible explanations for the losses. A "molehunt"—an effort to determine whether there was a human penetration, a spy, within CIA's ranks—was pursued more or less continuously and with varying degrees of intensity until Ames was convicted of espionage in 1994, nine years after the compromises began to occur.

3. The 1985-1986 compromises were first discussed in late 1985 with DCI William Casey, who directed that the Deputy Director for Operations (DDO) make every effort to determine the reason for them. In January 1986, SE Division (Soviet East European Division, later renamed Central Eurasia Division, directed operations related to the Soviet Union and its successor states) instituted new and extraordinary compartmentation measures to prevent further compromises. In the fall of 1986, a small Special Task Force (STF) of four officers operating under the direction of the Counter-intelligence Staff (CI Staff) was directed to begin an effort to determine the cause of the compromises. This effort, which was primarily analytic in nature, paralleled a separate FBI task force to determine whether the FBI had been penetrated. The FBI task force ended, and the CIA STF effort diminished significantly in 1988 as its participants became caught up in the creation of the Counterintelligence Center (CIC). Between 1988 and 1990, the CIA molehunt came to a low ebb as the officers involved concentrated on other CI matters that were believed to have higher priority.

4. In late 1989, after his return from Rome, Ames' lifestyle and spending habits had changed as a result of the large amounts of money he had received from the KGB in return for the information he provided. Ames made no special efforts to conceal his newly acquired wealth and, for example, paid cash for a $540,000 home. This unexplained affluence was brought to the attention of the molehunt team by a CIA employee in late 1989, and a CIC officer began a financial inquiry. The preliminary results of the financial inquiry indicated several large cash transactions but were not considered particularly significant at the time.

5. Nevertheless, information regarding Ames' finances was provided to the Office of Security (OS) by CIC in 1990. A background investigation (BI) was conducted and a polygraph examination was scheduled. The BI was very thorough and produced information that indicated further questions about Ames and his spending habits. However, this information was not made available to the polygraph examiners who tested him, and CIC did not take steps to ensure that the examiners would have full knowledge of all it knew about Ames at the time. In April 1991, OS determined that Ames had successfully completed the reinvestigation polygraph with no indications of deception, just as he had five years previously.

6. In 1991, CIA's molehunt was revitalized and rejuvenated. Two counterintelligence officers were assigned full-time to find the cause of the 1985–86 compromises. The FBI provided two officers to work as part of the molehunt team.

7. During this phase, attention was redirected at Ames and a number of other possible suspects. In March 1992, a decision was made to complete the financial inquiry of Ames that had been initiated in 1989. In August 1992, a correlation was made between bank deposits by Ames that were identified by the financial inquiry and meetings between Ames and a Soviet official that the Agency and FBI had authorized in 1985. The joint CIA/FBI analytic effort resulted in a report written in March 1993, which concluded that, among other things, there was a penetration of the CIA. It was expected by CIA and FBI officials that the report, which included lists of CIA employees who had access to the compromised cases, would be reviewed by the FBI in consideration of further investigative steps.

8. The totality of the information available to CIC and the FBI prompted the FBI to launch an intensive CI investigation of Ames. During this phase, the FBI attempted to gather sufficient information to determine whether Ames was in fact engaged in espionage, and the Agency molehunt team was relegated to a supporting role. Every effort was made to avoid alerting Ames to the FBI CI investigation. According to FBI and Agency officials, it was not until a search of Ames' residential trash in September 1993, which produced a copy of an operational note from Ames to the Russians, that they were certain Ames was a spy. After the FBI had gathered additional information, Ames was arrested on February 21, 1994 and pled guilty to espionage on April 28, 1994.

9. The two CIA officers and the two FBI officers who began working in earnest on the possibility of an Agency penetration in 1991 under the auspices of the Agency's CIC deserve credit for the ultimate identification of Ames as a hostile intelligence penetration of CIA. Without their efforts, it is possible that Ames might never have been successfully identified and prosecuted. Although proof of his espionage activities was not obtained until after the FBI began its CI investigation of Ames in 1993, the CIA molehunt team played a critical role in providing a context for the opening of an intensive investigation by the FBI. Moreover, although the CIA and the FBI have had disagreements and difficulties with coordination in other cases in the past, there is ample evidence to support statements by both FBI and CIA senior management that the Ames case was a model of CI cooperation between the two agencies.

10. From its beginnings in 1986, however, the management of CIA's molehunt effort was deficient in several respects. These management deficiencies contributed to the delay in identifying Ames as a possible penetration, even though he was a careless spy who was sloppy and inattentive to measures that would conceal his activities. Despite the persistence of the individuals who played a part in the molehunt, it suffered from insufficient senior management attention, a lack of proper resources, and an array of immediate and extended distractions. The existence and toleration of these deficiencies is difficult to understand in light of the seriousness of the 1985-86 compromises and especially when considered in the context of the series of other CI failures that the Agency suffered in the 1980s and the decade-long history of external attention to the weaknesses of the Agency's CI and security programs. The deficiencies reflect a CIA CI function that has not recovered its legitimacy since the excesses of James Angleton, which resulted in his involuntary retirement from CIA in 1974. Furthermore, to some extent, the "Angleton Syndrome" has become a canard that it used to downplay the role of CI in the Agency.

11. Even in this context, it is difficult to understand the repeated failure to focus more attention on Ames earlier when his name continued to come up throughout the investigation. He had access to all the compromised cases; his financial resources improved substantially for unestablished reasons; and his laziness and poor performance were rather widely known. All of these are CI indicators that should have drawn attention to Ames. Combined, they should have made him stand out. Arguably, these indicators played a role in the fact

Rosario Ames

that Ames was often named as a prime suspect by those involved in the molehunt.

12. One result of management inattention was the failure of CIA to bring a full range of potential resources to bear on this counterespionage investigation. There was an over-emphasis on operational analysis and the qualifications thought necessary to engage in such analysis, and a failure to employ fully such investigative techniques as financial analysis, the polygraph, behavioral analysis interviews, and the review of public and governmental records. These problems were exacerbated by the ambiguous division of the counterespionage function between CIC and OS and the continuing subordination by the Directorate of Operations (DO) of CI concerns to foreign intelligence collection interests. Excessive compartmentation has broadened the gap in communications between CIC and OS, and this problem has not been overcome despite efforts to improve coordination. CIC did not share information fully with OS or properly coordinate the OS investigative process.

13. These defects in the Agency's capability to conduct counterespionage investigations have been accompanied by a degradation of the security function within the Agency due to management policies and resource decisions during the past decade. These management policies emphasize generalization over expertise, quantity over quality, and accommodation rather than professionalism in the security field. This degradation of the security function has manifested itself in the reinvestigation and polygraph programs and appears to have contributed to Ames ability to complete polygraphs successfully in 1986 and 1991 after he began his espionage activities.

14. Beyond defects in counterespionage investigations and related security programs, the Ames case reflects significant deficiencies in the Agency's personnel management policies. No evidence has been found that any Agency manager knowingly and willfully aided Ames in his espionage activities. However, Ames continued to be selected for positions in SE Division, CIC and the Counternarcotics Center that gave him significant access to highly sensitive information despite strong evidence of performance and suitability problems and, in the last few years of his career, substantial suspicion regarding his trustworthiness. A psychological profile of Ames that was prepared as part of this investigation indicates a troubled employee with a significant potential to engage in harmful activities.

15. Although information regarding Ames' professional and personal failings may not have been available in the aggregate to all of his managers or in any complete and official record, little effort was made by those managers who were aware of Ames' poor performance and behavioral problems to identify the problems officially and deal with them. If Agency management had acted more responsibly and responsively as these problems arose, it is possible that the Ames case could have been avoided in that he might not have been placed in a position where he could give away such sensitive source information.

16. The principal deficiency in the Ames case was the failure to ensure that the Agency employed its best efforts and adequate resources in determining on a timely basis the cause, including the possibility of a human penetration, of the compromises in 1985–86 of essentially its entire cadre of Soviet sources. The individual officers who deserve recognition for their roles in the eventual identification of Ames were forced to overcome what appears to have been significant inattentiveness on the part of senior Agency management. As time wore on and other priorities intervened, the 1985–86 compromises received less and less senior management attention. The compromises were not addressed resolutely until the spring of 1991 when it was decided that a concerted effort was required to resolve them. Even then, it took nearly three years to identify and arrest Ames, not because he was careful and crafty, but because the Agency effort was inadequate.

17. Senior Agency management, including several DDOs, DO Division Chiefs, CIC and DO officials, should be held accountable for permitting an officer with obvious problems such as Ames to continue to be placed in sensitive positions where he was able to engage in activities that have caused great harm to the United States. Senior Agency management, including at least several DCIs, Deputy Directors, DO Division Chiefs, and senior CI and security officials, should also be held accountable for not ensuring that the Agency made a maximum effort to resolve the compromises quickly

through the conduct of a focused investigation conducted by adequate numbers of qualified personnel.

What was Ames' Career History with CIA?

18. In June 1962, Ames completed full processing for staff employment with the Agency and entered on duty as a GS-4 document analyst in the Records Integration Division (RID) of the DO. Within RID, Ames read, coded, filed, and retrieved documents related to clandestine operations against an East European target. He remained in this position for five years while attending George Washington University, on a part-time or full-time basis. In September 1967, Ames received his Bachelor of Arts degree in history with an average grade of B-.

19. Ames originally viewed his work with RID as a stopgap measure to finance his way through college. However, he grew increasingly fascinated by intelligence operations against Communist countries, and, influenced by other RID colleagues who were entering the Career Trainee (CT) program, he applied and was accepted as a CT in December 1967. When Ames completed this training nearly a year later, he was assigned to an SE Division branch. He remained there for several months before beginning Turkish language studies.

20. Ames' first overseas posting took place between 1969 and 1972. It was not a successful tour, and the last Performance Appraisal Report (PAR) of his tour stated, in effect, that Ames was unsuited for field work and should spend the remainder of his career at Headquarters. The PAR noted that Ames preferred "assignments that do not involve face-to-face situations with relatively unknown personalities who must be manipulated." Such a comment was devastating for an operations officer, and Ames was discouraged enough to consider leaving the Agency.

21. Ames spent the next four years, 1972-76, at Headquarters in SE Division. Managing the paperwork and planning associated with field operations at a distance was more comfortable for Ames than trying to recruit in the field himself, and he won generally enthusiastic reviews from his supervisors. One payoff from this improved performance was the decision in September 1974 to name Ames as both the Headquarters and field case officer to manage a highly valued Agency asset.

22. Ames' opportunity to expand his field experience came with his assignment to the New York Base of the DO's Foreign Resources Division from 1976 to 1981. The PARs that Ames received during the last four of his five years in New York were the strongest of his career. These PARs led Ames to be ranked in the top 10% of GS-13 DO operations officers ranked for promotion in early 1982. He was promoted to GS-14 in May 1982.

23. The career momentum Ames established in New York was not maintained during his 1981-83 tour in Mexico City. This assignment, like his earlier tour and his later tour in Rome, failed to play to Ames' strengths as a handler of established sources and emphasized instead an area where he was weak—the development and recruitment of new assets. In Mexico City, Ames spent little time working outside the Embassy, developed few assets, and was chronically late with his financial accountings. Further, Ames developed problems with alcohol abuse that worsened to the point that he often was able to accomplish little work after long, liquid lunches. His PARs focused heavily, and negatively, on his failure to maintain proper accountings and were generally unenthusiastic. In Mexico City, Ames also became involved in an intimate relationship with the Colombian cultural attache, Maria del Rosario Casas Dupuy.

24. Despite his lackluster performance in Mexico City, Ames returned to Headquarters in 1983 to a position that he valued highly. His appointment as Chief of a branch in an SE Division Group was recommended by the officer who had supervised Ames in New York and approved by Chief, SE Division and the DDO. This position gave him access to the Agency's worldwide Soviet operations. Ames completed this tour with SE Division by being selected by the SE Division Chief as one of the primary debriefers for the defector Vitaly Yurchenko from August to September 1985. For his work in the SE Division Group, Ames was ranked very near the lower quarter of DO operations officers at his grade at this time.

25. By early 1984, Ames was thinking ahead to his next field assignment and asked to go to Rome as Chief of a branch where he had access to information regarding many operations run or supported from that post. He left for Rome in 1986. He once again began to drink

heavily, particularly at lunch, did little work, sometimes slept at his desk in the afternoons, rarely initiated developmental activity, and often fell behind in accountings, reporting and other administrative matters. Ames was successful in managing liaison relations with U.S. military intelligence units in Italy, but he registered few other achievements.

26. Ames' mediocre performance for the Agency in Rome did not prevent his assignment upon his return to Headquarters in mid-1989 to head a branch of an SE Division Group. Here again he had access to many sensitive cases. When that position was eliminated in a December 1989 reorganization of SE Division, Ames became Chief of another SE Division branch, where he remained until late 1990. At this time, Ames was ranked in the bottom 10% of DO GS-14 operations officers. He appears to have been a weak manager who focused only on what interested him.

27. Ames moved to a position in the Counterintelligence Center in October 1990. In the CIC, where he remained until August 1991, he prepared analytical papers on issues relating to the KGB but also had access to sensitive data bases. Discussions between Ames and the Deputy Chief, SE Division, resulted in Ames temporary return to SE Division as head of a small KGB Working Group between August and November 1991.

28. In 1991, Chief SE Division requested that a counternarcotics program be established through liaison with the states of the former Soviet Union. Thereafter, Ames began a rotation to the Countenarcotics Center (CNC) in December 1991. At CNC, where Ames remained until his arrest, he worked primarily on developing a program for intelligence sharing between the United States and cooperating countries.

29. Ames was arrested on February 21, 1994. On that date, DCI Woolsey terminated his employment with the Agency.

What were Ames' Strengths, Weaknesses and Vulnerabilities?

Performance Problems
30. Ames appears to have been most successful and productive in assignments that drew on his:

Analytical skills, particularly collating myriad bits of information into coherent patterns;

Writing skills, both in drafting operational cables and crafting more intuitive thought pieces;

Intellectual curiosity and willingness to educate himself on issues that were beyond the scope of his immediate assignment; and

Creativity in conceiving and implementing sometimes complex operational schemes and liaison programs.

31. Ames was far less successful—and indeed was generally judged a failure—in overseas assignments where the development and recruitment of assets was the key measure of his performance. For most of his career, moreover, a number of work habits also had a dampening impact on his performance. These included:

Inattention to personal hygiene and a sometimes overbearing manner that aggravated the perception that he was a poor performer;

A lack of enthusiasm for handling routine administrative matters. By the late 1970's, when Ames was assigned to New York, this pattern of behavior was evident in his tardy filing of financial accountings and failure to document all of his meetings in contact reports. Ames' disdain for detail also manifested itself in his pack-rat amassing of paper and his failure, especially in Rome, to handle action cables appropriately and expeditiously; and

Selective enthusiasm. With the passage of time, Ames increasingly demonstrated zeal only for those few tasks that captured his imagination while ignoring elements of his job that were of little personal interest to him.

Sleeping on the Job
32. A significant number of individuals who have worked with Ames in both domestic and foreign assignments state that it was not uncommon for Ames to be seen asleep at his desk during working hours. This behavior often coincided, especially in Rome and at

Headquarters in the 1990's, with Ames having returned from lunch where he consumed alcohol.

Failure to File Required Reports

33. The Agency has an established system of reports of various kinds that serve administrative, operational, security, and counterintelligence purposes. Ames paid very little attention to a variety of these reporting requirements. His attention to these matters was by and large ignored, to the extent it was known by Agency management.

Foreign Travel

34. Over the course of several years, Ames failed to report foreign travel to OS as required by Headquarters Regulation. It is difficult to determine whether and to what extent management was aware of his unreported travel. The official record includes no mention, but fellow employees appear to have had some knowledge of his travels, especially in Rome.

Contact Reports

35. Ames also failed to file timely contact reports regarding many of his meetings with foreign officials. While this failure originally may have been related to his laziness and disdain for regulations, it became more calculated and had serious CI implications once he had volunteered to the Soviets in 1985. Ames states that he deliberately avoided filing complete and timely reports of his contacts with Soviet officials in Washington. If he had done so, he believes, Agency and FBI officials might have identified contradictions. Moreover, he believes they would have seen no operational advantage to the meetings, ceased the operation, and removed the ready pretext for his espionage activities. This also was true of his meetings with Soviets in Rome.

Financial Accountings

36. Throughout the course of Ames' career, managers reported that they frequently counseled and reprimanded him, or cited in his PAR Ames' refusal to provide timely accountings and properly maintain his revolving operational funds. This is more than a question of financial responsibility for DO officers. It also provides DO managers with another means of monitoring and verifying the activities of the operations officers they supervise.

Foreign National Contacts and Marriage

37. Ames also did not fully comply with Agency requirements in documenting his relationship with Rosario. He never reported his intimate relationship with her as a "close and continuing" one while he was in Mexico City. Management was aware generally of a relationship but not its intimate nature and did not pursue the reporting. He did follow proper procedures in

L to R: NACIC officers Rusty Capes and Anna Kline; FBI Special Agent Les Wiser; who was in charge of the Ames Investigation and NACIC Branch Chief Frank Rafalko.

obtaining approval for their marriage. However, Agency management did not accept or implement properly the CI Staff Chief's recommendation at the time that Ames be placed in less sensitive positions until Rosario became a U.S. citizen.

Security Problems

38. Ames also seemed predisposed to ignore and violate Agency security rules and regulations. In New York in 1976, he committed a potentially very serious security violation when he left a briefcase full of classified information on a New York subway train. In 1984, Ames brought Rosario to an Agency-provided apartment; a clear violation that compromised the cover of other operational officers. Ames also committed a breach of security by leaving a sensitive secure communications system unsecured at the FR/New York office. On July 2, 1985, Ames received the only official security violation that was issued to him when he left his office safe open and unlocked upon departure for the evening. Ames admits to using his home computer occasionally when in Rome between 1986 and 1989 to draft classified memoranda and cables that he would print out and take into the office the next day. In the most extreme example of his disregard for physical security regulations, of course, Ames wrapped up five to seven pounds of cable traffic in plastic bags in June 1985 and carried it out of Headquarters to deliver to the KGB.

Alcohol Abuse

39. Much has been made since his arrest of Ames' drinking habits. While it is clear that he drank too much too often and there is some basis to believe this may have clouded his judgment over time, he does not appear to have been an acute alcoholic who was constantly inebriated. Ames acknowledges the presence of a variety of symptoms of alcohol addition. The term "alcoholic" often conjures up images of broken individuals who spend their days helplessly craving a drink, becoming intoxicated beyond any self-control, and only breaking out of their intoxication with severe withdrawal symptoms. As explained in the psychological profile prepared by the psychologist detailed to the IG, alcohol addiction is, in reality, a more subtle, insidious process. This accounts for the fact that many of Ames' colleagues and a few supervisors were able to work with Ames without noticing his substance abuse problem.

40. In regard to why they did not deal with problems associated with Ames' alcohol abuse, several Agency managers say that alcohol abuse was not uncommon in the DO during the mid–to late–1980's and that Ames' drinking did not stand out since there were employees with much more serious alcohol cases. Other managers cite a lack of support from Headquarters in dealing with problem employees abroad.

41. Medical experts believe that alcohol, because it diminishes judgment, inhibitions, and long-term thinking ability, may play some role in the decision to commit espionage. At the same time, because the number of spies is so small relative to the fraction of the U.S. population that has an alcohol abuse problem, statistical correlation cannot be made. As a result, alcohol abuse cannot be said to have a predictive connection to espionage and, in and of itself, cannot be used as an indicator of any real CI significance.

Financial Problems

42. In 1983-85, Ames became exceedingly vulnerable to potential espionage as a result of his perception that he was facing severe financial problems. According to Ames, once Rosario moved in with him in December 1983 he had begun to feel a financial pinch. Ames describes being faced with a credit squeeze that included a new car loan, a signature loan that had been "tapped to the max," mounting credit card payments, and, finally, a divorce settlement that he believed threatened to bankrupt him.

43. Ames claims to have first contemplated espionage between December 1984 and February 1985 as a way out of his mounting financial dilemma. Confronting a divorce that he knew by that time was going to be financially draining, and facing added expenses connected with his imminent marriage to someone with already established extravagant spending habits, Ames claims that his financial predicament caused him to commit espionage for financial relief.

Why did Ames Commit Espionage?

44. Ames states that his primary motivating factor for his decision to commit espionage was his desperation regarding financial indebtedness he incurred at the time of his separation from his first wife, their divorce settlement and his cohabitation with Rosario. He also

says that several otherwise inhibiting "barriers" had been lowered by:

    a. the opportunity to meet Soviet officials under Agency sanction;

    b. the lack of concern that he would soon be subject to a reinvestigation polygraph;

    c. his fading respect for the value of his Agency work as a result of lengthy discussions with Soviet officials; and

    d. his belief that the rules that governed others did not apply to him.

Ames claims he conceived of a one-time "scam" directed against the Soviets to obtain the $50,000 he believed he needed to satisfy his outstanding debt in return for information about Agency operations he believed were actually controlled by the Soviets. He recognized subsequently that there was no turning back and acted to protect himself from the Soviet intelligence services by compromising Agency sources first in the June 1985 "big dump."

How were Indications of Substantial Changes in Ames Financial Situation Handled?

45. The financial inquiry regarding Ames began in November 1989 with the receipt of information from at least one Agency employee that Ames' financial situation had changed and he was living rather extravagantly. Upon his return from Rome, Ames purchased a home in Arlington for more than a half million dollars in cash and made plans to remodel the kitchen and landscape the yard, sparing no expense. Ames was also known to have purchased a Jaguar automobile and to have Filipino servants whom he had flown to and from the Philippines. Ames' lifestyle change was apparent to others as well as several employees state that they noticed at that time a marked improvement in Ames' physical appearance, including capped teeth and expensive Italian suits and shoes.

46. The financial inquiry faltered over resource limitations and priority conflicts, was reinvigorated in March 1992 and was not completed until mid-1993. The information obtained as a result of the Ames financial review, especially the correlation between deposits made by the Ameses and the operational meetings, was an essential element in shifting the focus of the molehunt toward Ames and paving the way, both psychologically and factually, for the further investigation that resulted in his arrest. Yet the financial review was permitted to stall for almost a year while other matters consumed the time and effort of the single CIC officer who possessed the interest and ability to necessary to conduct it. Technical management expertise to oversee the investigator's activities and help guide him was lacking. Given the responsibility that was placed on the investigator and his relative inexperience in conducting and analyzing financial information, he did a remarkable job. But there was clearly a lack of adequate resources and expertise available in CIC for this purpose.

47. If the financial inquiry had been pursued more rapidly and without interruption, significant information about Ames' finances would have been acquired earlier.

Was the Counterespionage Investigation Coordinated Properly with the FBI?

48. Under Executive Order 12333, CIA is authorized to conduct counterintelligence activities abroad and to coordinate the counterintelligence activities of other agencies abroad. The Order also authorizes CIA to conduct counterintelligence activities in the United States, provided these activities are coordinated with the FBI. Under a 1988 CIA-FBI Memorandum of Understanding (MOU) the FBI must be notified immediately when there is a reasonable belief that an individual may engage in activities harmful to the national security of the United States.

49. CIA-FBI cooperation in the Ames case after the spring of 1991 generally exceeded the coordination requirements under the 1988 MOU. The FBI could have taken over the Ames case completely in 1991 but apparently concluded that it did not have sufficient cause to open an intensive CI investigation directed specifically at Ames. The FBI officers who were part of the team were provided unprecedented access to CIA information related to Ames and to other CIA cases. These FBI officers indicate that they had full access to all of the CIA information they needed and requested. Once the FBI did take over the case in 1993, CIA cooperation with the Bureau was excellent, according to FBI and CIA accounts.

Were Sufficient Resources and Management Attention Devoted to the Ames Investigation?

50. In consideration whether the resources that were applied to the molehunt were sufficient, it is necessary to evaluate the need for secrecy and compartmentation. If alerting a potential mole to the investigation was to be avoided at all costs, then concerns about the size and discretion if any group undertaking the investigation would be paramount. Nevertheless there must be some balance between secrecy and progress. Despite the arguments for the small size of the molehunt team, many officers concede that more resources could have been brought to bear earlier on the Ames investigation.

51. Even accepting the argument that the team had to be small to maintain compartmentation and to manage a complex CI investigative process, the resource issue remains because the molehunt team members who were made available were not focused exclusively on the task, but were frequently diverted to other requirements. The limited size and diffused focus of the molehunt team does not support DO management's assertions that the 1985-86 compromised Soviet cases were "the biggest failure a spy Agency could have." Rather, the resources applied to the task force indicate lack of management attention to this most serious of intelligence failures.

52. The resources that the Agency devoted to the molehunt were inadequate from the outset, especially when considered in light of the fact that the 1985-86 compromises were the worst intelligence losses in CIA history.

Has Agency Use of Polygraphs and Background Investigations been Sufficient to Detect Possible Agency Counterintelligence Problems at the Earliest Time?

53. The fact that Ames conceived, executed and sustained an espionage enterprise for almost nine years makes it difficult to argue that Agency screening techniques functioned adequately to detect a CI problem at the earliest possible time. The question then becomes whether the screening techniques, particular the periodic polygraph examination, were adequate and why they did not detect Ames. The available evidence indicates that there were weaknesses in the polygraph methods that were used. However, it is difficult to conclude that the techniques themselves are inadequate since the major failing in the Ames case appears to be traceable to non-coordination and non-sharing of derogatory information concerning Ames.

54. Although this IG investigation necessarily focused on the Ames polygraph and background investigations, many employees of the Office of Security also raised generic problems in these programs. At a minimum, these expressions of concern about the Agency's polygraph program reflect a significant morale problem.

55. In light of the dominant role that the polygraph plays in the reinvestigation process, OS management came to be interested in production. For most of the time since 1986—when the five-year periodic reinvesti-

Ames arrest at his car.

gation program was begun—until the present, the reinvestigation program has been behind schedule. As a result, OS managers have stressed the successful completion of polygraph examinations. Many examiners believe that this requirement implicitly stressed quantity over quality. In addition to the pressures of production, the lack of experience in the polygraph corps has detrimentally affected the Agency's polygraph program. The 1988 IG inspection of the polygraph program noted this loss of experience. Many current and former OS polygraphers say that the OS policy of promoting generalists has caused the loss of experience. Many individuals also cite the lack of complete information on testing subjects as a defect in the Agency's polygraph program.

56. The 1986 polygraph of Ames was deficient and the 1991 polygraph sessions were not properly coordinated by CIC after they were requested. The Office of Security (OS) conducted a background investigation (BI) prior to Ames' polygraph examination in 1991. This 1991 BI is deemed by OS personnel to be a very professional and in-depth investigation of Ames' personal and professional activities. The investigator who conducted this BI deserves great credit for the competency and thoroughness of her efforts. Unfortunately, the results of this 1991 BI were not available to the polygraph examiners at the time they tested Ames nor was financial information that had been developed by CIC. Ultimately, the miscommunication between CIC and OS components that were involved led the individual examiners to conduct standard reinvestigation polygraph tests that Ames passed. Both examiners say that having such detailed information available could have significantly altered their approach to testing Ames.

To what Extent did Ames Use Computer Access and Capabilities to Engage in Espionage Activities?

57. Ames reports that he bought his first computer in the late winter or early spring of 1986 just prior to leaving for Rome. Ames' interest, however, was limited to computer applications rather than the technical aspects of computer science or programming. Ames admits to using his home computer occasionally when in Rome to draft classified memoranda and cables that he would print out and take into the office the next day. Ames admits to writing all his notes to the Soviets on his home computer using WordPerfect word processing software while in Rome. These notes, however, were passed only in paper form. Ames began preparing at home and passing computer disks to the Soviets after returning to Washington. These disks had been password-protected by the Russians. The information contained on the disks, according to Ames, consisted only of one or two-page messages from him to his handler. All other information he passed was in the form of paper copies of documents. The intent was for Ames to leave a disk at a drop site and have the same disk returned later at his pick-up site.

58. Ames says that passing disks and using passwords was entirely his idea. Although Ames admits to discussing Agency computer systems with the Soviets, he says it was obvious that his handlers had little or no expertise in basic computer skills. Ames describes his handlers as being "rather proud of their having been able to turn a machine on, crank up WordPerfect and get my message on it."

59. Ames states consistently that he did not use or abuse computer access as a means for enhancing his espionage capabilities. He explains that the computer systems to which he had access in CIC, SE/CE Division and Rome Station were "really no more than bona fide electric typewriters." He does say, however, that this changed after he was given access to the CNC Local Area Network (LAN). That LAN featured the DO's message delivery system (MDS). However, the CNC terminals differed from DO LANs in that the capability to download information to floppy disks had not been disabled in the CNC LAN. The combination of having the MDS system available on terminals that had floppy disk capabilities represented a serious system vulnerability.

60. Ames clearly viewed his access to the CNC LAN as a very significant event in his ability to conduct espionage. The broadened access, combined with the compactness of disks, greatly enhanced the volume of data he could carry out of Agency facilities with significant reduced risk. Fortunately, he was arrested before he could take full advantage of this system vulnerability.

61. No specific precautions were taken by Agency officials to minimize Ames' computer access to information within the scope of his official duties. In

fact, there is one instance where Ames was granted expanded computer access despite expressions of concern by CIC and SE Divison management at the time about his trustworthiness. Ames states he was surprised when he signed on and found that he had access to information about double agent cases. This allowed him to compromise a significant amount of sensitive data from the CIC to which he did not have an established need-to-know.

Is There any Merit to the Allegations in the "Poison Fax?"

62. In April 1994, an anonymous memorandum was faxed to the Senate Select Committee on Intelligence criticizing CIA counterintelligence policies and practices. That memorandum, which came to be known as the "poison fax," also alleged that an SE Division manager had warned Ames he was suspected of being a KGB mole and that a message from the field confirmed this. These allegations were featured in the press and raised questions in the Congress. No evidence has been found to substantiate these allegations.

Has CIA Been Effectively Organized to Detect Penetrations Such as Ames?

63. During the period of the Agency molehunt that led to Ames, the CI function and its counterespionage element was divided between the DO and OS. This division created problems that adversely affected the Agency's ability to focus on Ames. Although attempts were made to overcome these problems by written understandings and the assignment of OS officers to CIC, these attempts were not altogether successful.

64. Senior security officials have pointed out that there always has been a "fault line" in communications between the CIC, and its predecessors, and the OS. This division has created a number of problems, given the disparate cultures of the two organizations. Attempts are being made to employ CIC-OS teams to overcome these problems, but the problems are inherent to the division of CI responsibility for CI between CIC and OS interfered with a comprehensive approach to the molehunt. When financial leads were obtained in 1989 and 1990, CIC essentially turned the matter over to OS for Ames' investigation but failed to communicate all the relevant facts effectively with the OS personnel who were involved in the reinvestigation.

65. Many senior managers and other officers have strong opinions regarding whether the Agency's CI element, at least the portion that handles possible penetrations of the Agency, should report through the DDO. A number of officers believe that taking the CI function out of the DO would permit the addition of personnel who are not subject to the limitations of the DO culture and mindset. Other officers view the prospect of taking counterespionage outside the DO as impossible and potentially disastrous. Doing so, they argue, would never work because access to DO information would become more difficult. Some officers also argue that reporting directly to the DCI would be copying the KGB approach, which proved over the years to be unworkable. As a counter argument, however, former DCI Webster believes, in retrospect, that the CIC he created in 1988 should have reported to him directly with an informational reporting role to the DDO.

Were CIA Counterintelligence Personnel Who Conducted the Molehunt Properly Qualified by Training and Experience?

66. Of the four officers who were assigned to the STF in 1986, one remained when the molehunt team was established in CIC in 1991 to continue to pursue the cause of the 1985-86 compromises. That officer was chosen to head the effort primarily because she was an experienced SE Division officer, was familiar with the KGB and wanted to pursue the compromises. According to her supervisor, there were not many other employees who had the years of experience, the operational knowledge, the interest, the temperament, and the personality to persist in this effort. She was joined by another officer who had headed the Moscow Task Force inquiry charged with doing the DO damage assessment concerning the Lonetree/Bracy allegations. A third officer, who had been on rotation to CIC from the Office of Security was chosen to assist the team because of his background and CI experience, although he was not actually made a team member until June 1993. While this investigator was certainly not the only person in CIA who was capable of performing a financial analysis, he was the only one who was known to, and trusted by, the team leader. He was ideal in her view because of his previous work with her on other CI cases. In addition, two FBI officers were assigned to the effort.

67. Put most simply, the consensus view of those in CIC who were directly involved in the molehunt seems to be that good CI officers have both innate and learned characteristics that make them effective. In addition to innate CI ability, a good CI analyst needs a great deal of general and particular knowledge to make the mental connections necessary to conduct a CI investigation. General knowledge in the molehunt context refers to knowledge of the KGB, while particular knowledge refers to knowledge of the 1985-86 compromised cases. In addition, many CIC employees say that operational experience is essential to CI work. Although this general and particular knowledge can be acquired through study, for the most part it is obtained over years of experience actually working on foreign intelligence operations and CI cases in a particular subject area.

68. In the judgment of the IG, these criteria for qualifications as a CI analyst and for the process of conducting a CI investigation reflect a very narrow view of the scope and nature of CI investigations. In the Ames case, it was unduly cramped and justified an unfortunate resistance to adding more personnel to the molehunt unless they were deemed by the team leader to be qualified. Further, this view of counterespionage presents significant risks both to the Agency and successful prosecutions in the future. In the Ames investigation, the equities of any future prosecution were protected by the fact of FBI participation. Law enforcement officers bring an understanding of investigative procedure critical to building a successful prosecution. Without FBI participation, the risk of the narrow CIC view is that prosecutions may be jeopardized in future CI investigations. In addition to protecting Agency and prosecutive equities, training in law enforcement and other investigative techniques would expand the scope of information and techniques available to the Agency's CI investigators.

69. Despite these general shortcomings in CI training and methodology, the molehunters performed admirably. Their work included useful analysis that helped advance the resolution of the 1986-86 compromises significantly. On occasion, their work also went beyond the scope of what had been considered an adequate CI investigation to that point. Thus, they advanced the art form of CI investigations within the CIA. In the final analysis, they contributed substantially to catching a spy.

Was the Molehunt that led to Ames Managed Properly, and Who was Responsible?

70. Supervisors responsibility for the molehunt that eventually led to Ames shifted over time as managers, organizations and circumstances changed.

71. The primary responsibility for the molehunt within the Agency rested with officials in the CI Staff, later the CIC, as well as senior DO management. Management of the molehunt during the initial, analytic phase was inconsistent and sporadic. Although keen interest was expressed from time to time in determining what went wrong, the resources devoted to the molehunt were quite modest, especially considering the significance to the DO and the Agency of the rapid compromise of essentially all major Soviet sources. Those directly engaged in the molehunt also had to contend with competing assignments and were distracted from the molehunt by other possible explanations for the compromises, such as technical penetrations and the Lonetree/Bracy case, that eventually proved not to be fruitful. Senior CI managers at the time admit that they could, and probably should, have devoted more resources to the effort.

72. In the CI staff, the early years of the molehunt were primarily analytical and episodic, rather than investigative and comprehensive. Although information gathering and file review are important, little else appears to have been done during this time. A number of CI cases concerning Agency employees were opened based on suspicious activity, but none were brought to resolution. No comprehensive list of Agency officers with the requisite access was created and analyzed during this stage in an attempt to narrow the focus of the molehunt.

73. SE Division management must also assume some responsibility, given the fact that the 1985-86 compromises involved major SE Division assets. SE Division management should have insisted upon an extensive effort and added its own resources if necessary to determine the cause of the compromises. It is not sufficient to say, as these and many other officials now do, that they did not more closely monitor or encourage the molehunt effort because they knew they were suspects themselves and did not wish to appear to be attempting to influence the matter in an undue fashion. The distinction between encouraging a responsible effort

and improperly interfering in the process of that effort is considerable. In any event, another senior SE official who was not on the list could have been given the necessary authority and responsibility.

74. Given the importance of the compromises and the need to determine their cause, the DDOs during this phase also must bear responsibility for not paying more attention to and better managing the molehunt.

75. Beyond those in the DO and CIC who had direct responsibility for the molehunt during this phase, OS should have done a better job of developing leads that would have assisted the molehunt team in focusing its attention on Ames as early as 1986. In the mid-1980s, OS had fallen behind in its reinvestigation polygraphs, and many officers had not been repolygraphed for periods much longer than the required five-year intervals. Ames had not been polygraphed for almost ten years when he was scheduled for a reinvestigation polygraph in 1986. That polygraph raised several questions but failed to reveal any problems despite the fact he had begun spying for the Soviets a year earlier and he reports he was very apprehensive at the time about being exposed.

76. The reorganization of OS in 1986 was followed in 1988 by the creation of the CIC which included a large OS contingent as an integral part of the CIC. While one of the purposes of CIC was to consolidate all of the Agency's CI resources in a single component, the result was an overlap of missions, jurisdictional struggles at the highest levels of OS and CIC, and a failure to share information. According to a May 1991 Office of Inspector General Report of Inspection concerning OS, these problems were caused by the failure of Agency management to define the relative responsibilities of the two components, to provide a mechanism for a smooth flow of information between them, and to establish policy for managing cases of common interest.

77. CIC and the FBI can be credited for initiating a collaborative effort to revitalize the molehunt in April 1991. However, CIC management must also bear responsibility for not allocating sufficient dedicated resources to ensure that the effort was carried out thoroughly, professionally and expeditiously. The delay in the financial inquiry can be attributed largely to the lack of investigative resources allocated to the effort. The CIC investigator deserves a great deal of credit for his initiative and interest in financial analysis and it appears clear that an inquiry into Ames finances would not have occurred to anyone else in CIC had he not been available to suggest it and carry it out. However, the failure to either dedicate the investigator fully to this inquiry before 1992, or to bring in other officers who would have been able to conduct a similar or more thorough financial analysis of Ames, represents one of the most glaring shortcomings of the molehunt. This failure alone appears to have delayed the identification of Ames by at least two years.

78. In 1993, when the FBI opened an intensive CI investigation of Ames, the Agency was fully cooperative and provided excellent support to the FBI's investigation. CIA deferred to the FBI decisions regarding the investigation and allowed Ames continued access to classified information in order to avoid alerting him and to assist in developing evidence of his espionage. The common goal was to apprehend Ames, while safeguarding evidence for a successful prosecution. As has been stated earlier, the CIA/FBI working relationship during the FBI phases appears to have been a model of cooperation.

The White House

Office of the Press Secretary

For Immediate Release   May 3, 1994

Statement By The Press Secretary

U.S. Counterintelligence Effectiveness

President Clinton signed today a Presidential Decision Directive on U.S. counterintelligence effectiveness to foster increased cooperation, coordination and accountability among all U.S. counterintelligence agencies. The President has directed the creation of a new national counterintelligence policy structure under the auspices of the National Security Council. In addition, he has directed the creation of a new National Counterintelligence Center, initially to be led by a senior executive of the Federal Bureau of Investigation. Finally, the President's Decision Directive requires that exchange of senior managers between the CIA and the FBI to ensure timely and close coordination between the intelligence and law enforcement communities.

The President's decision to take these significant steps of restructuring U.S. counterintelligence policy and interagency coordination, followed a Presidential Review of U.S. counterintelligence in the wake of the Aldrich Ames espionage investigation. The President, in issuing this Directive, has taken immediate steps to improve our ability to counter both traditional and new threats to our nation's security in the post-Cold War era.

Fact Sheet:
U.S. Counterintelligence Effectiveness

Many threats to the national security of the United States have been significantly reduced by the break-up of the Soviet Union and the end of the Cold War. Core U.S. concepts—democracy and market economics—are more broadly accepted around the world than ever before. Nevertheless, recent events at home and abroad make clear that numerous threats to our national interests — terrorism, proliferating weapons of mass destruction, ethnic conflicts, sluggish economic growth— continue to exist and must be effectively addressed. In this context, it is critical that the U.S. maintain a highly effective and coordinated counterintelligence capability.

A review of U.S. counterintelligence effectiveness in the wake of the Ames case highlights the need for improvements in the coordination of our counterintelligence (CI) activities. The recent DCI and Attorney General Joint Task Force on Intelligence Community-Law Enforcement Relations noted that changes to the basic underlying legal authorities defining the relationship between the intelligence and law enforcement communities are not required. Rather, the task force concluded that what is needed..." is for the two communities to improve their understanding of their respective needs and operating practices...to cooperate earlier, more closely, and more consistently on matters in which they both have a separate but parallel interest." This Directive outlines specific steps which will be taken to achieve the objective of improved cooperation.

Executive Order 12333 designates the National Security Council (NSC) "as the highest Executive Branch entity that provides review of, guidance for and direction to the conduct of," among other things, counterintelligence policies and programs. Consistent with E.O. 12333, the President directed the creation of a new CI structure, under the direction of the NSC, for the coordination of CI policy matters in order to integrate more fully government-wide counterintelligence capabilities, to foster greater cooperation among the various departments and agencies with CI responsibilities and to establish greater accountability for the creation of CI policy and its execution. This new structure will ensure that all relevant departments and agencies have a full and free exchange of information necessary to achieve maximum effectiveness of the U.S. counterintelligence effort, consistent with U.S. law.

Nothing in this directive amends or changes the authorities and responsibilities of the DCI, Secretary of Defense, Secretary of State, Attorney General or Director of the FBI, as contained in the National Security Act of 1947, other existing laws and E.O. 12333.

The following specific initiatives will be undertaken to improve U.S. counterintelligence effectiveness:

National Counterintelligence Policy Coordination

A National Counterintelligence Policy Board (Policy Board) is hereby established and directed to report to the President through the Assistant to the President for National Security Affairs. The existing CI policy and

Keith Hall, first Chairman of National Counterintelligence Board.

coordination structure, the National Advisory Group for Counterintelligence, is hereby abolished and its CI functions transferred to the Policy Board.

The Policy Board will consist of one senior executive representative each from DCI/CIA; the FBI; the Departments of Defense, State, and Justice; a Military Department CI component; and the NSC, Special Assistant to the President and Senior Director for Intelligence Programs.

The Chairman of the Policy Board will be designated by the DCI in consultation with the Assistant to the President for National Security Affairs. The Chairman will serve for a period of two years. The position of Chairman of the Policy Board will be rotated among the CIA, FBI, and Department of Defense.

The Policy Board will consider, develop and recommend for implementation to the Assistant to the President for National Security Affairs policy and planning directives for U.S. counterintelligence. The Policy Board will be the principal mechanism for reviewing and proposing to the NSC staff legislative initiatives and executive orders pertaining to U.S. counterintelligence. This Board will coordinate the development of interagency agreements and resolve conflicts that may arise over the terms and implementation of these agreements.

A National Counterintelligence Operations Board (Operations Board) will be established under the Policy Board with senior CI representatives from CIA, FBI, DoD, the Military Department CI components, NSA, State, Justice, and Chief of the National CI Center established below.

The Chairman of the Operations Board will be appointed by the Policy Board from among the CIA, FBI, or DoD, and rotated every two years. The Chairmanship of the Policy Board and the Operations Board will not be held by the same agency at any one time. The Operations Board will discuss and develop from an operational perspective matters to be considered or already under consideration by the Policy Board. It will oversee all coordinating subgroups, resolve specific conflicts concerning CI operations and investigations and identify potential CI policy conflicts for referral to the Policy Board.

Counterintelligence Integration and Cooperation

The Policy Board, with the assistance of the DCI and the cooperation of the Director of the FBI, the Secretary of Defense, and the Secretary of State, will establish a National Counterintelligence Center within 90 days of this directive.

A senior FBI executive with CI operational and management experience will serve as the Chief of the National CI Center and a senior Military Department CI component executive will serve as the Deputy Chief of the National CI Center. These agencies will hold these positions for an initial period of 4 years, after which, with the approval of the National CI Policy Board and in consultation with the Assistant to the President for National Security Affairs, the leadership positions will rotate, for 2 year terms, among the FBI, DoD and CIA. At all such times that the FBI does not hold the position of Chief, it will hold the position of Deputy Chief.

The National Counterintelligence Center will be located, staffed and initially structured as recommended in PDD-44.

The National Counterintelligence Center will implement interagency CI activities as described in PDD-44 and report to the Policy Board.

The National Counterintelligence Center will serve as the interagency forum for complementary activities among CI agencies. The CIA's Counterintelligence Center will serve as the CI component for the CIA and execute on behalf of the DCI his authorities to coordinate all U.S. counterintelligence activities overseas.

The Chief of the CIA's Counterintelligence Center Counterespionage Group will be permanently staffed by a senior executive from the FBI.

CIA counterintelligence officers will permanently staff appropriate management positions in the FBI's National Security Division and/or FBI Field Offices.

The Policy Board will be responsible for the regular monitoring and review of the integration and coordination of U.S. counterintelligence programs. The Policy Board will provide an annual report to the Assistant to the President for National Security Affairs on U.S. counterintelligence effectiveness.

Preparing for the 21st Century: An Appraisal of U.S. Intelligence

Background

On 1 March 1996, the Commission on the Roles and Capabilities of the United States Intelligence Community—generally known as the Aspin-Brown Commission—released its final report entitled *Preparing for the 21st Century: An Appraisal of U.S. Intelligence*. This Commission was chartered by Congress in October 1994 to conduct a comprehensive review of American intelligence. The Commission began operation on 1 March 1995 and conducted a rigorous inquiry during the following year. A distinguished panel of 17 individuals composed the Commission, which was first chaired by Les Aspin until his untimely death on 21 May 1995 and then by Dr. Harold Brown. It reviewed 19 separate issues that were identified by Congress for assessment. The Commission received formal testimony from 84 witnesses, and its staff interviewed over 200 other individuals.

The mandate of the Commission was to review the efficacy and appropriateness of the activities of the US Intelligence Community (IC) in the post Cold War global environment and to make such recommendations as the Commission considered advisable. As required by law, the Chairman of the Commission—Dr. Harold Brown, former Secretary of Defense—submitted the report and its recommendations to the President and to the Congressional intelligence committees.

The Goal of the Report

This 200-page report contains a number of recommendations for action by the Executive and Legislative Branches that would, in the view of the Commission, produce a more effective, more efficient, and more responsive Intelligence Community to serve the nation's interests.

The unclassified report has concluded that the IC, with 14 separate agencies, is functioning well in its current form and performing a valuable service for the rest of the government. The report does, however, call for increased efficiencies in the organizations.

The Commission's View of Counterintelligence

The Commission stated that counterintelligence (CI) is a critical part of nearly all intelligence activities. When performed properly, the CI function is integral to the intelligence activity itself and part of the overall security of the organization. As the Ames case demonstrated, the consequences of poor CI can be disastrous and deadly.

In Chapter 2 of the report, the Commission first describes the basic CI functions of detecting and monitoring the activities of foreign intelligence services and investigating those suspected of espionage. CI, however, is an integral part of the entire intelligence process, and all agencies that undertake intelligence collection must be constantly on guard that what they collect is genuine. This requires continuous evaluation of their sources as well as the information gathered from them. Intelligence analysts who are familiar with the totality of information on a particular topic are often in a position to detect anomalies.

Three Overarching Themes

While the Commission's recommendations address a great many issues, there are three discernible overarching themes:

1. The need to better integrate intelligence into the policy community it serves. Intelligence cannot operate successfully in a vacuum. Its effectiveness is largely a function of its responsiveness, and its responsiveness is a function of the relationships it has with those it serves, from the President on down.

2. The need for intelligence agencies to operate as a "community." In times of crisis or war, intelligence agencies overcome the obstacles that separate them and pull together toward a common objective. By all accounts, it is in such situations that intelligence performs best. The challenge is to create the same level of performance in the absence of crisis.

3. The need to create greater efficiency. The Commission's report suggests a number of ways this might be done. Few will be easy. If the intelligence function is to retain its vitality, however, and if the confidence of the Congress and the public is to be restored, more rigor and modern management practices must be brought to the system.

The Commission concluded that intelligence agencies have not performed this crucial function very well. Virtually all have suffered severe losses because of a failure to recognize anomalous behavior on the part of their own employees. Some have also had problems recognizing anomalies in the behavior of their sources or in the appearance or actions of their targets. The Ames spy case revealed serious shortcomings in both categories.

In Chapter 6, the Commission concluded that, given the history of CI failures in CIA operations, the concern remains that the CI function may not have found its permanent place in CIA's overall foreign intelligence mission.

In Chapter 7, the Commission stated that the CI function is not readily amenable to budgetary trade-offs among the various agency CI staffs. However, they concluded that there is a need for an independent review of CI budgets to ensure that adequate resources are being allocated to this function consistent with national objectives and priorities. In the past, funding for CI activities has occasionally been a convenient place for agencies under budget pressures to find money for other activities. This must be assiduously prevented.

The Commission believes that funding for CI activities should remain a part of the National Foreign Intelligence Program. At the same time, it is useful to have the National Counterintelligence Policy Board (NACIPB) perform a separate review of CI budgets. This approach should provide assurance that funding is adequate to achieve national objectives and priorities as well as prevent CI funds being used for other purposes.

In the wake of the Ames case, the IC made sweeping changes to its CI infrastructure. A new NACIPB, which reports to the Assistant to the President for National Security Affairs, was created to coordinate CI activities and resolve interagency disagreements. In addition, the National Counterintelligence Center (NACIC) was created to share and evaluate information regarding foreign intelligence threats.

The Commission reported that the area of CI has undergone significant changes over the past two years. They question, however, whether these changes will have a long-term positive effect; the Commission believes it is still too early to evaluate this issue.

The Commission concluded that, because CI is so crucial to the success of the entire enterprise, the IC must sustain the renewed emphasis recently placed on this function. CI must be viewed not as an annoying intrusion, but rather as an integral part of the intelligence process. It must focus not only on protecting our own sensitive information but also equally on efforts to manipulate our collection and analysis through double agents or other means. This process requires a certain openness of mind and a willingness continually to balance the conclusions drawn from intelligence with the possibility of deliberate deception by a target.

Summary of the Commission's Key Recommendations

The Commission perceives four functional roles for intelligence agencies—collection, analysis, covert action, and CI—as well as a number of "missions" in terms of providing substantive support to particular governmental functions. In each of the 14 chapters of its report, the Brown Commission summarized its principal recommendations. Cited below are the Commission's key recommendations that are contained in each chapter.

Chapter 1. The Need To Maintain an Intelligence Capability

The Commission concludes that the United States should continue to maintain a strong intelligence capability. US intelligence has made, and continues to make, vital contributions to the nation's security. Its performance can be improved. Its can be made more efficient. But it must be preserved.

Chapter 2. The Role of Intelligence

The Commission concludes that a capability to conduct covert actions should be maintained to provide the president with an option short of military actions when diplomacy alone cannot do the job. The capability must be utilized only where essential to accomplishing important and identifiable foreign policy objectives and only where a compelling reason exists why US involvement cannot be disclosed.

Chapter 3. The Need for Policy Guidance

The Commission recommends a two-tier structure to carry out the institutional role of the National Security Council (NSC). A "Committee on Foreign Intelligence" should be created, chaired by the Assistant to the President for Nation Security Affairs and includes the DCI, the Deputy Secretary of Defense, and the Deputy Secretary of State. This Committee should meet at least semiannually and provide broad guidance on major issues. A subordinate "Consumers Committee," comprising representatives of the major consumers and producers of intelligence, should meet more frequently to provide ongoing guidance for collection and analysis and periodically to assess the performance of intelligence agencies in meeting the needs of the Federal Government.

Chapter 4. The Need for a Coordinated Response to Global Crime

The Commission recommends the establishment of a single element of the NSC—a Committee on Global Crime—chaired by the Assistant to the President for National Security Affairs and including, at a minimum, the Secretaries of State and Defense, the Attorney General, and the DCI to develop and coordinate appropriate strategies to counter such threats to national security.

For these strategies to be effective, the relationship between intelligence and law enforcement also must be substantially improved. In this regard, the Commission recommends:

1. The President should designate the Attorney General to serve as the spokesperson and coordinator of the law enforcement community for purposes of formulating the nation's law enforcement response to global crime.

2. The authority of intelligence agencies to collect information concerning foreign persons abroad for law enforcement purposes should be clarified by executive order.

3. The sharing of relevant information between the two communities should be expanded.

4. The coordination of law enforcement and intelligence activities overseas should be improved.

Chapter 5. The Organizational Arrangements for the IC

To improve the ability of the Director of Central Intelligence to manage the IC, the commission recommends that the current position of Deputy Director of Central Intelligence be replaced with two new deputies to the DCI: one deputy for the IC and one with day-to-day responsibility for managing the CIA. Both would be appointed by the president and confirmed by the Senate. The deputy for the CIA would be appointed for a fixed term. To give the DCI greater bureaucratic weight within the IC, the DCI would concur in the appointment or recommendation for appointment of the heads of national intelligence elements within the Department of Defense and would be consulted with respect to the appointment of other senior officials within the IC. The Directors of the National Security Agency and Central Imagery Office or its successor agency would be dual hatted as Assistant Directors of Central Intelligence for signals intelligence and imagery, respectively. Their performance in those capacities would be evaluated by the DCI as part of their rating by the Secretary of Defense. In addition, the DCI would be given new tools to carry out his responsibilities with respect to the intelligence budget and new authority over the intelligence personnel system.

Chapter 6. Central Intelligence Agency

To provide greater continuity in the management of the CIA, the Commission recommends that the Deputy DCI responsible for the CIA be appointed to a fixed term with an overall length of six years, renewable by the president at two-year intervals. To improve the quality of management, the Commission recommends a comprehensive approach to the selection, training, and career progression of CIA managers. Separate career tracks with appropriate opportunities for advancement ought to be provided for specialists who are not selected as managers. Clear guidelines should be issued regarding the types of information that should be brought to the attention of senior Agency managers, including the DCI and Deputy DCI.

Chapter 7. The Need for a More Effective Budget Structure and Process

The Commission recommends that the budget for national intelligence be substantially realigned. Programs grouping similar kinds of intelligence activities should be created under separate discipline managers reporting to the DCI. For example, all signals intelligence activities would be grouped under the discipline management of the Director of the National Security Agency. These discipline managers also would coordinate the funding of activities within their respective disciplines in the defense-wide or tactical aggregations of the DOD, thus bringing greater consistency to all intelligence spending. The DCI should be provided a sufficient staff capability to enable him to assess trade-offs between programs or program elements and should establish a uniform, communitywide resource database to serve as the principal information tool for resource management across the IC.

Chapter 8. Improving Intelligence Analysis

The Commission recommends that intelligence producers take a more systematic approach to building relationships with consumers in policy agencies. Key consumers should be identified and consulted individually with respect to the form of support they desire. Producers should offer to place analysts directly on the staffs of consumers at senior levels.

The Commission recommends that the skills and expertise of intelligence analysts be more consistently and extensively developed and that greater use be made of substantive experts outside the IC. A greater effort also should be made to better harness the vast universe of information now available from open sources. The systems establishing electronic links between producers and consumers currently being implemented should be given a higher priority.

The Commission recommends that the existing organization that prepares intelligence estimates, the National Intelligence Council, be restructured to become a more broadly based "National Assessments Center." It would remain under the purview of the DCI but be located outside the CIA to take advantage of a broader range of information and expertise.

Chapter 9. The Need to "Right-Size" and Rebuild the Community

The Commission recommends the enactment of new legislation giving the most severely affected intelligence agencies a one-year window to "right-size" their workforces to the needs of their organization. Such authority would be available only to the CIA and to intelligence agencies within the DOD that decide to reduce their civilian work force by 10 percent or more beyond the present Congressionally mandated level. Agencies that avail themselves of this authority would identify positions no longer needed for the health and viability of their organization. The incumbents of such positions, if close to retirement, would be allowed to retire with accelerated eligibility. If not close to retirement, they would be provided generous pay and benefits to leave the service of the agency concerned, or, with the concurrence of the agency affected, exchange positions with an employee not in a position identified for elimination who was close to retirement and would not be allowed to leave under the accelerated retirement provisions. New employees would be hired to fill some, but not all, of the vacancies created, providing the skills necessary to satisfy the current and future needs of the agency involved.

Four separate civilian personnel systems exist within the IC. These systems discourage rotation between intelligence agencies, which is key to functioning as a "community." In addition, many aspects of personnel and administration could be performed more efficiently if they were centralized.

The Commission recommends the DCI consolidate such functions where possible or, if centralization is not reasonable, issue uniform standards governing such functions. The Commission also recommends the creation of a single "Senior Executive Service" for the IC under the overall management of the DCI.

Chapter 10. Military Intelligence

The Commission did find that progress had been made in reducing duplication in military intelligence analysis and production, but that the size and functions of the numerous organizations performing these functions continued to raise concern. The Commission recommends that the Secretary of Defense undertake a comprehensive examination of the size and missions of these organizations.

The Commission recommends that the Director for Intelligence (J-2), who is now an officer assigned to the Defense Intelligence Agency, be constituted as part of the Joint Staff and be made responsible for providing intelligence support to joint war fighting and for executing the functions of the Joint Chiefs of Staff as they pertain to intelligence.

The Commission also found that a problem continued to exist with respect to how information produced by national and tactical intelligence systems is communicated to commanders in the field. Many organizations and coordinating entities within DOD are working on aspects of this problem, but no one, short of the Secretary of Defense, appears to be in charge. The Commission recommends that a single focal point be established on the staff of the Secretary of Defense to bring together all of the relevant players and interests to solve these problems. It considers the Assistant Secretary of Defense (Command, Control, Communication, and Intelligence) to be the appropriate official for this purpose.

The Commission recommends that the clandestine recruitment of human sources, now carried out by active-duty military officers assigned to the Defense HUMINT Service, be transferred to the CIA, utilizing military personnel on detail from the DOD as necessary.

Chapter 11. Space Reconnaissance and the Management of Technical Collection

The Commission recommends greater international cooperation in space reconnaissance through expanded government-to-government arrangements as a means of dealing with both the vulnerability and cost of US space systems. In this regard, the Commission proposes a two-tier approach as a model for such collaboration. The Commission also recommends that the President re-examine certain restrictions on the licensing of commercial imaging systems for foreign sale in order to encourage greater investment by US firms in such systems.

The Commission endorses greater coordination between the space programs of the DOD and IC in order to achieve economies of scale where possible but recommends the National Reconnaissance Office be preserved as a separate organization.

The Commission endorses the creation of a National Imagery and Mapping Agency as recently proposed by the DCI and the Secretary of Defense.

Chapter 12. International Cooperation

The Commission recommends that the DCI and the Secretaries of State and Defense develop a strategy that will serve as the normal basis for sharing information derived from intelligence in a multinational environment.

Chapter 13. Cost of Intelligence

The Commission recommends a number of actions that it believes would, if implemented, reduce the cost of intelligence. In particular, the Commission believes that, until the IC reforms its budget structure and process, as recommended in Chapter 7, it will remain poorly positioned to identify potential cost reductions.

Chapter 14. Accountability and Oversight

The Commission recommends that the president or his designee disclose the total amount of money appropriated for intelligence activities during the current fiscal year and the total amount being requested for the next fiscal year. The disclosure of additional detail should not be permitted.

The Commission recommends a comprehensive review of these arrangements by the Intelligence Oversight Board to ensure effective performance of the oversight function.

Robert Chaegon Kim

(The following are excerpts from the Affidavit in support of the arrest warrant and search warrant on Kim filed in the US District Court, Eastern District of Virginia, Case Number:96-00791-m.)

Robert Chaegon Kim, an employee of the Office of Naval Intelligence ("ONI"), is knowingly and without authorization transmitting classified documents, including materials classified at the "Secret" and "Top Secret" level, to Baek Dong-Il, a Naval Attaché for the Republic of Korea (hereafter "South Korea"). According to ONI officials, Kim has a computer at his desk which allows him access go government information systems such as the Electronic Collateral Support System (ELCSS); this system contains documents that the Office of Naval Intelligence receives from other U.S. intelligence agencies, including documents classified at the "Secret" and "Top Secret" level. Kim regularly searches the system to find classified documents relating to military, political and intelligence matters in the Asia-Pacific region. Kim copies and stores these documents in his work computer, removes classification markings, prints them on his office printer, and transmits them to Baek Don-IL.

This affidavit is not intended to be an exhaustive summary of the investigation against Kim, but is for the purpose of setting out probable cause in support of:

    a. an arrest warrant for Robert Chaegon Kim for violations of Title 50, United States Code Section 783(a);

    b. a search warrant for KIM's residence at 20765 Bank Way, Sterling, VA, in the Eastern District of Virginia;

    c. a search warrant for KIM's workspace, located in Room 2D225 at the Office of Naval Intelligence on Suitland Road in Suitland, MD.;

    d. a search warrant for KIM's vehicle, a dark red 1987 Volvo license plate BVY 893.

Pursuant to Executive Order 12958, information which, if disclosed without authorization, could reasonably be expected to cause "damage to national security," must be classified as Confidential and properly safeguarded. Information which, if disclosed without authorization, reasonably could be expected to cause "serious damage to the national security," must be classified as Secret and properly safeguarded. Information which, if disclosed without authorization, could reasonably be expected to cause "exceptionally grave damage to the national security," must be classified as Top Secret and properly safeguarded. When a classified document can be released to a particular foreign country, the originating agency will usually place markings at the top of the document to show that is releasable to that country.

A review of Robert Chaegon KIM's personnel file at the Office of Naval Intelligence shows that Kim was born on January 21, 1940 in Seoul, Korea. He became a naturalized American citizen in Baltimore, Maryland on May 21, 1974. Kim is employed as a computer specialist in the Maritime Systems Directorate of ONI, known as ONI-7, and has been employed by ONI since November 20, 1978. Kim has had a "Top Secret" security clearance, and access to "Sensitive Compartmented Information (SCI), since 1979. KIM's work involves classified information to such an extent that he physically works within a "Sensitive Compartmented Information Facility ("SCIF").

According to KIM's personnel file, KIM's primary job responsibility is to provide technical oversight regarding the design, development and maintenance of U.S. computer system known as the "Joint Maritime Information Element"(JMIE). This system monitors, tracks and stores information related to international maritime movement and maritime vessel identification. As a computer specialist, Kim does not ordinarily have duties relating to South Korea, though he has occasionally performed duties relating to that country under the specific direction of ONI officials.

(A review was made of) a document signed by defendant Robert Chaegon Kim entitled "Sensitive Compartmented Information Nondisclosure Agreement." In this document, Kim acknowledges that he has been granted access to Sensitive Compartmented Information as part of his employment, that any unauthorized disclosure of classified information is a violation of federal criminal law, and that any unauthorized disclosure of SCI information could irreparably injure the United States or provide an advantage to a foreign nation. In this signed document,

Robert Chaegon Kim

he agrees that he will never divulge classified information to anyone not authorized to receive it without prior written authorization from the United States.

According to information obtained from Department of State records, Baek Dong-Il is a Korean national, an O-6 Captain in the Korean Navy and an employee of the South Korean government. Baek arrived in the United States on October 1, 1994 to begin a three year tour as Naval Attaché assigned to the Embassy of the Republic of Korea. He works at the Embassy of South Korea in Washington, D.C. According to DMV and telephone records, Baek Dong-Il resides in Falls Church, VA, in the Eastern District of Virginia.

This affidavit will refer to information obtained from electronic surveillance, video surveillance and searches of KIM's workspace and mail. In each instance, the surveillance and searches were authorized by court order.

5/9/96 - Delivery of Documents

On or about May 1, 1996, video surveillance of KIM's workspace revealed Kim working on his computer while simultaneously creating a handwritten list, hereafter referred to as the "K list."

On or about May 5, 1996, the FBI conducted a court authorized search of KIM's work computer at KIM's workspace at the ONI in Suitland, MD. During the search, the FBI copied files stored on KIM's computer. One file, Titled "Baek.ltr" and dated 1/24/96, was a letter from Kim to Baek. In the letter, Kim offered his services to Baek and another South Korean official on the "OBU/OED business." (It is known) that the United States is involved in negotiations with South Korea to sell South Korea the "OBU" system, which is a computer software system used for tracking maritime vessels. (It is also known) that Kim has no official role in the negotiation or sale of this system. In the letter, Kim states that he hopes Baek has digested "the materials I have sent you" and warms him to "please be careful with these materials."

The May 5, 1996 computer search revealed that Kim had stored a number of "K" files, that is, files titled with as "K" followed by a number, such as "K10." Most of these "K" files contained copies of documents from agencies of the United States relating to North Korea, South Korea or other Asia-Pacific countries. Some of these "K" documents had their original classification markings removed. Using comparisons with the original documents, (it was determined), that at least some of these documents are classified at the "Confidential," "Secret" or "Top Secret" level. In addition to the "K" documents, there were other files containing U.S. agency documents relating to South Korea and other Asia-Pacific countries; some of these documents are also classified.

On or about May 7, 1996, video surveillance of KIM's desk at the Office of Naval Intelligence, Suitland, MD, revealed Kim working on his computer, moving to his left where his printer is located, and returning to his desk with papers in hand. While working on the computer, and while retrieving the documents, Kim was observed writing on a scratch pad similar to the one observed on May 1, 1996. This scratch pad contained a handwritten "K" list similar to the one found in his computer two days earlier, that, a list of numbers each preceded by the letter "K" such as "K-10." These activities went on for several hours. Kim placed the papers in a pile on his desk, and put the pile in an 8X11 manila envelope. Kim placed the envelope in his briefcase, and left work that day with the briefcase.

Video surveillance revealed a portion of three documents that were placed in the envelope. By comparing the surveillance photograph to an original document, (it was) determined that one document was a document found in the May 5, 1996 computer search of KIM's computer under the title "K10." This document is a United States agency document classified "Secret" which relates to North Korea. This classification heading had been removed from the copy seen on video surveillance. By comparing the surveillance photograph to an original document, (it was) determined that the second document is a document of a United States agency classified "Top Secret" which relates to North Korea. The classification headings were removed from the copy seen on video surveillance. The third document was unclassified.

On or about May 9, 1996, electronic surveillance revealed that Kim telephoned Baek, and stated that he had something for Baek. There was discussion about how the two could meet for a delivery of this item. Kim indicated that lunch would be difficult because Kim would be bringing "this thing" along, and the two joked about mailing it. Baek gave Kim directions so that Kim could drive to his house, and told Kim to give the package to his son, who was mowing the law.

On 10 May, 1996, Baek called Kim back, confirming he received "it" yesterday.

Early June, 1996 - Delivery of Documents
On or about June 3, 1996, video surveillance of KIM's desk at ONI revealed Kim working on his computer, moving to his left where the printer is located, and returning to his desk with papers in hand. Video surveillance revealed that one of these documents was a U.S. agency document with classification markings removed. Using comparisons with an original document, (it was) determined that this document is classified "Secret."

On or about June 4, 1996, video surveillance of KIM's workspace revealed, inside KIM's open briefcase, a manila enveloped addressed to Baek at Baek's home address.

On or about June 12, 1996, electronic surveillance revealed that Baek called Kim at KIM's office, and thanked Kim, adding that "what was shown to me" was interesting. The two then discussed a matter pertaining to negotiations between the United States and South Korea on a particular project. Baek asked Kim a question relating to "what you sent me," referring to information that Baek had received from Kim earlier. Kim indicated that he could not answer the question without reviewing the "original text again." "When I sent that," Kim added, "I cut it all off and threw it away." Based on an investigation, (It is) believe that this is a reference to KIM's practice of cutting off classification markings, as well as other identifying information found at the beginning and end of U.S. agency documents, before delivering documents to Baek. This practice makes it easier for Kim to remove documents undetected from his office.

After this June 12, 1996 conversation, video surveillance later that day revealed that Kim placed a document on his desk belonging to the United States classified "Secret" concerning the same U.S.-South Korea project that Kim had discussed with Baek that morning. Later that same day, electronic surveillance revealed another telephone conversation between Kim and Baek. In this conversation, Kim told Baek he reviewed the message again. Kim then summarized to Baek four paragraphs in this "Secret" document. Each individual paragraph that Kim described to Baek is classified at the "Confidential" or "Secret" level.

On or about June 16, 1996, agents of the FBI and the Naval Criminal Investigative Service (NCIS) performed a search of KIM's office space. This search revealed a document in KIM's "burn bag," written in Korean, containing excerpts from the above described "Secret" document.

6/17/96 - Mailing of Documents
On or about June 17, 1996, video surveillance of KIM's workspace revealed portions of three documents on KIM's desk. By reviewing the video, (it was) determined that these documents belong to agencies of the United States, and relate to South Korea. By comparing these documents to original documents, (it was) determined that the documents were altered, in that their classification markings were removed. Two of the original documents are classified "Secret," and the third classified "Confidential." Video surveillance showed Kim picking up these documents and placing them in his briefcase. Several hours later, video surveillance detected Kim leaving work with his briefcase.

A review of the outside of mail sent from KIM's residence revealed that on June 17, 1996, an 8X11 manila envelope was mailed from KIM's residence in Sterling, Virginia, in the Eastern district of Virginia, to Baek at his residence in Falls Church, Virginia, in the Eastern District of Virginia. The envelope had a return address label listing KIM's name and address as the sender, and was large enough to hold the documents that Kim removed from his office earlier in the day.

8/3/96 - Mailing of Documents
On or about August 2, 1996, video surveillance of KIM's workspace revealed portions of these three documents belonging to agencies of the United States and relating to Asia-Pacific countries on KIM's desk. Kim later moved these documents into his briefcase, and left the office with that briefcase.

25. On or about August 3, 1996, a mail cover revealed an 8X11 manila envelope postmarked from the Eastern District of Virginia to Baek's residence in the Eastern District of Virginia. The envelope had a return address in the name of Robert Kim with KIM's home address. FBI personnel opened the envelope, and found two of the three documents seen by video surveillance on KIM's desk on August 2, 1996. By comparing the documents to the original documents, it was determined that the classification markings had been removed. Both documents belong to agencies of the United States and are classified "Secret." According to markings on the original documents, portions of one of those documents had already been released to South Korean officials, but the remaining information in those documents was not releasable to South Korea. FBI personnel placed the two documents back in the envelope and returned it to the mail for delivery to Baek. Video surveillance has periodically detected the third document on KIM's desk or in his open briefcase, and to the best of my knowledge Kim has retained this document. Based on the video surveillance, this third document has had classification markings removed, and is classified "Secret."

On or about August 7, 1996, electronic surveillance revealed that Baek called Kim and stated that "the material you had sent me was safely received with thanks."

8/14/96 - Mailing of Documents
On or about August 9, 1996, video surveillance revealed that Kim was printing numerous materials and placing them on the corner of his desk. Portions of three documents were visible to video surveillance, and comparison to original documents showed that all three documents belong to agencies of the United States and are classified "Confidential." All three documents contain information relating to countries in the Asia-Pacific region near South Korea. According to classification markings on the documents, none of these documents may be released to South Korea.

On or about August 12, 1996, video surveillance detected Kim pick up unidentified documents from his desk and place them in is briefcase. Kim later left his office with that briefcase.

On or about August 14, 1996, mail coverage revealed that Kim mailed an 8X11 manila envelope postmarked in the Eastern District of Virginia addressed to Baek at Baek's Fall Church, VA address. The enveloped had KIM's name and home address on the return label. FBI personnel opened and searched the envelope, finding the three documents seen on KIM's desk on August 9, 1996. The classification markings had been removed from these documents. FBI personnel returned these documents to the envelope for delivery to Baek.

On or about August 17, 1996, electronic surveillance revealed that Baek called Kim at his residence, and left a message that he "truly gratefully and satisfactorily received the material that you sent me."

8/16/96 - Mailing of Documents
On or about August 14, 1996, video surveillance detected Kim printing numerous materials at his desk, and eventually placing them in his briefcase.

On or about August 16, 1996, mail coverage revealed that Kim mailed an 8X11 manila envelope postmarked from the Eastern District of Virginia addressed to Baek at Baek's Falls Church, VA address. The envelope had Kim's name and home address on the return label. FBI personnel searched the envelope, finding six documents belonging to agencies of the United States, all relating to countries and activities in the Asia-Pacific region near South Korea. The classification markings had been removed from these documents. Comparison to original documents shows that four of the documents are classified "Secret," and the other two unclassified. According to the classification markings, none of the four classified documents were releasable to South Korea. The documents were placed back in the envelope for delivery to Baek.

A note written in Korean was attached to one of the above documents. The note stated: "Captain Baek, used all the stamps, still have the envelopes. Thanks."

On or about August 21, 1996, electronic surveillance revealed that Baek called Kim at work and stated that he received the items. Kim stated that he was saving items for Baek.

8/28/96 - Mailing of Documents
On or about August 27, 1996, video surveillance of Kim's workspace revealed Kim printing numerous documents and placing them on a pile on his desk. Portions of 17 documents were visible to video surveillance. All of these documents were United States

agency documents relating to South Korea and other countries in the Asia-Pacific region.

On or about August 28, 1996, mail coverage revealed that Kim mailed an 8X11 manila envelope addressed to Baek at his Falls Church, VA residence. The return address label on the envelope had Kim's name and home address. FBI personnel searched the envelope, finding 19 documents. Seventeen of these documents appeared to be identical to those documents viewed by video surveillance on August 27, 1996. Comparison to original documents showed that all but four of the 19 documents are classified, many at the "Secret" level; according to the classification markings on the original documents, only 4 of the classified documents are releasable to South Korea. Classification headings had been removed from the classified documents. At the request of a U.S. agency, one of the documents was removed from the package, and the remaining 18 documents returned to the envelope for delivery for Baek.

On or about August 28, 1996, electronic surveillance revealed a telephone conversation between Kim and Baek. Kim confirmed that he had received the stamps and envelopes that Baek had sent him. Kim told Baek that he sent a high volume of "very hot items" Baek yesterday, and urged Baek to be very careful with the contents. Kim told Baek that he removed security markings on the documents by computer. Baek assured Kim that he is careful with the documents, shredding them after he translates them.

On or about August 31, 1996, electronic surveillance revealed that Baek contacted Kim and stated he had received the package.

9/6/96 - Mailing of Documents

On or about September 4, 1996, video surveillance of Kim's workspace revealed that Kim printed numerous documents on the office printer and placed them on his desk. Later, he placed these documents in his briefcase, and left the office with this briefcase. Portions of documents were visible to video surveillance, which revealed that the documents belonged to agencies of the United States. The documents related to South Korea and the Asia-Pacific region, and comparison to original documents revealed that all but one of the documents are classified, many at the "Secret" level. According to classification markings on the original documents, none of the documents were releasable to South Korea.

On or about September 6, 1996, mail coverage revealed that an 8X11 manila envelope addressed to Baek at Baek's address in Falls Church, VA, was received at a post office in Falls Church, VA. The return address label on the envelope had Kim's name and home address. FBI personnel opened and searched the envelope, finding eleven documents which were observed on Kim's desk on September 4, 1996. Classification markings had been removed from the documents. At the request of a U.S. agency, two documents were removed from the envelope. The remaining nine documents were placed back in the envelope for delivery to Baek.

Based on review of video surveillance, one of the documents that Kim printed on September 4, 1996 was not in the September 6, 1996 envelope. By comparing video surveillance to an original, I determined that this document belongs to an agency of the United States and is classified "Secret."

On or about September 7, 1996, surveillance at a golf course in Fort Meade, MD revealed that Kim, Baek, and two high ranking South Korean naval officials met and played golf together.

9/9/96 - Telefaxing of Document

On or about September 9, 1996, electronic surveillance revealed that Baek called Kim at Kim's office. Kim thanked Baek for his hospitality during the golf outing, and offered Baek information relating to the South Korean military, which Baek expressed an interest in receiving. A few minutes later, electronic surveillance revealed that a telefax of a United States agency document classified "Confidential" relating to South Korea was sent from Kim's office to Baek.

According to Department of the Navy officials, Kim has had no official duty nor liaison responsibilities relating to South Korea during the time period covered by this affidavit, and has not been authorized to disclose classified documents to South Korean officials. According to ONI regulations, Kim must report any "continuing association" with foreign nationals to his employer. According to ONI officials, Kim has not disclosed his association with Baek.

Based on surveillance, (it is known) that Kim normally drives between his home in the Eastern District of Virginia and his office in a car which, according to Department of Motor Vehicles, he owns. This car is a dark red 1987 Volvo, license plate BVY 893 VA. (It is planned) to search this vehicle while it is located in the Eastern District of Virginia.

Based on the above facts, there is probable cause to believe that Robert Chaegon Kim, an employee of any agency of the United States, has knowingly communicated classified information to an agent of a foreign government, the Republic of Korea, in violation of Title 50, United States Code Section 783(a).

(It was) asked that his affidavit with its accompanying warrants and complaint (not attached herein) be kept under seal until Kim's arrest on the morning of September 25, 1996, so that Kim will not be alerted to the searches before they occur.

From physical surveillance, It is known that Kim frequently leaves his home before 6 a.m. The plan is to arrest Kim after he has left his home within a mile of his home. Permission is asked to search his home immediately after his arrest to prevent any chance that the occupants of the home could become aware of the arrest and destroy evidence.

NOTE: On May 7, 1997, Robert Kim pleaded guilty to a low-level espionage charge. As part of a plea bargain, prosecutors dropped a more serious spying charge that carried a maximum life sentence. According to a federal grand jury indictment, Kim gave South Korea seven documents related to national defense. Six of the documents were classified Secret and one was Confidential. At the court hearing, Kim admitted passing Defense Department and Statement documents to South Korean Navy Captain Baek Dong-Il, an attaché at the South Korean Embassy who was later recalled to Seoul.

Robert Stephan Lipka

Robert Stephan Lipka, age 50, 17 Dublin Drive, Millersville, Pennsylvania, was arrested on 23 February 1996 without incident by Special Agents of the Federal Bureau of Investigation and charged with espionage. The complaint and warrant that was filed in the Eastern District of Pennsylvania today, is the first time in the history of this judicial district that anyone has been charged with espionage.

The complaint states that, between the years 1964 and 1974, Lipka conspired to deliver, communicate, and transmit to officers and agents of the Soviet Union information relating to the national defense. While Lipka was in the US Army, assigned to the National Security Agency (NSA) at Ft. Meade, Maryland, he was assigned to the Collections Bureau that has since been renamed the Priority Material Branch. His principal assignment was to remove classified NSA national defense documents from teleprinters and distribute them to the appropriate departments.

In an affidavit of probable cause accompanying the criminal complaint, the FBI alleges that Lipka often secured these classified documents on his person to escape detection from NSA security and used a common espionage technique known as a deaddrop to transfer these documents to the KGB and then retrieve payment at a prearranged site. The affidavit states that Lipka also possessed special spy cameras to clandestinely photograph sensitive documents.

Lipka left the military and moved to Lancaster, Pennsylvania, in August 1967, where he attended college at a local university. The affidavit stated that Lipka took NSA documents with him when he left his Army position and that he met with Soviet representatives as late as 1974.

UNITED STATES DISTRICT COURT EASTERN DISTRICT OF PENNSYLVANIA

UNITED STATES OF AMERICA
v.
ROBERT STEPHAN LIPKA,
A/K/A/ "ROOK"

Complainants's Statement of Facts Constituting the Offense or Violation

That, between in or around 1965 to in or around 1974, in Lancaster County, in the Eastern District of

Pennsylvania, and elsewhere, defendant ROBERT STEPHAN LIPKA, a/k/a "Rook," did unlawfully, knowingly and willfully conspire, combined, confederate and agree, with Peter Karl Fischer, Ingeborg Else Dora Fischer, and Artem Petrovich Shokin, who are not charged herein, and other persons known and unknown, to communicate, deliver, and transmit to the Soviet Union and to representatives, officers and agents thereof, information relating to the national defense, including but not limited to information directly concerning communications intelligence, with the intent and reason to believe that such information would be used to the injury of the United States and to the advantage of the Soviet Union, in violation of Title 18, United States Code, Section 794(c). Among the overt acts committed in furtherance of this conspiracy, in or around December 1968, after receiving a post card from a representative of the Soviet Union at his (Lipka's) residence, defendant LIPKA drove from Lancaster, in the Eastern District of Pennsylvania, to a location in the District to Maryland, to meet with a representative of the Soviet Union.

Affidavit Introduction: Deleted for brevity.

Robert Stephan Lipka and the National Security Agency (Highlights)

Robert Stephan Lipka was born on June 16, 1945, and enlisted in the U.S. Army on or about August 19, 1963. From October 1963 to January 1964, Lipka received Army training to be an intelligence analyst.

On December 30, 1963, Lipka was issued a "Top Secret" U.S. Government security clearance and received official authorization to have access to cryptographic U.S. government information.

On January 22, 1964, Lipka began working at NSA Headquarters at Fort Meade, Maryland.

From January 1964 to August 1967, Lipka worked in a NSA office which was known as the Collection Branch (CB) and was renamed the Priority Materials Branch (PMB) in October 1964.

From January 1964 to August 1967, the CB/PMB had two to four teleprinters dedicated to printing electrically transmitted classified reports. The CB/PMB also periodically received typewritten classified reports via courier from other DOD agencies and from other U.S. government agencies.

During this period, Lipka's principal assignment at CB/PMB was to remove the classified reports described above from the teleprinters and sort them for distribution to the appropriate NSA units. On occasion, he would also distribute the classified reports CB/PMB received via courier.

Lipka's military records show that in August 1967 he left active service and began residing in Lancaster, Pennsylvania.

Cooperating Witness

A cooperating witness (CW), advised s/he first met Lipka in 1965 and remained in frequent contact with him until the late 1970s. According to the CW, during the winter of 1966-67, Lipka admitted to the CW that he (Lipka) was taking things from NSA and selling them to the Russians. Lipka used the name "Ivan" to refer to his Russian contact.

The CW accompanied Lipka to a restaurant in Maryland during January 1967, where he delivered a package for "Ivan." Lipka told the CW he had placed a package in the toilet tank in the men's room. After placing the package, Lipka and the CW proceeded to a wooded area that night to retrieve a package of money. Lipka searched for the package but could not find it. He became frightened and they left the park hurriedly. The CW also remembers accompanying Lipka to other parks and fishing areas where Lipka would place or retrieve packages, usually wrapped in plastic and bound with tape.

In the summer of 1966, Lipka showed the CW three cameras, which he described as being used by spies to copy information. One was operated by being rolled over a document. The other two were very small; one was only an inch in height. At the time, Lipka told the CW that he had the cameras in connection with a NSA security project. (Note: There are no NSA or Army records of Lipka ever being assigned to any project that would require the use of these cameras.)

The CW stated that, after retrieving envelopes containing the money he was paid by the Russians for the NSA material he passed, Lipka would often count it in CW's presence. The CW recalled that Lipka received approximately $500 in U.S. currency as payment, except for two occasions when he received $1000.

The CW described how, sometime in December 1968, after Lipka had moved to Lancaster, Lipka told the CW that the Russians had contacted him via post card and that he was considering meeting with them. Lipka was no longer working at NSA, but he told the CW he had retained NSA documents in order to keep his options open.

A few days later, the CW and Lipka traveled to a store in Maryland, where they were required to be at a specific time. Lipka took some NSA documents with him. At the store, Lipka left the CW alone for a few minutes and then returned, telling the CW that he had met with the Russians but that no agreement had been reached.

The CW advised that Lipka's recognition signal or code word that he used in communicating with the Russians was *"Rook."* Lipka said he had an emergency plan and that if he were every caught, the Russians would get him out.

Artem Shokin and the Fischers' (Highlights)

Peter Karl Fischer and his wife, Ingeborg Else Dora Fischer (nee Ziegler), lawfully entered the United States from Canada to reside in Buffalo, NY, in February 1965. They moved from Buffalo to Philadelphia in 1966, and then to Upper Darby, in the Eastern District of Pennsylvania. They both claimed they were born in 1929, in what later became East Germany.

According to official U.S. records, Artem Petrovich Shokin, a citizen of the Soviet Union, was employed by the UN Secretariat at UN Headquarters in New York City from 1965 to 1970.

On April 13, 1968, the Fischers traveled by car to New York City where they delivered unidentified items through use of a KGB dead drop near Grant's Tomb. Later that day, Shokin traveled to the same area, ostensibly to service the dead drop. The Fischers were later heard in a conversation in which they discussed their mission and congratulated themselves on their success.

Other evidence suggests the Fischers were acting at the behest of the KGB. A search of their apartment disclosed two short-wave radios. An examination of bank records on six occasions between August 1965 and November 1966 showed deposits to the Fischers' U.S. joint bank accounts from Switzerland. The Fischers' recorded conversations also revealed an anti-U.S. and pro-Soviet bias, and the use of terminology commonly associated with Soviet communism. This activity lead investigators to the conclusion that Peter Fischer was a KGB illegal officer posing as a German immigrant to the United States, and that Ingeborg Fischer was his knowing and willing assistant. It was further concluded that Shokin was a KGB officer operating under cover of an employee of the UN Secretariat.

The Fischers' Contact with Lipka

Based on recorded conversations and an analysis of travel patterns, there is strong evidence the Fischers made contact with Lipka on April 21, 1968. Six days later, a piece of paper in Fischers' apartment was annotated with the world "ROECK." There is no German word spelled R-O-E-C-K., but it could more or less be pronounced as "rook." As noted above, the CW stated that Lipka's codeword signals was *Rook.*"

Undercover Investigation of Lipka

Between May 12 and December 8, 1993, an undercover FBI special agent, posing as "Segey Nikitin," an official of Russian military intelligence, had four meetings with Lipka and several instances of written correspondence.

Lipka was initially very uneasy with Nikitin because the special agent didn't know Lipka liked the game of chess or his code name. Before Nikitin was totally accepted, Lipka tested him in several areas involving his case history and past association with the KGB. The special agent was finally accepted, saying that the reason for his unfamiliarity with Lipka was because the case had been transferred from the KGB to the GRU.

Over time, Lipka and Nikitin discussed the circumstances and reasons for Lipka's breaks in contacts with the KGB, his access to and passage of materials to the Soviets, and his use of dead drops and meetings with his Soviet handlers.

Lipka pressed Nikitin for money for his prior espionage work, which he claimed he didn't receive due to missed drops. Lipka also said he still had documents he had taken from NSA and agreed to send them to Nikitin. He later said he took the NSA materials with him after he stopped working there in 1967.

The two men then began communicating through an accommodation address. Lipka was referred to as *en passant* (a chess term) and Nikitin was *Checkmate*. Lipka later told Nikitin he would refer to him as *"Carl Marx,"* a variation on the initial letters of the word checkmate. Lipka later signed a letter to Nikitin as *"Enrico Passante,"* a variation on the initial letters of Lipka's parole. The term "coins" was used in reference to the NSA material. Lipka was paid $5,000 and told that additional payments would be made.

Throughout their meetings and correspondence, Lipka expressed mistrust and doubts about Nikitin, and Lipka refused on several occasions to comply with instructions, discuss his training, or clear dead drops in a timely manner. He also professed to a memory problem and frequently claimed he was underpaid for his efforts.

Lipka's final meeting with Nikitin was on December 8 1993, in Lancaster. Before this final meeting ended, Nikitin gave Lipka emergency contact instructions with a new accommodation name, address and telephone number, and $5000 as the balance due for his past espionage activities.

On September 15, 1994, the FBI mailed Lipka a copy of *The First Directorate*, by former KGB Major General Oleg Kalugin. At page 82 *et seq.*, this book implicates Lipka in its detailed description of espionage committed by a "young soldier at NSA" who provided "reams of top secret material" to the KGB in the mid-1960s, prior to leave to go to college. In the letter, "Carl Marx" advised Lipka that if the need arises, he should activate the instructions for an emergency contact.

Conclusion

Based on the foregoing, the U.S. Government believed there was probable cause to believe that ROBERT STEPHAN LIPKA violated Title 28, United States Code, Section 794(c), conspiracy to commit espionage, as charged in the Criminal Complaint.

Note: On 23 May 1997, Robert S. Lipka pleaded guilty to one count of conspiracy to committee espionage and was sentenced to 18 years in prison and a fine of $10,000. The sentence came in a bargain for Lipka's plea of selling top-secret NSA documents for Soviet agents 30 years ago.

Phillip Tyler Seldon

IN THE UNITED STATES DISTRICT COURT FOR THE EASTERN DISTRICT OF VIRGINIA

Alexandria Division

UNITED STATES OF AMERICA

v.   CRIMINAL NO. 96-305-A

PHILLIP TYLER SELDON,

Defendant.

CRIMINAL INFORMATION

The United States Attorney Charges That:

from on or about November 6, 1992 through on or about July 10, 1993, in the Eastern District of Virginia and elsewhere, PHILLIP TYLER SELDON, then an officer and employee of the United States and the Department of Defense, did unlawfully, willfully and knowingly conspire, combine, confederate and agree with an officer in the air force of El Salvador to communicate to a person whom SELDON knew and had reason to know was an agent and representative of a foreign government, information which had been classified by the President as affecting the security of the United States, with defendant SELDON knowing and having reason to known such information to been so classified, and without defendant SELDON having been specifically authorized by the President and the head of the Department of Defense to make such disclosure of such information, in violation of Title 50, United States Code, section 783(b).

IN THE UNITED STATES DISTRICT COURT FOR THE EASTERN DISTRICT OF VIRGINIA

Alexandria Division

UNITED STATES OF AMERICA

v.   CRIMINAL NO. 96   -

PHILLIP TYLER SELDON,

Defendant.

STATEMENT OF FACTS

1. On or about May 14, 1983, defendant PHILLIP TYLER SELDON was commissioned as an officer in the U.S. Army.

2. On each of three occasions, on or about February 5, 1986, on or about November 30, 1987, and on or about July 17, 1992, defendant SELDON executed a Classified Information Nondisclosure Agreement (CINA) in which he acknowledged receiving a security briefing concerning (a) the nature and protection of classified information, and (b) the procedures to be followed in ascertaining whether or persons to whom he might contemplate disclosing classified information have been approved access to it. In each CINA defendant SELDON further acknowledged that he would never divulge classified information unless he had officially verified that the recipient had been properly authorized by the United States government to receive such information, or unless he (defendant SELDON) had been given prior written notice of such authorization from the U.S. government. In each CINA defendant SELDON further acknowledges that he was aware and had been advised that the unauthorized disclosure of classified information may constitute a violation of Title 50, United States Code, Section 783(b).

3. From on or bout July 2, 1987, through on or about May 25, 1994, Defendant SELDON held a "Top Secret" U.S. government security clearance.

Manner and Means

1. It was part of the conspiracy that defendant SELDON would use his authorized access to classified information to generate and gather classified documents in his office located in the Pentagon.

2. It was further a part of the conspiracy that defendant SELDON would remove classified documents from the Pentagon.

3. It was further a part of the conspiracy that defendant SELDON would deliver classified documents to an officer in the air force of the El Salvador through use of the U.S. Postal Service and by personally delivering the classified documents to the El Salvadoran air force officer in El Salvador.

Overt Acts

In furtherance of the conspiracy and in order to effect the objects and purposes thereof, defendant SELDON performed the following overt acts in the Eastern District of Virginia and elsewhere:

1. On or about November 6, 1992, in the Pentagon, within the Eastern District of Virginia, defendant SELDON mailed a package containing classified documents to El Salvador, with the intent that such documents would be delivered to an officer in the air force of El Salvador.

2. On or about May 31, 1993, in El Salvador, defendant SELDON personally delivered an envelope containing classified documents to an officer in the air force of El Salvador.

3. On or about July 10, 1993, in Stafford County, within the Eastern District of Virginia, defendant SELDON mailed a package containing classified documents to El Salvador, with the intent that such documents would be delivered to a officer in the air force of El Salvador.

All in violation of Title 18, United States Code, Section 371

/s/ 8/7/96 by AUSA Robert C. Chesnut.

4. From on or about February 22, 1991, through on or about July 6, 1992, defendant SELDON served with the U.S. Army in El Salvador. While in El Salvador, defendant SELDON came to know a certain officer in the air force of El Salvador.

5. On or about July 7, 1992, defendant SELDON began serving with the U.S. Army in the Pentagon as a military assistant to a senior executive of the Department of Defense.

6. A few months later, the El Salvadoran air force officer telephoned defendant SELDON from El Salvador and asked defendant SELDON to provide him with certain information that the air force officer believed defendant SELDON had access to pursuant to his new job duties. On several other occasions before on or about July 10, 1993, the El Salvadoran officer and defendant SELDON had additional telephone conversations in which the El Salvadoran officer made additional requests for information from defendant SELDON.

7. On or about November 6, 1992, defendant SELDON mailed a package containing, among other things, an envelope in which were enclosed several documents containing classified information originating from the Central Intelligence Agency and/or the Department of Defense. Defendant SELDON had obtained the documents through his employment at the Pentagon. Defendant SELDON mailed the package from a post office in the Pentagon in the Eastern District of Virginia. The package was received in El Salvador by a U.S. official who, on SELDON's instructions, subsequently transferred it to the El Salvadoran air force officer, the U.S. official now knowing the package contained classified documents.

8. On or about May 31, 1993, defendant SELDON traveled to El Salvador, met with the El Salvadoran air force officer and delivered to him an envelope enclosing several documents containing classified information originating from the Central Intelligence Agency and/or the Department of Defense. Defendant SELDON had also obtained these documents by virtue of his employment at the Pentagon.

9. On or about July 10, 1993, defendant SELDON mailed a package containing, among other things, an envelope containing several documents containing classified information originating from the Central Intelligence Agency and/or the Department of Defense. Again, defendant SELDON had obtained the documents through his employment at the Pentagon. Defendant SELDON mailed the package from a post office in Stafford, Virginia, in the Eastern District of Virginia. The package was received in El Salvador by a U.S. official who, on SELDON's instructions, subsequently transferred it to the El Salvadoran air force officer, the U.S. official now knowing the package contained classified documents.

10. On at least one occasion, the El Salvadoran air force officer, upon receiving classified documents from defendant SELDON, provided the documents to other officers in the El Salvadoran air force. SELDON was unaware of this transfer.

11. The United States learned of the criminal conduct when SELDON applied for another position with the United States which required a polygraph examination as a prerequisite to employment. Over a period of time and in response to a series of questioning, SELDON disclosed his transmittal of classified documents, which the United States confirmed through mailing records and interviews with individuals in El Salvador.

12. While admitting to the offense conducted, SELDON has voluntarily reviewed numerous documents, and identified documents that he believes he transmitted to the El Salvadoran officer. Many of these documents were classified, and some were classified "Secret." SELDON identified one document, which was classified "Top Secret," as a document that he believes that he may have passed. However, he cannot specifically recall passing this document, and is unsure that he passed it. The parties agree that the United States cannot prove beyond a reasonable doubt that any document classified "Top Secret" was passed, but the parties agree that documents classified "Secret" and below were passed.

All of the above described actions of defendant SELDON were performed knowingly and willfully, not by accident or mistake. Had this case gone to trial, the United States would have proven SELDON's illegal conduct beyond a reasonable doubt.

The Nicholson Chronology

June 1994: Stationed in Malaysia, Nicholson begins his espionage career for the Russians. Just prior to his return to the United States, he has several meetings with his KGB handlers. Immediately after these meetings, he deposits $12,000 to his credit union account in Oregon.

December 1994: Nicholson takes a three-week vacation to Asia. During and after the trip, he deposits money into his account and pays off credit card debts; the amount totals $28,000.

June-July 1995: Nicholson takes another Asia vacation and shows $24,000 in unexplained deposits and payments.

October 1995: Nicholson's polygraph examinations shows deception to questions of unauthorized foreign contacts.

December 1995: Nicholson takes a Christmas vacation in Thailand and again $27,000 shows up in his bank account.

January 1996: A CIA internal investigation focuses on Nicholson. FBI agents assigned to CIA Hqs detect a pattern of foreign travel and unexplained income.

March 1996: A Russian intelligence officer informs an FBI agent that the Russian Government has issued a worldwide task to obtain information on terrorism by Chechnya rebels.

April 1996: Nicholson, who is an instructor at a CIA training facility, attempts to obtain information on Chechnya although he has no need to know.

June 1996: FBI has Nicholson under surveillance. Vacationing in Singapore, he is observed entering a Russian diplomatic vehicle. Following his vacation, he gives his son $12,000 to buy a new car and distributes another $20,000 for purchases, credit payments, and savings.

July 1996: Nicholson is assigned to the Counterterrorism Center at CIA Hqs. An audit of his computer use shows him searching databases not related to his job. He is listed as a surfer.

1 August 1996: Nicholson mails an envelope with a false return address and a greeting card inside with an alias name. The FBI believes he was signaling the KGB that he had a new assignment at CIA Hqs.

11 August 1996: FBI agents search Nicholson's Chevy van. His laptop computer hard drive is analyzed along with a diskette. Both are loaded with classified documents.

23 September 1996: Nicholson is caught photographing documents by a hidden camera in his office.

9 October 1996: Nicholson is observed using a mail drop to signal a meeting in Switzerland in late November with his Russian handlers.

23 October 1996: An FBI search of Nicholson's residence fails to uncover any new evidence.

3 November 1996: A search of Nicholson's office at CIA by FBI agents turns up 40 documents on Russia, none of which were pertinent to his work.

12 November 1996: Nicholson is again observed photographing documents in his office.

16 November 1996: The FBI arrests Nicholson at Dulles International Airport.

Respectfully submitted,

HELEN F. FAHEY
UNITED STATES ATTORNEY

BY: Robert C. Chesnut
    Assistant United States Attorney
    Michael C. Liebman, Trial Attorney
    Internal Security Section
    Criminal Division
    U.S. Department of Justice

SEEN AND AGREE:
Phillip Tyler Seldon
Defendant

Joseph J. Bernard, Esquire
Counsel for the Defendant

(All signed: 8/7/96)

PLEA AGREEMENT HIGHLIGHTS

1. SELDON agrees to waive indictment and plead guilty to a one count criminal information filed with this agreement. The maximum penalty for this offense is five years of imprisonment, a fine of $250,00, full restitution, a special assessment, and two years of supervised release.

2. The Court may order the defendant to pay a fine sufficient to reimburse the government for the costs of imprisonment, term of release and probation, if so ordered.

3. The defendant is aware that his sentence will be imposed in accordance with the Sentencing Guidelines and Policy Statements concerning what sentence the defendant will receive. The defendant waives his right to appeal the sentence.

4. The United States will not further criminally prosecute defendant for this specific conduct

5. The defendant represents to the Court that he is satisfied that his attorney has rendered effective assistance.

6. The defendant adopts the Statement of Facts and agrees that the facts therein are accurate in every respect.

Harold J. Nicholson

(Excerts from the Affidavit in support of complaint, arrest warrant and search warrants update)

United States v. Harold J. Nicholson

As more fully described below, Harold James Nicholson, an American citizen and employee of the Central Intelligence Agency (CIA), has been acting clandestinely, corruptly and illegally as an agent of the *Russia*n Federation Foreign Intelligence Service, Sluzhba Vneshney Razvedki Rossii, commonly referred to within the U.S. intelligence community as SVRR. The SVRR is the direct successor to the Committee For State Security of the Union of Soviet Socialist Republics (hereafter USSR), known as the KGB. By his actions, Nicholson has committed violations of 18 U.S.C. 794(a) and (c), that is, with reason to believe that it would be used to the injury of the United States and the advantage of a foreign nation, he has unlawfully and knowingly conspired to communicate, transmit and deliver to representatives of a foreign government, specifically the Russian Federation, information relating to the national defense of the United States. The investigation reveals that the Russian Federation has paid Nicholson over $100,000 since June, 1994 for his unlawful acts.

Information in this affidavit is based on my personal knowledge and on information provided to me by other law enforcement officers. This affidavit also relies on information provided by the CIA, which has cooperated with the investigation. This affidavit is not intended to be an exhaustive summary of the investigation against Nicholson, but is for the purpose of setting out probable cause in support of:
. The U.S. makes no promise

   a. A complaint charging Harold J. Nicholson; with a violation of title 18, United States code section 794(c) (conspiracy to commit espionage);

   b. An arrest warrant for Harold J. Nicholson;

   c. A search warrant for Nicholson's residence at 5764 Burke Towne Court, Burke, Virginia, in the Eastern District of Virginia;

   d. A search warrant for Nicholson's workspace, located in room 6E2911, Old Hq. Building, CIA Headquarters, Langley, Va;

e. A search warrant for Nicholson's vehicle, a 1994 *Chevrolet Lumina* sports van, Virginia license plate 8888BAT;

f. A search warrant for a safe deposit box in the name of Harold J. Nicholson, Box #417, located at Selco Credit Union in Springfield, Oregon.

g. A search warrant for any luggage that Nicholson may be carrying or may check at *Dulles Airport* on November 16, 1996, the day of his arrest.

Background

Harold James Nicholson, was born on November 17, 1950, in Woodburn, Oregon. He is divorced, and has three children. Nicholson entered on duty as an employee of the CIA on October 20, 1980. According to CIA records, Nicholson took the oath of office on January 26, 1982, where he stated that "I will support and defend the Constitution of the United States against all enemies foreign and domestic; that I will bear true faith and allegiance to the same; that I take this obligation freely, without any mental reservation or purpose of evasion; and that I will well and faithfully discharge the duties of the office on which I am about to enter. so help me God."

I have reviewed Nicholson's CIA personnel and security files. These files reveal that throughout Nicholson's employment with the CIA, he has held a "Top Secret" security clearance, and had regular, frequent access to sensitive classified information. I have also reviewed a document signed by Harold J. Nicholson entitled "sensitive compartmented information nondisclosure agreement." In this document, Nicholson acknowledges that he has been granted access to sensitive compartmented information (SCI) as part of his employment, that any unauthorized disclosure of such highly classified information is a violation of federal criminal law. and that any unauthorized disclosure of SCI information could irreparably injure the United States or provide an advantage to a foreign nation. In this signed document, Nicholson agrees that he will never divulge classified information to anyone not authorized to receive it without prior written authorization from the United States.

In his career with the CIA, Nicholson has been assigned duties throughout the world. He has worked for the CIA as an operations officer specializing in intelligence operations against foreign intelligence services, including the intelligence services of the USSR and later, the Russian Federation. Specifically, from 1982-85, Nicholson worked for the CIA in Manila, where he had sustained, direct contacts with targeted Soviet officials. Nicholson worked for the CIA in Bangkok from 1985-87, and in Tokyo from 1987-89. From 1990-92, Nicholson was the CIA Chief of Station in Bucharest, Romania. From 1992 until 1994, Nicholson was the Deputy Chief of Station/operations officer in Kuala Lumpur, Malaysia, where, among other duties, he met with and targeted for recruitment Russian intelligence officers. From 1994 until July, 1996, Nicholson worked as an instructor at the classified CIA special training center ("STC") in the Eastern District of Virginia, teaching CIA trainees intelligence tradecraft. In July, 1996, Nicholson was assigned as a branch chief in the Counterterrorism Center, Directorate of Operations, at CIA headquarters in Langley, Virginia. this position carries a pay grade GS-15, and his current salary is approximately $73,000; it is the highest pay grade Nicholson has held during his CIA employment.

According to CIA records, Nicholson owns and currently resides in a townhouse at 5674 Burke Towne Court, Burke, Virginia, in the Eastern District of Virginia, Virginia department of motor vehicle records show that a *Chevrolet Lumina* sport van, Virginia plate no. 8888BAT, is registered to Harold J. Nicholson.

Harold J. Nicholson

The Investigation–Polygraphs

On or about October 16, 1995, and October 20, 1995, Nicholson underwent polygraph examinations administered by CIA polygraphers as part of his routine security update. A computerized review of the examination results indicated a .97 (out of 1.0) probability of deception on two questions: (1) are you hiding involvement with a foreign intelligence service? and (2) have you had unauthorized contact with a foreign intelligence service? During one the examinations, a CIA polygrapher deemed Nicholson's response "inconclusive" to the following question: "are you concealing contact with any foreign nationals"?

On or about December 4, 1995, Nicholson underwent a third polygraph examination administered by a CIA polygrapher. A computerized review of the examination revealed an .88 probability of deception on the following questions: (1) since 1990, have you had contact with a foreign intelligence service that you are trying to hide from the CIA? and (2) are you trying to hide any contact with a foreign intelligence service since 1990? The CIA examiner noted that Nicholson appeared to be trying to manipulate the test by taking deep breaths on the control questions, which stopped after a verbal warning.

By reviewing CIA records and Nicholson's frequent flyer records and financial records from 1994 through early 1996, the FBI uncovered a pattern of twice yearly foreign travel, followed by unexplained deposits and payments to Nicholson's accounts.

June 1994 Meeting with Russian and Unexplained Money

According to CIA records, Nicholson was assigned to Kuala Lumpur, Malaysia during 1992-94 as Deputy Chief of Station/operations officer. CIA records show that Nicholson met with an officer of the Russian Intelligence Service SVRR in Kuala Lumpur on four occasions during Nicholson's final months there; three of these meetings took place in the Russian Embassy in Kuala Lumpur. These meetings were authorized by the CIA and reported by Nicholson. On June 30, 1994, one day after Nicholson's last reported meeting with the SVRR officer, financial records show that $12,000 was wired into Nicholson's savings account #000026-1759/01 at Selco Credit Union, Eugene, Oregon.

Nicholson left Kuala Lumpur on July 5, 1994, and returned to the United States. The FBI has been unable to trace the source of this money to any legitimate source of income.

December 1994 Foreign Travel and Unexplained Money

According to Nicholson's travel records, Nicholson left the United States on personal travel on or about December 9, 1994. According to an itinerary he provided to the CIA, Nicholson planned to travel to London, New Delhi, Bangkok and Kuala Lumpur. Nicholson left Kuala Lumpur on December 28, 1994, returning to the United States on December 30, 1994.

According to financial records, after arriving in Kuala Lumpur, Nicholson made a $9,000 wire deposit from Malaysia to his Selco checking account #000026-1759/10, and a $6,000 cash payment to his American Express account #3728-128689-71001. Almost immediately after returning to the U.S., on December 31, 1994, Nicholson entered the Selco Credit Union in Eugene, Oregon, and, using 130 $100 bills, paid off a $3,000 loan at Selco (loan #86, Volkswagen), and paid $10,019.35 toward his Selco Visa account. The FBI has been unable to trace the source of the money in these transactions to any legitimate source of income.

June/July 1995 Foreign Travel and Unexplained Money

CIA leave records show that Nicholson took annual leave from June 15, 1995 through July 14, 1995. According to an itinerary Nicholson provided to the CIA, Nicholson left the United States on June 16, 1995, for Singapore, then traveled to Kuala Lumpur, where he stayed from June 17 through July 1, 1995. Nicholson returned to the United States through Hong Kong on July 1, 1995.

Analysis of financial records created during and shortly after the trip show the following financial transactions totaling $23,815.21 involving accounts in the name of Harold J. Nicholson and joint accounts he holds with his children. The FBI has been unable to trace these financial deposits and payments, which are set out below, to any legitimate source of income.

Date	Amount	Institution	Account
6/21/95	$6,300	American Express	3728-128689-71001
6/30/95	$1,000	Selco Credit Union money market	000026-1759/20
6/30/95	$4,715.21	Selco Credit Union Visa	4202-51000-261-7591
6/30/95	$1,000	Selco Credit Union	000029-1248
6/30/95	$1,000	Selco Credit Union	000034-2527
6/30/95	$1,000	Selco Credit Union	000029-1249
7/10/95	$1,000	Selco Credit Union checking	000026-1759/10
7/10/95	$1,000	Selco Credit Union money market	000026-1759/20
7/17/95	$3,000	Central Fidelity	7922119540
7/17/95	$1,000	Central Fidelity	7922119540
7/20/95	$1,400	USAA Mutual Fund	52900-468973
7/20/95	$1,400	USAA Mutual Fund	54900-278125

December 1995 Foreign Travel and Unexplained Money

According to CIA leave records and Nicholson's travel records, Nicholson left the United States for personal travel on December 18, 1995, and arrived in Bangkok, Thailand on December 20, 1995. Nicholson stayed in Bangkok until December 24, 1995, when he left for Phuket, Thailand. Nicholson returned to the United States on December 30, 1995.

Analysis of Nicholson's financial records during and shortly after this trip show the following financial transactions involving accounts in the name of Harold J. Nicholson totaling $26,900 which the FBI has been unable to trace to any legitimate source of income.

date	amount	institution	account
1/3/96	$4,000	Central Fidelity	7922119540
1/3/96	$4,400	Central Fidelity	7922119540
1/4/96	$3,000	Central Fidelity	7922119540
1/5/96	$1,900	Central Fidelity	7922119540
1/8/96	$1,000	USAA Mutual Fund	52900-468973
1/8/96	$1,000	USAA Mutual Fund	54900-278125
1/11/96	$900	Central Fidelity	7922119540
1/16/96	$2,000	Central Fidelity	7922119540
1/17/96	$1,400	Central Fidelity	7922119540
1/22/96	$900	Central Fidelity	7922119540
2/6/96	$1000	Central Fidelity	7922119540

June 1996 Meeting with Russians in Singapore and Cash Payment

On or about March 17, 1996, FBI officials were contacted by an SVRR liaison officer who asked for information about Chechnyan terrorism. The SVRR liaison officer added that his request was part of a global tasking by SVRR Headquarters to gather information about Chechnya.

On or about April 26, 1996, Nicholson traveled from his duty station at the CIA's special training center to CIA Headquarters in the Eastern District of Virginia. While at CIA headquarters, he asked several CIA employees for background information about Chechnya; Nicholson claimed that he needed the information for a training exercise at the training facility. However, according to CIA officials at the training facility, training exercises ongoing at that time were developed months in advance, and no training was planned or conducted regarding Chechnyan matters. Requests for changes to the exercises must be submitted to a board for review, and Nicholson did not submit any proposed changes.

According to CIA records, Nicholson left the United States on personal travel on June 25, 1996, arriving in Singapore on June 26, 1996. While Nicholson's checked luggage was searched and no evidence found, the FBI was unable to search Nicholson's carry on luggage, which included a camera bag.

At the time of his travel, Nicholson had applied for a position as CIA chief of station in a foreign country, and was being actively considered for that post.

Upon arrival in Singapore on June 26, 1996, Nicholson checked into the garden wing at the Shangri-La Hotel, where the cost of a room exceeds $300 per night.

Surveillance of Nicholson in Singapore on June 27, 1996, revealed that Nicholson left his hotel with his camera bag at approximately 10:11 a.m. for about four hours. During this four hour period, Nicholson made a "surveillance detection run," that is, a trip designed to detect surveillance. For example, Nicholson was observed taking numerous countersurveillance measures, such as backtracking his steps, watching glass panels of shops to look behind him, then entering and immediately exiting a subway station. During this excursion, Nicholson made no purchases and took no photographs.

Surveillance of Nicholson later on June 27, 1996, in Singapore revealed that Nicholson left his hotel with his camera bag at approximately 6:15 p.m., and retraced part of his route from earlier in the day, finally arriving at a subway station at 7:15 pm. Nicholson remained on the elevated area of the station until all other passengers had gone to the station's lower level. Nicholson then came down the escalator and sat on a stone seat at the end of the station near a taxi stand. After a few minutes, Nicholson got up and went back into the main concourse area of the station. While walking through the concourse area, he was met by a Caucasian male. The two men walked together toward a taxi stand. A car pulled up to the taxi stand. The trunk of the car opened, and Nicholson placed his camera bag in the trunk. Nicholson then got into the back seat of the vehicle. The vehicle bore diplomatic license plates which are registered to the Russian embassy in Singapore. The vehicle left the area. This meeting with Russian nationals was not authorized, nor did Nicholson report it to the CIA as required by agency regulations.

The next morning, on or about June 28, 1996, surveillance detected Nicholson leave his hotel and go to an American Express travel services center in Singapore, where he made an $8,300 cash payment to his American Express account. Several days later, Nicholson left Singapore for Bangkok, paying his $1,679.59 bill in cash.

On or about July 2, 1996, Nicholson left Bangkok for Honolulu with a female companion. In an August 21, 1996 letter to the CIA, Nicholson identified this woman as a foreign national currently residing in Thailand whom he intends to marry. According to a receipt found in a car search described below, Nicholson made a $762.93 cash payment to the Hanalei Bay Resort in Hawaii on July 5, 1996.

Records of Nicholson's financial transactions during and immediately after this Singapore trip reveal approximately $20,000 in purchases, deposits and payments. In addition, electronic surveillance has detected a telephone conversation between Nicholson and an acquaintance indicating that Nicholson gave his son approximately $12,000 to purchase a new car. I have seen a cash receipt found in Harold J. Nicholson's van dated July 12, 1996, issued to his son for $12,377.50 cash.

date	amount	institution	account
6/28/96	$8,300	American Express	3728-128689-71001
7/1/96	$ 820.58	Overseas Union Bank purchase gold coins	
7/1/96	$1,679.59	Shangri La Hotel	
7/5/96	$ 762.93	Hanalei Bay Resort	
7/8/96	$1,000	Selco Credit Union	000029-1248
7/8/96	$1,000	Selco Credit Union	000034-2527
7/14/96	$ 120	Dulles Airport parking	
7/29/96	$5,000	Selco Credit Union	000026-1759/10

Nicholson's Move to CIA Headquarters

On or about July 16, 1996, Nicholson reported to his new position at CIA headquarters in the Counterterrorism Center. Nicholson had applied for several foreign postings, including the chief of station position discussed above, all of which were denied.

On or about July 19, 1996, an audit of CIA computer information revealed that Nicholson was using his computer to conduct searches in CIA databases for information using the following key words:"Russia(n)" and "Chechnya." As a result of Nicholson's use of these key words to conduct searches, CIA cables, reports, and documents containing either of those key words would be routed to his computer where he could read them and print them. According to CIA officials, Nicholson has no need for such materials in his present position.

The audit also revealed that Nicholson attempted to access CIA databases that he had no authorization to access, including two attempts to access Central Eurasian Division databases which would contain information on Russia. This unauthorized activity led the CIA computer security personnel to list Nicholson as a "surfer."

On or about August 1, 1996, surveillance detected Nicholson approach a mailbox at 8283 Greensboro Drive, Tyson's Corner, in the Eastern District of Virginia. A sealed Hallmark greeting card envelope containing a postcard was subsequently retrieved from the mailbox A return address of 2206 Pimmit Run, Falls Church, 22041 was hand-printed on the envelope. Both the envelope and the postcard carried oversized commemorative stamps with a face value on $1, an amount in excess of the necessary postage. The postcard, which was addressed to a post office box in a foreign country, contained the following text:

Dear J. F.,

Just wanted to let you know that unfortunately I will not be in your neighbor as expected. Priorities at the home office resulted in my assignment to the management position there. Some travel to your general vicinity to visit field offices will occur, but not for more than a few days at a time. Still, the work at the home office should prove very beneficial - I know you would find it very attractive. I look forward to a possible ski vacation this winter. Will keep you informed. Until then, your friend,

Nevil R. Strachey

P.S. I am fine.

Investigation at 2206 Pimmit Run, Falls Church, Virginia, revealed no one at this address named Nevil R. Strachey. The zip code 22041 is not accurate for 2206 Pimmit Run, Falls Church. No listing for Nevil R. Strachey was found in telephone directories for Northern Virginia, the District of Columbia, Prince George's and Montgomery County (MD).

(It is believed) the foreign post office box to which the postcard was mailed is an "accommodation address." An accommodation address is a prearranged address where an intelligence officer can receive mail clandestinely from an agent. The accommodation address itself may be serviced by an intermediary. This post office box appears to be the method that Nicholson uses to communicate with his SVRR handlers. The contents of the postcard appear to inform the SVRR that Nicholson did not get the particular chief of station foreign posting that he had sought, but instead got a management position at CIA Headquarters.

Classified Documents Recovered From Nicholson's Notebook Computer

On or about August 11, 1996, the FBI conducted a search of a 1994 Chevrolet Lumina sports van which is registered to Nicholson; surveillance and DMV records confirm that this is Nicholson's only vehicle. In addition to cash receipts confirming some of the above financial transactions, the FBI discovered a personally-owned notebook computer in the van. An analysis of the hard drive showed that it contained numerous CIA classified documents relating to Russia. All of these files had been deleted from program directories, which in my training and experience indicates that they had already been copied on to a disk and transmitted to Russian Intelligence. This is corroborated by the fact that the original classified documents are all dated prior to Nicholson's June 1996 trip to Singapore. While the files had been deleted, the FBI recovered certain files and fragments of files from the notebook computer's hard drive. A brief summary of some of these documents follows:

a. A fragment recovered by the FBI describes the planned assignment of a CIA officer to a position in Moscow. Nicholson trained this officer at a CIA training facility. The text of the fragment includes the statement "(comment: please see biographic profile prepared previously on (name of officer) as well as updated assignment listings provided separately." According to the CIA, information about this officer's assignment was classified "Secret." The assignment was intended to be a covered slot, and the officer was trained in the use of a full range of intelligence collecting techniques. Collection targets included, but were not limited to, military preparedness of the Russian Federation, the Russian Federation's knowledge of U.S. national defense plans, and other important foreign intelligence and counterintelligence matters. The disclosure of this officer could have led to the losses of human sources and caused serious damage to U.S. intelligence capabilities. Further, the fragment indicates that Nicholson has provided the SVRR with biographic information and assignment listings of CIA case officers. This is confirmed by the fact that the hard drive also contained biographic information about CIA employees who were at the training facility during Nicholson's tenure there. Nicholson's position as a staff instructor at the CIA's special training center gave Nicholson access to highly sensitive information, including access to the biographical information and assignments for every CIA case officer trained during his two year tenure there. As a result of this disclosure, it will be difficult, if not impossible, for the CIA to place some of these newly trained case officers in certain sensitive foreign postings for the rest of their careers. Further, Nicholson communicated with other case officers who were instructors at the center, and may have heard descriptions of their work as part of training. The methods of training, and the techniques taught to future case officers, would be valuable information for foreign intelligence agencies.

b. A document concerning a closed briefing on Russian recruitment pitches to CIA case officers in the field. A CIA official has told the FBI that there was a briefing concerning recruitment pitches by Russian intelligence officers and that the briefing was classified "Secret." A CIA official said that information concerning how many recruitment pitches have been reported by CIA officers to CIA headquarters is classified "Secret."

c. A document concerning information on Chechnya. The information was a near verbatim copy of an actual "Secret" CIA report regarding Chechnya that had been provided to Nicholson by CIA officials. I believe that Nicholson gathered the Chechnyan information found on his computer in response to clandestine tasking from the SVRR, consistent with the SVRR's global tasking for such information as discussed above.

d. A document which included the statement "the following added notes were taken by me from the secret report from the CIA's Paris accountability review team, dated 16 June 1995...."

According to a CIA official, the notes contained in the electronic document came from a "Secret" CIA report dated June 16, 1995 regarding expulsions of CIA officers from Paris.

e. A document regarding information about the Moscow CIA station. The document gave the name of the Chief of Station, and set out staffing information for this CIA office. CIA officials advised that information concerning the location and staffing of any CIA station is classified "Secret." (It is known) that the Russian intelligence services attempt to identify U.S. intelligence officers to identify CIA intelligence operations and confidential human assets, some of whom report on the military intentions and military preparedness of foreign powers.

f. A document summarizing information obtained during the debriefing of convicted spy Aldrich Ames.

g. An extended description of Nicholson's polygraph examination, focusing on the questions Nicholson had been asked about any unauthorized contact with a foreign intelligence service and the CIA polygraphy's reaction to the test.

A 3.5 inch computer diskette was also found in the search of the vehicle. Unlike the hard drive, it contained an electronic document that had not been erased titled "Subject: Reporting From Access Agents to Russian Sources and Developmental." Access agents are individuals who are not employed by the federal government. Instead, they are individuals who work in a variety of private fields who, by the nature of their work, often travel and gain valuable intelligence information. These individuals voluntarily provide this information to the United States. The identity of these assets is classified, as they could be the target of reprisals if foreign countries were aware of their intelligence gathering activities. The access agent document contained seven summary reports concerning CIA human assets and their confidential reporting on foreign intelligence matters. The document noted: (comment: The following was gleaned from reporting accessions lists on Russian objectives.): the topics included intelligence information concerning the Russian banking system, efforts of a foreign country to acquire

Russian cruise missile technology, acquisition of Russian designed electric field suppression systems of interest to the U.S. Navy, sound-vibration insulation for diesel generator plants, high frequency radar research, submarine weapons systems design, and information concerning the Russian economy. In addition, the human sources of information, whose identities the DIA seeks to protect from disclosure, were identified in the document by their codenames, positions, and access to particular information. CIA officials told the FBI that the seven items were all apparent extracts from three actual CIA documents, each dated July 18, 1996, and classified "Secret." A CIA official who examined the extracts said that the information contained in the extracts was classified "Secret" and consisted of Russian matters selected from a broader compilation of CIA headquarters comments to three CIA stations concerning reporting by CIA assets of those CIA stations. The "comment" reported above was not found in the text of any of the three CIA documents.

(It is known) that agents of foreign intelligence services collect information on computers and transfer the information on diskettes. I know that classified CIA intelligence information concerning staffing in Moscow; reports from CIA assets about Russian banking, technology, and political information; and information about the number of Russian recruitment pitches reported by CIA officers is valuable intelligence information which is being sought by the Russian intelligence services, particularly the SVRR. Much of the information on the hard drive and the disk relates to the national defense of the United States.

On or about August 24, 1996, a search of Nicholson's safe deposit box #417 at Selco Credit Union in Springfield, Oregon, revealed a number of gold and commemorative coins, including the two gold coins Nicholson purchased in Singapore with cash on July 1, 1996.

Nicholson's Planned Meeting with Russians in November 1996

On or about September 23, 1996, electronic surveillance at Nicholson's workplace in Langley, Virginia revealed Nicholson removing a camera from his desk and holding it above papers on his lap, as if he were trying to photograph documents. Nicholson had requisitioned this camera and lenses from the CIA.

Later, Nicholson asked for a camera that folds down into a briefcase; ...this style camera is useful in photographing documents. According to CIA officials, Nicholson has no need for any camera in connection with his current official duties

On or about October 4, 1996, Nicholson made plans to travel to two foreign locations for official meetings with friendly foreign intelligence services, departing on November 16, 1996, and returning to the U.S. on November 26, 1996. Nicholson has informed travelling companions from the CIA that he plans to travel to Switzerland after the official meetings rather than return to the U.S. with them. Nicholson has made reservations to fly to Zurich, Switzerland.

On or about October 9, 1996, FBI surveillance observed Nicholson deposit an item in a mailbox at Gallows Road and Electric Avenue, Dunn Loring, Virginia. The FBI retrieved the item, a sealed airmail envelope which contained a postcard mailed to the same address and same foreign post office box as the August 1, 1996, postcard. Both the envelope and the postcard carried the same oversized commemorative style stamps with a face value of $1 as used on the August 1, 1996 postcard. The text of the postcard reads:

Hello Old Friend,

I hope it is possible that you will be my guest for a ski holiday this year on 23-24 November. A bit early but it would fit my schedule nicely. I am fine and all is well. Hope you are the same and can accept my invitation.

Best regards,
Nevil R. Strachey

P.S. The snow should be fine by then.

(It is believed) that Nicholson was informing an SVRR intelligence officer of his intention to meet in Switzerland on November 23 and November 24, 1996. (It is further believed) that the reference to "a bit early" refers to the fact that their prior semi-annual meetings have occurred in December.

On or about October 23, 1996, the FBI conducted a surreptitious search of Nicholson's residence. This search was very limited in that the FBI had little time to perform the search, and had to leave no trace of their entry or the search. Most of the search focused on Nicholson's home and notebook computers, which revealed no new evidence. They each revealed that Nicholson keeps his notebook computer in his bedroom, and electronic surveillance has detected the sounds of typing in the bedroom at night. The search also revealed that Nicholson has an electronic document scanner at home which would enable him to scan documents onto a computer disk.

On or about November 3, 1996, FBI agents conducted a search of Nicholson's office in Langley, Virginia. Approximately 40 documents relating to Russia were found on his desk, including documents classified at the "Secret," "Top Secret," and "SCI" levels. According to CIA officials, these documents contained information concerning, among other things, the intelligence capabilities and military preparedness of the Russian federation. The documents do not appear to be germane to Counterterrorism Center matters. Many of these documents relate to the national defense of the United States. The majority of these documents was located in a black folder on his desk.

Unlike his computer at previous CIA assignments, Nicholson's computer at Langley has no disk drive. This security feature makes it impossible for anyone to copy classified documents onto a disk for editing, removal or transfer.

On or about November 9, 1996, electronic surveillance of Nicholson's workspace revealed Nicholson removing documents from the black folder on his desk, and removing classification markings from the tops and bottoms of documents. I believe that the no disk drive security feature of Nicholson's computer is forcing Nicholson to print out these documents and edit them by hand.

On or about November 12, 1996, in response to Nicholson's request, individuals from the CIA's Office of Technical Services delivered a document camera to Nicholson's office. Immediately Nicholson closed his door and placed the camera under his desk. Nicholson took some of the documents relating to Russia from the black folder, placed them under the desk, knelt on the floor, and began photographing the documents. Nicholson photographed documents for about 30 minutes on the morning of November 12, 1996.

Surveillance detected Nicholson photographing documents under his desk later that same evening, and on the morning of November 13, 1996.

According to a personal financial statement that Harold J. Nicholson signed and filed with the CIA in 1995, Nicholson has no outside business interests or sources of income that account for the income described in connection with his foreign travel. His federal tax returns for the 1994 and 1995 tax years do not appear to declare the income described above that Nicholson has deposited in his accounts or used to pay debts.

Based on the above information, there is probable cause to believe that Nicholson is engaged in a conspiracy to commit espionage in violation of Title 18, United States Code Section 794 (c).

Items to be Searched for and Seized

a. Agents of foreign intelligence services maintain national defense and classified documents and materials, clandestine communications devices and instructions, contact instructions, codes, telephone numbers, maps, photographs, other papers and materials relating to communications procedures, proceeds of illegal espionage transactions, records, notes, bank records, financial statements, calendars, journals, and other papers or documents relating to: 1) the transmittal of national defense and classified intelligence information to foreign governments and intelligence services; 2) the identities of other foreign espionage agents and intelligence officers; 3) financial transactions including payments from governments and hidden financial accounts; 4) records of previous illicit espionage transactions; 5) the source and disposition of national defense and classified intelligence information.

b. Agents of foreign intelligence services often utilize espionage paraphernalia, including devices designed to conceal and transmit classified and intelligence information. These paraphernalia and devices include materials used by espionage agents to communicate between each other and with a foreign government, such as computer disks or photographic film.

c. It is common for agents of foreign intelligence services to secrete national defense and classified documents and materials, clandestine communications devices and instructions, contact instructions, codes, telephone numbers, maps, photographs, other papers and materials relating to communications procedures, proceeds of illegal espionage transactions, records, notes, bank records, financial statements, calendars, journals, espionage paraphernalia, and other papers or documents on their persons and in secure, hidden locations and compartments within or near their residences, at places of employment, in safe deposit boxes, and in motor vehicles, including hidden compartments within motor vehicles, for ready access and to conceal such items from law enforcement authorities.

d. Agents of foreign intelligence services routinely maintain or conceal in and near their residences or in safe deposit boxes large amounts of U.S. and foreign currency, financial instruments, precious metals, jewelry, and other items of value and/or proceeds of illegal espionage transactions. They also conceal records relating to hidden foreign and domestic bank and financial accounts, including accounts in fictitious names.

e. Agents of foreign intelligence services are not unlike any other individual in our society in that they maintain documents and records. These documents and records will normally be maintained for long periods of time regardless of whether their value to the agent has diminished. These persons maintain documents and records which will identify and corroborate travel both in the U.S. and abroad made in connection with clandestine espionage activity, including personal meets with foreign intelligence officers. These documents and records include passports, visas, calendars, journals, date books, telephone numbers, address books, credit cards, hotel receipts, airline records, correspondence, carbon copies of money orders and cashier's checks evidencing large cash expenditures, and accounts and records in fictitious names.

f. Agents of foreign intelligence services often maintain and conceal identity documents, including those utilizing fictitious identities, U.S. and foreign currency, instructions, maps, photographs, U.S. and foreign bank account access numbers and instructions, and other papers and materials relating to emergency contact procedures and escape plans.

Description of Items and Places to be Searched

(It is planned to) arrest Nicholson on November 16, 1996 at Dulles Airport in the Eastern District of Virginia just prior to his scheduled departure. In his past travel, Nicholson has checked luggage with the airline and also carried, hand luggage, including a camera bag, onto the airplane. Based on the above information, there is probable cause to believe that Nicholson will have classified information in some form on his person or secreted in his luggage for delivery to his SVRR handlers. Accordingly, should Nicholson check any items with the airline for transportation with his flight, or should he have any carry on items prior to boarding the aircraft.

NOTE: On 31 March 1997 Harold J. Nicholson, the highest-ranking CIA agent ever charged with spying for Russia, pled guilty to espionage. Nicholson admitted to a federal court that he sold Top-Secret U.S. intelligence information to the Russians for $180,000. On 5 June 1997, Nicholson was sentenced to 23½ years in prison. He did not get life imprisonment because of his cooperation with federal authorities.

Pitts Affidavit

Subject: Earl Edwin Pitts Affidavit
Category: Pitts Case

The following information is UNCLASSIFIED.

UNITED STATES DISTRICT COURT
EASTERN DISTRICT OF VIRGINIA

UNDER SEAL
UNITED STATES OF AMERICA

CRIMINAL COMPLAINT
v.
CASE NUMBER: 96-1041-M

EARL EDWIN PITTS
(Name and Address of Defendant)

I, the undersigned complainant being duly sworn state the following it true and correct to the best of my knowledge and belief. From on or about July, 1987 - December, 1996 in Arlington and Stafford Counties in the Eastern District of Virginia Defendent(s) did, (Track Statutory Language of Offense)

commit a violation of Title 18, U.S.C. Section 794 (c), that, with reason to believe that it would be used to the injury of the United States and the advantage of a foreign nation, Earl Edwin Pitts did unlawfully and knowingly conspire with others to communicate, transmit and deliver to representatives of a foreign government, specifically the U.S.S.R. and the Russian Federation, information relating to the national defense of the United States, and did overt acts to effect the object of said conspiracy, including but not limited to the following: Earl Edwin Pitts did travel on March 24, 1992 from National Airport, in the Eastern District of Virginia, to New York City; and did

commit a violation of Title 18, U.S.C. Section 794 (a), that is, with reason to believe that it would be used to the injury of the United States and the advantage of a foreign nation, Earl Edwin Pitts did unlawfully and knowingly attempt to communicate, transmit and deliver to representatives of a foreign government, specifically the Russian Federation, information relating to the national defense of the United States; and did

commit a violation of Title 50, U.S.C. Section 783 (a), that is, communication of classified information without authority by Government officer or employee to a person he had reason to believe was an agent of a foreign government; and did commit a violation of Title 18, U.S.C. Section 641, that is, conveyance without authority of property of the United States.

In violation of Title 18 United States Code, Section(s) 794 (a) and (c), and 641, and Title 50, U.S.C. § 783(a).

I further state that I am a Special Agent, FBI and that this complaint is based on the following facts:

_____

Signature of Complainant
David G. Lambert, Special
Agent Federal Bureau of Investigation

Reviewing AUSA - Randy I. Bellows
Sworn to before me and subscribed in my presence, December 17, 1996 at Alexandria, Virginia

Date _____ City and State _____

Thomas Rawles Jones, Jr.
United States Magistrate Judge

Name & Title of Judicial Officer

_____

Signature of Judicial Officer

AFFIDAVIT IN SUPPORT OF CRIMINAL COMPLAINT, ARREST WARRANT, AND SEARCH WARRANTS

UNITED STATES v. EARL EDWIN PITTS

I, David G. Lambert, being duly sworn, depose and state as follows:

1. I am presently employed as a Special Agent of the Federal Bureau of Investigation (FBI) and am assigned to the Washington Field Office in the District of Columbia. I have been employed as an FBI Special Agent for approximately 9 years. I have been assigned to foreign counterintelligence (FCI) investigations for approximately 7 years. As a result of my training and experience, I am familiar with the tactics, methods, and techniques of foreign intelligence services and their agents.

Earl Edwin Pitts

2. This affidavit is in support of the following:

   a. Complaint and Arrest Warrant for:
   EARL EDWIN PITTS,
   DOB: September 23, 1953
   SSAN: 486-62-7841,

for the following violations of federal criminal law.

   a. Conspiracy to commit espionage
   (Title 18, United States Code, Section 794(c)); and

   b. Attempted Espionage
   (Title 18, United States Code, Section 794(a)); and

   c. Communication of Classified Information by Government, Officer or Employee
   (Title 50, United States Code, Section 783(a)).

3. The information stated below is based on personal knowledge, training and experience, including training and experience I have gained while assigned to FCI investigations, and information provided to me by others as noted herein.

Summary

4. This affidavit concerns an investigation by the FBI into the compromise of FBI intelligence operations and information. During this investigation, I and others have conducted interviews, physical and electronic surveillance, financial analysis, and other forms of investigation.

5. The results of this investigation to date indicate there is probable cause to believe that:

   a. EARL EDWIN PITTS (hereafter, "PITTS"), a United States citizen, is an agent of the Sluzhba Vneshney Rasvedi Rossii (hereafter, "SVRR"), which is the intelligence service of the Russian Federation. The SVRR is the direct successor of the Union of Soviet Socialist Republics' Committee for State Security, known hereafter as the "KGB." An agent of a foreign intelligence service is one, other than an intelligence officer or employee, who clandestinely and illegally acts on behalf of that service. Prior to being an agent of the SVRR, there is probable cause to believe PITTS was an agent of the KGB.

   b. From in or about July, 1987, through the present, PITTS conspired with officers of the KGB and SVRR to commit espionage. This included numerous trips which PITTS made from the Eastern District of Virginia to the New York area in connection with his espionage activities. From in or about October, 1992, to the present, to the best of my knowledge and belief, PITTS remained an agent of the SVRR in a dormant capacity.

   c. During PITTS' espionage activities between 1987 and 1992, PITTS received from the KGB and SVRR in excess of $224,000, including over $100,000 set aside for PITTS in a "reserve" account (according to PITTS).

   d. From in or about August, 1995, through the present, PITTS attempted to commit espionage and committed numerous other violations of federal criminal law in connection with his contact with certain individuals who he believed were agents of the SVRR but who were, in fact, undercover personnel employed by, or operating on the instructions of the FBI. During this "false flag" operation, described in greater detail below, PITTS gave persons he believed to be SVRR officers sensitive and Secret classified documents related to the national defense, gave "SVRR [FBI]" handlers personal, medical and family information about fellow FBI special agents, proposed strategies by which the SVRR might recruit additional agents, made plans to smuggle into the FBI Academy an SVRR technical expert, provided his "SVRR [FBI]" handlers an FBI cipher lock combination, an FBI key and his own FBI identification badge in order to facilitate the smuggling operation, stole from the FBI a handset to a telecommunications device used to transmit classified information, and divulged a variety of classified information to his "SVRR [FBI]" handlers. PITTS did this for money. During the "false flag" operation, PITTS accepted $65,000 for his espionage activities and his attempt to compromise FBI intelligence activities.

Background on Earl Edwin Pitts

6. EARL EDWIN PITTS is a United States citizen, presently employed as a Supervisory Special Agent of the FBI. PITTS is 43 years old and is an attorney. PITTS and his wife, Mary, were married in 1985. PITTS resides with his wife at a single family dwelling located at 13415 Fox Chase Lane, Spotsylvania, Virginia, 22553.

7. On September 18, 1983, PITTS entered on duty with the FBI and, on September 19, 1983, took the following Oath of Office:

> I will support and defend the Constitution of the United States against all enemies, foreign and domestic; that I will bear true faith and allegiance to the same; that I take this obligation freely, without any mental reservation or purpose of evasion; and that I will well and faithfully discharge the duties of the office on which I am about to enter. So help me God.

8. On September 20, 1983, PITTS signed an FBI Employment Agreement, which included the following provisions:

> That I am hereby advised and I understand that Federal law such as Title 18, United States Code, Sections 793, 794, and 798 . . . prohibit loss, misuse, or unauthorized disclosure or production of national security information, other classified information and other nonclassified information in the files of the FBI;
>
> I understand that unauthorized disclosure of information in the files of the FBI or information I may acquire as an employee of the FBI could result in impairment of national security, place human life in jeopardy, or result in the denial of due process to a person or persons who are subjects of an FBI investigation, or prevent the FBI from effectively discharging its responsibilities. I understand the need for this secrecy agreement; therefore, as consideration for employment, I agree that I will never divulge, publish, or reveal either by word or conduct, or by other means disclose to any unauthorized recipient without official written authorization by the Director of the FBI or his delegate, any information from the investigatory files of the FBI or any information relating to material contained in the files, or disclose any information or produce any material acquired as a part of the performance of my official duties or because of my official status.
>
> That I understand unauthorized disclosure may be a violation of Federal law and prosecuted as a criminal offense.

9. On October 22, 1984, PITTS signed the Classified Information Nondisclosure Agreement, which reads in part:

> I have been advised and am aware that direct or indirect unauthorized disclosure unauthorized retention or negligent handling of classified information by me could cause irreparable injury to the United States or could be used to advantage by a foreign nation. I hereby agree that I will never divulge such information unless I have officially verified the recipient has been properly authorized by United States Government to receive it or I have been given prior written notice of authorization from the United States Government Department or Agency (hereinafter Department or Agency) last granting me a security clearance that such disclosure is permitted. I further understand that I am obligated to comply with laws and regulations that prohibit the unauthorized disclosure of classified information.
>
> I have been advised and am aware that any breach of this Agreement may result in the termination of any security clearances I hold; removal from any position of special confidence and trust requiring such clearances; and the termination of my employment or other relationships with the Departments or Agencies that granted my security clearance or clearances. In addition, I have been advised and am aware that any unauthorized disclosure of classified information by me may constitute a violation of United States criminal laws including the provisions of Sections 641, 793, 794, 798, and...the provisions of Section 783(b), Title 50, United States Code, and the provisions of the Intelligence Identities Protection Act of 1982.

10. PITTS currently holds a "Top Secret" security clearance. From November 15, 1989 until November 18, 1996, PITTS held certain additional "code word" clearances for access to sensitive compartmented information.

11. Upon graduation from the FBI Academy, he was assigned to the FBI's Alexandria Field Office where he worked applicant, white collar crime and narcotics investigations. PITTS was assigned to the Fredericksburg Resident Agency within the Alexandria Field Office from March 18, 1985 through January 21, 1987.

12. PITTS was assigned to the New York Field Office from January 31, 1987 to August 13, 1989. He worked FCI investigations including investigations concerning KGB officials assigned to the (then) Soviet Mission to the United Nations.

13. In August 1989 PITTS was promoted to Supervisory Special Agent and transferred to the Document Classification Authority Affidavit Unit within the Operations Section of the Records Management Division at FBI Headquarters, in Washington, DC. Upon assignment to the Records Management Division, PITTS was granted access to Sensitive Compartmented Information. In 1991, he was reassigned to the Security Programs Section, where he was responsible for supervising personnel security investigations.

14. On or about October 18, 1992, PITTS was transferred to the Legal Counsel Division at FBI Headquarters, where he worked in DNA Legal Assistance and was then assigned to civil litigation matters. PITTS worked in FBI office space located within a building at 601 Pennsylvania Avenue, NW, Suite 750, Washington, DC.

15. On or about January 23, 1995, PITTS began working in the Behavioral Science Unit, FBI Academy in Quantico, Virginia, where he remains at present. Among his responsibilities at the FBI Academy is to conduct security briefings for FBI personnel.

16. Since PITTS' assignment to the FBI Academy, PITTS had no duty or responsibility that would have required or necessitated ongoing contact with Russian citizens in a foreign counterintelligence capacity. PITTS was not authorized in 1995 or 1996 to meet with agents of foreign counterintelligence services. In addition, PITTS was required by FBI policy and procedure to accurately and fully report such contacts, which he did not do.

17. This affidavit refers to information obtained from electronic surveillance, video surveillance and searches of various places and things. In each instance, the searches and surveillance described in this affidavit were authorized by court order, or by consensual monitoring.

Espionage-Related Activities (1987-1992)

18. In January, 1987, PITTS began his duties with the New York Division, assigned to a squad responsible for various FCI investigations. Between January, 1987 and August, 1989, PITTS had access to a wide range of sensitive and highly classified operations. These included the following: recruitment operations involving Russian intelligence officers, double agent operations, operations targeting Russian intelligence officers, true identities of human assets, operations against Russian illegals, true identities of defector sources, surveillance schedules of known meet sites, internal policies, documents, and procedures concerning surveillance of Russian intelligence officers, and the identification targeting and reporting on known and suspected KGB intelligence officers in the New York area.

19. In 1988, PITTS described his duties in New York as follows:

> my current duties in NY include investigations concerning Soviet intelligence officers, Soviet establishments, Soviet emigres, espionage matters and developing assets. These duties have afforded me an opportunity to investigate some highly complex and sensitive cases, including identification of Soviet intelligence officers, identifying Soviet efforts directed at the emigre community and participation in recruitment efforts.

The July 1987 Letter

20. In or about late July 1987, a cooperating witness (hereafter, "CW"), who is known to be reliable and credible, received a letter addressed to the CW at the (then) Soviet Mission to the United Nations. At the time, the CW was a citizen of the Soviet Union assigned

to the Soviet Mission to the United Nations. The letter provided surveillance information concerning the CW's recent activities.

21. Specifically, CW recalled that the letter received from the writer contained reference to a trip which CW had made to a New York City airport to meet two high-ranking KGB officials several days earlier. Review of FBI records indicates that on July 15, 1987—one week before it is believed the letter was sent to CW—PITTS conducted surveillance on the CW at another New York City airport and later reported the surveillance in a memorandum classified Secret.

22. Based on the foregoing, the CW concluded that the writer was an FBI employee. In the letter, the writer requested a meeting with the CW or, if the CW was not a KGB officer, with an actual KGB officer.   uring the summer of 1987, several Special Agents on the counterintelligence squad to which PITTS was assigned, wrongly concluded the CW was a senior KGB officer. PITTS, himself, told the CW in December, 1995, that he had chosen the CW to meet with because the CW had been "misidentified" [as a KGB officer].)

23. The CW provided the letter to the Mission Security Officer, Vadim Voytenko (hereafter, "Voytenko"). Later, the CW met with Voytenko and Aleksandr Vasilyevich Karpov (hereafter, "Karpov").

24. Based upon investigation and analysis, Aleksandr Vasilyevich Karpov has been identified by the FBI as an officer of the SVRR and, formerly the KGB. From 1987 through 1990, he was the New York Chief of Line KR. Line KR, the counterintelligence component of the KGB, was responsible for penetrating the intelligence and security services of foreign nations, including those of the United States, by human and technical means. The FBI was one of the intelligence/security services targeted by Line KR.

The Meeting at the New York Public Library

25. The CW was instructed by Voytenko to meet with the writer of the letter at the New York Public Library, located at Fifth Avenue and 42nd Street in New York City. The CW briefly met the writer inside the library, and then introduced the writer to Karpov.

26. Based upon statements made by PITTS during the "false flag" operation, information provided by the CW, and based upon PITTS' subsequent conduct and on other investigative activities, I believe that the writer of the letter to the CW was PITTS and that PITTS was the U.S. intelligence officer who met with the CW and Karpov at the New York Public Library.

Disclosure of Classified Material

27. The meeting between Karpov and PITTS at the New York Public Library was the beginning of five years of active espionage activity by PITTS on behalf of the KGB and SVRR.

28. I believe that among the classified documents and information which PITTS conveyed to the KGB in the course of his espionage activity in return for money were the following:

> a. A document known as the "Soviet Administrative List." The "Soviet Administrative List" was the FBI's computerized, alphabetical compilation of all Soviet officials posted or assigned to the United States. It is classified "Secret" and is related to the national defense. The "Secret" classification is applied to information whose unauthorized disclosure reasonably could be expected to cause serious damage to the national security. The list contains the names, dates of birth, posting, in-country/travel/out-country status, file number, FBI office of origin, FBI squad, FBI case agent, and the known or suspected intelligence affiliation of each Soviet official assigned to Soviet legations in the United States, including the Soviet Embassy in Washington, D.C., and the Soviet Mission to the United Nations in New York, New York.
>
> PITTS was not authorized to deliver the "Soviet Administrative List" to any person not employed by the FBI nor to any person within the FBI who did not have an official need to know the information contained in the list.
>
> b. A letter to CW, then suspected by the FBI of being a KGB officer, containing surveillance information concerning CW. Specifically, PITTS disclosed classified Secret information concerning FBI surveillance of CW.

c. Secret information concerning an FBI asset who reported covertly on Russian intelligence matters.

Information Obtained in the "False Flag" Operation Concerning PITTS' 1987-1992 Espionage Activity

29. The FBI conducted an analysis of PITTS' financial affairs and travel records and conducted additional investigation, including the debriefing of CW by the FBI. In or about August 1995, a "false flag" operation was initiated. A "false flag" operation is an operation intended to persuade a target of the operation that he is working for one country when, in fact, he is working for another. The purpose of this "false flag" operation was to confirm PITTS' 1987-1992 suspected espionage activities and, most importantly, to determine what FBI information, projects and operations PITTS had compromised by divulging them to the KGB and SVRR during the course of his espionage activities.

30. Specifically the "false flag" operation was designed to persuade PITTS through the use of the CW, and through the use of U.S. government personnel posing as SVRR officers, that he was being contacted again by the SVRR and then, in the course of conducting current espionage-type activites, ascertain the scope and content of his past espionage activities. In fact, during the course of the "false flag" operation, PITTS made numerous incriminating statements concerning his prior espionage activites, including the following:

a. On or about September 8, 1995, PITTS wrote a letter to the person he believed to be his new SVRR handler in which he apologized for missing a meeting with his old SVRR handler in New York and stated that he was "very pleased to hear from you again."

b. In the same September 8, 1995 letter described above, PITTS indicated that he did not have information concerning a certain KGB official and stated: "Shortly after I last met with Alex, I left the operational side of the business and became more of an administrator and researcher." The reference to "Alex" is believed to be a reference to one of PITTS handlers, Aleksandr Karpov.

c. In the same September 8, 1995 letter described above, PITTS stated: "I have no additional material to pass along as collections ceased when I missed your friend in New York."

d. On or about November 2, 1995, PITTS wrote a letter to the person he believed to be his SVRR handler. In this letter, PITTS made reference to "previous exchanges." (This letter was not in fact sent due to PITTS' discovery of a surveillance device.)

e. In the same November 2, 1995 letter, PITTS asked for $35,000 to $40,000 from "my account" to fund an escape plan. It is believed that this reference to "my account" is a reference to an account set up in Russia on PITTS" behalf.

f. On December 17, 1995, a telephone call took place between PITTS and the person he believed to be his SVRR handler. In that call, the "SVRR [FBI]" handler told PITTS that PITTS needed to have a face-to-face meeting with PITTS' friend from Moscow. The "SVRR [FBI]" handler told PITTS that "you must come to the place where you first requested to meet in 1987." PITTS acknowledged that he remembered the place [the New York Public Library] and the section in the place where the 1987 meeting had occurred.

g. On December 28, 1995, a telephone call took place between PITTS and the person he believed to be his SVRR handler. The call concerned the fact that the meeting scheduled for earlier that day in New York had not taken place as planned. After the "SVRR [FBI]" handler told PITTS that his friend had been waiting in one section of the library for PITTS, PITTS stated that this section was "not where we first met" and that their first meeting had been in a different section of the library. I believe this is a reference to PITTS' first meeting with the CW in or about July, 1987.

h. In a December 29, 1995 meeting with a person he believed to be his SVRR handler, PITTS was asked if he had brought anything for the handler. PITTS said he had not because "before" we were "never supposed to exchange two things." I believe this is a reference to the procedures PITTS used during his espionage activity between 1987 and 1992.

i. In the same December 29, 1995 meeting, PITTS said: "I feel very uneasy compared to last time, it's, uh, I'm much more out of out of touch with what's going on." I believe this is a reference to PITTS' espionage activity between 1987 and 1992.

j. In the same December 29, 1995 meeting, the following exchange took place between an Undercover officer ["UCO"], who was posing as an SVRR officer, and PITTS:

UCO: Edwin, does your wife know anything about our present project?

PITTS: No, No. She doesn't know about any of the Projects but she....

UCO: Did she know anything about the project when you worked with Alex in the old days in New York?

PITTS: No, unless she suspected. She has great deals of suspicions.

UCO: You had no problem with that then in New York at the time?

PITTS: No.

k. In the same December 29, 1995 meeting, the following exchange took place:

UCO: Do you remember the last date when you met Alex [Karpov]?
PITTS: No.

UCO: You don't? The year?

PITTS: Oh, the year? The year would have been, um, uh, 1988.

l. In the same December 29, 1995 meeting, the following exchange took place:

UCO: ...the money you got in the past... there was some doubt that you perhaps did not get all the money which was coming to you, to your account.

PITTS: No, I didn't. No . . . but,

UCO: No. You . . .

PITTS: But, I mean, I understand, we had to break contact.

UCO: Yeah, but I understand those people who did bring you money at the time or that money which was passed to you . . .

PITTS: Um Hum.

UCO: They, well, tried to reach us, establish to see if your account is up to date. We have an account, you know this?

PITTS: Um Hum. Yes.

UCO: Are you aware of the account?

PITTS: Well, Yeah, I've been told about it.

UCO: Yeah, did ever mention how much it is, in the account?

PITTS: Alex did, but I, I don't remember the amount.

UCO: You don't remember?

PITTS: No. I've tried to put those things out of my head.

m. On July 9, 1986, PITTS wrote a letter to the person he believed to be his SVRR handler, which reads in part:

If it is possible, please make payment for my most recent deliveries (or withdraw from my reserve account) . . .

n. On or about August 14, 1996, PITTS wrote a letter to the person he believed to be his SVRR handler, which reads in part:

Regarding my reserve, I do not know the amount and it is my understanding that you do not. When I last met with Alex, it was over 100,000.

o. In the same August 14, 1996 letter, PITTS stated that it might be appropriate for the SVRR to pay him out of his "reserves" because "much of the information I have recently provided is not of the quality I have provided in the past

p. On or about September 18, 1996, PITTS made additional statements in a letter to the person he believed to be his SVRR handler concerning moneys he had received in the course of his espionage activities during the 1987 to 1992 time period. In this excerpt, PITTS made reference to an SVRR officer who handled PITTS after Alexander Karpov:

> During the time I knew him, two payments were made but I can not remember if they were in round numbers. He never spoke of the size of the reserve fund or how much I was to expect in payment. The greatest difficulty was the distance between our locations and the absence of an alternate means of communicating meeting dates and alternate dates. The distance and time between meetings made it impossible to plan for unforeseen circumstances. The nature of the information changed because of the type of work I was assigned. I only met him two, or maybe three, times after my posting to Washington (in 1989).

q. On December 13, 1996, in a communication to the persons he believed to be his SVRR handlers, PITTS stated that he no longer had "direct access" to the files from his New York assignment (1987-1989) but "I believe I have provided you with everything that I was aware of."

r. In the same December 13, 1996 communication, PITTS stated that he wished "to draw on reserve funds" on January 6, 1991 and February 6, 1997. I believe this to be a reference to the Russian account set up on behalf of PITTS, as described, above.

Trips to New York City in 1990-1992
31. In August 1989, PITTS was transferred from the New York Field Office of the FBI to FBI Headquarters. Beginning in February 1990, and continuing to October 1992, PITTS made a series of nine brief trips to New York City, most of which were one day trips, all such trips taken to or from National Airport, in the Eastern District of Virginia. Financial analysis indicates a pattern of unusual monetary deposits following these trips. believe that PITTS made all or most of these trips for the purpose of continuing his espionage activities.

Financial Analysis
32. The FBI has conducted a financial analysis of PITTS for the time period in which it is believed PITTS was actively involved in espionage activities on behalf of the KGB and SVRR. This financial analysis indicates that PITTS acquired substantial money during this period of time which cannot be traced to legitimate sources of funds.

33. PITTS' only known source of substantial income during the period from 1987 to 1992 was from his employment and his wife's employment with the FBI. PITTS made frequent deposits of cash and/or money accounts or as payments on credit card accounts. This activity was unusual as compared to PITTS' normal financial banking activity prior to July, 1987 and subsequent to June, 1992. Furthermore, examination of when money orders were purchased and when groupings of deposits were made, revealed a pattern linking such deposits to the dates of PITTS' New York trips.

34. From 1987 to 1992, these unexplained deposits and credit card payments resulted in an enhancement of PITTS' wealth by over one hundred thousand dollars, as follows:

YEAR	TOTAL VALUE OF DEPOSITS
1987	$2,775.00
1988	5,024.48
1989	23,414.31
1990	35,520.00
1991	29,115.21
1992	28,375.66
TOTAL	**$124,224.66**

This sum of money does not include any funds PITTS may have received which were not deposited into one of his accounts or used to pay bills. Nor does it include the account in Russia which, according to PITTS' statement, was funded with "over $100,000."

35. PITTS utilized a number of financial institutions and accounts to hide his receipt of this unexplained wealth, including several accounts at financial institutions in the Eastern District of Virginia. The deposits to these accounts were small, no larger than

$1,100.00, and spread out over several days within a month. To further conceal the receipt of illegal funds, PITTS rented a post office box in Washington, D.C., which received the American Security Bank statements, he made innumerable deposits, withdrawals, and transfers via automated teller machines, and he purchased multiple money orders for deposits into his bank accounts and for payments on credit and accounts. For example, in the years 1987-1992, over 50 money orders were purchased by PITTS.

36. The following is a summary of activity concerning the specific accounts listed above that have led me to believe these accounts contain proceeds of PITTS' espionage activity:

a. Name/Company: PENTAGON FEDERAL CREDIT UNION
Address: Alexandria, Virginia
Account #: 587571-027
In name of: EARL EDWIN PITTS and Mary Colombara Pitts
Activity: From July 1987 through May 1992, there were thirty-five known deposits to this account totaling, approximately $10,595, all unexplained by PITTS' known income.

Account #: 587571 019
In name of: EARL EDWIN PITTS and Mary Colombaro Pitts
Activity: From September 1987 through April 1992, there were thirty-two known deposits to this account totaling approximately $8,419, all unexplained by PITTS known income.

b. Name/Company: CENTRAL FIDELITY BANK
Address: Richmond, Virginia
Account #: 1018713721
In name of: EARL EDWIN PITTS and Mary Colombaro Pitts
Activity: From July 1989 through July 1992, there were twelve known deposits to this account totaling approximately $4,591, all unexplained by PITTS' known income.

Account #: 7919862232
In name of: EARL EDWIN PITTS and Mary Colombaro Pitts
Activity: From July 1989 through October 1992, there were one hundred fifty one known deposits to this account totalling approximately $38,612, all unexplained by PITTS known income.

Name/Company: KEY OF NEW YORK
Address: Albany, New York
Account: 342928376
In name of: EARL EDWIN PITTS and Mary Colombaro Pitts
Activity: From June 1988 through August 1989, there were fifty-three known deposits to this account totalling approximately $10,488 all unexplained by PITTS known incomes.

Account #: 347009151
In name of: EARL EDWIN PITTS and Mary Colombaro Pitts
Activity: From September 1988 through June 1989, there were nineteen known deposits to this account totalling approximately $1,354, all unexplained by PITTS' known income.

d. Name/Company: CHEMICAL BANK (MANUFACTURERS HANOVER)
Address: New York, New York
Account #: 0630264
In name of: EARL EDWIN PITTS and Mary Colombaro Pitts
Activity: From January 1989 through August 1989, there were thirty-two known deposits to this account totaling approximately $8,027, all unexplained by PITTS' known income.

e. Name/Company: NATIONS BANK (AMERICAN SECURITY)
Address: Baltimore, Maryland
Account #: 11661881

In name of: EARL EDWIN PITTS
Activity: From March 1990 through August 1992, there were one-hundred twenty known deposits to this account totaling approximately $33,735, all unexplained by PITTS' known income

Espionage–Related Activities (1995-1996)

37. In August 1995, the FBI initiated the "false flag" operation described above. It began with correspondence, postmarked in New York, New York, and sent to PITTS' residence. There was no response.

The August 26, 1995 Meeting

38. On or about August 26, 1995, at approximately 2:30 p.m., the CW went to the PITTS residence and met PITTS at the door. He told PITTS:

There is a guest visiting me. He wanted to see you. He's in my car. He's from Moscow.

39. PITTS agreed to meet with the CW and the "guest from Moscow" one hour later at the Chancellorsville Battlefield Visitor Center.

40. At approximately 3:20 p.m. that same day, PITTS met the "guest from Moscow," an undercover intelligence officer (hereafter, "UCO"), at the Chancellorsville Battlefield Visitor Center.

41. The UCO told PITTS that the reason he was there was to advise him of a mutual problem. The UCO indicated that the "SVRR" was worried about the behavior of a Resident [a senior SVRR official] who had been recently assigned in the United States and requested PITTS' assistance.

The UCO asked PITTS:

UCO: Have you brought anything for me, with you? Anything you can give me? Maybe you have some.

PITTS: I, I have nothing. I wasn't expecting you.

42. The UCO stated that his superiors were very happy with PITTS and highly appreciative of PITTS' help and asked if PITTS would help them. PITTS responded: "I'll help you if I can." PITTS added that he was in "another line now," and did not have good access.

43. The UCO provided a sealed envelope to PITTS which contained written instructions to PITTS describing how PITTS should make a "dead drop" at a particular location code-named "POLE" on September 9, 1995 in the Clifton, Virginia area. (A "dead drop" is a prearranged location where a clandestine foreign agent or intelligence officer may utilize impersonal, clandestine means of communication to transfer tangible objects between them.) PITTS was also instructed to mark a signal site, codenamed "GRADE," in this same area once the "dead drop" had been put down. Also included in the envelope was "SVRR [FBI]" tasking for PITTS to accomplish and provide in the future.

44. The UCO asked PITTS about his financial situation and indicated that money was available if PITTS needed it. PITTS responded by asking if the UCO had the money with him. The UCO told PITTS that he did have the money with him and PITTS stated that he "could" use the money. The UCO gave PITTS a sealed envelope containing $15,000.00 in used, unmarked, non-sequential, $100 bills. PITTS placed the envelopes in his pants' pocket.

45. The meeting ended with PITTS stating, "I'll do what I can."

Mary Pitts' Suspicions

46. On August 26, 1995, the day of the first "false flag" contact, Mary Pitts talked to her sister on three occasions. She said that on that day a man with a foreign accent came to the house and asked for PITTS, after which PITTS left the house in a "panic." Mary Pitts warned that she didn't want to talk about it over the phone, but she confronted PITTS with what she found. (She searched PITTS' home office while he was meeting with the "SVRR [FBI]".) Her sister then asked if that included "the secret stuff" and Mary Pitts answered affirmatively.

47. On or about August 29, 1995, at approximately 8:00 a.m., Mary Pitts telephoned Special Agent Tom Carter at the Fredericksburg Resident Agency, and asked him to meet with her on an urgent and confidential matter

concerning her husband. Special Agent Carter met with Mary Pitts for approximately an hour and obtained statements from her regarding PITTS' suspicious activities on August 26, 1995 and a copy of the initial "false flag" letter referred to above. Special Agent Carter advised Mary Pitts that he would look into the matter for her, and that he would get back to her as soon as possible.

48. Later that day, Mary Pitts had a telephone conversation with a neighbor in which she expressed concerns about PITTS' conduct and her own decision to report her husband to the FBI:

Mary: I probably shouldn't gone to the Bureau and it will probably be the end of my marriage either way it goes because if he find . . . If he is on the up and up and he finds out that I went behind his back we're finished.

Neighbor: Ahm, the thing of it is Mary. You did what you had to do at the time and there is no point in beating yourself.

Mary: There is no going, there is no going back now . . .
Neighbor: No, no beating yourself over that...

Mary: What price for national security.

Neighbor: Were you worrying about national security really?

Mary: Yeah, part of me is.

Neighbor: Yes.

Mary: Because, you know I have… There is things wrong with this country but it's still my country.

Neighbor: Yeah.

Mary: And passing information to a foreign national or a foreigner, a foreign country…

Neighbor: Well if it turns out to be the case then you know you did the right thing. You did the only thing.

Mary: Even though maybe he would have stopped in a, in a while? What you would have stopped at my request and we could have gone on with our wonderful life?
Neighbor: Don't know, uh see…

Mary: Could I have gone on with my regular and wonderful life? It's over, my life is over.

Events of August 29, 1995– August 30, 1995

49. At approximately 9:00 a.m., on or about August 29, 1995, while sitting in his office, PITTS took from his gym bag, under his desk, an envelope believed to contain the operational instructions given to him by the UCO on August 26, 1995. PITTS read the instructions, consulted his calendar, and returned them to the envelope, which he put in his desk drawer.

50. At approximately 1:00 p.m., on or about August 29, 1995, PITTS took an envelope of money from his gym bag under his desk and proceeded to count and separate the money into stacks of ten bills. PITTS placed each stack into a white letter size envelope, 15 envelopes in all. PITTS sealed each envelope and placed the envelopes into one large manila envelope, along with what appeared to be the written instructions for the "dead drop" site, and placed the large envelope into his desk drawer.

51. At approximately 8:00 a.m., on or about August 30, 1995, PITTS concealed a large manila envelope in a ceiling panel of his office. The envelope contained the money and instructions previously furnished to PITTS by the UCO on August 26, 1995.

PITTS' Meeting with Agent Carter

52. After learning from his wife that she had talked to Special Agent Carter about her suspicions, PITTS asked for a meeting with Special Agent Carter. At approximately 10:52 a.m., on or about August 30, 1995, PITTS meet with Special Agent Carter in PITTS' office space. PITTS was calm and made a series of statements to Special Agent Carter to explain the situation which transpired between himself and his wife on August 26, 1995, as follows: A man visited their home on August 26, 1995, who PITTS explained was an asset he knew while working in the New York Division. The name provided by PITTS to Special Agent Carter was the

name of a person other than the CW. Due to their previous relationship and the fact that PITTS was a lawyer, the asset sent PITTS a note asking him to come to New York. Because of the asset's drunken state when the asset appeared at PITTS' residence, PITTS met the asset at the Walmart near his home to render legal advice. These statements were false.

53. At approximately 4:30 p.m., on August 31, 1995, in PITTS' office, PITTS took a white letter-sized envelope out of his filing cabinet and opened it. He took from the envelope ten bills and proceeded to examine each bill by placing them up against the light. PITTS returned nine of the bills to the envelope and placed the envelope back in his filing cabinet. He placed one bill into his wallet.

Office Search on August 31, 1995

54. A search was conducted on August 31, 1995 of PITTS' office space at the FBI Academy, Quantico. The search revealed the following: a legal size manila envelope found inside a five drawer filing cabinet, located behind PITTS' desk, which contained 15 sealed white, letter-sized envelopes, and one manila, letter-sized envelope that was folded but not sealed. The manila envelope contained the written "dead drop" instructions provided to PITTS by the UCO on August 1995. Each one of the 15 white envelopes were sealed and contained money in what appeared to be denominations of $100.00. The serial number of one bill in each envelope, which could be seen through the envelopes, matched those provided to PITTS by the UCO on August 26, 1995.

Events of September 7–8, 1995

55. At approximately 8:33 a.m., on September 7, 1995, PITTS retrieved the "dead drop" instructions furnished to him by the UCO on August 26, 1995 from his hardcover briefcase. He placed the instruction in plastic pockets of a dark colored binder, and discarded the envelope from which they came.

56. At approximately 11:49 a.m., on the same day PITTS took a large manila envelope from his legal attaché case. PITTS took a smaller, white envelope out of the manila envelope and withdrew cash from it, afterwards marking on the white envelope. PITTS placed the cash in a pre-addressed, small, white envelope. He also took money from his money clip and placed this into the pre-addressed envelope as well. PITTS then placed the pre-addressed envelope and the money envelopes into a stenotype folder on top of his desk.

57. On or about September 8, 1995, PITTS arrived at his work place at approximately 7:18 a.m. At approximately 7:29 a.m., PITTS began typing on his laptop computer.

58. At approximately 7:38 a.m., PITTS took out a Northern Virginia map and the "dead drop" instructions which were stored in a dark colored binder. PITTS studied both the map and the instructions, then placed the binder into his bottom, right desk drawer.

59. At approximately 10:43 a.m., PITTS put on a pair of gloves. PITTS then retrieved a 3.5" computer disk, wiped the disk off with the gloves and placed it into the hard drive of his laptop computer and began typing. At approximately 10:32 a.m., PITTS looked at the dead drop instructions contained in the dark colored binder. PITTS continued to glance at the instructions intermittently while typing. At approximately 10:46 a.m., PITTS took out a small piece of paper and briefly wrote on it, while wearing gloves. At approximately 12:37 p.m., PITTS took the disk out of his laptop hard drive and replace it with another one. One minute later, PITTS exchanged the disks again, replacing the new one with the original. At approximately 12:39 p.m., PITTS took a map out and looked at it. At approximately 12:40 p.m., he took a plastic bag from his briefcase, and placed one disk into the plastic bag. This disk was placed into his briefcase, while another disk was placed into a disk storage container, taped shut, then placed in a file cabinet. At approximately 12:44 p.m., PITTS reviewed a map and then the dead drop instructions in the binder. PITTS departed his office at approximately 12:53 p.m.

60. PITTS entered the Clifton, Virginia, area at approximately 2:11 p.m. PITTS proceeded directly to the "dead drop" location in Clifton, arriving at the "dead drop" site at approximately 2:30 p.m. PITTS placed a package containing a 3.5" computer disk into the "dead drop." The disk was wrapped in a plastic sandwich bag, which was then concealed in a paper bag.

61. PITTS proceeded to signal site "Grade," and at approximately 2:40 p.m. marked the signal site as previously instructed. PITTS departed the Clifton area at approximately 3:10 p.m. and proceeded back to his work place.

62. The package retrieved from dead drop "Pole" contained a note with the signature, "Edwin Pearl" [a code name for PITTS] and a computer disk which contained a file named "Alex" which, in part, said:

> I was very pleased to hear from you again. I'm sorry I missed your friend when I was in New York. I discovered I had gone to the wrong location and by the time I realized my mistake I missed the get together. Unfortunately, I did not have ready access to a telephone number or address where I could contact you and could not invite you or your friends to any future get togethers.

It is my belief that PITTS was referring to a missed meeting with his SVRR handler in New York.

63. The file also contained the following statement by PITTS:

> I appreciate your concern for my well being, but there should be no great concern on your part. It appears to me that there are several aspects about our system that are greatly different from your concept of our system. It is possible to insulate one's self from real harm even if all security systems fail. There are certain legal and political factors one can rely on to prevent a serious threat to one's safety. Therefore, I strongly recommend you take no dramatic action on my behalf, even if you have had a total problem within your system. My sudden movement would only confirm suspicions if they exist and could seriously harm the degree of cordiality that is being developed between our principals. If I am confronted, I can use certain procedures to protect myself from any long term harm.

Office Search on September 13, 1995
64. On September 13, 1995, a search was conducted at PITTS' office space at Quantico. The search revealed the following: a dark colored binder was located in PITTS' file cabinet which contained the "dead drop" instruction note furnished to PITTS by the UCO on August 26, 1995. A sheet of paper containing the alias signature "Edwin Pearl" was also located in the binder.

October 18, 1995 Drop by "SVRR [FBI]" and Pick Up by PITTS
65. At approximately 5:12 a.m., on October 18, 1995, the FBI posing as the "SVRR," placed a 3.5" computer disk, wrapped in plastic, at the appointed drop site in Fairfax County, Virginia. The disk contained tasking for PITTS and operational planning for future-drop activities.

66. PITTS left his residence at approximately 8:00 a.m. He drove to his work place and entered his office at approximately 8:45 a.m. He took a dark colored binder from his file cabinet and several envelopes, and then left his office at 9:60 a.m. During the next two hours, PITTS drove to various locations in what I believe to be an effort to detect surveillance.

67. Technical coverage at the drop site revealed that PITTS arrived from a westerly direction on Yates Ford Road, at approximately 11:21 a.m. He left the drop site at approximately 11:27 a.m. and left the area, heading north on Highway 123 to the signal site. Instead of turning right at Burke Center Parkway, as would be the most direct route, PITTS continued north on Highway 123, .25 miles north of Burke Center Parkway. He turned left into Fairfax Station Square Shopping Center at approximately 11:46 a.m. PITTS exited his vehicle and walked toward one of the stores. PITTS was next seen in a southbound direction on Highway 123, turning left onto Burke Center Parkway. He turned left into Burke Center Shopping Center and parked in the western end of the parking lot. He entered CVS Pharmacy, exited and walked toward Baskin Robbins. He entered Baskin Robbins, bought an ice cream cone and stayed in the store for approximately ten minutes. He exited the store, looked around the area, walked across the street and marked the signal on a fire hydrant as he passed by. He then walked through the parking lot back toward his vehicle. Before reaching his vehicle he returned (through the parking lot) to the area of the signal site. He once again looked around, looked at the signal site from across the street (in front of Baskin Robbins), then walked down the sidewalk and back to his vehicle, leaving the shopping center at approximately 12:03 p.m.

Events of November 1, 1995–November 3, 1995

68. On or about November 1, 1995, PITTS was observed typing on a laptop computer in his office, looking through and writing in spiral notebooks, looking at a dark colored binder and handling and reviewing documents marked "Secret." These activities collectively lasted approximately 176 minutes.

69. On or about November 2, 1995, PITTS spent approximately 95 minutes typing on his laptop computer in his office at work.

70. On or about November 2, 1995 at approximately 8:26 p.m., a search of PITTS' office revealed the following items of interest: a handwritten note with names of FBI Special Agents recently transferred to the National Security Division at FBI Headquarters; a handwritten note describing a Northern Virginia Public storage facility at 7400 Alban Station Boulevard, with telephone number (703) 569-6926; a 3.51" computer disk labeled "PITTS" which contained the information passed via "dead drop" on September 8, 1995; and a dark colored binder containing, in part, "dead drop" and signal site locations and a photocopy of the note with the name "EDWIN PEARL" on it.

71. During the same search on November 2, 1995, the hard drive on PITTS' personal notebook computer was searched. It contained a six page, single spaced, letter to PITTS' "SVRR handlers."

This letter included the following:

Information concerning past and current FCI operations in New York, Los Angeles and Washington, D.C., identifying information concerning eight FBI agents, including himself, including such information as home address, current assignment, and number of children. (PITTS made reference to himself in this letter in the third person, as if the letter had been composed by someone else.)

Information concerning an "emergency escape plan in the event it needs to be used on short notice."

Information concerning PITTS' plan to provide and receive information via a computer disk left in a storage facility in the Springfield, Virginia, area.

72. I believe that PITTS was preparing this document to pass via computer disk to persons he believed to be the SVRR on the scheduled drop dates of either November 1, November 2, or November 3, 1995. (This document was not in fact passed due to the discovery by PITTS of a surveillance device.)

73. On November 3, 1995, it was determined that PITTS had discarded the following, among other items:

1) ten typewritten pages with classified markings cut off;

2) ten pieces of paper stamped "Secret" which appeared to be from the cut off tops of a document;

3) ten pieces of paper stamped "Secret" which appeared to be cut off from the bottom portion of a document.

November 16, 1995 Telephone Contact

74. On or about November 16, 1995, PITTS was telephonically contacted by an undercover FBI Special Agent (hereinafter "UCA") posing as an SVRR officer. PITTS received the call at a public telephone near the FasMart Convenience Store, located at the intersection of Kilarney Drive and Route 3, Fredericksburg, Virginia.

75. During the telephone conversation, the UCA instructed PITTS to retrieve two keys and a slip of paper from a magnetic box located underneath the telephone. PITTS was told the keys were for a mailbox and the address of the mailbox was on the paper. The keys open Box 318, located at a Mailboxes Etc., facility in the Eastern District of Virginia, hereafter referred to as "Box 318."

November 17, 1995 Drop

76. On or about November 17, 1995, PITTS placed a computer disk in Box 318. This disk contained a letter to the person PITTS believed to be his SVRR handler. The letter included the following: apologies for missing the last meeting, information regarding the discovery and arrest of Aldrich Ames, and the risks associated with exchanging information via a mailbox.

77. On or about November 17, 1995, PITTS was paid $10,000.00 by what he believed to be the SVRR via Box 318.

December 13, 1995 Drop

78. On or about December 13, 1995, PITTS delivered a computer disk via Box 318. This disk contained a letter to the person PITTS believed to be his SVRR handler. The letter included the following: information regarding technical penetrations in use by the FBI, his use of surveillance detection routes, and the identities of FBI agents who had access to operations conducted against the KGB while PITTS was assigned to the New York office and their current assignments.

Events of December 17, 1995, December 28, 1995 and December 29, 1995

79. On December 17, 1995, PITTS had a telephone conversation with the person he believed to be his SVRR handler. In fact, the person posing as an SVRR officer was an FBI Undercover Agent (hereafter, "UCA"). In the conversation, the UCA and PITTS set up a meet. Significantly, PITTS was never told precisely where the meet was to take place; rather, he was told to meet at the same location where he had first met the CW in 1987 (i.e., the New York Public Library]:

UCA: Okay. Edwin. Thank you for your package and your signal was received and ah, ah, listen Edwin. Ah, your friend from Moscow has come and he must speak to you face-to-face to discuss some important matters and give you something substantial from your account and a Christmas bonus also, okay?

PITTS: Okay.

UCA: Okay. Now, Edwin. Ah, you must come to the place where you first requested to meet in 1987. Do you remember this place?

PITTS: Ah, yes.

UCA: Okay, good. Now you remember the section where you came?

PITTS: Ah, I believe so. Yes.

UCA: Good. Good. Okay, Edwin. We will meet you there, okay?

PITTS: Okay.

UCA: Go to the same place you first requested to meet and arrive there at thirteen hundred hours. One three zero zero.

PITTS: Okay.

UCA: At the same table, in the same section at this place.

PITTS: Okay.

UCA: And you will see somebody, someone you already know. Somebody already known to you. Okay?

PITTS: Okay.

UCA: This person will give you instructions.

PITTS: Okay.

The meet was set for December 28, 1995 at 1 p.m.

80. The meet described above did not take place. PITTS traveled to New York City and followed a surveillance detection route provided to him by his "SVRR [FBI]" handler. He then went to the New York City Public Library and spent approximately 30 minutes in several rooms of the library. PITTS then left the library and returned to Virginia.

81. At 5:35 p.m., on December 28, 1995, PITTS and the undercover agent spoke on the telephone:

UCA: Edwin, what happened?

PITTS: Uh, I was there in the room. I, I, none of your friends were there.

UCA: Okay. Now, uh, a friend that you know, a person whom you know waited for you and was seated at the table in the Law Section of Room 228, and waiting for you.

PITTS: Okay. That's not where we first met.

UCA: It is not where you met?

PITTS: No.

UCA: Oh, where did you meet? You know I, I thought that this is the place that you met. Where did you meet him the first time?

PITTS: No, it was in the uh, uh, I think it is called the Public Affairs and Economics.

UCA: Public Affairs and Economics you think that is where you met him?
PITTS: Yes.

UCA: Because my people thought that you met him in the Law Section, in Room 228.

PITTS: No, it, it was around the corner. I, I thought there might be some confusion. I looked around uh, but I couldn't find him anywhere, I, I must have missed him in that section.

A second meeting was scheduled for the next day at National Airport. PITTS stated that he would do "everything I can" to make the meet and would "treat it importantly" but that he did not have "complete control" over his schedule. PITTS was told that the meet would be with "somebody that you know uh, somebody that knows you...."

82. On December 29, 1995, at approximately 10 a.m., PITTS arrived at National Airport and met with CW (the person to whom PITTS had written the 1987 letter):

PITTS: Hi. I'm sorry I, didn't, uh, like yesterday I couldn't find you inside the . . .

CW: You couldn't find the place, yes?

CW: I mean uh, you didn't remember the place, yes? Actually I went to this, the, the library where you took me for the first time after how many years have passed? (laughs)

PITTS: Well, I'm trying to remember.

CW: (laughs)

PITTS: Yeah, we met down on the, on the second floor . . .

CW: . . . how much time did you wait?

PITTS: No, I looked through the (word or two unclear) half an hour or so.

CW: And uh . . .

PITTS: I looked through the library, and I looked through other areas, but uh . . .

CW: But it was changed, you know? Because . . .

PITTS: Yeah.

CW: . . . when you invited me, then those computers were not in.

PITTS: Yeah, that's, that's what caused the confusion, really, the library had changed considerably, and it's full of computers now.

CW: Uh-huh, uh-huh! Well, I didn't say Merry Christmas, sir!

PITTS: Yes, also Merry Christmas to you.

CW: I have one funny question to ask you.

PITTS: Yes?

CW: Why did you select me? (laughs) You had that whole bunch of people in the, in the Embassy.

PITTS: Ah, it's because you were ah, you were misidentified [as a KGB officer].

83. CW then took PITTS to a parked car, where PITTS met with the undercover officer (hereafter, "UCO") posing as an SVRR official from Moscow. The UCO tasked PITTS, on behalf of the "SVRR [FBI]," to obtain a list of all our [SVRR] people from our services . . . who is known to your [FBI] people. By name and their avocation, what they really deal with. When asked if he understood the tasking, PITTS responded, "You, you, want a list of uh, of people with their, their overt cover and, and what we have them classified as." PITTS

was told that "should you provide this list to us, we are willing to pay you fifteen thousand dollars for this list."

84. On or about December 29, 1995, PITTS accepted $20,000.00 in payment for services from what he believed to be the "SVRR." The money was passed to PITTS by his "SVRR [FBI]" handler in a meeting which took place in a vehicle parked at National Airport, in the Eastern District of Virginia.

February 13, 1996 Drop

85. On or about January 29 and January 30, 1996, PITTS made arrangements with a pager company to buy a pager, which he picked up on or about February 1, 1996. PITTS purchased this pager to use for covert communication with what he believed to be his "SVRR" handlers. A paging system was established so the need to physically mark a signal site was eliminated and intentions to make a drop or a telephone call could be relayed via the pager. PITTS purchased this pager in furtherance of his espionage activities while using the pager issued to him by the FBI for other purposes.

86. On or about February 13, 1996, PITTS deposited a manila envelope in Box 318. The envelope contained an FBI document entitled: "Russian Administrative List," dated 10/20/95 consisting of 91 pages (pages 71 through 91 were repeated). The "Russian Administrative List" was marked "Secret" at the top and bottom of each page. In my opinion, this document is related to the national defense as that term is used in Title 18, United States Code, Section 794. This list was made available to PITTS in early November 1995 in the course of PITTS' regular duties at the FBI. While PITTS came into possession the "Russian Administrative List" in a lawful manner, he had no authority to duplicate the list for the purpose of conveying it to persons he did not believe to be authorized recipients.

87. On or about March 21, 1996, PITTS paged the "SVRR [FBI]" to his cellular phone and reported that he was not able to make his drop as planned, but would do so on the first, second or third of April. The following was part of this conversation:

> PITTS: Uh, yes, everything is fine uh, I'm making some progress on your request uh some of the things are more difficult than I thought but I have several avenues to explore so . . .

> UCA: Yes.

> PITTS: Ah I'll explain that in more detail uh when uh you get my package.

April 3, 1996 Drop

88. On or about April 3, 1996, PITTS placed an envelope in Box 318. The envelope contained a computer disk which contained a letter to the person he believed to be his SVRR handler. The letter included the following: information regarding numerous FBI Special Agents who had recently been given transfer orders to various FBI Field offices and Headquarters, a description of various FBI units within the National Security Division, and the names of FBI or other agency personnel who he said were assigned to national security related investigations.

89. In the same April 3, 1996 letter, PITTS promised his "SVRR [FBI]" handler that he would "attempt to gain an inroad" into a unit responsible for reviewing sensitive national security operations.

April 16, 1996 Drop

90. On or about April 16, 1996, PITTS placed an envelope in Box 318. The envelope contained three hundred fifty two pages. Included in the envelope were FBI telephone directories from The FBI Training Academy, FBI Headquarters, the Washington Metropolitan Field Office, FBI Field offices throughout the United States and FBI Legal Attaché Offices throughout the world. The envelope also contained FBI organizational charts from FBI Headquarters.

91. Such telephone directories including the FBI Headquarters directory referred to above, often contained on their front cover the following warning prohibiting unauthorized dissemination:

> This document is for internal use within the FBI, is to be provided appropriate security, and disposed of in official trash receptacles when no longer current.

April 24, 1996 Telephone Conversation

92. On or about April 2, 1996, PITTS paged the "SVRR [FBI]" and, during the telephone conversation that followed, the UCA and PITTS spoke substantially as follows:

PITTS: I was wondering if it would be able ah, if it would be possible for me to pick up a payment, ah, sometime in the near future?

UCA: Ok, ah, what are your needs, Edwin?

PITTS: Ah just for the material that I've ah, delivered.

UCA: Right. Did you have a certain amount in mind?

PITTS: Ah, well, ah, I believe uh, I have the list you gave me ah, whatever you feel is equitable.

Later in the conversation they continue substantially as follows:

UCA: Is, is eh, equitable. Ok, ok, I will tell this to my superiors. And, ah, is everything ok with you?

PITTS: Ah, yes. Everything is going well. I'm continuing on our project. There's some an… unanticipated uh, difficulty in just locating uh, the information but uh, I'll continue. I…I'll send a progress report with my next uh… report on…on what I found or haven't been able to find.

Later in the conversation they continue substantially as follows:

UCA: Ok. By the by, we received your recent shipment and I understand it was very interesting information.

PITTS: I hope it's ah, good.

93. On or about May 6, 1996, the "SVRR [FBI]" paid PITTS $5,000.00 via Box 318.

May 16, 1996 Drop
94. On or about May 15, 1996, PITTS paged the "SVRR[FBI]," indicating that he would make a drop the next day on or about May 16, 1906. PITTS placed an envelope in Box 318. This envelope contained a videotape classified "Secret." The videotape was of a presentation by an FBI Special Agent to a counterintelligence training class at the FBI Academy in Quantico, Virginia.

June 28, 1996 Drop
95. On or about June 27, 1996, PITTS paged the "SVRR [FBI]" to let them know that he would make a drop the next day. On or about June 28, 1996, he placed an envelope in Box 318. This envelope contained a personnel list for certain FBI employees in the Washington, D.C. area and a computer disk. This disk contained a letter to the person PITTS believed to be his SVRR handler. The letter contained information about three FBI Special Agents who had participated in a particular counterintelligence operation while PITTS was in New York. The letter included the FBI Special Agents home addresses, current office assignments and PITTS' assessment of their personalities. The latter included information such as job satisfaction and, as to one agent, her medical condition. I am aware that the SVRR targets persons with vulnerabilities, such as job dissatisfaction, and that these vulnerabilities can be exploited for recruitment purposes.

The disk also contained lists of FBI personnel being trained at the FBI Academy and the training received; and transfers within the Intelligence Division of the FBI. Finally, PITTS' letter to his "SVRR [FBI]" handler contains the following statements concerning two telecommunications devices:

The secure telephone model III (STU III) is capable of encrypting telephone conversations and facsimile transmissions up to Top Secret level.

I need to know how long you need access to the telephone. I also need to know if you will need access to the key. Finally, I need to know if it will be necessary for me to deliver the telephone to you, or if it can be examined on site.

I can get into a protected area that houses a telephone, but I don't know if I'll be able to disconnect it once inside. I know the location of the key for the unit, but do not have access to where it is located. Access can be gained by manipulating a common tumbler lock, but I do not have those skills. If you have someone who is skilled in entry, I have several preliminary plans for getting them to the location undected [sic]. The key planning factor is how long the examination will take, as it will only be a matter of hours before the unit is missed. Please advise.

I have located several ciphered radios, but they are closely accounted for. Access to the area is closely controlled, so a direct theft of one of the radios would be a very high-risk manuver [sic]. If it is possible to make a facsimile of a radio, it is possible that the facsimile could be substituted for the actual radio, delaying discovery that it is missing. Once the discovery is noticed, security measures will increase dramatically, making future operations much more difficult or impossible. My own assessment is that a direct theft poses greater risks than the potential rewards, but it is a possibility.

I will continue to look for an alternative means of securing a radio that poses fewer operational risks.

July 9, 1996 Drop

96. On or about July 8, 1996, PITTS paged the "SVRR [FBI]" indicating that he would make a drop the next day. As indicated on July 9, 1996, he placed an envelope in Box 318 which contained a computer disk and 112 pages of an FBI Headquarters manual titled "Informal FBI Headquarters Supervisors Manual - Intelligence Division (INTD)." The document was clearly classified "Secret" on the cover, and on numerous internal pages.

The letter on the disk explained that this was only a portion of the manual and the rest would be delivered later (due to the size of the manual). He also requested payment during the week of July 15, 1996.

97. On or about July 22, 1996, the "SVRR [FBI]" paged PITTS, indicating that they would make a drop the following day. This drop included a payment of $5,000.00.

July 25, 1996 Drop

98. On or about July 24, 1996, PITTS paged the "SVRR" indicating that he would make a drop on the following day. As indicated on July 25, 1996 he placed an envelope in Box 318. This envelope contained 110 pages of the Secret FBI manual described above. The drop also contained a computer disk, containing a letter to PITTS' "SVRR [FBI]" handlers. In the letter, PITTS apologized for missing "my appointment last week"; noted that his schedule was unpredictable but believed it could be "managed to avoid unreasonable disruption to our mutual interests"; promised to provide the SVRR "details concerning the [STU-III] telephone you have requested as soon as possible"; and suggested that the Thanksgiving holiday would offer an "excellent window of opportunity" [to smuggle into the FBI Academy an SVRR technical expert].

July 31, 1996 Drop

99. On or about July 30, 1996, PITTS paged the "SVRR [FBI]" indicating that he would make a drop the following day. As indicated, on July 31, 1996, he placed an envelope in Box 318 which contained 192 pages of the Secret FBI manual described above.

August 14, 1996 Drop

100. On or about August 13, 1996, PITTS paged the "SVRR [FBI]" to indicate that he would make a drop the next day. As indicated, on August 14, 1996, he placed an envelope in Box 318. This drop included a computer disk which contained a six page letter. Among "Personnel Actions of Interests," PITTS described a recently retired FBI Special Agent as one whose "knowledge of operations and sources of information over a number of years would be valuable in assessing any past or present security breaches. If the opportunity arises to make an indirect approach, it should be worth the effort." As stated above, vulnerabilities are a key to assessing potential recruitment targets. PITTS also wrote that this agent "tends to be talkative, and appears to be somewhat lonely and isolated. At the time I knew him, most of his social activities revolved around work relationships. Now that he is retired, he will probably feel cut off socially and may be approachable as an indirect source of information."

101. Other information contained on the disk dealt primarily with PITTS' continued efforts toward assisting the "SVRR [FBI]" in gaining access to a STU-III telephone. He told of the location of the STU-III he considered most appropriate, and gave the "SVRR [FBI]" the cypher lock combination to the door of the room housing the telephone. Vehicle and foot access into the Academy were detailed, as well as the possibility of "covert placement (by SVRR personnel] in a class" at the Academy.

102. In this communication, PITTS also noted his desire for a "steady stream of payments," and his concern about being able to "mask" his payments received from the SVRR:

Regarding my reserve, I do not know the amount and it is my understanding that you do not. When I last met with Alex, it was over $100,000. I do not recall discussing the matter with Alex's friends who I met later. The amount of the reserve is not the key point I was trying to raise in my recent communication. I believe I am being treated fairly even though circumstances have made our working relationship more difficult.

My purpose in requesting the recent payments, even if they came from reserve, was to keep a steady stream of payments in place. Given the difficulties we have had maintaining contact in the past, changes in your organizational structure and current conditions, large reserves are of very little current use to me. There are also practical problems that I must deal with if your payments are made in only a few lump sums. It is very difficult to make use of large sums, (over $10,000) without leaving traces of its source. It also is not wise to leave large sums of cash unused, as holding large amounts of cash raises immediate suspicions. The safest way to deal with this is to create a situation where smaller amounts of money can be hidden in assets that are not easily observable but, that can accumulate over a longer period of time. To do this, it is better to deal in smaller amounts but to do so regularly. Regular patterns of spending are difficult to detect, but erratic patterns stand out regardless of the amounts involved. Transactions involving large amounts of money are difficult to hide, even if they are done in cash. Therefore, it is important to my purposes that smaller amounts of cash can regularly be infused into the structures I am using to mask your payments. I suggested use of the reserves because much of the information I have recently provided is not of the quality I have provided in the past and did not wish to imply I expected the same level of payment. However, it is also important that I create and maintain a structure that can accomodate [sic] and mask payments for higher quality material, such as the project we are working on now.

With both my needs and your needs (both monetary and security) in mind, I would ask you to make payments on the material I have provided on either the 10th or 11th of next month. I anticipate I will need one more payment before the end of this year (probablly [sic] November) after additional material is delivered to you.

103. The envelope provided to the "SVRR [FBI]" on August 14, 1996, also contained a color slide of an aerial view of the FBI Training Academy at Quantico, Virginia; eighty seven (87) pages of a Federal Bureau of Investigation manual titled "The Federal Bureau of Investigation Emergency Response Plans, FBI Academy, Quantico, Virginia, Training Division, April, 1996"; and ten (10) FBI Directories.

August 29, 1996 Drop
104. On or about August 29, 1996, PITTS placed an envelope in Box 318. This envelope contained a computer disk and four maps which correlated with information on the disk. On the disk, PITTS gave the exact location of "the device you are interested in" [the STU-III telephone detailed above], information concerning security devices near and on the way to the telephone, and various routes to the phone from the outside of the Academy. He gave the pros and cons for each route, stated which he recommended, and marked the routes on the accompanying maps.

105. On or about September 9, 1996, the "SVRR [FBI]" paged PITTS, indicating there would be a drop made on the following day. On or about September 10, 1996, PITTS was paid $5,000.00 by the "SVRR [FBI]."

September 18, 1996 Drop
106. On or about September 17, 1996, PITTS paged the "SVRR [FBI]" to indicate that he would make a drop the following day. On September 18, 1996, as indicated, PITTS placed an envelope in Box 318. This envelope contained a computer disk and five pages of technical information relating to FBI radios and telephones, including radio frequencies and channels used at the FBI Academy, FBI Headquarters, Washington Field Office, Philadelphia, Pittsburgh, Richmond and New York Divisions.

107. The disk contained information regarding transfers within the FBI Intelligence Division and National Security Division training instructors and attendees at the FBI Academy, including some home addresses and telephone numbers. PITTS highlighted

one individual as someone who "may be of significant interest to you." PITTS also gave extensive information on an FBI espionage investigation of an individual who passed "Top Secret" military information to the Soviets. PITTS continued in his efforts to plan the compromise of a STU-III telephone by recommending a date and method of entry for the SVRR technician, including a particular method to smuggle in the SVRR technician.

September 25, 1996 Drop

108. On or about September 24, 1996, PITTS paged the "SVRR [FBI]" indicating that he would be making a drop the following day. As indicated on or about September 25, 1996, PITTS placed an envelope in Box 318. This envelope contained a computer disk and several telephone directories for the FBI and it's field divisions.

The disk contained detailed information about the STU-III telephone and the best dates for the SVRR technician to enter the FBI Academy. PITTS offered a key to the Academy and a coded card which would allow unaccompanied access to the Academy.

October 6, 1996 Drop

109. On or about October 5, 1996 PITTS paged the "SVRR [FBI]" to indicate that he would make a drop the following day. On or about October 6, 1996, PITTS placed an envelope in Box 318. This envelope contained a computer disk containing a letter which detailed PITTS' continued planning for the entry of the SVRR technician. PITTS stated that "he was in the process of assessing security measures" for the building containing the STU-III. Also enclosed in the envelope were telephone directories and assignment charts for various divisions within the FBI.

110. In this same drop, PITTS enclosed a nineteen page FBI Intelligence Division report titled "Counterintelligence Techniques: Identifying an Intelligence Officer." This document is classified "Secret" in its entirety and, in my opinion, is related to the national defense, as that term is used in Title 18, United States Code, Section 794.

October 16, 1996 Drop

111. On or about October 15, 1996, PITTS paged the "SVRR [FBI]," indicating that he would be making a drop the next day. On or about October 16, 1996, PITTS placed an envelope in Box 318. The envelope contained a computer disk, a key, a hand drawn map with "target" written on it, and a printed FBI Academy map with handwritten notes. An FBI Special Agent verified that the key unlocked an outside door to the FBI Academy.

112. The disk contained information on the best date and time for the SVRR technician to enter the academy, according to staffing and security procedures around the "target area," and suggested a pick up point for the SVRR technician. PITTS offered to obtain an identification card and uniform for the technician to ensure the success of the operation.

113. On or about November 4, 1996, the "SVRR [FBI]" paged PITTS to indicate that there would be a drop for him the next day. On or about November 5, 1996, the "SVRR [FBI]" paid PITTS $5,000.00 via Box 318.

114. Along with the November 5, 1995, payment was a computer disk containing a letter from PITTS' "SVRR [FBI]" handlers. In the letter, the "SVRR [FBI]" told PITTS that it wished to have PITTS' assistance in a "related effort to defeat secure telephones" and that PITTS would be provided a device for this purpose.

115. On November 10, 1996, PITTS was provided by his "SVRR [FBI]" handlers a STU-III handset which PITTS was told had been "modified." PITTS was requested to exchange it with the STU-III handset at the FBI Academy and to deliver the handset "through normal method" for "modifications."

November 12, 1996 Drop

116. On or about November 12, 1996, PITTS placed an envelope in Box 318. This envelope contained an FBI Intelligence Division identification badge, number 784046. The badge is identifiable as PITTS' by his name and photo on the front. This type of badge is used by FBI employees and is considered to be Bureau property. This badge allows entry onto the FBI Academy grounds, as well as unaccompanied entry into the Academy buildings. It also provides bonafides for a person while walking through the Academy as all students, instructors, and visitors are required to wear a badge of some type while inside the Academy.

November 26, 1996 Drop

117. On or about November 26, 1996, PITTS placed an envelope in Box 318. It contained a computer disk

containing a letter to the person PITTS believed to be his SVRR handler. In the letter, PITTS referred to the STU-III handset and said:

> The device has been recieved [sic] and is ready for installation. A window of opportunity exists to install the device, and expect installation by December 2 or 3.

Stealing the STU-III Handset

118. On or about November 29, 1996, PITTS stole a handset from a STU-III telecommunications device from the FBI Academy and replaced it with the supposedly "modified" handset provided to him by his "SVRR [FBI]" handlers.

December 4, 1996 Drop

119. On or about December 3, 1996, PITTS paged the "SVRR [FBI]" to indicate that he would make a drop the next day. On or about December 4, 1996, PITTS made a drop via Box 318. The box he dropped included the handset which he had stolen from the FBI Academy.

The Final Drop

120. On December 12, 1996, PITTS paged the "SVRR [FBI]" indicating that he would make a drop the next day. On December 13, 1996, PITTS placed an envelope in Box 318. In the envelope was a computer disk containing a letter to PITTS' "SVRR [FBI]" handler. Among other things, the letter said:

> Please understand I no longer have direct access to the files concerning the events that took place during that period [of his New York assignment] and I believe I have provided you with everything that I was aware of.

121. The "false flag" operation described above began on or about August 12, 1995, and continued to on or about December 13, 1996. During this 16 month time period, PITTS made 22 drops of FBI internal information and documents, of both a classified and unclassified nature, held nine telephone conversations and two face-to-face meetings with his "SVRR [FBI]" handlers, and accepted payment of $65,000 for these services. At no time was PITTS authorized to divulge or convey such documents and information to unauthorized persons or to persons he believed to be unauthorized persons, or to attempt to compromise the security of this information.

Intent to Escape

122. On or about November 2, 1995, during a physical search of Room B-103, FBI Academy, Quantico Marine Base, Quantico, Virginia, the following information relating to an escape plan was found in the hard drive of PITTS' personally owned computer [typed, as in the original]:

> Personal security is a greater concern now due to suspicions that may have been raised by our direct communication and the greater possibility of security breakdowns since our previous exchanges. I am developing an emergency escape plan, in the event it needs to be used on short notice. If you wish me to contact you in such an event, please advise me of a point of contact, preferably outside this country, where I should make the contact. Under my working plan, it will take five to six weeks between instituting the plan and being in a position to make contact. To avoid possible security breaches, I will take total responsibility for extracting myself, and only need to know any final point at which you want me to arrive. If it can be passed, I need 35 to 40K from my account to fund the plan and use as a reserve to be used if the plan must be put into effect. Let me emphasize that my plan will only be put into effect as a final extreme measure when all other safeguards

123. In a December 6, 1996, telephone conversation between PITTS and his "SVRR [FBI]" handler, PITTS indicated that it was getting "close to that time" when he would need a passport prepared by the SVRR, and that he would provide the SVRR with a photograph.

124. Based on the above facts and circumstances I believe there is probable cause that EARL EDWIN PITTS committed the following violations of federal criminal law:

  A. Conspiracy to Commit Espionage, in violation of Title 18 United States Code Section 794(c);

  B. Attempted Espionage in violation of Title 18 United States Code Section 794(a);

C. Communication of Classified Information by Government Officer of Employee, in violation of Title 50 United States Code Section 783(a); and

D. Conveyance Without Authority of Government Property, in violation of Title 18 United States Code Section 641.

Items to be Searched and Seized

125. Based on my training and experience, I know that:

a. Agents of foreign intelligence services maintain records, notes, bank records, financial statements, calendars, journals, maps, instructions, classified documents, and other papers or documents relating to the transmittal of national defense and classified intelligence information to foreign governments and intelligence services. The aforementioned records, notes, bank records, financial statements, calendars, journals, maps, instructions, classified documents, and other papers or documents are maintained, albeit often secreted, on their persons, in and around their residences, places of employment, in home and office computers, automobiles, and in other remote locations, such as safe deposit boxes and storage facilities.

b. Agents of foreign intelligence services often utilize espionage paraphernalia, including devices designed to conceal and transmit national defense and classified intelligence information. These paraphernalia and devices include materials used by espionage agents to communicate between each other and with a foreign government, to wit: coded pads, secret writing paper, microdots, microfiche together with instructions in the use of these materials, recording and electronic transmittal equipment, chemicals used to develop coded and secret messages, computers, computer disks, cameras, film, books, records, documents, and papers. The information which is frequently passed or recorded through such methods often includes:

1) national defense and classified intelligence information;

2) the identities of other foreign espionage agents and intelligence officers;.

3) financial transactions including payments to foreign espionage agents and hidden financial accounts;

4) Records of previous illicit espionage transactions; and

5) the source and disposition of national defense and classified intelligence information.

c. Agents of foreign intelligence services routinely conceal in their residences large amounts of U.S. and foreign currency, financial instruments, precious metals, jewelry, and other items of value and/or proceeds of illegal espionage transactions. They also conceal records relating to hidden foreign and domestic bank and financial accounts, including accounts in fictitious names.

d. It is common for agents of foreign intelligence services to secrete national defense and classified documents and materials, clandestine communications devices and instructions, contact instructions, codes, telephone numbers, maps, photographs, other papers and materials relating to communications procedures, and proceeds and records of illegal espionage transactions in secure, hidden locations and compartments within their residences, places of employment, safe deposit boxes, and/or motor vehicles, including hidden compartments within motor vehicles, for ready access and to conceal such items from law enforcement authorities.

e. Agents of foreign intelligence services are not unlike any other individual in our society in that they maintain documents and records. These documents and records will normally be maintained for long periods of time regardless of whether their value to the agent has diminished. These persons maintain documents and records which will identify and corroborate travel both in the United states and abroad made in connection with foreign intelligence activity, including personal meets with foreign intelligence officers. These documents and records include passports, visas, calendars, journals, date books, telephone numbers, credit cards, hotel receipts, airline records, correspondence, carbon copies of money orders and cashier's checks evidencing large cash expenditures, and accounts and records in fictitious names.

f. Agents of foreign intelligence services often maintain identity documents, including those utilizing fictitious identities, U.S. and foreign currency, instructions, maps, photographs, U.S. and foreign bank accounts access numbers and instructions, and other papers and materials relating emergency contact procedures and escape plans.

126. Based on the foregoing, I believe there is probable cause that evidence, fruits, instrumentality's, and proceeds of this offense/these offenses are located in:

a. Premises known and described as a single family residence located at 13415 Fox Chase Lane, Spotsylvania, Virginia, 22553 (as more fully described in Attachment A), which is within the Eastern District of Virginia;

b. Premises known and described as Room B-103, Building 19, Behavioral Science Unit, FBI Academy, Quantico Marine Base, Quantico, Virginia (as more fully described in Attachment B) which is within the Eastern District of Virginia;

c. One 1992 Chevrolet S-10 Pick-up Truck, bearing Virginia registration KVI-582, VIN:lGCCS19R7N2l48561, which based on recent observation by FBI Special Agents and surveillance personnel presently is located at 13415 Fox Chase Lane, Spotsylvania, Virginia, 22553;

d. One 1996 Honda Accord, bearing Virginia reg. OXK-347, VIN:lHGCD5636TA1.12429, which based on recent observation by FBI Special Agents and surveillance personnel presently is located at 13415 Fox Chase Lane, Spotsylvania, Virginia, 22553;

e. One storage unit, numbered A425, located at 7400 Alban Station Boulevard, Springfield, Virginia, 22150 (as more fully described in Attachment C);

f. One storage unit,, numbered D13, located at U-Stor-It Mini Storage, 3662 1/2 Jefferson Davis Highway, Fredericksburg, Virginia, 22408 (as more fully described in Attachment D); and

g. One safety deposit box, numbered 114, located at the Central Fidelity Bank, 4230 Plank Road, Fredericksburg, Virginia, 22407.

Warrants Requested

127. Based on the foregoing, I respectfully request the following:

a. Warrant for the Arrest of:
EARL EDWIN PITTS
DOB: September 23, 1953,
SSAN: 486-62-7841;

for violations of Title 18, United States Code (USC), Sections 794(a), 794(c) and 641, and Title 50, United States Code, Section 783(a).

b. Search Warrants for:

1) Premises known and described as a single family residence located at 13415 Fox Chase Laner Spotslvania, Virginia, 22553 (as more fully described in Attachment A), which is within the Eastern District of Virginia;

2) Premises known and described as Room B-103, Building 19, Behavioral Science Unit FBI Academy, Quantico Marine Base, Quantico, Virginia (as more fully described in Attachment B), which is within the Eastern District of Virginia;

3) One 1992 Chevrolet S-10 Pick-up truck, bearing Virginia registration NVI-582, VIN:lGCCS19R7N2l48561 which based on recent observation by FBI Special Agents and surveillance personnel is presently located at 13415 Fox Chase Lane, Spotsylvania, Virginia 22553;

4) One 1996 Honda Accord sedan, bearing Virginia registration OXK-347,

VIN:1HGCD5636TA112429, which based on recent observation by FBI Special Agents and surveillance personnel is presently located at 13415 Fox Chase Lane, Spotsylvania, Virginia, 22553;

5) One storage unit, numbered A425, located at Public Storage, 7400 Alban Station Boulevard, Springfleld, Virginia, 22150 (as more fully described in Attachment C);

6) One storage unit, numbered D13, located at U-Stor-It Mini Storage, 3662 1/2 Jefferson Davis Highway, Fredericksburg, Virginia, 22408 (as more fully described in Attachment D); and

7) One safety deposit box, numbered 114, located at the Central Fidelity Bank, 4230 Plank Road, Fredericksburg, Virginia 22407.

Items to be searched for are more fully described in Attachment E.

128. The above facts are true and correct to the best of my knowledge and belief.

David G. Lambert, Special Agent
Federal Bureau of Investigation
Subscribed to and
Sworn before me this
17th day of December, 1996

Hon. Thomas Rawles Jones, Jr.
UNITED STATES MAGISTRATE JUDGE

Alexandria, Virginia

ATTACHMENT A
(Residence of EARL EDWIN PITTS)

The residence located on two and one half acres of land with the address 13415 Fox Chase Lane, Spotsylvania, Virginia. It is a single family dwelling facing Fox Chase Lane. The home has two levels above ground and an unfinished basement. The outside of the residence is finished with tan siding and brick and has a two-car garage attached.

The residence is accessed via a paved driveway that extends 215 feet from Fox Chase Lane. The house number "13415" is located on a mailbox at the street.

ATTACHMENT B
(Office space of EARL EDWIN PITTS)

Room B-103, Building 19, Behavioral Science Unit, is located on the 3rd level beneath the gun vault at the FBI Academy, Quantico Marine Base, Quantico, Virginia. The room is accessed by descending in the elevator located in the firearms cleaning area to "3B." On the wall beside B-103 is a sign, "Earl E. Pitts." The office has a single, wooden door and is approximately 15 feet long and 10 feet wide. The office walls are blue; the ceiling is white.

ATTACHMENT C
(Storage space of EARL EDWIN PITTS)

One storage unit, numbered A425, located at Public Storage, 7400 Alban Station Boulevard, Springfield, Virginia, 22150.

Directions to this unit are as follows: go through a locked gate that requires a keypad code. Facing the storage building, turn left and approximately 35-50 yards on the right is a door to enter the building. Take the elevator to the third floor, exit and take two lefts. Unit A425 is on the right.

ATTACHMENT D
(Storage Space of EARL EDWIN PITTS)

One storage unit, numbered D13, located at U-Stor-It Mini Storage, 3662 1/2 Jefferson Davis Highway, Fredericksburg, Virginia, 22408.

The storage facility is located on the Route 1 Bypass, behind Purvis Ford. The facility is surrounded by a 7'-8' fence. Turn left after entering the facility and go to the end of the two buildings.

Unit D13 is in the western-most building on the north end.

ATTACHMENT E
(Items of EARL EDWIN PITTS to be searched)

1) records, notes, bank records, financial statements, calendars, journals, maps, instructions, classified documents, and other papers or documents relating to the transmittal of national defense and classified intelligence information to foreign governments;

2) espionage paraphernalia, including devices designed to conceal and transmit national defense and

classified intelligence information and materials used by espionage agents to communicate among each other and with a foreign government, to wit: coded pads, secret writing paper, microdots, microfiche together with instructions in the use of these materials, recording and electronic transmittal equipment, chemicals used to develop coded or secret messages, computers, computer disks, cameras, film, books, records, documents, and papers which reflect:

    a) national defense and classified intelligence information,

    b) the identities of other foreign espionage agents and intelligence officers,

    c) financial transactions including payments to foreign espionage agents and hidden financial accounts

    d) records of previous illicit espionage transactions, and

    e) the source and disposition of national defense and classified intelligence information;

3) large amounts of U.S. and foreign currency financial instruments, precious metals, jewelry, and other items of value and/or proceeds of illegal espionage transactions.

4) national defense and classified documents and materials, clandestine communications devices and instructions, contact instructions, codes, telephone numbers, maps, photographs, other papers and materials relating to communications procedures and proceeds and records of illegal espionage transactions;

5) passports, visas, calendars, journals, date books, telephone numbers, address books, credit cards, hotel receipts, airline records, correspondence, carbon copies of money orders and cashier's checks evidencing large cash expenditures, and accounts and records in fictitious names;

6) identity documents, including those utilizing fictitious identities, U.S. and foreign currency, instructions, maps, photographs, U.S. and foreign bank account access numbers and instructions, and other papers and materials relating emergency contact procedures and escape routes;

7) foreign and domestic bank records, including canceled checks, monthly statements, deposit slips, withdrawal slips, wire transfer requests and confirmations, account numbers, addresses, signature cards, credit cards, and credit card statements, and all other financial statements;

8) safety deposit box records, including signature cards, bills, and payment records;

9) financial and investment account records, including statements, investment confirmations, withdrawal and dividend records, and all other-related account records;

10) federal, state, and local tax returns, work sheets, W-2 forms, W-4 forms, 1099 forms, and all related schedules; and

11) records concerning real property purchases, sales, transfers, in the U.S. and foreign countries, including but not limited to deeds, deeds of trust, land contracts, promissory notes, settlement statements, and mortgage documents.

Russian Commentary on Pitts' Arrest

Analysis by Igor Korotchenko under the general headline: "Yet another agent arrested in the United States....This is the way the FBI 'congratulated' the Russian Chekists on their professional holiday." (FBIS translated text from Moscow Nezavisimaya Gazeta (NG), 20 December 1997.)

In line with existing practice, the official spokesman of Russia's Foreign Intelligence Service (SVR) traditionally declined all comment on the arrest in the United States of FBI employee Earl Edwin Pitts of charges of spying for Moscow. Admittedly, Tatyana Smolis, press secretary of the SVR Director, uttered a very remarkable phrase talking with your NG correspondent: "Irrespective of this case, I can say that even having carried out a considerable reduction of our apparatus abroad, we have not lost the high quality of work inherent in our service. It is sometimes possible to score a greater effect with a smaller number of people."

It will be recalled that this disgraceful episode happened soon after the case of CIA officer Harold Nicholson accused of cooperation for many years with the KGB's PGU (First Main Department) and the SVR was taken to court.

Although the SVR gave up "globalism" after 1991 and closed more than 30 of its stations in Africa, South East Asia, and Latin America, Russian intelligence doctrine still lists the United States among the objects of prime attention. True, the term "Main Adversary" with regard to Washington is no longer used in the official documents of the intelligence service. At the present time, the man in charge of the American area in the SVR's activities is Lt. Gen. Grigoriy Rapota who has the rank of Deputy Director of this Special Service. He keeps daily tabs on the operational subdivisions abroad subordinated to him. The SVR has three "legal" stations operating in the United States under the cover of official Russian institutions in New York, Washington, and San Francisco. Each of them includes several dozen staff members and has a direct channel of coded communication with the SVR headquarters in Yasenevo. The work of diplomatic stations is organized and carried out in three main area—political, economic, and technical-scientific spying.

Furthermore, according to existing expert assessments, the Foreign Intelligence Service has created anywhere from three to seven major illegal stations in the United States and Canada, each of which is in contact with a corresponding Directorate in Yasenevo. The SVR's Foreign Counterintelligence Directorate also has its own apparatus of agents in the United States who operate independently.

Obviously, in order to localize what is already the second exposure of a valuable Russian spy, Yasenevo will set up a special commission to thoroughly investigate the circumstances of what happened. However, the circumstance that the date of Pitt's arrest was not a random choice is now already conspicuous; it comes shortly before 20 December, the day of the Workers of Russian Federation State Security. American counterintelligence has in this manner "congratulated" Russian Chekists on their professional holiday. FBI Director Louis Freeh must have been strongly impressed by the recent press conference of FSB (Federal Security Service) head Nikolay Kovalev where he announced the catching of 39 agents, Russian citizens recruited by Western special services. This was, perhaps, the other reason why the FBI urgently detained Earl Edwin Pitts, who had been actively watched by American counterintelligence.

Economic Espionage Act of 1996

SECTION 1. SHORT TITLE.

This Act may be cited as the "Economic Espionage Act of 1996."

Sec. 101. PROTECTION OF TRADE SECRETS.

(a) IN GENERAL.–Title 18, United States Code, is amended by inserting after chapter 89 the following:

"CHAPTER 90–PROTECTION OF TRADE SECRETS

Sec.
1831. Economic espionage.
1832. Theft of trade secrets.
1833. Exceptions to prohibitions.
1834. Criminal forfeiture.
1835. Orders to preserve confidentiality.
1836. Civil proceedings to enjoin violations.
1837. Conduct outside the United States.
1838. Construction with other laws.
1839. Definitions.
1831. Economic espionage

(a) IN GENERAL.–Whoever, intending or knowing that the offense will benefit any foreign government, foreign instrumentality, or foreign agent, knowingly—

(1) steals, or without authorization appropriates, takes, carries away, or conceals, or by fraud, artifice, or deception obtains a trade secret;

(2) without authorization copies, duplicates, sketches, draws, photographs, downloads, uploads, alters, destroys, photocopies, replicates, transmits, delivers, sends, mails, communicates, or conveys a trade secret;

(3) receives, buys, or possesses a trade secret, knowing the same to have been stolen or appropriated, obtained, or converted without authorization;

(4) attempts to commit any offense described in any of paragraphs (1) through (3); or

(5) conspires with one or more others persons to commit any offense described in any of paragraphs (1) through (4), and one or more of such persons do any act to effect the object of the conspiracy, shall, except as provided in subsection (b), be fined not more than $500,000 or imprisoned not more than 15 years, or both.

(b) ORGANIZATIONS.—Any organization that commits any offense described in subsection (a) shall be fined not more than $10,000,000.

1832. Theft of trade secrets

(a) Whoever, with intent to convert a trade secret, that is related to or included in a product that is produced for or placed in interstate of foreign commerce, to the economic benefit of anyone other than the owner thereof, and intending or knowing that the offense will, injure any owner of that trade secret, knowingly—

(1) steals, or without authorization appropriates, takes, carries away, or conceals, or by fraud, artifice, or deception obtains a trade secret;

(2) without authorization copies, duplicates, sketches, draws, photographs, downloads, uploads, alters, destroys, photocopies, replicates, transmits, delivers, sends, mails, communicates, or conveys such information;

(3) receives, buys, or possesses such information, knowing the same to have been stolen or appropriated, obtained, or converted without authorization;

(4) attempts to commit any offense described in any of paragraphs (1) through (3); or

(5) conspires with one or more others persons to commit any offense described in any of paragraphs (1) through (3), and one or more of such persons do any act to effect the object of the conspiracy, shall, except as provided in subsection (b), be fined under this title or imprisoned not more than 10 years, or both.

(b) Any organization that commits any offense described in subsection (a) shall be fined not more than $5,000,000.

1833. Exceptions to prohibitions

"This chapter does not prohibit—

"(1) any otherwise lawful activity conducted by a government entity of the United States, a State, or a political subdivision of a State; or

"(2) the reporting of a suspected violation of law to any government entity of the United States, a State, or a political subdivision of a State, if such entity has lawful authority with respect to that violation.

1834. Criminal forfeiture

(a)   The court, in imposing sentence on a person for a violation of this chapter, shall order, in addition to any other sentenced imposed, that the person forfeit to the United States—

(1) any property constituting, or derived from, any proceeds the person obtained, directly or indirectly, as the result of such violation; and

(2) any of the person's property used, or intended to be used, in any manner or part, to commit or facilitate the commission of such violation, if the court in its discretion so determines, taking into consideration the nature, scope, and proportionality of the use of the property in the offense.

(b) Property subject to forfeiture under this section, any seizure and disposition thereof, and any administrative or judicial proceedings in relation thereto, shall be governed by section 413 of the Comprehensive Drug Abuse Prevention and Control Act of 1970 (21 U.S.C. 853), except for subsections (d) and (j) of such section, which shall not apply to forfeitures under this section.

1835. Orders to preserve confidentiality

In any prosecution or other proceeding under this chapter, the court shall enter such orders and take such other action as may be necessary and appropriate to preserve the confidentiality of trade secrets, consistent with the requirements of the Federal Rules of Criminal and Civil Procedure, the federal rules of Evidence, and all other applicable laws. An interlocutory appeal by the United States shall lie from a decision or order of a district court authorizing or directing the disclosure of any trade secret.

1836. Civil proceedings to enjoin violations

(a) The Attorney general may, in a civil action, obtain appropriate injunctive relief against any violation of this section.

(b) The district courts of the United States shall have exclusive original jurisdiction of civil actions under this subsection.

1837. Applicability to conduct outside the United States

This chapter also applies to conduct occurring outside the United States if—

(1) the offender is a natural person who is a citizen or permanent resident alien of the United States, or an organization organized under the laws of the United States or a State or political subdivision thereof; or

(2) an act in furtherance of the offense was committed in the United States.

1838. Construction with other laws

This chapter shall not be construed to preempt or displace any other remedies, whether civil or criminal, provided by United States Federal, State, commonwealth, possession, or territory law for the misappropriation of a trade secret, or to affect the otherwise lawful, disclosure of information by any Government employee under section 552 of title 5 (commonly known as the Freedom of Information Act).

1839. Definitions

As used in this chapter—

(1) the term 'foreign instrumentality' means any agency, bureau, ministry, component, institution, association, or any legal, commercial, or business organization, corporation, firm, or entity that is substantially owned, controlled, sponsored, commanded, managed, or dominated by a foreign government;

(2) the term 'foreign agent' means any officer, employee, proxy, servant, delegate, or representative of a foreign government;

(3) the term 'trade secret' means all forms and types of financial, business, scientific, technical, economic, or engineering information, including patterns, plans, compilations, program devices, formulas, designs, prototypes, methods, techniques, processes, procedures, programs, or codes, whether tangible or intangible, and whether or how stored, compiled, or memorialized physically, electronically, graphically, photographically or in writing if—

(A) the owner thereof has taken reasonable measures to keep such information secret; and

(B) the information derives independent economic value, actual or potential, from not being generally known to, and not being readily ascertainable through proper means by, the public; and

(4) the term 'owner', with respect to a trade secret, means the person or entity in which or in which rightful legal or equitable title to, or license in, the trade secret is reposed."

(b) CLERICAL AMENDMENT.—The table of chapters at the beginning part 1 of title 18, United States Code, is amended by inserting after the item relating to chapter 89 the following:

(c) REPORTS.–Not later than 2 years and 4 years after the date of the enactment of this Act, the Attorney General shall report to Congress on the amounts received and distributed from fines for offenses under this chapter deposited in the Crime Victims Fund established by section 1402 of the Victims of Crime Act of 1984 (42 U.S.C. 10601).

Cold War Espionage in Germany

(*This report has been lightly edited and all classified data deleted.*)

This assessment was tasked by the Department of Defense Damage Assessment Committee, chaired by Mr. John Grimes DASD (CI&SCM)/C3I. This report describes Soviet and East German intelligence agency Cold War espionage, which targeted German industry and how those activities evolved to serious dimensions for Western security. It examines the ongoing Russian espionage efforts still targeting German industry, which cause the loss of key US defense-related technologies provided in bilateral military exchange programs. Finally, the paper raises concerns over the future implications of this continuing harm to the basic security of the nation, providing policy perspectives for decisionmakers.

There was and continues to be a natural tension between the policies that increase international military sales and commercial trade and the security policies that limit nonproliferation and technology transfer. During the Cold War we accepted risk of compromise with military exchange programs. We still accept a high degree of risk with the same programs, while expecting no immediate change to the threat.

For the future there is every indication that additional espionage and resulting loss of key US defense-related technologies will occur. How severe the risk turns out to be can still be affected by a proactive US Governmentwide response, which must ensure a better balance between risk and potential gain.

Many German defense companies have access to US defense technology information. This information is typically transferred to Germany for weapon system coproduction or for the marketing of US defense goods and services through host-nation companies. Defense technology transfers to Germany represent important material support for its key role in the North Atlantic Treaty Organization. During the Cold War, West Germany's eastern border marked the "front line" of the NATO central region. Germany was, and remains, a principal provider of military forces and weapons to the alliance.

The report makes several judgements and observations:

The espionage threat posed by the East German intelligence services during the 1980's evolved from a collection effort directed primarily at weapon system "hardware." The focus was expanded to high technology applications as well as to hardware.

The combination of high-tech espionage and US budgetary restraint may narrow the qualitative edge of our future military forces to a surprising and dangerous degree.

Even if the possibility of war with Russia is remote, war between the US and other regional powers is quite plausible. Compromised US technology, marketed to these powers by entrepreneurial Russians, is not unthinkable.

And there are economic consequences. Much of the technology stolen is the valuable proprietary information of US companies. These companies depend upon proprietary information for their competitiveness, profitability, even survival.

DASA's Legacy of Spies

MBB is a major subsidiary of Deutsche Aerospace AG (DASA), the aircraft, defense and satellites division of Daimler Benz. DASA was formed in early 1989 to build a "technology group" on the foundations of the Mercedes Benz automotive business. DASA immediately began a series of corporate acquisitions and new joint ventures. Joint ventures already under way included the "Eurofighter" project with British, Italian, Spanish, and other German companies.

In 1991, DASA's defense sales accounted for 50 percent of the corporation's revenue according to press reporting. By 1993 defense sales generated only about 27 percent of revenue. DASA was sharply and adversely affected by the Cold War's end, by efforts to reduce the German Government budget deficit, and by the long-running global recession. In addition to the Eurofighter, DASA's major remaining military programs include a joint venture guided-missile program with France and close links with Aerospatiale in the European military/civilian helicopter project.

MBB: one Company–Many Spies

Dirk Peter Meyer surrendered to the BfV in 1982 and confessed he had been an agent for the MfS for one year.

Dieter Klimm's espionage career ended with his death in February 1990. He had spied for the MfS since April 1983.

Lothar and Katharina Straube were arrested on 11 December 1990 for spying for the MfS for 19 years (1963 to 1982).

Franz Musalik was arrested in October 1990 on espionage charges.

Peter Kraut and his wife Heindrun were arrested for espionage on 1 January 1992.

Manfred Rotsch was arrested in September 1984 as a KGB spy. Rotsch was probably the most productive known KGB spy at MBB. He had been spying for more than 30 years, the last 15 of them at MBB. Three weeks after Rotsch's September 1984 arrest, FRG authorities arrested a second MBB employee and two workers from other West German defense contracting companies. All three were native East Germans suspected of spying for the KGB. Two of the three, including the MBB employee, were released due to lack of criminal evidence.

Helmut Kolasch's espionage career ended in 1984 with the discovery at MBB, which netted Manfred Rotsch and the others. Kolasch went to work in 1978 on a special project Siemens had contracted with Dornier. Siemens was employed by Dornier to collaborate on a study for a test concept of the tactical fighter jet of the 1990s (TFK-90). The TFK-90 was a forerunner of the European Fighter Aircraft (EFA)—now called the Eurofighter 2000. The project with Dornier was similar to the AFT work with MBB.

Something New for the KGB

The Manfred Rotsch case illustrates the excellent ability of the KGB and MfS to obtain sensitive Western military technology information through human sources actually placed within Western defense industries. The Kolasch case indicates a refinement in the KGB's collection objectives during the early 1980s. The KGB wanted data on high-technology applications, as well as the traditional data on hardware Rotsch and his fellow spies at MBB provided so well for so long.

Espionage for State Profit

Werner Stiller, an East German intelligence officer who defected in 1979, reportedly told Western officials the "game plan." By investing about $2 million in spy operations, East Germany could gain about $130 million worth of technology it would otherwise have to buy. Much of the take was reportedly passed along to the Soviet Union.

An excellent example of such espionage against MTU involved Juergen and Marietta Reichwald from 1973 to 1980. Juergen Reichwald was an MTU engineer. MTU jointly manufactured the engine for the Tornado Multi-role Combat Aircraft, along with Britain's Rolls-Royce and Italy's Fiat. The Tornado was a joint venture of the German, British, and West German aerospace industries. In 1980, the Tornado promised to be Western Europe's most advanced war plane. For delivery in 1988, the FRG had ordered 322 of the aircraft, Britain at least 305, and Italy 100. The Reichwalds were sentenced in 1982 to six and a half years (him) and 15 months (her). At the Reichwald's trial, the presiding judge said the couple had betrayed some of West Germany's most sensitive military secrets "because of their lust for money." The court estimated they received at least $60,000 deutsche marks (about US $470 in monthly payments) from 1973 to 1980.

The KGB Takes Over at MTU

The MfS disintegrated in May 1990. At least one well-placed MfS spy in the MTU company immediately agreed to continue spying directly for the KGB. Karlheinz Steppan, who was arrested October 9, 1990 for espionage on behalf of the MFS from 1972 until May 5, 1990, apparently agreed to work for the KGB. He was arrested before beginning to work for his new masters. The Steppan case makes clear that the threat to military-related high technology in German industry did not expire with the demise of the East German espionage apparatus.

Undetected Spies

In an October 1990 magazine interview, Kurt Stavenhagen, the oversight official for all German intelligence agencies reported that a number of former

East German operatives were currently working for the KGB. The KGB had also reportedly taken over entire East German spy nets and operational files.

According to Stavenhagen, the MfS and the KGB had always worked closely. The MfS reportedly had placed about 4,000 active spies in West Germany. Many of the former MfS—now KGB spies—were presently dormant. Others were reportedly active and would remain active. Many had not been detected.

A Spy at DLR

The KGB net extended to another high-technology facility affiliated with Deutsche Aerospace—the German Aviation Research Establishment—better known by the acronym "DLR." On September 4, 1992 a 56-year-old unnamed employee of the DLR Aviation and Space Flight Test Center at Goettingen was charged with intelligence activities.

The accused man reportedly confessed to having MfS contacts after his incrimination by a former MfS case officer. The accused was reportedly employed by the Goettingen Test Center for more than 20 years and was recruited by the MfS in the mid–1970s.

Both the Federal German prosecutors' office and a spokesman for the DLR head office stated that the accused was the first MfS spy to be detected within the DLR. The DLR spokesman reported, however, that the accused had not been authorized access to any "classified matters."

The DLR is the largest engineering research and development organization in the FRG. It conducts research at facilities in Oberpfaffenhofen near Munich, Braunschweig, Goettingen, Cologne and Stuttgart. Germany-wide, DLR employs about 4,200, to include more than 1,000 scientists. It has an annual operating budget of approximately $600 million deutsche marks (US $375 million).

The DLR is a hybrid organization, carrying out largely government-funded research and development. It is also obliged to transfer the technology developed to industry for commercial application. A principal industrial beneficiary of the DLR is Deutsche Aerospace AG.

The DLR carries out an impressive array of activities, all involving application of aerospace technology in such areas as flight safety, aerodynamics, and propulsion engineering. The DLR is the focus of the FRG's space programs and contributes to the FRG's participation in the European Space Shuttle Program.

An Underestimated Threat?

The nature of the DLR is such that even a spy with no access to classified material is bound to find unclassified material of interest, especially after working there for 20 years. The accused DLR employee with the MfS contacts showed that agents can be found in "unproductive" areas, and may be far more productive than they seem.

The OLMOS System: A Case Study in Technology Application

The OLMOS Maintenance Support Fatigue Monitoring System permits the German Luftwaffe to monitor the life cycle fatigue values of wear items in the engines and airframe of the Tornado aircraft. It will eventually be expanded to helicopters. The OLMOS system permits "on condition" maintenance—an efficiency-increasing and cost-saving innovation— over the old method of maintenance and repair based upon time-change intervals.

Under the old method, parts that are still fully operational must be exchanged for safety reasons. "On condition" maintenance permits part exchanges only when wear—which is dependent on operation—requires. Knowing the wear lessens the number of unforeseeable part failures and renders unnecessary a preventive parts exchange based upon operating hours.

The Dornier OLMOS Fatigue Monitoring System calculates wear with mathematical algorithms of recorded signals and stores the results as cumulative fatigue values on board the aircraft. Because operating costs are the largest part of the total cost of a complex weapons system, automated "on condition" maintenance permits a considerable reduction in total cost.

New Reasons to Spy

Knowing about OLMOS could not help the Soviets shoot down any Tornados if war broke out. However, theft of Western high-technology applications is motivated by economic as well as military considerations.

Knowledge of OLMOS helped the Soviet Union reduce the desperately high cost of operating its own military aircraft fleet. A Soviet version of OLMOS might have been sold to client militaries around the world bringing in much needed hard currency.

According to press reporting "most present-day (1992) Russian intelligence activity against Germany is concentrated on industrial and economic"— not military—secrets. "A special division of the main Russian service run by Yevgeny Primakov is dedicated exclusively to collecting information on economic conditions and developments in Germany, the US and other leading industrial nations."

A Matter of Competition

The recently issued BfV (German Counterintelligence) 1992 annual report squarely addresses the issue of Russian spying on the West for economic reasons. "Western companies, banks, think tanks and economic journals (now) enjoy the status of top priority targets," said the report. "The aim is to acquire information to modernize Russian enterprises and improve their ability to compete in world markets."

"Since 1991, numerous Russian intelligence officers assigned to Germany have left the service and tried to establish themselves in private enterprise in Russia or in Germany," the BfV report continued. "Not all of these persons have broken with their former employer." According to German Interior Minister Manfred Kanther, Russian intelligence services reduced their "legal" agents in consulates and the embassy (in Bonn) by about a third in 1992. However, the remaining ones "are still believed to be working hard."

The Story of "John" and "Elizabeth Anne"

Of no less concern are the "illegals"— spies who do not work out of embassies, but run networks of agents under cover or false identities.

On April 23, 1992, a man and a woman claiming to be British disembarked from an Aeroflot plane in Helsinki, Finland. Officials became suspicious when both of the "Brits" (identified as "John David A." and "Elizabeth Anne G.") spoke with heavy Eastern European accents. They were carrying $30,000 in cash, a modified short-range radio receiver, and materials used for writing coded messages. Under questioning, the "Brits" admitted to being Russians and Finnish officials expelled them to Russia.

"The two were either going on an assignment for a foreign intelligence service as 'illegals,' or were on their way back from a consultation in Moscow," the 1992 BfV report concluded. "Articles in their luggage that were made in Germany strongly indicated that this could have been their operational area."

The "Hannover Hackers"

From 1986-88, an eight-member ring of German computer "hackers" created a new form of espionage. The Hannover, Germany-based computer enthusiasts, gained access to passwords and codes at some of the West's most sensitive technical research and military installations. They sold the passwords and codes to the KGB. This was the first international computer espionage case to show how much damage could be done by gathering and selling unclassified data.

The "Hannover Hackers" (collectively known herein as the Hackers) started innocently enough. They soon realized, however, that the information they were collecting might be worth something. They all needed the extra money, some to support drug habits. At first they thought about selling the stolen industrial and research data to competing companies. They focused, however, on a potentially more profitable strategy— obtaining the computer access authorizations with the highest privileges at targeted companies and institutions. They commenced operations, approached the Soviets in East Berlin, and began delivering the data.

The Hackers penetrated Dornier, DLR, MBB, and many other German companies and institutions. The KGB gained full knowledge of the computers at these companies and institutions, and how to break into them. The Hackers showed particular interest in Western research institutions potentially associated with weapons of mass destruction (nuclear, chemical, biological)— and in information about atomic accidents, decontamination zones, toxicological experiments, weapons production, and the contents of weapons depots.

The Hackers' downfall began with an accounting error of 75 cents in a computer billing program at LBL in California. A newly assigned astronomer decided to investigate the 75-cent problem and discovered that a previous user had added a new account. He then began tracking down the user.

LBL officials established a monitoring system to observe the user, identified as "Sventenk." Over the next year, Sventenk attacked about 450 computer systems around the United States, gaining entry into more than 30. He searched for military and defense-related items, and, when successful, copied data from them.

Sventenk was patient and methodical. He usually followed a pattern: attempting to gain super-user access, then searching for keywords, then for the password file, and finally for other network connections. He would regularly check the system status to see what jobs were running—and who was on line—as if to avoid detection by system administrators.

After tracing was accomplished, several of the Hackers under suspicion were brought in for interrogation by FRG authorities. After the necessary work with other governments, the principal Hackers were formally arrested in March 1989. Two of them cooperated with the authorities to avoid prosecution. (An excellent treatment of the whole story of the Hackers is contained in *The Cuckoo's Egg*, by Cliff Stoll.)

And... Spies at The Ministry of Defense
Wolf-Heinrich Prellwitz and Ulrich Steinmann were longtime KGB and MfS spies in the FRG MOD. Prellwitz served 21 years in the Armaments Division In May 1992, Prellwitz was sentenced to 10 years imprisonment for committing "particularly severe acts of treason" and for "corruption." The 58-year-old "former Federal Defense Ministry Official" had reportedly supplied "particularly sensitive Ministry documents to the former GDR for 21 years."

The Prellwitz and Steinmann cases demonstrate that by the mid-1980s, the GDR intelligence services had penetrated the German MOD as well as the industrial sectors. The GDR services, the KGB, and the Russian Foreign Intelligence Service received considerable amounts of high-quality high-technology information of US origin.

The GDR spent 40 years building the intelligence networks that produced the government spies Prellwitz and Steinmann, and the company spies at MBB, Dornier, MTU, and the DLR. From a GDR point of view, it was a considerable success.

Conclusion: Why This Problem Still Matters to the United States
The July 1992 DoD Key Technologies Plan lists eleven "Technology Areas." These areas are considered vital to achieving success in seven Scientific and Technical (S&T) "thrusts." These thrusts are in turn considered crucial toward making significant improvement in US warfighting capability.

The following lists the eleven technology areas:

1. Computers: High performance computing systems (and their software operating systems) providing orders-of-magnitude communications capabilities as a result of improvements in hardware, architectural designs, networking, and computational methods.

2. Software: The tools and techniques that facilitate the timely generation, maintenance, and enhancement of affordable including sofftware for distributed systems, data base software, artificial intelligence, and neural nets.

3. Sensors: Active sensors (with emitters, such as radar and sonar), passive ("silent') sensors (e.g., thermal imagers, systems), and the associated signal and image processing.

4. Communications Networks: The timely, reliable, and secure production and worldwide dissemination of information, using DoD consumers, in support of joint—Service mission planning, simulation, rehearsal, and execution.

5. Electronic: Ultra-small (nano-scale) electronic and devices optoelectronic devices, combined with electronic packaging and photonics, for high speed computers, data storage modules, communication systems, advanced sensors, signal processing, radar, imaging systems, and automatic control.

6. Environmental Effects: The study, modeling, and simulation of atmospheric, oceanic, terrestrial, and space environmental effects, both natural and man-made, including the interaction of a weapon system with its operating medium and man-produced phenomena such as obscurants found on the battlefield.

7. Materials and Processes: Development of man-made materials (e.g., composites, electronic and photonic materials, smart materials) for improved structures, higher temperature engines, signature reduction, and electronics, and the synthesis and processing required for their application.

8. Energy Storage: The safe, compact storage of electrical or chemical energy, inluding energetic materials for military systems.

9. Propulsion and Energy Conversion: The efficient conversion of stored energy into usable forms, as in fuel efficient aircraft turbine engines and hypersonic systems.

10. Design Automation: Computer-aided design, concurrent engineering, Automation simulation, and modeling; including the computational aspects of fluid dynamics, electromagnetics, advanced structures, structural dynamics, and other automated design processes.

11. Human-System: The machine integration and interpretation of interfaces data and its presentation in a form convenient to the human operator; displays; human intelligence emulated in computational devices; and simulation and synthetic environments.

Exploiting the US Strategy

US Defense S&T Strategy places the highest priority on achieving goals in six technology areas. The six areas (and thrusts) are:

Software (Precision Strike)

Sensors (Air Superiority and Defense/Sea Control and Undersea Superiority)

Communications Networking (Global Surveillance and Communications)

Materials and Processes (Advanced Land Combat)

Design Automation (Technology for Affordability)

Human-System Interface (Synthetic Environments)

Keeping the Game Close

There are at least several possible explanations for the apparent correspondence between our S&T Strategy and their collection objectives. Soviet and GDR leaders apparently intended their espionage to help prevent the West from secretly developing any potentially war-winning military technologies. They also apparently wanted to help prevent or reduce any "technology gaps" between the military forces of the West and East. Such gaps could be used by the West to the political disadvantage of the East.

The evidence indicates the Soviet and GDR leadership wanted to avoid spending the time and money associated with high-technology research and development. They also apparently wanted to apply selected technologies to their own military and commercial products.

Yesterday's Problem?

There is an urge to conclude that the problem of residual KGB and MfS spies in Germany now represents a very manageable risk for US national security. Reasons for such a conclusion may include:

The Warsaw Pact has "gone away." Chances for a major war in Europe presently appear low.

Unification of Germany, and the demise of KGB and MfS, mean that the problem will go away by itself. As the old spies die off, espionage will peter out.

Current political and economic developments in the Russia are not unfavorable. However, if hostile forces emerge to control Russia and if

Russia presents a major new military threat we will know about it well in advance.

If a serious threat develops, any US key technology stolen by spies in earlier years will be more than matched by continuing advances in US defense technology. Our military forces will still possess a significant qualitative edge.

The political, military, and economic future of the former Soviet Union and Warsaw Pact countries is far from certain. Prudence dictates caution about Russia and the East for the next several years. If Russia again presents a serious military threat, the threat may not appear clearly and with sufficient warning. Military threats are often protracted and ambiguous. In the future, serious and continuing losses of US key technologies through espionage and other means could be an important factor undermining international security. This could contribute to military confrontation and increased risk of war.

Even if war with Russia is now remote, war between the US and other regional powers is far more plausible. Stolen United States key technology, marketed to other powers by entrepreneurial Russians, is not unthinkable.

The qualitative edge our military forces have traditionally enjoyed over adversaries is the product of a long-term national commitment to developing key technologies for defense. In today's US budgetary climate, there is no guarantee the nation will be able to sustain the traditional commitment; the future qualitative edge of our military forces is far from assured. The combination of high-tech espionage and budgetary restraint may narrow the qualitative edge of our future forces to a surprising and dangerous degree.

Much of the stolen technology constitutes the valuable proprietary information of US companies. These companies depend upon proprietary information for their competitiveness, profitability, even survival. Much of the capital used by these companies to develop the technologies originated with the US taxpayer.

Department of Defense Directive

May 22, 1997

SUBJECT: DoD Counterintelligence (CI)
References: (a) DoD Directive 5240.2, subject as above, June 6, 1983 (hereby canceled)

(b) Executive Order 12333, "United States Intelligence Activities," December 4, 1981

(c) Presidential Decision Directive/NSC-24, "U.S. Counterintelligence Effectiveness," May 3, 1994

(d) DoD Directive 5137.1, "Assistant Secretary of Defense for Command, Control, Communications and Intelligence (ASD(C3I))," February 12, 1992

(e) through (bb), see enclosure 1

A. REISSUANCE AND PURPOSE

1. Reissues reference (a) and implements Section 1.11 of reference (b) as it pertains to the assignment of CI responsibilities to the Defense Intelligence Agency (DIA), National Security Agency (ASA), the Military Departments, and offices referenced in that section.

2. Integrates DoD CI capabilities and coordination procedures into a national CI structure under the direction of the National Security Council (NSC) under reference (c).

3. Establishes and maintains a comprehensive, integrated, and coordinated CI effort within the Department of Defense, pursuant to the responsibilities and authorities assigned to the Assistant Secretary of Defense for Command, Control, Communications and Intelligence (ASD9C3I)) in reference (d).

4. Assigns responsibilities to the DoD Components for the direction, management, coordination, and control of CI activities conducted under the authority of references (b), (d), (e) and this Directive.

5. Establishes the Defense Counterintelligence Board (DCIB).

B. APPLICABILITY

This Directive applies to the Office of the Secretary of Defense (OSD), the Military Departments, the Chairman of the Joint Chiefs of Staff, the Combatant Commands, the Defense Agencies, and the DoD Field Activities (hereafter referred to collectively as "the DoD Components").

C. DEFINITIONS

Terms used in this Directive are defined in enclosure 2.

D. POLICY

It is DoD policy that:

1. CI activities shall be undertaken to detect, assess, exploit, and counter or neutralize the intelligence collection efforts, other intelligence activities, sabotage, terrorist activities, and assassination efforts of foreign powers, organizations, or persons directed against the Department of Defense, its personnel, information, materiel, facilities and activities.

2. CI activities shall be conducted in accordance with applicable statutes, E.O. 12333 (reference (b)) and DoD issuances that govern and establish guidelines and restrictions for these activities, to include procedures issued under DoD Directive 5240.1 (reference (f)) that govern, among other things, CI activities that affect U.S. persons, as contained in DoD 5240.1-R.

3. CI activities shall be coordinated and conducted within the United States in accordance with the Memorandum of Agreement (MOA) and its supplement between the Attorney General and the Secretary of Defense (references (h) and (i)), and outside the United States between the Secretary of Defense and Director of Central Intelligence in accordance with the Director of Central Intelligence Directive 5/1 and its supplement (references (j) and (k)).

4. Military Department CI elements are under the command and control of their respective Military Department Secretaries, so as to carry out their statutory authorities and responsibilities under 10 U.S.C.162(a)(2) (reference (1)) and 10 U.S.C.3013(c)(7), 5013(c)(7), and 8013(c)(7) (reference (m)).

5. Combatant Commanders may choose to exercise staff coordination authority over Military Department CI elements deployed in an overseas theater. Staff coordination authority is intended to encompass deconfliction of activities and assurance of unity of effort in attaining the Military Department Secretaries and Combatant Commander's objectives relating to CI. This coordination will normally be accompanied through the assigned CI Staff Officer (CISO), as found in DoD Instruction 5240.10 (reference (n)).

6. If a military operation plan or operation order so specifies, a Combatant Commander or the Combatant Commander's designated joint force commander, may, upon National Command Authority-directed execution, assume operational control of Military Department CI elements assigned to support the operation for the duration of the operation, to include pre-deployment, deployment, and redeployment phases. Under this circumstance, these CI elements come under the Combatant Commander's combatant command authority. However, law enforcement and CI investigations and attendant matters carried out by CI elements remain part of the Military Department's administrative responsibilities. Likewise, for joint training exercise purposes, the joint force commander may assume operational control of assigned CI elements for the purpose and duration of the exercise.

7. The Deputy Assistant Secretary of Defense (Intelligence and Security) (DASD(I&S)) will resolve CI issues, where a Military Department CI entity and a Combatant Commander disagree and when one or both appeal the matter through an appropriate channel to the OSD.

8. CI activities shall be inspected in accordance with DoD Directive 5148.11 (reference (o)).

9. There shall be a DCIB, as described in enclosure 3.

E. RESPONSIBILITIES

1. The <u>Assistant Secretary of Defense for Command, Control, Communications, and Intelligence</u> shall delegate to the DASD(I&S) the authority to act for the ASD(C3I) in carrying out CI responsibilities assigned by DoD Directive 5137.1 (reference (d)), as follows:

a. The DASD(I&S) shall:

(1) Oversee development and management of the DoD Foreign CI Program.

(2) Establish and monitor management procedures to improve the effectiveness and efficiency of CI and resource management.

(3) Serve as the OSD Tactical Intelligence and Related Activities (TIARA) Functional Manager for CI programs.

(4) Serve as the Functional Manager for information management matters related to designated CI systems.

(5) Represent DoD CI interests on the National CI Policy Board (NACIPB) under PDD/NSC-24 (reference (c)), when necessary.

(6) Delegate to the Director, CI, the following authority and functions:

(a) Develop DoD CI policy and exercise policy supervision and management of DoD CI programs and activities as defined in this Directive.

b) Act as program manager for DoD FCIP resources, which include resources for the Military Departments, On-Site Inspection Agency (OSIA), DIA, and Defense Investigation Service (DIS).

(c) Serve as functional CI manager to include reviewing and monitoring the progress and effectiveness of CI investigations, offensive operations, collection, analysis and production. Conduct or provide for the conduct of inspections of DoD CI Components; staff oversight of DoD CI components and resolve conflicts between those components; and assign special tasks to the DoD Components as may be necessary to accomplish DoD CI objectives.

(d) Chair the DCIB.

(e) Coordinate DoD CI programs and activities with other U.S. Government organizations.

(f) Ensure adequate CI support is provided to the DoD Components, as necessary, to include support to Special Access Programs and support to Human Intelligence (HUMINT).

(g) Support the DASD(I&S) role as the Functional Manager in areas relating to CI.

(h) Support the DASD(I&S) role as the Functional Manager for the Defense CI Information System.

(i) Be the U.S. National CI Advisor to the Allied Command Europe, for the purposes of consultation and coordination of policy matters.

(j) Support or provide DoD representation on the National CI Policy Board, National CI Operations Board, Operations Chiefs Working Group, Investigations Working Group, and representation to the other national-level CI agencies in accordance with PDD/NSC-24 (reference (c)); and represent the ASD(C3I) on the Secretary's Board on Investigations in accordance with DoD Directive 5105.59 (reference (p)).

(k) Approve or refer to the NSC or NACIPB operations or other CI matters that involve significant policy issues.

b. The Director, DIA, shall:

(1) Conduct analysis and production on foreign intelligence and terrorist threats to meet customer needs within Department of Defense, and contribute to national products of these types as appropriate, in accordance with E.O. 12333 (reference (b)), and within the scope of assigned responsibilities and functions of DIA as described in DoD Directive 5105.21 (reference (q)).

(2) Coordinate the CI production of all DoD CI components as requested by the Director of CI.

(3) Provide CI analytic, production, and database support to the Services as requested.

(4) Serve as the DoD CI Collection Requirements Manager as requested by the Director of CI.

(5) Provide CI staff support to the Chairman of the Joint Chiefs of Staff and the Combatant Commanders as requested by the Director of CI and in conformance with DoD Instruction 5240.10 (reference (n)).

(6) Provide CI staff support to the DoD HUMINT Manager as described in DoD Directive 5200.37 (reference (r)) and ensure CI support is provided to the DoD HUMINT collection program.

(7) Develop, implement and maintain intelligence and CI capabilities designed to assist Commanders in the protection of DoD personnel and facilities from terrorism, in accordance with DoD Directive 0-2000.12 (reference (s)).

(8) Conduct threat and vulnerability analysis and support decisions by commanders or program managers in the implementation of appropriate Operations Security (OPSEC) measures in accordance with DoD Directive 5205.2 (t).

(9) Assess and provide information systems security threat and vulnerability information to support information operations requirements.

(10) Participate on DoD, national, international, and interdepartmental boards, committees, and other organizations involving CI as requested by the Director of CI.

c. The Director, DIS, shall:

(1) Integrate CI principles and experience into the DIS security countermeasures missions, which consist of conducting personnel security investigations and serving as the cognizant DoD security authority for the National Industrial Security Program, pursuant to E.O. 12829 (reference (u)).

(2) Assist the defense industry in the recognition and reporting of foreign contacts and collection attempts, and the application of threat-appropriate security countermeasures.

(3) Provide pertinent information on the defense industry to support the production of multidisciplinary intelligence threat analyses as required.

(4) Assist the Military Departments' CI organizations in the protection of critical DoD technologies.

(5) Perform those CI-related responsibilities assigned by the OSD, to include the investigative support to the DoD Components (exclusive of Military Departments) relative to unauthorized disclosures of classified information to the public in accordance with DoD Directive 5210.50 (reference (v)).

(6) Participate in national, international, and interdepartmental boards, committees, and other organizations as requested by the Director of CI.

d. The <u>Command, Control, Communications, Computers and Intelligence Integration Support Activity</u> shall:

(1) Provide CI programmatic analyses and expertise to ASD(C3I) and DASD(I&S) in accordance with DoD Directive 5100.81 (reference (w)), to include consolidation of Military Department and Defense Agency Foreign CI Program submissions and participation in Congressional Budget Justification Book production.

(2) Support planning for CI capabilities, communications, and architectures.

2. The <u>Secretaries of the Military Departments</u> shall:

a. Provide for the conduct, direction, management, coordination, and control of CI activities as outlined in paragraphs E.2.b through E.2.j, below; E.O. 12333 (reference (b)); 10 U.S.C.3013, 5013, 8013 (reference (m)); 10 U.S.C. 535 (reference (x)); Pub.L. 99-145(1985), Section 1223.(reference (y)); and DoD Instruction 5505.3 (reference (z)).

b. Conduct CI investigations of Active and Reserve military personnel and, as provided for in agreements with the Attorney General (references (h) and (i)), DoD civilian employees, who may be subject to judicial and/

or administrative action under applicable Federal law and regulations, including the Uniform Code of Military Justice, 10 U.S.C.801-940 (reference (aa)).

c. Conduct CI operations against foreign intelligence services and organizations.

d. Collect, process, exploit and report information of CI significance to satisfy validated national and tactical CI collection requirements.

e. Conduct CI analysis focusing on support to DoD CI operations and investigations, military operations and force protection, security countermeasures, and national policy and programs.

f. Produce CI assessments, studies, estimates, and other finished products, to support U.S. military commanders, the Department of Defense, and the U.S. Intelligence Community.

g. Develop, implement and maintain antiterrorism programs designed to assist Commanders in the protection of DoD personnel and facilities, in accordance with DoD Directive 0-2000.12 (reference (s)).

h. Conduct threat and vulnerability analysis and support decisions by commanders or program managers in the implementation of appropriate OPSEC measures in accordance with DoD Directive 5205.2 (reference (t)).

i. Assess and provide information systems security threat and vulnerability information to support information operations requirements.

j. Prescribe regulations providing to their military investigative organizations the authority to initiate, conduct, delay, suspend or terminate investigations and ensure Commanders outside those specified CI military organizations do not impede the use of military techniques permissible under law or regulation.

k. Maintain, operate, and manage their respective CI components, in accordance with the authorities and responsibilities assigned by this Directive, and provide personnel, equipment, and facilities that CI missions require.

l. Establish Military Department plans, programs, policies, and procedures to accomplish authorized CI functions.

m. Establish and maintain a worldwide CI capability for the purposes outlined in paragraphs E.2.b through E.2.j., above.

n. Develop CI techniques, methods, and equipment required for CI activities and provide basic and specialized training to CI personnel.

o. Provide CI support to the Combatant Commands, other DoD Components, U.S. Government organizations, and foreign CI and security agencies as provided for in this Directive.

p. Inform periodically the Combatant Commanders on CI investigations and operations through the appropriate CI entity and in coordination with the command CISO to fulfill briefing requirements set forth in this Directive and DoD Instruction 5240.10 (reference (n)).

q. Submit CI operational and investigative data and prepare CI analyses as required by the Director for CI.

r. Establish and maintain liaison with U.S. and foreign CI, security, and law enforcement agencies in accordance with policies formulated in E.O. 12333 (reference (b)); the MOA and its supplement between the Attorney General and the Secretary of Defense (references (h) and (i)); DCID5/1 (reference (j) and the CIA/DoD MOA (reference (k)); and coordinate Military Department programs with other U.S. Government organizations.

s. Participate on DoD, national, international, and interdepartmental boards, committees, and other organizations involving CI as requested by the Director for CI.

3. The <u>Chairman of the Joint Chiefs of Staff</u> shall integrate, where appropriate, CI support into all joint planning programs, systems, exercises, doctrine, strategies, policies, and architectures.

4. The <u>Commanders of the Combatant Commands</u> shall integrate, where appropriate, CI support into all

command planning programs, systems, exercises, doctrine, strategies, policies, and architectures.

5. The <u>Under Secretary of Defense for Acquisition and Technology</u> shall ensure that the Director, OSIA, shall:

a. Provide for the internal security of OSIA's inspection, escort and portal monitoring teams.

b. Participate in the production of multidisciplinary intelligence threat analyses as required.

c. Participate on national, international, and interdepartmental boards, committees, and other organizations involving CI as required by the Director for CI.

6. The <u>Director, National Security Agency/Chief, Central Security Service</u> shall:

a. Collect, process, and disseminate signals intelligence information for CI purposes.

b. Participate in the production of multidisciplinary intelligence threat analyses, as required.

c. Participate on national, international, and interdepartmental boards, committees, and other organizations involving CI as requested by the Director for CI.

7. The <u>Director, National Reconnaissance Office</u>, shall:

a. Utilize its systems to support CI activities and requirements.

b. Support the production of multidisciplinary intelligence threat analyses as required.

c. Participate on DoD, national, and interdepartmental boards, committees, and other organizations involving CI as requested by the Director for CI.

8. The <u>Heads of Other DoD Components</u> shall:

a. Refer to the applicable Military Department CI Agency any CI information involving military personnel assigned to their Components for investigation and disposition. Refer reported CI information involving civilian employees by their Components in the United States to their servicing Military Department CI Agency and, when overseas, to the Military Department responsible for providing administrative and logistical support, in accordance with DoD Directive 5240.6 (reference (bb)).

b. Contact the nearest Military Department CI Agency office for guidance should a question arise as where to refer reported CI information.

F. EFFECTIVE DATE
This Directive is effective immediately.

/s/ John P. White
Deputy Secretary of Defense

ENCLOSURE 1

REFERENCES (continued)

(e) Title 10, United States Code, "Armed Forces."

(f) DoD Directive 5240.1, "DoD Intelligence Activities," April 25, 1988.

(g) DoD 5240.1-R, "Activities of DoD Intelligence Components that Affect United States Persons," December 1982, authorized by DoD Directive 5240.1, April 24, 1988.

(h) "Agreement Governing the Conduct of Defense Department Counterintelligence Activities in Conjunction wit the Federal Bureau of Investigation," between the Attorney General and the Secretary of Defense, April 5, 1979.

(i) Supplement to 1979 FBI/DoD Memorandum of Understanding: "Coordination of Counter-intelligence Matters Between FBI and DoD," June 3, and June 20, 1966.

(j) Director of Central Intelligence Directive 5/1, "Espionage and Counterintelligence Activities Abroad," December 19, 1984.

(k) Memorandum of Agreement Between the Central Intelligence Agency and the Department of Defense regarding counterintelligence activities abroad, February 3, 1995.

(l) Section 162 et seq. of title 10, United States Code.

(m) Sections 3013, 5013, and 8013 of title 10, United States Code.

(n) DoD Instruction 5240.10, "DoD Counterintelligence Support to Unified and Specified Commands, May 18, 1990.

(o) DoD Directive 5148.11, "Assistant to the Secretary of Defense for Intelligence Oversight," July 1, 1992.

(p) DoD Directive 5105.59, "The Secretary's Board on Investigations," September 25, 1995.

(q) DoD Directive 5105.21, "Defense Intelligence Agency," May 19, 1977.

(r) DoD Directive 5200.37, "Centralized Management of the Department of Defense Human Intelligence (HUMINT) Operations," December 18, 1992.

(s) DoD Directive 0-2000.12, "DoD Combating Terrorism Program," September 15, 1996.

(t) DoD 5205.2 "DoD Operations Security Program," July 7, 1983

(u) Executive Order 12829, "National Industrial Security Program," January 6, 1993.

(v) DoD Directive 5210.50, "Unauthorized Disclosure of Classified Information to the Public," February 27, 1992.

(w) DoD Directive 5100.81, "Department of Defense Support Activities," December 5, 1991.

(x) Section 535 of title 10, United States Code.

(y) Section 1223 of Public Law 99-145, "Authority for Independent Criminal Investigations by Navy and Air Force Investigative Units," November 8, 1985.

(z) DoD Instruction 5505.3, "Initiation of Investigations by Military Criminal Investigative Organizations," July 11, 1986.

(aa) Sections 801-940 of title 10, United States Code, "Uniform Code of Military Justice."

(bb) DoD Directive 5240.6, "Counterintelligence Awareness and Briefing Program," July 16, 1996.

ENCLOSURE 2

DEFINITIONS

1. <u>Counterintelligence (CI)</u>
and activities conducted to protect against espionage, other intelligence activities, sabotage, or assassinations conducted by or on behalf of foreign governments or elements thereof, foreign organizations, or foreign persons, or international terrorist activities.

2. <u>Counterintelligence (CI) Analysis.</u> CI analysis is the function of assimilating, evaluating, and interpreting information about areas of CI proponency and responsibility. Information derived from all available sources is considered and integrated in the analytical process.

3. <u>Counterintelligence (CI) Collection.</u> The systematic acquisition of information concerning espionage, sabotage, terrorism, and related foreign activities conducted for or on behalf of foreign nations, entities, organizations, or persons and that are directed against or threaten DoD interest.

4. <u>Counterintelligence (CI) Investigation.</u> Includes inquiries and other activities undertaken to determine whether a particular person is acting for, or on behalf of, a foreign power for espionage, treason, spying, sedition, subversion, sabotage, assassinations, international terrorist activities, and actions to neutralize such acts.

5. <u>Counterintelligence (CI) Operation.</u> Actions taken against foreign intelligence services to counter espionage and other clandestine intelligence activities damaging to the national security.

6. <u>Counterintelligence (CI) Production.</u> The process of analyzing all-source information developed into final product and disseminated—irrespective of media—concerning espionage, other foreign intelligence collection threats, sabotage, terrorism, and other related

threats, to U.S. military commanders, the Department of Defense, and the U.S. intelligence community.

7. <u>Counterintelligence (CI) Support to DoD HUMINT.</u> The application of CI information, knowledge, and experience to prevent foreign intelligence or security services from detecting, neutralizing, or controlling DoD HUMINT plans and operations.

8. Military Department <u>Counterintelligence (CI) Agency.</u> The Military Department CI Agencies include Army CI, the Naval Criminal Investigative Service, and the Air Force Office of Special Investigations.

ENCLOSURE 3

DEFENSE COUNTERINTELLIGENCE (CI) BOARD

1. Organization and Management

a. The DCIB shall be convened and chaired by the Director of CI, Office of the Deputy Assistant Secretary of Defense (Intelligence and Security). The DCIB membership shall include representatives from the OSD; Senior Deputy General Counsel (International Affairs and Intelligence); the Assistant to the Secretary of Defense (Intelligence Oversight); one representative from each of the Military Department CI Agencies; the Defense Investigative Service (DS), the On-Site Inspection Agency (OSIA); and the Defense Intelligence Agency (DIA). Associate DCIB members are the National Security Agency/Central Security Service (NSA/CSS); the National Reconnaissance Office (NRO); Marine Corps Counterintelligence/Human Intelligence (HUMINT) Branch; Joint Staff, J-38/IW Special Technical Operations Division/TSB; DIA's Joint CI Support Branch; Counterintelligence Support Officers (CISOs), as described in DoD Instruction 5240.10 (reference (n)); and a representative of the C4I Integration Support Activity (CISA).

b. The DCIB shall be supported by subcommittees or panels, with participation from those organizations represented on the DCIB. The subcommittee and panel chairs shall be appointed by the chair, DCIB.

2. Functions

a. The DCIB shall advise and assist the DASD(I&S) on CI matters within the purview of E.O.12333 (reference (b)), PDD/NSC-24 (reference (c)), and this Directive; e.g. overseeing the implementation of CI policy; advising on the need for and allocation of CI resources; monitoring and evaluating support functions, such as automated data processing; carrying out specific tasks as outlined by the Chair; and reviewing and evaluating reforms of CI entities, to include functional consolidation, integration, and collocation.

b. The DCIB membership will coordinate their respective CI activities, under the guidance of the DCIB chairman.

Spies

Charles Lee Francis Anzalone

Charles Lee Francis Anzalone, a 23-year-old Marine corporal stationed in Yuma, Arizona, was arrested February 13, 1991, after a four-month investigation and charged with suspicion of attempted espionage.

In November 1990, Anzalone, a telephone linemen, called the Soviet Embassy in Washington to offer his services as a spy (under the pretext of asking about a college scholarship). An FBI agent posing as a KGB officer contacted Anzalone who passed him two technical manuals about cryptographic equipment, a security badge, and guard schedules. Anzalone, who is part Mohawk, told the agents that he hated capitalism, the American Government, and held a grudge against the nation's treatment of native Americans. Anzalone testified that his offering to spy was a ruse to get money from the Soviets.

Charles Lee Francis Anzalone

On May 3, 1991, Anzalone was found guilty of attempted espionage. He was also convicted of adultery with the wife of another Marine stationed in the Persian Gulf and of possession and use of marijuana. He was sentenced to 15 years in prison.

Joseph Garfield Brown and Virginia Jean Baynes

On 27 December 1992, FBI agents arrested Joseph Garfield Brown, former US airman and martial arts instructor and charged him with spying for the Philippine Government. Brown allegedly provided an official there with illegally obtained Secret CIA documents on Iraqi terrorist activities during the Persian Gulf War and assassination plans by a Philippine insurgent group.

The former US airman was arrested at Dulles International Airport after being lured to the United States from the Philippines by undercover FBI agents with the promise of a job teaching self-defense tactics to CIA agents. On the following day he was indicted on three counts of espionage in Federal Court, Alexandria, Virginia.

Brown enlisted in the US Air Force in 1966 and served until 1968. He continued to reside in the Philippines, working as a martial arts instructor for the Department of Tourism until the time of his arrest.

He was accused of obtaining classified documents in 1990 and 1991 in Manila from CIA secretary Virginia Jean Baynes and passing them to a Philippine Government official. An FBI spokesman stated that Baynes pleaded guilty to espionage in Federal Court on 22 May 1992 and is serving a 41-month prison term.

The FBI began its investigation in April 1991, after an internal CIA inquiry determined that Baynes, who joined the Agency in 1987 and who was assigned two years later to the American Embassy in Manila, had passed two or three classified documents to Brown. Baynes had met Brown when she enrolled in a karate class which he taught at an embassy annex. According to Baynes, as the friendship between her and Brown grew in the late summer of 1990, he asked her to obtain CIA information on assassinations planned by an insurgent group that were to be carried out in the Philippines. Baynes, who held a Top Secret clearance, complied with his request by removing secret documents from the embassy.

Jeffrey M. Carney

Jeffrey M. Carney, a former intelligence specialist with the Air Force, was sentenced at a General Court Martial December 1991, to 38 years. He pleaded guilty to charges of espionage, conspiracy, and desertion.

Carney entered the Air Force in Berlin where he was a linguist. While at Tempelhof, he began copying classified documents, which he then provided to the East German Ministry for State Security (Stasi). In 1984 he was transferred to Goodfellow AFB in Texas where he worked as an instructor while continuing to spy for East Germany.

After defecting to East Germany in 1985, he continued to aid the Communists by intercepting and translating official telephone communications of US military commanders and embassy officials in Berlin. Carney is a complex personality who became disillusioned with the Air Force. He originally intended to defect to East Germany, but allowed himself to be drawn into espionage by East German agents who expertly manipulated him and claimed his complete loyalty. He was apprehended in Berlin in April 1991 by Air Force Office of Special Investigation agents.

Mark Goldberg

In the late 1980s, a French computer engineer, Mark Goldberg, came to the United States under a program run by the French Ministry of Foreign Affairs that arranged for young Frenchmen to do alternative military service overseas. He was paid a stipend by the French Government, and part of his responsibility under the program was to write reports for the French Government about his work experiences. He worked for a brief period of time for a software company in Connecticut, a wholly owned subsidiary of the French state-owned firm Thompson. Then he joined Renaissance Software, Inc., of Palto Alto, California, a start-up company with fewer than 20 employees specializing in risk management software used by financial traders and banks.

One night, not long before Goldberg was scheduled to return to France on 8 July 1990, he came to the office and copied Renaissance's computer source code. Not long before this, company officials had become suspicious of Goldberg and rigged the computer system and copying machine to detect any theft attempts. The next day, company officials were able to trace exactly what Goldberg had downloaded.

Goldberg was arrested at the San Francisco airport while waiting for a Paris-bound flight. On 17 July 1990, the Assistant US Attorney Northern District of California, declined to prosecute Goldberg because Goldberg did not place the stolen computer codes into interstate commerce. The US Attorney recommended that the case could be more appropriately prosecuted locally.

On 3 December 1990, Goldberg pleaded guilty in California court to two felony counts of theft and attempted theft of trade secrets. He received a suspended sentence and was allowed to return to France in March 1991 to complete the remaining 400 hours of his 1,000-hour sentence of community service. It never became completely clear whether Goldberg was working for the French Government to steal US technology, but there are many indicators pointing to that possibility.

Douglas Frederick Groat

On 3 April 1998, the FBI arrested Douglas Frederick Groat, a 50-year old former CIA employee, on charges of espionage. Groat is accused of providing information to two foreign governments on how US intelligence successfully cracked their codes.

At a news conference, following Groat's arraignment, US Attorney Wilma A. Lewis said that during his 16-year career with the CIA, Groat "participated in classified covert operations." Other US officials said that Groat worked in units that broke or stole foreign codes.

Groat joined the CIA in 1980. Prior to his CIA employment, he spent five years in the army and held jobs as a police officer, prison guard, process server and deputy US marshal. Groat is the third former or current CIA employee arrested for espionage in the last four years.

Groat was actually indicted on October 31, 1996 in the United States District Court for the District of Columbia. In the indictment, the Grand Jury charged that:

Count One—From on or about March 24, 1997, until in or about April 1997, in the District of Columbia and elsewhere, the defendant, Douglas Fred Groat, did knowingly and willfully communicate, deliver and transmit, and attempt to communicate, deliver, and transmit to "Foreign Government A," and to representatives, officers and agents thereof, a document, writing and information relating to the national defense, that is, information concerning the targeting and compromise of the cryptographic systems of "Foreign Country A" by the United States, with intent and reason to believe that said information was to be used to the injury of the United States and to the advantage of a foreign nation, that is, "Foreign Government A."

Count Two—From on or about March 24, 1997 until in or about April 1997, in the District of Columbia and elsewhere, the defendant, Douglas Fred Groat, did knowingly and willfully communicate, furnish, transmit, and otherwise make available to an unauthorized person, namely representatives, agents and employees of "Foreign Government A," classified information concerning the nature, preparation and use of the cryptographic systems of "Foreign Government A," specifically, the targeting and compromise of the cryptographic systems of "Foreign Government A' by the United States,

(Communications of Cryptographic System Information to a Foreign Government, in violation of Title 18, United States Code, Section 798(a)(1))

Count Three—From on or about March 24, 1997, until in or about April 1997, in the District of Columbia and elsewhere, the defendant, Douglas Fred Groat, did knowingly and willfully communicate, deliver and transmit, and attempt to communicate, deliver, and transmit to "Foreign Government B," and to representatives, officers and agents thereof, a document, writing and information relating to the national defense, that is, information concerning the targeting and compromise of the cryptographic systems of "Foreign Country B" by the United States, with intent and reason to believe that said information was to be used to the injury of the United States and to the advantage of a foreign nation, that is, "Foreign Government B."

Count Four—From on or about March 24, 1997 until in or about April 1997, in the District of Columbia and elsewhere, the defendant, Douglas Fred Groat, did knowingly and willfully communicate, furnish, transmit, and otherwise make available to an unauthorized person, namely representatives, agents and employees of "Foreign Government B," classified information concerning the nature, preparation and use of the cryptographic systems of "Foreign Government B," specifically, the targeting and compromise of the cryptographic systems of "Foreign Government B" by the United States,

(Communications of Cryptographic System Information to a Foreign Government, in violation of Title 18, United States Code, Section 798(a)(1))

Count Five—From on or about March 24, 1997 until in or about April 1997, in the District of Columbia and elsewhere, the defendant, Douglas Fred Groat, did knowingly and unlawfully attempt to obstruct, delay and affect commerce by extortion, as that term is defined in Title 18, United States Code, Section 1951, in that the defendant, Douglas Fred Groat, did attempt to obtain property of the Central Intelligence Agency, an agency of the United States Government engaged in activities in and affecting foreign commerce by attempting to induce the consent of the Central Intelligence Agency by the wrongful use of actual and threatened fear, including fear of economic and on-economic harm, that is, the defendant did threaten to interfere with Central Intelligence Agency intelligence activities and methods known to him as a result of his employment with the Central Intelligence Agency, by revealing those activities and methods to foreign governments, unless the Central Intelligence (Agency) paid the defendants for his silence in excess of five hundred thousand dollars ($500,000).

(Interference with Commerce by Extortion, in violation of Title 18, United States Code, Section 1951(a))

On 16 April 1998, federal prosecutors said in court that classified documents were found in Groat's recreational vehicle during a FBI search, following his arrest. The prosecutors also said that Groat has "recently considered traveling abroad to seek employment with foreign governments interested in purchasing his classified cryptographic knowledge. The prosecutors' arguments were made in response to Groat's motion to gain release from jail before his trial. The US District Judge, Thomas F. Hogan, rejected the motion and ordered Groat kept in jail.

Groat did not receive any money for his information and did not act out of greed. Rather, this case if one of revenge. The press cites a senior federal official who said that Groat felt slighted and abused by the CIA because he had never been given the assignments he believed he deserved.

A date of 23 September 1998 was set for Groat's trial and arguments concerning legal issues. Groat pleaded not guilty to the five-count indictment, however on 27 July 1998, Grout appeared in the US District Court to plead quilty to one count of attempted extortion. His plea agreement called for a maximum sentence of five years in prison, followed by three years' probation.

Jeff E. Gregory

Jeff E. Gregory, a US Army Staff Sergeant, was arrested on 29 April 1993 at Fort Richardson, Alaska. His arrest resulted from a joint investigation between the FBI and the US Army Intelligence and Security Command. Gregory was the sixth active or former US service member charged with espionage in connection with the Clyde Lee Conrad espionage network that sold US and NATO military secrets to Hungary and Czechoslovakia when those countries were part of the Soviet Bloc.

Gregory is alleged to have been a member of the spy ring which operated out of the 8th Infantry Division, Bad Kreuznach, Germany in the mid-1980s. Gregory was recruited into the spy ring by Roderick James Ramsay, also a former Army sergeant at Bad Kreuznach.

According to the federal complaint against Gregory, while assigned to the 8th Infantry Division in Germany from March 1984 to October 1986, "he helped procure extremely sensitive, classified documents relating to national defense, for transmittal to one or more foreign powers." At the time, Gregory was a staff driver at Bad Kreuznach and helped maintain the commanding general's mobile command center. He was also in charge of updating maps showing military maneuvers and had access to classified messages and correspondence.

According to an FBI official, Gregory once took a military flight bag stuffed with 20 pounds of classified documents. The documents included "war plans" for the United States and NATO. On 28 March 1994, Gregory pleaded guilty to espionage charges.

Frederick Christopher Hamilton

Frederick Christopher Hamilton, a former Defense Intelligence Agency (DIA) analyst, pleaded guilty on 5 February 1993 to the charge of passing to Ecuadorian officials classified US intelligence reports evaluating the military readiness of Peruvian security forces. At the time, Hamilton was a DIA research technician in the defense attache's office in Lima, Peru, a post which he held from 1989 to 1991. He apparently believed that the disclosures could help avert a possible conflict between the two countries. Peru and Ecuador have been disputing territory, sometimes violently, along their mutual border for over 50 years.

Hamilton holds advanced degrees in Spanish and Portuguese. At the time of his arrest, he was employed as a language instructor at a military academy in Virginia. His activities were uncovered by US intelligence agencies after receiving information from a confidential source indicating secrets were being leaked.

Hamilton, who held a Top Secret security clearance while with the DIA, met Ecuadorian representatives in their embassy in Lima on 13 February and 20 May 1991. He passed extremely sensitive information, which disclosed US intelligence operations and the identity of US sources in the region.

"He didn't get any money," said a U.S. official. "He was a very naïve individual who was flattered by the (Ecuadorians)." Hamilton's attorney stated that, "What he thought he was trying to do was prevent a war.... The purpose of disclosing documents that he did was to show the country that was concerned about being attacked that the other country had neither the intent nor the ability to attack."

Hamilton reportedly passed five Secret intelligence reports and orally disclosed the contents of four other classified reports. Under a court agreement, the former DIA employee pleaded guilty to two counts of unlawfully communicating classified information to a foreign country. The agreement specified Hamilton may not appeal the sentence and the Justice Department will not prosecute him for espionage-related crimes.

On 16 April 1993, he was sentenced to 37 months in prison.

Geneva Jones and Dominic Ntube

Geneva Jones, a secretary with a Top Secret clearance in the Department of State's Bureau of Politico-Military Affairs, was arrested on 3 August 1993. On 4 August, the FBI arrested West African journalist Dominic Ntube. On 31 August, she was indicted on 21 counts of theft of government property and one count of transmission of defense information to unauthorized persons. FBI officials said she smuggled classified documents for two years to Ntube, indicted at the same time.

Jones was carrying classified documents with her at the time of arrest. A search of Ntube's apartment by FBI agents discovered thousands of classified cables and 39 CIA documents marked Secret, including documents relating to US military operations in Somalia and Iraq. Some of the material apparently made its way to West African magazines, which had been publishing classified State Department cables for several months.

FBI agents indicated they wiretapped Jones's telephone after several classified US documents were found 10 months earlier in the West African command post of Charles Taylor, leader of a faction seeking to overthrow the Liberian Government. Ntube reportedly faxed 14 documents he received from Jones to the Liberian rebels.

The former State Department employee told the FBI she had been giving Ntube classified cables for about 18 months. In a preliminary hearing, the FBI testified that agents watched her on 16 occasions take documents from the State Department and hide them in newspapers or a grocery bag. During the month she was under surveillance, she allegedly took more than 130 classified documents from her office.

On 31 August, 1993, Ntube was indicted with Jones for receiving stolen property and for transmitting national defense information to unauthorized persons. On 3 September, 1993, Jones pleaded not guilty to the charges in Federal District Court.

Peter H. Lee

On 8 December 1997, US Attorney Nora M. Manella announced that a physicist pleaded guilty that day to transmitting classified national defense information to representatives of the People's Republic of China. Dr.

Peter H. Lee, 58, of Manhattan Beach, California, admitted that in 1985, while working as a research physicist at Los Alamos National Laboratory, he traveled to the People's Republic of China. At the time of his trip, Lee, an expert on laser energy, was working on classified projects relating to the simulation of nuclear detonations, which required that he have a security clearance. During meetings with Chinese scientists, Lee provided detailed information about the use of lasers to simulate nuclear detonations, even though Lee knew that this information was classified.

The motive, authorities believe, was not money but national loyalties. Lee "wanted to help the Chinese Government and the Chinese scientists and to do something to advance what he considered to be a poorer, less technologically advanced scientific community," said one law enforcement source. The source further added that "I would characterize (Lee's motives) as an empathy and a sympathy for that country based on his ancestry. He seemed to be eager to help friends back there."

In pleading guilty, Lee admitted that he knew the information was classified, and that by transmitting the information he intended to help the Chinese. "One of the nation's greatest resources is the knowledge possessed by our top scientists," Manella said. "The security of our nation depends on our scientists safeguarding that knowledge. Doctor Lee failed in his duty to protect the information entrusted to him."

In addition to pleading guilty to transmitting national defense information, Lee admitted making a false statement to a government agency. The second charge related to conduct in 1997, when Lee again traveled to the People's Republic of China and lectured on various topics relating to his current employment as a research scientist for TRW, Inc. Following his return to the United States, Lee lied on a security form when he denied that he gave technical talks to the Chinese.

According to Assistant United States Attorney Jonathan S. Shipiro, the information Lee passed in 1985 had important military applications related to nuclear weapons. The information was later declassified.

Lee entered his guilty pleas before US District Judge Terry J. Hatter, who scheduled a sentencing hearing for February 23, 1998. The defendant faces a maximum sentence of 15 years in federal prison and a fine of $250,000. A plea agreement in this case has been filed under seal pursuant to an agreement of the parties.

Kurt G. Lessenthien

After he admitted to trying to sell military secrets to Russia, Petty Officer Kurt G. Lessenthien, a nuclear submarine crewman and instructor at the US Navy's Nuclear Power School in Orlando, Florida, was sentenced to 27 years in prison on 28 October 1996. After Lessenthien made a deal with prosecutors in Norfolk, Virginia, he decided to let a jury determine his sentence hoping it would result in a lighter sentence. Instead, the jury recommended the maximum sentence. He will be eligible for parole after nine years.

Lessenthien had contacted the Russian Embassy in Washington, DC, in March and offered to sell classified nuclear submarine information. Shortly thereafter, an FBI agent posing as a spy contacted Lessenthien and agreed to pay $11,000 for two packages of classified information.

A Navy psychiatrist testified that Lessenthien has a personality disorder making him dependent on women and obsessive about his relationships; however, a Navy prosecutor said Lessenthien spied for money and excitement.

Aluru J. Prasad

An Indian businessman, Aluru J. Prasad, was sentenced on 9 December 1996 to 15 months in prison for spying for the former Soviet Union during the 1980s. The suspected spy pleaded no contest to trying to gather secrets about the US "Star Wars" anti-missile defense system, the stealth bomber, and other classified defense projects.

At the plea hearing, Prasad admitted to working with Subtrahmanyan Kota of Northboro, Massachusetts— an Indian-born software engineer—to steal high-tech information from the Mitre Corporation, including formulas for the paint used to cloak the stealth bomber form radar detection. Earlier in the year, Kota had testified against Prasad and pleaded guilty to wire fraud, three counts of tax evasion, and a charge relating to biotech theft.

Yen Men Kao

On 3 December 1993, the FBI arrested Yen Men Kao, a Chinese national, in Charlotte, North Carolina, as a suspect in a spy ring that unsuccessfully sought secrets on an advanced Navy torpedo and a jet engine. The arrest of Yen by the FBI and Immigration and Naturalization Service agents concluded a six-and-a-half-year investigation that determined that Kao and several other Chinese nationals conspired to steal and export classified and embargoed high-technology items. The attempted espionage targeted the Navy's MK 48 Advanced Capability Torpedo and the F404-400 General Electric jet engine used to power the Navy's Hornet fighter.

According to the FBI, the investigation yielded a significant amount of counterintelligence information, including the identities of numerous suspected intelligence operatives and commercial entities involved in Kao's alleged attempts to illegally acquire US technology. Kao was charged with violating US immigration laws, specifically, a section of the Immigration and Nationality Act that provides for deporting a foreigner involved in any espionage or sabotage activity or seeking to illegally acquire US technology.

Steven J. Lalas

On 3 May 1993, the FBI arrested Steven J. Lalas, a former Department of State communications officer stationed at the US Embassy in Athens, Greece. He was charged with passing sensitive military information to Greek officials. Lalas originally claimed that a Greek military official recruited him in 1991. Lalas said he agreed to cooperate because he feared for the welfare of relatives living in Greece. American authorities later stated that he began spying for the Greek Government in 1977 when he was with the US Army.

American authorities estimate that he passed 700 highly classified documents, including papers dealing with plans and readiness for US military strategy in the Balkans and a US assessment of Greece's intentions toward the former Yugoslav. Athens was Lalas' fourth communications posting with the State Department. He had previously served in Belgrade, Istanbul, and in Taiwan.

During his espionage career, he earned a steady income stealing, then selling, Defense Intelligence Agency reports about troop strength, political analyses, and military discussions contained in cables between the US Embassy in Athens and the White House, FBI communications about counterterrorism efforts, and the names and job descriptions of CIA agents stationed overseas. Greek handlers allegedly paid him $20,000 to provide about 240 documents from 1991 to 1993.

The US Government first learned of the espionage activities in February 1993, when an official of the Greek Embassy in the United States made a statement to a State Department officer indicating that he knew the contents of a Secret communication from the US Embassy in Athens to the State Department. Lalas was later identified (through a video monitoring system) stealing documents intended for destruction.

In June 1993, Lalas pleaded guilty to one count of conspiracy to commit espionage and on September 16th was sentenced to 14 years in federal prison without possibility of parole. Prosecutors had recommended the 14-year sentence in return for Lalas' promise to reveal what documents he turned over and to whom. The full extent of his espionage activity was revealed prior to sentencing only after he failed two FBI polygraph examinations.

Roderick James Ramsay

Roderick James Ramsay, a former US Army sergeant, was arrested in Tampa, Florida, on 7 June 1990 and charged with conspiracy to commit espionage.

Roderick James Ramsay

Ramsay joined the Army in 1981 and was transferred to West Germany in June 1983 where he was recruited by then, Army Sgt. Clyde Lee Conrad. Ramsay received $20,000 for selling military secrets that could have caused the collapse of NATO, Top Secret plans for the defense of Central Europe, the location and use of NATO tactical nuclear weapons, and the ability of NATO's military communications that were passed to Hungary and Czechoslovakia. An FBI official said, "It's one of the most serious breaches ever, it's unprecedented what went over to the other side. The ability to defend ourselves is neutralized because they have all our plans."

Ramsay initially used a 35-mm camera to photograph classified documents, but then switched to more effective videotape. He reportedly recorded a total of about 45 hours of videotape. Ramsay is said to have a high IQ, is multilingual, and has the "ability to recall minute details, facts, and figures from hundreds of volumes of documents." The FBI described him as "brilliant and erratic."

In West Germany he worked as a clerk-typist in the 8th Infantry Division. When arrested he was unemployed, living sometimes at his mother's house and sometimes in his car.

In September 1991 he pleaded guilty and agreed to cooperate with prosecutors. On 28 August 1992 he was sentenced to 36 years in prison. The sentence reflects his cooperation with investigators.

Jeffrey Stephen Rondeau

On 22 October 1992, Jeffrey Stephen Rondeau, a US Army sergeant stationed at Bangor, Maine, was arrested in Tampa, Florida. He was charged with espionage for providing US Army and NATO defense secrets, including tactical nuclear weapons' plans, to Hungarian and Czechoslovak intelligence agents from 1985 through 1988. Rondeau was part of the Clyde Lee Conrad spy ring, which operated out the 8th Infantry Division, Bad Kreuznach, Germany, in the mid-1980s.

The inquiry into Rondeau's involvement was aided by the cooperation of Roderick James Ramsay. As a recognition signal, Ramsay reportedly gave Rondeau a torn dollar bill to use when dealing with others in the plot. The US Attorney for the Middle District of Florida said, "The espionage charge in this case is especially serious because it's related to the allied defense of Central Europe, including the use of tactical nuclear weapons and military communications."

The three-count indictment of Rondeau charged that he conspired with Conrad, Ramsay and others to "copy, steal, photopgrah and videotape" documents and sell them to Hungary and Czechoslovakia. The indictment did not specify what amount of money he may have received. On 28 March 1994, Rondeau pleaded guilty to espionage.

Albert T. Sombolay

Albert T. Sombolay, a specialist 4th class with the US Army artillery, pleaded guilty in July 1991 to espionage and aiding the enemy. He was tried by a military judge in Baumholder, Germany, and sentenced to confinement at hard labor for 34 years, reduced to E-1, forfeited all pay and allowances, and received a dishonorable discharge.

Sombolay was born in Zaire, Africa. He became a naturalized US citizen in 1978 and entered the Army in 1985 as a cannon crewman. In December 1990, assigned to the 8th Infantry Division in Baumholder, he contacted the Iraqi and Jordanian Embassies to volunteer his services in support of the "Arab cause." To the Jordanian Embassy in Brussels, he passed information on US troop readiness and promised more information to include videotapes of US equipment and positions in Saudi Arabia. He told the Jordanians that he would be

Albert T. Sombolay

deployed to Saudi Arabia and could provide them with useful information. To the Iraqi Embassy in Bonn, Germany, he offered the same services, but they did not respond.

On 29 December 1990, Sombolay's unit was deployed to Saudi Arabia, as part of Desert Sheild, without him. Still in Germany, Sombolay continued to contact the Iraqis and provided a Jordanian representative several items of chemical warfare equipment (chemical suit, boots, gloves, and decontamination gear).

His activity was discovered by US Army Military Intelligence. After Sombolay's arrest in March 1991, he admitted to providing Desert Sheild deployment information, military identification cards, and chemical protection equipment to Jordanian officials. He was motivated by money.

Jeffrey Schevitz

In November 1995, a German court in Stuttgart convicted Jeffrey Schevitz, an American systems analyst, of spying for East Germany. At the trial, Schevitz admitted to passing information about West Germany's nuclear policies to the East German intelligence agency between 1977 and 1990. He also claimed that he was working for the Central Intelligence Agency (CIA) as a double agent with the objective of learning Stasi modus operandi. The CIA denied any involvement with Schevitz and a German intelligence officer testified that his service found no connection between CIA and Schevitz.

The prosecutors at the trial revealed that the Stasi gave Schevitz the codename "Robert." During his espionage activities, Schevitz provided information about German nuclear and nonproliferation policies. He obtained his information from contacts with German Government and other officials during his teaching at Berlin's Free University during the 1970s and later when employed as a systems analyst at Germany's Nuclear Research Center in Karlsruhe from 1980 to 1994. Schevitz delivered his information during personal meetings with Stasi officers and by using a dead drop aboard the express train from Basel to Berlin.

The five judge panel announced a suspended sentence of 18 months but did give him three years probation, allowing Schevitz to go free. The court fined him $10,000, which will go to charity, and court costs. Schevitz's plea for leniency influenced the judges. He said that he was attempting to ease the potential conflicts between East and West during the tense 1970s. The prosecutors's statement that the information passed was of little importance also helped.

The German authorities arrested Schevitz's wife, Beatrice Altman, but dropped the charges when she agreed to pay a fine of $7,000.

Three Taiwan Nationals Indicted for Espionage

Kai-Lo Hsu, Technical Director of the Yuen Foong Paper Co. Ltd., in Taipai, and Chester S. Ho, a professor at the National Chiao Tung University, were arrested in Philadelphia on 14 June 1997 on charges relating to an alleged plan to steal trade secrets from the pharmaceutical firm, Bristol-Myers Squibb Company. The two are being held in home detention under a $1 million bond secured by real estate and bank accounts. An arrest warrant was also issued for a third person, Jessica Chou, identified as a manager for business development in Yuen Foong. Her exact location was unknown.

According to the arrest warrant and multiple open sources, Hsu and Ho conspired to illegally acquire, through an FBI undercover agent, plant cell culture technology used to make Taxol, an anticancer drug used to treat ovarian cancer. The 11-count indictment charges that two of the three accused agreed to make a preliminary payment of $400,000 in cash, stock, and royalties to a corrupt Bristol-Myers scientist and a man they thought was a technology-information broker. The broker was an undercover FBI agent and the supposedly corrupt scientist was working with the government.

Hsu was charged with six counts of mail fraud, one count of conspiracy to steal trade secrets, one count of attempted theft of trade secrets, and other violations. Ho was charged with one count of conspiracy to steal trade secrets, one count of attempted theft of trade secrets, and other violations. Chou was charged with mail fraud, conspiracy to steal trade secrets, and other charges. Maximum penalties for the charges range up to 60 years in prison and up to a $2,500,000 fine.

It is uncertain if the attempted deal was sanctioned by high-level executives at Yuen Foong, however, Hsu allegedly made the comment that his company was diversifying its interests into the area of biotechnology and working on a government project on Taxol technology. A spokesman for Bristol-Myers noted that Taxol is a billion-dollar product around the world and that the cost of losing the technology would have been significant.

A federal judge in October 1997, ordered prosecutors to turn over to the defendants and their lawyers the very documents the defendants are accused of trying to steal. The judge ruled that they needed the information to prepare their defense, and that their right to a fair trial overrides the rights of a company to projtect its trade secrets. Prosecutors are appealing the ruling.

Daniel and Patrick Worthing

On April 18, 1997, Daniel Worthing, of New Kensington, Pennsylvania, became the first person in the United States to be convicted under the Economic Espionage Act. Convicted in February 1997 of conspiracy to possess and deliver trade secrets, Worthing was sentenced to five years' probation, with six months' home confinement. He was also ordered to complete 100 hours of community service and pay a special assessment of $100.

The plot involving the two brothers began unraveling in mid-November 1996 when the chief executive officer of Owens-Corning received a letter from "Dane Davis," offering to sell 19 items of PPG Industries' trade secrets for $1,000. The trade secrets were later identified as customer lists, secret fiberglass formulas, videos of machine operations, blueprints, photographs, and product samples. Unknown to the sender, the Owens-Corning executive forwarded the letter to PPG officials, who contacted the FBI.

On 3 December 1996, the Owens-Corning Company executive received a three-page fax from "Dane Davis," outlining more PPG insider information. A small memo automatically typed on the fax by the sending machine identified it as being sent from PPG's offices. The executive was asked to page the sender if he was interested.

The sender turned out to be Patrick Worthing, who used his own pager number in the fax. Patrick supervised a maintenance crew of about 50 workers who cleaned PPG's fiberglass research center and supplied people to operate prototype machines in suburban Pittsburgh. The crew allegedly had complete access to every office in the facility.

On 7 December 1996, believing they were to meet with a Owens-Corning representative, Patrick and Daniel Worthing were arrested by the FBI. Daniel Worthing, a garbage hauler by trade, said he got involved to protect his brother and to get a percentage of the profits.

Patrick Worthing was sentenced to a 15-month federal prison term in May 1997 for his ill-fated attempt to steal trade secrets from PPG Industries. He was free on bond until he reported to prison.

Charles Schoof and John Haeger

Two US Navy men stationed aboard a ship at the US Naval Amphibious Base at Little Creek, Virginia, received lengthy jail sentences after pleading guilty to conspiring to sell classified information to the Soviets. In proceedings held at the Navy Legal Service Office in Norfolk, Haeger pleaded guilty to conspiracy to commit espionage on 23 April 1990 and on 24 April was sentenced to 19 years in prison, reduction in rate to E-1, forfeiture of all pay and allowances, and a dishonorable discharge. On 24 April, Schoof pleaded guilty to conspiracy to commit espionage and was sentenced to 25 years in prison, reduction in rate to E-1, forfeiture of all pay and allowances, and a dishonorable discharge. Charles Edward Schoof, age

Charles Schoof

21, and John Joseph Haeger, age 20, both Operations Specialists (OS3) were arrested on 1 December 1989 by Naval Criminal Investigative Service (NCIS) special agents.

Both men, assigned to the USS *Fairfax County*, became the focus of an investigation when one of their fellow crewmembers reported what he believed to be suspicious activity by them to the ship's commanding officer. Upon hearing the crewmember's suspicions, the commanding officer immediately initiated an inventory of classified material abroad the vessel. The inventory revealed that classified microfiche containing Secret and NATO Secret material were missing.

After confirming that classified material was missing, the commanding officer notified NCIS. NCIS agents arrested Schoof on board the ship and found him in possession of 12 pieces of microfiche containing six separate publications. An hour later, Haeger was arrested aboard the ship. NCIS later learned that Schoof was planning to either destroy the material or take it to the Soviet Embassy in Washington, DC, that weekend. Schoof was actually preparing to leave the ship when he was arrested.

John Haeger

CI at the End of the 20th Century
Bibliography

Andrew, Christopher. *For the President's Eyes Only: Secret Intelligence and the American Presidency from Washington to Bush*. New York: Harper Collins, 1995.

Bar-Joseph, Uri. *Intelligence Intervention in the Politics of Democratic States: The United States, Israel and Britain*. University Park, PA: The Pennsylvania State University Press, 1995.

Beans, James D. "Marine Corps Counterintelligence: 1990-2000." *American Intelligence Journal* 10:2 (1989): 47-50.

Boren, David L. "Counterintelligence for the 1990's," *American Intelligence Journal* 10:2 (1989): 9-14.

Costello, John and Oleg Tsarev. *Deadly Illusions*. New York: Crown Publishers, 1993.

Deriabin, Peter and T. H. Bagley. *The KGB: Masters of the Soviet Union,* New York: Hippocrene Books, 1990.

Early, Pete. *Confessions of a Spy: The Real Story of Aldrich Ames*. New York: G.P. Putnam's Sons, 1997.

Eftimiades, Nicholas. *Chinese Intelligence Operations*. Annapolis, MD: Naval Institute Press, 1994.

Fialka, John. *War By Other Means: Economic Espionage in America*. New York: W.W. Norton & Company, 1997.

Kalaris, George and Leonard McCoy. "Counterintelligence for the 1990's," *International Journal of Intelligence and Counterintelligence* 2:2 (1988): 179-187.

Maas, Peter. *Killer Spy: The Inside Story of the FBI's Pursuit and Capture of Aldrich Ames, America's Deadliest Spy*. New York: Warner Books, 1995.

MacKenzie, Angus. *Secrets: The CIA's War at Home*. Berkeley, CA: University of California Press, 1997.

Milano, James V. *Soldiers, Spies and the Rat-Line: America's Undeclared War Against the Soviets*. Washington: Brassey's, 1995.

O'Toole, G.J.A. *Honorable Treachery*. New York: Atlantic Monthly Press, 1991.

Porch, Douglas. *The French Secret Service: A History of French Intelligence From the Dreyfus Affair to the Gulf War*. New York: Farrar, Strauss and Giroux, 1995.

Richelson, Jeffrey T. *A Century of Spies: Intelligence in the Twentieth Century*. New York: Oxford University Press, 1995.

Riebling, Mark. *Wedge, The Secret War Between the FBI and CIA*. New York: Alfred A. Knopf, 1994.

Schachte, W.L., Jr. "NISCOM Counterintelligence Strategy for the 1990's," *American Intelligence Journal* 10:2 (1989) 43-45.

Sessions, William S. "The Evolving Threat. Meeting the Counterintelligence Challenges of the 1990's: A Strategic Issue Facing Our Nation." *American Intelligence Journal* 10:2 (1989): 19-23.

U.S. Congress. Senate. Select Committee on Intelligence. *An Assessment of the Aldrich H. Ames Espionage Case and its Implications for US Intelligence: A Report of the US Senate Select Committee on Intelligence*. Washington, DC: GPO, 1994.

Weiner, Tim, David Johnston and Neil A. Lewis. *Betrayal: The Story of Aldrich Ames, An American Spy*. New York: Random House, 1995.

Weinstein, Sidney T. "The Role of U.S. Counterintelligence in the Next Decade," *American Intelligence Journal* 10:2 (1989): 33-36.

Westerfield, H. Bradford, ed. *Inside CIA's Private World: Declassified Articles From the Agency's Internal Journal 1955-1992*. New Haven, CT: Yale University Press, 1955.

Wise, David. *Nightmover: How Aldrich Ames Sold the CIA to the KGB for $4.6 Million*. New York: Harper Collins, 1995.

CI at the End of the 20th Century

IMPORTANT DATES AND COUNTERINTELLIGENCE EVENTS
CLOSING THE 20TH CENTURY
1990-PRESENT

1990	7 June	Roderick Ramsey, US Army, arrested for spying for Hungary and Czechoslovakia.
	12 June	Clyde Lee Conrad, U.S. Army Sergeant, is convicted of espionage and given life imprisonment.
	16 July	President Bush restructures the President's Foreign Intelligence Advisory Board by shrinking the membership from 15 to six.
	5 October	President George Bush signs off on National Security Directive-47, which tasks CIA, FBI, NSA and the departments of State, Defense and Justice to continue to rebuild US counterintelligence programs.
	5 November	The State department dismisses foreign service officer Felix Bloch who is suspected of spying for the Soviet Union since the early 1970s.
1991	29 March	A major fire damages the US embassy in Moscow.
	22 April	Jeffrey M. Carney, USAF, is arrested for spying for the East German Ministry of State Security.
	30 September	Yevgeniy Primakov named director of the SVRR, the renamed First Chief Directorate, which was the foreign intelligence arm of the old KGB.
	25 December	The Soviet Union dissolves.
1992	21 January	Douglas Tsou, FBI, sentenced to 10 years in prison for spying for Taiwan.
	22 May	Virginia J. Baynes, a CIA employee, pleaded guilty to one count of espionage and was sentenced in October 1992 to 41 months in prison.
	18 September	The existence of the National Reconnaissance Office officially acknowledged.
	22 October	Jeffrey Stephen Rondeau, U.S. Army, arrested and indicted on three counts of espionage. He is believed to be a member of the Clyde Lee Conrad espionage ring.
	27 December	Joseph G. Brown was arrested and charged with passing classified information he received from Virginia J. Baynes to the Philippine Government.

CI at the End of the 20th Century

IMPORTANT DATES AND COUNTERINTELLIGENCE EVENTS

CLOSING THE 20TH CENTURY
1990-PRESENT

1993	5 February	Frederick C. Hamilton, DIA official who was arrested for espionage, pled guilty to two counts of espionage and is sentenced to 37 months imprisonment.
	16 April	Frederick Hamilton, Defense Intelligence Agency, sentenced to 37 months in prison for spying for Ecuador.
	29 April	Jeff E. Gregory, Army Staff Sergeant, arrested for espionage. He is believed to be a part of the Clyde Lee Conrad espionage ring.
	30 April	Steven J. Lalas, a Department of State employee, is arrested and charged with passing sensitive military, political, and economic information to Greek officials.
	3 August	Geneva Jones, U.S. Department of State, arrested for Unauthorized Possession of National Defense Information.
1994	21 February	Aldrich "Rick" Ames, CIA officer, arrested for espionage.
	6 May	Richard Miller, the FBI agent arrested for espionage on 3 October 1984, is released from prison.
	4 July	FBI opens a legal attache office in Moscow.
	1 August	The National Counterintelligence Center is established by Presidential Executive Order.
1995	23 June	Morris Cohen, 84, who also used the name Peter Kroger, died in a Moscow hospital. Cohen spied for the Soviet Union and was instrumental in relaying U.S. atomic bomb secrets to the Kremlin in the 1940s.
	12 September	George Kalaris, who succeeded James Angleton as chief of counterintelligence at CIA, dies.
	8 October	John Cairncross, 82, the so-called "fifth man" in the ring of spies recruited at Cambridge University in the 1930s to work for Moscow, died in Western England after a stroke. The other four spies were Kim Philby, Guy Burgess, Donald Maclean and Anthony Blunt.
1996	23 February	Robert Lipka, former National Security Agency clerk, is arrested by the FBI on espionage charges.

CLOSING THE 20TH CENTURY
1990-PRESENT

1996	27 February	Former Sgt Clayton Lonetree, the only US Marine ever convicted of espionage, is released from prison.
	1 March	The Commission on the Roles and Capabilities of the United States Intelligence Community—known as the Aspin-Brown Commission—released its final report entitled *Preparing for the 21st Century: An Appraisal of U.S. Intelligence.*
	14 June	President signed and forwarded to Congress the first Annual Report to Congress on Foreign Economic Collection and Industrial Espionage, prepared by NACIC.
	24 September	Pavel Sudoplatov, a former senior KGB officer, who claimed to have engineered the stealing of the atomic bomb secrets from the United States, died.
	25 September	Robert C. Kim, a civilian computer expert at the Office of Naval Intelligence, is arrested for passing documents to a South Korean Embassy official.
	15 November	Alger Hiss died. He was the center of controversy over his espionage activities on behalf of the GRU for which he was never tried. Instead, he spent four years in prison for perjury when he lied to a grand jury in 1950.
	16 November	CIA officer Harold James Nicholson is arrested for spying for the Russians.
	18 November	John Vassall, a former British naval attaché, who admitted to spying for the KGB and sent to prison in 1962, died in London at age 71.
	7 December	Patrick and Daniel Worthing are arrested by the FBI. On April 18, 1997, Daniel Worthing became the first person in the US to be convicted under the Economic Espionage Act of 1996.
	18 December	Earl Edwin Pitts, an FBI agent, is arrested for spying for Russia.
1997	3 March	Harold James Nicholson plead guilty to espionage and was sentenced on 5 June 1997 to 23½ years in federal prison.
	30 April	Donald Ratcliffe, head of Far Eastern Operations for Litton Industries Inc., arrested by South Korean intelligence on charges of obtaining classified information.

CI at the End of the 20th Century

CLOSING THE 20TH CENTURY
1990-PRESENT

1997

4 June — Kai-Lo Hsu, Technical Director of the Yeun Foong Paper Co. Ltd., in Taipei, and Chester S. Ho, a professor at the National Chiao Tung University, are arrested in Philadelphia on charges relating to an alleged plan to steal trade secrets from the pharmaceutical firm Bristol-Myers Squibb Company.

5 June — Patrick Worthing convicted under Economic Espionage Act of 1996 for trying to sell PPG Industries trade secrets to Owens-Corning Fiberglass of Toledo, Ohio.

10 June — Kelly Therese Warren, former U.S. Army clerk, arrested for espionage. She was the fifth person to be charged in connection with the Clyde Lee Conrad espionage ring as a result of a 10-year probe by the FBI and Army intelligence.

23 June — Earl E. Pitts, former FBI agent, sentenced to 27 years in prison.

11 July — Robert C. Kim, former Navy computer specialist, sentenced to nine years in prison for passing classified material to officials in South Korea.

25 July — Donald Ratcliffe, the first American defense contractor to be arrested in South Korean on espionage charges, convicted and given a suspended two-year sentence.

24 September — Ex-NSA employee Robert S. Lipka is sentenced to 18 years in prison and fined $10,000 for selling top-secret documents to the Soviet Union three decades ago.

4 October — Theresa Squillacote, Kurt Stand, and James Michael Clark are arrested and charged with spying for East Germany and Russia in an espionage operation that began in 1972.

3 November — Harold C. Worden, a retired Eastman Kodak manager, is sentenced to a year in prison and fined $30,000 for stealing formulas, drawings and blueprints from the company.

8 December — Peter S. Lee, a nuclear physicist, pleaded guilty to willfully passing national defense information to Chinese scientists during a 1985 visit to China.

CI at the End of the 20th Century

IMPORTANT DATES AND COUNTERINTELLIGENCE EVENTS
CLOSING THE 20TH CENTURY
1990-PRESENT

1998	8 January	Clyde Lee Conrad, a former US Army Sergeant who was convicted of treason in 1990, died in a German prison where he was serving a life sentence.
	26 January	Steven L. Davis pleaded guilty to federal charges that he stole and disclosed Gillette Company trade secrets. He was sentenced on 17 April 1998 to 27 months in prison.
	3 April	FBI arrests CIA employee Douglas Frederick Groat on charges of espionage.
	11 May	Israel officially acknowledged for the first time that Jonathan Pollard was an Israeli agent.
	3 June	James Clark, a one-time campus radical and former US Army paralegal, pleaded guilty to conspiracy to commit espionage.
	15 June	The French magazine Le Point reported that France systematically listens in on the telephone conversations and cable traffic of many businesses based in the United States and other nations.
	17 June	Department of Defense declassified its first reconnaissance satellite, which was launched shortly after the 1 May 1960 shoot-down of Francis Gary Powers' U-2 over the Soviet Union.
	27 July	CIA employee Douglas Frederick Groat pleads guilty to one count of attempted extortion after a plea agreement.
	28 July	FBI arrests Huang Dao Pei, a Chinese-born naturalized US citizen on charges he tried to steal trade secrets for a hepatitis C monitoring kit from Roche Diagnostics from 1992 to 1995 and sell it to China.
	1 August	Joel Barr, an American Communist and friend of Julius and Ethel Rosenberg, who barely eluded the FBI before he could be arrested for espionage in 1950, died of complications of diabetes in a hospital in Moscow.

ACKNOWLEDGMENTS

I wish to express my gratitude to everyone who contributed to making the Counterintelligence Reader a reality. I must single out the Director of the National Counterintelligence Center, Michael J. Waguespack, who gave his approval to this project and supported it during the months it took to bring it to fruition.

I also want to thank Dr. Louis R. Sadler, head of the History Department at New Mexico State University, for his insightful comments and helpful advice and Emma Sullivan, CIA's Historical Intelligence Collection librarian, who helped to locate some of the research material for the Reader and to find the data to fill in those hard-to-find dates in the chronologies.

I am again grateful to Dr. Sadler and to Dr. Charles H. Harris III, also from New Mexico State University, Dr. Timothy Naftali, of Yale University, and Wayne Goldstein, Naval Criminal Investigative Service, who gave permission to use their writings; to Dan Lovelace, former CIA officer, Louise Sayre, National Security Agency, Christopher Lyons, Department of State, and Eric Rafalko at Radford University, for writing articles for the Reader.

To the CTX Corporation crew; Connie Yarab who designed and formatted the Reader and put up with the many changes and last minute additions; John Rutledge who took the photographs and made them usable for insertion into the text; Timothy Cox who provided his expert advice and helped locate and prepare the photographs at the beginning of each chapter; and to CIA's Mark Hernandez who designed the cover and the layout for the chronologies, I owe special thanks. In addition, Tom Shirey of the CIA and Charles Emmling, a former CIA officer, made contributions for which I am appreciative. I am deeply indebted to CIA's Lisa Lupton who painstakingly read and edited Volumes II and III.

My staff at the National Counterintelligence Center's Community Training Branch has been extraordinarily helpful, particularly in helping prepare the articles and doing all the small things to bring the Reader together. I would like to thank SA G. Anna Kline, Air Force Office of Special Investigations, who prepared the bibliographies and searched for those missing chronology dates; SA Robert Breitenbach and SA Catherine M. Kiser, Federal Bureau of Investigation (FBI), who obtained FBI data or provided FBI photographs; Diane Harper, Central Intelligence Agency and Thomas Xenakis, Defense Security Service, who helped proofread; and Stephen Argubright, Naval Criminal Investigative Service, who read my introductions to each chapter and large parts of the manuscript. As always, his perceptiveness was sharp, his questions penetrating and his criticisms helpful. Jeana Herrmann, a student from the University of Maryland, who worked in the office for the summer, was absolutely indispensable in helping type articles.

www.ingramcontent.com/pod-product-compliance
Lightning Source LLC
Chambersburg PA
CBHW080437170426
43195CB00017B/2802